A ROMANIZED HINDUSTANI AND ENGLISH DICTIONARY

DESIGNED FOR

THE USE OF SCHOOLS,

AND FOR VERNACULAR STUDENTS OF THE LANGUAGE

A ROMANIZED HINDUSTANI AND ENGLISH DICTIONARY

DESIGNED FOR THE USE OF SCHOOLS, AND FOR VERNACULAR STUDENTS OF THE LANGUAGE

COMPILED BY

NATHANIEL BRICE

A NEW EDITION, REVISED AND ENLARGED

ENTERED AT STATIONERS' HALL

GYAN

Published by

GYAN

Gyan Publishing House
5, Ansari Road
Daryaganj, New Delhi-110002
Phone: 011-47034999, 9811692060
E-mail: books@gyanbooks.com

Distribution Network
gyanbooks.com
India, USA, Canada, UK, Australia, France

ISBN : 978-81-212-4421-3 (PB)
First Published, 1864

2nd Impression 2020

Printed at: Gyan Press, Delhi.

A Romanized
Hindustani and English Dictionary Designed for
the use of Schools, and for Vernacular Students of the Language
Compiled by: Nathaniel Brice

A ROMANIZED
HINDÚSTÁNÍ AND ENGLISH
DICTIONARY,

DESIGNED FOR

THE USE OF SCHOOLS,

AND FOR VERNACULAR STUDENTS OF THE LANGUAGE.

COMPILED BY

NATHANIEL BRICE.

A NEW EDITION, REVISED AND ENLARGED.

LONDON:

TRÜBNER & CO., 60 PATERNOSTER ROW; R. C. LEPAGE & CO.,
AND OTHER BOOKSELLERS, CALCUTTA;
AND
NATHANIEL BRICE, DINAPORE.
1864.

PREFACE TO THE FIRST EDITION.

SINCE the time when the practicability of applying the Roman Character to the languages of India, and particularly to the Urdú, or Hindústání, was brought to the test by Mr. Trevelyan and his coadjutors, a considerable number of Books has been published in Romanized Hindústání, and introduced into Schools, particularly in Upper India; but with the exception of the English and Romanized Hindústání and Bangálí Dictionary, published some twelve years ago by Mr. P. S. D'Rozario, nothing has been done to provide those engaged in learning or teaching the language through the medium of Romanized books, with a Dictionary in that character, or at least prepared on the same system of orthography. At an early period the want of such a Dictionary was strongly felt, and every year has added new proofs of the necessity that one should be provided. It was with a view to supply this desideratum, and furnish schools and the public with a Dictionary small in dimension, but comprehensive in matter and cheap in price, that this work was undertaken.

It has been the author's endeavour to render the Dictionary as complete as possible, he has therefore not scrupled to introduce many words of Hindí or Sanskrit origin which he found current either in books or the spoken language.

The author commends the little work to the favourable regard of the public generally, and particularly to the long-tried friends and advocates of the Roman character, as applicable to the Hindústání language, of the immense advantage of which this little Dictionary is no mean evidence. In the compass of 346 duodecimo pages, the author has been able to introduce upwards of 20,000 Hindústání words with their renderings in English, which in the native character would in all probability have filled four times that number of pages.

NATHANIEL BRICE.

Dinapore.

PREFACE TO THE PRESENT EDITION.

THE first edition of my Romanized Hindústání and English Dictionary having been appreciated by the public in India, and copies of it being no longer procurable, I have availed myself of my visit to England to republish it in a more compact and portable form; and whilst the number of pages are but few in excess of the former edition, by economizing space, several more current and useful words have been added, with the view of making it more useful.

The object I had in view in the compilation was to furnish a Dictionary of only the words in most general use; and it is believed that there is scarcely a word in it but is most useful in the acquisition of the vernacular language.

Great attention has been given to have this edition orthographically correct; yet there are some mistakes which in the correction of proofs escaped detection. These are noted in a list of "corrections," and by it any one might, in a few minutes, with a pen and by erasures, make the necessary corrections. This step will prevent any one being afterwards misled by an incorrect orthography; and it is of importance, as a correct orthography in accordance with the system used, is a sure guide to correct pronunciation, as each letter is a representative of only one sound.

It is probable that all copies have not some of the orthographical errors in the list of "Corrections," as in the process of printing diacritical *marks* occasionally break off. In cases where the letter *ı* has no dot it is most probable that it is properly *ı*.

NATHANIEL BRICE.

THE ANGLO-HINDÚSTÁNÍ ALPHABET,

WITH

THE POWERS OF THE LETTERS.

Capital	Small		Power
A	a	pronounced as	*a* in w*o*man.
Á	á	,,	*a* in *a*rt.
AI	ai	,,	*ai* in *ai*sle.
AU	au	,,	*ou* in *ou*r.
B	b	,,	*b* in *b*ut.
CH	ch	,,	*ch* in *ch*urch.
D	d	,,	with the point of the tongue pressed on the upper fore teeth, similar to *d* in "*d*ew."
Ḍ	ḍ	,,	with the point of the tongue struck back on the palate, similar to *d* in ba*d*.
E	e	,,	*e* in th*e*re.
F	f	,,	*f* in *f*ind.
G	g	,,	*g* in *g*o.
G̣H	g̣h	,,	somewhat like *g* in *g*ar*g*le. It represents the Arabic letter ghain, and has a peculiar guttural sound.
H	h	,,	*h* in *h*ouse.
I	i	,,	*i* in p*i*n.
Í	í	,,	*i* in pol*i*ce.
J	j	,,	*j* in *j*ust.
ḲH	ḳh	,,	somewhat similar to the Scotch *ch* in lo*ch*. It represents the Persian letter ḳhe, and has a peculiar guttural sound.
L	l	,,	*l* in *l*ane.
M	m	,,	*m* in *m*an.
N	n	,,	*n* in *n*oo*n*.
Ṇ	ṇ	pronounced as	*n* in the French words sans, bon.
O	o	,,	*o* in no.
P	p	,,	*p* in *p*un.
Q	q	,,	somewhat like *q* in quoit, and uttered by pressing back the root of the tongue on the throat.
R	r	,,	*r* in *r*an.
Ṛ	ṛ	,,	similar to *r* in ete*r*nal, and uttered by striking the point of the tongue on the palate.
S	s	,,	*s* in sin.
SH	sh	,,	*sh* in *sh*ine.
T	t	,,	with the point of the tongue pressed on the upper fore teeth, and nearly as *t* in *t*ake.
Ṭ	ṭ	,,	with the point of the tongue struck back on the palate, and nearly as *t* in *t*ub.
U	u	,,	*u* in bull.
Ú	ú	,,	*u* in rule.
V	v	,,	*v* in vine.
W	w	,,	somewhat like *w* in *w*as, and having a power between the English v and w.
Y	y	,,	*y* in *y*ear.
Z	z	,,	*z* in zeal.
ZH	zh	,,	*zh* in a*zh*ure.

Note 1.—The vowels, whether long or short, with the point under thus—ạ, ạ́, ị, ị́, ụ, ụ́, represent the letter ạin, and have a peculiar guttural sound.

Note 2.—Bh, chh, dh, ḍh, gh, jh, kh, ph, ṛh, th, ṭh, are respectively the aspirates of b, ch, d, ḍ, g, j, k, p, ṛ, t, and ṭ, and are pronounced as one letter.

The following are the initial letters or abbreviations for the parts of speech, grammatical terms and other purposes :—

s. or *subst.* for substantive.
v. for verb.
adj. for adjective.
conj. for conjunction.
adv. for adverb.
part. for participle.
pron. for pronoun.
prep. for preposition.
postpos. for postposition.
interj. for interjection.
m. or *mas.* for masculine.
f. for feminine.
a. for active.
n. for neuter.
poss. or *posses.* for possessive.
sing. for singular.
pl. or *plur.* for plural.
compar. for comparative.
superl. for superlative.
corrupt. for corruption.
compos. for composition.
contract. for contraction.
inflect. for inflection.
met. for metonymically.
fig. for figuratively.
prop. for properly.
improp. for improperly.
vulg. for vulgarly.
rel. for relative.
correl. for correlative.
dem. for demonstrative.
indef. for indefinite.
interrog. for interrogative.
imper. for imperative.
neg. for negative.
pass. for passive.
object. for objective.
gen. for gender.
pers. for person.
Eng. for English.

CORRECTIONS.

Page.	Col.	Line.	for	read
2	1	15,	*for* Áb-i-ghost,	*read* Áb i gosht.
5	2	15	Agház	Ágház.
6	2	14	blackhead	blockhead.
7	2	2	Ạ́jís	Ạ́jis.
7	2	18	Ȧjogya	Ȧjogya.
8	1	43	Ạláhidá	Ạláhida.
9	2	13	Ạ̇mber	Ȧmbar.
11	2	44	Ạ́nkh	Ánkh.
12	1	41	Anṭachit	Anṭáchit.
12	1	43	Anṭaghar	Anṭágha r.
13	1	48	Ạr	Ạ́r.
16	2	20	Áṭhwán	Áṭhwáṇ.
17	1	2	Aṭna	Aṭná.
20	2	4	márna	márná.
20	2	10	Bághícha	Bághícha.
23	1	1	azmáí	ázmáí.
24	2	19	best	plot.
25	1	25	thanná	ṭhanná.
28	2	22	Bátís	Ḃatís.
29	1	1	Báṭṭá	Baṭṭá.
32	2	48	Be ehuụ́r	Be shuụ́r.
33	1	17	Be tạ́lím	Be tạlím.
33	1	31	Be tawaqqú	Be tawaqqụ.
33	2	3	Be wástá	Be wásta.
46	2	27	Champáṭ	Champaṭ.
47	2	33	Chapqualish	Chapqalish.
47	2	41	Chapṭa	Chapṭá.
49	2	44	slate	slab.
57	1	18	Chonḍa	Chonḍá.
61	2	14	Ḍáiya	Dạiya.
66	2	24	Ḍ̇áṭná	Ḍaṭná.
66	2	25	Ḍ̇aṭná	Ḍ̇áṭná.
69	1	4	Ḍ̇hamádham	Ḋhamádham.
69	1	33	Ḋhá á	Dháná.
77	1	4	Dumba	Dumba.
79	2	8	Ḟáham	Faham.
81	2	32	Fáṭákhá	Faṭákhá.
82	1	41	Fiạl	Fiạ́l.
82	1	43	Fiạ́l	Fiạl.
82	2	13	Fildandán	Fíldandán.
82	2	47	Firga	Firqa.
83	2	6	Phútá	Phúṭá.
90	2	27	G̣hamgin	G̣hamgín.
91	1	30	G̣har	Ġhar.
91	2	36	G̣harib	G̣haríb.
91	2	40	G̣harib	G̣haríb.

Page.	Col.	Line.		
104	2	25,	*for* Halfá	*read* Halfa.
105	2	11	Humára	Hamárá.
109	2	5	mạ́múl	mạmúl.
121	2	3	mạ́ní	mạní.
123	1	45	Jạ́farí	Jạfarí.
125	2	12	Jálsáz	Jạlsáz.
125	2	13	Jálsází	Jạlsází.
126	1	24	Jámíṉḍár	Jamíṉḍár.
138	1	7	Jura	Jurá.
142	1	16	Qaím	Qáim.
145	1	47	Kámij	Kamíj.
146	2	25	Khachaní	Kanchaní.
153	2	28	Kauṛa	Kauṛá.
169	1	32	Kishtikárí	Kishtkárí.
173	2	5	Kunwárí	Kuṉwárí.
176	1	38	Lagwaná	Lagwáná.
177	1	42	Laḳharáj	Láḳharáj.
182	1	37	Lí'e	Li'e.
185	1	22	Mạ́búd	Mạbúd.
190	2	6	Mạ́lúm	Mạlúm.
190	2	9	Mạ́lúm	Mạlúm.
190	2	10	Mạ́lúm	Mạlúm.
190	2	48	Mạ́lúm	Mạlúm.
194	2	23	Mạ́rifat	Mạrifat.
195	2	1	Mạ́rúf	Mạrúf.
195	2	3	Mạ́rúz	Mạrúz.
199	1	23	Mạ́zúr	Mạzúr.
204	2	20	Muddáị	Muddaị.
205	1	30	dafter	daftar.
217	1	43	Námumkín	Námumkin.
225	2	44	Níranjan	Niranjan.
232	1	33	Paisna	Paisná.
250	1	39	Phnṭ	Phuṭ.
255	1	38	Pajárí	Pujárí.
256	1	24	Pushtánga	Pushṭanga.
286	1	1	Sarsaráhat	Sarsaráhaṭ.
291	1	11	Shánáma	Sháhnáma.
295	2	31	Shamár	Shumár.
297	1	26	Sikná	Síkná.
297	1	26	Sikhná	Síkhná.
299	2	38	Sivarátrí	Sivarátri.
303	1	2	Suj	Súj.
308	1	7	Tabị	Tabị.
302	1	8	Tabịat	Tabíạt.
315	2	14	Tamṭam	Ṭamṭam.
325	1	23	Teroas	Teoras.
328	2	35	Thiliyá	Ṭhiliyá.
349	1	26	Wazir	Wazír.
350	2	30	altogether	all together.
357	2	7	Zulmíyal	Zulmíyat.

ROMANIZED

SCHOOL DICTIONARY,

HINDUSTÁNÍ AND ENGLISH.

A, a short vowel, pronounced as *u* in *up*. In composition it gives the word it precedes a privative, negative or diminutive meaning: *an* is substituted for it when it precedes a vowel. In Hindí words at the end, it may be used to form the diminutive of a noun, or adjectives from substantives.

Á, a long vowel, pronounced as *a* in father: *(imper. sing.* of áná), come.

Ab, *adv.* now, presently, just now.

Áb, *s. m.* water; splendour, dignity, honour; lustre or water, (in gems;) temper, (of steel, &c.) and edge or sharpness, (of a sword.)

Ábá, *s.* (*plur.* of ab), fathers.

Ábábíl, *s. m.* a swallow.

Abad, *s. m.* eternity, without end.

Ábád, *adj.* populous, civilized, cultivated, inhabited; prosperous: in *compos.* a city.

Ábádí, *s.* population.

Abadí, *adj.* eternal, without end.

Ábád karná, *v. a.* to build, to cultivate, to civilize, to make a place habitable.

Ạbas, *adj.* vain, absurd, profitless: *adv.* in vain, idly.

Ạbd, *s. m.* a servant (of God), a slave.

Ábdána, *s. m.* drink and food.

Ábdár, *s. m.* the person entrusted with the charge of water for drinking: *adj.* well-tempered, (as steel.)

Ábdárí, *s. f.* brilliancy, (of gems;) temper or polish, (of steel.)

Ábdárk͟hána, *s. m.* a room where water for drinking is kept.

Ábdast, *s. m.* the ablution or washing after easing nature.

Ábdída, *adj.* in tears.

Abe, *interj.* hollo, you fellow, you rascal!

Aber, *s. f.* delay, lateness.

Abe tabe karná, to thee and thou a person.

Abhág, *s. m.* misfortune.

Abhágá, } *adj.* unfortunate, destitute.
Abhágí, }

Ab-hí, *adv.* just now, exactly now, immediately.

Abhidán, *s. m.* a dictionary.

Abhilák, *s. m.* wish, desire.

Abhimán, *s. m.* pride haughtiness, arrogance.

Abhimání, *adj.* proud, haughty.

Abhipráya, *s. m.* meaning, intention, design.

Abhishek, *s. m.* installation to office, usually by anointing.

Abhishikt, *adj.* anointed to office, installed.

Ābhúkhan, *s. m.* jewels, ornaments.

Abhyás, *s. m.* study, practice, experience.

Abhyásí, *adj.* studious.

Ābí, *adj.* aquatic, watery.

Abibek, *s. m.* want of discrimination, indiscretion.

Abibekí, *adj.* indiscreet, inconsiderate.

Abichár, *s. m.* want of consideration, injustice.

Abichárí, *adj.* inconsiderate, unjust.

Ạbid, *s. m.* an adorer, a votary, a devotee.

Āb-i-ghost, *s. m.* gravy, broth.

Āb-i-hayát, *s.* water of life.

Ābila, *s. m.* a blister.

Abinásí, *adj.* incorruptible, imperishable, eternal.

Ạbír, *s. m.* a red powder, thrown about in the Holí.

Abiswás, *s. m.* want of confidence, distrust.

Abiswásí, *m.*
Abiswásin, *f.*
Abiswásiní, *f.* } *adj.* without confidence, distrustful.

Abká, abke, abkí, *adj.* of the present time, now.

Ābkár, *s. m.* a seller or distiller of wine; a water-carrier.

Ābkárí, *s. f.* the business of a distiller, or water-carrier; duty levied on distilleries.

Ābḳhúra, *s. m.* a narrow-mouthed vessel for drinking out of.

Ablah, *adj.* foolish, silly.

Ablahí, *s. f.* folly, silliness.

Ablaq, *adj.* pyebald, black and white.

Ablaqá, *s. m.* a bird of the mainá kind, a starling.

Ābnús, *s. m.* ebony.

Ābnúsí, *adj.* made of ebony.

Āb-o-dána, *s. m.* drink and food.

Āb-o-hawá, *s. f.* air, atmosphere, climate.

Abr, *s. m.* a cloud.

Abrá, *s. m.* the outer fold of a double garment.

Abrak, *s. m.* talc, mica.

Abrí, *adj.* clouded, variegated.

Abrú, *s. f.* eyebrow.

Ābrú, *s. f.* honour, character, renown.

Ābrú barbád dení, *v. a.* to lose one's own character, to destroy one's character.

Ābrú dení, *v. a.* to impart honour or reputation to any one.

Ābrú lení, *v. a.* to take away character or reputation.

Ābrú utární, *v. a.* to dishonour, to disgrace.

Ab se, *adj.* hence, from this time.

Ābshora, *s.* water cooled with saltpetre.

Ābtáb, *s. f.* splendour.

Ab tab, *adv.* presently.

Ab tab honá, to be at the point of death.

Ab taiṇ,
Ab tak,
Ab talak, } *adv.* till now, hitherto, yet.

Abtar, *adj.* ruined, spoiled, worthless, dissolute.

Abtarí, *s. f.* worthlessness, &c.

Ab teṇ, *adv.* from this time, henceforth.

Ab torí, *adv.* till now, hitherto, yet.

Achakke meṇ, all at once, suddenly.

Achal, *adj.* immoveable, incapable of motion.

Āchaman, *s. m.* sipping water before religious ceremonies, meals, &c. from the palm of the hand and spitting it out again.

Achambhá, *s. m.* wonderful things, astonishment.

Achaná, *v. a.* to rinse the mouth after eating.

Achának,
Achánchak, } *adv.* suddenly, unawares, unexpectedly.

Āchár,
Achár, } *s. m.* pickles.

Acháraj, *s. m.* a Hindú doctor, a learned paṇḍit.

Āchár, banáná, *v. a.* to pickle.

Achchhá,
Āchchhá, } *adj.* good, excellent, healthy, well, sound.

Achchhá honá, *v. n.* to recover.
Achchhá karná, *v. a.* to cure.
Achchhá lagná, to become, to beseem, to be pleasing.
Achchhar, *s. m.* a letter of the alphabet.
Achchhat, *s. m.* whole rice used in religious ceremonies.
Achchhe, se achchhá, *adj. superl.* best, best of all.
Achchhí, tarah, well, right, properly.
Achhen, *adj. plur.* good.
Achet, *adj.* out of mind or senses, senselesss, stupified.
Achhrauṭí, *s. f.* orthography.
Achhtáná pachhtáná, *v. n.* to repent, to grieve, to be sorry.
Achhwání, *s. f.* caudle.
Achraj, *s. m.* wonder, admiration.
Achtáná pachtáná, *v. n.* to repent, to lament some neglect, to grieve.
Achúk, *adj.* unerring, undeviating.
Ad, in *compos.* half.
Aḍá, *s. m.* a perch for pigeons, the perch in a bird cage, an iron perch to which parrots are chained; a police station in the country; a fixed place for unemployed pálkí bearers and qúlís.
Ádá, *s. m.* ginger in the undried state.
Adá, *s. f.* performance, payment.
Adab, *s. m.* politeness, civility, courtesy, urbanity, rule.
Ádáb, *s. m.* (*plur.* of adab), ceremonies, politeness, civilities, institutes, rules.
Adab bajáláná, to pay one's respects, to behave courteously.
Adab karná, to respect, to behave politely.
Ạdad, *s. m.* number.
Adá honá, to be performed, to be discharged, (a debt, &c.)
Adáí, *s. f.* performance, payment.
Adá karná, to perform, to discharge (a debt), to pay.
Ạdálat, *s. f.* a court of justice, justice, law, equity.
Ádam, *n. prop.* Adam, the first man; man.
Ádamkhor, *adj.* a cannibal.
Ádamzád, *s. m. f.* man, mankind.
Ạdan, *s. f.* Eden, paradise.
Ádar, *s. m.* respect, veneration, esteem.
Ádarmán, *s. m.* respect and honour.
Adarsá, *s. m.* a sweetmeat.
Ạdat, *s. f.* habit, custom, usage.
Ạdat karná, to adopt a habit, to introduce a custom, to accustom.
Ạdáwat, *s. f.* enmity, hatred, strife, spite.
Adh, Ádh, } in *compos.* half.
Addhí, *s. f.* half a damṛí.
Ádhá, *adj.* half: in *compos.* it becomes ádh, or adh, or ad.
Adham, *adj.* inferior, low, vile, despicable.
Adhan, *s. m.* boiling water.
Adhangí, *adj.* palsied, paralytic.
Ádhár, *s. m.* food, aliment, victuals.
Adhar, *s. m.* the lower lip; the space between heaven and earth.
Adharm, *s. m.* injustice, irreligion, impiety, sin.
Adharmí, *adj.* unjust, sinful, criminal, immoral.
Adharmpaná, *s. m.* injustice, crime.
Adharsá, *s. m.* name of a sort of cloth.
Adhásísí, *s. f.* pain affecting the half of the head, hemicrania.
Adhauṛí, *s. f.* half of a hide (of a thick strong kind.)
Adhelá, *s. m.* half a paisá.
Adhelí, *s. f.* half a rupee.
Ad-heṛ, *adj.* middle-aged, just past the prime of life.
Adhik, *adj.* exceeding, greater, more, additional, extra.
Adhikáí, *s. f.* increase, augmentation, abundance, excess.
Adhikár, *s. m.* possession, right, dominion.
Adhikárí, *adj.* possessor of a right, title or privilege.

Adhín, } *adj.* obedient, dependent,
Ādhín, } submissive, humble, docile, subject.

Adhínatá, } *s. f.* submission, obedi-
Ādhínatá, } ence, servility, humility.

Adhíní, *s. f.* submission, humbleness.

Adhíraj, *s. m.* confusedness, unsteadiness: *adj.* unsteady, impatient.

Ādhírát, *s. f.* midnight.

Adhkachchá, *adj.* half-ripe, half-dressed.

Adhkahá, *adj.* half-spoken, half-uttered.

Adhkapálí, } *s. f.* a pain affecting
Adhkapárí, } half the head, hemicrania.

Adhmúá, *adj.* half-dead.

Adhotar, *s. f.* a thin kind of cloth.

Adhpakká, *adj.* half-ripe, half-cooked.

Adhúrá, *adj.* unfinished, half-ready.

Adhwáṛ, *s. f.* a half (generally applied to pieces of cloth.)

Adhyáná, *v. a.* to halve, to divide.

Ādi, *adj.* first, prior: in *compos.* other, etcetera.

Adíb, *s. m.* a teacher of polite manners, urbanity, &c.

Ạdil, *adj.* just, equitable, righteous.

Ādhkhilá, *adj.* half-blown, (a flower, &c.)

Adkhulá, *adj.* half-open.

Ạdl, *s. m.* justice, equity.

Ādlá badlá, *s. m.* exchange, alteration.

Adlá badlá karná, } to exchange, to
Adlá badlí karná, } swop or barter.

Adl badl, *s. m.* exchange, alteration.

Adlí badlí karní, *v.* to exchange, to swop or barter.

Admará, *adj.* half-dead.

Ādmí, *s. m. f.* a human being (man or woman), an individual.

Ādmíyat, *s. f.* humanity, civility, good breeding.

Ādmíyat meṉ láná, to civilize.

Ādmíyat pakaṛní, to become civilized.

Ādmíyat sikhláni, to civilize.

Admúá, *adj.* half-dead.

Adná, *adj.* inferior, lowest; a person of no consequence.

Adrak, *s. f.* ginger in an undried state.

Adrakí, *s. f.* a kind of sweetmeat.

Adrishya, *adj.* invisible.

Adwait, *adj.* unique, alone.

Adwán, } *s. f.* braces for tighten-
Adwáyan, } ing the cords of a chárpáí.

Āfat, *s. f.* calamity, misfortune.

Afghán, *n. prop.* a people, called also Paṭháns.

Afím, *s. f.* opium.

Afíman, *f.* }
Afímchí, *m.* } *adj.* an opium-eater; *fig.* a sot.
Afímí, *m.* }

Aflák, *s.* (*plur.* of falak), the heavens, heavenly bodies.

Aflátún, *n. prop.* Plato.

Āfrín, *s. f.* praise: *interj.* bravo! well done!

Āfrínish, *s. f.* creation.

Āfrín karná, *v. a.* to praise, to applaud.

Afsána, *s. m.* a fable, a story.

Afshán, in *compos.* scattering, strewing, shedding, &c.

Afshání kághaz, sprinkled (with gold, &c.) paper.

Afsos, *s. m.* sorrow, concern, vexation, a pity: *interj.* ah! alas!

Afsún, *s. m.* incantation, a spell.

Āftáb, *s. m.* the sun.

Āftába, *s. m.* a kind of ewer.

Āftábparast, *s.* a worshipper of the sun.

Āftábparastí, *s. f.* worship of the sun.

Ạfú, *s. m.* absolution, forgiveness.

Āfwáh, *s. f.* doubtful news; fame, report.

Afzá, in *compos.* increasing.

Afzáish, *s. f.* increase.

Afzal, *adj. compar.* more or most excellent.
Afzúd, *adj.* increasing, more.
Ág, *s. f.* fire, passion.
Ágá, *s. m.* the front, the forepart.
Agádh, *adj.* unfathomable, deep.
Ágáh, *adj.* informed of, acquainted with, aware.
Ágáhí, *s. f.* information, intelligence, vigilance.
Agal, *adv.* before.
Agalbagal rakhná, to put one side.
Agal jáná, to go out of the way.
Agam, *adj.* impassable, unfathomable, bottomless.
Ágam, *s. m.* futurity.
Ágambidyá, *s. f.* the art or science of foretelling or divining.
Ágamgnyání, *s. m.* a prognosticator.
Aganit, *adj.* innumerable.
Ágá píchhá karná, *v. n.* to hesitate, to waver.
Agar, *s. m.* wood of aloes.
Agar, *conj.* if.
Agaráná, *v. n.* to be conceited, to give one's self airs.
Agaŗ bagaŗ, *s. m.* trifling employment or talk, trumpery, trash
Agarchi, *conj.* although, though.
Agáŗí, *adv.* before, in front, further on: *s. f.* the ropes with which a horse's forefeet are tied.
Agáŗí pichháŗí lagáná, to confine a horse.
Agarwálá, *s. m.* a cast of merchants of the Vaisya tribe.
Agáú jáná, to go to meet a person.
Agauní, *s. f.* the going or sending forward to meet and receive a visitant with honour.
Ág barasná, *v. n.* to rain fire (applied to the extreme heat of the sun, &c.)
Ág dená, *v. a.* to burn a Hindú corpse.
Áge, *adv.* before, in front, beyond, formerly, onwards, hence, forwards, in future.
Age, *interj.* voc. O! used to a female.
Áge dhar lená, to get before, to outstrip, to surpass.
Áge jáná, to go before.
Áge láná, to bring forward.
Aggyá, } Ággyá, } *s. f.* command, order, permission.
Aggyákárí, *adj.* obedient.
Ághá, *s. m.* lord, chief, master.
Aghan, *s. m.* the eighth Hindú month.
Agháná, *v. n.* to be satiated.
Aghárí, *adj.* greedy.
Agház, *s. m.* beginning, commencement.
Aghlab, *adv.* most likely, probably.
Ág honá, *s.* to get into a passion.
Aghorí, *s. m.* See Aghorpanthí.
Aghorpanth, *s. m.* a particular religious order among Hindús.
Aghorpanthí, *s. m.* a faqír who eats everything however filthy, even human carcases.
Agin, *s. m.* name of a bird, a kind of lark.
Aginboţ, *s.* a steamer.
Aglá, *adj.* prior, first, former; ancestor; other, next.
Ág lagáná, *v. a.* to set on fire, to inflame; to enrage.
Ág lagná, *v. n.* to be enraged, to be hungry.
Ág men pání ḍálná, to extinguish a fire; to appease a tumult.
Agní, *s. f.* fire.
Agoriyá, *s. m.* a watchman.
Agorná, *v. a.* to watch.
Agŗam bagŗam, *s. m.* odds and ends, trash.
Ág sulgáná, *v. a.* to blow up a fire.
Agú, *adj.* forward: *adv.* before, heretofore.
Agúá, *s. m.* a guide, one who adjusts a marriage.
Agúá jáná, to go to meet a person.
Ág uţháná, *v. a.* to enrage.
Agwá, *s. m.* a guide, a forerunner, harbinger.

Agwáhí, *s. f.* conflagration.
Agwái, *s. f.* guidance.
Agwáṛá, *s. m.* the front, the forepart, the space in the front of a house.
Agyán, } *adj.* witless, ignorant; a
Agyání, } simpleton.
Agyánpan, *s. m.* ignorance, foolishness, stupidity.
Agyárí, *s. f.* kindling the fire by Hindús at the time of worshipping.
Áh, *s. f.* a sigh: *interj.* alas!
Aháháhá, *interj.* expressive of surprize, pain, pleasure, &c. Ah! aha!
Áhan, *s. m.* a mixture of straw and earth for building walls.
Áhaní, *adj.* of iron, made of iron.
Ahankár, *s. m.* pride, haughtiness, conceit.
Ahankárí, *adj.* haughty, arrogant, proud, an egotist.
Ahár, *s. m.* aliment, food, victuals; starch.
Áhaṭ, *s. m.* sound, noise.
Áh bharná, *v. n.* to sigh, to sob.
Ạhd, *s. m. f.* contract, compact, promise, treaty; time.
Ạhdnáma, *s. m.* contract, an agreement in writing.
Ahe, *interj.* voc. O! holla.
Aher, *s. f.* prey, game, the chase, hunting.
Aherí, } *s. m.* a sportsman, a
Aheriyá, } hunter.
Ahír, *s. m.* a cowherd, a caste whose business it is to attend on cows.
Ahírí, *s. f.* a female of the Ahír caste.
Áhista, *adv.* gently, slowly, softly, tenderly.
Áhistagí, *s. f.* gentleness, softness, slowness.
Áhiste, } *adv.* gently, softly.
Áhiste áhiste, }
Ahkám, *s.* (*plur.* of hukm), orders, commands, decrees.

Ahl, *s. m.* people: *adj.* fit, capable, worthy: in *compos.* possessed of, endowed with.
Ahl i ạql, wise.
Ahl i ilm, scientific.
Ahl i kár, a workman, a clerk.
Ahl i kitáb, a learned man, a person of any religion revealed and contained in books.
Ahl i sharạ, a legislator, a lawyer, one who observes the law of Muhammad.
Ahmaq, *adj.* very or most foolish, fool, blackhead.
Ahmaqána, *adv.* foolishly, stupidly.
Ahmaqí, *s. f.* } folly, stupidity.
Ahmaqpan, *s. m.* }
Áh márná, *v. n.* to groan, to sigh.
Aho, *m. interj.* voc. O! holla!
Ahra, *s. m.* a reservoir for collecting rain water to water the fields.
Áhut, *s. m.* incense used in burnt-offerings.
Ahwál, *s. m.* condition, circumstances, events, state.
Ahwál batláná, to state one's condition.
Ahwál púchhná, to inquire after health, &c.
Ai, *interj.* O! used in calling to or addressing.
Ạib, *s. m.* fault, defect, a vice, blemish.
Ạibgírí, *s. f.* finding fault.
Ạibí, *adj.* faulty.
Ạib lagáná, to defame, to slander.
Áigun, *s. m.* defect, blemish, vice.
Ạin, *adj.* the very, exact, intrinsic, real.
Áín, *s. m.* regulation, institute, common law.
Áína, *s. m.* a mirror, a looking-glass.
Ạinak, *s. f.* spectacles, glasses to assist the sight.
Ainchná, *v. a.* to draw, to attract.
Ainí baini karná, to do eye-service.
Ainṭh, *s. f.* twisting, tightening, twist, coil.

Ainṭhná, *v. a.* to tighten : *v. n.* to writhe, to cramp, to twist; to strut.
A̤in waqat, the exact time.
Aisá, *adj.* such, this-like, so; resembling, like.
Aisá waisá, *adj.* of little moment, middling.
Aise, *adv.* thus.
Aise meṉ, in the mean time.
A̤ish, *s. m.* pleasure, delight.
A̤ish o a̤shrat, *s. f.* pleasure, luxury, profligacy.
Ais jais, *s.* profligacy, voluptuousness.
Aisoṉ, *adv.* this year.
Aiswarj, *s. m.* glory, splendour.
Aiyám, *s. m.* season, weather.
A̤iyár, *adj.* cunning, sly.
A̤iyásh, *adj.* luxurious.
A̤iyáshí, *s. f.* luxury, profligacy.
Ãj, *adv.* to-day.
Ãjá, *s. m.* a paternal grandfather.
A̤jab, } *adj.* rare, wonderful,
A̤jab tarah, } strange.
A̤jáib, } *s.* (*plur.* of a̤jíb), wonders,
A̤jáibát, } curiosities.
A̤jáib o gharáib, wonders, curiosities, strange things.
Ajal, *s. f.* a natural death.
Aján, *adj.* ignorant, simple.
Ãjáná, *v. n.* to come suddenly, to befall, to happen, to come unawares.
Ajas, *adj.* infamous, disreputable.
Aját, *adj.* expelled from his caste (a man.)
Ajdád, *s.* (*plur.* of jadd), ancestors.
Ajgar, *s. m.* a large serpent, the boa constrictor.
Ajgut, *adj.* extraordinary, surprising.
Aj-hú, *adv.* yet, immediately.
Aj-húṉ, *adv.* yet, hitherto, this very day.
Ají, *an interjection* to call or bespeak attention.
A̤jíb, *adj.* wonderful, astonishing, rare.

Ajíran, *s. m.* indigestion.
Ajít, *adj.* invincible.
Ã̤jíz, *adj.* impotent, weak, exhausted, helpless.
Ã̤jizí, *s. f.* weakness, humility, hopelessness.
Ãj ke din, } to-day.
Ãj ke roz, }
Ãjkal, *adv.* now-a-days, in a few days.
Ãjkal batáná, } to procrastinate.
Ãjkal karná, }
Ãj kí rát, to-night.
Ajnabí, *adj.* foreign, strange, unknown (person.)
Ajnás, *s.* (*plur.* of jins), kinds, sorts, species.
Ajogya, *adj.* improper, unbecoming.
Ajoṛ, *adj.* without joining.
Ãjr, *s. m.* retribution, hire, fare.
Ajúra, *s. m.* hire, rent, wages, fare.
Ajúradár, *s. m.* a labourer for hire.
Ajwáyan, *s. f.* the seed of a plant of the dill kind.
A̤jz, *s. m.* weakness, wretchedness.
Ãkál, } *s. m.* famine, scarcity, pinch.
Akál, }
Ãkár, *s. m.* form, shape.
Akaṛ, *s. f.* crookedness; strut.
Akárath, *adj.* profitless, in vain.
Akárath, or Akárthe marná, *v. n.* to die by accident.
Akaṛbáí, *s. f.* the cramp.
Akaṛbáz, *s. m.* an affected person, a fop.
Akaṛbází, *s. f.* swaggering, strutting.
Akarm, *s. m.* bad action, sin, vice, wickedness.
Akarmak, *adj.* intransitive, (a verb.)
Akarmí, *adj.* wretch, unprincipled.
Akaṛná, *v. n.* to writhe, to ache, to be cramped, to strut.
Akás, } *s. m.* the sky, the atmo-
Ãkás, } sphere, the heavens, firmament, space.
Ãkásbání, *s. f.* a voice from heaven.
Ãkásdiyá, *s. m.* a lamp raised in the air by the Hindús in the month of Kártik.

Akasmát, *adv.* immediately, suddenly.
Akbar, *adj.* greater, very great, greatest.
Akelá, *adj.* alone, single, solitary.
Akhá, *s. m.* a bag in which grain is carried on bullocks.
Akháṛá, *s. m.* a place for wrestling.
Akhbár, *s.* (*plur.* of khabar), news, a newspaper.
Ákhír, *s. m.* the end, completion.
Ákhir, *adj.* last, latter: *s. m.* end, issue: *adv.* at last, finally.
Ákhirash, *adv.* at the end of it, finally, after all.
Ákhirat, *s. f.* futurity, a future state.
Ákhirí, *adj.* last, final.
Akhláq, *s.* (*plur.* of khulq), virtues.
Ákhor, *s. f.* refuse, offal, filth.
Akhroṭ, *s. m.* a walnut.
Ákhta, Akhta, } *adj.* a gelding.
Akhta murgh, *s. m.* a capon.
Aks, *s. m.* the contrary, opposite; spite, opposition.
Aksar, *adv.* generally, for the most part, usually, often.
Aksar auqát, at most times, generally, frequently.
Akuláná, *v. n.* to be agitated, to be confused, to be distracted.
Akwand, *s. m.* the swallow wort.
Akwár, *s. f.* embrace.
Akwár bheṭ, *s. f.* meeting and embracing.
Ál, prop. Yál, *s. f.* a horse's mane; the name of a tree from which a red colour is extracted.
Alá, *adv.* above, on, upon.
Alag, *adj.* separate, apart, distinct.
Alag alag, *adv.* separately.
Alag karná, to separate.
Aláhidá, *adj.* or *adv.* separate, apart, distinct.
Alaihi, on him.
Alaihim, on them.
Alaihis salám, blessing on him.
Áláish, *s. f.* pollution, contamination, filth.
Alakh, *adj.* invisible, unseen.
Álam, *s. m.* the world, universe, concourse.
Alam, *s. m.* colours, standard.
Alambardár, *s. m.* standard-bearer.
Alamán, *s. m.* a German.
Alámat, *s. f.* a mark, a sign, symptom.
Álan, *s.* straw, &c. mixed in earth for building.
Álán, *s. m.* the brushwood used for creepers to run on.
Alang, *s. f.* side, way, quarter.
Aláo, *s. m.* a bonfire.
Álápna, *v. a.* to pitch the voice, to sing.
Álas, *s. m.* laziness, slowth, drowsiness.
Álasyí, *adj.* drowsy, slothful.
Aláwa, *adv.* besides, in addition.
Álaya, *s. m.* an affix signifying the abode of; as, Himálaya, the abode of snow.
Albatta, *adv.* certainly, indeed, verily.
Albelá, *adj.* a simpleton.
Albelpaná, *s. m.* a piece of folly, foolishness.
Alfáz, *s. m.* (*plur.* of lafz), words, articulate sounds, terms.
Alfin, *s. m.* a pin.
Algáí, *s. f.* separation.
Algáná, *v. a.* to separate, to put on one side.
Alganí, *s. f.* a line for hanging clothes on.
Algharaz, *adv.* in short, upon the whole, in a word.
Algojá, *s. m.* a whistle, pipe, flageolet.
Alhamdu lilláhi, God be praised.
Alhaṛ, *adj.* young, untaught, unskilful.
Alí, a proper name, Muhammad's son-in-law.
Alif be, *s. f.* the alphabet.
Alíl, *adj.* indisposed, weak, sick.
Álim, *adj.* learned, knowing.
Alláh, *s. m.* God.

Alláh alláh! an interjection expressive of surprise and approbation.
Alláhu akbar, God is great.
Alláh re, O God! my God!
Allam ghallam, *s. m.* random, &c.
Almás, *s. m.* a diamond.
Almásí, *adj.* cut into facets (like a diamond.)
Almásí rang, *s. m.* a bright clear white colour.
Al o atfál, *s. f.* family.
Alol kalol, *s. f.* gambols, playsomeness, wantonness.
Aloná, *adj.* not salt, fresh, insipid.
Alop honá, *v. n.* to disappear, to vanish.
Ālpin, *s. m.* a pin.
Alqissa, *adv.* in short, in a word.
Alsáná, *v. n.* to be drowsy, to be lazy.
Alsí, *s. f.* linseed.
Ālú, *s. m.* an esculent root, a potato.
Ālú, Buḳhárá, *s. m.* a kind of plum.
Ālúda, *adj.* defiled, foul, smeared; covered.
Ām, *s. m.* the mango fruit; the mango tree.
Āmad, *s. f.* arrival, income, coming.
Āmad o raft, }
Āmad o shud, }
Āmad raft, }
Āmad shud, } *s. f.* coming and going, access and egress, intercourse.
Amal, *s. m.* intoxication.
Ạmal, *s. m.* action, work, practice, use.
Ạmala, }
Ạmala fáil, } the native officers in civil courts.
Ạmaldár, *s. m.* a native subaltern, an officer in the army.
Ạmaldárí, *s. f.* the business of an ạmaldár.
Ạmalí, *adj.* artificial, practical.
Ȧmán, *s. f.* safety, security, protection, quarter.
Amáná, *v. n.* to be contained, to go in.
Amánat, *s. f.* deposit, any thing given in trust.
Amánatdár, *s. m.* a trustee.
Amánatdárí, *s. f.* guardianship, agency, trust.
Amánya, *adj.* undeserving of credit.
Amar, *adj.* immortal, deathless, everlasting.
Amarpad, *s. m.* the state of an immortal, immortality.
Amáwas, *s. f.* the day of the new moon.
Amáwaṭ, *s, m.* the inspissated juice of the mango.
Ạmber, *s. m.* ambergris.
Ạmbarí, *adj.* odour of ambergris.
Ȧmbárí, *s. f.* a covered litter for an elephant.
Ambiyá, *s. f.* a small unripe mango: *s.* (*plur.* of nabí), prophets.
Amboh, *s. m.* a crowd, multitude, mob, concourse.
Amchúr, *s. m.* parings of the mango dried in the sun.
Ạmdan, *adv.* purposely, designedly.
Āmdaní, *s. f.* import, income, revenue.
Āmez, in *compos.* mixed, mixing.
Āmezish, *s. f.* mixture, intercourse.
Āmín, *adj.* amen, so be it.
Amín, *s. m.* a commissioner, a trustree, an overseer and investigator, a superintendent.
Amíní, *s. f.* the office of a commissioner, overseer, &c.
Ạmíq, *adj.* deep, profound.
Ȧmír *s. m.* a nobleman, a grandee, a person of eminence.
Amírána, *adj.* princely, lordly.
Amírí, *s. f.* nobility, greatness, sway, lordship.
Amírzáda, nobly born.
Amiṭ, *adj.* indelible.
Ạml karná, to act, to operate.
Ȧmmá, *s. f.* mother.
Amn, *s. m.* security, safety.
Āmná sámná, *s. m.* confronting.
Āmne sámne, *adv.* opposite, face to face.
Amr, *s. m.* the imperative mood in grammar; an affair, a transaction.

Amṛá, *s. m.* the hog-plum.
Amrit, *s. m.* nectar.
Amrúd, *s. m.* a guava.
An, a prefix of negation, privation, or diminution.
Ăn, *adj.* other, another.
Ăná, *v. n.* to come: *s. m.* the sixteenth part of a rupee, or generally a sixteenth part.
Anádar, *s. m.* disrespect, affront.
Anádi, *adj.* without beginning, eternal.
Anáj, *s. m.* grain, corn.
Ănákání, *s. f.* turning a deaf ear.
Ănákání karná, to overlook, to turn a deaf ear, to connive at.
Ănand, *s. m. f.* happiness, joy, ease.
Ănandit, *adj.* joyful, glad.
Anannás, *s. m.* a pine-apple.
Anannásí, *adj.* made like a pine-apple.
Anant, *adj.* boundless, endless: *s. m.* a cord with fourteen knots which the Hindús tie on the arm on the fourteenth day of Bhádoṉ.
Anár, *s. m.* a pomegranate; a kind of fire-works.
Anárí, } **Anáṛí**, } *adj.* unskilful, clumsy, inexpert.
Anárpan, *s. m.* unskilfulness, clumsiness, ignorance.
Anarth, *adj.* absurd, improper.
Anáth, *adj.* husbandless, destitute, forlorn, orphan.
Anbiyáhá, *adj.* unmarried.
Ănch, *s. f.* heat, flame of a fire (not of a candle.)
Anchal, } **Ănchal**, } *s. m.* the end or border of a cloth, veil, shawl, &c.
Anchit, *adv.* unawares, suddenly.
Anchlá, *s. m.* see Anchal.
Anḍá, *s. m.* an egg.
Anḍá dená, to lay an egg.
Anḍaj, *adj.* oviparous.
Andar, *prep.* within, in the inside.
Andarsá, *s. m.* a kind of fried sweetmeat.
Anḍá, sewná, to incubate.
Andáz, *s. m.* measure, weighing, conjecture, guess. In *compos.* throwing.
Andáza, *s. m.* measure, valuation, guess.
Andekhá, *adj.* unseen, invisible.
Anḍel, *adj.* oviparous; with egg (a bird.)
Andesha, *s. m.* thought, concern, care.
Andesha karná, to reflect, to hesitate, to fear.
Andhá, *adj.* blind, dark.
Andhá dhund luṭáná, to squander, to spend extravagantly.
Andhá kúá, *s. m.* a dry well.
Andhan, *s. m.* wealth in both grain and specie.
Andher, *s. m.* injustice, violence.
Andherá, *adj.* dark: *s. m.* darkness.
Ăndhí, *s. f.* storm, gale, tempest.
Andhkár, *s. m.* darkness.
Andhlá, *adj.* blind.
Andhlápan, *s. m.* blindness; intellectual blindness.
Andhoá, *adj.* unwashed, unclean.
Andhyárá, *adj.* dark, blind: *s. m.* darkness.
Anek, *adj.* many, much, abundant.
Ang, *s. m.* the body, a limb, a member.
Angá, *s. m.* a coat, a kind of spencer.
Ăngan, *s. m.* a court-yard.
Angárá, *s. m.* embers, a firebrand.
Angaṛhá, *adj.* unformed, unwrought.
Angarkhá, *s. m.* a kind of jacket.
Angeṭhí, *s. f.* a chafing-dish.
Angez, in *compos.* exciting.
Angíkár, *s. m.* an agreement, a promise, acceptance of a proposal.
Anginá, } **Angint**, } **Angintí**, } *adj.* numberless, innumerable.
Angiyá, *s. f.* bodice, stays.

Angná, *s. m.* } a court-yard.
Angnái, *s. f.* }

Angochhá, *s. m.* a cloth with which Hindús wipe themselves after bathing; a towel.

Angṛái, *s. f.* stretching the limbs, a yawning.

Angṛáná, *v. n.* to stretch the limbs, to yawn.

Angrezí, *adj.* English, the English language.

Angul, *s. m.* a finger's breadth.

Angulí, *s. f.* a finger or toe.

Angúr, *s. m.* a grape; granulations in a healing sore.

Angúrí, *adj.* of or relating to the grape.

Angurí, } *s. f.* a finger.
Angusht, }

Angushtnumá, one who is pointed at.

Angushtána, *s. m.* a thimble, a ring.

Angúṭhá, *s. m.* the thumb,

Angúṭhí, *s. f.* a ring worn on the finger.

Anhoná, *adj.* impossible, not to be.

Anhwáná, *v. a.* to cause to be bathed.

Aní, *s. f.* the point or edge of any thing sharp.

Aníti, *s. f.* unmannerliness, rudeness, injustice, impropriety.

Anjalí, *s. f.* the cavity formed by putting the two hands together.

Anjám, *s. m.* end, termination.

Anjan, *s. m.* a collyrium or application to the eyelids when inflamed, or to improve them.

Anján, *adj.* unwitting, unintentional: *s.* a stranger.

Anjáná, *adj.* unknown, ignorant.

Anjáne, *a.* } *adv.* ignorantly, unwittingly.
Anján se, }

Anjír, *s. m.* a fig.

Ank, } *s. m.* figure, number, mark on cloth to show the price.
Ảnk, }

Ảnkh, *s. f.* the eye.

Ảnkh ání, to be blear-eyed, to have an inflammation in the eyes.

Ảnkh bacháná, to steal away privately and unseen.

Ảnkh badalná, to withdraw one's favour or affection from any one.

Ảnkh band kar lení, to turn from another; to die.

Ảnkh bharke dekhná, to look till one's curiosity is fully satisfied.

Ảnkh bhar láná, to be ready to cry.

Ảnkh chír chír dekhná, } to look with great attention and deep meditation, or with anger.
Ảnkh chírke dekhná, }

Ảnkh churání, to avert the eyes through shame, to avoid the sight of any one.

Ảnkh ḍabḍabáná, to be in tears.

Ảnkh dikhlání, to frighten, to browbeat.

Ảnkh ghurakná, to look at with anger.

Ảnkh lagání, to fall in love, to contract friendship for any one.

Ảnkh mární, to wink.

Ảnkh michaulí, *s. f.* } blindman's buff.
Ảnkh michauwal, *s. m.* }

Ảnkhon men charbí chháná, to be wilfully blind, to pretend from pride not to know one's old acquaintance.

Ảnkhon men ḳhák ḍální, to commend or puff wares of an inferior quality; to pilfer and snatch away anything quickly and privately.

Ảnkhon men kharakná, to be seen with envy and dislike.

Ảnkh pasárná, to open one's eyes, to stare.

Ảnkh pher lená, to turn away the eyes (as from grief, displeasure, &c.)

Ạnkh phoṛá, *s. m.* a midge said to fly in the eyes.

Ảnkh phoṛní, to make blind.

Aukná, *v. n.* to be valued, to be prized, to be marked.

Ánkná, *v. a.* to value, to prize, to mark (the price on cloth.)

Ankṛsí, *s. f.* a hook, tenter.

Ankur, } *s. m.* a sprout.
Ankúrá, }

Ankus, *s. m.* the hook or iron with which elephants are driven.

Ankwár, *s. f.* embrace.

Anmel, *adj.* discordant, heterogeneous.

Anmol, *adj.* invaluable, beyond price.

Ann, *s. m.* food, victuals, grain.

Ánná, *v. a.* to bring.

Anní, *s. f.* a nurse for a child.

Annjal, } *s. m.* victuals and
Annpání, } drink.

Anokhá, *adj.* rare, uncommon, wonderful.

Anpaṛhá, *adj.* illiterate, uninformed.

Án paṛná, *v. n.* to happen, to come suddenly.

Anqabút, *s. f.* a spider.

Anqaríb, *adv.* near, soon, shortly, nearly.

Anrít, *s. f.* unmannerliness, ill behaviour.

Ans, *s. m.* part, division, share.

Ansamjhá, *adj.* not understood, not knowing.

Ansamjh karná, to pretend not to understand.

Ansdhárí, *adj.* becoming incarnate.

Áṉsú, *s. m.* a tear.

Ansuná, *adj.* unheard.

Ansuní karná, to pretend not to hear.

Ant, *s. m.* end, completion: *adv.* after all, at last.

Ánt, *s. f.* entrails, gut, tripe.

Anṭá, *s. m.* a ball, a marble.

Anṭachit honá, to trip up, to fall down.

Anṭaghar, *s. m.* a billiard-room.

Antakaran, *s. m.* the understanding.

Antarbed, *n. prop.* name of the country between the Gangá and Jamuná rivers.

Antardhyán, out of sight, vanished, disappeared.

Antaríchh, *s. m.* vanishing.

Antaríchh ho jáná, to vanish.

Antarjámí, *adj.* knowing the heart.

Ánṭhí, *s. f.* stone of fruit.

Ánṭí, *s. f.* a skein of thread, a bundle of grass, &c., a small faggot.

Antkál, *s. m.* dying moment, hour of death.

Anṭná, *v. n.* to be contained.

Antṛí, *s. f.* entrails, intestine, bowels, gut.

Antṛiyáṉ jalná, } to be very
Antṛiyoṉ meṉ ág lagná, } hungry.

Anṭwáná, *v. a.* to make contain.

Anuchit, *adj.* improper.

Anugrah, *s. m.* favour, grace, kindness.

Anúp, *adj.* incomparable.

Anúṭhá, *adj.* rare, wonderful, uncommon.

Áṉw, *s. m.* the glutinous whitish matter or mucus voided by people afflicted with a tenesmus.

Áṉw girná, *v. n.* to void white glutinous stools.

Anyáe, } *s. m.* injustice, oppres-
Anyáya, } sion.

Anyáyí, *adj.* unjust, oppressive.

Áp, *pron.* self, selves, yourself, you sir, used respectfully and politely instead of the second personal pronoun.

Apáhaj, *adj.* cripple.

Apajas, *s. m.* ignominy, dishonour.

Apajasí, *adj.* ignominious.

Apamán, *s. m.* contempt, disrespect.

Ápan, *pron. recip.* self.

Apár, *adj.* boundless, excessive.

Aparádh, *s. m.* transgression, crime.

Aparádhí, *s. m.* } a criminal, sinner,
Aparádhin, *s. f.* } offender.

Aparampár, *adj.* boundless, infinite.

Ápas, *pron. recip.* themselves, one another.

Ápas meṉ, mutually, among ourselves, themselves, &c.

Apavitr, *adj.* unclean, defiled, impure.

Apavitratá, *s. f.* uncleanness, defilement, impurity.

Apharná, *v. n.* to gormandize.

Áp'hí, } *adv.* spontaneously.
Áp'hí áp, }

Aphím, *s. f.* opium.

Ápkáj, } *adj.* attending to one's own
Ápkájí, } business, engaged in one's own affairs.

Apná, *pron. poss.* of or belonging to self, own.

Apnáná, *v. a.* to make a thing one's own, to convert to one's own use.

Apnáyat, *s. f.* family relations, kindred.

Apramán, *adj.* without proof, untrue.

Áprúp, *s. m.* and *adj.* self, self-formed, the Deity.

Áp se, } *adv.* spontaneously.
Áp se áp, }

Ápswárth, *s. m.* selfishness.

Ápswárthí, *adj.* selfish, seeking the interest of self.

Áqá, *s. m.* master, owner.

Ạqab, *adv.* behind, after: *s. m.* the rear.

Ạqd, *s. m.* a knot; a marriage-compact, agreement.

Ạqibat, *s. f.* the end, future state.

Ạqibatandesh, *adj.* prudent, looking into futurity.

Ạ́qil, *adj.* wise, sensible: *s. m.* a sage.

Ạql, *s. f.* reason, intellect, sense, wisdom.

Ạqlan, *adv.* reasonably.

Ạql dauṛáná, to speculate, to think.

Ạqlí, *adj.* reasonable, of or relating to intellect.

Ạqlmand, *adj.* sensible, intellectual, wise.

Ạqlmandí, *s. f.* sense, intelligence.

Aqsám, *s. f.* (*plur.* of qism), sorts, kinds.

Áṛ, *s. f.* a skreen, shelter, protection, stop, hindrance.

Ạr, *s. m.* shame, modesty.

Aṛ, *s. f.* contention, contrariety, obstinacy.

Áṛá, *adj.* oblique, crooked, across.

Árá, *s. m.* a saw; the name of a district.

Ạrab, *s. m.* Arabia; an Arabian horse.

Ạrabí, *adj.* Arabian, Arabic; the Arabic (language), an Arab (horse.)

Árádhná, *v. a.* to celebrate the praises of God.

Áráish, *s. f.* embellishment.

Arajná, *v. a.* to earn, to acquire.

Árákash, *s. m.* a sawyer.

Árám, *s. m.* ease, rest, relief, repose, comfort.

Árambh, *s. m.* beginning, prologue.

Árámgáh, *s. f.* a resting-place; a bed-chamber.

Árámí, *adj.* a lover of ease; idle, slothful.

Árám karná, *v. n.* to rest, to repose.

Árám páná, *v. n.* to recover.

Aṛang, *s. f.* a depôt.

Ạraq, *s. m.* juice, essence, spirit, sap, sweat.

Aṛáṛá, *s. m.* high steep banks of a river.

Árásta, *adj.* prepared, dressed, adorned, embellished, decked out.

Árástagí, *s. f.* preparation, decoration, arrangement.

Árbal, *s. f.* age.

Aṛbaṛ, *s. m.* unmeaning words, &c.; rugged, uneven.

Aṛbaṛ bakná, *v. a.* to talk nonsensically, to rave.

Ardalí, from orderly, *s. f.* the persons who run before the pálkí, &c. of a rich man.

Ardáwá, *s. m.* coarsely ground meal, made of parched barley and other grain.

Ardháng, *s. m.* half the body; hemiplegia.

Ardhángí, *adj.* one afflicted with hemiplegia.

Are, *m.* interjection used in calling to or addressing, commonly in a disrespectful way, Holla! ho! O! hear you!

Arganí, *s. f.* a line for hanging clothes on to dry.

Arghá, *s. m.* a vessel used by the Hindús for performing libations in their devotions.

Argh dená, to pour out water to the sun.

Aṛhái, two and half; or when used with a noun of number, twice and half the aggregate number.

Aṛhaiyá, *s. m.* a weight of two and a half sers, a measure containing two and a half sers.

Arhar, *s. f.* a species of pulse.

Áṛhat, *s. f.* sale by commission, commission.

Áṛhatiyá, *s. m.* a broker, one who sells on commission.

Árí, *s. f.* a small saw, a hand-saw.

Arí, *interj. f.* see Are.

Ạriyat, *s. f.* a loan, anything borrowed.

Ạriyatí, *adj.* borrowed, assumed.

Arjan, *s. m.* gain, earning.

Arkáṭí, *s. m.* a pilot.

Arman, *n. prop.* Armenia.

Armaní, *adj.* Armenian.

Aṛná, *v. n.* to stop, to be restive or halt (as a horse.)

Arná, *s. m.* a wild buffalo.

Arní, *s. f.* a female wild buffalo.

Aṛos paṛos, *s. m.* neighbourhood.

Aṛosí paṛosí, *s.* neighbour.

Arpan, *s. m.* an offering.

Ạrsa, *s. m.* a space of time, period, interval.

Aṛsaṭh, *adj.* sixty-eight.

Ạrsh, *s. m.* a throne; the ninth heaven.

Ársí, *s. f.* a mirror (particularly one worn on the thumb.)

Ártá, *s. m.* a ceremony attending marriage.

Arspars, *s. m.* touching.

Aṛtálá, *s. m.* screen, shelter, a covert.

Aṛtális, *adj.* forty-eight.

Arth, *s. m.* intention, object, meaning.

Arthát, *adv.* namely, that is to say, videlicet.

Ártí, *s. f.* a ceremony performed with a lamp in adoration of the gods.

Aṛtís, *adj.* thirty-eight.

Aru, *conj.* and; more, again.

Ạrús, *s. f.* bride.

Ârwáh, *s.* (*plur.* of rúh), spirits, soul.

Arwí, *s. f.* a vegetable, the root of which is used in food.

Ạrz, *s. f.* a petition, request, representation; breadth, latitude.

Arzán, *adj.* cheap.

Arzání, *s. f.* cheapness, abundance of provisions.

Ạrzdár, *adj.* broad; a petitioner.

Ạrzí, *s. f.* a representation, memorial, a written petition.

Ạrz karná, to represent, to offer, to propose.

Ârzú, *s. f.* wish, desire.

Ârzúmand, *adj.* desirous, eager, longing.

Ás, Ásá, } *s. f.* hope, desire, trust, reliance.

Ạsá, *s. m.* a staff, mace.

Ạsábardár, *s.* a mace-bearer.

Ạsad, *s. m.* the lion, Leo (the sign of the zodiac.)

Asal, *s. f.* see Asl.

Asálatan házir honá, to be present in person.

Asámí, *s. m.* or *f.* a defendant (in a lawsuit), a tenant, renter, client.

Ásan, *s. m.* a stool, a seat, a carpet to sit on; attitude, posture, especially those adopted by jogís in their devotional exercises; the name of a tree on which the tasar silkworm feeds.

Ásán, *adj*. easy, convenient, commodious.
Ásaní, *s. f.* a small carpet on which Hindús sit at worship.
Ásání, Ásániyat, } *s. f.* facility, easiness.
Asar, *s. m.* an impression, effect.
Asáṛh, *s. m.* the name of the third Hindú month.
Asás ul bait, household furniture.
Asat, *adj*. untrue, false.
Asbáb, *s. m.* goods and chattels, furniture, apparatus, baggage.
Asganí, *s. f.* a line for hanging clothes on.
Asharfí, *s. f.* see Ashrafí.
Áshcharj, *s. m.* amazement, astonishment, surprise.
Ásh i jau, barley-water, water-gruel.
Ạ́shiq, *s.* a lover.
Ạ́shiqána, *adj*. amorous, lover-like.
Ạ́shiqí, *s. f.* making love, love.
Ashk, *s. m.* a tear, tears.
Áshkár, Áshkárá, } *adj*. apparent, clear, revealed, known, public.
Ashlok, *s. m.* verse, distich.
Áshná, *s. m. f.* an acquaintance, lover, friend.
Áshnáí, *s. f.* acquaintance, friendship.
Áshnáí karná, *v. a.* to associate, to unite.
Áshnáí lagná, *v. n.* to become intimate.
Ashnán, *s. m.* bathing.
Áshnáyána, *adv.* in a friendly way, through friendship.
Ashráf, *s.* (*plur.* of sharíf), nobles, gentry, gentlemen.
Ashrafí, *s. f.* a gold coin so called: improperly called asharfí.
Ạshrat, (properly Ịshrat), *s. f.* society; pleasure, delight, enjoyment, mirth.
Ashṭ, *adj*. eight.
Ashṭam, *s. m.* the eighth day of the increase or decrease of the moon; date.

Áshufta, *adj*. distressed.
Ạ́sí, *adj*. disobedient, rebellious: *s. m.* and *f.* a rebel, a sinner.
Ásikh, *s. m.* blessing, benediction.
Asíl, *adj*. well-born, noble, genuine: *s. f.* a kind of lady's maid.
Ásin, *s. m.* the sixth Hindú month.
Asír, *s. m.* a prisoner, a captive.
Ásirbád, Asírbád, } *s. m.* a benediction, a salutation, blessing.
Asírí, *s. f.* imprisonment, captivity.
Asís, Ásís, } *s. f.* blessing, benediction.
Áskat, *s. f.* laziness, tardiness.
Áskatáná, *v. n.* to be lazy.
Áskatí, *adj*. lazy, remiss.
Asl, *s. f.* root, origin, lineage; capital, stock in trade.
Aslan, *adv.* by no means, never.
Aslí, *adj*. original, radical, essential, genuine, fundamental.
Ásmán, *s. m.* the sky, the firmament, heaven.
Ásmání, *adj*. heavenly, celestial, azure, sky-coloured.
Ásmání rang, *adj*. sky-blue.
Asnán, *s. m.* bathing.
Asoṉ, *adv.* this year.
Áspás, *s. m.* vicinity, circumference: *adj*. around, on all sides.
Ạsr, *s. m.* time, age; the time of prayer before sunset.
Ásrá, *s. m.* trust, reliance, hope, asylum, retreat, hiding-place.
Ásrait, *adj*. an expectant.
Assí, *adj*. eighty.
Ast, *s. m.* setting of the sun.
Astabal, *s. m.* a stable.
Astaghfir ulláh, I entreat forgiveness of God, (an expression signifying a negation.)
Ástán, Ástána, } *s. m.* a threshold.
Astar, *s. m.* lining.
Áste, *adj*. gently, softly.
Asṭh, *adj*. eight.
Asṭham, *adj*. the eighth.
Ashṭamí, *s. f.* the eighth day of the lunar fortnight.

Asthán, *s. m.* place, abode, residence.

Asthir, *adj.* properly restless, unsteady, but generally used in the sense of at rest, at peace.

Ast honá, to set (the sun.)

Ástín, *s. f.* a sleeve.

Astut, *s. f.* praise, a song of praise.

Ásúda, *adj.* at rest, quiet, tranquil, satisfied, contented.

Ásúdadil, *adv.* quiet or easy in mind, composed.

Ásúdagí, *s. f.* quiet, peace, content.

Ásúdahál, full, at ease, contented.

Asudh, *adj.* unholy, incorrect.

Asudhtá, *s. f.* impurity, an error, a mistake.

Asugan, *s. m.* bad omen.

Asur, *s. m.* a sort of evil spirit.

Aswár, *s. m.* cavalry, a horseman; riding on any thing (as a ship, &c.)

Aswárí, *s. f.* a cavalcade, horsemanship, riding.

Átá, *s. m.* a kind of custard apple.

Atá, *s. f.* a gift, present, favour.

Áṭá, *s. m.* flour, meal.

Aṭak, *s. f.* prevention, stop, obstruction, obstacle.

Aṭakná, *v. n.* to be stopped, to be prevented, to stick, to stop.

Aṭal, *adj.* immoveable, steadfast.

Aṭál, *s. f.* a stack, a rick (of grass, corn, &c.), a heap of baggage, &c.

Aṭálá, *s. m.* a heap; furniture.

Aṭárí, *s. f.* a thatched upper room.

Átash, *s. f.* fire; anger.

Átashak, *s. f.* the venereal disease.

Átashbáz, *s. m.* a player or maker of fireworks.

Átashbází, *s. f.* exhibition of fireworks.

Átashdán, *s. m.* a chafing-dish, any receptacle for fire.

Átashmizáj, *adj.* fiery-tempered.

Átashparast, *s. m.* a worshipper of fire.

Átashparastí, *s. f.* the worship of fire.

Atfál, *s.* (*plur.* of tifl), children.

Áṭh, *adj.* eight.

Atháh, *adj.* bottomless, unfordable, unfathomable.

Aṭháis, *adj.* twenty-eight.

Aṭhánavwe, *adj.* ninety-eight.

Aṭhárah, *adj.* eighteen.

Aṭhásí, *adj.* eighty-eight.

Athavá, *conj.* or.

Aṭháwan, *adj.* fifty-eight.

Aṭhhattar, *adj.* seventy-eight.

Áṭhoṇ pahar, } day and night, constantly.
Áṭhpahar, }

Aṭhsaṭh, *adj.* sixty-eight; more commonly arsaṭh.

Aṭhtális, *adj.* forty-eight.

Aṭhtís, *adj.* thirty-eight.

Áṭhwán, *adj.* eighth.

Aṭhwára, *s. m.* the eighth day after any other; a week.

Aṭhwáṭí khaṭwáṭí, *s. f.* the state of being confined to bed through sickness, &c.

Ati, } *prep.* exceeding, surpassing, very.
Atí, }

Atisár, *s. m.* dysentery, diarrhœa.

Atít, *s. m.* a wanderer, pilgrim, a Hindú faqír.

Aṭká, *s. m.* name of the pot in which victuals are dressed at Jagannáth.

Aṭkal, *s. f.* conjecture, opinion, guess.

Aṭkalbáz, *adj.* adroit at guessing; an appraiser.

Aṭkalná, *v. a.* to guess, to conjecture, to judge, to think.

Aṭkal pachchú, *s. m.* one who guesses at a venture or without ground on which to judge: *adv.* at random.

Aṭkáná, *v. a.* to stop, to prevent, to hinder, to restrain, to detain.

Aṭkáo, } *s. m.* stop, prevention, hindrance.
Aṭkáoná, }

Atlas, *s. m.* satin.

Átmá, *s. f.* the soul, the spirit, the mind.

Átmik, *adj*. spiritual.
Aṭna, *v. n.* to be contained, to be filled.
Aṭpaṭángí, *adj*. inconsiderate, irregular.
Aṭpaṭí bát, nonsense, prevarication.
Ạtr (*prop.* ịtr), *s. m.* perfume, fragrance, essence, ottar (of roses, &c.)
Atráf, *s. f.* (*plur.* of taraf), sides, environs, skirts, districts.
Ạtrdán, *s. m.* a perfume box, or receptacle for perfume.
Ạttár, *s. m.* a perfumer, a druggist.
Ạttárí, *s. f.* the business of a perfumer or druggist.
Átur, *adj*. annoyed, distracted, perplexed.
Aṭwáṭ khaṭwáṭ, *s. f.* the state of a person who in great affliction remains bed-rid.
Atyant, *adj*. very much, excessive, great.
Au, *conj*. and.
Aubásh, *s. m.* a rake, a debauchee.
Aubaṭ, *adj*. unfrequented (road.)
Aubhagat, *s. f.* civil reception or salutation.
Auchaṭ, *adj*. suddenly, unawares.
Audhút, *s. m.* a class of faqírs.
Aughaṭ, *adj*. unfrequented.
Augun, *s. m.* defect, blemish, vice.
Aukás, see Avakás.
Aukhad, *s. f.* remedy, medicine.
Aulá, *adj*. better.
Aulád, *s. f.* children, offspring, progeny.
Aulátar, *adj*. better, best.
Auliyá, *s.* (*plur.* of walí), the saints, the holy.
Aundhá, *adj*. upside down, overturned, inverted.
Aundháná, *v. a.* to turn upside down, to reverse, to overturn.
Aunehár, *adj*. future.
Aune paune, *adv*. more or less.
Auṇṭná, *v. n.* to boil (as milk), to evaporate over a fire.
Auqát, *s. f.* (*plur.* of waqt), times, circumstances.
Auqátbasarí, *s. f.* pastime, amusement, employment.
Aur, *conj*. and, also: *adj*. more, other.
Auras chauras, *s. m.* level.
Ạurat, *s. f.* a woman, a wife.
Aur hí, quite different.
Aur koí, any one else, other.
Aur kyá, *adv*. certainly, what else.
Aur nahíṇ, *adv*. only, no more.
Aur nahíṇ to, and otherwise.
Ausán, *s. m.* courage, presence of mind.
Ausar, *s. m.* occasion, opportunity, leisure.
Auṭáná, *v. a.* to cause to boil, to make hot.
Autár, *s. m.* birth, descent incarnation of the Deity.
Auṭná, *v. a.* see Auṇṭná.
Auwal, *adj*. first, best, prime: *s. m.* beginning: *adv*. at first, in the first place.
Auwalíyat, *s. f.* priority, pre-eminence, excellence.
Auzár, *s. plur.* arms, tools, apparatus; sickness, disease.
Avakás, alias Aukás, *s. m.* leisure, opportunity.
Avardá, *s. f.* age.
Avashya, *adv*. certainly, necessarily, positively.
Avasthá, *s. f.* state, condition, stage of life.
Avatár, *s. m.* see Autár.
Áwá, *s. m.* a potter's kiln.
Awadh, *s. f.* agreement, engagement.
Áwájáí, } *s. f.* coming and
Áwágaman, } going.
Áwágawan, *s. m.* transmigration.
Áwámm, *s. plur.* the vulgar, the populace.
Áwar, in *compos.* bringing, bearing.
Áwára, *adj*. vagabond, wanderer.

Áwáz, *s. f.* voice, sound, report, fame, echo.
Áwáz uṭháná, to raise the voice.
Áyá, *s. f.* a lady's maid, a nurse.
Ayál, *s. f.* a horse's mane.
Ạyán, *adj.* manifest.
Áyanda, coming, future: *adv.* in future.
Áyat, *s. f.* a sign; a sentence; verse or paragraph of the Qurán.
Az, *prep.* from, of, by, with.
Ạzáb, *s. m.* pain, torment, punishment.
Ázád, *adj.* free, liberated: *s. m.* a kind of faqír who shaves his beard, &c. &c.
Ázádagí, } *s. f.* freedom, independence, release; conduct of an *Ázád*.
Ázádí, }
Azal, *s. f.* eternity, without beginning.
Azalí, *adj.* eternal, from all eternity.
Ạzamat, *s. f.* greatness, magnificence, magnitude.
Azán, *s. f.* summons to prayers.
Ázár, *s. m.* sickness, disorder, disease, affliction.
Ázárí, *adj.* sick, a sick person.
Az baski, whereas.
Azhdahá, *s. m.* a large snake, a dragon.
Azhdhát, *s.* name of a mixed metal, bell-metal.
Ạzím, *adj.* great, high in dignity.
Azíyat, *s. f.* distress, harm, affliction, vexation.
Ạzíz, *adj.* dear, darling, beloved, precious friend.
Ázmáish, *s. f.* trial, proof, examination.
Ázmáná, *v. a.* to try, to prove, to examine, to touch gold, &c., on the touchstone.
Ázmúda, *adj.* tried, proved, examined.
Ázmúdakár, experienced in business.
Ázú bázú, *adv.* on all sides, all about or around.
Ázurda, *adj.* afflicted, sad, dispirited, sorrowful, vexed.
Ázurdadil, vexed, offended, disgusted.
Ázurdagí, *s. f.* affliction, displeasure, vexation.
Ázurdaḳhátir, vexed, offended, disgusted.

B.

Ba, *prep.* with, by, in, &c.
Bá, *prep.* with.
Báb, *s. m.* a chapter; subject, head, affair.
Bábá, *s. m.* father, sire, sir! child. Faqírs are so addressed.
Babar, *s. m.* a tiger.
Babarchí, *s.* a cook.
Babarchí-ḳhána, *s. m.* a cook-room.
Bábat, *s. f.* account, matter; on account (of.)
Babesí, *s. f.* the piles.
Babrí, *s. f.* having cropped hair.
Bábú, *s. m.* a child; a prince; master, a title given by Hindús equivalent to Mr. or Esquire.
Babúl, } *s. f.* the name of a tree of the mimosa kind.
Babúr, }
Baburí, }
Bach, *s. f.* orris root.
Bachá, *s. m.* a child, the young of any animal.
Báchá, *s. f.* promise.
Bachan, *s. m.* speech, talk, word; promise, agreement.
Bacháná, *v. a.* to save, to preserve, to spare, to guard.
Bachan band karná, to bind by promise.
Bachan dená, to promise.
Bachan hárná, to promise, to give one's word.
Bachan lená, to receive a promise.
Bachan mánná, to obey.
Bachan nibháná, } to abide by a promise.
Bachan pálná, }
Bacháo, *s. m.* protection, defence.
Bachcha, *s. m.* an infant, a child, the young of any creature.
Bachchagána, *adj.* fit for children, puerile.
Bachchí, *s. f.* see Bachcha.
Báchhá, *s. m.* a calf.

Bachheṛá, *s. m.* a colt.
Bachheṛí, *s. f.* a filly.
Bachhiyá, *s. f.* } a calf.
Bachhrá, *s. m.* }
Bachhrú, *s. m.* }
Bachkáná, *adj.* small (generally applied to shoes and clothes.)
Bachná, *v. n.* to be saved, to escape, to remain unexpended, to recover.
Bachpan, *s. m.* childhood, infancy.
Bád, *s. f.* wind, air, breeze, gale: *s. m.* rheumatism; a deduction.
Bạd, *post.* after, afterwards, subsequent.
Bad, *adj.* evil, bad.
Badá, *adj.* predestined.
Baḍá, *adj.* great.
Bádal, *s. m.* a cloud.
Badal, *s. m.* exchange, substitution.
Badal lená, *v. a.* to exchange, to take in exchange.
Badalná, *v. n.* to change, to alter.
Bádám, *s. m.* an almond.
Bádámí, *adj.* almond-coloured, almond-shaped.
Badan, *s. m.* the body.
Bad andesh, *adj.* evil-minded, inimical.
Bádar, *s. m.* a cloud.
Badastúr, as usual, according to custom.
Bad atwár, *adj.* ill-mannered.
Badaulat, by the auspices, by the bounty, by the means.
Bad baḳht, *adj.* unlucky, unfortunate.
Bad bú, *adj.* fetid: *s. f.* an offensive smell.
Bad chálí, *s. f.* bad conduct, misconduct.
Bad dastúr, *s. m.* an evil custom or habit.
Baddhí, *s. f.* a kind of sash.
Bad duạ, *s. f.* a curse, imprecation.
Bad fiạl, *s. m.* evil deeds: *adj.* of bad habits.
Bad fiạlí, *s. f.* evil deeds.
Bad go, *adj.* evil speaking, slanderous.
Bad goí, *s. f.* slander, evil speaking.
Bad gumán *adj.* suspicious.
Bad gumání, *s. f.* suspicion.
Badh, *s. m.* killing, slaying, slaughter.
Bad hál, *adj.* ill-conditioned.
Bad hazmí, *s. f.* indigestion.
Badháwá, *s. m.* a song in congratulation.
Bad hawáss, *adj.* senseless.
Badhiyá, *s. f.* any castrated animal.
Badhná, *v. a.* to kill, to smite: *s. m.* a kind of pot with a spout to it.
Bádí, *adj.* flatulent, windy.
Badí, *s. f.* badness, wickedness; the wane of the moon.
Bad kár, *adj.* evil-doer, sinful.
Bad kárí, *s. f.* wickedness, evil doing.
Bád karná, *v. a.* to argue; to deduct, to subtract.
Bad ḳhatt, *adj.* writing ill.
Bad ḳhiyál, *s. m.* evil machination.
Bad ḳho, *adj.* of bad habits, ill-disposed.
Bad ḳhwáh, *adj.* wishing evil.
Bad ḳhwáhí, *s. f.* ill-will, enmity.
Badlá, *s. m.* exchange, stead, recompense, revenge, compensation.
Bádlá, *s. m.* gold or silver thread.
Badláí, *s. f.* price of exchange.
Badlá lena, *v. a.* to alter; to take revenge.
Badláná, *v. a.* to cause to alter, to change.
Badle, in exchange, in return for.
Badlí, *s. f.* exchange, substitute, relief (of watches); cloudiness.
Bad maạsh, *adj.* a rakish profligate person.
Bad mazá, *adj.* bad-flavoured, out of humour.
Bad mizáj, *adj.* ill-tempered.
Bad muạmala, *adj.* unfair in dealing.
Bad muạmalí, *s. f.* unfairness in dealing.
Badná, *v. a.* to wager, to bet, to settle.

Bad nám, *adj.* infamous, ignominious.
Bad námí, *s. f.* infamy, ignominy, scandal.
Bad nám karná, to asperse, to traduce.
Bad nasíb, *adj.* unfortunate.
Bad numá, *adj.* ill-looking.
Bad parhez, *adj.* not controlling one's inclinations.
Bad ráh, *adj.* wicked, sinful.
Bad sáạt, *s. f.* an unlucky moment.
Bádsháh, *s. m.* a king, a sovereign.
Bádsháhána, *adj.* imperial: *adv.* royally, princely.
Bádsháhat, *s. f.* kingdom, government.
Bádsháhí, *adj.* royal: *s. f.* royalty, reign, sovereignty.
Bad shakl, *adj.* ill-shaped, ugly.
Bad sulúk, *adj.* behaving ill.
Bad sulúkí, *s. f.* bad behaviour.
Bad súrat, *adj.* ugly, ill-conditioned.
Bad tínat, *adj.* malevolent.
Bádur, *s. m.* a large kind of bat.
Bad zabán, *adj.* abusive.
Bad zabání, *s. f.* indecent language, abuse.
Bad zát, *adj.* low-born, of bad breed, wicked, vicious.
Bad zátí, *s. f.* baseness, wickedness, viciousness.
Bad zeb. *adj.* ungraceful.
Báe, *s. f.* wind, flatulency, rheumatism.
Bág, *s. f.* the rein of a bridle.
Bágá, *s. m.* a dress for a bridegroom, &c.
Bagadná, *v. n.* to be spoiled.
Bagdáná, *v. a.* to spoil.
Bágḍor, *s. f.* a long leading rein.
Bágh, *s. m.* a garden, orchard, grove.
Bágh, } *s. m.* a tiger.
Bághá, }
Baghair, *part.* without, except, besides: *improp.* Bigar.
Baghal, *s. f.* the armpit, embrace.
Baghal hojáná *or* **jáná**, *v. n.* to go out of the way.
Baghal meṉ dabáná, } to conceal under one's arms.
Baghal meṉ márna, }
Bághan, *s. f.* a tigress.
Baghár, *s. m.* seasoning.
Bagharná, *v. a.* to season.
Bághbán, *s. m.* a gardener.
Bághbání, *s. f.* gardening.
Baghícha, *s. m.* a garden.
Bághní, *s. f.* a tigress.
Bagí, *s. f.* a gig with a hood, a buggy.
Baglá, *s. m.* name of a bird, a species of heron.
Baglá bhagat, a hypocrite.
Bág moṛná, *v. a.* to turn the reins.
Bahá bahá phirná, *v. n.* to wander, to be in a distressed condition.
Bahá dená, *v. a.* to destroy, to ruin.
Bahádur, *adj.* brave: *s. m.* a hero, a champion.
Bahádurí, *s. f.* bravery, valour.
Bahakná, *v. n.* to be deceived, to stray.
Bahal, *s. f.* a two-wheeled vehicle for riding on.
Bahál honá, to be reinstated.
Bahál karná, to reinstate.
Bahalná, *v. n.* to be diverted, to be amused.
Báham, } *adv.* together, one with another.
Baham, }
Baham áná *or* **pahunchná**, *v. a.* to get, to acquire.
Bahan, *s. f.* a sister.
Báhan, *s. m.* a vehicle, any animal or conveyance on which a person rides.
Bahána, *s. m.* pretence, evasion, contrivance.
Baháná, *v. a.* to make flow, to launch; to pour forth.
Bahangí, *s. f.* a stick with ropes hanging from each end for slinging baggage to, which is carried on the shoulder.

Bahá phirná, *v. n.* to wander, to be in a distressed condition.

Bahar, *s. f.* a fleet of boats.

Bahár, *s. f.* spring, prime, bloom, beauty, enjoyment.

Báhar, *adv.* without, abroad.

Baharhál, *adv.* by every means, somehow or other.

Bahárí, *adj.* vernal, of the spring.

Bahasná, *v. a.* to argue, to dispute.

Bahattar, *adj.* seventy-two.

Baheliyá, *s. m.* a fowler.

Bahí, *s. f.* a book stitched at the ends for keeping accounts, an account book.

Bahi jáná, *v. n.* see Bahjáná.

Bahilá, *adj. f.* barren.

Bahin, *s. f.* sister.

Báhir, *adv.* without, abroad.

Bahír, } *s. f.* the baggage, &c., of an
Bahíṛ, } army.

Bahirá, *adj.* deaf.

Báhirí, *adj.* outward, foreign.

Bahjáná, *v. n.* to flow, to go or swim with the stream; to be ruined.

Bahkáná, *v. a.* to balk, to disappoint, to mislead, to deceive.

Bahláná, *v. a.* to divert, to amuse.

Báhman. *s. m.* a bráhman.

Báhamaní. *s. f.* the wife of a bráhman.

Bahná, *v. a.* to flow, to glide; to float; to blow.

Bahnoí, *s. m.* a sister's husband, a brother-in-law.

Bahr, *s. m.* a sea; a fleet.

Bahrá, *adj.* deaf.

Bahrí, *adj.* maritime, belonging to the sea: *s. f.* a falcon.

Bahs, } *s. f.* discussion, alter-
Bahsábahsí, } cation, controversy.

Bahtá, *part. act.* running (water), afloat.

Bahú, *s. f.* a daughter-in-law, a son's wife.

Bahu, *adj.* much, many.

Bahubachan, *adj.* plural.

Bahuráná, *v. a.* to bring back, to cause to return.

Bahurangí, *adj.* various or variable (in colour); changeable.

Bahuriyá, *s. f.* a daughter-in-law.

Bahurná, *v. n.* to return, to come back.

Bahurúpiyá, *s. m.* an actor, a mimic.

Bahutát, } *s. f.* excess, plenty,
Bahutáyat, } abundance.

Bahuterá, *adj.* many, very much.

Báí, *s. f.* a dancing girl; rheumatism.

Baiána, *s. m.* earnest money.

Baid, *s. m.* a physician.

Baíd, *adj.* far, distant, remote.

Baidáí, *s. f.* practice of physic.

Baigan, *s. m.* the egg-plant.

Bai karná, *v. a.* to sell.

Baikunṭh, *s. m.* paradise, elysium.

Bail, *s. m.* a bull, an ox; (*metaph.*) a blockhead.

Baindruma, *s. m.* bill or deed of sale.

Baingan, *s. m.* the egg-plant.

Baipár, *s. m.* traffic, trade.

Baipárí, *s. m.* a merchant.

Bair, *s. m.* enmity, revenge.

Bairág, *s. m.* a kind of austerity.

Bairágan, *s. f.* a female bairágí.

Bairágí, *s. m.* one who has professedly no sensual passions.

Bairan, *s. f.* a female enemy.

Bairí, *s. m.* an enemy.

Báís, *adj.* twenty-two.

Báis, *s. m.* reason, cause.

Bais, *s. m.* the third of the four Hindú castes; age.

Baisákh, *s. m.* the first solar month of the Hindús.

Baisaní, *s. f.* the female of the Bais caste.

Baishnav, *adj.* a worshipper of Vishnu.

Bait, *s. f.* a couplet, a verse (in poetry.)

Baitál, *s. m.* name of a demon.

Baitará, *s. f.* dry ginger.

Baiṭhak, *s. f.* a kind of saloon, a place where people meet to sit and converse, a bench, a room where natives receive their visitors.

Baiṭhálná, } *v. a.* to cause to sit down, to seat, to place.
Baiṭháná,
Baiṭhárná,

Baiṭhká, *s. m.* a bench, &c. See Baiṭhak.

Baiṭhná, *v. a.* to sit, to be unemployed or idle.

Bait ul mál, *s. m.* an escheat.

Baiza, *s. m.* an egg.

Báj, *s. m.* a tax, duty, toll, tribute.

Bájá, *s. m.* a musical instrument.

Bajá, *adj.* in place; fit, accurate, true.

Bajá láná, *v. n.* to perform, to accomplish, obey.

Bájan, *s. m.* musical instruments.

Bajáná, *v. a.* to sound, to play upon an instrument of music, to perform (music.)

Bajbajáná, *v. n.* to effervesce with noise in putrefying.

Bájdár, *s. m.* a tax-gatherer, a collector of revenue or tribute.

Bajháná, *v. n.* to entangle, to ensnare, to entrap (as game).

Bajhná, *v. n.* to be ensnared, to be caught (as game.)

Bajidd honá, to be importunate.

Bajins, by kind, in detail, particularly.

Bajná, } *v. n.* to be sounded, to sound.
Bájná,

Bajr, *s. m.* a thunderbolt.

Bájrá, *s. m.* a kind of grain, millet.

Bajrá, *s. m.* a kind of pleasure boat.

Bajr paṛe us par, may lightning fall on him, (an expression used in cursing any one.)

Bajuz, *prep.* with the exception, besides.

Bajwáná, *v. a.* to cause to play on an instrument of music.

Bak, *s. f.* prattle, chat, foolish talk.

Bákal, *s.* the outside cut of a piece of timber.

Bakáyan, *s. f.* name of a tree.

Bakbak, *s. f.* see Bak.

Bakbakáná, } *v. n.* to prattle, to chatter.
Bakbak karná,

Bakhán, *s. m.* explanation, praise, description.

Bakhánná, *v. a.* to praise, to commend; to explain, to define.

Bakhár, *s. m.* } a granary.
Bakhárí, *s. f.*

Bakheṛá, *s. m.* wrangling, a tumult, contention, dispute.

Bakheṛiyá, *adj.* quarrelsome, a wrangler.

Bakheṛná, *v. a.* to scatter.

Bakhí, *s. f.* the side under the armpit.

Baḳhíl, *adj.* miser, niggard.

Baḳhílí, *s. f.* stinginess, niggardliness.

Bakhiya, } *s. m.* kind of stitch, strong quilting stitching.
Bakhiyá,

Bakhiyáná, *v. a.* to stitch, to quilt.

Baḳhrá, *s. m.* share, portion.

Baḳhrait, *adj.* sharer.

Baḳhsh, in *compos.* imparting, bestowing, forgiving.

Baḳhsháná, *v. a.* to cause to give, to procure pardon for another.

Baḳhsh dená, *v. a.* to give, to bestow, to forgive.

Baḳhshí, *improp.* Baksí, *s. m.* a paymaster.

Baḳhshí ḳhána, *s. m.* pay office.

Baḳhshiuda, *part. act.* giving, giver, bestower, pardoner.

Baḳhshí sáhib, *s. m.* paymaster.

Baḳhshish, *s. f.* gift, grant, forgiveness.

Baḳhshish dená, *v. a.* to give a present, to reward.

Baḳhshná, *v. a.* to give, to forgive.

Baḳht, *s. m.* fortune, luck, prosperity.

Baḳhtáwar, *adj.* fortunate.

Baḳht azmáí, *s. f.* the trying one's fortune.
Baḳhúbí, well, in a good manner.
Baḳhúd, in self, by self, of self.
Baḳhúdáná, *v. n.* to come to (one's) self.
Baklá, *s. m.* rind (of fruit, &c.)
Bakná, *v. n.* to prate, to chatter.
Bakoṭná, *v. a.* to scratch (with nails.)
Bakrá, *s. m.* a he-goat.
Bakrí, *s. f.* a she-goat.
Baksúá, *s. m.* a buckle.
Baktá, *s. m.* a speaker in general: *adj.* loquacious, eloquent.
Baktar, *s. m.* a coat of mail.
Bakwád, *s. f.* foolish talk.
Bakwádí, Bakwáhá, Bakwáhí, } *adj.* a chatterer, an idle talker.
Bakwás, *s. f.* prattle.
Bal, *s. m.* a coil, twist; power, strength; an offering, a sacrifice.
Bál, *s. m.* hair: *s. f.* an ear of corn; a crack in a cup or glass.
Balá, *s. f.* a calamity, misfortune.
Bálá, *prep.* above, up: *adj.* high.
Bálábar, *s. m.* the part of a dress that laps over the thighs.
Baláeṇ lená, to draw the hands over the head of another in token of taking all his misfortunes upon himself.
Bálak, *s. m.* a young child, an infant.
Bálakpan, Bálakpaná, } *s. m.* childhood.
Báláḳhána, *s. m.* an upper room, a balcony.
Bálánishín, occupying the chief seat, a president.
Bálápan, *s. m.* childhood, infancy.
Báláposh, *s. m.* a coverlet, a quilt.
Bálbachche, *s. plur.* children, brats.
Bálbál, *adv.* hair by hair, every hair, every whit.
Baldár, *adj.* crooked, twisted, coiled.
Bal dená, *v. a.* to sacrifice.
Balgham, *s. m.* phlegm, a running at the nose from cold.
Balghamí, *adj.* phlegmatic.
Balí, *adj.* strong, powerful.
Balidán, *s. m.* an offering.
Básligh, *s.* a youth just arrived at the age of maturity; an adult.
Bálisht, *s. f.* a span.
Balki, *adv.* moreover, but, nay.
Ballá, *s. m.* Ballí, *s. f.* } a prop, a pole.
Ballam, *s. m.* a spear.
Ballambardár, *s. m.* a spearman.
Balná, *v. n.* to burn.
Bálná, *v. a.* to kindle.
Baltoṛ, Báltoṛ, } *s. m.* a pimple, a boil.
Bálú, *s. f.* sand.
Balúá, *adj.* sandy.
Balwálá, Balwán, Balwant, } *adj.* powerful, strong.
Bam, *s. f.* a fountain; a fathom; a measuring rod; shaft (of a carriage, &c.), an interjection addressed to Shiva.
Bám, *s. f.* an eel.
Baman, *s. m.* vomit, emetic.
Baman karná, *v. a.* to vomit.
Bámhní, *s. f.* a stye on the eyelids; a lizard; the wife of a bráhman.
Bamújib, by reason.
Bán, *s. m.* an arrow; a rocket used in battle: *s. f.* habit; (used as an affix in *compos.* only), keeper, guardian.
Ban, *s. f.* a forest, a wood.
Báná, *s. m.* dress, fashion; the woof in weaving; a kind of weapon: *v. a.* to open.
Baná, *part.* of banná, made, prepared.
Baná banáyá, ready made.
Báṇáṇ, *adj.* left (hand.) See Báyáṇ.
Banáná, *v. a.* to make, to prepare, to build, to invent, to fabricate, to adjust, to dress (victuals), to mend.

Ban áná, *v. n.* to prosper, to succeed.

Banáo, *s. m.* preparation, make, invention.

Banáoná, *v. a.* to make, to prepare. See Banáná.

Baná rahná, to remain waiting.

Banáwaṭ, *s. f.* make, invention, contrivance. See Banáo.

Banáyá jáná, *v. n.* to be making, to be in hand.

Bánát, } *s. f.* broad cloth, woollen
Banát, } cloth.

Bánátí, } *adj.* woollen, made of
Banátí, } broad cloth.

Banbás, *s. m.* living in the forest.

Banbásí, *adj.* inhabiting the forest.

Banbiláo, *s. m,* a wild cat.

Banchná, *v. n.* to be read or perused.

Bánchná, *v. a.* to read.

Band, *s. m. f.* a fastening, imprisonment, belt, joint, knuckle, a tie. See Bándh.

Banda, } *s. m.* a slave, a servant.
Bandá, }

Bandagí, *s. f.* slavery, service, devotion, respects; a mode of salutation.

Bandanawáz, *s.* a patron, Sir, Your worship.

Bándár, *s. m.* a rocket-thrower.

Bandar, *s. m.* a monkey.

Bandariyá, *s. f.* a female monkey.

Bánavwe, } *adj.* ninety-two.
Bánawe, }

Banderí, *s. f.* a ridge-pole.

Bándh, *s. n.* an embankment, a mound raised round land to retain water for transplanting rice, &c.

Bandh, *s. m. f.* binding, bandage, bondage.

Bandhái, *s. f.* price paid for tying.

Bandhak, *s. m.* a pledge, a pawn.

Bandhan, *s. m.* fastening, bandage, bondage.

Bandhán, *s. m.* a fixed allowance made to any one.

Bandháni, *s. m.* one who carries stone, timber, &c., by slinging it on the shoulder.

Bandhná, *v. n.* to be tied, to be fastened, to be bound, to be enclosed.

Bándhná, *v. a.* to bind, to tie, to fasten, to shut, to embank, to settle.

Bandhú, } *s. m.* a friend; a pri-
Bandhúá, } soner, one bound.

Bándí, *s. f.* a female slave.

Bandí, *s. f.* slave, servant.

Bandíḳhána, *s. m.* a prison.

Band karná, *v. a.* to fasten, bind, close, shut, stop, to obstruct.

Bandish, *s. f.* contrivance.

Bandish bándhná, *v. a.* to contrive a best.

Bandobast, *s. m.* settlement, regulation, arrangement, economy, management, government.

Bandobastí, *s. f.* arrangement, economy.

Bandrí, *s. f.* a female monkey.

Bandúá, *s. m.* a prisoner, a captive.

Bandúq, *s. f.* a musket, a gun.

Bandúqchí, *s. f.* a small musket: *s. m.* a musketeer.

Banelá, *adj.* wild.

Bang, *s. f.* hemp; an intoxicating potion made from the leaves of hemp.

Báng, *s. f.* voice, crying out; the voice of the muazzin calling Muhammadans to prayer; the crowing of a cock.

Bángá, *s. m.* the cotton plant.

Bangálá, *n. prop.* name of Bengal.

Báng dená, *v. a.* to call Muhammadans to prayer, to crow (a cock.)

Bangí, *s. m.* one who intoxicates himself with bang.

Bángí, *s. f.* a pattern, a muster.

Banglá, *s. m.* a kind of thatched or tiled house.

Báng márná, *v. n.* to cry out, to call.

Báṇh, *s. f.* the arm.
Báṇh pakaṛná, *v. a.* to protect.
Bání, *s. f.* speech, language.
Baní, *s. m.* (*plur.* of ibn), sons.
Baní Ádam, sons of Adam; men.
Baní Isráíl, children of Israel, Israelites.
Báníkár, *s. m.* an architect.
Banjárá, *s. m.* a grain-merchant, a carrier of grain.
Bánjh, *adj.* barren.
Ban jháṛná, to beat the forests.
Bánk, *s. m.* a bending; a reach or turning of a river; an ornament worn (half circle) on the arms; a kind of dagger.
Bánká, *s. m.* a fop, a coxcomb: *adj.* crooked, foppish.
Bankái, *s. f.* bending, curvature.
Bánkpan, *s. m.* foppishness.
Banmánukh, Banmánus, } *s. m.* a wild man, an orang-outang.
Banná, *v. n.* to be made, to be mended; to answer, to succeed.
Banná thanná, adorned, decked out.
Ban paṛná, *v. n.* to succeed, to answer, to suit.
Bans, *s. m.* lineage, race, offspring.
Báṇs, *s. m.* a bamboo; a measure of about ten feet.
Bansáwalí, *s. f.* a genealogy.
Bansí, *s. f.* a flute; a fishing-hook.
Báṇslí, *s. f.* a flute, &c.
Baṇsphoṛ, *s. m.* name of a caste who work on bamboos.
Báṇsrí, *s. f.* a flute, fife, pipe.
Báṇṭ, *s. m.* share, distribution.
Banṭáná, *v. a.* to share, to divide.
Báṇṭ chonṭ, *s. m.* share, distribution.
Báṇṭná, *v. a.* to share, to distribute, to divide.
Banṭwáná, *v. a.* to distribute, to cause to be shared.
Banwái, *s. f.* price paid for making anything.
Banwaiyá, *s. m.* a maker.
Banwáná, *v. a.* to cause to make or to prepare or to build, &c.

Banyá, *s. m.*, Banyáin, *s. f.*, Banyáṇ, *s. m.*, Banyá baqqál, *s. m.* } a retailer of corn, &c.
Báogolá, *s. m.* the colic.
Báojhak, *adv.* a trifling foolish talker.
Báolá, *adj.* mad, insane, crazy.
Báolí, *s. f.* a large (pakká) well into which people descend to get water.
Báoná, *adj.* dwarfish.
Báorá, *adj.* mad, insane.
Báp, *s. m.* father.
Baphárá, *s. m.* vapour, vapour or steam bath.
Bápre, Báprebáp, } *interj.* expressive of grief, surprise, &c.
Baqá, *s. f.* duration, permanence, immortality.
Baqar-íd, *s. m.* a Muhammadan festival in commemoration of Abraham's offering his son Ismáíl, (as they say.)
Báqí, *adj.* remaining, permanent, eternal: *s. f.* remnant, remainder, balance.
Báqí rahná, to remain, to be left, to be saved.
Baqíya, *s. m.* remainder, balance.
Baqla, *s.* a pot-herb.
Bar, *s. m.* a blessing, a bridegroom.
Baṛ, *s. m.* the banyan tree.
Bár, *s. f.* time: *s. m.* a day of the week.
Báṛ, *s. f.* edge; a fence, a hedge; name of a place near Mongir; a valley.
Bara, *s. m.* a lamb, a kid.
Baṛá, *adj.* large, great.
Barábar, *adj.* abreast, even, uniform, smooth, like, equal, exact, straight: *adv.* straight on, up to.
Barábarí, *s. f.* equality, competition.
Barábar karná, *v. a.* to smoothe, to compose.
Barad, *s. m.* a bull.
Baráe, *adv.* for the sake of.

Báráh, *s. m.* a hog.
Bárah, *adj.* twelve.
Bárahsingá, *s. m.* a stag.
Bárahwáṉ, *adj.* twelfth.
Baṛáí, *s. f.* greatness, excellence; boasting.
Baṛáí dená, *v. a.* to honour.
Baṛáí karná, *v. a.* to extol, to boast.
Barajná, *v. a.* to forbid, to prohibit.
Baṛá karná, *v. a.* to enlarge, to exalt, to promote.
Barakat, *s. f.* blessing, abundance, prosperity.
Barakat dená, to bless, to prosper.
Barakhná, *v. n.* to rain.
Barámad, *s. f.* accusation, calumny.
Barámada, *s. m.* a verandah, balcony, porch.
Baran, *s. m.* one of the four tribes among the Hindús.
Bárán, *s. m.* rain.
Baráná, *v. n.* to be successful.
Barangá, *s. m.* a small rafter.
Báráni, *s. f.* a great-coat or cloak for keeping off the rain: *vulg.* Brándí.
Baraní, *s. f.* an eyelash; a broom.
Baras, *s. m.* rain; a year.
Barasná, *v. n.* to rain.
Baraswáṉ, *adj.* annual.
Barat, *s. m.* a fast, a religious rite.
Barát, *s. f.* marriage company.
Barátí, *s. m. f.* an attendant at a marriage feast.
Baratná, *v. a.* to use.
Barbád, *adj.* given (to the winds); thrown away, destroyed, ruined.
Bárbár, *adv.* repeatedly, often.
Baṛbaṛ, *s. f.* muttering, senseless talk.
Baṛbaṛáná, *v. a.* to mutter, to chatter nonsense.
Baṛbaṛiyá, *s. m.* a mutterer, a chatterer.
Barbat, *s. f.* a kind of harp or lute.
Barchhá, *s. m.* a spear, a javelin.
Barchhá-bardár, *s. m.* a spearman.
Barchhí, *s. f.* a spear, a javelin.
Barchhi-bardár, *s. m.* a spearman.
Bardár, in *compos.* taker up, carrier, bearer.
Bardárí, *s. f.* in *compos.* the act of bearing, carrying, &c.
Bardásht, *s. f.* endurance, patience.
Báṛ dená, to sharpen by grinding.
Báre, *adv.* at last, at length.
Baṛe-miyáṉ, an old man. Sir, (applied to an elderly man.)
Baṛerá, *s. m.* / Baṛerí, *s. f.* } a ridge pole.
Barf, *s. f. m.* ice, snow.
Barfí, *s. f.* a kind of sweetmeat: *adj.* icy, snowy.
Barg, *s. m.* a class of letters pronounced on the same part of the mouth.
Bargashta, *adj.* apostatized.
Barguzída, *adj.* chosen, selected.
Báṛh, *s. f.* a flood; promotion, increase.
Bárhá, *adv.* often, repeatedly.
Baṛhaí, *s. m.* a carpenter.
Baṛhal, *s. m.* the name of a small round fruit.
Baṛhá láná, *v. a.* to bring forward, to lead on (an army.)
Barham, *adj.* confused, angry.
Barham darham, *adj.* confused, topsy-turvy.
Baṛhan, *s. f.* a carpenter's wife.
Baṛháná, *v. a.* to increase, to lengthen, to cause to advance, to promote; to shut up (a shop); to remove the table-cloth.
Barhaqq, in truth, true, just.
Baṛháwá, *s. m.* flattery.
Baṛhiyá, *adj.* high priced, dear, of good quality.
Baṛhná, *v. n.* to increase, to proceed, to advance, to grow, to be promoted.
Baṛhní, *s. f.* a broom.
Baṛhtá, *s. m.* / Baṛhtí, *s. f.* } increase, overplus, more, promotion.
Barí, *s. f.* quicklime; a dish made of pulse.

Bárí, *s. f.* time, tour, turn; a garden, an orchard: *s. m.* the Deity, the Creator.
Báríḳ, *adj.* fine, slender, minute, subtile.
Báríkí, *s. f.* subtilty, minuteness.
Bárish, *s. f.* rain.
Bárí-taālá, *s. m.* the most high God.
Baṛká, *adj.* great.
Barḳhást, *s. f.* rising up.
Barḳhiláf, *adj.* contrary, opposed to, false, untrue.
Barḳhiláfí, *s. f.* opposition, contrariety.
Barmá, *s. m.* a bore worked with a string.
Barmáná, *v. a.* to bore with the barmá.
Barmhá, *n. prop.* the name of a country, Burmah; the people are called Barmhá.
Barná, *v. n.* to burn.
Bárná, *v. a.* to light, to kindle; to prohibit.
Barnan, *s. m.* description, explanation, praise.
Barnan karná, *v. a.* to explain, to describe, to praise.
Barngá, *s. m.* a small rafter.
Barpá honá, *v. n.* to be raised, pitched or established.
Barpá karná, *v. a.* to raise, to pitch, to establish.
Barq, *s. f.* lightning.
Barqandáz, *s. m.* an armed policeman.
Barqarár, *s. f.* rest, steadfastness, firmness.
Báṛ rakhná, *v. a.* to sharpen by grinding.
Barráná, *v. a.* to talk in one's sleep.
Barsáná, *v. a.* to cause to rain.
Barsát, *s. f.* the rainy season, the rains.
Barsátí, *s. f.* produced in the rains; a disease in horses and cows in the rains.
Barsí, *s. m.* annual ceremony in commemoration of deceased relations.
Bartamán, *adj.* present; the present tense.
Bartan, *s. m.* a dish, a plate, a vessel, &c.
Bartáná, *s. m.* old clothes used for wadding in turbans.
Bartaraf honá, *v. n.* to be dismissed, discharged or turned off.
Bartarafí, *s. f.* dismission, discharge.
Bartaraf karná, *v. a.* to dismiss, discharge, turn off.
Bárú, *s. f.* sand.
Bárúd, *s. f.* gunpowder.
Bárúdḳhána, *s. m.* a magazine for gunpowder, a powder manufactory.
Báṛ uṛáná, *v. a.* to fire a volley.
Bárút, *s. f.* gunpowder.
Baryár, Baryárí, } *adj.* strong, violent.
Bás, *s. f.* smell, scent, odour: *s. m.* abode, residence.
Bas, *adj.* enough, plenty: *s. m.* power, subjection, control, authority.
Básá, *s. m.* a dwelling, residence.
Basabab, by reason, on account.
Básan, *s. m.* a plate, dish, a vessel, &c.
Basáná, *v. a.* to people, to colonize.
Bas áná, *v. n.* to be obtained, to come into one's power.
Basant, *s. f.* the spring, from the middle of March to the middle of May.
Basantí, *adj.* a light-yellow colour.
Basar áná, *v. n.* to come to an end, to be accomplished.
Basar honá, *v. n.* to be ended, to be finished.
Basar karná, *v. n.* to bring to an end, to spend, to pass.
Básaṭh, *adj.* sixty-two.
Baserá, *s. m.* a night's lodging; a bird's roost.

Baserá karná, *v. n.* to roost.
Basgít, *s. f.* residence.
Bashar, *s. m.* man, mankind, a human being.
Bashárat, *s. f.* news, intelligence.
Basharteki, on condition that, provided that.
Bashiddat, with violence, excessively, violently.
Báshinda, *s.* inhabitant: *adj.* residing.
Bashrí, *adj.* human, relating to man.
Básí, *adj.* stale, fusty; perfumed: *s.* an inhabitant.
Básí karná, *v. a.* to make stale.
Bas karná, *v. n.* to overpower, to bring to submission; to stop, to have done.
Basná, *v. n.* to dwell, to abide, to be peopled.
Bast, *s. f.* chattels, things, baggage.
Basta, } *s. m.* the cloth in which a
Bastá, } bundle is tied up, a wrapper,
Bastar, *s. m.* cloth, raiment.
Bastí. *s. f.* a small town, a village.
Basúlá, *s. m.* a kind of axe used by carpenters, an adze.
Basúlí, *s. f.* an instrument for cutting bricks.
Bát, *s. f.* speech, word; account, subject, thing, affair, matter.
Báṭ, *s. f.* a road, a highway: *s. m.* a weight.
Baṭ, *s. m.* the banyan tree.
Batá, *s. m.* a lath made of the large kind of bamboo.
Baṭáí, *s. f.* hire paid for twisting ropes, &c,
Batak, *s. f.* a goose, a duck.
Batáná, *v. a.* to point out, to explain, to teach.
Batang honá, to be distressed.
Batar, *adj.* very bad, worse.
Bataraf, aside, apart.
Bataráná, *v. n.* to talk, to converse.
Batariq, by the way.
Batás, *s. f.* wind, air.
Batásá, *s. m.* a kind of sweetmeat.
Bataur, by the way, in the manner.
Bát banáná, to make excuses.
Bát baṛháná, *v. n.* to prolong a contest.
Bát bigáṛná, to spoil, to mar a plot.
Bát chaláná, to start a subject.
Bátchít, *s. f.* conversation, chitchat.
Báteṇ sunáná, to abuse.
Baṭer, *s. f.* a kind of quail, a partridge.
Bathúá, *s. m.* a kind of potherb.
Bátí, *s. f.* the wick of a lamp; a tent or bougie put into a wound to keep it open.
Batí, *s. f.* a lath made of the small kind of bamboo. See also **Batá.**
Báṭiká, *s. m.* a garden.
Bátil, *adj.* false, vain, useless.
Bátin, } *adj.* internal.
Bátiní, }
Bátin meṇ, *adv.* internally.
Bátís, *adj.* thirty-two.
Batiyáná, *v. a.* to speak, to talk, to converse.
Bát ká batakkaṛ karná, to talk much on little.
Bátkahá, *adj.* conversable.
Bát karná, to converse, to talk.
Bát káṭná, *v. a.* to interrupt, to contradict.
Baṭkhará, *s. m.* a weight.
Bát kí bát meṇ, in an instant.
Bát lagáná, to calumniate.
Batláná, *v. a.* to shew, to explain, to teach, to inform.
Baṭlohí, *s. f.* a brass vessel in which Hindús cook.
Báṭmár, *s. m.* a highwayman.
Baṭná, *v. a.* to twist (as ropes, &c.): *v. n.* to be divided; to be twisted.
Baṭohí, *s. m.* a traveller.
Baṭor, *s. m.* a gathering, a crowd.
Baṭorná, *v. a.* to gather up, to collect, to purse.
Bát pherná, to equivocate.
Bát rahná, to succeed, to get the better in an argument.
Bát rakhná, to comply.

Bâṭṭá, *s. m.* deficiency; discount; defect, injury.
Bát ṭálná, *v.* to put off, to excuse one's self.
Baṭṭebáz, a juggler, a cheat.
Baṭṭebází, *s. f.* jugglery, deception, sleight of hand.
Battí, *s. f.* a candle, a wick.
Battís, *adj.* thirty-two.
Baṭúá, *s. m.* a purse, a small bag used for betel-nut, &c.; a Hindú brass vessel.
Bátúní, *adj.* talkative.
Baṭwáná, *v. a.* to cause, to twist.
Baṭwárá, *s. m.* a share.
Bauchhár, *s. f.* driving rain, wind and rain.
Baul, *s. m.* urine.
Baulá, *adj.* mad, insane.
Bauná, *s. m.* a dwarf.
Bauní, a female dwarf.
Baunḍiyáná, *v. n.* to run irregularly, to stagger as a drunken man.
Baurá, *adj.* mad, insane.
Baurái, *s. f.* madness, insanity.
Bauráná, *v. n.* to be mad, to madden.
Baurápan, *s. m.* madness.
Bawáhá, *adj.* affected with the venereal disease,
Báwan, *adj.* fifty-two.
Bawanḍar, *s. m.* a whirlwind.
Báwar, *s. m.* belief, credit.
Báwarchí, *s. m.* a cook.
Báwarchíḳhána, *s. m.* a kitchen, a cook-room.
Bayábán, *s. m.* a desert, a wilderness.
Bayábání, *adj.* of the desert, &c., wild.
Bayán, *s. m.* explanation, relation.
Bayán karná, *v. a.* to explain, to relate.
Bayár, *s. f.* wind, air.
Bayáz, *s. f.* a common-place book.
Báz, *s. m.* a hawk, a female falcon.
Báz áná, to decline, to leave off, to desist from.
Bázár, *s. m.* public streets containing shops.
Bázárí, *adj.* common, wares made for sale; a market person.
Bází, *s. f.* play, sport, a tumble over (as pigeons do.)
Bázígar, *s. m.* } a tumbler, one who
Bázígarní, *s. f.* } exhibits feats of activity.
Bází hárná, } to lose (as a bet.)
Bází khoná, }
Bází lagáná, to bet.
Bází lejáná, to win.
Bázḳhwást, *s. f.* investigation.
Báz rakhná, to hold back, to prevent.
Bázú, *s. m.* the arm; door-jambs; the side of a bedstead.
Bazzáz, *s. m.* a cloth-merchant, a mercer.
Be, a *priv. particle* or *prepos.* without. When prefixed to words it is equivalent to the English in, un, im, ir, less, &c.
Be ábrú, *adj.* disgraced, dishonoured.
Be adab, *adj.* rude, ill-mannered.
Be adabí, *s. f.* rudeness, ill-manners.
Be ạdad, *adj.* not counted or calculated.
Be ạdl, *adj.* unjust.
Be ahwál, *adj.* wretched.
Be ạib, *adj.* faultless, without blemish.
Be ajal, *adj.* untimely (death.)
Be ạláqa, *adj.* unconnected with, not related to.
Beálís, *adj.* forty-two.
Be andáz, *adj.* immoderate.
Be ạql, *adj.* ignorant, stupid: *adv.* unmannerly.
Be aqúf, *prop.* Be wuqúf, which see.
Be aqúfí, *prop.* Be wuqúfí, which see.
Be árám, *adj.* restless, uneasy.
Be árámí, *s. f.* restlessness.
Be asar, *adj.* without impression or effect, ineffectual.
Be aulád, *adj.* without offspring.
Be auládí, *s. f.* childlessness.

Be áyámí, being out of time or season.
Be bák, *adj.* fearless.
Be bandobast, *adj.* unsettled, without order.
Be báq, *adj.* completely paid off or settled.
Be barakat, *adj.* without a blessing.
Be bas, *adj.* without power, helpless.
Be chain, *adj.* uneasy.
Be chainí, *s. f.* uneasiness.
Be chál, *adj.* unprincipled.
Be chára, *adj.* without remedy, helpless, poor.
Be charágh, *adj.* desolate, childless, (from bereavement.)
Bechná, *v. a.* to sell.
Be choba, *s. m.* a kind of tent, pitched without a pole.
Bed, *s. m.* the name of the four Hindú Scriptures.
Be dágh, *adj.* spotless, sound (as a horse.)
Be dahshat, *adj.* fearless.
Be dakhl karná, *v. a.* to dispossess.
Be dam, *adj.* breathless.
Be damí, *s. f.* breathlessness.
Bedaná, *s. f.* pain, ache, pains of child-birth,
Bedánt, *s. m.* the name of a Hindú philosophical system.
Bedántí, *s. m.* one who is conversant in the Bedánt system.
Bedár, *adj.* watchful, wakeful, on the alert.
Be dard, *adj.* unfeeling.
Be dardí, *s. f.* unfeelingness.
Be dastkhatt, *adj.* without signature, unsigned.
Be dast o pá, *adj.* helpless, without power.
Be dastúr, *adj.* not customary, unusual.
Be ḍaul, *adj.* shapeless, ill-bred.
Be daulat, *adj.* unfortunate.
Be dawá, *adj.* incurable.
Bedh, *s. m.* a hole bored.
Be ḍhab, *adj.* ill-shaped, awkward.
Bedharak, *adj.* without fear or doubt, fearless.
Bedhná, *v. a.* to pierce. to perforate.
Bedí, *s. f.* an altar.
Be dil, *adj.* heartless.
Be dilí, *s. f.* heartlessness.
Be dín, *adj.* irreligious.
Be diyánat, *adj.* unfaithful, unworthy of trust.
Be fáida, *adj.* profitless, useless, vain.
Be fikr, *adj.* thoughtless, unconcerned; in independent circumstances.
Be fikrí, *s. f.* thoughtlessness.
Beg, *s. m.* a moghal title corresponding with the English, Lord: *adv.* soon, quickly.
Begam, *s. f.* a lady, a queen.
Begána, *adj.* not related, a stranger.
Begánagí, *s. f.* the not being related or acquainted.
Begár, *s. m.* a person forced to work with or without pay.
Begárí, *s. f.* the act of pressing or forcing to work.
Begárí pakarná, *v. a.* to take forcibly or press, with or without pay.
Be ghairat, *adj.* shameless, impudent, rude.
Be gham, *adj.* without anxiety.
Be gharaz, *adj.* disinterested, independent.
Be ghaur, *adj.* without consideration.
Be gunáh, *adj.* innocent, guiltless.
Be gunáhí, *s. f.* innocence.
Be hadd, *adj.* boundless, infinite.
Be hál, *adj.* ill-circumstanced, indisposed.
Behar, *adj.* uneven, rugged.
Beharí, *s. f.* a subscription.
Be hásil, *adj.* unproductive, unsuccessful.
Be hawáss, *adj.* senseless from intoxication or any other cause.
Be háyá, *adj.* shameless, impudent.

Be hijáb, *adj*. immodest, shameless.

Be himmat, *adj*. without spirit, miserly.

Be hosh, *adj*. senseless, stupid, intoxicated.

Be hoshí, *s*. *f*. senselessness, stupidity, intoxication.

Behúda, *adj*. absurd, vain, fruitless, unprofitable.

Behúdagí, *s*. *f*. absurdity, nonsense, foolery.

Be hukm, *adj*. contrary to or without orders.

Be hunar, *adj*. unskilful, unskilled.

Be hurmat, *adj*. disgraced.

Be hurmatí, *s*. *f*. disgrace.

Be ịtibár, *adj*. of no credit or estimation.

Be ịtibárí, *s*. *f*. faithlessness.

Be ịtiqád, *adj*. incredulous, disbelieving.

Be ịtiqádí, *s*. *f*. incredulity, unbelief.

Be ikhtiyár, *adj*. without choice, helpless.

Be ímán, *adj*. faithless, dishonest.

Be ímání, *s*. *f*. dishonesty, shuffling, irreligion.

Be imtiyáz, *adj*. rude, impertinent, unmannerly.

Be insáf, *adj*. unjust, not equitable.

Be insáfí, *s*. *f*. injustice.

Be istịmál, *adj*. not accustomed to.

Be intihá, *adj*. boundless, infinite.

Be ịzzat, *adj*. without honour, disgraced.

Be ịzzatí, *s*. *f*. dishonour, disgrace.

Be já, *adj*. ill-placed, ill-timed, improper: *adv*. inopportunely, improperly.

Be ján, *adj*. faint, lifeless; intrepid, brave.

Be káj, *adj*. useless.

Be kal, *adj*. restless, uneasy.

Be kalí, *s*. *f*. restlessness.

Be kám, *adj*. unemployed.

Be kár, *adj*. unemployed.

Be kárí, *s*. *f*. want of employment.

Be kas, *adj*. friendless.

Bekh, *s*. *m*. habit, dress, appearance.

Be khabar, *adj*. incautious, careless, uninformed.

Be khabarí, *s*. *f*. imprudence, carelessness, heedlessness.

Be khamír, *adj*. unleavened (as bread or tobacco.)

Be kharch, not yet brought into use.

Be kharchá, *adj*. without money for expenses.

Be khatar, } *adj*. free from danger,
Be khatra, } safe, out of danger, (a sick person.)

Be kháwind, a widow.

Be khúd, *adj*. beside one's self, out of one's mind, enraptured, senseless.

Bel, *s*. *m*. the name of a fruit: *s*. *f*. a creeper, a climber, tendril (of a vine.)

Belá, *s*. *f*. name of a shrub; a fiddle; a while, a time.

Be lagáo, *adj*. unconnected.

Be láj, *adj*. shameless.

Belan, *s*. *m*. rolling-pin.

Belcha, *s*. *m*. a kind of hoe.

Beldár, *s*. *m*. a pioneer, a digger.

Be liház, *adj*. ill-bred, unmannerly.

Belná, *s*. *m*. a rolling-pin: *v*. *a*. to spread out.

Be madad, *adj*. without assistance.

Be mahsúl, *adj*. free from postage or custom duties.

Be mạlúm, *adj*. unknown.

Be maqdúr, *adj*. without authority, poor, miserable.

Be marammat, *adj*. not mended, unrepaired, out of repair.

Be mauqạ *adj*. unseasonable, out of place.

Be mausim, *adj*. out of season (as fruit.)

Be mazá, *adj*. tasteless, insipid.

Be mịád, *adj*. not confined to a stipulated time.

Be mújib, *adj*. causeless, without reason.

Be munaffa, *adj.* unprofitable.
Be munásib, *adj.* improper, unfit.
Be muqábala, not confronted.
Be murúwat, *adj.* uncourteous.
Ben, *s. f.* a pipe, a flute.
Bená, *s. m.* a fan.
Be namak, *adj.* saltless, insipid; ugly.
Be nám o nishán, *adj.* an unknown person.
Be nasíb, *adj.* unfortunate.
Be nazír, *adj.* incomparable.
Benchná, *v. a.* to sell.
Benḍá, *adj.* crooked.
Beng, *s. m.* a frog, toad.
Bení, *s. m.* the hair twisted behind.
Be niháyat, *adj.* without bound.
Benṭ, *s. m.* a handle.
Be parda, *adj.* unveiled, immodest, openly.
Be parwá, *adj.* fearless, independent.
Be parwáí, *s. f.* fearlessness, independence.
Be pasand, *adj.* disapproved of.
Be qáida, *adj.* ungrammatical.
Be qánún, *adj.* without rule or law.
Be qarár, *adj.* unsettled, restless, uneasy.
Be qaul, *adj.* faithless, perfidious.
Be qiyás, *adj.* inconceivable, incomprehensible.
Be qusúr, *adj.* faultless, innocent.
Be qúwat, *adj.* destitute of power or strength, weak.
Ber, *s. m.* the name of a fruit and tree; time, turn, while.
Beṛá, *s. m.* a raft, a float, the raft which is floated by Muhammadans in honour of Ḳhwája Ḳhizr.
Be rabt, *adj.* contrary to rule.
Be ráh, *adj.* erring, dissolute, unprincipled.
Be rahm, *adj.* merciless, cruel.
Be rahmí, *s. f.* cruelty.
Be rází, *adj.* dissatisfied, disapproving.
Berber, *adv.* often, frequently, repeatedly.
Be resha, *adj.* without fibres (as mangoes.)
Beṛhá, *adj.* crooked.
Beṛhná, *v. n.* to distrain, to drive away cattle.
Beṛí, *s. f.* irons fastened to the legs (of criminals, elephants, &c.); fetters.
Be rozgár, *adj.* without employ.
Be sabab, *adj.* without reason, causeless.
Be sabar, *adj.* impatient, restless.
Be sabarí, *s. f.* impatience.
Be saláh, *adj.* without counsel or advice.
Be salíqa, *adj.* without method, awkward.
Besan, *s. m.* the flour of pulse (particularly of chaná). The natives use it to wash themselves instead of soap.
Besaní, *adj.* made of or mixed with besan.
Besar, *s. f.* a small ring worn in the nose.
Be sar o pá, *adj.* destitute, very wretched.
Be sarposh, *adj.* without a cover.
Be sawál, *adj.* unasked.
Besh, *adj.* more; good, proper, well, excellent.
Be shakk, } *adj.* doubtless,
Be shakk o shubh, } indubitable, certain.
Be sharm, *adj.* shameless, impudent.
Be sharmí, *s. f.* shamelessness.
Beshí, *s. f.* excess, surplus.
Besh o kam, *adj.* not so much, a moderate quantity, more or less.
Besh qímat, *adj.* of great price or value.
Beshtar, *adj.* exceeding, more, frequently.
Be shubh, see Be shakk o shubh.
Be shumár, *adj.* countless, numberless, much.
Be shuụr, *adj.* not clever, not intelligent.

Be sifárish, *adj.* without a recommendation.
Be súd, *adv.* without interest.
Beswá, Besyá, } *s. f.* a prostitute.
Bet, *s. f.* a cane, a ratan.
Beṭá, *s. m.* a son, a child.
Be taạlluq, *adj.* without connexion.
Be taammul, *adj.* inconsiderate, rash.
Be táb, *adj.* faint, restless.
Be tadbír, *adj.* irremediable, without deliberation.
Be tajwíz, *adj.* without examination or scrutiny.
Be takalluf, without ceremony.
Be tál, *adj.* out of time (in music.)
Be tạlím, *adj.* uninstructed, untaught.
Be tamạ, *adj.* free from covetousness.
Be tamíz, *adj.* indiscreet.
Be táqat, *adj.* weak.
Be taqsír, *adj.* innocent.
Be tarah, *adj.* ill-mannered, unmannerly, uncivil, rude, awkward.
Be tarbiyat, *adj.* uneducated, uninstructed.
Be tásír, *adj.* ineffectual.
Be taur, *adj.* see Be tarah.
Be tawaqqú, *adj.* hopeless.
Beṭhan, *s. m.* pack-cloth, wrapper.
Be ṭhaur, Be ṭhikáná, } *adj.* uncertain, random.
Beṭí, *s. f.* a daughter.
Be tijárat, without trade or commerce.
Be ulfat, *adj.* void of friendship or attachment.
Bewa, Bewá, } *s. f.* a widow.
Be wafá, *adj.* faithless.
Be wajh, *adj.* without cause or reason.
Be wálí, *adj.* without a protector.
Be wáqif, *adj.* ignorant.
Be waqt, *adj.* out of season, at an unusual hour, premature.
Be wáris, *adj.* destitute of a master not claimable by an heir.
Be wástá, *adv.* without cause or reason.
Be watan, *adj.* of another country.
Be wazan, *adj.* unweighed, unmeasured.
Be wuqúf, *adj.* ignorant, inexpert, stupid.
Be wuqúfí, *s. f.* ignorance, stupidity.
Be zar, *adj.* without money.
Bezár, *adj.* displeased, angry, out of humour.
Bezárí, *s. f.* anger, bad humour, displeasure.
Be zín, *adj.* unsaddled.
Be zor, *adj.* weak, impotent.
Bhabakná, *v. n.* to rage (as fire.)
Bhabhar, *s. m.* a sudden fright, a panic.
Bhabharáná, *v. n.* to swell (particularly the face.)
Bhabhúká, *adj.* red (as a coal.)
Bhabhút, *s. f.* ashes of cow-dung which fakírs rub over their bodies.
Bhabká, *s. m.* a distilling machine.
Bhabkí, *s. f.* a threat.
Bhachakná, *v. n.* to be astonished or amazed.
Bhachh, *s. m.* food.
Bhad, *s. f.* Bhadák, *s. m.* Bhadáká, *s. m.* Bhad bhad, *s.* } the noise of the falling of fruit, &c.
Bhaddá, *adj.* stupid, senseless; dull.
Bhádoṉ *s. m.* the Hindú fifth solar month.
Bhadrá, *s. f.* an unlucky moment, hour, day, &c.
Bhadr honá, *v. n.* to be shaved.
Bhág, *s. m.* share, portion; chance, fortune, destiny.
Bhagal, *s. m.* deception, imposture.
Bhágalpúrí, *s. m.* a kind of cloth from Bhágalpúr.
Bhagandar, *s. m.* a fistula.
Bhaggú, *adj.* a runaway.

Bhagáná, *v. a.* to cause to flee, or run away.
Bhagat, *s. m.* a devotee, an adorer.
Bhagawat, *s. m.* God, the Deity, the Supreme Being.
Bhágí, *s. m.* a partner, a sharer, an accomplice: *adj.* fortunate.
Bhagini, *s. f.* a niece, a sister's daughter.
Bhág jáná, *v. n.* to run away, to flee.
Bhágmán, *adj.* fortunate, rich.
Bhágmání, *s. f.* good fortune, prosperity.
Bhágná, *v. n.* to flee, to run away.
Bhagoṛá, *s. m.* a runaway, a deserter.
Bhagtáí, *s. f.* piety, devotion, religion.
Bhagwán, *s. m.* God, the Supreme Being.
Bhágwán, *adj.* fortunate, rich.
Bhai, *s. m.* fear.
Bháí, *s. m.* a brother.
Bháíband, *s. m.* brothers, relations, people of the same caste.
Bháíchárá, *s. m.* brotherhood, fraternity.
Bhai kháná, *v. n.* to be frightened or afraid.
Bhaimán, *adj.* terrified, afraid.
Bhaiṇs, *s. f.* a female buffalo.
Bhaiṇsá, *s. m.* a male buffalo.
Bhaiyá, *s. m.* brother.
Bhajan, *s. m.* adoration, worship; a hymn.
Bhajan karná, *v. a.* to sing, to worship, &c.
Bhájí, *s. f.* greens.
Bhájná, *v. n.* to flee, to run away: *v. a.* to fry.
Bhajná, *v. a.* to worship, to count one's beads, to adore: *v. n.* to flee, to run away.
Bhajník, *s. m.* a singer.
Bhak, *s. m.* flash in the pan, or explosion (of a gun, &c.)
Bhákhá, *s. f.* speech, language, dialect.
Bhakosná, *v. a.* to devour, to stuff.
Bhaksí, *s. f.* a dungeon.
Bhakt, *s. m.* an adorer, a devotee, &c.
Bhakti, *s. f.* religion, faith, devotedness.
Bhakúá, *adj.* foolish.
Bhakuáná, *v. n.* to be stupified.
Bhal, *adj.* good, well: *s. m.* side direction.
Bhál, *s. f.* the point of an arrow: *s. m.* a bear.
Bhálá, *s. m.* a spear.
Bhalá, *adj.* good, healthy, virtuous, sound (as a horse, &c.)
Bhalá ádmí, *s. m.* a gentleman; (ironically) a silly fellow.
Bhalá changá, *adj.* in good order, in health.
Bhaláí, *s. f.* goodness, welfare.
Bhálait, *s. m.* a spearman.
Bhalá mánná, to take well.
Bhalá mánus, *adj.* courteous, polite.
Bhalmansí, Bhalmansát, } *s. f.* good-nature, good manners, civility.
Bhalmánus, *adj.* courteous, polite.
Bhálná, *v. a.* to see, to perceive.
Bhálú, Bháluk, } *s. m.* a bear.
Bhambherí, *s. f.* a red butterfly.
Bhambhoṛná, *v. a.* to bite and mumble (as a dog), to worry.
Bháná, *v. n.* to like, to be approved of.
Bhanak, *s. f.* a distant sound.
Bhanbhanáná, *v. n.* to hum (as a bee), to buzz (as a fly, &c.)
Bháṇḍ, *s. m.* a mimic, an actor.
Bhaṇḍá phúṭná, to be disclosed (a secret.)
Bhaṇḍár, *s. m.* a store, a storehouse.
Bhaṇḍárí, *s. m.* a house steward, a treasurer.
Bhaṇḍelá, *s. m.* an actor.
Bhaṇḍelan, Bháṇḍin, } *s. f.* an actress.
Bháṇḍná, *v. a.* to abuse.
Bhang, *s. f.* the leaf and liquor of the hemp plant.

Bháng, *s. f.* the hemp plant and the liquor extracted from its leaves.
Bhangan, *s. f.* the wife of a sweeper (halálkhor); a female drinker of bhang.
Bhangerá, *s. m.* a vender of bhang or bháng.
Bhangeran, *s. f.* a female seller of bhang.
Bhangí, *s. m.* a cast of sweepers or halálkhors; a drinker of bhang.
Bhánjá, *s. m.* a sister's son, nephew.
Bhanjáná, *v. a.* to change money.
Bhánjí, *s. f.* a sister's daughter; niece; interruption, hindrance, tale-bearing.
Bhánjí dená *or* márná, *v. a.* to interrupt, to put a stop to.
Bhánjíkhor, *s. m.* an interrupter, a tale-bearer.
Bhánjná, *v. a.* to put into circular motion, to lathe.
Bhanjwáná, *v. a.* to cause to change money.
Bhanmatí, *s. f.* a female juggler.
Bhansná, *v. n.* to float.
Bhánt, *s. f.* manner, kind, sort.
Bhánt bhánt, *adj.* various.
Bhánwar, *s. f.* revolution, circulation.
Bhanwar, *s. m.* a whirlpool, an eddy; a large black bee.
Bhanwarkalí, *s. f.* a collar (for a dog, goat, &c.)
Bhanwrá, *s. m.* a large black bee.
Bhánwrí phirná, *v. a.* to make a circuit, to go round.
Bháo, *s. m.* rate; friendship.
Bháo batáná, *v. a.* to gesticulate in dancing.
Bháph, *s. f.* steam, vapour.
Bhaphárá, *s. m.* steam, vapour.
Bhár, *s. m.* a load or burden, weight; a charge, trust.
Bhár, *s. m.* a furnace, kiln (particularly for parching grain); price of fornication.
Bhar, *adj.* full, as much as, whole.
Bhar, *s. m.* a large boat, a lighter.
Bhárá, *s. m.* hire, the rent of any thing.
Bhará, *adj.* full.
Bharábhar, *adj.* completely full.
Bharaití, *s. m.* a tenant.
Bharak, *s. f.* splendour, show; starting, shyness (in animals.)
Bharakná, *v. n.* to start, to shrink, to be alarmed; to blaze forth (fire.)
Bharam, *s. m.* error, mistake, doubt; credit, reputation.
Bharam ganwáná, *v. a.* to lose character.
Bharáná, *v. a.* to fill, to cause to fill; to cover (a mare.)
Bharariyá, *s. m.* a fortune-teller.
Bharáwat, *s. f.* filling, stuffing.
Bharbharáná. *v. n.* to swell and be glossy (particularly the face.)
Bharbhariyá, *adj.* open-hearted.
Bharbhúnjá, *s. m.* a man who parches grain.
Bharbhúnjan, *s. f.* a woman who parches grain.
Bhar dená, *v. a.* to fill, to pay, to reimburse; to darn.
Bhárí, *adj.* heavy, weighty; important, big, fat, strong, loud, burdensome, sad, serious.
Bharí, *s. f.* the weight of a rupee.
Bharjáná, *v. a.* to be filled, to be fatigued; to be covered (a mare, &c.)
Bharká, *s. m.* slaked lime.
Bharkáná, *v. a.* to slake (lime.)
Bharkáná, *v. a.* to frighten; to blow up into a flame, to kindle (a fire.)
Bharkel, *adj.* shy, coy, wild, untamed.
Bhár khána, *v. a.* to live on the wages and means of prostitution.
Bharkí, *s. f.* slaked lime.
Bharkílá, *adj.* splendid, glittering.
Bhar kos, a full kos.

Bharmáná, *v. a.* to deceive.

Bhar maqdúr, to the best of one's power.

Bharná, *v. a.* to fill, to satisfy; to pay, to liquidate or discharge a debt, fine, &c.: *v. n.* to be filled.

Bharní, *s. f.* weft, woof.

Bharosá, *s. m.* hope, dependence, faith.

Bharosá karná, *v. a.* to confide, to hope, to rely (on.)

Bhar páná, *v. a.* to be paid, to receive the full amount.

Bharpúr, } *adj.* full, brimful.
Bharpúran, }

Bhart, *s. m.* a mixed metal.

Bhartá, *s. m.* boiled or fried vegetables.

Bhartí, *s. f.* loading, filling; completion; recruiting.

Bhartí honá, *v. n.* to enlist.

Bhartí karná, *v. a.* to recruit, to employ (a servant.)

Bhaṛúá, *s. m.* a pimp, one who lives on what a prostitute earns.

Bhaṛúáí. *s. f.* pimping, the wages of prostitution.

Bharwáná, *v. a.* to cause to fill.

Bhasam, *s f.* ashes.

Bhasam karná, *v. a.* to consume, to reduce to ashes.

Bhasáná, *v. a.* to launch, to set afloat.

Bhasbhasá, *adj.* weak (as a man, house, &c.)

Bhasná, *v. n.* to float.

Bhát, *s. m.* boiled rice.

Bháṭ, *s. m.* a bard; name of a tribe.

Bhaṭakná, *v. n.* to go astray, to wander, to miss the right path, to lose (the way.)

Bhatár, *s. m.* a husband.

Bháṭhá, *s. m.* a current or stream, the ebb-tide.

Bháthí, *s. f.* bellows.

Bháṭhí, *s. f.* down the river, with the stream.

Bhaṭhí, *s. f.* a furnace for distilling.

Bhaṭhiyál, *adj.* with the current, *i.e.*, down the river and not with the flood tide (as boats, &c.)

Bhaṭhiyáná, *v. n.* to go down the river; to ebb (the tide.)

Bhaṭhiyárá, *s. m.* an inn-keeper, one who prepares victuals for travellers in a sará.

Bhaṭhiyárin, *s. f.* a hostess, the wife of a bhaṭhiyárá.

Bhaṭhiyárkhána, *s. m.* an inn, a caravansary.

Bhaṭhiyárpan, *s. m.* inn-keeping.

Bhatijá, *s. m.* nephew, brother's son.

Bhatijí, *s. f.* a niece, brother's daughter.

Bhaṭká, *adj.* astray, lost.

Bhaṭkáná, *v. a.* to mislead, to deceive, to cause to wander.

Bhaṭkatáí, } *s. f.* the name of a prickly plant.
Bhaṭkataiyá, }

Bhatta, *s. m.* an extra allowance to troops on service.

Bhaṭṭhá, *s. f.* furnace, brick-kiln.

Bhaujáí, } *s. f.* a brother's wife, sister-in-law.
Bhaují, }

Bhauṉ, *s. f.* the eye-brow.

Bhaunkná, *v. n.* to bark, to talk foolishly.

Bhauṉrá, *s. m.* a large black bee.

Bhauṉrí, *s. f.* name of a defect in horses; a large black bee.

Bhauṉriyáná, *v. a.* to whirl, to turn.

Bhauṉrkalí, *s. f.* a kind of halter for horses or dogs.

Bháúságar, the ocean of the world or existence.

Bháwaj, *s. f.* a brother's wife.

Bhawan, *s. m.* a house.

Bhawání, *s. f.* name of a Hindú goddess.

Bhayá, was, became, become.

Bhayának, *adj.* terrifying, frightful, formidable, dreadful.

Bhayankar, *adj.* terrific, terrible.

Bhed, *s. m.* separation, difference, secrecy, mystery.

Bhedí, } *s. m.* a scout, a secret-
Bhediyá, } keeper.
Bhed lená, *v. a.* to spy, to pry into.
Bhedú, *s.* a confidant, a spy.
Bhejá, *s. m.* the brain.
Bhejná, *v. a.* to send, to transmit.
Bhekh, *s. m.* disguise, assumed appearance, dress, &c.
Bhelá, *s. m.* a nut used for marking clothes.
Bhelí, *s. f.* a large lump of coarse sugar (or guṛ.)
Bhená, *s. f.* sister.
Bhenṭ, *s. f.* interview, visit; a present at meeting.
Bhenṭná, *v. a.* to meet with, to visit.
Bheṛ, *s. f.* sheep, ewe.
Bheṛá, *s. m.* a ram.
Bheṛí, *s. f.* a ewe.
Bheṛí ká gosht, mutton.
Bheṛiyá, *s. m.* a wolf.
Bheṛiyá dhasán, *s. m.* the act of following the example of another.
Bheṛ ká gosht, mutton.
Bheṛná, *v. a.* to shut, to close.
Bhes, *s. m.* assumed likeness, counterfeit dress.
Bheṭ, *s. f.* meeting, interview; a present to a superior.
Bheṭí, *s. m.* a present sent to a person, &c.
Bheṭná, *v. a.* to join, to meet; to make a present to a superior.
Bhí, *conj.* also, too, even.
Bhichchhuk, *s. m.* a beggar.
Bhigáná, *v. a.* to wet, to moisten, to steep.
Bhígná, *v. n.* to be wet.
Bhigoná, *v. a.* to wet, to steep.
Bhijáná, *v. a.* to wet, to moisten; to cause to send.
Bhíjná, *v. n.* to be wet.
Bhijwáná, *v. a.* to cause to send a person.
Bhíkh, *s. f.* begging, charity, alms.
Bhikhárí, *s. m.* a beggar.
Bhíkh máṅgná, *v. a.* to beg, to ask alms.
Bhíl, *s. m.* name of a race of mountaineers.
Bhiláwáṉ, *s. m.* a nut used for marking clothes, &c.
Bhimbhináná, *v. n.* to buzz (as a fly.)
Bhímsení, *s. f.* a kind of camphire.
Bhinakná, *v. n.* to be covered with flies.
Bhíngná, *v. n.* to be wet.
Bhinn, *adj.* separate, different.
Bhinnáná, *v. n.* to have a singing in the ears from a blow.
Bhinsár, *s. m.* dawn of day.
Bhinsáre, *adv.* in the morning, at dawn.
Bhíṛ, *s. f.* multitude, crowd, mob; a press of work, trouble, difficulty.
Bhiṛáná, *v. a.* to join, to place close to, to close; to cause to fight.
Bhiṛbháṛ, *s. f.* } a crowd, a
Bhíṛbhaṛakká, *s. m.* } multitude, bustle.
Bhiṛná, *v. n.* to close (as two armies), to come together, to be joined, to join.
Bhít, *s. f.* a wall, or breadth of a wall.
Bhítar, *adv.* within.
Bhítariyá, *s. m.* a domestic priest a cook.
Bhíṭhá, *s. m.* a house in ruins.
Bhiṭní, *s. f.* a nipple.
Bhítrí, *adj.* inward, inside, internal
Bhog, *s. m.* enjoyment, suffering; victuals.
Bhogí, *adj.* jovial, jolly.
Bhog karná, } *v. a.* to enjoy, to suf-
Bhogná, } fer.
Bhoí, *s. m.* a pálkí-bearer.
Bhoj, *s. m.* a feast after the death of a relation.
Bhojan, *s. m.* the act of eating a meal, food.

Bhojan karná, *v. a.* to eat.
Bhokhná, *v. a.* to bark.
Bholá, *adj.* simple, artless, innocent.
Bholánáth, *s. m.* a name of Mahádeva.
Bholí, *adj. f.* artless, innocent.
Bholí báteṇ, innocent prattle.
Bhondú, *adj.* silly, artless, simple.
Bhonkná, *v. a.* to thrust at, to stab.
Bhor, *s. f.* dawn of day: *adv.* early.
Bhore, *adv.* in the morning, at dawn.
Bhotá, *adj.* blunt.
Bhrasht, *adj.* out of caste, depraved, seduced.
Bhrasht honá, *v. n.* to be ruined, to be polluted, to be seduced.
Bhrasht karná, *v. a.* to pollute, to seduce.
Bhúá, *s. f.* a worm with bristly hair.
Bhúbhal, *s. m.* hot ashes, embers.
Bhuch, *adj.* ignorant, a person unacquainted with the language.
Bhugatná, *v. a.* to enjoy, to receive the punishment of a crime.
Bhugtán, *s. m.* settlement of accounts.
Bhugtáná, Bhugtán karná, } *v. a.* to settle accounts.
Bhúíṇ, *s. f.* the earth, ground.
Bhúíṇdol, *s. m.* an earthquake.
Bhuj, Bhujá, } *s. f.* the arm (above the elbow.)
Bhúkamp, *s. m.* an earthquake.
Bhúkh, *s. f.* hunger.
Bhúkhá, *adj.* hungry.
Bhúkhoṇ marná, *v. n.* to die with hunger.
Bhúl, *s. f.* forgetfulness, an error, blunder.
Bhúlábhaṭká, *adj.* missing the road.
Bhuláná, *v. a.* to cause to forget, to mislead, to fascinate, to coax.
Bhulasná, *v. n.* to be singed or scorched.
Bhuláwá, *s. m.* deception, imposture.
Bhuláwá dená, *v. n.* to deceive, to play a trick.
Bhúlná, *v. n.* to forget, to err, to miss, to omit, to stray.
Bhúm, Bhúmi, } *s. f.* land, earth, ground, the earth.
Bhuná, *adj.* fried, parched.
Bhúṇchál, *s. m.* an earthquake.
Bhunná, *v. n.* to be parched, grilled, fried, broiled.
Bhúnná, *v. a.* to parch, to grill, to broil, to toast, to fry.
Bhúrá, *adj.* fair, auburn or brownish (as hair): *s. m.* a kind of coarse sugar.
Bhuráná, *v. a.* to wheedle.
Bhurbhurá, *adj.* dry and in the state of powder.
Bhurbhuráná, *v. a.* to throw or sprinkle sugar or salt upon meat.
Bhus, *s. m.* bran, husk, chaff.
Bhusauṇṛá, *s. m.* a receptacle for chaff.
Bhúsí, *s. f.* bran, husk, chaff.
Bhút, *s. m.* the past preterite tense; an impure spirit.
Bhutáhá, *adj.* haunted, devilish.
Bhutiyáná, *v. n.* to be furious.
Bhútkál, *s. m.* the past tense.
Bhutná. *s. m.* a small devil, an imp.
Bhutní, Bhútní, } *s. f.* an impure spirit of the female kind.
Bhuṭṭá, *s. m.* Indian corn.
Bíar, *s. m.* a hole (of a rat, &c.)
Bíaṛ, *s. f.* seed-bed, seed-plot.
Bibád, *s. m.* quarrel, altercation.
Bibádí, *s. m.* a disputant.
Bibáh, *s. m.* a wedding, marriage.
Bibek, *s. m.* discrimination; compassion.
Bibekí, *adj.* discreet; compassionate.
Bibhau, *s. m.* power, grandeur.
Bíbí, *s. f.* a lady, a wife, a dame.
Bíbíána, *adj.* belonging to or fit for a lady.

Bích, *adv.* in, among, between: *s. m.* middle, centre, difference.
Bíchábích, middlemost, in the very middle, central.
Bichálí, *s. f.* straw, rice-straw.
Bichalná, *v. n.* to slip; to break one's promise.
Bichár, *s. m.* consideration, reflection.
Bichárá, } *adj.* helpless.
Bichára, }
Bichárná, *v. a.* to consider, to reflect, to investigate.
Bichchhú, *s. m.* a scorpion; name of a firework.
Bichhá dená, *v. a.* to spread; to knock down.
Bichhalná, *v. n.* to be separated, to slip, to slip out of place.
Bichháná, *v. a.* to spread.
Bichhauná, *s. m.* bedding, bed, carpetting.
Bichhná, *v. n.* to be spread.
Bichhoná, *s. m.* see Bichhauná.
Bichhúá, *s. m.* a scorpion; a sort of dagger; an ornament worn on the toes.
Bichhwáná, *v. a.* to cause to spread.
Bíchoṉ bích, *s. m.* the very middle, the very midst.
Bích paṛná, *v. n.* to differ.
Bíchwání, *s. m.* a mediator, an arbitrator.
Bidá, *s. f.* taking leave, farewell.
Bidáhná, *v. a.* to plough after sowing, to cover the seed, or after the seed is sprung up; to clean (a well.)
Bidá karná, *v. a.* to bid farewell, to dismiss.
Bidạt, *s. f.* violence, oppression.
Bidạtí, *adj.*, a tyrant, an oppressor.
Bides, *s. m.* a foreign or distant country, a distant part of the same country.
Bidesí, *adj.* foreign, strange: *s.* a foreigner.
Bidh, *s. f.* manner, mode.
Bidorná, *v. a.* to laugh at.
Bidún, *prep.* without, besides.
Bidyá, *s. f.* knowledge, science, philosophy.
Bidyárthí, *s. m.* a student.
Bidyáwán, *adj.* scientific, learned.
Bigáná, } *adj.* strange.
Bigána, }
Bigar, *prop.* Baghair, without, except, besides.
Bigáṛ, *s. m.* a misunderstanding, falling out.
Bigaṛná, *v. n.* to fall out with.
Bigáṛná, *v. a.* to spoil, to damage; to cause misunderstanding between friends, to break (a custom.)
Bíghá, *s. m.* a measure of land varying in different parts.
Bígná, *v. a.* to throw away.
Bigṛí, *s. f.* a quarrel.
Bihan, *s. m.* seed.
Bihán, *s. m.* to-morrow morning.
Biháne, *adv.* early in the morning.
Bihár, *n. prop.* name of a province: *s. m.* diversion, amusement. See Sair.
Bihasná, *v. n.* to smile, to laugh; to crack of itself (as an earthen vessel.)
Bíhaṛ, *adj.* uneven, rugged.
Bihí, *s. f.* a quince.
Bihin, *s. m.* seed. See Bihan.
Bihphai, *s. m.* Thursday. See B:-phai.
Bihrí, *s. f.* a subscription, contribution.
Bihisht, *s. f.* Paradise.
Bihishtí, *s. m.* a Muhammadan water-carrier.
Bihtar, *adj. compar.* better, well, very good, preferable.
Bihtarí, *s. f.* welfare, advantage.
Bij, *s. m.* seed, stone of fruit.
Bijak, *s. m.* mark on cloth, &c., to show the price.
Bijhkáná, *v. a.* to frighten.
Bijlí, *s. f.* lightning, a thunderbolt.

Bijog, *s. m.* separation, misfortune.
Bikal, *adj.* restless, uneasy.
Bikáná,-*v. a.* to sell.
Bikár, *s. m.* deterioration, sickness.
Bikáú, *adj.* saleable, for sale.
Bikh, *s. m.* venom, poison.
Bikhai, *s. m.* an object of sense; affair, matter.
Bikhaí, *adj.* sensual.
Bikná, *v. n.* to be sold, to sell.
Bikrál, } *adj.* terrific, ugly.
Bikrár, }
Bikrí, *s. f.* sale, a sale.
Bikwáná, *v. a.* to cause to be sold.
Bil, *s. m.* a hole, burrow.
Bilá, *prep.* without.
Bilaband, *s. m.* settlement, regulation.
Bilahrá, *s. m.* a basket for holding pán.
Biláí, *s. f.* a she-cat.
Bilakná, *v. n.* to sob (as a child.)
Bilallá, *adj.* foolish, silly.
Bilamb, } *s. m.* delay.
Bilambh, }
Bilambná, *v. n.* to stay, to tarry.
Biláná, *v. n.* to disappear, to be lost, to be extinguished.
Biláo, *s. m.* a tom-cat.
Biláp, *s. m.* lamentation, a loud mourning.
Bilás, *s. m.* pleasure, delight.
Bilasht, *s. f.* a span.
Bilásí, *adj.* voluptuous, addicted to pleasure.
Bilaṭná, *v. n.* to become bad.
Biláyat, *s. f. prop.* Wiláyat; a country; it is often applied to Europe, and sometimes only to England.
Biláyatí, *ad.* belonging to a country, European, English.
Bilbiláná, *v. n.* to lament, to be restless from pain: to weep.
Bildár, *s. m. prop.* Beldar, a pioneer, a digger.
Bil-fiạl, *adv.* now.
Bilisht, *s. f.* a span.
Bilkull, *adv.* entirely, wholly.
Billá, *s. m.* a tom-cat; a large bolt for a door.
Billár, *s. m.* a tom-cat.
Billaur, *s. m.* a kind of stone, crystal.
Billaurí, *adj.* made of crystal or glass.
Billí, *s. f.* a she-cat; the bolt of a door.
Bilmáná, *v. a.* to delay.
Bilní. *s. f.* a sty or stithe.
Biloná, *v. a.* to churn.
Bímá, *s. m.* insurance.
Bímár, *adj.* sick, indisposed.
Bímárí, *s. f.* sickness.
Bímárḳhána, *s. m.* a hospital.
Bimukh, *adj.* unfavourable to an object, having the face turned from an object, averse.
Bín, *s. f.* a lute, a kind of fiddle; in *compos.* seeing, looking.
Bin, } *adv.* without, except, unless.
Biná, }
Bíná, *adj.* clear-sighted, intelligent.
Bínáí, *s. f.* sight.
Binás, *s. m.* destruction,
Binaulá, *s. m.* the seed of the cotton tree.
Binaulí, *s. f.* hail.
Bináwaṭ, *s. f.* weaving, texture.
Binḍá, *s. f.* see Bínṭhá.
Bindhná, *v. n.* to sting, to bite.
Binná, *v. a.* to knit, to weave.
Bínṭhá, *s. m.* a roll of cloth or straw put on the head by those who carry burdens, a roll of straw upon which pots are set to keep them steady.
Bintí, *s. f.* an apology, solicitation, request.
Binwáí, *s. f.* price paid for weaving.
Bipat, *s. f.* adversity, calamity, misfortune.
Biphai, *s. m.* Thursday.
Bipharná, *v. n.* to be excited.
Bír, *s. m.* a champion, a hero, a valiant man.
Bíṛá, *s. f.* seed-bed, seed-plot: *s. m.*

a betel-leaf made up with spice, &c.
Birádar, *s. m.* a brother.
Birádarána, *adj.* brotherly.
Birádarí, *s. f.* brotherhood, relationship.
Birah, *s. m.* absence (especially of lovers); distance, loneliness.
Birájná, *v. n.* to be conspicuous; to reside; to live in health, ease, content and independence.
Biráná, *adj.* strange, foreign, belonging to another: *v. a.* to mock.
Biránawe, *adj.* ninety-two.
Birásí, *adj.* eighty-two.
Bíṛá uṭháná, *v. a.* to undertake a business.
Bírbahutí, *s. f.* a scarlet insect.
Birinj, *s. m.* rice.
Birinjí, *adj.* brazen, of brass.
Biriyán, *s. f.* a time.
Birlá, *adj.* scarce, rare, uncommon.
Birní, *s. f.* a wasp.
Birodh, *s. m.* opposition, contrariety.
Birodhí, *adj.* opposed to.
Biruá, *s. f.* see Bínṭhá.
Biruddh, *adj.* contrary to, hostile to, against.
Birúp, *adj.* disfigured, deformed, ugly.
Biryán, *adj.* fried, roasted, grilled.
Bis, *s. m.* poison, venom of reptiles, &c.
Bís, *adj.* twenty.
Bisáhind, *s. f.* fetidness, stink.
Bisáhindá, *adj.* fetid, stinking.
Bisáhná, *v. a.* to buy, to purchase.
Bisárná, *v. a.* to forget.
Bisarná, *v. n.* to forget.
Bisát, *s. f.* means, ability, difference, consequence.
Bisátí, *s. m.* a pedlar, one who sells every kind of things.
Bisbisáná, *v. n.* to burn (as a wound.)
Bisekh, *adv.* particularly, specially.
Bishá, *adj.* venomous (as reptiles.)
Bishai, *adj.* sensual, worldly.
Bishan, *n. prop.* the Deity in the character of Preserver.
Bishṭhá, *s. f.* ordure.
Bísí, *s. f.* a score.
Bismilláh, in the name of God.
Bismilláh karná, *v. a.* to begin, to commence.
Bisní, *s. m.* a rake, a debauchee.
Bisrám, *s. m.* refreshment, ease, rest after fatigue.
Bisrám lená, *v. n.* to rest, to pass the night.
Bisráná, *v. a.* to cause, to forget, to mislead.
Bistar, *s. m.* bedding, carpetting, a bed, &c.
Bistará, *s. m.* a bed, &c., peculiar to faqírs; the abode of a faqír.
Bistárí, *adj.* extensive, diffuse.
Bístí, *improper:* see Bihishtí.
Biswa, } *s. m.* the twentieth part.
Biswá, }
Biswás, *s. m.* trust, confidence, faith, credence.
Biswásí, *adj.* confidential, trustworthy.
Bíṭ, *s. f.* dung of any animal.
Biṭáná, *v. n.* to pass.
Biṭawá, *s. m.* a little son.
Biṭháná, *v. a.* to cause to sit down, to sit, to seat.
Bitharná, *v. n.* to be scattered or sprinkled.
Bithárná, *v. a.* to cause to scatter or sprinkle.
Biṭhláná, *v. a.* to seat, to cause to sit.
Biṭhráná, *v. a.* to scatter, to sprinkle.
Biṭiyá, *s. f.* a daughter.
Bitná, } *v. n.* to pass.
Bítná, }
Biṭoná, *s. m.* a son.
Bittá, *s. m.* a span.
Biwái, *s. f.* a blister or chop on the foot.
Biyá, *s. m.* seed.
Biyáhná, *v. n.* see Byáhná.
Bo, *s. f. corrup.* of bú, smell, odour.

Boáí, *s. f.* sowing, seed time.
Boáná, *v. a.* to cause to sow: *v. n.* to stink.
Boch, *s. m.* an alligator.
Bochá, *s. m.* a kind of sedan.
Bodá, *adj.* weak, low-spirited.
Bodár, *adj.* scented.
Bodh, *s. m.* understanding, comfort.
Bodlí, *adj. f.* a simple woman.
Bohní, *s. f.* the first sale in the morning for ready money.
Bojh, *s. m.* a load, a burden.
Bojháí, *s. f.* a cargo, a load, the loading of a boat or ship.
Bojhel, *adj.* loaded.
Bojhná, *v. a.* to load.
Bol, *s. m.* word, speech, talk, conversation.
Bolbálá honá, to prosper.
Boláchálí, } *s. f.* conversation, talk.
Bolchál, }
Bolí, *s. f.* a language, a dialect, conversation.
Bolí ṭholí márná, to jeer.
Bolná, *v. n.* to speak, to tell, to say.
Bolná chálná, *v. n.* to converse.
Boltá, *s. m.* the faculty of speech; the rational soul.
Boná, *v. a.* to sow.
Boní, *s. f.* the season of sowing.
Boqla, *s. m.* a pot-herb.
Borá, *s. m.* a canvas bag for carrying grain, &c., a kind of bean.
Boriyá, *s. m.* a mat.
Boṛná, *v. a.* to dip, to dye.
Boro, *s. m.* the rainbow; name of a kind of rice.
Bosa, *s. m.* a kiss.
Bostán, *s. m.* a flower-garden; name of a Persian book.
Boṭ, *s. f. Eng.* a boat.
Botám, *s. m.* a button.
Boṭí, *s. f.* a small lump of meat.
Botú, *s. m.* a he-goat (not castrated.)
Brahm, *s. m.* God.
Brahmá, *s. m.* the Deity in the character of Creator.
Bráhman, *s. m.* a Hindú priest, a brahman.
Bráhmaní, *s. f.* a brahmaness.
Braj, *s. m.* the name of a district.
Braj bhákhá, *s. f.* the language of Braj.
Bránḍí, *prop.* Baráni, which see.
Bratí, *s. m.* one who fasts.
Brichchh, *s. m.* a tree, a plant.
Briddh, *adj.* old.
Brihaspatí, *n. prop.* the planet Jupiter; Thursday.
Brithá, *adj.* vain, in vain.
Brittánt, *s. m.* history, narration.
Bú, *s. m.* smell, odour.
Búá, *s. f.* a sister.
Búchá, *m.* } *adj.* ear-cropt.
Búchí, *f.* }
Búdbásh, *s. f.* residence, abode.
Buddhi, *s. f.* cleverness, quickness of apprehension, understanding.
Buddhimán, } *adj.* intelligent, sagacious.
Buddhiwán, }
Budh, *s. m.* Wednesday; the planet Mercury.
Buḍhá, *adj.* old man.
Buḍhí, *adj.* old woman.
Búd o básh, *s. f.* residence, abode.
Bughára, *vulg.* Bugárá, *s. m.* a pit, a deep wound.
Bughdá, *s. m.* a cleaver.
Bughz, *s. m.* malice, hatred.
Buháran, *s. f.* sweepings.
Buhárí, *s. f.* a broom.
Buhárná, *v. a.* to sweep.
Buhární, *s. f.* a broom.
Buhárú, *s. m.* a sweeper.
Buhní, *s. f.* handsel, first sale in the morning for ready money.
Buhrí, *s. f.* fried or parched barley.
Búí, *s. f.* a word used to frighten children, a goblin.
Bújh, *s. f.* understanding, comprehension.
Bujhail, *adj.* laden; beasts, &c. of burthen.
Bujháná, *v. a.* to explain, to make comprehend, to demonstrate, to persuade; to extinguish to put out.

Bujhná, *v. n.* to be extinguished, put out; quenched (thirst.)
Bújhná, *v. a.* to understand, to comprehend, to think.
Buk, *s. m.* a blow with the fist.
Bukhár, *s. m.* fever.
Bukhár nikálná, to break out (as an irruption on the skin.)
Bukká, *s. m.* a handful.
Bukkaṭ, *s. m.* a claw.
Bukkí, *s. f.* a cloth brought over the shoulders under the armpits and tied behind; a handful.
Búkná, *v. a.* to reduce to powder, to pulverize.
Bukní, *s. f.* powder.
Bulá bhejná, *v. a.* to send for.
Buláhaṭ, *s. f.* calling, a summons.
Bulá láná, *v. a.* to summons.
Bulána, to call, to invite, to bid.
Buland, *adj.* high, exalted, sublime, tall.
Bulandí, *s. f.* height, elevation, exaltation.
Bulbul, *s. f.* a species of bird erroneously called the nightingale.
Bulbulá, Bullá, } *s. m.* a bubble.
Bulwáná, *v. a.* to cause to call or to send for.
Búnd, *adj.* high, soaring, (generally applied to kites): *s. f.* a drop.
Bundá, *s. m.* a dot.
Búndá, *s. m.* a large drop.
Búndí, *s. f.* drops of rain.
Bundiyá, *s. f.* a kind of sweetmeat (like drops.)
Búnṭ, *s. m.* a kind of pulse, gram.
Bunyád, *s. f.* foundation, basis, origin, groundwork.
Buqcha, *s. m.* a wrapper.
Búrá, *s. m.* coarse kind of sugar, sand-dust.
Burá, *adj.* bad, worse, abominable.
Buráda, *s. m.* filings.
Burái, *s. f.* mischief, evil, wickedness.
Burái par kamar bándhná, Burái par uṭhná, } to resolve on mischief.
Burá lagná, *v. n.* to be unpleasant.
Burá mánná, *v. a.* to take amiss, to be displeased.
Buṛáná, *v. a.* to cause to sink.
Búṛhá, *adj.* old, an old man.
Buṛhápá, *s. m.* old age.
Buṛhbhas, *adj.* affecting in old age the manners of youth.
Buṛhí, Buṛhiyá, } *s. f.* an old woman.
Burj, *s. m.* a bastion, a tower; a sign of the zodiac; a large track-rope.
Burjí, *s. f.* a small tower, a turret.
Búṛ marná, *v. n.* to be drowned, to drown.
Búṛná, *v. n.* to drown.
Burqa, *s. m.* a dress or kind of veil with eye holes to it.
Burqaposh, one who wears a burqa.
But, *s. m.* an idol, an image.
Búṭ, *s. m.* a kind of pulse (for cattle, &c.) gram. See Búnṭ.
Bútá, *s. m.* strength, power, ability.
Búṭá, *s. m.* flowers wrought in cloth.
Butáoná, *v. a.* to extinguish.
Bútát, *s. m.* household expenses.
Búṭedár, *adj.* flowered (cloth.)
Búṭí, *s. f.* medicinal roots; flowers or sprigs wrought on muslin.
Butkhána, *s. m.* an idol-temple.
Butparast, *s.* an idolater.
Butparastí, *s. f.* idolatry.
Buttá dená, *v. a.* to take a person in.
Buttarásh, *s. m.* an idol sculptor.
Buttaráshí, *s. f.* idol sculpture.
Buzurg, *adj.* great: *s.* an ancestor, a senior, a saint.
Buzurgí, *s. f.* greatness, eminence.
Buzurgwár, *adj.* elder; great (a man.)
Byádh, *s. m.* disease, sickness.
Byádhá, *s. m.* a fowler.

Byádhí, *adj.* ill, sick.
Byáh, *s. m.* marriage.
Byáhá, *adj.* married.
Byáhanjog, *adj.* marriageable.
Byáh láná, *v. a.* to bring home a wife.
Byáhná, *v. n.* to be delivered of young (an animal) : *v. a.* to give or take in marriage.
Byáh racháná, *v. a.* to celebrate a marriage.
Byáhtá, *adj.* married.
Byáj, *s. m.* interest on money.
Byájkhor, *s. m.* one who takes interest, a usurer.
Byájú, *s. m.* the principal sum put out to interest.
Byákaran, *s. m.* grammar.
Byákarní, *s. m.* a grammarian.
Byákul, *adj.* perplexed, disturbed, restless, agitated (in mind), uneasy.
Byán, *s. m.* the giving of young.
Byáná, *v. n.* to be delivered of young (animals.)
Byápná, *v. a.* to pervade, to occupy space, to penetrate.
Byárí, *s. f.* supper.
Byárth, *adj.* vain.
Byásí, *adj.* eighty-two.
Byohár, *s. m.* trade, calling, profession.
Byontná, *v. a.* to cut or shape clothes.

C.

Cha, a particle fixed to Persian nouns to form diminutives, as Bághícha, a little garden.
Chá, *s. f.* tea.
Chabáná, *v. a.* to chew, to masticate, to bite (the lip.)
Chabená, *s. m.* } parched, grain.
Chabení, *s. f.* } parched, grain.
Chábí, *s. f.* a key.
Chabláná, *v. a.* to chew slowly.
Chábná, *v. a.* to chew, to masticate, to gnaw.
Chábuk, *s. m.* a horse-whip, a whip, a scourge.
Chábuk márná, *v. a.* to whip, to lash.
Chábuk phatkárná, *v. a.* to crack a whip.
Chábuksawár, *s. m.* a horse-breaker, a jockey, a good rider.
Chábuksawárí, *s. f.* jockeyship.
Chabútara, *s. m.* a terrace, &c. to sit and converse on, a police office.
Chabwáná, *v. a.* to cause to chew, &c.
Cháchá, } *s. m.* an uncle, a father's brother.
Chachá, } *s. m.* an uncle, a father's brother.
Chacherá, *adj.* descended from or related to a paternal uncle.
Chacherá bhái, cousin, son of a paternal uncle.
Chacherí bahin, daughter of a paternal uncle.
Cháchí, } *s. f.* a father's brother's wife, an aunt.
Chachí, } *s. f.* a father's brother's wife, an aunt.
Chachorná, *v. a.* to scratch.
Chádán, *s. m.* a tea-box.
Chádar, *s. f.* a sheet, a covering or bed-sheet.
Chádar bichháná, to lay the cloth.
Chaddar, *s. f.* a sheet, a table-cloth, a cloth of more than one breadth.
Chaddar bichháná, to lay the cloth.
Chaddhá, *s. m.* the groin; a bubo.
Cháh, *s. f.* desire, wish, want, love, affection, choice : *s. m.* a well.
Chahakná, *v. n.* to whistle or chirp (as birds.)
Chahar, *s.* the large kind of bamboo.
Chahár. *adj.* four.
Chahárum, *adj.* the fourth.
Chahbachcha, *s. m.* a vat, a cistern.
Chahchahá, *s. m.* the song of a bird.
Chahchahábat, *s. f.* the singing, &c. of birds.
Chahchaháná, *v. n.* to sing (as a nightingale), to whistle (as birds.)
Chahchahe márná, *v. n.* to sing (as birds.)
Cháhe, *conj.* either, or.
Cháhítá, *s. m.* a sweetheart.

Cháhítí, *s. f.* a mistress, a sweetheart.
Chahkárná, *v. n.* to whistle or chirp (as birds.)
Cháhná, *v. a.* to love, to desire, to choose, to look for, to require.
Chahlá, *s. m.* mud, ooze, slime.
Cháho, Cháhoṉ, *conj.* either, or.
Chailá, *s. m.* a small billet of wood cut for burning.
Chailí, *s. f.* chips.
Chain, *s. m.* ease, relief, repose, tranquillity.
Cháiṉ, *s. m.* name of a low caste of Hindús; seed of the tamarind; a thief.
Chait, *s. m.* name of a Hindú month, containing a part of March and April.
Chaitanya, *s. m.* a sentient being.
Chák, *s. m.* a potter's wheel, a narrow opening intentionally left in clothes; a rent; a fissure: *adj.* rent.
Chak, *s. m.* landed property, a farm.
Chakaí, *s. f.* the name of a plaything, a whirligig; the name of a bird.
Chákar, *s. m.* a servant.
Chakarbá, *s. m.* noise, a squabble.
Chakarbá macháná, to make a noise or uproar.
Chákarí, *s. f.* service.
Chakariyá, *s. m.* a servant.
Chakar makar, *s. m.* evasion, trick, subterfuge, shuffle.
Chakchakí, *s. f.* a kind of musical instrument made of wood.
Chaḳh, *s. f.* quarrel, strife, contest.
Chaḳháchaḳhí, *s. f.* discord; a bribe.
Chakháchaundh, *s. f.* the state of being dazzled.
Chakháná, *v. a.* to cause to taste.
Chaḳhe, begone, away, avaunt.
Chakhná, *v. a.* to enjoy, to relish, to taste.
Chakká, *s. m.* coagulated milk, curd; a carriage-wheel, a wheel: *adj.* thick (as dahí.)

Chakkar, *s. m.* a whirlwind, a whirlpool; a wheel; a revolution, a circular course; a sharp circular missile weapon.
Chakkar dená, to make a horse run round in a circle.
Chakkar márná, to wheel round, to wheel; to lounge a horse.
Chák karná, *v. a.* to rend, to tear, to split, to rip.
Chakkí, *s. m.* a mill, a hand-mill; the kneepan.
Chakkú, *s. m.* a clasp-knife, a penknife.
Chaklá, *s. m.* a brothel; a district, a province, a number of villages: *adj.* wide, broad.
Chakledár, *s. m.* the governor of a chaklá.
Chakmák, } *s. f.* the steel for striking a light.
Chakmak, }
Chakmakpathrí, *s. f.* a flint.
Chaknáchúr, *s. m.* scraps, small pieces, atoms.
Chakotra, *s. m.* a fruit of the lime kind.
Chakriyá, *s. m.* servitude.
Chaktí, *s. f.* ring of leather for putting on the axle of wheels; a patch; a round plate of metal, &c.
Chakwá, *s. m.* } the ruddy goose.
Chakwí, *s. f.* }
Chál, *s. f.* conduct, behaviour, walk, pace, gait, custom, practice.
Chaláchal, } *s. f.* the bustle of setting out on a journey, &c.; setting about any thing.
Chaláchalí, }
Chalá jáná, to go along, to go away, to be off, to depart.
Chálák, *adj.* expert, active, dexterous, nimble.
Chálákí, *s. f.* activity, dexterity, nimbleness.
Chalan, *s. m.* habit, behaviour, deportment, currency.
Chalán, *s. f.* clearance (of a ship), despatching of goods, an invoice

for goods, bringing before the magistrate, &c.
Chaláná, *v. a.* to impel, to make to go or pass, to drive, to set a machine a going, to fire off a gun, &c.; to brandish (a sword, &c.); to throw stone, &c.
Chalansár, *adj.* current, customary.
Chalauná, *s. m.* a small stick by which a spinning or potter's wheel is turned, or by which liquids are stirred.
Chaláwá, *s. m.* habit, custom.
Chalbichal, *s. m.* alteration; purloining.
Chalchaláo, *s. m.* preparation for journey or departure.
Chál chalná, to behave.
Chal dená, *v. a.* to retreat (as an army), to flee, to run away.
Chale chalná, to go along.
Chálí, *s. f.* the bamboo work on the floor of a boat.
Chális, *adj.* forty.
Cháliswán, *adj.* fortieth; the fortieth day after childbirth, &c.
Chál karná, to call to or after.
Chalná, *v. n.* to move, to go, to proceed, to go off, to pass (as coin), to blow, to sail; to discharge as a gun, &c.
Chálná, *v. a.* to sift.
Chalní, *s. f.* a sieve.
Chal nikalná, to exceed bounds.
Chalo, *interj.* away! begone!
Chál pakaṛná, to imitate.
Chaltí chíz, *s. f.* saleable goods, passable (coin, &c.)
Chalwá, *s. f.* a kind of fish.
Chám, *s. m.* hide, skin, leather.
Chamach, *s. m.* *prop.* Chamcha, a spoon.
Chamak, *s. f.* glitter, splendour.
Chamakná, *v. n.* to glitter, to shine, to startle, to be angry.
Chaman, *s. m.* a bed in a garden.
Chamár, *s. m.* a worker in leather, a shoemaker, tanner, currier.
Chamáún, *s. f.* a kind of patten.
Chambá, *s. m.* a tribe of beggars who scarify their skin.
Chambelí, *s. f.* the name of a flower.
Chamcha, *s. m.* a spoon.
Chamchabhar, *adj.* a spoonful.
Chameṭá, *s. m.* a slap, a box.
Chamgádaṛ, *s. m.* }
Chamgídaṛ, *s. m.* } a bat.
Chamgúdṛí, *s. f.* }
Chamkáhaṭ, *s. f.* glitter, splendour, lustre.
Chamkáná, *v. a.* to cause to glitter, to brighten, to brandish.
Chamlá, *s. m.* }
Chamlí, *s. f.* } a beggar's cup.
Chammal, *s. m.* }
Chamoṭá, *s. m.* }
Chamoṭí, *s. f.* } a razor-strop.
Chámp, *s. f.* the lock of a gun; the name of a tree.
Champá, *s. m.* the name of a flower tree; a kind of oar.
Champákalí, *s. f.* an ornament for the neck.
Champákelá, a kind of plantain.
Champáṭ hojáná *or* honá, *v. n.* to vanish, to scamper away.
Chámpná, *v. a.* to press, to shampoo.
Chamṛá, *s. m.* leather, a hide, a skin.
Chamṛá chhuṛáná, *v. a.* to flay, to skin.
Chamrakh, *s. f.* the apparatus of a spinning wheel.
Chamṛá khainchná, }
Chamṛá nikálná, } *v. a.* to flay, to skin.
Chamṛá udheṛná, }
Chaná, *s. m.* a kind of pulse, a sort of vetch, gram.
Chanak, *s. f.* crack in a vessel, &c.: the bursting of the husk of a seed by exposure to the sun.
Chanakná, *v. n.* to crack (as an earthen vessel); to burst and fall out (as a seed from the husk.)
Chanchal, *adj.* fickle, restless, inconstant, transitory.

Chanchanáná, *v. n.* to make a noise (as in parching of grain, &c.)
Chand, *adj.* some, a few; (in *compos.*) quantity, as much, many.
Chánd, *s. m.* the moon; name of an ornament; a target (to shoot at); a white spot in the forehead (of an animal.)
Chandá, *s. m.* contribution, subscription.
Chanḍál, *s. m.* a wicked man, a wretch, a miser.
Chanḍálin, *s. f.* the wife of a chanḍál.
Chandan, *s. m.* sandal-wood.
Chandarmá, *s. m.* the moon.
Chande, *adj.* some, a few, a little, sometime, a while.
Chándí, *s. f.* silver (pure), plate; the crown of the head.
Chandiyá, *s. f.* the crown of the head.
Chándmárí, *s. f.* a place of target practice.
Chánd márná, *v. a.* to fire at a mark or target.
Chándní, *s. f.* an awning, a cloth ceiling, a cloth spread on a carpet; the moonbeams.
Chándní rát, a moonlight night.
Chandmukh, *s. m.* a face bright and beautiful as the moon.
Chandmukhí, *adj.* having a countenance splendid as the moon.
Chanḍol, *s. m.* a sort of sedan.
Chandramukhí, *adj.* see Chandmukhí.
Chand roz, / Chand roza, } *adj.* of a few days.
Chandwá, *s. m.* a small canopy, an awning.
Chang, *s. f.* a kind of paper kite with a tail.
Changá, *adj.* healthy, recovered (from a disease), sound.
Changá banáná, *v. a.* to correct, to punish, to chastise.
Changá karná, *v. a.* to cure.
Changer, *s. f.* a flower-pot.
Changerá, *s. m.* / Changerí, *s. f.* } a large basket, a tray or trough.
Changul, *s. m.* talons, claws, hand, clutch, grasp.
Chanṭ, *s. m.* a miser.
Cháṇwal, *s. m.* rice.
Chaṇwar, *s. f.* an instrument for driving away flies, a fly-flapper.
Chapaṛ chapaṛ, an imitative sound of the mouth in eating.
Chapaṛná, *v. a.* to varnish, to anoint, to besmear.
Chapátí, *s. f.* a thin cake of unleavened bread.
Chapaṭná, *v. n.* to be flattened.
Chapeṭ, *s. f.* a slap, a flat palm; a sudden misfortune.
Chapeṭá, *s. m.* a slap, a blow.
Chapkan, *s. f.* a kind of vest, a sort of coat.
Chapkáná, *v. a.* to make adhere, to stick on.
Cháplús, *s. m.* a flatterer, a wheedler.
Cháplúsí, *s. f.* flattery, wheedling.
Chápochí, *s. f.* a tea-pot.
Chapná, *v. n.* to be abashed, to blush: *s. m.* a lid or cover.
Chapní, *s. f.* a lid or cover (small.)
Chappan, *s. m.* a lid or cover (large.)
Chappí, *s. f.* kneading the limbs.
Chapqualish, *s. f.* crowding, want of room.
Chapṛá, *s. m.* a kind of lac.
Chapṛáná, *v. a.* to seal.
Chaprás, *s. f.* a buckle, a breastplate, a badge.
Chaprásí, *s. m.* a servant wearing a chaprás, a peon.
Chapṭa karná, / Chapṭáná, } *v. n.* to flatten.
Cháqú, *s. m.* a clasp-knife, a penknife.
Chár, *adj.* four.
Char, *s. m.* a shoal, an island.
Chaṛ, *s. m.* sound made by breaking a branch.

Chára, } s. m. remedy, cure, help,
Chárá, } aid.

Chára, s. m. forage, fodder, food for cattle; bait for fish; a seedling, a plant.

Chára ḍálná, v. a. to bait.

Charáí, s. f. the price paid for pasturage; grazing, feeding.

Charak, s. m. white leprous spots.

Charan, s. m. the foot, a poetical foot.

Charáná, v. a. to graze, to pasture.

Charand, } s. m. a beast, an ani-
Charanda, } mal that grazes.

Charas, s. m. a kind of intoxicating drug.

Charbí, s. f. fat, suet, grease.

Charbídár, adj. fat, not lean.

Charbí kí jhillí, s. f. caul.

Charchá, s. m. f. talking over past events, mention, mentioning.

Charchar, s. m. prating, chattering.

Charcharáná, } v. n. to crack, to
Chaṛchaṛáná, } sputter (as wood in the fire.)

Chárdíwárí, s. f. the wall by which a court-yard is enclosed.

Chárguná, adj. four-fold.

Chaṛháí, s. f. ascent, acclivity, embarkation, attack; price paid for ascending, riding, embarking, &c.

Chaṛháná, v. a. to make ascend, embark, &c.; to offer up oblations; to string a bow; to brace a drum.

Chaṛhandár, s. m. a passenger, a supercargo.

Chaṛháo, s. m. ascent, acclivity, attack.

Chaṛhná, v. n. to ascend, mount, advance, embark, climb, soar, ride.

Chaṛhtá, s. m. increase of price.

Chaṛhtí, s. f. advantage, gain.

Chaṛhwaiyá, s. m. one who ascends, mounts, &c., a rider.

Chaṛhwáṇ, adj. rising up (a shoe over the heel of the wearer.)

Chaṛhwáná, v. a. to cause others to raise or to make ascend or to pull on, &c.

Charit, } s. m. conduct, custom.
Charitr, }

Chárjáma, s. m. a kind of saddle.

Charká, adj. white spotted (as from a leprosy): s. m. a small wound, scratch.

Charkaṭá, s. m. the person who cuts forage for elephants.

Charkh, s. m. a wheel, circular motion.

Charkhá, s. m. a spinning wheel, a reel.

Chárkhána, s. m. cloth ornamented with squares, check muslin.

Charkhí, s. f. a spinning-wheel, a cotton machine, a kind of firework.

Charkh márná, v. n. to turn round, to wheel.

Charkhpújá, s. f. the religious ceremony of swinging with iron hooks passed through the muscles of the back.

Charná, v. n. to graze, to feed: s. m. half trowsers.

Chárpáí, s. f. a bedstead.

Charpará, adj. acrid, hot (as pepper); smart (in conversation.)

Charparáná, v. n. to smart.

Charpariyá, adj. active, ingenious.

Chárpáya, s. m. a quadruped.

Charráná, v. n. to burst, to ache, to smart.

Charsá, s. m. a hide, a skin.

Chartí, s. m. one who does not fast.

Charúá, s. m. a large earthen pot.

Chárungal, s. m. the breadth of four fingers.

Chárwá, s. m. a horse.

Charwáhá, s. m. a grazier, a shepherd.

Charwáí, s. f. price paid for pasturage, keeping or feeding cattle.

Charwáná, v. a. to graze, to pasture.

Chárzánú, a mode of sitting, as tailors sit at work.
Chás, *s. f.* ploughing.
Chásá, *s. m.* a ploughman, a husbandman.
Chashm, *s. m. f.* the eye.
Chashma, *s. m.* spectacles; a fountain.
Chashní, *s. f.* a specimen; syrup.
Chás karná, } *v. a.* to plough.
Chásná, }
Chaṭ, *adv.* quickly, instantly: *s. f.* an excoriation, a sore.
Cháṭ, *s. f.* relish, taste for.
Chaṭái, *s. f.* a mat.
Chaṭak, *s. f.* glitter, splendour.
Chaṭák, *s. f.* a crash, an explosion.
Chaṭakná, *v. n.* to crackle, to crack as a whip, to splinter, to split.
Chaṭán, *s. f.* block of stone, rock.
Chaṭáná, *v. a.* to make lick or lap up.
Chaṭiyá, *s. m.* a pupil or scholar.
Chaṭká, *s. m.* a habit.
Chaṭkaná, *s. m.* a slap, a box, a cuff.
Chaṭkáná, *v. a.* to crack (as a whip); to snap the fingers (in rejoicing); to enrage.
Chaṭkárná, *v. a.* to urge cattle by the cracking noise made by drawing the tongue from the palate.
Chaṭkílá, *adj.* splendid, gaudy.
Cháṭ lená, *v. a.* to lick up, to lap.
Cháṭná, *v. a.* to lick up: *adj.* voracious (man.)
Chaṭní, *s. f.* a kind of acid or pungent sauce: *adj. f.* voracious (woman.)
Chaṭorá, *s. m.* an epicure.
Chaṭpaṭ, *adv.* hastily, in a hurry, instantly.
Chaṭpaṭáhaṭ, *s. f.* agitation, flurry, flutter, palpitation.
Chaṭpaṭáná, *v. n.* to be agitated, to flutter, to wince.
Chaṭpaṭí, *s. f.* haste, hurry, quickness, agility.
Chaṭpaṭiyá, *adj.* active, quick, alert.
Chaṭṭán, *s. f.* block of stone, rock.
Chatur, } *adj.* intelligent, cunning,
Chaturá, } clever, shrewd.
Chaturái, } *s. f.* slyness, cleverness,
Chaturtá, } ingenuity.
Chaṭwáná, *v. a.* to cause to lick or lap up.
Chau, *s. m.* a back tooth; (in *compos.*) four.
Chaube, *s. m.* a kind of brahman.
Chaubís, *adj.* twenty-four.
Chaudah, *adj.* fourteen.
Chaudawáṉ, *adj.* fourteenth.
Chaudawíṉ rát, fourteenth night of the moon.
Chaudání, *s. f.* } an ornament
Chaudániyá, *s. m.* } worn in the ear.
Chaudas, *s. f.* the fourteenth day of the moon.
Chaudharái, *s. f.* the business of a Chaudharí.
Chaudharí, *s. m.* the head man of a trade.
Chaugán, *s. m.* a plain; name of a game.
Chaugána, } *adj.* quadruple, fourfold.
Chaughará, *s. m.* a small box of gold or silver, with four partitions for holding perfumes.
Chaugird, *adv.* on all sides.
Chauguná, *adj.* fourfold.
Chauhán, *s. m.* a caste of Rájpúts.
Chauhaṭṭá, *s. m.* a place where four streets meet.
Chauhattar, *adj.* seventy-four.
Chauk, *s. m.* a market, a square, a court-yard.
Chauká, *s. m.* a square plot of ground marked out, in which a Hindú dresses his food; a square slate of marble, &c.
Chaukaṛí, *s. f.* a bound, a spring, a bounce.
Chaukaṛí bharná, to leap, bound, bounce.

Chaukas, *adj.* circumspect, attentive, vigilant, clever; full weight.
Chaukasí, *s. f.* circumspection, attention, vigilance, watchfulness.
Chaukaṭ, } *s. m.* a door-frame, the
Chaukhaṭ, } lower piece of a frame of a door.
Chaukhúnṭá, *adj.* four-cornered, square.
Chaukí, *s. f.* a chair, a bench, a stool; guard, watch; the post where a guard is stationed.
Chaukídár, *s. m.* a watchman, a sentinel.
Chaukídárí, *s. f.* a tax levied for supporting watches, the pay or office of a watchman.
Chaukí dená, *v. a.* to mount guard, to watch.
Chaukí márná, *v. a.* to smuggle.
Chaukoná, } *adj.* four-cornered,
Chaukor, } square.
Chauláí, *s. f.* a kind of vegetable.
Chaulaṛá, *s. m.* } a necklace of four
Chaulaṛí, *s. f.* } strings.
Chaumásá, *s. m.* the rainy season.
Chaumukh, *s. m.* a lamp-stand with partitions.
Chaumukhá, *adj.* having four burners, &c. (a lamp.)
Chaundhiyáná, *v. n.* to be confused, to be out of one's senses.
Chauṇḍol, *s. m.* a kind of sedan with two poles.
Chaunḍú, *s. m.* a blockhead.
Chaungí, *s. f.* wheedling.
Chaungíbáz, *s. m.* a wheedler.
Chaunk, *s. f.* the act of starting.
Chaunkel, *adj.* shy, timid (as an animal.)
Chaunkná, *v. n.* to start, to start up from sleep, to start up at.
Chaunk paṛná, *v. n.* to bounce, to start up.
Chaunk uṭhná, *v. n.* to start, to wince.
Chauṇrí, *s. f.* an instrument for driving away flies, a fly-flapper.
Chauṇsar, *s. m.* the name of a game.
Chauṇsaṭh, *adj.* sixty-four.
Chauṇtará, *s. m.* a terrace, &c. See Chabútara.
Chauṇtís, *adj.* thirty-four.
Chauwá, *s. m.* a hand-breadth.
Chauwan, *adj.* fifty-four.
Cháwal, *s. m.* rice separated from the husk but not cooked.
Chawálís, } *adj.* forty-four.
Chawáṇlís, }
Chawaṇr, *s. f.* see chauṇrí.
Chechak, *s. f.* the small-pox.
Chelá, *s. m.* a pupil, a disciple, a slave brought up in the house.
Chelí, *s. f.* a slave-girl.
Cheṇcheṇ karná, *v. n.* to chatter, to chirp.
Cherá, *s. m.* a slave-boy.
Cherí, *s. f.* slave-girl.
Chet, *s. m.* memory, remembrance, thought.
Chetan, *s. m.* a sentient or rational being.
Chetná, *v. a.* to remember, to think of, to reflect, to recover the senses, to be roused.
Chha, *adj.* six.
Chhab, *s. f.* beauty, splendour, shape, form.
Chhabbís, *adj.* twenty-six.
Chhabílá, *adj.* handsome, comely.
Chhabís, *adj.* twenty-six.
Chháchh, *s. f.* buttermilk.
Chhadám, *s. m.* the fourth part of a paisá.
Chhail, }
Chhailá, } *s. m.* fop, beau, a coxcomb.
Chhailchikniyá, }
Chhajjá, *s. m.* gallery.
Chhairog, } *s. m.* consumption.
Chhaírog, }
Chhá jáná, *v. n.* to be spread; to be thatched; to be overcast (the clouds.)
Chhakáná, *v. a.* to pamper, to cloy, to satiate.
Chhakkápanja karná, to deceive, to play tricks.

Chhakkaṛ, *s. f.* a slap, a blow, a cuff.

Chhakṛá, *s. m.* a cart, a wheel carriage.

Chhal, *s. m.* fraud, a stratagem, pretence, artifice, a trick, a plot.

Chhál, *s. f.* peel, skin, rind, bark.

Chhálá, *s. m.* a blister, skin.

Chhalak, *s. f.* running over.

Chhalakná, *v. n.* to be spilt, to overflow.

Chhal bal, *s. m.* force and fraud, stratagem, trick.

Chhalchhaláná, *v. n.* to undulate.

Chhal dená, *v. a.* to deceive, to cheat.

Chhal karná, to practice deceit.

Chhá lená, *v. a.* to cloud, to overspread, to darken; to thatch.

Chhalí, **Chhaliyá**, } *adj.* deceitful, fraudulent, treacherous, artful, false, perfidious.

Chháliyá, *s. f.* a kind of betel-nut.

Chhalkáná, *v. a.* to spill.

Chhallá, *s. m.* a ring worn on the toe or finger.

Chhalní, *s. f.* a sieve.

Chhalorí, *s. f.* a whitlow; felon.

Chhál utárná, *v. a.* to peel, to decorticate.

Chhamchhamáná, *v. n.* to shine, to glitter; to sound.

Chhan, *s. m.* a sound made by the falling of a drop of water upon a warm plate; a moment or instant.

Chhán, *s. f.* a roof, a frame of bamboo for thatching.

Chháná, *v. a.* to thatch, to tile, to roof, to shade, to cover, to spread.

Chhanák, *s.* the sound (hissing) of a drop of water falling on a hot plate; the sound of the breaking of earthenware.

Chhanchhanáná, *v. n.* to smart, to pain, to simmer, to crackle (as in frying.)

Chhánd, *s. f.* a tether, a trammel, a net.

Chhándá, **Chhandá**, } *s. m.* a share, part.

Chhándná, *v. n.* to tether, to fasten, to tie, to bind.

Chháṇh, *s. f.* shade, shadow; the reflection of any object in a mirror.

Chhán lená, *v. a.* to choose, to select.

Chhán márná, *v. a.* to search, to rummage.

Chhanná, *v. n.* to be strained: *s. m.* a sieve, a cloth through which any thing is strained or sifted.

Chhánná, *v. a.* to strain, to sift, to search.

Chháṇoṇ, *s. f.* shade, shadow. See Chháṇh.

Chhánṭ, *s. f.* refuse.

Chhánṭ karná, *v. a.* to vomit, to disgorge.

Chhánṭ lená, to elect, to choose.

Chhanṭná, *v. n.* to be extracted, or separated (by pounding.)

Chhánṭná, *v. a.* to husk rice, to wash (clothes) by beating; to pare, to prune, to lop, to crop, to trim, to select; to vomit.

Chhanṭwáná, *v. a.* to cause to husk rice or wash clothes; to cause to pare, crop, trim, &c.

Chháṇw, *s. f.* shade, shadow. See Chháṇh.

Chhanwáná, *v. a.* to cause to sift.

Chhánve, *adj.* ninety-six.

Chháoná, *v. a.* to thatch, tile, &c. See Chháná.

Chháoní, *s. f.* cantonments, barracks or huts for soldiers; thatching, tiling, &c.

Chháp, *s. f.* stamp, print, copy, a seal, impression.

Chhápá, *s. m.* edition, print, seal: *adj.* printed.

Chhapáí, *s. f.* edition, the price of printing.

Chhapáká, *s. m.* the sound produced by striking water, squash.

Chhapáná, *v. a.* to cause to print; to conceal, to hide.
Chhápekhána, *s. m.* a printing office.
Chhápewálá, *s. m.* a printer, a pressman.
Chhápná, *v. a.* to print, to impress a figure, to stamp.
Chhapna, *v. n.* to be printed, to be concealed, to lie hid, to disappear.
Chhappan, *adj.* fifty-six.
Chhappar, *s. m.* a thatched roof.
Chhapparband, *s. m.* a thatcher.
Chhapparbandí, *s. f.* thatching.
Chhapparkhaṭ, } *s. m.* a bed with
Chhapparkháṭ, } curtains.
Chhapwáná, *v. a.* to cause to print.
Chhár, *s. f.* the pole of a spear.
Chhaṛá, } *adj.* alone.
Chhaṛáchaṭánk, }
Chharchobí, *s. f.* a privy, a necessary.
Chhaṛí, *s. f.* a switch, a twig, a thin stick.
Chharrá, *s. m.* small shot.
Chha sát, trick, cheat, juggle.
Chhat, *s. f.* a roof, a cloth ceiling.
Chhát, *s. f.* the roof of a house.
Chhátá, *s. m.* an umbrella.
Chhaṭahá, *adj.* waspish, peevish.
Chhaṭánk, *s. f.* the sixteenth part of a ser, two ounces.
Chhat banáná, *v. a.* to ceil, to cover the inner roof a building.
Chhaṭh, name of a fast.
Chhaṭhá, *adj.* sixth.
Chhaṭhí, *adj. f.* sixth: *s. f.* a religious ceremony performed on the sixth day after childbirth.
Chhátí, *s. f.* the breast, the bosom.
Chhátí bhar, *adj.* breast-high.
Chhátí jalná, to have the heartburn.
Chhátí lagáná, *v. n.* to clasp to the breast, to fondle.
Chhátí kholke milná, to meet frankly.
Chhátí nikálke chalná, to stalk, to strut.
Chhátí par patthar rakhná, to have patience.
Chhátí phaṭní, to break the heart with grief or sorrow.
Chhátí píṭná, to beat the breast from sorrow.
Chhátí se lagáná, to fondle.
Chhátí ṭhaṇḍí honá, to be pleased or overjoyed.
Chhat lagáná, } *v. a.* to ceil, to cover
Chhat páṭná, } the inner part of a building.
Chhaṭpaṭáná, *v. n.* to toss, to tumble about, to flounder.
Chhatrí, *s. f.* a small umbrella; an awning; a frame made of bamboo for pigeons to settle upon: *s. m.* a man of the second or Military tribe of Hindús.
Chhatrídár, *adj.* having a hood or covering (as a carriage, &c.)
Chhattá, *s. m.* a honeycomb.
Chhattar, *s. m.* an umbrella, a place of pilgrimage.
Chhattís, *adj.* thirty-six,
Chhattísí, *adj. f.* prude, prudish.
Chhaṭwáṇ, *adj.* sixth.
Chhauná, *s. m.* young (of any animal.)
Chhauní, *s. f.* barracks, cantonments.
Chhaunkná, *v. a.* to season.
Chhawaiyá, *s. m.* a thatcher.
Chhed, *s. m.* a hole, an orifice.
Chhedná, *v. a.* to pierce, to bore.
Chhekná, *v. a.* to detain, to stop, &c. See Chhenkná.
Chhem, } *s. f.* welfare.
Chhemkushal, }
Chhenk leṇá, *v, a.* to distrain (for rent, &c.), to confiscate.
Chhení, *s. f.* a chisel for cutting iron or stone.
Chhenkṇá, *v. a.* to prevent, to stop, to retain, to restrain, to distrain (for rent, &c.)
Chhenkwaiyá, *s. m.* a preventer, a confiscator.

Chheo, *s. f.* a mark, a cut, a piece of wood cut off.

Chheo márná, *v. a.* to line out, to mark.

Chheoná, *v. a.* to pierce or to bleed a tár, to extract tárí; to mark.

Chher, *s. f.* the act of irritating, vexing, &c.

Chherí, *s. f.* a goat.

Chherná, *v. a.* to irritate, to exasperate, to annoy, to trouble.

Chhetr, *s. m.* a pure or sacred spot, a place of pilgrimage.

Chhí, } *interj.* fye! for shame!
Chhí chhí, }

Chhichhorá, *adj.* trifling, puerile, airy.

Chhíchhrá, *s. m.* the skinny and rejected part of meat, a piece of flesh.

Chhidáná, *v. a.* to cause to pierce, to perforate.

Chhidná, *v. n.* to be pierced or bored.

Chhihattar, *adj.* seventy-six.

Chhíká, *s. m.* a sling for carrying baskets. See Chhínká.

Chhikuní, *s. f.* a wand, stick.

Chhílan, *s. f.* parings.

Chhíl chhál karná, *v. a.* to pare, to peel.

Chhilká, *s. m.* crust, husk, shell, peel, scale, rind, bark, skin.

Chhilká utárná, } *v. a.* to peel, to skin, to pare.
Chhílná, }

Chhilná, *v. n.* to be excoriated.

Chhilwáná, *v. a.* to cause to skin or excoriate, &c.

Chhimá, *s. f.* pardon, forgiveness.

Chhimá karná, *a.* to pardon, to forgive.

Chhímí, *s. f.* a pod, legume.

Chhin, } *s. m.* moment or instant.
Chhín, }

Chhínáchhání karná, *v. a.* to scramble.

Chhinál, *s. f.* a harlot, a strumpet, an adulteress.

Chhinalá, *s. m.* a fornicator.

Chhinálá, *s. m.* fornication, whoredom.

Chhinálá karná, *v. a.* to play the harlot.

Chhinálpan, } *s. m.* harlotry, prostitution.
Chhinálpaná, }

Chhináná, *v. a.* to cause to seize, snatch, pluck, &c.

Chhin bhar men, in a moment.

Chhingulí, *s. f.* a little finger (the fifth.)

Chhínk, *s. f.* sneezing, sneeze.

Chhínká, *s. m.* a network of cords to hang any thing on, the cords of a bahangí.

Chhínkná, *v. n.* to sneeze.

Chhín lená, *v. a.* to snatch away, to forcibly take away, to seize.

Chhínná, *v. a.* to pull away, to tear away, to take or snatch away.

Chhínt, *s. f.* chintz.

Chhíntá, *s. m.* spot, splash.

Chhíntá márná, *v. a.* to sprinkle, to splash.

Chhíntná, *v. a.* to sprinkle, to sow.

Chhinwáná, *v. a.* to cause to snatch.

Chhíp, *s. f.* a fishing-rod.

Chhipá, *adj.* close, hidden, concealed.

Chhipáchhipí, *adj.* underhand, secretly.

Chhipáná, *v. a.* to conceal, to hide.

Chhipá rahná, to abscond.

Chhípí, *s. m.* cloth-printer.

Chhip jáná, *v. n.* to retire, to withdraw.

Chhipkalí, *s. f.* a lizard.

Chhipná, *v. n.* to be concealed, to be absent, to disappear, to lurk.

Chhirakkar bechná, *v. a.* to puff off goods.

Chhirakná, *v. a.* to sprinkle.

Chhirakwáná, } *v. a.* to cause another to sprinkle.
Chhirkáná, }

Chhirkáo, *s. m.* sprinkling, watering.

Chhít, *s. f.* spot, speck; chintz.

Chhitakná, *v. n.* to be scattered or dissipated, to spread.

Chhiṭkáná, *v. a.* to disperse, to scatter, to sprinkle.
Chhiṭkaní, *s. f.* a bolt.
Chhiṭkí, *s. f.* speck, spitting or dashing of rains.
Chhíṭná, *v. a.* to scatter, to sprinkle.
Chhitráná, *v. a.* to scatter, to spread.
Chhiyális, *adj.* forty-six.
Chhiyánauwe, *adj.* ninety-six.
Chhiyásaṭh, *adj.* sixty-six.
Chhiyásí, *adj.* eighty-six.
Chhoá, *s. m.* treacle.
Chhokrá, *s. m.* a boy.
Chhokrí, *s. f.* a girl.
Chholná, *v. a.* to pare, to scrape.
Chholní, *s. f.* a scraper.
Chhop, *s. m.* a coat of paint, plaster &c., a colour.
Chhop chháp karná, } *v. a.* to plaster or re-
Chhopná, } pair a wall.
Chhoṛá, *s. m.* a boy.
Chhoṛá, } *s. m.* release, omission,
Chhoṛáo, } deliverance, letting
Chhoṛáwá, } go.
Chhoṛná, *v. a.* to let go, to forsake, desert, pardon, release; shoot.
Chhoṭá, *adj.* little, small, younger, mean, low.
Chhoṭá baṛá, *adj.* varied, variegated, great and small.
Chhoṭáí, *s. f.* smallness.
Chhoṭpaná, *s. m.* minority, childhood.
Chhúáná, *v. a.* to cause to touch.
Chhúchhá, *adj.* empty, hollow: *s. m.* conjuration.
Chhúchhí, *adj.* empty, mean.
Chhuchhúndar, *s. f.* a musk rat.
Chhuchhúndarí, *s. f.* a squib.
Chhuchkárná, *v. n.* to whistle.
Chhudr, *adj.* mean, low.
Chhuhárá, *s. m.* a dry date.
Chhulakná, *v. n.* to make water slowly (as mares, &c., in heat.)
Chhuláná, *v. a.* to cause to touch.
Chhulchhuláná, *v. n.* see Chhulakná.
Chhúná, *v. a.* to touch, to meddle with, to feel.
Chhurá, *s. m.* a large knife.
Chhuṛáná, *v. a.* to set free, to deliver, to dismiss, to separate, to except.
Chhuṛáwá, *s. m.* a deliverer, setter free.
Chhurí, *s. f.* a knife.
Chhurí tale dam lená, to be patient in difficulties.
Chhuṛwáná, *v. a.* to cause to let go or set free.
Chhút, *s. f.* defilement, contamination, touch.
Chhutahrá, *adj.* defiled by touching, polluted (as persons or vessels.)
Chhuṭká, *adj.* see Chhoṭá.
Chhuṭkárá, *s. m.* deliverance, salvation, exemption, liberty.
Chhuṭná, } *v. n.* to be adrift, to be
Chhúṭná, } discharged, to escape, to be liberated, to be loose, to cease, to leave, to remain, to slip away, to spout.
Chhuṭpaná, *s. m.* childhood, infancy.
Chhuṭṭí, *s. f.* discharge, leave, leisure, disengagement, permission, freedom.
Chibil, } *adj.* childish, boyish.
Chibillá, }
Chichindá, *s. m.* the name of a vegetable.
Chichiyáná, *v. n.* to squeak, to shriek, to bleat.
Chihra, *s. m.* face, visage, countenance, description roll.
Chihra likháná, *v. a.* to enlist; to take service and horses.
Chihra likhná, *v. a.* to write a description roll (soldier's.)
Chik, *s. m.* a butcher who kills only goats, sheep, kids, and lambs.
Chikan, *s. m. f.* embroidery on muslin or cloth.
Chikandoz, *s. m.* an embroiderer.
Chikárná, *v. n.* to squeak.
Chíkaṭ, *s. f.* a mixture of oil and dust, greasy or dusty (as clothes.)
Chíkh, *s. f.* a scream, a screech, a shriek.

Chíkh márná, *v. n.* to scream, to screech, to roar, to cry.
Chíkhná, *v. a.* to taste.
Chikkaṭ, *adj.* filthy, covered with grease and dirt.
Chikkí, *s. f.* a rotten betel-nut.
Chikná, *adj.* beautiful; greasy, oily: *s. m.* oil, lard.
Chiknáhaṭ, *s. f.* cleanness, smoothness, polish; greasiness; beauty.
Chiknáí, *s. f.* fat of meat; gloss, smoothness.
Chiknáná, *v. a.* to clean, to polish, to smooth.
Chikní máṭí, } *s. f.* clay, potter's
Chikní miṭṭí, } clay.
Chikní supárí, *s. f.* a kind of betel-nut prepared by boiling.
Chikṭhá, *adj.* filthy, greasy.
Chíl, *s. f.* a kite.
Chilam, *s. f.* the part of a huqqa which contains the tobacco and fire.
Chilamchí, *s. f.* a metal washing-bason.
Chilchiláná, *v. n.* to shreik, to scream, to screech.
Chilghoza, *s. m.* a kind of nut.
Chílhaṛ, *s. f.* a louse.
Chilhwáṇs, *s. m.* screaming like a kite.
Chíl jhapaṭṭá márná, to snatch away (as kites.)
Chillá, *s. m.* quarantine; the string of a bow.
Chillá chaṛháná, *v. a.* to bend a bow.
Chilláhaṭ, *s. f.* cry, outcry, scream.
Chillá khainchná, *v. a.* to bend a bow; to prepare for battle; to keep quarantine.
Chilláná, *v. n.* to scream, to shriek.
Chillaṛ, *s. f.* a louse.
Chilṛáhá, *adj.* lousy.
Chilta, *s. f.* a coat of mail.
Chilwan, *s. f.* a screen for keeping out the glare, a venetian blind, a lattice.
Chimaṛná, *v. n.* to be tough, to grow tough.
Chimaṭná, *v. n.* to adhere, to stick.
Chimṛá, *adj.* tough, flexible.
Chimṛáná, *v. n.* to toughen, to grow tough.
Chimṛí, *adj.* infrangible (as a quill), hard.
Chimṭá, *s. m.* tongs, forceps or pincers, a pair of nippers.
Chimṭáná, *v. n.* to adhere, to cling to.
Chimṭhá, *adj.* elastic, tough.
Chimṭí káṭná, *v. a.* to pinch.
Chín, *s. m.* China.
Chindí, *s.* piece, fragment, &c.
Chindí chindí karná, to break or tear to pieces.
Chingárí, *s. f.* a spark or coal (of fire.)
Chinghár, *s. f.* scream, screech, clamour.
Chinghároṇ márná, to scream, to roar.
Chinghárná, *v. n.* to scream, to screech (applied properly to the elephant.)
Chingí, *s. f.* spark (of fire.)
Chingí jhaṛná, } *v. n.* to sparkle.
Chingí nikalná, }
Chingní, *s. f.* a chicken.
Chingṛá, *s. m.* a prawn, a shrimp.
Chinh, } *s. m.* a scar, a mark, sign,
Chính, } symbol, token by which anything is known; signature.
Chínhá, } *s. m.* an acquaintance.
Chínhá parchá, }
Chinhár, }
Chinhárí, *s. f.* acquaintance.
Chínhná, *v. a.* to know, to recognise.
Chíní, *s. f.* sugar; Chinese; earthenware.
Chintá, *s. f.* thoughtfulness, care, anxiety, a thought, risk, peril, danger.
Chínṭí, *s. f.* a small ant.

Chipakná, } v. n. to stick, to adhere.
Chipaṭná, }

Chipchipáná, v. n. to adhere, to cohere.

Chipná, v. n. to be concealed.

Chípná, v. a. to squeeze, to express the juice from a fruit, to press out.

Chippí, s. f. a patch on paper.

Chiprí, s. f. cakes of cow-dung.

Chipṭáná, v. a. to stick to, to apply patches.

Chiq, s. f. a kind of lattice used as a blind to windows or doors.

Chír, s. m. rent, split, strip, crack.

Chiṛ, s. f. vexation, irritation; aversion, antipathy.

Chírá, s. m. a turban.

Chirágh, s. m. a lamp, a light.

Chirágh baṛháná, v. a. to put out, to extinguish (a lamp.)

Chirághdán, s. m. a stand for a lamp.

Chirághí, s. f. a present made to the Mullá for offering oblations at the tomb of a saint, &c.

Chirághpá, adj. rearing (a horse.)

Chirakná, v. n. to have a scanty stool.

Chiráná, v. a. to cause to tear or be torn, to cause to split.

Chiṛáná, v. a. to vex, irritate, provoke, offend, mock, gibe, jeer.

Chiranjí, adj. long-lived.

Chiṛh, s. f. abhorrence, abomination, dislike, vexation.

Chiṛímár, s. m. a bird-catcher, a fowler.

Chiṛiyá, s. f. a bird, a kind of sewing, a hen sparrow.

Chiṛiyáḳhána, s. m. an aviary.

Chirk, s. m. dirt, filth, ordure, matter from a wound, pus.

Chirkuṭ, s. m. a rag, a piece.

Chirkuṭiyá, adj. tattered, ragged.

Chirná, v. n. to be rent or split.

Chírná, v. a. to rend, to split, to cleave, to saw, to plough the water (as a ship.)

Chír nikálná, v. a. to break through troops.

Chironjí, s. f. a kind of nut.

Chirwáná, v. a. see Chiráná.

Chit, s. m. the mind, the attention, memory: adj. lying flat on the back.

Chiṭ, s. f. rag, scrap.

Chitá, s. f. a funeral pile.

Chítá, s. m. a leopard or panther; a kind of snake: adj. spotted, speckled.

Chitáná, } v. a. to caution, warn,
Chitáoná, } admonish.

Chitáoní, s. f. a token, admonition, warning.

Chit dená, v. a. to pay attention.

Chithaṛiyá, adj. tattered, ragged, clothed in rags.

Chíṭhí, s f. a letter, a note, an assignment.

Chithṛá, } s. m. a rag.
Chíthṛá, }

Chitkabrá, adj. piebald, speckled.

Chítná, v. a. to draw, to paint.

Chitrbichitr, adj. of various colours, variegated.

Chiṭṭá, adj. white: s. a rupee.

Chiṭṭhá, s. m. a memorandum of money paid.

Chiṭṭhí, s. f. a note, a letter.

Chiṭṭi, s. f. the hen of the little birds called Amaduvades.

Chittí, s. f. a spot, a freckle.

Chittídár, adj. speckled, spotted.

Chiṭ ukhaṛná, v. n. to splinter, or have small pieces knocked off furniture.

Chíz, s. f. thing, commodity, any thing.

Chízbast, s. f. chattels, baggage, furniture.

Choá, s. m. the name of a perfume.

Choáná, v. a. to cause to drip, to distil, to filter.

Chob, s. f. a drumstick.

Chobchíní, s. f. the name of a medicine, Chiná-root.

Chobdár, *s. m.* a servant whose business it is to announce the arrival of visitors, a mace-bearer.

Chobhá, *s. m.* a kind of victuals given upon special occasions, marriages, &c.

Chobkárí, *s. f.* a kind of embroidery.

Chochlá, *s. m.* playfulness, coquetry, toyish.

Chokaṛ, *s. m.* bran.

Chokhá, *adj.* pure, unadulterated, genuine, good, fine, sharp.

Cholá, *s. m.* the body.

Cholí, *s. f.* a sort of bodice worn by females.

Chonch, *s. f.* a beak, bill.

Choṇchlá, *s. m.* see Chochlá.

Choṇḍa, *s. m.* hair braided on the top of the head.

Chondhlá, *adj.* dim, purblind, dim-sighted.

Chondhláná, *v. n.* to be purblind, to see dimly.

Chonglá, *s. m.* a joint of bamboos used to send letters in.

Chonthná, *v. a.* to scratch, to claw.

Choṇṭí, *s. f.* pinnacle, top, summit, the hair braided behind.

Choráná, *v. a.* to steal, to rob.

Chor, } *s. m.* a thief, a robber.
Chorchakár, }

Chorí, *s. f.* theft, robbery, thievery.

Chorí chorí, *adv.* by stealth, clandestinely.

Chorḳhána, *s. m.* a secret drawer.

Choṭ, *s. f.* a blow, a contusion, a stroke.

Choṭí, *s. f.* the plait or tie of hair behind, a summit of a hill.

Choṭ kháná, *v. n.* to be hurt, to receive a blow, to suffer loss.

Choṭ par choṭ, one misfortune follows another.

Choṭṭá, *s. m.* a thief, a robber.

Chúbh, *s. m.* prick, puncture.

Chubháná, *v. a.* to stick into, to pierce, to goad, to stab, to prick.

Chubhná, } *v. n.* to be stuck into, to be pierced, goaded, stabbed, to penetrate.
Chúbhná, }

Chubhoná, *v. a.* see Chubháná.

Chubkí, *s. f.* a plunge in water, dip.

Chúchí, *s. f.* breast.

Chuchkárná, *v. n.* to fondle, to chirp to.

Chuchuháná, *v. n.* to sing, whistle, warble (as birds); to glow as a colour, to dye a deep colour.

Chugáná, *v. a.* to cause to peck (as a hen her chickens.)

Chughlí, *s. f.* tale-bearing, backbiting.

Chughlí kháná, *v. n.* to backbite, to tell tales, to inform.

Chughul, } *s. m.* a tell-tale, tale-bearer, backbiter, informer.
Chughulḳhor, }

Chughulḳhorí, *s. f.* the act of backbiting.

Chug lená, *v. a.* to select, to choose.

Chugná, *v. n.* to peck, to pick up food with the beak.

Chúhá, *s. m.* a rat, a mouse.

Chuhal, *s. f.* cheer, jollity, mirth, festivals.

Chuhal karná, *v. n.* to make merry, &c.

Chúhedán, *s. m.* a mouse or rat trap.

Chúhemár, *s. m.* a rat-catcher.

Chúhí, *s. f.* a mouse.

Chuhiyá, *s.* a little mouse.

Chúhṛá, *s. m.* } a sweeper, halálḳhor.
Chúhṛí, *s. f.* }

Chúk, *s. f.* an error, fault, a blunder, an oversight, a mistake; name of a medicine for indigestion.

Chukáná, *v. a.* to finish, to complete, to settle, to adjust, to fix the price of.

Chukautá, *s. m.* a task, agreement, settlement.

Chukká, } *s. m.* an earthen pot for drinking spirituous liquors out of.
Chukkaṛ, }

Chukkí, *s. f.* deceit, fraud.

Chukkí dená, *v. a.* to deceive, to play tricks.

Chukná, *v. n.* to be finished, to be completed; to be agreed upon (as price, &c.)

Chúkná, *v. n.* to blunder, to mistake, to depart from, to err.

Chuktí, *s. f.* settlement.

Chúl, *s. f.* the part of a joiner's work which fits into another (as dovetail); a pivot upon which a door turns.

Chuláná, *v. a.* to distil, to cause to drip, &c.

Chulbulá, *adj.* restless, fickle, unsteady.

Chulbuláná, *v. n.* to be restless or inconstant.

Chulchul, *s. m.* wantonness, inconstancy.

Chulchuláná, *v. n.* to itch, to titillate.

Chulchulí, *s. f.* see Chulchul.

Chúlhá, *s. m.* } a fire-place, a portable hearth.
Chúlhí, *s. f.* }

Chullú, *s. m.* a handful, the palm of the hand contracted so as to hold water.

Chumá, } *s. m.* a kiss.
Chúmá, }

Chúmácháṭí, *s. f.* dalliance.

Chúmakpatthar, *s. m.* a magnet, a loadstone.

Chumáná, *v. a.* to cause to kiss.

Chumbak, *s. m.* a magnet.

Chumkár, *s. f.* a sound with the lips by which dogs and horses are called.

Chumkárná, *v. a.* to coax, to speak kindly to, to soothe.

Chummá, *s. m.* a kiss.

Chummak, *s. m.* a loadstone.

Chúmná, *v. a.* to kiss.

Chúná, *v. n.* to leak, to be filtered; to drop from the tree when ripe: *s. m.* lime.

Chuná lená, *v. a.* to plait (cloth.)

Chunan, *s. m.* rumple, crease.

Chunáná, *v. a.* to cause to pick, choose, &c.

Chunánchi, *adv.* so that, such, such as that.

Chunáṉ chuníṉ, *adv.* in this and that manner; (*met.*) evasion, subterfuge.

Chunat, *s. f.* plaiting (cloths), plaits.

Chunauṭá, *s. m.* } a box for holding the lime used to chew with betel.
Chunauṭí, *s. f.* }

Chunáwaṭ, *s. f.* a plait.

Chúnchí, *s. f.* breast.

Chunchunáná, *v. n.* to throb (as the body from heat.)

Chundhá, } *adj.* dim, purblind, dim-sighted.
Chúndhá, }

Chundhláná, *v. n.* to be purblind, to see dimly.

Chungí *s. f.* tax, toll, duty, a tax gathered from grain merchants by faqírs, being as much grain as a man can grasp in his hand.

Chungná, *v. a.* to pick up food as birds.

Chúní, *s. f.* pulse split or ground very coarsely; a small ruby or other gem.

Chunná, *v. a.* to gather, to pick, to choose, to pick up food as birds; to place in order; to plait: *s. m.* lime.

Chunní, *s. f.* a small ruby.

Chúnṭá, *s. m.* a large ant.

Chúnṭí, *s. f.* a small ant; a pinch.

Chúnṭná, *v. a.* to pinch, to claw.

Chunwáná, *v. a.* to cause to pick, select, put in order, &c.

Chup, *adj.* silent, quiet: *interj.* silence! be quiet!

Chúpaṛ, *s. m.* grease.

Chúpcháp, *adj.* silent: *adv.* silently, secretly.

Chupchupáte, *adv.* silently, secretly.

Chupká, } *adj.* silent.
Chupkí, }

Chuppí, *s. f.* silence.

Chupṛá, *adj.* plausible though false.

Chup rah, silence, be still, be quiet.
Chupṛí, *adj. f.* oiled, greasy; smooth, plausible.
Chupṛí bát, flattery, soft words.
Chupṛí roṭí, cakes rich with clarified butter.
Chuqundur, *s. m.* beet, beet-root.
Chúr, *s. m.* powder, filings, atoms: *adj.* bruised.
Chúrá, *s. m.* filings, saw-dust.
Chúṛá, *s. m.* flattened rice; a kind of bracelet.
Churail, *s. f.* the ghost of a woman who died when pregnant; a hag, a fury; a dirty woman, a slut.
Chúran, *s. m.* compounded powder for promoting digestion.
Churáná, *v. a.* to filch, to steal, to rob.
Chúrchár, } *adj.* broken to atoms:
Chúrchúr, } *s. m.* pieces and fragments.
Chúr honá, *v. n.* to be broken into small pieces.
Chúṛí, } *s. f.* a kind of bracelet.
Churí, }
Chúr karná, *v. a.* to reduce to very small pieces or to atoms.
Churkí, *s. f.* lock of hair.
Chúrná, *v. a.* to reduce to very small pieces or to atoms.
Churúá, *s. m.* a dish prepared from parched rice.
Churugná, *v. n.* to gabble, to prattle.
Chúsná, *v. a.* to suck.
Chúsní, *s. f.* a coral or other plaything for little children to suck.
Chuṭálná, *v. a.* to wound.
Chútaṛ, *s. m.* the buttocks, the backside, breech.
Chuṭílá, *adj.* wounded, bruised.
Chuṭiyáná, *v. a.* to wound.
Chuṭkí, *s. f.* a pinch; snapping of the fingers.
Chuṭkí káṭná, *v. a.* to pinch.
Chuṭkiyá, *s. f.* a lock of hair left on the head when the rest is shaved.
Chuṭkiyoṇ meṇ uṛáná, to turn into ridicule.
Chúza, *s. m.* a chicken.
Chúzabáz, *s. f.* an old woman fond of striplings.
Chyúnṭá, *s. m.* a black ant.
Chyúnṭí, *s. m.* a small ant.

D.

Ḍab, *s. m.* a small leathern vessel for holding oil.
Ḍáb, *s. m.* a sword-belt; unripe cocoanut.
Dabak baiṭhná, } *v. n.* to crouch, to
Dabakná, } lie in ambush.
Dabá lená, to encroach upon.
Dabá márná, to overcome, to crush to death.
Dabáná, *v. a.* to press down; to chide, to keep under.
Dabang, } *adj.* ill-bred, brutish,
Dabangá, } clownish.
Dabáo, *s. m.* submissiveness; overladen.
Ḍabbá, *s. m.* a leathern vessel for holding oil.
Ḍabbú, *s. m.* a large iron spoon.
Ḍabḍabáná, *v. a.* to fill with tears.
Dabel, *s. m.* subject, person under dominion.
Dabe páoṇ, *adj.* with silent steps, softly, gently.
Ḍabgar, *s. m.* the person who makes the ḍab or ḍabbá.
Dabjáná, to be mortified, to be suppressed.
Dabkáná, *v. a.* to conceal, to hide.
Ḍabká, *s. m.* fresh water drawn from a well.
Dabkí márná, to lie in ambush.
Dab marná, to be crushed to death.
Dabná, *v. n.* to be snubbed, to crouch, to be pressed down, to be awed, to be concealed.
Dábná, *v. a.* to press down, to suppress; to subdue the passions; to squeeze.
Ḍabrá, *s. m.* marshy land, a puddle.

Dáb rakhná, *v. a.* to conceal, to steal and conceal, to press (particularly with the thighs), to retain by pressure.
Dachhiná, *s. f.* a fee given to a bráhman.
Dád, *s. f.* gift; justice; complaint; in *compos.* given.
Dád, *s. m.* the ringworm, herpes.
Dadá, *s. f.* a nurse.
Dádá, *s. m.* paternal grandfather.
Dád dihish, *s. f.* liberality, beneficence.
Dádí, *s. f.* paternal grandmother.
Dád faryád, *s. f.* complaint.
Dádí faryádí, *s.* a plaintiff, a complainant.
Dád ḳhwáh, *s.* a plaintiff, a petitioner for justice.
Dád ko pahunchná, to obtain justice.
Dád lení, *v.* to take revenge.
Dád milní, *v. n.* to obtain redress.
Dádní, *s. f.* advances (of money), for work or goods.
Dád o bedár, crying out for help or justice.
Dadoṛá, *s. m.* a bump (occasioned by the bite of an insect.)
Dádrá, *s. m.* a kind of song.
Dádur, Dádurwá, } *s. m.* a frog.
Dáejá, *s. m.* dowry, dower.
Ḍaen, *s. f.* a witch.
Dáeṉ báeṉ, on the right and left.
Daf, *s. m.* a small tambourin.
Dafạ, *s. m.* repulsion, averting, warding off: *s. f.* a time, a turn.
Dafạ ba dafạ, *adv.* from time to time, repeatedly.
Dafạdár, *s. m.* an officer placed over an affair.
Dafạ karná, *v. a.* to repel, to ward off, to remove.
Dafálí, *s. m.* a player on the tambourin or daf.
Dafla, *s. m.* a tambourin.
Dafnáná, *v. a.* to bury, to inter.
Dafn honá, *v. n.* to be buried.
Dafn karná, *v. a.* to bury, to inter.
Daftar, *s. m.* record, register, a parcel of account books or papers.
Daftarí, *s. m.* one who in an office makes and mends the office books and pens, and rules lines, &c.
Daftarḳhána, *s. m.* a record-office, a counting-house.
Daftín, *s. f.* the boards of the binding of a book, pasteboard.
Ḍagar, *s. f.* a road, a highway.
Ḍagḍagáná, *v. n.* to shake, to burn brightly, to burn clear (charcoal.)
Ḍaggá, *s. m.* a thin long-legged person or animal.
Dágh, *s. m.* mark, scar, spot, stain, a mark made by burning with a hot iron, a brand.
Daghá, *s. f.* deceit, imposture, treachery, fraud.
Daghábáz, *s.* a cheat, a traitor, an impostor.
Daghábází, *s. f.* fraud, deceit, villany.
Daghá dení, to cheat, to impose upon.
Daghá kháni, to be deceived, &c.
Daghal fasal, treachery, deceit, depravity.
Dagháná, *v. a.* to cause to fire a gun; to cause any thing to be marked.
Daghdaghá, Daghdagha, } *s. m.* alarm, fear, dread, awe.
Dághdár, *adj.* spotted, stained, cauterized, marked.
Dágh dená, *v. a.* to mark by burning with a hot iron, to brand, to cauterize.
Dághí, *adj.* spotted, stained, marked, blotted.
Dághí karná, *v. a.* to stain, to blemish.
Daghilá, *adj.* stained, spotted.
Dágh lagáná, *v. a.* to vilify.
Dágh lagná, *v. n.* to be damaged; to get a bad name.

Dághná, *v. a.* to cauterize, to mark by burning with a hot iron; to fire (a gun, &c.)
Daghná, *v. n.* to be marked; to be fired off (as a gun, &c.)
Dághrezí, *s. f.* the repairing of cracks, &c., in the terrace, roofs, &c., of buildings.
Daglá, *s. m.* a kind of quilted coat.
Dagmagáná, **Ḍagmagáná**, } *v. n.* to tremble, to totter, to stagger, to shake (the hand.)
Ḍagrá *s. m.* a kind of tray made of bamboo.
Dáh, *s. m.* malice, spite, envy.
Dahá, *s. m.* the first ten days of the Muharram.
Dahakná, *v. n.* to burn, to be burnt.
Dahalná, *v. n.* to shake, to tremble, to fear.
Dahána, *s. m.* the mouth, mouth of a water-bag.
Dáh dená, to light the funeral pile.
Dahez, *s. m.* a dowry, a portion, everything a wife carries with her to her husband.
Dahí, *s. m.* curdled sour milk.
Ḍáhí, *adj.* spiteful, malicious.
Dáhiná, *adj.* right (the opposite to left.)
Dahíwálá, *s. m.* **Dahíwálí**, *s. f.* } a seller of dahí.
Dahkáná, *v. a.* to burn to kindle.
Dalíz, *s. f.* a portico.
Dahná, *adj.* right (the opposite of left.)
Dáhná, *v. a.* to burn: *adj.* see Dahiná.
Dahserá, *s. m.* a measure of ten ser.
Ḍahrá, *s. m.* the bottom of a boat where the water accumulates.
Dahshat, *s. f.* fear, terror, dread, awe.
Dahshat dení, to frighten, terrify, alarm.
Dáí, *s. f.* a milk-nurse, a midwife: *s. m.* in *compos.* giver, giving.
Dáíjanáí, *s. f.* a midwife.
Dáígarí, *s. f.* midwifery.
Dáíkhiláí, *s. f.* a dry-nurse.
Dáí ko sompná, to put out to nurse.
Ḍáin, *s. f.* a witch.
Ḍainá, *s. m.* a wing.
Ḍáinpaná, *s. m.* witchcraft.
Dáípiláí, *s. f.* a wet-nurse.
Dáira, *s. m.* a circle, circumference, orbit.
Dáir o sáir, going the circuit (judges, &c.); absolute, invested with authority.
Ḍáiya, *s. m.* petition, plaint.
Daiyá, *s. f.* a mother, a nurse.
Ḍák, *s. f.* a post (for the conveyance of letters and parcels; also a relay of horses or of pálkí-bearers.)
Ḍáká, *s. m.* an attack by robbers.
Ḍáká dená, *v. a.* to rob, to plunder.
Ḍakait, *s. m.* a robber, a pirate.
Dakaití, *s. f.* robbery, piracy.
Ḍakár, *s. f.* a belch.
Ḍakár baiṭhná, **Ḍakár jáná**, } *v. n.* to embezzle.
Ḍakárná, *v. n.* to belch; to bellow, to low.
Ḍáká paṛná, *v. n.* to be robbed.
Ḍák bahangí, *s. f.* a post conveyance of parcels.
Ḍák chaukí, *s. f.* a place where the post is changed.
Ḍák ghar, *s. m.* a post-office.
Dakhan, *s. m.* south, the southern part of India.
Dakhaní, *adj.* southern (generally things or persons from the south.)
Dáḳhil, *s. m.* the delivering of goods, the payment of money; entering, arriving: *adj.* entered, received.
Dáḳhilá, *s. m.* a receipt for money, &c.
Dáḳhil honá, *v. n.* to enter, to be inserted.
Dáḳhil, karná, *v. a.* to hand in (as money into the treasury), to enter

(as accounts), to insert, to cause to enter or arrive.

Daḳhil, *s. m.* entrance; interference, the meddling with an affair; possession, income.

Daḳhl karná, *v. a.* to meddle, to interfere, to concern one's self, to take possession, to enter.

Daḳhl páná, *v. a.* to have access.

Dakhná, *adj.* southern: *s. f.* southerly wind.

Dakkhan, } *s. m.* south, the southern part of India.
Dakkhin, }

Dakkhiná, *adj.* southern: *s. f.* southerly wind.

Ḍák mahsúl, *s. m.* the postage of a letter or parcel.

Ḍák piyáda, *s. m.* a postman, a letter-carrier.

Ḍákú, *s. m.* a robber, a pirate.

Ḍákwálá, *s. m.* a postman, a letter-carrier.

Dal, *s. m.* thickness.

Ḍál, *s. f.* a branch, a bough.

Dál, *s. f.* pulse or vetches, or peas split.

Ḍálá, *s. m.* a large basket, a tray of wicker-work.

Dalá, *s. m.* a large lump, a clod.

Daláil, *s.* (*plur.* of Dalíl), proofs, arguments.

Dálán, *s. m.* a hall.

Dalbádal, *s. m.* a mass of clouds; a large army; a large tent.

Dálchíní, *s. f.* cinnamon.

Daldal, *s. f.* a quagmire, a bog.

Daldalá, *adj.* swampy, quaggy, boggy.

Daldaláhaṭ, *s. f.* tremor.

Daldaláná, *v. n.* to shake.

Daldalí, *adj.* see Daldalá.

Daldár, *adj.* thick.

Ḍál dená, *v. a.* to throw away.

Dalhárá, *s. m.* }
Dalháran, *s. f.* } one who sells dál.
Dalhárí, *s. f.* }

Ḍalí, *s. f.* a lump (of sugar, meat, &c.)

Ḍálí, *s. f.* a basket full of any articles, or of fruits, &c., for a present; a branch, a bough.

Dalidr, } *s. m.* wretchedness, poverty, indigency.
Dálidr, }

Dalidrí, } *adj.* poor, wretched, indigent, unfortunate.
Dálidrí, }

Dalíl, *s. f.* argument, proof, demonstration.

Dalílí, *adj.* argumentative: *s. m.* a good arguer.

Ḍaliyá, *s. m.* a basket (without a cover, like a tray.)

Dallál, *s. m.* a broker, an appraiser.

Dallálí, *s. f.* brokerage, the business of a broker.

Dal masal karná, *v. a.* to thrash, to crumple, to rumple, to ruffle.

Dalná, *v. a.* to grind coarsely, to split pulse.

Ḍálná, *v. a.* to throw down, to fling, to cast, to pour, to thrust, to throw away.

Ḍalwá, *s. m.* a large basket (without a lid.)

Dalwaiyá, *s. m.* one who grinds.

Dalwáná, *v. a.* to cause to be coarsely ground.

Dám, *s. m.* a net, a snare; the twenty-fourth part of a paisá; the price of a thing, value.

Dam, *s. m.* breath, life; boasting; a moment; deceit.

Dama, *s. m.* asthma.

Dámád, *s. m.* a son-in-law.

Dámádí, *s. f.* state, quality or right of a son-in-láw.

Damak, *s. f.* glitter.

Damakná, *v. n.* to shine.

Damámá, } *s. m.* a kettle-drum.
Damáma, }

Dáman, *s. m.* the skirt of a garment; *fig.* protection; the foot of a mountain.

Dámangír, *adj.* attached to, an adherent, a dependent.

Dámangírí, *s. f.* dependence.

Dáman pakaṛná, *v. a.* to take protection.

Ḍámar, *s. m.* resin.
Ḍamarú, *s. m.* a sort of drum beaten with the fingers.
Dam ba dam, *adj.* every moment, constantly.
Dambáz, *s. m.* a wheedler, a deceiver.
Dam bází, *s. f.* wheedling, deceiving.
Dam bharná, to boast.
Dam chaṛhná, *v. a.* to pant, to respire.
Dam chhoṛná, *v. a.* to expire.
Dam dená, *v. a.* to coax, to deceive, to keep warm (as meat after having been cooked.)
Damdilásá, *s. m.* encouragement, comfort, soothing, coaxing.
Dam honá, *v. n.* to be left on the fire after cooling (as a puláo.)
Dáminí, *s. f.* lightning.
Dáminí damakná, *v. n.* to lighten.
Damkalá, *s. m.* a screw-jack used to raise weights; a fire-engine.
Dam karná, to blow (as a conjuror when juggling or exorcising.)
Dam khá jáná, } to remain silent,
Dam kháná, } to bear insults patiently and without retaliating.
Dam lená, *v. n.* to take breath, to rest.
Dam márná, *v. n.* to waste one's breath in speaking; to boast.
Dam nák meṉ áná, to be fatigued to death, to gasp for life.
Dam nikalná, *v. n.* to die.
Dam phúlná, *v. n.* to breathe short.
Damṛí, *s. f.* the eighth part of a paisá.
Damṛí ke tín tín honá, to be ruined.
Dam sádhná, *v. n.* to stop one's breath when feigning death.
Dam ṭúṭná, to die.
Dán, *s. m.* a donation, a gift, a present, alms; an affix denoting the receptacle, place or stand.
Dáná, *adj.* wise, prudent.
Dána, *s. m.* a grain, seed, corn, speck, pimple.
Dána badalná, *v. a.* to caress as birds do by joining bills, to bill.
Dána badlauwal, billing, caressing as birds do by joining bills.
Dánadár, having the appearance of being granulated.
Dánáí, *s. f.* wisdom.
Dána pání, *s. m.* food, victuals, meat and drink.
Danḍ, } *s. m.* fine, punishment.
Dánḍ, }
Ḍanḍ, *s. m.* the arm above the elbow; a kind of bodily exercise.
Ḍánḍ, *s. m.* retaliation, punishment, penalty; an oar; the backbone.
Dánḍá, *s. m.* landmarks.
Ḍanḍá, *s. m.* a staff, an ensign staff, the posts of a bedstead.
Dandanáná, *v. n.* to enjoy one's self, to live at one's ease.
Danḍawat, *s. f.* Hindú salutation, bow, obeisance.
Dánḍ bharná, *v. a.* to pay a fine.
Ḍánḍí, *s. m.* a rower, a boatman.
Ḍanḍí, *s. f.* a handle; the beam of a pair of scales.
Ḍanḍídár, *s. m.* a weigher.
Ḍanḍiyá, *s. m.* a collector of market duties.
Ḍánḍ lená, to take a fine, to fine.
Ḍanḍpel, *adj.* one who exercises himself at the ḍanḍ.
Dándrá, *s. m.* landmarks.
Ḍanḍwat, } *s. f.* Hindú salutation,
Dánḍwat, } bow, obeisance.
Dang, *adj.* astonished.
Dangá, } *s. m.* wrangling, mu-
Dangá fasád, } tiny, sedition, a disturbance, an uproar.
Dangal, *s. f.* a crowd.
Ḍángar, *adj.* thin, lean: *s. m.* a lean beast, a starveling.
Dangebáz, *adj.* mutinous, turbulent.
Dání, *adj.* charitable, liberal, bountiful: *s. f.* in *compos. dimin.* of dán, receptacle, stand, place, &c.
Dánish, *s. f.* wisdom, knowledge.

Dánishmand, *adj.* wise, sensible.
Dánishmandí, *s. f.* learning, wisdom.
Dánist, *s. f.* knowledge, opinion.
Ḍank, *s. m.* the sting of a reptile, particularly of a scorpion.
Ḍanká, *s. m.* a double kettledrum.
Ḍaukiní, *s. f.* a witch.
Ḍank márná, *v. a.* to sting, (as a reptile.)
Dánpattar, *s. m.* a deed of gift.
Dánpun, *s. m.* charity, alms.
Ḍáṇr, *s. m.* an oar.
Ḍáṇrí, *s. m.* a rower, a boatman.
Ḍaṇs, } *s. m.* the sting of a reptile;
Ḍáṇs, } a large musquito.
Dánt, *s. m.* a tooth.
Dántákilkil, *s. f.* a quarrel.
Ḍáuṭhí, *s. f.* a straw, stubble, stalk.
Dántí, *s. f.* the tooth of a saw or other instrument.
Dántí lagná, to have a locked jaw.
Dánt kachkacháná, } *v. n.* to grind
Dánt kaṭkaṭáná, } the teeth.
Dánt lagná, to have a locked jaw.
Ḍánṭná, *v. a.* to snub, to rebuke, to threaten, to browbeat.
Dánt nikálná, *v. n.* to laugh, to grin.
Dánt nikalná *v. n.* to teeth.
Dantpír, *s. f.* the tooth-ache.
Dánt písná, to gnash the teeth.
Dáṇw, *s. m.* ambuscade, ambush; opportunity; a stake, a wager.
Ḍáṇwáṇḍol, *s. m.* wandering without house or home.
Dáṇw chaláná, *v. a.* to take advantage of.
Dáṇw chalná, to have the advantage.
Ḍáṇwrú, *s. m.* a tiger's cub or whelp.
Dáo, *s. m.* a bill-hook, a sickle.
Dáoná, *v. a.* to thrash.
Dapaṭ, *s. f.* course, gallop.
Dapaṭná, *v. n.* to gallop, to rush; to rebuke, to reprimand.
Dapdapáná, } *v. a.* to shine.
Dapdap karná, }
Dapṭáná, *v. a.* to gallop.
Dár, *s. m.* a dwelling, a mansion, an abode; a gibbet, a gallows: *s. f.* pulse, vetches; in *compos.* having, possessing, master, keeper, lord.
Ḍár, *s. f.* branch, bough.
Dar, *s. m.* a door; price, rate: *prep.* in, at, on, into.
Ḍar, *s. m.* fear, dread, awe.
Daráj, *s. m. Eng.* drawers.
Daṛakná, *v. n.* to split, to rend, to be torn, to crack.
Daraḳht, *s. m.* a tree.
Dar áná, *v. n.* to come in, to engage (in), to arrive, to penetrate.
Ḍaráná, *v. a.* to frighten, to scare, to alarm, to deter: *adj.* frightful, terrible.
Darántí, *s. f.* a sickle.
Darár, *s. m.* a crack, a fissure, rent.
Ḍaráwná, *v. a.* to frighten: *adj.* frightful, terrifying.
Daráz, *adj.* long.
Darází, *s. f.* length, extension.
Darb, *s. m.* wealth, property; metal.
Dar ba dar, from door to door.
Darbán, *s. m.* a door-keeper, a porter.
Darbání, *s. f.* the office of a door-keeper.
Darbár, *s. m.* a court, a hall of audience, house; the holding of a court.
Darbár bándná, to bribe, to give bribes.
Darbárí, *s. m.* a courtier: *adj.* attending court.
Dárchíní, *s. f.* cinnamon.
Dard, *s. m.* pain, affliction; pity, sympathy, compassion.
Dardálán, *s. m.* an outer hall.
Dard áná *v. n.* to be affected with compassion.
Dardará, *adj.* half-pounded, coarsely ground.
Dard i sar, *s. m.* the head-ache.
Dard i shikham, *s. m.* colic.
Dard kháná, *v. a.* to feel compas-

sion or pity, to feel the pains of child-birth.

Dard lagná, *v. n.* to feel the pains of child-birth.

Dardmand, *adj.* compassionate, sympathizing.

Dardmandí, *s. f.* compassion, feeling.

Daregh, *s. m.* a sigh, sorrow, repugnance.

Dargáh, *s. f.* a palace, court, threshold, door; a mosque; presence.

Darguzar karná, *v. a.* to pass over, to neglect, to excuse.

Darguzarná, *v. n.* to decline, to leave off, to refrain from, to pass by.

Ḍáṛh, *s. f.* a jaw-tooth or grinder.

Dáṛhí, Ḍáṛhí, } *s. f.* beard.

Ḍáṛhí banáná, Ḍáṛhí múndná, } *v. a.* to shave.

Ḍaṛhiyal, *adj.* having a long beard.

Ḍaṛhmuṇḍá, *adj.* beard-shaven.

Ḍarí, *s. f.* a small carpet.

Dárí, *s. f.* in *compos.* the having, holding, possessing.

Darícha, *s. m.* a window.

Daridr, Dáridr, } *s. m.* wretchedness, poverty, indigency.

Daridrí, Dáridri, } *adj.* poor, wretched, indigent.

Darind, Darinda, } *adj.* rapacious, fierce, ravenous: *s.* ravenous beast.

Darj, *s. m. prop.* Darz, a crack, cleft, flaw (in wood.)

Darja, *s. m.* step, stair, degree, rank; a degree of a circle.

Darja ba darja, *adv.* step by step, gradually.

Darjawáb, *s. m.* a reply, a rejoinder.

Darkár, *adj.* necessary, wanting, requisite.

Darḳhwást, *s. f.* request, petition, appeal or petition of appeal; wish, desire.

Darmáhá, *s. m.* monthly wages, salary.

Darmáhádár, *s.* one who receives monthly wages.

Darmándagí, *s. f.* misery, distress, penury, misfortune.

Darmiyán, *s. m.* interval, middle: *adv. postpos.* or *prepos.* in the midst, between.

Darmiyán dená, to employ as a mediator.

Darmiyání, *s. m.* a mediator.

Ḍarná, *v. n.* to fear, to be frightened.

Ḍarobast, *adj.* whole, all, entire.

Darodgar, *s. m.* a carpenter.

Darogh, *s. m.* a lie, falsehood: *adj.* false.

Dárogha, Darogha, } *s. m.* a peace-officer, the name of an officer in charge of the police, a superintendent.

Daroghgo, *s. m.* a liar.

Daroghgoí, *s. f.* lying, false speaking.

Darpai, in the footstep, in pursuit, intent on, following.

Darpai honá, to follow, to be in pursuit or in search.

Darpan, *s. m.* a mirror.

Darparda, *adj.* concealed, secretly.

Darpesh, in front, before, in the presence.

Darpesh honá, *v. n.* to be in front, to be necessary, to be in hand.

Darpesh láná, to adduce.

Ḍarpokná, *adj.* a coward.

Ḍarráná, *adj.* going straight and quickly.

Darsan, *s. m.* interview, a visit, vision.

Darsaní hunḍí, *s. f.* a bill of exchange payable at sight.

Darsúrat, *adv.* a cant word, in case, provided.

Dárú, *s. f.* spirituous liquors; medicine.

Dárú darman, application of medicine, medicine.

Darúd bhejná, to bless.

Dárussaltanat, *s. m.* the seat of

empire, the royal residence, the capital.

Darwán, *s. m.* a door-keeper, a porter.

Darwání, *s. f.* the office of a door-keeper.

Darwáza, *s. m.* a door, a gate.

Darwáza chunná, to close a door with bricks.

Darwáza mạmúr karná, to close or shut a door.

Darwáza ṭhokná, *v. a.* to knock at the door, or gate.

Darwesh, *s. m.* a dervis, a Muhammadan devotee.

Daryá, *s. m.* the sea, a river.

Daryáí, *adj.* of the sea or river, maritime.

Daryáft, *s. f.* conceiving, understanding, discovery.

Daryáft honá, *v. n.* to be discovered.

Daryáft karná, *v. a.* to conceive, to understand, to discover.

Darz, *s. m.* see Darj.

Darzí, *s. m.* a tailor.

Das, *adj.* ten.

Dás, *s. m.* a male slave, or servant.

Dásá, *s. m.* a small rafter.

Dasá, *s. f.* condition, state, circumstances.

Dasahrá, *s. m.* name of a Hindú feast.

Dasamí, *s. f.* the tenth day of the lunar fortnight.

Dasarath, *n. prop.* name of an ancient Rájá, father of Ráma.

Dásí, *s. f.* a maidservant.

Daskhatt, *s. m.* signature.

Ḍasná, *v. a.* to bite or sting (as a venomous animal.)

Dason disá, the ten regions, sides or quarters.

Dast, *s. m.* the hand; stool, purge, evacuation.

Dasta, *s. m.* a handle; a pestle; a quire of paper.

Dastak, *s. f.* a pass for goods, a passport, a writ.

Dástán, *s. f.* a story, fable, tale.

Dastána, *s. m.* a glove.

Dastár, *s. f.* a turban.

Dastárband, *s. m.* a person whose business it is to make up the turban.

Dastarkhwán, *s. m.* a table-cloth.

Dastawez, *s. f.* a note of hand, bond, title-deed, certificate, &c.

Dastkhatt, *s. m.* a signature; a manuscript.

Dastkhatt karná, *v. a.* to sign.

Dastmál, *s. m.* a handkerchief.

Dastpanáh, *s. m.* tongs.

Dastúr, *s. m.* custom, fashion, usage, manner, regulation.

Dastúrí, *s. f.* custom, perquisites paid to servants by one who sells to their masters.

Daswán, *adj.* tenth.

Dátá, *s. m.* a giver, a liberal or bountiful person.

Ḍaṭhá, *s. m.* a stalk.

Ḍáṭná, *v. n.* to stand still.

Ḍaṭná, *v. a.* to snub, to check, to threaten, to browbeat.

Datwan, *s. m.* a tooth-brush made from the branch of a tree.

Dáúd, *n. prop.* name of the prophet David.

Dáúdí, *s. f.* a shrub that bears a flower like camomiles, a kind of firework.

Ḍaul, *s. m.* manner, method, mode, shape.

Daulat, *s. f.* wealth, treasure, riches.

Daulatkhána, *s. m.* a mansion, a palace, a house.

Daulatmand, / **Daulatwálá**, } *adj.* rich, wealthy, opulent.

Dauná, *s. m.* a leaf folded up to hold a parcel of betel, flowers, food, &c.

Dauṛ, *s. f.* a race, a career, a running, endeavour, attack, assault.

Daur, *s. m.* time, age, revolution (of time or any body), circular motion.

Daurá, *s. m.* a large basket (without cover); going the circuit (judges.)

Dauṛádauṛí, *s. f.* exertion in running, hurry.

Dauṛáhá, *s. m.* a messenger, a courier, a guide.

Dauṛáná, *v. a.* to cause to run, to drive, to expedite.

Dauṛdhúp, *s. f.* labour and fatigue.

Dauṛdhúp karná, *v. a.* to use great labour and exertion for the accomplishment of any thing.

Ḍauṛhá, *m.* } *adj.* half as much
Ḍauṛhí, *f.* } again.

Daurí, *s. f.* a basket (without a lid), a rope wherewith a string of cattle are bound together.

Dauṛná, *v. n.* to run, to gallop, to invade.

Dauṛná dhúpná, *v. n.* to run violently, to use great exertion, to toil.

Ḍawá, *s. m.* a large wooden spoon.

Dawá, *s. f. vulg.* Dawáí, medicine, a remedy.

Dạwá, *s. m.* a lawsuit, claim, pretension, plaint.

Dawáí, *s. f.* see Dawá.

Dawá karná, *v. a.* to administer medicine.

Dawáḳhána, *s. m.* a room for medicines, an apothecary's shop, dispensary.

Ḍáwáṇḍol, *adj.* see Ḍáṇwáṇḍol.

Dawát, *s. f.* an inkstand.

Dạwat, *s. f.* invitation.

Dạwat karní, to invite.

Dạwídár, *s. m.* a plaintiff, a claimant.

Dayá, *s. f.* pity, compassion, kindness, tenderness.

Dáyak, *s. m.* in *compos.* giver, donor, giving.

Dayál, *adj.* pitiful, gracious, compassionate.

Ḍáyan, *s. f.* a witch.

Dayáwant, *adj.* charitable, merciful, kind.

Debí, *s. f.* a Hindú goddess.

Deg, *s. f.* a kettle, pot, caldron.

Ḍeg, *s. m.* step, pace.

Degcha, *s. m.* a pot, a small caldron.

Deh, *s. f.* the body.

Dekhádekhí, *adv.* within sight: *s. f.* the imitation of another person; competition.

Dekhláná, *v. a.* to show, to exhibit, to point out.

Dekhná, *v. a.* to see, to look at, to observe, to inspect, to behold, to perceive.

Dekhná bhálná, *v. a.* to see, to look at.

Dekhwaiyá, *s. m.* a spectator, an observer.

Ḍelá, *s. m.* see Ḍhelá.

De márná, *v. a.* to dash on the ground, to throw, to stamp.

Dená, *v. a.* to give, to grant, to yield; to lay (eggs.)

Denápáná, *s. m.* traffic, profit and loss.

Ḍengí, *s. f.* a small boat, a wherry.

Ḍengíwálá, *s. m.* a boatman.

Denlen, *s. m.* debts and credit, traffic, barter.

Der, *s. f.* delay, tardiness, a long time: *adj.* late, slow.

Derá, *s. m.* a dwelling, a tent.

Ḍerá, *s. m.* a dwelling, a tent *adj.* squint-eyed.

Ḍeṛh, *adj.* one and a half.

Ḍeṛh páo, *s. m.* three-eighths, ⅜.

Ḍeṛh pauwá, *s. m.* a weight three-eighths of a ser.

Derí, *s. f.* lateness, delay, slowness.

Derí honá *or* **lagná**, *v. n.* to be late, slow, &c.

Derí karná, *v. a.* to delay, to dally.

Der tak, } for a long time, till
Der talak, } late.

Des, *s. m.* country, territory, religion.

Desáwar, *s. m.* a foreign country.

Desí, *adj.* belonging to a country, indigenous, home-made.

Desnikálá, an exile.
Deví, *s. f.* a Hindú goddess.
Dew, } *s. m.* a god, a demon, a
Dewá, } heathen god.
Dewálá, *s. m.* bankruptcy.
Dewálí, *s. f.* a Hindú festival.
Dewáliyá, *adj.* bankrupt.
Dewar, *s. m.* husband's younger brother.
Dewasthán, *s. f.* a place of idols, a temple.
Dewhrá, *s. m.* a temple where idols are worshipped.
Dewlí, *s. f.* the scab of small-pox.
Dewrání, *s. f.* husband's younger brother's wife.
Ḍewṛhá, *s. m.* half as much again, a mode of reckoning.
Ḍewṛháná, *v. a.* to take once and a half.
Ḍewṛhí, *s. f.* a threshold, a door.
Ḍewṛhídár, } *s. m.* a door-keeper, a
Ḍewṛíwán, } porter.
Dewtá, *s. f.* a heathen god, a divinity.
Dewthán, *s. f.* a place of idols, a temple.
Ḍhab, *s. m.* shape, manners, behaviour, method, fashion, position.
Ḍhábá, *s. m.* a net, the eaves of a house, extending three or four cubits beyond the wall.
Ḍhabbús, *adj.* fat, corpulent, awkward, uncouth.
Ḍhabúá, *s. m.* a copper coin equal to a paisá.
Dhadhakná, *v. n.* to blaze.
Dháeṇ dháeṇ, *s. f.* the report of a cannon heard at a distance.
Dhágá, *s. m.* thread.
Dhaggaṛ, } *s. m.* a paramour.
Dhagṛá, }
Ḍhái, *adj.* two and a half.
Ḍhaí dená, *v. a.* to force an invitation, by fixing one's self in a house till dinner comes on table.
Ḍhaiyá, *s. m.* a measure or weight of two and a half ser.

Dhaj, *s. m.* shape, attitude, figure, appearance.
Dhajá, *s. f.* a slip of cloth, a standard, a flag.
Dhajjí, *s. f.* a slip of cloth or paper.
Dhajjí karná, } to tear to pieces.
Dhajjiyáṇ karná, }
Ḍhák, *s. m.* name of a tree.
Ḍhákar, *s. m.* a clown who is tall and stout.
Ḍhakár, *s. f.* a belch.
Ḍhakár lená, *v. n.* to belch.
Ḍhakdhakáná, *v. n.* to palpitate.
Dhakel, } *s. m.* a shove, a push, a
Ḍhakel, } thrust.
Dhakel *or* Ḍhakel dená, *v. a.* to push, to precipitate.
Dhakelná, } *v. a.* to shove, to push,
Ḍhakelná, } to jostle.
Dhakká, *s. m.* a shove, jolt, push.
Dhakká dená, *v. a.* to shove, to push.
Dhakkamdhakká, *s. m.* shoving and jostling.
Ḍhakná, *v. a.* to cover, to conceal: *s. m.* a lid, a cover, a pot-lid.
Ḍhakní, *s. f.* a lid, cover (of a pot.)
Dhakiyáná, *v. a.* to shove, to thrust forwards.
Ḍhál, *s. m.* declivity, slope: *s. f.* shield, target.
Ḍhalait, *s. m.* a person armed with sword and buckler.
Ḍhalakná, *v. n.* to roll.
Ḍhaláná, *v. a.* to cause to cast (metal), to cause to pour.
Ḍhalkáná, *v. a.* to tilt, to overturn, to spill, to pour, to roll.
Ḍhalmaláná, *v. n.* to move from side to side, to stagger, to totter.
Ḍhalná, *v. n.* to be cast (as metal), to be poured out, to spill, to decline (the day.)
Ḍhálná, *v. a.* to cast (metal in fusion); to pour out, to spill.
Ḍhálú, *adj.* slant, sloping: *s. m.* one who casts metals.
Ḍhálwáṇ, *adj.* sloping, declivity; (cast metal.)

Dhám, *s. m.* a dwelling, a house, a place.

Dhamáchaukṛí, *s. f.* noise, tumult.

Ḍhamádham, *s. m.* the sound of stamping, thumping.

Dhamdhúsar, *adj.* corpulent.

Dhamak, *s. f.* noise of footsteps over-head, thumping, &c.

Dhamáká, *s. m.* a kind of cannon carried on an elephant.

Dhamakná, *v. n.* to throb, to shoot (as the pain of a headache); to thump; to palpitate.

Dhamdhamáná, *v. a.* to make a noise (as over-head with the feet); to be feverish.

Dhámin, *s. m.* a harmless kind of serpent.

Dhamkáná, *v. a.* to threaten, to chide, to snub.

Dhamkí, *s. f.* threat, menace.

Ḍhamláná, *v. n.* to roll.

Dhammál, *s. n.* running through fire on religious occasion (among Musalmán faqírs.)

Ḍhámpná, *v. a.* to cover, to conceal.

Dhan, *s. m.* wealth, property, riches; an expression of praise, thanks.

Dhán, *s. m.* the rice plant, or rice in husk.

Dhá á, *v. n.* to run, to make haste.

Ḍhaná, *v. n.* to be demolished, razed, destroyed.

Ḍháná, *v. a.* to break, to knock down or raze (a building, &c.); to demolish.

Dhanak, *s. f.* embroidery.

Dhanattar, *adj.* opulent, powerful.

Dháncliá, *s. m.* a frame, a plan.

Dhandá, } **Dhandhá**, } *s. m.* business, employment, occupation.

Dhándhal, *s. f.* } **Dhándhalpaná**, *s. m.* } trick, cheating, chicanery.

Dhándhlí, *s. m.* a cheat.

Ḍhanḍhorá, *s. m.* publication or proclamation by beat of drum.

Ḍhanḍhoriyá, *s. m.* a crier, a proclaimer by beat of drum.

Ḍhang, *s. m.* behaviour, manners, mode, manner.

Dhángar, *s. m.* a caste whose business is to dig the earth, and to do other laborious work.

Dhanhá, *adj.* (of land) in which rice is cultivated.

Dhání, *s. f.* a kind of rice in the husk; a light green colour.

Dhaní, *adj.* rich, wealthy, fortunate: *s. m.* owner, proprietor.

Dhaniyá, *s. m.* coriander seed.

Dhankaṭí, *s. f.* the season for cutting rice.

Dhán káṭná, *v. a.* to reap or cut rice.

Dhánkná, *v. a.* to cover, to shut.

Dhankuṭṭí, the place where the rice is separated from the husk.

Dhanmán, *adj.* affluent, rich.

Dhan mánná, *v. a.* to thank.

Dhannáseṭh, *adj.* successful.

Dhanpatr, *s. m.* an inventory of property.

Dhaṉaná, *v. n.* to sink, to enter.

Dháṉsná, *v. n.* to cough.

Dhanuk, *s. f.* a bow.

Dhánuk, *s. m.* name of a caste of hill people.

Dhanukí, *s. f.* the bow with which cotton is cleaned.

Dhanwán, } **Dhanwant**, } *adj.* wealthy, affluent, rich.

Dhap, *s.* voice, sound, noise, crack.

Ḍhapná, *v. n.* to be covered: *s. m.* a cover, covering.

Ḍhapḍhapáná, *v. a.* to thump a drum (as children do.)

Dhappá, *s. m.* false accusation, slander; a stain; a blow.

Dhár, *s. f.* a line, lineament, stream, current; edge of a sword; sharpness.

Dhaṛ, *s. m.* the body.

Dhárá, *s. f.* a water-course, a stream, a current.

Dháṛá, } **Dhaṛá**, } *s. m.* a weight.

Dháŗá bándhná, } v. a. to make up
Dhaŗá bándhná, } a standard to weigh by, with bricks, &c.

Dhaŗak, s. f. palpitation, fear.

Dhaŗáká, s. m. a crash, report of a gun, explosion.

Dharam, s. m. see Dharm.

Dharan, s. f. a beam.

Dharáná, v. a. to owe.

Ḍháŗas, s. m. f. firmness of mind, confidence, animation, encouragement, comfort.

Ḍháŗas bándhná, v. a. to encourage, to comfort, to keep in spirits.

Ḍháŗas dená, v. a. to animate.

Dhaŗdhaŗ jalná, v. n. to burn with great fury.

Dhaŗí, s. f. a line, the black lines made on the lips with missí; the quantity weighed at once.

Ḍháŗí, s. m. a kind of musician, a singer.

Dhárí, s. f. a line, a lineament; in *compos.* bearing, holding, having, wearing.

Ḍháŗin, s. f. female of a Ḍháŗí.

Dhaŗká, s. m. fear.

Dharm, s. m. religious merit, virtue, duty, righteousness.

Dharmátmá, *adj.* virtuous, holy, pious, just.

Dharmautár, } s. m. an incarnation
Dharmavatár } of justice or virtue: this word is often used as a term of flattery by Hindús.

Dharm báp, s. m. an adopted father, a god-father.

Dharm beṭá, s. m. an adopted son.

Dharmí, *adj.* virtuous, righteous, just, honest.

Dharmráj karná, to govern justly.

Dharmsálá, s. m. a place where beggars are allowed to lodge and are fed.

Dharmshástar, s. m. the great body of Hindú law.

Dharna, v. a. to place, to put down, to assume, to put on, to give in charge; to seize, to hold; to owe.

Dharohar, s. f. a trust, a charge, any thing given in charge.

Dhartí, s. f. the earth.

Dharwáná, v. a. to cause to place, &c.

Dhasakná, v. n. to give way, to sink (as a quagmire or slough.)

Dhasan, s. f. a quagmire.

Dhasán, s. m. a slough, bog, quagmire, a swamp.

Dhasáná, v. a. to cause to be thrust into, to sink.

Dhasáo, s. m. see Dhasán.

Dhasná, v. n. to be stuck into, to sink, to enter.

Dhat, s. m. a word used to encourage elephants.

Dhát, s. m. ore, mineral; the Sanscrit root.

Ḍháṭá, s. m. a handkerchief tied over the turban and ears.

Ḍháṭhí, s. f. a noose fastened on the nose of an animal.

Dhaṭíngar, *adj.* clownish: s. f. a clown, tall and stout.

Dhatkárná, v. a. to reprove, to reprimand.

Dhatúrá, s. m. name of a poisonous plant.

Dhaul, s. f. a thump, a rap, a slap.

Dhaulá, *adj.* white.

Dhauldhappá, s. m. thumping and slapping.

Dhaulágir, s. m. name of a mountain.

Dhauliyáná, } v. a. to thump, to
Dhaul jaŗná, } box, to slap.
Dhaul lagáná, }

Dhaul lagná, v. n. to suffer loss.

Dhaul márná, v. a. to thump.

Dhaunj, s. f. thought, consideration, reflection.

Dhaunkná, v. a. to blow with bellows, &c.

Dhaunkní, s. f. bellows.

Dhaurá, *adj.* white.

Dhauntál, *adj.* strong, stout; vicious, mischievous.

Dhauntálí. s. f. viciousness, mischievousness.

Dháwá, *s. m.* running, overrunning an enemy's country.

Dháwá márná, *v. a.* to go expeditiously from a different country, to run on or about.

Ḍhawáná, *v. a.* to cause to raze or pull down.

Dhelá, *s. m.* half a paisá (a small coin.)

Ḍhelá, *s. m.* a clod of earth, a lump of clay, chalk, &c.

Ḍhelá márná, *v. a.* to pelt.

Dhengámushṭí, *s. f.* fisticuffs.

Ḍhenkí, *s. f.* a machine for pounding with.

Ḍhenkul, *s. m.* a machine for drawing water.

Ḍhenṛí, *s. f.* a pod, poppy-head.

Ḍher, *s. m.* a heap: *adj.* much, abundant, enough.

Ḍherá, *adj.* squinting, squint-eyed.

Ḍherí, *s. f.* a heap.

Ḍheú, *s. m.* a wave.

Dhí, *s. f.* a daughter.

Ḍhíhá, *s. m.* a rising ground.

Dhikkár, *s. m.* curse, anathema, reproach.

Dhikkárí, *adj.* cursed, condemned, reproached.

Dhikkárná, *v. a.* to curse, to reproach.

Ḍhíl, *s. f.* looseness; remissness; laziness, inattention.

Ḍhílá, *adj.* loose, not tight; remiss; lazy, inattentive.

Ḍhíláí, *s. f.* looseness; remissness.

Dhímá, *adj.* slow, lazy; gentle, mild, dispassionate.

Ḍhimḍhimí, *s. f.* a kind of tambourin.

Dhíme dhíme, *adj.* gently, softly.

Dhíṉwar, *s. m.* a fisherman, name of a caste of fishermen.

Dhír, *adj.* gentle, patient, tranquil, serene: *s. m.* patience, forbearance.

Dhírá, *adj.* gentle, patient, deliberate, sedate, grave.

Dhiráj, *s. m.* a potentate, a monarch.

Dhíraj, *s. m.* patience, forbearance.

Dhírajwán, *adj.* patient, mild, gentle.

Dhiráná, *v. a.* to threaten, to bully.

Dhíratá, *s. f.* patience, sedateness.

Dhirkár, *s. m.* curse, reproach.

Ḍhíth, } *adj.* forward, impudent,
Ḍhíṭhá, } presumptuous.

Dhíwar, *s. m.* see Dhíṉwar.

Dhiyá, *s. f.* a daughter.

Ḍhiṭháí, *s. f.* forwardness, impudence, petulance.

Dhob, *s. m.* a washing.

Dhobí, *s. m.* a washerman.

Dhobin, *s. f.* a washerwoman.

Dhoendhí ḍakár, *s. f.* a sour belch.

Dhokhá, *s. m.* deceit, deception, doubt, hesitation; anything imaginary, not real; a vapour resembling water at a distance.

Dhokhá dená, *v. a.* to deceive.

Dhokhá kháná, *v. n.* to be deceived.

Ḍhokná, *v. a.* to drink, to tope.

Ḍhol, *s. m.* a large drum.

Dholáí, *s. f.* see Dhuláí.

Ḍholak, *s. f.* a small drum.

Ḍholí, *s. f.* a bundle of two hundred betel-leaves.

Ḍholkí, *s. f.* a small drum.

Ḍholkiyá, *s. m.* a person who plays on the Ḍholak.

Ḍhoná, *v. a.* to carry.

Dhoná, *v. a.* to wash, to rinse.

Dhondhá, *s. m.* a ball of earth made for building walls.

Dhotí, *s. f.* a cloth worn round the waist, passing between the legs and fastening behind.

Ḍhúá, *s. m.* a bank, a mound.

Dhublá, *s. m.* a petticoat or any loose garment for covering the legs.

Ḍhukáná, *v. a.* to cause to enter or go in.

Dhukdhukí, *s. f.* perturbation, anxiety, apprehension; an ornament worn on the breast.

Dhukaṛí, *s. f.* a beggar's bag.

Dhukkí lagáná, *v. a.* to take aim.

Ḍhukná, } v. n. to go into, to enter,
Ḍhúkná, } to take aim.

Ḍhukuṛ pukuṛ, s. palpitation, agitation.

Dhúl, s. f. dust.

Dhuláí, s. f. washing; price of washing.

Ḍhuláí, s. f. act of carrying; price paid for carrying.

Ḍhuláná, v. a. to cause to be carried.

Dhuláná, } v. a. to cause to wash.
Dhúláná, }

Dhulenḍí, s. f. the second day of the holí.

Ḍhúlí, s. f. a bundle of one hundred betel-leaves.

Dhúlí, s. f. dust.

Dhúlkhelí, see Dhulenḍí.

Dhulwáná, v. a. to cause others to wash.

Ḍhulwáná, v. a. to cause to be carried.

Dhúm, s. f. tumult, bustle, noise, fame.

Dhúmdhám, s. f. pomp, parade, tumult, bustle, noise.

Dhun, s. f. sound, musical sound.

Dhúná, s. m. rosin.

Dhunakná, v. a. to card or comb cotton.

Dhúnáṉ, s. m. smoke.

Dhund, s. thought.

Dhundh, s. m. dim-sightedness; haziness.

Ḍhúnḍh ḍhánḍ, s. m. search.

Dhúndhúṉkál, } s. m. strong tem-
Dhúndhúṉkár, } pestuous wind.

Dhundhlá, adj. foggy, misty, dull.

Dhúnḍhná, } v. a to seek, to search
Ḍhúnḍhná, } for.

Ḍhúnḍhná ḍhánḍhná, v. a. to seek for, to search.

Dhúndhrá, adj. foggy, dull, gloomy.

Dhundhráná, v. n. to be dull, misty.

Ḍhunḍhwáná, v. a. to cause to seek or search.

Dhungár, s. m. seasoning.

Dhúní, s. f. a fire over which a Hindú faqír sits.

Dhuniyá, s. m. a carder of cotton, a comber.

Dhunná, v. a. to comb, to card (cotton); to beat (the head.)

Ḍhúṉṛḍháṉṛ, s. m. search.

Ḍhúṉṛhná, v. a. to seek for, to search.

Dhúp, s. f. sunshine, the solar rays, the solar heat; incense, a perfume burnt by Hindús.

Dhúpdání, s. f. a pot for keeping Dhúp.

Dhúpkálá, s. m. the hot weather.

Dhúpná, v. a. to perfume with incense.

Dhúr, s. f. dust.

Dhurí, } s. f. an axle-tree.
Dhúrí, }

Dhuriyáná, v. a. to throw dust in order to deceive.

Dhúrsanjhá, s. m. evening.

Dhussá, s. m. a kind of coarse stuff made of shawl-wool.

Dhwajá, s. f. a standard, a ship's pendant, a flag.

Dhyán, s. m. meditation, contemplation, reflection, thought.

Dhyán karná, } to think, consider,
Dhyán lagáná, } reflect, contemplate, meditate.

Dhyán meṉ honá, to be in meditation.

Díbája, s. m. preface, introduction, exordium.

Ḍibbá, s. m. a round box.

Ḍibbí, s. f. a very small round box.

Ḍibiyá, s. f. a small round box.

Dída, s. m. the eye, sight.

Dídár, s. m. sight, interview.

Dídarezí, s. f. fatiguing to the eye (as minute objects, &c.)

Digar, adj. another, other.

Dighí, s. f. a pond or lake.

Ḍigrí, s. Eng. decree; a judicial decree.

Dih, s. m. a village.

Ḍíh, } s. m. a bank, a mound.
Ḍíhá, }

Dihát, s. m. the country.

Dihátí, *s. m.* a countryman
Dihqán, *s. m.* a villager, a husbandman.
Dihqání, *s. m. f.* a villager, a husbandman; agriculture, husbandry.
Dihlí, *s. f.* a threshold: *s. m.* name of a city. See Dillí.
Dihinda, *part. act.* giving, giver.
Dihurá, *s. m.* an idol temple.
Dikháí dená, *v. n.* to appear.
Dikháná, *v. a.* to show, to exhibit.
Dikhláí dená, *v. n.* to appear, to be apparent, to seem.
Dikhláná, *v. a.* to show, to exhibit.
Ḍíl, *s. m.* stature, body, bulk, size.
Dil, *s. m.* heart, mind, soul.
Diláná, *v. a.* to cause to give, to occasion, to cause to give up.
Dilásá, *s. m.* comfort, encouragement, consolation.
Diláwar, *adj.* brave, intrepid.
Diláwarí, *s. f.* bravery, intrepidity, boldness.
Dil bahalná *v. n.* to be amused, diverted.
Dil bahláná, *v. a.* to amuse, to divert.
Diler, *adj.* brave, intrepid, bold, heroic.
Dilerána, *adv.* boldly, intrepidly, heroically.
Dilerí, *s. m.* intrepidity, boldness, valour.
Dilgír, *adj.* melancholic, sad, dispirited.
Dilgírí, *s. f.* melancholy, sadness, sorrow, concern.
Dil haṭ jáná, *v. n.* to be averse.
Dilí, *adj.* hearty, cordial, of the heart.
Diljamạ, collected in mind, cheerful.
Diljamạí, *s. f.* ease of mind, confidence, content.
Dil ká phapholá phoṛná, *v. a.* to rip up old sores, to renew a half-forgotten grief.
Dil lagáná, to apply the mind.
Dillagí, *s. f.* application of mind, attention, diversion, amusement.
Dil lagná, *v. n.* to apply, to be attentive.
Dillí, *s. f.* name of a city, called also Sháhjahánábád.
Dil o ján *s.* heart and soul.
Dil o ján se, *adv.* with heart and soul, heartily.
Dil páná, *v. a.* to find out what is pleasing to any one.
Dilwaiyá, *s. m.* one who causes to give or pay.
Dilwáná, *v. a.* to cause to give or pay.
Dimágh, *s. m.* the brain; pride, conceit, egotism.
Dimághdár, *adj.* proud, haughty.
Dimágh honá, to be vain, haughty, proud.
Dimágh karná, to act proudly, &c.
Dímak, *s. f.* white ant.
Din, *s. m.* day.
Dín, *s. m.* faith, religion: *adj.* poor, needy, indigent, humble.
Dináí, *s. m.* a tetter, a ringworm.
Din ba din, *adv.* day by day, daily.
Din chaṛháná, *v.* to commence any business late in the day.
Din chaṛhná, to be far advanced (the day.)
Díndár, *adj.* virtuous, religious.
Díndárí, *s. f.* attention to religion.
Díndayál, *adj.* protector of the poor.
Din din, *adv.* daily.
Din ḍhalná, *v. n.* to grow late, to decline (the sun.)
Din gaṇwáná, *v. a.* to spend time carelessly.
Ḍíngí, *s. f.* a small boat.
Ḍíngíwálá, *s. m.* a boatman.
Ḍíng márná, *v. a.* to boast.
Diní, *adj.* aged, old (generally applied to animals.)
Din káṭná, *v.* to pass time with difficulty.
Din ko din rát ko rát na jánná, or samajhná, to be totally absorbed in thought or business.

Din phirná, *v.* to begin to prosper (after adversity.)
Díntá, } *s. f.* poverty, indigence,
Díntáí, } humility.
Díṇyak, *s. f.* white ant.
Ḍioṛhí, *s. f.* threshold, entrance, door.
Ḍioṛhídár, *s. m.* a door-keeper.
Díp, *s. m.* an island, a continent, a lamp.
Dípak, *s. m.* a light; a kind of firework.
Diqq, *s. m.* vexation, trouble, a hectic fever.
Diqqat, *s. f.* uneasiness, trouble, difficulty.
Diqqdár, *adj.* troublesome, vexatious.
Diqqdárí, *s. f.* trouble, vexation, distress.
Diqq honá, *v.* to be irritated, &c.
Diqq karná, *v. a.* to perplex, to plague, to tease, to incommode, to irritate.
Diram, *s. m.* money.
Dirangí, *s. f.* lateness, tardiness.
Disá, *s. f.* a quarter of the heavens.
Disáwar, *s. m.* country (foreign.)
Disáwarí, *adj.* foreign: *s. m.* a kind of betel-leaf.
Dista, *s. m.* a quire of paper.
Díwál, *s. f.* a wall.
Diwálá, *s. m.* bankruptcy.
Díwálgír, *s. f.* a bracket fixed on the wall for a shade.
Diwálí, *s. f.* a Hindú festival; a leathern strap, a belt.
Diwáliyá, *adj.* bankrupt.
Díwán, *s. m.* a steward, a minister or secretary.
Diwáná }
Diwána, } *adj.* mad, insane.
Díwána, }
Diwánapan, } *s. m.* madness, in-
Díwánapan, } sanity.
Díwání, *s. f.* office of a Díwán: *adj.* civil (in opposition to criminal suit.)
Díwání ạdálat, *s. f.* a civil court.
Díwánḳhána, *s. m.* the office where a steward keeps his accounts and transacts business, a hall of audience.
Díwár, *s. f.* a wall.
Díwárgír, *s. f.* see Díwálgír.
Díwaṭ, *s. f.* a lamp-stand.
Diyá, *s. m.* a lamp.
Diyánat, *s. f.* conscience, honesty, integrity, piety, virtue.
Diyánatdár, *adj.* honest, just, conscientious.
Diyárá, *s. m.* the land by the riverside overflowed in the rains, but which is cultivated after the river subsides.
Diyásaláí, *s. f.* a match.
Do, *adj.* two.
Ḍob, *s. m.* a dip (in dye or colour.)
Do ba do, face to face, tête-à-tête.
Dobar, *adj.* double.
Dobár, *adj.* twice.
Dobárá, *adj.* twice double, again.
Dobáz, *s. m.* a piebald pigeon, a child's kite.
Ḍob dená, *v. a.* to dip in dye or colouring.
Dobe, *s. m.* a title of bráhmans.
Dobháshiyá, *s. m.* an interpreter.
Dochoba, *adj.* two-poled (tent.)
Dodhárá, *adj.* two-edged (sword.)
Dodila, *adj.* wavering, doubtful, in suspense.
Dodná, *v. a.* to deny.
Doghla, *adj.* mongrel.
Dohá, *s. m.* a couplet, a particular kind of verse.
Doháí, *s. f.* crying out for justice.
Dohar, *s. m.* a double sheet.
Dohatthaṛ, *s. f.* a slap or pat with both hands.
Dohná, *v. a.* to milk.
Dohrá, *s. m.* a distich: *adj.* double.
Dohráná, *v. a.* to repeat.
Ḍoí, *s. f.* a wooden spoon.
Ḍojiyá, *adj.* pregnant.
Dokasí, *adj.* fit for two persons (as vessels.)

Dokh, *s. m.* a crime, fault, blame, vice.
Dokhná, *v. a.* to accuse, to calumniate, to blame.
Ḍol, *s. m.* a bucket for drawing water.
Ḍolá, *s. m.* a kind of sedan, a swing.
Dolará, *s. m.* a necklace of two strings.
Ḍolchí, *s. f.* a small bucket for drawing water.
Ḍolí, *s. f.* a kind of sedan (for women); a meat-safe, &c.
Ḍolná, *v. n.* to move, to shake, to swing.
Ḍom, *s. m.* a low caste of Hindús who remove carcases.
Ḍomanpaná, *s. m.* the art or practice of a male or female of the Ḍom caste.
Ḍomní, *s. f.* a female of the Ḍom caste; a woman who sings at weddings, &c.
Doná, *s. m.* see Dauná.
Donálí, *adj.* double-barrelled (a gun.)
Ḍongá, *s. m.* } a trough.
Ḍongí, *s. f.* }
Dono, } *adj.* both.
Donon, }
Donon waqt milne, expresses the evening twilight, when day and night meet.
Dour, } *s. m.* name of a species of snake.
Ḍonr, }
Ḍonrá, *s. m.* a purse.
Dopahar, *s. f.* midday, noon.
Dopastá, *adj.* pregnant.
Dopaṭṭá, *s. m.* a piece of linen of two breadths, thrown loosely over the shoulders or head.
Dopiyázá, } *s. m.* a kind of dish without gravy, meat dressed dry with onions.
Dopiyáza, }
Ḍor, *s. f.* } string, cord, thread, line, rope.
Ḍorá, *s. m.* }
Ḍorí, *s. f.* }

Ḍoriyá, *s. m.* striped muslin; a dog-keeper.
Dos, *s. m.* see Dokh.
Dosád, *s. m.* a low caste of Hindús.
Dosála, *adj.* of two years, two years old.
Dos dená, *v. a.* see Dokhná.
Dosh, *s. m.* see Dokh.
Doshála, *s. m.* a pair of shawls.
Doshí, } *adj.* faulty, criminal.
Dosí, }
Dosná, *v. a.* to accuse, to blame.
Dost, *s. m.* a friend, a lover, a sweet-heart.
Dostdár, *s. m.* a friend.
Dostdárí, } *s. f.* friendship, love.
Dostí, }
Dostí karná, *v. a.* to form acquaintance.
Dost mohím, *s. m.* a friend, an acquaintance.
Dost rakhná, to like, to hold dear.
Dotahí, *s. f.* cloths that are lined.
Doṭuk, *adj.* clear, plain.
Doyam, *adj.* second; inferior, second sort or quality.
Doz, *part. act.* in *compos.* sewing, one who sews.
Dozakh, *s. m.* hell, (met.) belly.
Dozakh bharná, *v. n.* to be enough for support.
Dozakhí, *adj.* hellish, damned; a glutton.
Dozakh, mánná, to be satisfied with.
Dozánú baiṭhná, *v. n.* to kneel and sit on the two feet behind.
Driṛh, *adj.* firm, strong.
Drishṭ, *s. f.* sight, view.
Drishṭánt, *s. m.* parable, simile, example.
Duá, *s. f.* benediction, blessing, prayer.
Duá dená, to give a blessing, to bless or pray for.
Duágo, one who blesses or prays.
Duá karná, to pray.
Dúálí, *s. f.* a leathern strap, or belt.

Dúb, *s. f.* name of a grass.
Ḍubá dená, Ḍubáná, Ḍúbáná, *v. a.* to cause to sink, to immerse, to drown; to ruin, to destroy.
Dú ba dú, face to face.
Ḍúbáo, *adj.* out of man's depth, deep (enough to drown in.)
Dúbar, *adj.* weak, lean.
Dubára, *adj.* twice.
Dubdhá, *s. f.* doubt, suspense, uncertainty.
Ḍubkí, *s. f.* a dip, a dive, a plunge.
Ḍubkí dená, *v. a.* to dip, to immerse.
Dublá, *adj.* thin, lean, poor, barren, weak.
Dublápá, Dublápaná, *s. m.* thinness, leanness.
Ḍubná, Ḍúbná, *v. n.* to drive, to be drowned, to be immerged or deluged; to set, to sink; to be absorbed in business or study.
Ḍubo dená, *v. a.* to exhaust, to ruin, to demolish; to drown.
Dubṛú ghusṛú, *adj.* under obligation, dependent.
Ḍubwáná, *v. a.* to cause to drown, &c.
Ḍuchit, Duchitá, *adj.* of two minds, wavering.
Dúdh, *s. m.* milk, the juice (or milk) of certain trees and bushes.
Dúdh baṛháná, *v. a.* to wean.
Dudhail, Dudhár, Dúdhár, *adj.* milch, giving milk.
Dúdhbhái, *s. m.* a foster-brother.
Dúdhhaṇḍí, *s. f.* a milk-pan, a milk-pail.
Dúdhí, Dúdhiyá, *adj.* milky, containing milky juice.
Dúdhiyá patthar, *a.* kind of white stone.
Dúdh kí chiknáí, cream.
Dúdhpiláí, *s. f.* a wet-nurse.
Dúdh piláná, *v. a.* to suckle.
Dúdh píná, *v. n.* to suck.
Dugána, *s. m.* two prostrations at prayer.
Dugdugí, *s. f.* pit or hole at the bottom of the throat.
Dugná, Dúguná, *adj.* double, two-fold.
Duháí tiháí karná, to make reiterated complaints.
Duháná, *v. a.* to cause to milk.
Duhná, *v. n.* to be milked.
Duhrá, *adj.* double.
Duhráná, *v. a.* to fold, to double, to repeat.
Duk, *s. m.* a blow with the fist.
Dukán, Dúkán, *s. f.* a shop.
Dúkándár, *s. m.* a shopkeeper.
Dúkándárí, *s. f.* shopkeeping.
Dúkání, *adj.* what is sold in shops.
Dukh, *s. m.* affliction, distress, trouble, annoyance, suffering, labour, fatigue.
Dukháná, *v. a.* to inflict pain, to torment, to grieve.
Dukh dená, *v. a.* to afflict, to cause distress.
Dukhí, Dukhit, Dukhiyá, Dukhiyárá, Dukhiyárí, Dukh ká márá, *adj.* afflicted, distressed, wretched, miserable.
Dukhná, *v. n.* to ache, to pain, to smart.
Dukh páná, to be afflicted.
Dukhṛá, *s. m.* labour; misfortune.
Dukhtar, *s. f.* a daughter.
Dukṛá, *s. m.* the fourth part of a paisá.
Ḍuláná, *v. a.* to move, to shake, to swing.
Dulár, *s. m.* love, affection.
Dulárá, *adj.* beloved.
Dulaṛá, *s. m.* Dulaṛí, *s. f.* a necklace of two rows or strings.
Dulhá, Dúlhá, *s. m.* a bridegroom.
Dulhan, Dulhin, *s. f.* a bride.
Dulkí, *s. f.* trot.

Dulkí chalná, } v. n. to trot.
Dulkí jáná, }

Dum, s. f. a tail.

Ḍumba, s. m. a species of sheep with a thick tail.

Dumbal, s. m. a bile, a boil, a bubo.

Dumchí, s. f. a crupper; a small tail.

Dum dabájáná, v. n. to run away.

Dum dabáná, v. n. to run away, to put the tail between the legs.

Dummal, s. m. a bile, a boil, a swelling; a felon.

Dumuṇhá, adj. having two mouths: s. m. name of a snake which has two mouths.

Dúná, adj. double, two-fold.

Dunyá, s. f. the world, the universe.

Dunyádár, adj. worldly, engaged in business.

Dunyádárí, s. f. worldliness, attention to the concerns of the world.

Dunyáwí, } adj. worldly, belonging to this world.
Dunyawí, }

Dupahriyá, s. m. a kind of flower; mid-day, noon.

Dupaṭṭá, } s. m. a piece of linen of two breadths worn thrown over the shoulders or head.
Dupṭá, }

Dur, prep. bad, evil, ill, with difficulty: interj. avaunt!

Dúr, s. f. distance: adj. far, distant, remote.

Duráchár, s. m. a backbiter.

Duráchárí, s. f. backbiting.

Dúrandesh, adj. provident, foreseeing, sagacious, wise, prudent.

Dúrandeshí, s. f. foresight, circumspection, sagacity.

Durbachan, s. m. abuse.

Durbal, adj. weak, infirm, faint, poor.

Dúr bhágná, to abstain from, to abhor, to avoid.

Dúrbín, s. m. a spy-glass, a telescope.

Dúrdaráz, adj. far, distant, long.

Durgá, s. f. a Hindú goddess, one of the names of Bhawání.

Durgandh, s. f. stink, stench.

Dúr ho, begone, avaunt, be off!

Dúr honá, v. n. to be removed.

Ḍuriyá lená, } v. a. to lead about (as a horse), to lead in the hand.
Ḍuriyáná, }

Dúr karná, v. a. to remove, to dispel, to reject, to keep at a distance.

Durmus, s. m. an instrument for beating floors, &c., a rammer.

Durr, s. m. a pearl.

Durust, adj. right, proper, true, accurate, sound.

Durustí, s. f. rectitude, propriety, soundness.

Durust karná, v. a. to arrange, to adjust, to put in order, to rectify, to mend.

Dushála, s. m. two shawls (worn together by natives.)

Dushman, s. m. f. an enemy.

Dushmanágí, s. f. enmity, hatred.

Dushmaní, s. f. hatred, hostility, enmity.

Dushman i jání, s. a deadly foe.

Dushmanijání, s. f. deadly enmity.

Dushṭ, adj. bad, wicked.

Dushṭ bachan, bad word, speech, or language.

Dushwár, adj. difficult, arduous.

Dushwárí, s. f. difficulty, trouble.

Dúsrá, adj. second, other.

Dusútí, s. f. a coarse cloth made of double threads.

Duṭ, interj. away, begone, avaunt!

Dút, s. m. a messenger, an ambassador, an angel.

Dutkár, s. m. } reproof.
Dutkárí, s. f. }

Dutkárná, v. a. to reprove.

Duzd, s. m. a thief, a robber.

Duzdí, s. f. theft, robbery.

Dwápar, s. m. the third age according to the Hindús.

Dwár, s. m. a door, a gateway.

Dwárá, s. m. a door: adj. by, through, by means of.

Dwáriká, *s. f.* the name of a city renowned to have been the residence of Krishna.
Dwárikánáth, *s. m.* a name of Krishna.
Dwárpál, *s. m.* a doorkeeper.

E.

E, a vowel; pronounced invariably as *a* in name; one.
Egána, *s. m.* relation, kindred.
Egániyat, *s. f.* relationship.
Ego, one person or piece.
Ek, *adj.* a, an, one, only, single; when used after a numeral it signifies about, as, bís ek, about twenty.
Ekád, *adj.* some, some few.
Ekáek, } *adv.* all at once, sudden-
Ekáekí, } ly.
Ekaís, *adj.* twenty-one.
Ekánt, } *adv.* aside, apart, a-
Ekánt men, } lone.
Ekánwe, *adj.* ninety-one.
Ekásí, *adj.* eighty-one.
Ekaṭṭhá karná, to gather, to collect.
Ek aur, *adj.* another, one more.
Ekáwan, *adj.* fifty-one.
Ekbachan, *adj.* singular (number).
Ekbaghal, *adv.* on one side.
Ekbár, }
Ekbárgí, } *adv.* once, all at once.
Ekber, }
Ek bís, *adj.* twenty, a score.
Ekchobá, one-poled (a tent.)
Ekdafa, *adv.* once, all at once.
Ekḍál, *adj.* of one piece, without joining.
Ekdam, one moment, one breath.
Ekḍaul, *adj.* uniform, of one make.
Ekdesí, *adj.* belonging to the same place or country.
Ekdil, *adj.* unanimous, of one mind.
Ek ek, *adv.* severally, one by one.
Ekelá, *adj.* alone, single, unmarried.
Ekelá dukelá, *adv.* one or two together.
Ek'hará, *adj.* single, one.
Ekhaṭṭá, in one place, together.
Ekhattar, *adj.* seventy-one.
Ekhí, *adj.* alike, similar, the same, the self-same.
Ekín, *prop.* Yaqín, confidence, assurance.
Ekíndár, *adj. prop.* Yaqíndár, true, honest, trusty.
Ekís, *adj.* twenty-one.
Ekjá, in one place, together.
Ekján, one soul, a true friend.
Ekjoṛ, *adj.* of two pieces (a table, &c.)
Ekká, *s. m.* a one-horse vehicle.
Ek koṛí, a score, a corge.
Eklá, *adj.* alone, single, solitary.
Ekláí, *s. f.* veil, cloak, sheet or plaid.
Eklakht, *adj.* of one piece, without joining.
Eklautá, *adj.* only, single (child.)
Eklohiyá, made of one piece (of iron.)
Ekmaná, *s. m.* a bag holding a maund; of a maund weight.
Ekmat, *adj.* unanimous, of one accord.
Ekmushṭ, } all at once, prompt pay-
Ekmúṭh, } ment.
Ekmuwáfiq, *adj.* alike, similar.
Ek na ek, one or other.
Ek pal men, in a twinkling.
Ekpechá, } *adj.* opening at one
Ekpenchá, } turning (applied to a lock.)
Ekpet, *adj.* unanimous, of one mind.
Ekqalam, one hand-writing (a letter or book); all, entirely, altogether.
Ekrang, *adj.* of one colour; sincere.
Ekrúp, *adj.* like, similar, resembling.
Eksamán, *adj.* uniform, even, smooth.
Eksán, *adj.* alike, similar, level.
Eksang, } together.
Eksáth, }
Eksaṭh, *adj.* sixty-one.

Ektá, *adj*. unrivalled, unparalleled.
Ektálá, *adj*. having only one floor or story.
Ektális, *adj*. forty-one.
Ektaraf, *adj*. on the same side, partial.
Ekṭhá, *adj*. together, collected: *s. m.* a small boat made of a tree scooped out.
Ekṭháiṉ, together.
Ekṭhá karná, *v*. to gather, to collect.
Ekṭháṉ, one, one place, together.
Ekthán, in one piece.
Ektís, *adj*. thirty-one.
Ekwaqt, *adj*. simultaneous, coeval, at one time.
Ekzabán, of one voice or tongue.
Eláchí, *s. f.* cardamum.
Eláchídána, *s. m.* a kind of comfits.
Eláj, *s. m. f. prop*. Iláj, medicine, remedy.
Elchí, *s. m.* an ambassador, envoy.
Emán, *s. m. prop*. Imán, faith, belief, conscience.
Emándár, *adj*. trusty, honest, conscientious.
Em kí sál, *prop*. Imsál, this year.
Enḍıbenḍí, *s. f.* trick, subterfuge, laziness.
Enḍíbenḍí karná, to do eye service.
Eṛ, *s. f.* striking with the heel, spurring, spur.
Erápher, *s. m.* } exchange, interchange, dancing attendance.
Erápherí, *s. f.* }
Erí, *interj*. a vocative particle for females.
Eṛí, *s. f.* the heel.
Eṛ márná, to spur.
Etá, *adj*. so much, so many, so.
Eṭháiṉ, *adv*. here.
Ethí, what do you call it (used when the name of a thing is not remembered.)
Etíber, so late, yet, now.
Ètná, *adj*. so much, so many, so.
Etwár, *s. m.* Sunday.
Ewaj, *s. m. prop*. Iwaz, a substitute, a change, exchange.
Ewají, *prop*. Iwazí, *adv*. instead of, in lieu: *s. m.* a substitute.

F.

Faguá, see Phaguá.
Fágun, *s. m.* see Phágun.
Fáham, *prop*. Fahm, *s. m.* understanding, intellect, comprehension.
Fáida, *s. m.* profit, gain, advantage, utility.
Fáida honá, to reap benefit.
Fáida karná, to benefit, to profit.
Fáidamand, *adj*. profitable, useful.
Fáidamandí, *s. f.* profit, advantage.
Fáida uṭháná, to reap benefit.
Failáná, *v. a. prop*. Phailáná, to spread, expand, widen, publish, branch out.
Failná, *v. n. prop*. Phailná, to be spread, &c.
Failsúf, *s. m.* a philosopher: *adj*. cunning, artful, crafty.
Failsúfí, *s. f.* cunning, artfulness.
Faisal, } *s. m.* decision, decree.
Faisala, }
Faisala honá, to be decided or settled.
Faisala karná, to settle, to decide, to adjust.
Fajr, *s. f.* morning, dawn of day, early.
Fák, *s. m.* see Phák.
Faḳhr, *s. m.* boasting, pride, ostentation.
Fáḳhtai, *s. f.* dove-colour.
Fáḳhta uṛjáná, to be confounded.
Fal, *s. m. prop*. Phal, fruit.
Fál, *s. f.* an omen, presage; enchantment.
Falak, *s. m.* the heavens, the sky, the firmament.
Falakí, *adj*. heavenly, celestial.
Falána, see Fulána.
Falátún, *n. prop*. Plato.
Falíta, *s. m.* match, torch, wick.
Falná, *s. m. prop*. Phalná, to bear fruit.

Fáltú, *s. m.* spare, surplus, extra.
Fálúda, *s. m.* a kind of flummery.
Faná, *s. f.* mortality, frailty, death.
Faná hojáná, to perish, to die.
Fandá, *s. m. prop.* Phandá, perplexity, difficulty.
Fání, *adj.* frail, transitory, perishable.
Fánk, *s. f.* see Phánk.
Fanká, *s. m. prop.* Phanká, which see.
Fanká márná, *prop.* Phanká márná, which see.
Fánkná, *v. n. prop.* Phánkná, which see.
Fann, *s. m.* science, art, skill, sagacity.
Fannfareb, *s. m.* art and cunning.
Fannfarebí, *adj.* artful, cunning.
Fáṇsí, *prop.* Pháṇsí, a noose, strangulation.
Fáṇsí dená, *v. a. prop.* Pháṇsí dená, to hang.
Fáṇsí paṛná, *v. n. prop.* Pháṇsí paṛṇa, to be hanged.
Faṇsná, *v. n. prop.* Phaṇsná, to be entangled, to stick.
Faṇswáná, *v. a. prop.* Phaṇswáná, to cause to strangle, to cause to be ensnared or entrapped, &c.
Fánús, *s. f.* a table-shade, a kind of lantern.
Fáqa, *s. m.* poverty, necessity, want, fasting (from want.)
Fáqa karná, to fast from necessity or ill-health.
Fáqakash, *adj.* one who fasts, famished.
Fáqakashí, *s. f.* fasting, endurance of hunger.
Fáqa khainchná, *v. n.* to starve.
Fáqamast, one who is starving.
Faqat, *adj.* merely, simply, only, solely.
Faqír, *s. m.* a beggar, a dervis : *adj.* poor, indigent.
Faqírána, *adv.* poorly, beggarly.
Faqírdost, friendly to the poor.
Faqír fuqará, *s. plur.* beggars, dervises, &c.
Faqírí, *s. f.* poverty, indigence, life of a dervis or beggar.
Faqírní, *s. f.* a female beggar.
Fáqoṇ marná, *v. n.* to die with hunger.
Faqr fáqa, *s. m.* poverty.
Farághat, *s. f.* leisure, disengagement, abundance, affluence, freedom from care, repose.
Farághat karná, to finish and cease (from.)
Farámosh, *adj.* forgotten, forgetful.
Farámoshí, *s. f.* forgetfulness.
Farang, *s. m.* Europe.
Farangí, *s. m.* a Frank, a European.
Farangistán, *s. m.* Europe.
Faraq. See Farq.
Faraq karná, to make distinction or difference, to separate.
Fáras, *s. m.* Persia.
Farásís, *adj.* French.
Farbih, } *adj.* fat, corpulent.
Farbihdár, }
Fard, *s. f.* a sheet (of paper): *adj.* one, single, odd.
Fareb, *s. m.* deceit, fraud, deception, roguery.
Fareb dená, to deceive, to delude, to allure, to cheat, to beguile.
Farebí, *s. m.* a cheat, an impostor, an artful person.
Fareb kháná, to be deceived or deluded.
Farghúl, *s. f.* a great-coat, a cloak.
Farhang, *s. f.* a dictionary, a vocabulary.
Fárigh, *adj.* free, disengaged, at leisure, absolved, discharged.
Fárigh honá, to be at leisure.
Fárighkhattí, *s. f.* a deed of release or discharge.
Farmáish, *s. f.* an order (particularly for goods, &c.), commission.
Farmáishí, *adj.* particularly ordered (any thing excellent), made to order.

Farmá, *s. Eng.* a mould, a form.
Farmán, *s. m.* a mandate, command, order.
Farmáná, *v. n.* to order, to command (speaking with great respect), to say.
Farmánbardár, *adj.* subject to orders, obedient, a servant.
Farmánbardárí, *s. f.* obedience, subjection, allegiance.
Fáṛná, *v. a. prop.* Pháṛná, which see.
Farokht, *s. f.* sale, selling.
Farokht karná, *v. a.* to sell.
Farosh, in *compos.* selling, a seller.
Faroshí, in *compos. s. f.* selling.
Farotan, *adj.* humble.
Farotaní, *s. f.* humility.
Farq, *s. m.* difference, distance, dispersion: *adj.* distant, separate, distinct: *interj.* away! aside!
Farrásh, *s. m.* a servant who cleans the shades, spreads the carpets, &c.
Farráshí, *s. f.* the business of a farrásh.
Farráshkhána, *s. m.* the room where carpets, shades, &c., are kept.
Farráṭá, *s. m.* the sound of anything rushing or fluttering in the air; a piece of bamboo.
Fárs, *s. m.* Persia.
Farsh, *s. m.* a carpet, a floorcloth.
Farshí, *s. f.* a kind of huqqa.
Farsh karná, to spread.
Fársí, *s. f.* the Persian language: *adj.* Persian.
Faryád, *s. f.* complaint, lamentation, cry for help.
Faryádí, *s. m.* a complainant, plaintiff.
Faryád karná, to complain, to cry out for assistance.
Farz, *s. m.* a divine command, a positive duty.
Farzand, *s. m. f.* a child, son or daughter.
Farzandí, *s. f.* the state or condition of a child.
Farzandí men láná, to adopt.
Farz honá, to be incumbent.
Farz karná, *v. a.* to consider as a positive duty, to grant, to admit.
Fasád, *s. m.* depravity, sedition, rebellion.
Fasádí, *adj.* quarrelsome, vicious, wicked.
Fasal, see Fasl.
Fasáná, *v. a.* see Phasáná.
Fasd, *s. f.* opening a vein, bleeding.
Fasd kholná, *v. a.* to bleed.
Fásh, *adj.* apparent, manifest, known.
Fásh karná, to divulge, to reveal, to disclose.
Fasíh, *adj.* eloquent, sweet-tongued.
Fásila, *s. m,* space, distance.
Fasl, *s. f.* season, crops, harvest.
Fasná, *v. n.* see Phasná.
Fatah, *prop.* Fath, *s. f.* victory, conquest.
Fatah honá, to be conquered.
Fatah karná, to conquer.
Fatahmand, *adj.* victorious.
Fatahmandí, *s. f.* victory, conquest.
Fatahnishán, *s. m.* a victorious standard.
Fatahpech, a mode of tying the turban, a kind of huqqa snake.
Fáṭak, *s. m.* see Pháṭak.
Fáṭákhá, *s. m.* see Phaṭákhá.
Fátiha, *s. f.* oblations made to dead saints.
Fatíla, *s. m.* a match, a wick.
Fatílasoz, *s. m.* a peculiar kind of candlestick.
Faṭná, *v. n.* see Phaṭná.
Fatúhí, *s. f.* a kind of jacket without sleeves.
Fatwá, *s. m.* a judicial decree, judgment, sentence.
Fatwá dená, to give judgment, to decree.
Fauj, *s. f.* an army, a multitude.
Faujdárí, *adj.* belonging to the police, criminal, opposed to Díwání (civil.)

Fauṛá, *s. m. prop.* Phauṛá, a mattock, a hoe.
Fauran, *adv.* quickly, suddenly, instantly.
Faut, *s. f.* death.
Faut honá, *v. n.* to die.
Fauwára, *s. m.* a fountain, a jet, a spring.
Fauwára chhúṭná, *v. n.* to burst forth a jet d'eau.
Fazal, see Fazl.
Fazíhat, *s. f.* disgrace, ignominy, infamy.
Fazíhat honá, to be disgraced, to become infamous.
Fazíhatí, *adj.* disgraceful, infamous.
Fazíhat karná, to disgrace, to defame.
Fázil, *adj.* learned.
Fazl, *s. m.* gift, favour, grace.
Fazúl, *adj.* redundant.
Fazúlḳharch, extravagant, profuse.
Fen, *s. m.* see Phen.
Fenk dená, *v. a. prop.* Phenk dená, which see.
Fenkná, *v. a. prop.* Phenkná, which see.
Fer, *s. m. prop.* Pher, which see.
Fer dená, *prop.* Pher dená, which see.
Ferí, *s. f.* see Pherí.
Feríwálá, *s. m. prop.* Pheríwálá, a pedlar.
Fer kháná, *prop.* Pher kháná, which see.
Ferná, *v. a. prop.* Pherná, which see.
Fí, each (or for each), per.
Fiạl, *s. m.* action, work, operation; verb.
Fiạl, *plur.* of fiạl, actions, deeds, works.
Fiạl i lázimí, a verb neuter.
Fiạl i mutaaddí, a verb active, transitive or casual.
Fidá, *s. f.* sacrifice, redemption, ransom.
Fidá karná, to devote, to sacrifice.
Fidwí, *adj.* devoted (your devoted servant.)
Fihrist, *s. f.* an inventory, list, index.
Fíká, *adj. prop.* Phíká, which see.
Fikr, *s. f. m.* thought, consideration, solicitude, anxiety.
Fikr karná, to consider, to reflect, to be thoughtful or anxious, to care.
Fikrmand, *adj.* thoughtful, anxious.
Fíl, *s. m.* an elephant.
Fílbán, *s. m.* an elephant-driver.
Fíldandán, *s. m.* ivory.
Filfaur, *adv.* now, immediately.
Filhál, instantly.
Filhaqíqat, *adv.* really, truly, in effect, in fact.
Fílḳhána, *s. m.* elephant-house.
Filmasal, *adv.* allegorically.
Fílmurgh, *s. m.* a turkey.
Fílnishín, one who rides on an elephant.
Fílpá, *adj.* having a swelling in the leg (the elephantiasis.)
Fílpáí, *s. f.* elephantiasis.
Fílpáya, *s. m.* a pillar.
Filwáqí, *adv.* in fact.
Fí man, per maund.
Finkná, *v. n. prop.* Phinkná, to be thrown.
Finkwáná, *v. a. prop.* Phinkwáná, to cause to fling or throw.
Fiqra, *s. m.* a line, a sentence.
Fiqrabandí, *s. f.* arrangement, eloquence.
Fir, *adv*, again, then; *prop.* Phir.
Firáná, *v. a. prop.* Phiráná, which see.
Firạun, *n. prop.* Pharaoh.
Firishta, *s. m.* an angel.
Fir jáná, *v. n.* see Phir jáná.
Firná, *v. n. prop.* Phirná, which see.
Firní, *s. f.* a dish resembling hasty-pudding, ground rice and milk.
Firoza, *s. m.* a peculiar kind of stone, a turkois.
Firqa, *s. m.* a sect, tribe, troop, company.

Firtá rahná, *v. n. prop.* Phirtá rahná, which see.

Firtí, *s. f. prop.* Phirtí, return, homeward bound.

Firtí ká bháṛá, the hire of a return boat, carriage, &c.

Firwáná, *v. a.* see Phirwáná.

Fishán } in *compos.* scattering,
Fisháni, } shedding, strewing.

Fita, *s. m.* ribbon, tape.

Fiṭkirí, *s. f. prop.* Phiṭkirí, alum.

Fitna, *s. m.* sedition, mutiny, mischief.

Fitnaangez, a fomenter of disturbances, a mischief-maker.

Fitratí, *adj.* sagacious, cunning.

Fonk, *adj.* see Phonk.

Fúl, *s. m. prop.* Phúl, a flower, a blossom, a swelling.

Fúlád, *s. f.* steel.

Fúládí, *adj.* made of steel.

Fulána, or *vulg.* Falána, *s. m.* such a one or thing, such a, a certain; a term used when referring to a person or speaking of one of whose name we are ignorant.

Fuláná, *v. a.* see Phuláná.

Fúljhaṛí, *s. f. prop.* Phúljhaṛí, a kind of firework like a fountain.

Fúlkobí, *s. f. prop.* Phúlkobí, a cauliflower.

Fúlná, *v. n. prop.* Phúlná, to blossom, to blow.

Fúlwárí, *s. f. prop.* Phúlwárí, a flower-garden.

Fungí, *s. f.* see Phungí.

Fúnkná, *v. a.* see Phúnkná.

Fúnk dená, *prop.* Phúnk dená, to set on fire.

Funkná, *v. n.* see Phunkná.

Funkwáná, *v. a.* see Phunkwáná.

Funsí, *s. f.* for Phunsí, a pimple.

Furát, *n. prop.* the river Euphrates.

Furqán, *s. m.* Qurán.

Fursat, *s. f.* leisure, opportunity, time, convenience.

Furtí, *s. f. prop.* Phurtí, activity, quickness.

Furtílá, *adj. prop.* Phurtílá, quick, nimble, active, &c.

Fusláná, *v. a. prop.* Phusláná, to coax, to wheedle, &c.

Fúṭ, *adj. prop.* Phúṭ, odd, unpaired.

Fúṭá, *adj.* see Phúṭá.

Fúṭná, *v. n.* see Phúṭná.

Fuzalá, *s. plur.* of fázil; the excellent, the learned.

G.

Gáb, *s. m.* name of a tree, the juice of the fruit of which is used to smear the bottom of boats.

Gabbar, *adj.* proud, haughty.

Gábh, *s. m.* pregnancy.

Gábhin, *adj.* pregnant.

Gabhrú, } *s. m.* a fine and handsome
Gabrú, } young man.

Gach, *s. m.* mortar, cement, old mortar knocked off walls, &c., a floor made of mortar.

Gáchh, *s. m.* a tree.

Gáchhmirch, *s. f.* cayenne pepper.

Gachpach, *adj.* crowded, stuffed together, close, thick.

Gád. *s. f.* lees, dregs, sediment.

Gadá, *s. m.* a beggar: *adj.* poor, indigent.

Gadáí, *s. f.* begging, mendicity, poverty.

Gadáí karná, to beg.

Gaḍariyá, *s. m.* a shepherd.

Gaḍbaḍ, *s. f.* higgledy-piggledy, confusion.

Gaddar, *adj.* turbid, muddy, dirty.

Gaddí, *s. f.* a cushion, a pad, anything stuffed, a seat, a throne.

Gaḍḍí, *s. f.* a bundle of paper containing ten quires.

Gadelá, *s. m.* a thick bedding; an elephant's saddle.

Gadhá *s. m.* an ass.

Gadhágadhí, *s. f.* a sport among children.

Gadhí, *s. f.* a she-ass.

Gadká, *s. m.* a foil for fencing with.

Gadlá, *adj.* turbid, muddy, dull

dirty : *s. m.* a kind of warm garment.
Gadláí, *s. f.* muddiness, dulness.
Gadrá, *adj.* half ripe (fruit.)
Gáe, *s. f.* a cow.
Gáedum, *adj.* see Gáwdum.
Gáegosht, } *s. m.* beef.
Gáe ká gosht, }
Gáfil, *adj. prop.* Ghâfil, which see.
Gaflat, *s. f. prop.* Ghaflat, carelessness, negligence, neglect.
Gagarí, *s. f.* a water-pot.
Gagrá, *s. m.* a brass water-pot.
Gáh, *s. f.* time; in *compos.* place.
Gáhak, *s. m.* a chapman, a purchaser.
Gahan, *s. m.* an eclipse.
Gáhbegáh, *adv.* in season and out of season.
Gáhe, *adv.* one time, at any time, sometime.
Gáhegáhe, *adv.* at times, sometimes, now and then.
Gaheṇr, *s. f.* a flock or herd, a crowd.
Gaheṇr ká gaheṇr, crowd upon crowd.
Gáhgáh, *adv.* now and then, sometimes.
Gáhgáhe, *adv.* sometime or other, at times.
Gáhí, *s. f.* an aggregate made up of five parts, five.
Gahkí, *s. f.* a purchaser.
Gáhná, *v. a.* to calk.
Gahná, *s. m.* jewels, ornaments : *v. a.* to lay hold of, to seize, to catch, to take.
Gahní, *s. f.* oakum, act of calking.
Gahní karná, to calk (a boat, &c.)
Gahrá, *adj.* deep.
Gahrá rang, deep colour.
Gáib, *adj. prop.* Ghâib, absent, concealed, invisible.
Gáin, *s.* a singer.
Gainá, *s. m.* a small kind of bullock.
Gainḍá, *s. m.* a rhinoceros.
Gainí, *s. f.* a small kind of cow.
Gairí, *s. f.* demurrage.
Gaint, } *s. f.* a pick-axe.
Gaintí, }
Gaj, *s. m. prop.* Gaz, a yard, a ramrod, a carpenter's rule; the perpendicular bars of a gate, &c.; a pale.
Gájá, *s. m.* the sound or clangour of various musical instruments.
Gajab, *s. m. prop.* Ghazab, which see.
Gajar, *s. m.* the chimes rung at the expiration of a watch or *pahar* of the day or night.
Gájar, *s. f.* a carrot.
Gají, *s. f. prop.* Gazí, a kind of coarse cloth.
Gajrá, *s. m.* a carrot.
Gajráhár, *s. m.* a wreath, or necklace, or bracelet of flowers.
Gál, *s. m.* the cheek.
Gálá, *s. m.* a ball of carded cotton.
Galá, *s. m.* the throat, neck, the neck of a pitcher or jar: *adj.* rotten, melted.
Galá baiṭhná, to be hoarse.
Galáband, *s. m.* neckcloth, a cravat, a stock.
Galá bandháná, *v. a.* to ensnare one's self, especially in love.
Galá dabáná, *v. a.* to strangle.
Galá dená, *v. a.* to waste.
Galá ghonṭná, } *v. a.* to throttle, to choke, to hold by the throat.
Galá ghoṭná, }
Galahí, *s. f.* the forecastle (of a boat, &c.), prow.
Galá káṭná, *v. a.* to cut the throat.
Galáná, *v. a.* to melt, to dissolve, to soften.
Galat, *adj.* prop. Ghalat, wrong, erroneous: *s. m.* error, mistake.
Galatí, *s. m.* prop. Ghalatí, a mistake, an error.
Galá ṭípná, *v. a.* to throttle.
Galá uṭháná, *v. n.* to raise the voice (in singing.)
Galáwaṭ, *s. f.* solution, dissolving.
Gal dená, *v. a.* to throttle, to choke, to hang (a man.)

Gale lagáná, *v. a.* to embrace.
Gale lagná, *v. n.* to embrace.
Gale manḍhná, to insist upon one's buying (a thing.)
Gale paṛná, to seek the friendship of one who is averse from it.
Galgaláhaṭ, *s. f.* softness.
Galgaláná, *v. a.* to soften, to mollify.
Galhaiyá, *s. m.* forecastle-man, boatswain.
Gálí, *s. f.* abuse.
Galí, *s. f.* a lane, a street.
Gálib, *adj. prop.* Ghálib, which see.
Galí ba galí, from street to street.
Gálib honá, *v. n. prop.* Ghálib honá, to overcome or defeat.
Galícha, } Gálícha, } *s. m. prop.* Ghálícha, a particular sort of carpet.
Gálí dení, to abuse, to revile, to call names.
Gálígalauj, *s. f.* reciprocal abuse.
Galíkúcha, *s. m.* a narrow lane.
Gáliyáṉ, *s. f. plur.* indecent songs sung at marriages.
Galiyáná, *v. a.* to abuse.
Galiyárá, *s. m.* a narrow street or lane.
Galíz, *prop.* Ghalíz, *adj.* dirty, filthy: *s. m.* mud, filth; human dung.
Gal jáná, see Galná.
Galla, *s. m.* a flock, a herd; *corrupt.* of Ghalla, grain or corn (in general.)
Gallabán, *s. m.* pastor, shepherd.
Gallabání, *s. f.* keeping of a flock.
Gallafarosh, *s. m.* prop. Ghallafarosh, a grain-merchant, a cornchandler.
Galmochhá, } Galmúchhá, } *s. m.* whiskers.
Galná, *v. n.* to melt, to be dissolved, to be wasted away.
Galphaṛá, *s. m.* the jaws, the angle of the mouth.
Galphaṭákí karná, to scold, to lie.
Galphúlá, *adj.* chubby.
Galtakiya, *s. m.* a small round pillow for the neck or cheek.
Galtí, *s. f. prop.* Ghaltí, a mistake, an error.
Gám, *s. m.* a village.
Gam, *s. m. prop.* Gham, grief, sorrow, concern.
Gamak, *s. f.* smell, fragrance.
Gamakná, *v. n.* to smell, to stink.
Gaman, } Gamaná, } *s. m.* going, the act of going.
Gambhír, } Gambhírá, } *adj.* deep (as water), serious, thoughtful, sedate, grave.
Gamchhá, *s. m.* a towel.
Gamgín, *adj. prop.* Ghamgín, sorrowful, dispirited.
Gamí, *prop.* Ghamí, *adj.* sorrowful, grieved: *s. f.* grief, sorrow.
Gam kháná, *prop.* Gham kháná, to grieve, to mourn, to have patience.
Gamkílá, *adj.* spicy, fragrant, odoriferous.
Gamlá, *s. m.* a pot in which flowers, &c., are planted.
Gan, *s. m.* a troop, tribe, flock, class, multitude.
Gáná, *v. a.* to sing, to chant.
Gand, *s. f.* stink, filth, ordure, smell.
Gánḍ, *s. f.* the anus.
Ganda, } Gandá, } *adj.* stinking, filthy, rotten (an egg.)
Ganḍá, *s. m.* a knotted string tied round the neck of a child, &c., as a charm; it denotes also the number four.
Gandabiroza, *s. m.* see Gandafiroza.
Gandadahan, *adj.* stinking breath.
Gandafiroza, *s. m.* the name of a drug, a kind of resin.
Gandak, *s. f.* brimstone.
Ganḍerí, *s. f.* a cut or portion of the sugar-cane.
Gánḍghalat, *adj.* dead, stupid.
Gandh, *s. f.* perfume, odour, scent.
Gandhak, *s. f.* brimstone.
Gandhak ká ạtr, sulphuric acid.

Gandhí, *s. m.* a bug, a flying bug; a druggist, a perfumer.
Gandhílá, *adj.* stinking.
Gánḍú, *s. m.* a catamite.
Gandum, *s. m.* wheat.
Gandum rang, *adj.* swarthy, brown, russet.
Ganes, *s. m.* the Hindú god of wisdom.
Gang, *s. f.* a river, a stream. Do-gang, in two streams (a river.)
Gangá, *s. f.* the sacred river of the Hindús, the Ganges.
Gangábásí, *adj.* residing near the Ganges.
Gangá jal, *s. m.* the water of the Ganges.
Gangájalí, *s. f.* swearing by the water of the Ganges.
Gangájalí uṭháná, } to swear by the
Gangájal uṭháná, } water of the Ganges.
Gangájamní, *s. f.* a kind of ornamental work.
Gangákinárá, } *s. m.* the shore or
Gangákináre, } bank of the Ganges.
Gangápár, *s. m.* the opposite side of the Ganges.
Gangáságar, *s. m.* the place where the Ganges disembogues itself into the ocean.
Gangásnán, *s. m.* ablution in the Ganges.
Gangátír, *s. m.* the shore or bank of the Ganges.
Ganí, *adj. prop.* Ghaní, rich, wealthy, independent.
Ganj, *s. m.* a granary, heap, treasure, market, mart.
Ganjá, *adj.* scald-headed, bald.
Gánjá, *s. m.* the hemp plant.
Gánjáwálá, *s. m.* a seller of hemp.
Gánjhá, *s. m.* the hemp plant.
Ganjhail, *adj.* addicted to the use of gánjhá.
Ganjifa, } *s. m.* a pack of cards;
Ganjífa, } a game at cards.
Ganjífa khelná, to play cards.
Ganjína, *s. m.* a treasure, a magazine.
Ganjiyá, *s. f.* the bag in an Ekká in which the driver carries things.
Ganná. *s. m.* sugar-cane: *v. a.* to count, to reckon, to number.
Gáṇṛ, *s. f.* the anus.
Gáṇṛú, *s. m.* a catamite.
Gáṇsá, *s. m.* the space at the root where the finger and toes separate.
Gánṭ, } *s. f.* a knot, a joint.
Gánṭh, }
Gánṭhdár, *adj.* knotty.
Gánṭhí, *s. f.* a knot.
Ganṭhjoṛá, knot-joining.
Ganṭhjoṛá bándhná, to tie together the skirts of the mantles of the bride and bridegroom.
Gánṭh ká púrá, rich, wealthy.
Ganṭhkaṭá, *s. m.* a cut-purse.
Gánthná, *v. a.* to lay bricks in mortar; to string.
Gáṇw, *s. m.* a village, a town.
Gaṇwáná, } *v. a.* to lose, to throw
Gaṇwánná, } away, to get rid of, to squander, to pass, to trifle.
Gaṇwár, *s. m.* a countryman, a clown, a stupid person: *adj.* ignorant, clownish.
Gaṇwárí, *adj.* country (language.)
Gaṇwáú, *adj.* squanderer.
Gaṇwíṇ, } *s. m.* a village.
Gaṇwíṇgáṇw, }
Gáoghap, *s. m. f.* deceit, artifice.
Gap, *s. f.* prattle, tattle, a story, an idle report.
Gapakná, *v.* to swallow, to gulp.
Gap márná, *v. a.* to prattle, to tattle.
Gappí, *s.* a tattler, an idle talker.
Gapshap, *s. f.* prattle, chit-chat.
Gar, in *compos.* a maker or workman: *conj.* if; *corrupt.* of Ghar, which see.
Gár, *s. f.* abuse: in *compos.* doer, agent.
Gárá, *s. m.* mud prepared and used as mortar.

Garabh, *s. m.* pregnancy.
Garaj, *s. f. prop.* Ghạraz, which see.
Garají, *adj. prop.* Ghạrzí, interested, selfish, designing.
Garajná *v. n.* to thunder, to roar, to bellow.
Gaṛákú, *s. m.* a kind of prepared tobacco.
Garam, *adj. prop.* Garm, which see.
Gaṛáná, *v. a.* to cause to penetrate.
Gaṛariyá, *s. f.* a shepherd or goatherd.
Gárat, *s. f. prop.* Ghạ́rat, which see.
Gárat karná, *v. a. prop.* Ghạ́rat karná, to plunder, to ravage, to spoil.
Gaṛbaṛ, *s. m.* confusion, disorder, a tumult, hubbub.
Gaṛbaṛáná, *v. n.* to rumble (the bowels.)
Gaṛbaṛ honá, to be confused or alarmed.
Gaṛbaṛí, *s. f.* confusion, alarm, fright.
Garbh, *s. m.* pregnancy.
Garbhwantí, *adj.* pregnant.
Garchi, *conj.* although.
Gard, *s. f.* dust.
Gardálúd, } *adj.* defiled with dust,
Gardálúda, } dusty.
Gardán, *s. f.* conjugation, declension (in grammar.)
Gardan, *s. f.* the neck.
Gardaná, *s. m.* the neck of an animal.
Gardaní, *s. f.* a horse-cloth; a blow on the neck.
Gardaní dená, *v. a.* to drive a man by the neck, to turn one out of doors.
Gardankash, *adj.* proud, haughty, insolent, refractory.
Gardankashí, *s. f.* insolence, haughtiness, rebelliousness.
Gardankashí karná, *v.* to rebel.
Gardan káṭná, *v. a.* to decapitate, to behead.
Gardan márná, *v. a.* to behead, to put to death.
Gardánná, *v. a.* to conjugate, to turn, to inflect.
Gardish, *s. f.* revolution, vicissitude.
Gaṛerí, *s. m.* a shepherd.
Gaṛgaṛaná, *v. n.* to thunder, to make a noise (as the huqqa.)
Gargaráná, *v. n.* to gargle, to thunder, to roar (as a tiger), to rumble.
Gaṛgúdaṛ, *s. m.* old clothes of all kinds.
Gaṛh, *s. m.* a castle, a fort.
Gáṛh, *s. f.* difficulty.
Gaṛhá, *s. m.* a cavity, a hole, a pit, an abyss.
Gáṛhá *adj.* thick, close, strong (as tea.)
Gaṛhaiyá, *s. f.* a small pond.
Garhájir, *adj. prop.* Ghạirházir, absent.
Garhájirí, *s. f. prop.* Ghạirházirí, absence.
Gaṛháná, *v. a.* to cause to form by hammering, to cause to make.
Gaṛhant, } *s. f.* form, make, fashion.
Gaṛhat, }
Gaṛhí, *s. f.* a small fort or castle; a small pit.
Gaṛhná, *v. a.* to malleate, to form by hammering, to make, to fashion: *v. n.* to be made, formed or fashioned.
Garí, *s. f.* the kernel of a cocoanut: in *compos.* acting, making, office.
Gárí, *s. f.* abuse: in *compos.* doing, making.
Gáṛí, *s. f.* a cart, a carriage, a hackery.
Garíb, *adj. prop.* Ghạríb, poor, needy, mild, humble, meek; free from vice (a horse).
Garíbána, *adj. prop.* Ghạríbána, fit for the poor.
Garíbí, *s. f. prop.* Ghạríbí, poverty, humility, mildness.
Garíbmár, *s. f. prop.* Ghạríbmár, which see.

Garíbnawáj *adj.* see Ghạríbnawáz,

Garíbnawájí, *s. f. prop.* Ghạríbnawází, hospitality.

Garíbparwar, *adj. prop.* Ghạríbparwar, cherishing the poor, charitable.

Gáṛíwán, *s. m.* a carter, a coachman.

Garjan, *s. m.* a kind of tree which produces oil.

Garjí, } *adj.* see Ghạrzí.
Garjú, }

Garm, *adj.* hot, warm, fervent; passionate, fiery, ardent; thronged or crowded (as a market.)

Garmágarm, *adj.* hot and hot.

Garmáná, *v. n.* to be angry; to become enlivened; to become warm.

Garmbázár, *s. m.* } throng or much
Garmbázárí, *s. f.* } business in a market.

Garm bolná, to speak roughly and angrily.

Garm honá, *v. n.* to be angry; to become hot; to be thronged (a market.)

Garmí, *s. f.* the hot season; warmth, ardour, heat; the venereal disease.

Garmjoshí, *s. f.* warmth, affection, cordiality.

Garm karná, to warm, to make hot.

Garmmizáj, *adj.* passionate, hotheaded.

Garmumkin, *prop.* Ghạirmumkin, *adj.* impossible.

Gaṛná, *v. n.* to penetrate, to be driven into the earth (as a stake), to be buried.

Gáṛná *v. a.* to bury, to set, to drive down, to fix.

Gárná, *v. a.* to strain, to squeeze, to milk.

Garoh, see Guroh.

Gaṛoná, *v. a.* to pierce, to perforate, to bore, to stick into.

Gáṛthop, *s. f.* burying, burial.

Gaṛúr, *s. m.* a large kind of heron, gigantic crane or adjutant bird.

Garwájibí, *adj. prop.* Ghạirwájibí, wrong, improper, unjust.

Gaṛwáná, *v. a.* to cause to be buried or driven into the earth.

Gas, *s. m. prop.* Ghạsh, stupor, fainting.

Gas áná, *v. n. prop.* Ghạsh áná, to faint.

Gasht, *s. m.* walking, going round (especially of guards.)

Gashtí, } *s. m.* watch, sentinel,
Gashtiyá, } patrol.

Gas paṛná, *prop.* Ghạsh paṛná, to faint, to swoon.

Gast, *s. m. prop.* Gasht.

Gastángar, *adj.* clownish, ignorant, foolish.

Gat, *s. f.* state, condition; salvation.

Gátá, *s. m.* pasteboard.

Gaṭarmal, *s. m.* a nickname for a monkey.

Gaṭhar, *s. m.* a large bundle, a bale, a pack.

Gaṭhbandhan, *s. m.* tying the knot, a Hindú ceremony attending marriage in which the mantles of the bride and bridegroom are fastened together.

Gaṭhí, *s. f.* a bale, pack.

Gaṭhílá, *adj.* knotty, robust.

Gaṭhiyá, *s. f.* pains in the joints; a bag, sack.

Gaṭhiyábáo *s. f.* rheumatism.

Gaṭhjoṛá, *s. m.* see Gaṭhbandhan.

Gaṭhrí, *s. f.* a bundle, packet, parcel.

Gaṭhrí bándhná, *v. a.* to pack up.

Gaṭhrí karná, *v. a.* to add (figures).

Gaṭhúá, *s. m.* knots in cloths.

Gati, *s. f.* state, condition; salvation.

Gaṭiyá, *s. f.* a small bundle.

Gaṭpaṭ, *s. f.* higgledy-piggledy, confusion.

Gaṭṭá, *s. m.* the part of the pipe which fixes into the top of the metal part of a huqqa.

Gaṭṭhá, *s. m.* a bundle, package, pack; root of onion, &c.

Gau, *s. f.* a cow.

Gauchí, *s. f.* a hole or pit.
Gaudán, *s. m.* gift of a cow.
Gaugá, *s. m. prop.* Ghaughá, noise, disturbance, uproar, clamour.
Gauhar, *s. m.* essence, substance; a pearl, a jewel, a gem.
Gaukh, *s. m.* a portico.
Gaun, *s. f.* opportunity, advantage.
Gauná, *s. m.* bringing home a wife.
Gaunghát, *s. f.* power, opportunity.
Gaur, *s. m.* an ancient city, formerly the capital of Bengal.
Gaur, *s. f. prop.* Ghaur, which see.
Gaurá, *s. f.* a name of the goddess Párwatí: *s. m.* a cock-sparrow.
Gauraiyá, *s. f.* a hen-sparrow; a *huqqa* made of earth.
Gaurí, *s. f.* a name of the goddess Párwatí.
Gaur karná, *v. a. prop.* Ghaur karná, to reflect, consider, meditate.
Gausálá, *s. f.* a cow-house.
Gaut, *s.* fodder.
Gáw, *s. f.* a cow.
Gáwá ghí, *s. m.* cow's clarified butter.
Gawáh, *s. m.* a witness, an evidence.
Gawáhí, *s. f.* evidence, testimony, witness.
Gawáhí dená, to witness, to testify.
Gawaiyá, *s. m.* a singer.
Gawáná, *v. a.* to cause to sing.
Gawára, } *adj.* palatable, agreeable,
Gawárá, } pleasant.
Gawárá karna, to choose, to like, to take upon one's self trouble, &c.
Gáwdí, *adj.* a simpleton, blockhead.
Gáwdída, *s. m.* a kind of bread.
Gáwdum, *adj.* thick at the one end and thin at the other, taper: *s. f.* a cone.
Gáwgosht, *s. m.* beef.
Gáwtakya, *s. m.* a largo pillow or bolster.
Gáwzabán, *s. f.* a kind of bread.
Gayá, *s. f.* the name of a city in Bihár; past. part. (of jáná) gone, went.
Gáyak, *s. m.* } a singer.
Gáyan, *s. f.* }
Gáyatrí, *s. f.* a prayer repeated by bráhmans with a rosary.
Gayáwál, *s. m.* a class of Gayá bráhmans, who officiate in certain religious ceremonies performed by pilgrims at that place.
Gaz, *s. m.* a yard, a wand to measure cloth, a ramrod, a carpenter's rule, the perpendicular bars of a gate, &c.
Gazak, *s. f.* a relish (eaten with wine, &c.)
Gazí, *s. f.* a coarse kind of cloth (of cotton.)
Gedá, *s. m.* a young unfledged bird, a nestling: *adj.* stupid, ignorant.
Gedlá, *adj.* stupid, ignorant, silly.
Geglí, *s. f.* a trollop.
Gehúán, *s. m.* the colour of wheat: *adj.* of the colour of wheat.
Gehún, *s. m.* wheat.
Gend, *s. f.* a ball (to play with.)
Gendá, *s. m.* marigold.
Genrá, *s. m.* a rhinoceros.
Gerú, *s. m.* a kind of red earth or ochre.
Gerúá, *adj.* covered with or coloured like Gerú.
Gerúí, *adj.* of the colour of Gerú.
Getam, *s. m.* a kind of cloth used as ticking or horse cloth.
Ghábrá, *adj.* confused, confounded, timorous.
Ghabráhat, *s. f.* confusion, perplexity, agitation, alarm.
Ghabráná, *v. n.* to be confused, perplexed, agitated, embarrassed; to falter.
Ghachágach, *adj.* thick.
Ghachí, *s. f.* a hole made in the ground by boys for playing at tipcat.
Ghachípára, *s. m.* name of a game, [tipcat.
Ghác, *s. m.* a wound, a sore.
Ghaffár, *adj.* forgiving (the deity.)
Ghấfil, *adj.* negligent, indolent, remiss, careless, thoughtless.
Ghấfil honá, *v. n.* to be negligent, indolent, senseless.

Ġháfilí, } s. f. carelessness, negli-
Ġhaflat, } gence, neglect.
Ġhafs, adj. thick, close (as cloth), compact, substantial.
Ġhafúr, adj. clement, merciful, forgiving.
Ghágas, s. m. a large kind of fowl.
Ghágh, adj. old, aged, sly, wily, shrewd.
Ghaghrá, } s. m. a petticoat.
Ghághrá, }
Ghái, s. f. number five (in reckoning), the interval between the fingers or toes.
Ġháib, adj. absent, concealed, invisible; (substantively) the third person in grammar.
Ġhaib. adj. latent, concealed, absent, invisible, mysterious.
Ġhaibdán, adj. skilled in discovering mysteries; omniscient.
Ġhaibdání, s. f. knowledge of mysteries.
Ġhaibghullá honá, prop. Ġhaibghulelá honá, to be lost or absent.
Ghaib honá, to vanish, to disappear.
Ġhaibí, adj. absent, invisible.
Ġháil, adj. wounded.
Ġhair, adj. improp. Gar, other, different, foreign: adv. besides, without, except.
Ġhairat, s. f. modesty.
Ġhairatmand, adj. modest, bashful.
Ġhairházir, adj. absent, away.
Ġhairházirí, s. f. absence, non-appearance, non-attendance.
Ġhairmumkin, adj. impossible.
Ġhairmunásib, adj. unfit, improper.
Ġhairwájib, adj. wrong, unjust, unreasonable.
Ġhairwájibí, s. f. injustice, unreasonableness.
Ġhalaba, s. m. superiority, pre-eminence, conquest.
Ġhalaba, karná, to overcome, to conquer.
Ġhalat, adj. wrong, erroneous: s. m. error, mistake.
Ġhalatfahamí, s. f. mistake, misconception.
Ġhalatí, s. f. a mistake, an error.
Ġhálib, adj overcoming, victorious, predominant.
Ġhálib honá, to overcome, to conquer, to excel.
Ġhalícha, } s. m. a particular kind
Ġhálícha, } of carpet.
Ġhalíz, adj. dirty, filthy: s. m. filth, mud, dirt, human excrement.
Ġhalla, s. m. grain or corn (in general.)
Ġhallafarosh, s. m. a grain-merchant.
Ghálmel, adj. jumbled.
Ghálná, v. a. to make water, &c., muddy by stirring it.
Ġhaltí, s. f. a mistake, an error.
Ghám, s. f. sunbeams, sunshine.
Ġham, s. f. grief, sorrow, concern.
Ġhamálúda, adj. grieved.
Ġhamáná, v. n. to sun, to bask in the sun.
Ghamanḍ, s. m. pride, haughtiness.
Ghamanḍí, adj. haughty, proud.
Ghámar, adj. simple, artless; a blockhead.
Ġhamdída, adj. accustomed to grief, afflicted.
Ġhamgín, adj. sorrowful, dispirited.
Ġhamgusár, an alleviator of grief, an intimate friend.
Ġhamgusárí, s. f. alleviation of grief, friendship.
Ġhamí, adj. sorrowful, grieved: s. f. grief, sorrow.
Ghamír, } adj. patient, enduring;
Ghamírá, } deep (as water.)
Ġham karná, to lament, to grieve.
Ġham kháná, to grieve, to mourn, to have patience.
Ġhamḳhwár, adj. condoling, pitying, a comforter; afflicted, sad; an intimate friend.
Ġhamḳhwári, s. f. affliction, commiseration.
Ġhamnák, adj. sorrowful, sad.
Ġhamnákí, s. f. sorrowfulness, sadness.
Ghamorí, s. f. the prickly heat.
Ġhamrasída, adj. afflicted.
Ghamsán, s. m. battle engagement.
Ġham uṭháná, to suffer grief.

Ghamzada, *adj.* grieved, afflicted.
Ghán, *s. f.* as much as is thrown in at one time into a mill or mortar, &c.
Ghan, *s. m.* a sledge-hammer.
Ghaná, *adj.* thick, close, confused, numerous, many.
Ghanerá, *adj.* much, many.
Ghangholná, *v. a.* to rinse; to mix any liquid by stirring it about.
Ghání, *s. f.* see Ghán.
Ghaní, *adj.* rich, wealthy, independent.
Ghaním, *s. m.* an enemy, an adversary.
Ghanímat, *s. f.* plunder, gain, good fortune, a blessing.
Ghanímat jánná, *v. a.* to regard as prey, or as what cost nothing.
Gháns, *s. m.* grass, straw, hay, fodder.
Ghanṭá, *s. m.* a bell, clock, hour.
Ghanṭálí, Ghanṭí, } *s. f.* a small bell.
Gháo, *s. m.* wound, sore.
Ghap, *s. m.* brag, boast.
Ghapí, boaster, bragger.
Ghap márná, to brag, to boast, to swagger.
Ghar, *s. m.* house, apartment, partition (in a box, &c.), drawer, groove.
Ghár, *s. m.* a cavern, a cave, a grotto, a pit.
Ghaṛá, *s. m.* a water-pot, an earthen-pot, a pitcher.
Gharámí, *s. m.* a thatcher, a hut-builder.
Gharáná, *s. m.* family, household.
Gharára, *s. m.* a large sack.
Ghárat, *s. f.* rapine, plunder, devastation, ruin, destruction.
Gháratgar, *s. m.* a plunderer, an oppressor.
Ghárat karná, *v. a.* to plunder, to ravage, to spoil.
Gharaundá, *s. m.* a small house which children make to play in.
Gharaz, *s. f.* wish, view, design, occasion, interestedness; *adv.* in short, in fine.
Gharaz nikalná, to be successful in a design.
Gharaz nikálná, to make a design, succeed.
Gharazámez, Gharazáshná, } *adj.* designing, selfish, interested.
Gharb, *s. m.* the setting of the sun; the west.
Ghar ba ghar, *adj.* from house to house.
Ghar baiṭhná, to be tumbled down (as a house); to be out of employ.
Gharbár, *s. m.* family.
Gharbár basáná, *v. a.* to consummate a marriage, to establish a family.
Gharbár honá, *v. n.* to undergo the consummation of a marriage.
Gharbárí, *s. f.* housewifery, domestic concerns.
Ghar basáná, to establish a family.
Gharbí, *adj.* western, occidental.
Ghar ḍúbná, to be ruined.
Ghar ḍuboná, *v. a.* to ruin one's self and children.
Gharelá, *adj.* domestic, tame.
Gharghálú, *adj.* ruining.
Ghar ghar, *adv.* from house to house.
Ghaṛí, *s. f.* a clock, a watch, an hour, the space of twenty-four minutes.
Gharíb, *adj.* poor, needy, mild, meek, humble, quiet, free from vice (a horse); *s. m.* a stranger.
Gharíbána, *adj.* for the poor.
Gharíb ghuraba, the poor.
Gharíbí, *s. f.* humility, mildness, meekness, poverty.
Gharíbmár, *s. f.* oppression, tyranny, oppression of the poor.
Gharíbnawáz, *adj.* courteous to strangers, kind to the poor, hospitable.
Gharíbnawází, *s. f.* hospitality.

Gharíbparwar, *adj.* cherisher of the poor, charitable.

Gharíbparwarí, *s. f.* cherishing the poor.

Ghaṛisáz, } *s. m.* a watch-maker.
Ghaṛíwálá, }

Ghaṛiyá, *s. f.* a crucible.

Ghaṛiyál, *s. m.* a crocodile.

Ghaṛiyálí, *s. m.* the person who attends the Ghaṛí and strikes the time.

Ghar karná, to fix, to settle, to establish a family.

Ghar kí log, a wife, family, household.

Ghaṛná, *v. a.* to make, to form, to forge, to work (metals.)

Gharnaí, *s. f.* a raft made of pots, a float (of pots.)

Ghaṛonchá, *s. m.* } a stand for water-
Ghaṛonchí, *s. f.* } pots, &c.

Ghár paṛ jáná, } to become pits or
Ghár paṛná, } caverns (spoken of wounds that become great.)

Gharq, *adj.* drowned.

Gharqáb, *s. m.* deep water.

Gharq honá, to be drowned.

Gharqí, *s. f.* flooding lands, inundation.

Gharrá, *s. m.* a rattling noise in the throat which dying people are afflicted with, pain, agony, pang.

Gharrá, *s. m.* pride.

Gharúr, *s. m.* pride, vain-glory.

Gharúr meṇ áná, to become proud.

Gharwálá, *s. m.* a housekeeper, a master of a house.

Gharzí, *adj.* interested, selfish, designing.

Ghás, *s. f.* grass, straw, hay, fodder.

Ghasab, *s. m.* violence, oppression, injustice.

Ghash, *s. m.* stupor, fainting.

Ghash áná, } *v. n.* to faint, to
Ghash paṛná, } swoon.

Ghasiṭná, *v. n.* to be dragged, to be trailed.

Ghasíṭná, *v. a.* to pull, to drag, to trail.

Ghasiyárá, *s. m.* a grass-cutter.

Ghasiyárin, *s. f.* a female grass-cutter.

Ghasná, *v. n.* to be rubbed: *v. a.* to rub.

Gháspát, *s. m.* sweepings.

Ghassál, *s. m.* one whose business it is to wash the bodies of the dead.

Ghát, *s. f.* aim, design, snare, ambuscade; killing, slaughter.

Gháṭ, *adj.* deficient (as in weight), dear (rate), low (price): *s. m.* a landing-place, ferry, a quay, a bathing-place on a river-side.

Ghaṭ. *s. f.* mind, heart, soul, thought: *adj.* dear (rate), low (price.)

Ghaṭá, *s. f.* cloudiness, clouds.

Gháṭá, *s. m.* deficiency, abatement, reduction.

Ghaṭáná, *v. a.* to decrease, to diminish, to allay, to lessen.

Ghaṭáo, *s. m.* reduction, falling (as of a river or of the price of any thing.)

Ghaṭarghúṇ, *s.* cooing (as of doves.)

Ghaṭarghúṇ karná, to coo, to bill.

Ghaṭáṭop, *s. m.* a covering of a pálkí or carriage.

Ghaṭáwná, *v. a*, to reduce, to cause to subside or fall.

Ghaṭ baṛh, *adv.* more or less.

Gháṭí, *s. f.* a strait, a pass (in a mountain, &c.)

Ghaṭí. *s. f.* diminution, decrease, abatement, loss (in trade.)

Ghaṭiyá, *adj.* low-priced.

Gháṭiyá, *s. m.* a bráhman who sits in a Gháṭ to keep the clothes, &c. of those who resort to make ablution.

Ghát karná, *v. a.* to kill, to waylay, to lie in ambush.

Gháṭmár, *s. m.* a smuggler.

Ghaṭná, *v. n.* to abate, to decrease, to lessen, to be depressed.

Ghaṭpaṭ, *s. m.* congression, shock, conflict.

Ghaṭṭá, *s. m.* a corn (on the foot.)
Ghaṭṭí, *s. f.* decrease, alleviation, abatement, loss (in trade, &c.)
Ghátú, *adj.* deceitful, treacherous.
Ghaṭwál, } *s. m.* wharfinger, a ferry-
Ghaṭwár, } man.
Ghaud, *s. f.* a bunch or cluster of grapes, dates or plantains.
Ġhaughá, *s. m.* noise, disturbance, uproar, clamour, alarm.
Ġhaugháí, *adj.* noisy, clamorous : *s. m.* a disturber ; name of a bird.
Gháúghap, *adj.* deceitful, knavish.
Ġhaur, *s. f.* reflection, consideration, deliberation, meditation.
Ġhaur karná, *v. a.* to reflect, consider, meditate.
Ġhaurpardáḳht, *s. f.* attention to, attention on.
Gháw, *s. m.* a wound, a sore.
Gháyal, *adj.* wounded.
Ġhazab, *s. m.* violence, oppression, vengeance, anger, curse, calamity.
Ġhazab karná, *v. a.* to oppress, to tyrannise (over) ; to offer a low price for any thing.
Ġhazal, *s. f.* an ode, an amatory poem.
Ġhází, *s. m.* a conqueror, a hero ; one who fights against infidels.
Ġházímard, *s. m.* a hero, a horse.
Ġhegá, } *s. m.* a swollen or Derby-
Gheghá, } shire neck.
Ghenchná, *v. a.* to pull, to draw, to tighten, to paint.
Ghepná, *v. a.* to mix, to mingle, to unite into a paste (as flour and water.)
Gher, *adj.* round, surrounding, loose (as a robe), winding : *s. m.* circuit, circumference.
Gherá, *adj.* round, surrounded : *s. m.* a circle, a fence, a siege ; a hoop.
Gherá ḍálná, *v. a.* to surround, to lay a siege.
Gherdár, *adj.* full, loose (as a robe), circular, extensive.
Ghere meṉ paṛná, to be surrounded.
Gher ghár karná, *v. a.* to surround, to stop or hinder.
Gherná, *v. a.* to surround, to encircle, to fence, to enclose, to blockade.
Gherní, *s. f.* a handle for turning a spinning-wheel.
Ghetlá, *s. m.* a kind of shoe.
Ghewar, *s. f.* a kind of sweetmeat.
Ġhíbat, *s. f.* speaking ill of any one behind his back, backbiting, slander.
Ġhíbat karná, to slander, to traduce.
Ghichpich, *adj.* thick, confused, muddy.
Ghigáná, *v. n.* see Ghighiyáná.
Ghighí bandh jáná, *v. n.* to falter, to be unable to speak (from shame or fear, &c.)
Ghighiyáná, *v. n.* to falter ; to appear very humble ; to coax, to wheedle ; to implore.
Ghíkuwár, *s. m.* name of a medicinal plant.
Ġhiláf, *s. m.* a case, a cover, a sheath, an outer garment.
Ghin, *s. f.* disgust, shame, bashfulness.
Ghináná, *v. n.* to be disgusted.
Ghinauná, *adj.* disgusting, abominable, fulsome.
Ghínchná, *v. a.* to pull, to draw, to tighten.
Ghin kháná, *v. n.* to be disgusted, to have the stomach turned.
Ghiráná, *v. a.* to cause to surround or enclose.
Ghirná, *v. n.* to be surrounded or enclosed ; to gather (as the clouds.)
Ghirní, *s. f.* a pulley, an instrument for twisting ropes.
Ghirní kháná, to go round.
Ghisáná, *v. n.* to cause to rub, to wear.
Ghisáo, *s. m.* } attrition, rubbing,
Ghisáwaṭ, *s. f.* } friction.
Ghisiyáná, *v. a.* to trail, to drag.

Ghisná, *v. n.* to be rubbed, to be abraded: *v. a.* to rub, to whet, to beat.
Ghiyá, *s. m.* name of a vegetable, a pumpkin.
Ġhizá, *s. f.* aliment, diet, provision, food.
Ghol, *s. m.* butter-milk.
Ġhol, *s. m.* a crowd, a gang.
Gholá, *s. m.* an intoxicating potion made of bhang or opium.
Ġhol ká ghol, crowd upon crowd.
Gholmel, *s. m.* mixture, mixing.
Gholná, *v. a.* to mix with a liquid, to dissolve.
Ghompná, *v. a.* to thrust, to stab.
Ghongá, *s. m.* a cockle, a cockle-shell, a snail.
Ghoṇslá, *s. m.* a bird's-nest.
Ghonṭí, *s. f.* a decoction for infants.
Ghoṇṭná, *v. a.* to polish by rubbing; to investigate; to strangle.
Ghor, *adj.* gloomy, dark, horrible, awful.
Ghoṛá, *s. m.* a horse; the cock (of a gun), the knight (at chess.)
Ghoṛá chaṛháná, to cock a gun.
Ghoṛe ko sarpaṭ phenkná, to force a horse to his utmost speed.
Ghoṛesawár, *s. m.* a horseman.
Ghoṛí, *s. f.* a mare.
Ghos, *s. m.* name of a caste, a cowherd.
Ghosí, *s. m.* a Muhammadan milkman, a cowherd.
Ghoṭ, *s. f.* polish.
Ġhota, *s. m.* dipping, diving; a dip, a dive.
Ġhotabáz, *s. m.* a diver.
Ġhota dená, *v. a.* to dip, to plunge under water, to baptize.
Ġhota kháná, *v. n.* to be dipt, to dive, to dip.
Ġhotaḳhor, *s. m.* a diver.
Ġhotaḳhorí, *s. f.* dipping, being dipt.
Ġhota márná, see Ġhota kháná.
Ġhotam gháta, *s. m.* a game in which swimmers dip one another under water.
Ġhot márná, to disappear.
Ġhot meṇ áná, Ġhot meṇ jáná, } to faint.
Ghoṭná, *v. a.* to polish, to shave.
Ghoṭní, *s. f.* a rubber.
Ġhubár, *s. m.* dust, clouds of dust.
Ġhubára, *s. m.* a kind of firework.
Ġhubárálúd, Ġhubárálúda, } covered or polluted, with dust.
Ghughú, *s. m.* an owl; a blockhead.
Ġhul, *s. m. f.* noise, din, outcry, tumult.
Ġhulám, *s. m.* a slave, servant.
Ġhulám honá, to be a slave.
Ġhulámí, *s. f.* service, slavery.
Ghuláná, Ghúláná, } *v. a.* to allure, to deceive, to dissolve, to melt.
Ġhulel, *s. f.* a pellet-bow.
Ġhulela, Ġhulelá, } *s. m.* a pellet.
Ġhulelbáz, *s. m.* a pelleter (with a bow.)
Ġhulelbází, *s. f.* pelleting.
Ġhulghapára, *s. m.* clamour, disturbance.
Ġhul macháná, to make a noise, outcry or tumult; to hoot.
Ghulná, *v. n.* to melt, to be dissolved; to rot (as fruit); to become lean, to waste.
Ghulwáná, *v. a.* to cause to mix with a liquid, to cause to dissolve.
Ghúm, back, round, about.
Ghumáná, *v. a.* to turn round, to whirl round, to circulate, to encircle; to delude.
Ghumáná phiráná, to prevaricate.
Ghumghumálá, *adj.* loose (as a robe); full.
Ghúmná, *v. n.* to go round, to revolve, to turn, to roll, to wheel, to whirl.
Ghumrí, *s. f.* the vertigo, swimming of the head.
Ghun, *s. m.* name of an insect destructive to wood, grain, &c., a weevil.
Ghuná, *adj.* wood, grain, &c. destroyed by the Ghun; weevil-eaten.

Ghuncha, *s. m.* a bud, blossom.
Ghunchadahan, *s. m.* with a mouth like a rosebud.
Ghunda, *s. m.* a fop.
Ghundí *s. f.* a button.
Ghúngar, *s. m.* a curl.
Ghúngarwálá bál, curled hair.
Ghungchí, *s. f.* a small red and black seed.
Ghúnghaṭ, *s. f.* a veil.
Ghúnghaṭ káṛhná, to draw a veil over the face.
Ghúnghaṭ karná, to veil.
Ghúnghchí, *s. f.* a small red and black seed.
Ghunghunáná, *v. n.* to hum, to buzz.
Ghúngní, *s. f.* a sort of stir-about, or grain of any kind (pulse or wheat, &c.) boiled whole with sugar.
Ghúngrú, *s, m.* name of an ornament worn round the ankles, with bells fastened to it; a small bell.
Ghunná, *v. n.* to become worm or weevil eaten (as wood, grain, &c.): *adj.* reserve (as a person.)
Ghunna, *s. m.* a sound through the nose, the buzzing of flies: *adj.* quiescent, nasal (the letter n.)
Ghúns, *s. m.* a bandicote rat; a bribe.
Ghúnsá, *s. m.* the clinched fist.
Ghúns dená, to give bribes.
Ghúnse laṛná, to fight with the fists, to box.
Ghúns kkáná, } to take bribes.
Ghúns lená, }
Ghúnṭ, *s. m.* a gulp, a draught, pull.
Ghúnṭí, *s. f.* a decoction for infants.
Ghúnṭná, *v. a.* to gulp, to drink, to swallow.
Ghup, *adj.* dark.
Ghupchup, *adj.* silent, mute.
Ghuṛ, *s. m. contract.* of Ghoṛá, a horse, used in composition.
Ghúrá, *s. m.* a dunghill, a heap of sweepings.
Ghuraba, *s. pl.* (of gharíb), strangers, the poor.

Ghurakná, *v. a.* to browbeat, to reprimand, to frown at.
Ghuṛbahal, *s. f.* a four-wheeled carriage drawn by horses.
Ghuṛchaṛhá, *s. m.* } a rider, one on
Ghuṛchaṛhí, *s. f.* } horseback.
Ghuṛdauṛ, *s. f.* a race-course.
Ghurghurá, *s. m.* the mole-cricket.
Ghurkí, *s. f.* rebuff, browbeating, rebuke, frowning at.
Ghuṛmuṇhá, *adj.* horse-faced.
Ghúrná, *v. a.* to stare at, to fix the eyes on, to look at angrily.
Ghurra, *s. m.* the first day the new moon is seen: *adj.* vacant, void, unemployed.
Ghurráná, *v. n.* to frown.
Ghurráz, *adj.* frowning, haughty.
Ghuṛsál, } *s. m.* a stable.
Ghuṛsálá, }
Ghurúb, *s. m.* setting (of the sun, &c.); the west.
Ghurúb honá, *v. n.* to be set (the sun, moon, &c.)
Ghurúr, *s. m.* } pride, haughtiness,
Ghurúrí, *s. f.* }
Ghús, *s. m.* a bandicote rat; a bribe.
Ghúsá, *s. m.* the clinched fist.
Ghusal, *s. m*, see Ghusl.
Ghúsamghúsá, *s. m.* thumping and pulling, boxing.
Ghusáná, *v. a.* to thrust in, to stuff in, to cram, to force in.
Ghuseṛná, *v. a.* to cram, to thrust, to stuff, to force.
Ghusiṛná, *v. n.* to be thrust or stuffed in.
Ghusl, *s. m.* bathing, ablution.
Ghusl karná, to bathe.
Ghuslkhána, *s. m.* a bath, a bathing room.
Ghusná, *v. n.* to be thrust in, to enter, to penetrate, to meddle.
Ghuspaiṭh, *s. f.* access.
Ghussa, *s. m.* anger, passion, rage.
Ghussa honá, to be in a passion, to be angry.

Ghussa karná, to rage.
Ghussanák, } adj. passionate, hot-
Ghussawar, } headed.
Ghusse, *adj.* angry.
Ghusse se, angrily.
Ghusse se bhút hojáná, to rage like a fiend.
Ghúṭ, *s. m.* gulp, draught.
Ghuṭáí, *s. f.* polish.
Ghuṭáná, *v. a.* to shave clean, to polish.
Ghúṭí, *s. f.* the ankle.
Ghúṭná, *v. a.* to gulp, to drink, to guzzle.
Ghuṭná, *s. m.* the knee: *v. n.* to be rubbed.
Ghuṭní chalná, } *v. n.* to walk
Ghuṭnon chalná, } on the knees, to crawl about on the knees (as a child.)
Ghuṭṭí, *s. f.* the ankle.
Ghuwá, *s. m.* a coarse kind of cotton.
Gídaṛ, *s. m.* a jackal.
Gídaṛbhabkí, *s. f.* bullying, bluster, bravado.
Giddh, *s. m.* a vulture.
Gila, } *s. m.* complaint, lamentation,
Gilá, } reproach, blame.
Gílá, *adj.* moist, damp, wet.
Gilahrí, *s. f.* a squirrel.
Gilaurí, *s. f.* betel-leaf prepared and folded up.
Gilí, *adj.* of earth or clay, earthen.
Gilláwá, *s. m.* prepared mud for plaster.
Gilṭí, *adj.* gilded.
Gimṭí, *s. f.* a kind of cloth.
Gín, a particle which added to nouns, denotes possessed of, full of, affected with.
Gináná, *v. a.* to cause to count, &c.
Gínjná, *v. n.* to crumble, to rub with the hands.
Ginná, *v. a.* to count, to reckon, to number, to calculate, to compute.
Gintí, *s. f.* number, reckoning, account, muster; the first day of the month.
Gintí karná, to muster, to count.
Gintí lená, to have anything counted, to have muster taken.
Ginwáná, *v. a.* to cause to count.
Gír, in *compos.* taking, seizing, holding, holder, catcher, conqueror.
Girá dená, see Giráná.
Girah, *s. f.* see Girih.
Girahbáz, *s. m.* a kind of pigeon.
Girah paṛná, dissension arising between two people.
Girán, *adj.* heavy, important, precious, dear.
Giráná, *v. a.* to cause to fall, to let down, to throw down, to spill.
Girání, *s. f.* scarcity, dearth; weight, importance.
Girau, *s. m. improp.* Giro, a pledge, a pawn.
Gird, *s. m.* round, circuit, circumference, environs.
Girdá, *s. m.* a circle, a circular form, a ring, a hoop; a round cake of bread, a wafer: *adj.* round.
Girdágird, } *s. m.* all round,
Girdbagird, } round about, around, about.
Girdnawáh, *s. f.* environs.
Girebán, *s. m.* a collar (of a garment), cape.
Girebán men muṇh ḍálná, to confess and be ashamed of one's faults.
Girewán, *s. m.* see Girebán.
Girgiṛáná, *v. a.* to beseech, to implore earnestly and humbly.
Girgiṭ, *s. m.* a large kind of lizard.
Girhast. *s. m.* a householder, a peasant, a husbandman.
Girhastí, *s. f.* husbandry, housekeeping.
Girhist, *s. m.* see Girhast.
Girhistí, *s. f.* see Girhastí.
Gírí, *s. f.* in *compos.* taking, seizing.

Girift, *s. f.* taking, capture, seizure; an objection, criticism.
Giriftár, *adj. vulg.* Giripdár, arrested, seized, captive, prisoner, involved (in trouble, &c.)
Giriftár honá, to become a prisoner.
Giriftárí, *s. f.* seizure, imprisonment, embarrassment.
Giriftár karná, to arrest, to seize, to capture, to captivate.
Giriftár pakaṛná, to catch a runaway prisoner.
Girih, *s. f.* a knot, knuckle, joint; a division of a *gaz* or yard.
Giripdár, *adj.* see Giriftár.
Giripdár karná, see Giriftár karná.
Giriya, *s. m.* crying, weeping, lamentation, plaint.
Giriya karná, to weep, to cry, to lament.
Giriya o zárí, *s. f.* bewailing.
Girja, *s. m.* a Christian place of worship, divine service, preaching, prayer.
Girná, *v. n.* to fall, to drop, to sink, to tumble down.
Giro, *s. m.* see Girau.
Gir paṛná, *v. n.* to fall or tumble down.
Girte paṛte, with difficulty, with much ado.
Girwáná, *v. a.* to cause to throw down, &c.
Girwí, **Girwín**, } *adj.* pledged, pawned.
Gít, *s. m.* song, an ode, a hymn, singing.
Gítá, *s.* the name of a poem held in high estimation by the Hindús.
Gít gáná, to sing.
Giṭháná, *s. m.* a shoal, a shallow.
Giṭkarí, *s. f.* a particular vocal sound in singing; quavering, shake.
Glás, *Eng.* days of grace on bills of exchange, &c.
Go, in *compos.* speaking, speaker: *s. m.* piece or person: *s. f.* a cow.
Goáhí, *s. f. prop.* Gawáhí, evidence, testimony, witness.
Gobar, *s. m.* fresh cow-dung.
Gobarganes, *adj.* fat and lazy, one who is not able to endure hardship; bad-flavoured (meat.)
Gobar khàná, to do penance (by eating cow-dung.)
Gobind, *s. m.* a name of Krishna.
Gobrí, *s. f.* plaster made of cow-dung.
God, *s. f.* the lap, bosom, embrace.
Godám, *s. m.* a warehouse, a magazine, a storehouse, the back part of a boat.
Godí, *s. f.* the lap, bosom, embrace.
God lená, to adopt (a child.)
Godná, *v. a.* to prick, to tattoo: *s. m.* marks of tattooing.
God pasárná, to ask, to beg.
Goeṭhá, *s. m.* dried cow-dung.
Goh, *s. m.* the name of an animal.
Gohúm, *s. m.* wheat.
Goí, *s. f.* in *compos.* speaking.
Goinda, *s. m.* a scout, a spy, an informer.
Gojí, *s. f.* a stick, a walking-stick.
Gokhrú, *s. m.* name of a plant.
Goki, *conj.* although.
Gokul, *n. prop.* the place where Krishna was brought up.
Gol, *adj.* round, circular: *s. m.* a blockhead.
Gola, *s. m.* a cannon-ball.
Golá, *s. m.* a granary; a cannon-ball; a kind of pigeon; a large beam of wood; the kernel of a cocoa-nut.
Goládár, *s. m.* a grain-merchant, a corn-chandler.
Goládárí, *s. f.* merchandize in grain.
Golái, *s. f.* roundness.
Golandáz, *s. m* a gunner.
Golandází, *s. f.* gunnery.
Golí, *s. f.* a bullet, a ball, a pill, a marble (for playing with.)
Golíḍanḍá, *s. m.* name of a game.

Golí márná, to shoot a ball (at.)
Golmirch, *s. f.* black pepper.
Golsá, *adj.* roundish.
Gomútr, *s. m.* the urine of a cow.
Gon, *s. f.* a sack, bag (of coarse canvas), the sacks in which bullocks carry grain.
Gond, *s. f.* gum.
Gonddání, *s. f.* a vessel for holding gum.
Gonṭhá, *s. m.* dried cow-dung.
Gop, *s. m.* a cowherd, a dairyman: *s. f.* a gold necklace.
Gopál, *s. m.* a cowherd, one of the names of Krishna.
Gophan, *s. f.* a sling (for throwing with.)
Gopí, *s. f.* the female of Gop.
Gor, *s. f.* a tomb or grave.
Goṛ, *s. m.* the leg, foot.
Gorá, *adj.* white, fair (complexioned): *s. m.* a European soldier.
Goṛait, *s. m.* a watchman.
Goras, *s. m.* milk, butter-milk, curdled milk.
Goṛh, *s. m.* the leg, foot.
Goṛí, *s. f.* taking away.
Gor-i-gharíbán, a burying-ground for strangers.
Goṛí karná, to take away, to steal, to walk off with.
Goristán, *s. m.* a burying-ground.
Gorkan, *s. m.* a grave-digger.
Gorkhar, *s. m.* a wild ass.
Gorú, *s. m. f.* an ox, a cow.
Gorúáḍhukán, *s. m.* evening twilight.
Gosá, *adj. prop.* Ġhussa, which see.
Gosáín, *s. m.* the Deity, a saint, a holy person.
Gosainyá, *s. m.* the Deity.
Gosfand, *s. f.* a goat.
Gosh, *s. m.* the ear; *corrup.* of Gosht, meat, flesh.
Gosha, *s. m.* a corner, closet, cell, retirement, an angle.
Goshagír, *s. m.* a hermit.
Goshanishín, retired, a hermit, solitary.
Goshanishíní, *s. f.* life of a hermit.
Gosh guzár honá, to be heard.
Gosh guzár karná, to make pass into the ear, to hear, or to make to hear.
Goshmálí, *s. f.* rebuke, chastisement by pulling the ears.
Gosht, *s. m.* meat, flesh.
Goshwar, *adj. prop.* Ġhussawar, passionate, hot-headed.
Goshwárá, *s. m.* an ear-ring; boring the ears (of female children); an abstract of an account.
Gospand, *s. f.* a goat.
Goṭ, *s. f.* the hem of a garment; a counter piece or man at backgammon, chess, &c.
Got, *s. m.* parentage, lineage, pedigree.
Gota, *s. m. prop.* Ġhota, dipping, diving, a dip, a dive.
Goṭá, *s. m.* gold or silver lace or edging; person.
Gota kháná, see Ġhota kháná *or* márná.
Gotakhor, *s. m. prop.* Ġhotakhor, a diver.
Ġota márná, see Ġhota kháná.
Goṭí, *s. f.* the small-pox, a pock.
Gotiyá, *s. m.* a relation, a kinsman.
Goyá, *part. act.* speaker: *adv.* as you would say, as if, one would say, thus.
Goyáí, *s. f.* conversation, eloquence.
Goz, *s. m.* a fart.
Grah, *s. m.* a planet.
Grahan, *s. m.* an eclipse; seizing, taking, accepting.
Grahan karná, *v. a.* to accept, to consent to.
Granth, *s. f.* a book, particularly the book of the Sikh religion.
Gú, *s. f.* human excrement, dung, filth.
Gubháná,} *v. a.* to thrust, to stick
Gubhoná,} into.
Guchchha, *s. m.* a cluster (of fruit), a bunch (of keys.)

Gúdá, *s. m.* brain, marrow, kernel, pith, crumb.

Gudakṛá, *s. m.* lap, bosom, embrace.

Gudál, *s. f.* a tumult, a noise, uproar.

Gudám, *s. m.* a warehouse, a godown, a magazine, a storehouse.

Gudaṛ, *s. m.* a quilt, a bundle of old clothes, old tattered clothes; a kind of silk stuff.

Gudára, *s. m. prop.* Guzára, a ferry, a ferry-boat.

Gudaṛdás, see Gudaṛiyá.

Gudáre ká gháṭ, landing-place of a ferry-boat.

Gudáre kí náo, a ferry-boat.

Gudaṛiyá, *adj.* clothed in patched garments or in rags.

Gudaṛ síná, *v. a.* to make patchwork.

Gudast, *s. m. prop.* Guzasht, the past.

Guḍḍí, *s. f.* a child's kite.

Guddí, *s. f.* see Gudí.

Gudgudá, *adj.* soft, plump.

Gudgudáhaṭ, Gudgudáí, } *s. f.* titillation.

Gudgudáná, *v. a.* to tickle, to titillate.

Gudgudí, *s. f.* titillation.

Gudí, *s. f.* nape of the neck; the kernel or pith of a nut or grain; a dock, a place usually made by the river side for the purpose of reparing and caulking boats.

Gudíkarná, *v. a.* to dock (a boat.)

Gúdná, *v. a.* to prick, to puncture. See Godná.

Gudṛí, *s. f.* a quilt, a poor man's bedding, a patched quilt worn by a kind of faqír (Gudaṛdás); *corrupt.* of Guzri, a daily market.

Gufta, spoken, told.

Guftagú, Guftár, Guftgú, Guftogú, Guft o shaníd, Guft o shanúd, } *s. f.* conversation, discourse, chitchat.

Gúgal, *s. m.* name of a gum.

Gúh, *s. f.* human excrement, dung, filth.

Guhár, *s. f.* a fight with clubs or sticks.

Gúhaṛiyá, *s. m.* dung-hill, a place where excrement is thrown.

Gúiyáṉ, *s. m.* a partner (at a game.)

Gújar, *s. m.* a name of a low caste among Hindús.

Gujára, *s. m. prop.* Guzára, subsistence, livelihood.

Gujarát, *s.* name of a district of India, Guzarat.

Gújarí, *s. f.* the female of Gújar; name of an ornament.

Gujrán, *s. f. prop.* Guzrán, subsistence, livelihood.

Gul, *s. m.* rose, a flower; the snuff of a candle; balls of charcoal used for burning the tobacco in a huqqa; a mark made by burning, brand; *prop.* Ghul, noise, din, outcry, tumult.

Guláb, *s. m.* a rose; rosewater.

Gul ạbbás, *s. m.* the name of a plant and flower.

Gulábí, *adj.* pink, rosy.

Gulábíjáṛá, *s. m.* the spring season.

Gulábjáman, *s. f.* the rose-apple; a kind of sweetmeat.

Gulábpásh, *s. f.* a bottle for sprinkling rosewater.

Gulál, *s. m.* a red powder which Hindús throw on each other in the Holí.

Gulálí, *adj.* of the colour of the Gulál, or stained with it.

Gulám, *s. m. prop.* Ghulám, a slave, a servant.

Gulámí, *s. f.* slavery, service.

Gulandáz, *s. m.* a gunner.

Gulandází, *s. f.* gunnery.

Gúlar, *s. f.* a sort of fig.

Gulbadan, *s. m.* a kind of silk-cloth: *adj.* with a body like the rose, handsome.

Gul chharre uṛáná, to be addicted to pleasure, to live expensively.

Guldár, *adj.* spotted.
Guldasta, *s. m.* a nosegay.
Gul dená, *v. a.* to sear, to brand.
Guldum, *s. m.* name of a bird.
Gulel, *s. m. prop.* Ghulel, a pellet-bow.
Gulgasht, *s. m.* walking in the garden.
Gulgulá, *s. m.* sweet cakes fried in butter, ghí, &c.
Gulhattí, *s. f.* rice-gruel, or rice and water boiled together and seasoned with salt.
Gul honá, *v. n.* to be extinguished (a candle.)
Gul i ạbbás, *s. m.* the name of a plant and flower.
Gul i anár, *s. m.* the flower of the pomegranate.
Gul i ḳhairú, *s. m.* a hollyhock.
Gulistán, *s. m.* a rose garden; the name of a celebrated work.
Gulkárí, *s. f.* flowering, painting of flowers.
Gul karná, *v. a.* to extinguish (a candle or lamp); *prop.* Ghul karná, to make a noise or outcry.
Gul káṭná, *v. a.* to snuff a candle.
Gul kháná, to be cauterized or branded.
Gullá, *s. m.* a pellet-shot from a pellet-bow.
Gul lená, to snuff a candle.
Gul macháná, *prop.* Ghul macháná, to make a noise, outcry or tumult, to hoot.
Gulmeḳh, *s. f.* a tack, a nail.
Gulmihndí, *s. f.* name of a flower.
Gulnár, *s. m.* the flower of the pomegranate, scarlet (colour.)
Gulnárí rang, *s. m.* the colour of the Gulnár, carnation colour.
Gulqand, *s. m.* conserve of roses.
Gulrez, *s.* a sort of firework.
Gulrú, Gulruḳh, Gulruḳhsár, } *adj.* rosy-cheeked.
Gulshakarí, *s. f.* conserve of roses.
Gultarásh, *s. m.* snuffers.
Gulúband, *s. m.* a neckcloth, a cravat; a horse's collar.
Gum, *adj.* lost, wanting, missing, silent, sultry, close (no wind.)
Gúmá, *s. m.* name of a plant.
Gumán, *s. m.* doubt, suspicion, supposition, conjecture, conceit, pride.
Gumán karná, to imagine, to fancy.
Gumáshta, *s. m.* an agent, a factor.
Gumasná, *v. n.* to become musty or putrid.
Gumásta, *s. m.* see Gumáshta.
Gumbaz, *s. m.* cupola, dome.
Gumbazdár, *adj.* vaulted, arched.
Gumbazí, *s. f.* a small cupola or dome.
Gum karná, to lose.
Gumnám, *adj.* obscure (a person.)
Gumṛá, *s. m.* a protuberance, a hump, a swelling.
Gumráh, *adj.* erring, wandering, depraved, abandoned.
Gumráh honá, to be lost or wandering; to apostatize.
Gumráhí, *s. f.* error, depravity.
Gumráh karná, to turn aside, to make to err.
Gumsá, *adj.* musty.
Gún, in *compos.* implies colour, like in colour.
Gun, *s. m.* a quality, a property, an attribute, virtue, power, effect, an advantage; a small track-rope.
Guná, Gúná, } in *compos.* when preceded by a numeral it signifies as many times, fold, &c.
Gúnágún, *adj.* of different colour or kinds, various, variegated.
Gunah, Gunáh, } *s. m.* a fault, crime, sin.
Gunahgár, Gunáhgár, } *s. m.* sinner, a culprit, a criminal.
Gunahgárí, *s. f.* criminality, sinfulness; a fine, a penalty.
Gunáh karná, *v.* to sin, to commit sin.
Gundháwaṭ, *s. f.* plaiting, braiding.

Gundhná, *v. n.* to be kneaded, plaited, &c.
Gúndhná, *v. a.* to knead, to braid, to plait.
Gungá, }
Gúngá, } *adj.* dumb.
Gun gáná, to praise, to acknowledge a favour.
Gúngán karná, to prattle (as infants.)
Gungunú, *adj.* snuffling, muttering.
Gungunáná, *v. n.* to mutter, to grumble, to snuffle, to sing slowly or with a low voice.
Guní, *adj.* possessed of any quality or art: *s. m.* a snake-catcher, a sorcerer, a conjuror.
Gúnj, *s. f.* echo, resounding, hollow noise.
Gunjáish, *s. f.* capacity, room; containing, holding; livelihood.
Gunján, *adj.* thick, close.
Gunjání, *s. f.* thickness, closeness.
Gúnjná, *v. n.* to resound, to echo.
Gun karná, to benefit.
Gun mánná, to acknowledge a favour.
Gúnthná, *v. a.* to string, to make a garland.
Gunthwáná, *v. a.* to cause to string, &c.
Gunwán, }
Gunwant, }
Gunwantá, } *adj.* skilful, clever, ingenious.
Gunwantí, }
Gupatmár, *s.* kicking and cuffing.
Gupchup, *adj.* silent, mute: *s.* a kind of sugar-plums.
Guphpá, *s. f.* a cave, a grotto, cupola, a dome.
Gupt, *adj.* hidden.
Guptí, *s. f.* a sword-stick.
Guṛ, *s. m.* molasses, coarse raw sugar.
Gurakhá, *s. m.* a mast.
Guṛamba, *s. m.* mangoes boiled with meat and sugar.
Guraṇkhá, *s. m.* a mast.
Gurdá, *s. m.* a kidney; courage.
Gurgá, *s. m.* a servant boy.
Gurgábí, *s. f.* a kind of slipper.
Guṛguṛáná, *v. n.* to rumble (the bowels, a huqqa, &c.)
Guṛguṛí, *s. f.* a small huqqa, a kind of pipe for smoking.
Guṛhá, *s. m.* a beam of a ship, the cross timbers of a boat.
Guṛiyá, *s. m.* a doll.
Gurmukh honá, *v. n.* to become a disciple or scholar.
Guroh, *s. m. f.* a band, a troop, company, crew, gang, group.
Gurú, }*s. m.* a spiritual guide, tutor,
Gúrú, } teacher, schoolmaster.
Gurumukh honá, *v. n.* to become a scholar or disciple.
Gusal, *s. m. prop.* Ghusal, bathing, ablution.
Gusal karná, *prop.* Ghusal karná, to bathe.
Gusalkhána, *s. m. prop.* Ghusalkhána, a bath, a bathing-room.
Gussá, *s. m. prop.* Ghussa, anger, passion, rage.
Gusse, *adj. prop.* Ghusse, angry.
Gustákh, *adj.* presumptuous, rude, insolent, saucy, uncivil.
Gustákhí, *s. f.* presumption, insolence, sauciness, rudeness.
Gustákhí karná, to presume, to be arrogant, rude, &c.
Guṭakná, *v. n.* to swallow; to coo.
Guṭhlá, *adj.* being set on an edge (the teeth): *s. m.* swelling (from a blow.)
Guṭhlí, *s. f.* the stone of a fruit, a ball or pellet of anything.
Gúthná, *v. a.* to string (pearls, &c.); to spit or put on a spit.
Guthná, *v. n.* to be strung.
Guṭká, *s. m.* a pill.
Guzar, *s. m.* admission, approach.
Guzár, in *compos.* performing, executing, paying.
Guzára, *s. m. vulg.* Gudára, a ferry, a passage; subsistence, livelihood.
Guzaránná, *v. a.* to present, to offer.

Guzárish, *s. f.* representation.
Guzárish karná, to state politely.
Guzar jáná, to pass away, to elapse; to die.
Guzarná, *v. n.* to pass, to go, to pass by or over; to die.
Guzasht, } *part. pass. past. s. m.*
Guzashta, } the past.
Guzrán, *s. f.* subsistence, livelihood.
Guzrán karná, to pass or spend life or time, to live, to subsist.
Guzráná, to present, to offer.
Guzrí, *s. f. vulg.* Gudṛí, a daily market.
Gwálá, *s. m.* a cowherd, name of a caste.
Gwálin, *s. f.* a female of the Gwálá [caste.
Gyán, *s. m.* knowledge, wisdom, intellect, understanding.
Gyán dauṛáná, to meditate deeply.
Gyání, *adj.* wise, intelligent, judicious.
Gyánmán, } *adj.* a wise and intelli-
Gyánwán, } gent man.
Gyárah, *adj.* eleven.
Gyárahwáṉ, *adj.* eleventh.

H.

Habash, *n. prop.* the people or race of Abyssinians.
Habíb, *s.* a lover, a sweetheart, a favourite, a friend.
Habsh, *s. m.* Abyssinia.
Habshaní, *s. f.* a female Ethiopian.
Habshí, *adj.* an Ethiopian, a Caffre, a negro.
Habuáná, *v. n.* to itch.
Hachar machar, *s. m.* dispute, cavil, excuse.
Hachkolá, *s. m.* a jolt.
Hadas, *s. m.* fear, terror; fart.
Hadasáná, *v. a.* to frighten.
Hadas honá, to break wind.
Hadasná, *v. n.* to fear.
Hadd, *s. f.* boundary, limit, extremity, bounds.
Haḍḍá, *s. m.* a kind of wasp; a large bone.
Hadd bándhná, to bound, to terminate.
Hadd bharná, to do one's best.
Haḍḍí, *s. f.* a bone.
Haḍḍí haḍḍí honá, to pine away, to become lean.
Haḍḍílá, *adj.* bony.
Hadd maqdúr, *adv.* to the extent of power.
Hadd se báhar, } beyond bounds,
Hadd se ziyáda, } extremely.
Hádí, *s. m.* a director, leader, guide.
Hadís, *s. m. f.* a tradition, the traditional sayings of Muhammad.
Hádisa, *s. m.* a calamity, misfortune.
Hadíya, *s. m.* the price of a Qurán.
Hadiyáhá, *adj.* timid, timorous.
Hadíya karná, to sell.
Hadiyáná, *v. n.* to be alarmed, to shrink, to be disturbed, to be impatient.
Háe, } *interj.* alas! *s. f.* a sigh.
Háe háe, }
Háe márná, to sigh.
Háfiz, *s. m.* a guardian, having a good memory; one who has the whole Qurán by heart.
Háfiza, *s. m.* a retentive memory.
Hafta, *s. m.* a week.
Hafte ká din, the last day of the week.
Hagáná, *v. a.* to cause to go to stool (*vulg.*)
Hagás, *s. f.* inclination to go to stool (*vulg.*)
Hagná, *v. n.* to go to stool, to dung [(*vulg.*)
Hagneṭí, *s. f.* the podex.
Háhá, *s. m.* laughing at, ha, ha! interjection of surprise, or grief, or pain.
Háhá híhí, *s. f.* laughing.
Háhá híhí karná, } to laugh, to
Háhá karná, } joke.
Hai, *interj.* alas! strange! wonderful!
Hai'at, *s. f.* appearance or outward form.
Haibat, *s. f.* fright, panic, dread, awe.

Haibatzada, aghast, appalled.
Haidar, *adj*. brave, courageous: *s. m.* a name of Ạlí, son-in-law of Muhammad.
Haidarí, *s. f.* bravery, courage.
Haif, *interj.* ah! alas!
Haigá, is, must, may, shall or will be; an expression of consent, probably, suppose so, doubtless.
Hai hai, *interj.* alas! a-lack-a-day! &c.
Haija, *s. m. prop.* Haiza, which see.
Haikal, *s. f.* an ornament worn round the neck; the temple of Jerusalem.
Hainge, are, may be, must be, will be, &c.
Hairán, *adj.* astonished, confounded, disturbed, perplexed, fatigued.
Hairán honá, to be astonished, to be perplexed.
Hairání, *s. f.* astonishment, perturbation, distress.
Hairán karná, to annoy, to perplex.
Hairán pareshán, distressed.
Hairat, *s. f.* stupor and perturbation of mind, astonishment.
Hairatzada, *adj.* struck with astonishment.
Haisiyat, *s. f.* capacity, ability.
Haiwán, *s. m.* an animal, a beast, a brute.
Haiwánát, *s. plur.* of Haiwán, animals, brutes.
Haiza, *s. m.* the cholera, a flux and vomit.
Hajam, *s. m. prop.* Hazm, digestion.
Hajámat, *s. f.* shaving.
Hajámat banáná, } to shave.
Hajámat karná, }
Hajam honá, *prop.* Hazm honá, to be digested.
Hajár, *adj. prop.* Hazár, a thousand.
Hajárhá, *prop.* Hazárhá, thousands, by thousands.
Hajárí bájárí, *prop.* Hazárí bázárí, which see.
Hájat, *s. f.* need, want, necessity.
Hájatmand, *adj.* necessitous, indigent.
Hájat rafạ karná, to go to the necessary.
Hájí, *s. m.* a pilgrim to Mecca.
Hájir, *adj. prop.* Házir, which see.
Hájír honá, *prop.* Házir honá, which see.
Hájirí, *s. f. prop.* Házirí, which see.
Hájirí kháná, *prop.* Házirí kháná, to breakfast.
Hájir jawáb, *adj. prop.* Házir jawáb, pert, answering wittingly.
Hájir o nájir, *prop.* Házir o názir, present and seeing.
Hájir rahná, *prop.* Házir rahná, to attend, to wait on.
Hájir jámin, *s. m. prop.* Házir zámin, which see.
Hájir jáminí, *s. f. prop.* Házir záminí, which see.
Hajj, *s. m.* pilgrimage to Mecca.
Hajjám, *s. m.* a barber, a shaver.
Hajjámin, *s. f.* a barber's wife, a female of the barber caste.
Hajm, *s. m. prop.* Hazm, digestion.
Hajm karná, *prop.* Hazm karná, to digest, to embezzle.
Hajo, *s. f.* satire.
Hajo karná, to satirize.
Hajrat. *prop.* Hazrat, which see.
Hajrat Ịsá, *prop.* Hazrat Ịsá, Jesus Christ.
Hajrat salámat, *prop.* Hazrat salámat, which see.
Hak, *prop.* Haqq, which see.
Hak adá karná, *prop.* Haqq, &c., which see.
Hakbakáná, *v. n.* to be confused, to be aghast.
Hakdár, *prop.* Haqqdár, having right or claim to.
Hakíkat, *s. f. prop.* Haqíqat, which see.
Hakíkat men̤, *prop.* Haqíqat men̤, in reality.
Hákim, *s. m.* a ruler, a governor, a master.

Hakím, *s. m.* a doctor, a physician.
Hákim honá, to become a ruler.
Hakímí, *s. f.* the practice of medicine.
Hákimí, *s. f.* rule, government, dominion.
Hákimwaqt, the present ruler or rulers.
Hakkábakká, *adj.* confused (when any thing is to be done.)
Hakkák, *s. m.* a cutter and polisher of precious stones, &c.
Hakláhá, *s. m.* a stammerer.
Hakláná, *v. n.* to stutter, to stammer, to falter.
Hak márná, *prop.* Haqq, &c., to deprive one of his rights.
Hak meṉ, *prop.* Haqq meṉ, with respect to, in behalf
Hak ná hak, *prop.* Haqq, &c., *adv.* right or wrong, for nothing.
Hal, *s. m.* a plough.
Hál, *s. m.* state, condition, the present time; ecstacy; tire (of a wheel): *adv.* now, soon.
Hála, *s. m.* a halo, or circle round the moon.
Halabí, *adj.* from or belonging to Aleppo.
Halabí áina, *s. m.* a kind of looking-glass of very thick glass.
Haláhal, *s. m.* poison.
Hálá hálí chalná, to go or walk in haste or quickly.
Halák, *adj.* lost, destroyed: *s. m.* perdition, ruin, destruction, death.
Halákat, *s. f.* ruin, destruction, death.
Halák honá, *v. n.* to be killed, to perish, to be fatigued.
Halákí, *s. f.* perdition, ruin, destruction.
Halák karná, *v. a.* to destroy, to distress, to kill.
Halál, *adj.* legal, lawful, allowable, (to eat, &c.)
Halál karná, *v. a.* to slay according to the forms prescribed by the Muhammadan religion, to slaughter; to marry.
Halálkhor, *s. m.* a Muhammadan sweeper; a person of the lowest caste who cleans the privy, &c.
Halálkhorin, *s. f.* a Muhammadan female sweeper.
Hál áná, to be thrown into ecstacies.
Hálánki, *adv.* whereas, though, although, notwithstanding.
Halapná, *v. n.* to toss and tumble about, to shudder in a fever.
Halaq, *s. m* the windpipe.
Hálat, *s. f.* state, condition, posture of one's affairs or case.
Hálát, *s.* (*plur.* of Hálat), states, &c.
Haláwat, *s. f.* sweetness, freshness; condition, strength.
Halbalálat, *s. f.* hurry, confusion.
Halbaláná, *v. n.* to hurry, to be confused.
Hál be hál honá, to be out of condition, to be in bad circumstances.
Hál charháná, to tire (a wheel.)
Haldí, *s. f.* turmeric.
Half, *s.* an oath.
Halfá, *s. m.* a billow, a wave, a surge.
Halfa márná, to billow, to wave.
Half utháná, to swear (by the Qurán.)
Halhaláná, *v. n.* to shake or tremble from the effect of an ague, &c.
Halhalí, *s. f.* an ague.
Hálí, *adj.* modern, new: *adv.* now, soon.
Hálí hálí chalná, to go or walk in haste or quickly.
Hálí hálí karná, to make haste, to work expeditiously.
Hálim, *s. m.* cress, cresses.
Halím, *adj.* mild, meek, gentle: *s. m.* a kind of food.
Haljotá, *s. m.* a tiller, a ploughman.
Hal jotná, *v. a.* to plough.
Halká, *s. m.* *prop.* Halqa, which see.
Halká, *adj.* light (in weight or character); mean, lively, silly, easy, cheap.
Halkáí, *s. f.* lightness, levity.
Halká jánná, to disdain to disesteem.

Halká karná, to lighten, to ease, to debase, to abase, to affront.
Halkán, *adj.* confounded, confused, tired, wearied.
Halkápan, *s. m.* despicableness, meanness.
Halkhor, *s. m. prop.* Halálkhor, which see.
Halkorná, *v. a.* to gather, to collect.
Halla, } *s. m.* uproar, tumult, assault,
Hallá, } attack.
Hallákallá, *s. m.* loquacity, foolish talk.
Hallá karná, to make an uproar, to assault, to attack.
Hall karná, to dissolve, to pulverize, to discuss, to solve (a question or difficulty.)
Hál o qál áná, to be thrown into ecstacies.
Halorá, *s. m.* wave, billow, surge.
Halorná, *v. a.* to collect, to gather.
Halphá, *s. m* a billow, a wave.
Halq, *s. m.* the windpipe.
Halqa, *s. m.* a hoop; a horse's collar; a string of cattle.
Halq par chhuri chalána, to annoy (for payment), to dun.
Hál sál, this year.
Hál se behál honá, to be out of condition, to be in bad circumstances.
Hál shikasta, *adj.* ruined, distressed, wretched.
Haluk, *adj.* see Halká.
Haluk jánná, see Halká jánná.
Halukpan, see Halkápan.
Halwá, *s. m.* a kind of sweetmeat made of flour, ghí, and sugar.
Halwáhá, *s. m.* a ploughman.
Halwáhí, *s. f.* tillage, ploughing.
Halwái, *s. m.* a confectioner.
Halwán, *s. m.* a kid, a lamb.
Halwá nikálná, to beat severely.
Halwán ká gosht, the flesh of kid or lamb.
Halwásohan, *s. m.* a kind of sweetmeat.
Halwáyan, *s. f.* a confectioner's wife, a female of the confectioner caste.
Hám, *n. prop.* Ham, son of Noah.
Ham, *pron. plur.* we; in *compos.* together with, mutual, similar, same, equal.
Hamáil, *s. f.* a small Qurán suspended to the neck as an amulet.
Hamal, *s. m.* Aries.
Humára, } *pron. possess.*
Hamárau (in Braj), } *plur.* our.
Hamáwáz, *s. f.* of the same tone or voice, consonant.
Hambistar, lying on the same bed.
Hambistar honá, to cohabit.
Hamd, *s. f.* praise.
Hamdam, *s. m. f.* an intimate, a friend, a companion, a bosom friend.
Hamdard, a partner in adversity, sympathetical.
Hamdil, of the same mind; a friend.
Hamd karná, to praise or bless (God.)
Hameṉ, *pron. plur.* in the objective case, us, to us.
Hames, } *adv.* always, ever, con-
Hamesha, } tinually, perpetually.
Hameshagí, *s. f.* eternity, perpetuity.
Hamesha ká, eternal.
Hámí, *s. m.* a protector, a defender.
Hámí bharná, to become responsible, to take one's part.
Hámí honá, to become a friend and protector.
Hámila, *adj. f.* pregnant.
Hámila honá, to conceive, to be pregnant.
Hámil se, pregnant.
Hámil se honá, to be pregnant.
Hamíṉ, we ourselves.
Hamjawár, a townsman, a neighbour.
Hamjins, of the same kind or species; homogeneous, fellow-creature.

Hamjolí, equal, peer, coeval.
Hamkalám, conversing together.
Hamkinár, embracing.
Hamkhwábí, a bed-fellow, spouse.
Haml, *s. m.* pregnancy.
Hamla, *s. m.* an attack, an assault.
Hamla karná, to attack, to assault, to assail.
Hammaktab, a schoolfellow.
Hammám, *s. m.* a bath, a hot bath.
Hammashwarat, *adj.* of the same counsel, confederate.
Hammaslahat, confederated,
Hammazhab, of the same religion.
Hamnám, a namesake, of the same name.
Hamnasl, of the same breed.
Hamnawála, a messmate.
Hamnishín, one who sits with another, a companion.
Hamnishíní, *s. f.* companionship.
Hampesha, of the same trade.
Hamphail, *adj.* short-winded.
Hamphná, Hámphná, } *v. n.* to be out of breath, to pant.
Hampiyála, a pot-companion.
Hámpná, *v. n.* to be out of breath, to pant.
Hamqadd, of equal stature.
Hamqaum, of the same tribe.
Hamráh, *s. m.* a fellow-traveller: *adv.* with, together with, along with.
Hamráhí, *s. f.* company, society in travelling.
Hamrang, *adj.* of the same colour or disposition.
Hamráz, acquainted with one another's secrets, agreed.
Hamrikáb, fellow-rider, attendant.
Hamsabaq, a class-fellow.
Hamsafar, a fellow-traveller.
Hamsar, an equal, a peer.
Hamsáya, a neighbour, neighbouring.
Hamsáyagí, *s. f.* neighbourhood.
Hamshahrí, a fellow-citizen.
Hamshakl, of the same appearance, alike.
Hamshír, Hamshíra, } a sister.
Hamsinn, of equal age.
Hamsuhbat, of the same society.
Hamumr, of the same age, coeval.
Hamwár, *adj.* even, level, smooth.
Hamwára, *adv.* always.
Hamwár karná, to level, to smooth.
Hamwatan, a fellow-countryman.
Hamwataní, the being of the same country.
Hamwazn, of the same weight.
Hamyání, *s. f.* a purse.
Hamzabán, of the same language.
Hamzát, of the same caste.
Hamzulf, a wife's sister's husband.
Háṉ, *adv.* yes, ay, indeed.
Hanḍá, *s. m.* a cauldron.
Handasa, *s. m.* geometry, arithmetic.
Hánḍí, Hanḍí, } *s. f.* an earthen pot, a small cauldron; a kind of a hanging lamp.
Hangáma, *s. m.* a crowd, tumult, uproar, riot, disturbance, assault.
Hangáma karná, to raise a tumult, to riot.
Hánk, *s. f.* cry, bawling, calling to, driving.
Hánkáhánk, *s. m.* driving.
Háṉ kahná, to agree.
Hankáná, *v. a.* to drive away.
Hankárí, *adj.* proud, self-conceited.
Hankárná, *v. a.* to drive away, to expel, to bawl, to call; to hoist sails, &c.
Hánk láná, to fetch (a flock or herd.)
Hankláná, *v. n.* to stammer, to stutter, to speak with difficulty.
Hánk márná, to bawl after, to call to.
Hánkná, to drive; to bawl to.
Hánk paṛná, to call after.
Hánkpukár, *s. f.* calling out, calling for.
Hanoz, *adv.* yet, hitherto, still.
Háṉṛí, Haṉṛiyá, } *s. f.* an earthen pot, small cauldron.

Hans, Háns, } *s. m.* a swan, a goose.

Hansái, *s. f.* ridicule.

Hansáná, *v. a.* to turn into ridicule, to cause to laugh, to please.

Hánsí, Hansí, Hansí ṭhaṭṭhá, } *s. f.* laughter, laughing, joke, fun, sport, derision, jesting, ridicule, scorn.

Hansí ṭhaṭṭhá karná, to make fun or sport of, to make light of, to ridicule.

Hansiyá, *s. m.* a sickle.

Hanslí, *s. f.* the collar-bone, a collar of gold or silver, &c., worn round the neck.

Hansmukh, *adj.* cheerful, merry, facetious, jovial, blithe.

Hansná, *v. n.* to laugh, to deride.

Hansoṛ, *adj.* see Hansmukh.

Hansoṛpan, *s. m.* facetiousness, mirth.

Hanúmán, *s. m.* the deified monkey who was the ally of Rám; a species of monkey.

Haphhapháná, *v. n.* to pant, to be out of breath.

Haqíqat, *s. f.* account, narration, state, condition, ability; truth, reality, fact.

Haqíqatan, *adv.* really, truly.

Haqíqat men, in reality.

Haqíqí, *adj.* real, true; own.

Haqíqí bhái, a full brother.

Haqír, *adj.* mean, contemptible.

Haqír jánná, to contemn, to despise.

Haqq, *adj.* just, right, true: *s. m.* the Deity; the truth; justice, rectitude, right, due, just claim.

Haqq adá karná, to render every one his due; to perform social or domestic duties.

Haqqdár, having right or claim to.

Haqq guzár, *adj.* one who does what is just and right.

Haqq haqq karná, to be very hungry.

Haqq márná, *v. a.* to deprive one of his rights.

Haqq men, with respect to, for, in behalf.

Haqq ná haqq, *adv.* right or wrong; for nothing.

Haqq shinás, *adj.* knowing one's duty.

Haqq taạlá, Almighty God.

Har, *adj.* every, any: *s. m.* a plough.

Hár, in *compos.* means the performer of any act: *s. m.* a necklace of pearls, &c.: *s. f.* loss, forfeiture, discomfiture.

Háṛ, *s. m.* a bone.

Hará, *adj.* green, fresh, verdant.

Hárá, in *compos.* denotes the performer of any act, dealer in any article.

Harái, *s. f.* greenness, freshness, verdure.

Harakat, *s. f.* motion, procedure, action, (usually improper); prevention; hindrance; a short vowel.

Harakát, *s.* (*plur.* of Harakat); vowel points, &c.

Harakatí, *s. m.* an interrupter.

Harakat karná, to interrupt, to hinder, to do or commit an improper action.

Haram, *s. f.* concubine; seraglio.

Harám, *adj.* unlawful (to eat), prohibited, sacred, illegitimate.

Harámí, *s. m.* a bastard; a rascal.

Harámí pillá, *s. m.* a bastard.

Harámkár, *s. m.* a fornicator.

Haramkárí, Harámkárí, } *s. f.* fornication, adultery.

Harám khána, to receive or live on the wages of iniquity.

Harámkhor, *s. m.* one who lives on the wages of iniquity.

Harámmaghz, spinal marrow.

Haramwál, *adj.* illegitimate.

Haramzáda, *adj.* unlawfully begotten, bastard; vicious (a horse); mischievous: *s. m.* a wicked rogue, rascal.

Haramzadagí, *s. f.* rascality, baseness, villany.
Haramzadagí karná, to behave ill, to behave in a rascally manner.
Haran, *s. m.* a deer, an antelope, a hart.
Haṛáná, *v. a.* to win, to overcome, to beat (at a game), to weary, to worst.
Harárat, *s. f.* heat, warmth, burning fever.
Harauṭí, *s. f.* a cane, a staff; a kind of bamboo.
Harba, *s. m.* arms, warlike apparatus.
Har báb, every chapter, every circumstance.
Harbábí, master of knowledge of every kind; a factotum.
Harba karná, to attack, to thrust at.
Har bár, every time.
Haṛbaṛáná, *v. n.* to be confused, to hurry.
Haṛbaṛí, *s. f.* hurry, confusion, hastiness.
Haṛbaṛiyá, *adj.* easily agitated, irritable.
Harchand, *adv.* howmuchsoever, howsoever, although.
Harchandki, *adv.* notwithstanding, although.
Har dam, every moment.
Hardwár, *s. prop.* a famous place of pilgrimage.
Har ek, every one, each.
Harerá, *adj.* green.
Harf, *s. m.* a letter of the alphabet; a particle (in grammar); blame, censure, infamy.
Harfáleuṛí, see Harpharauṛí.
Harf áná, to be incurred (infamy, &c.)
Harf áshná, being just able to read, knowing the letters.
Harf baiṭhálná, } to compose for
Harf jamáná, } printing.
Harf láná, to asperse, to defame.
Harf pakaṛná, to censure, to criticise.

Har gáh, *adv.* whenever, wherever, everywhere.
Har ghaṛí, *adv.* at every hour, often.
Hargiz, *adv.* ever.
Hargiz nahíṇ, never.
Harguní, *adj.* skilful, clever.
Haṛhaṛáhaṭ, *s. f.* a crack, crash, sound.
Haṛhaṛáná, *v. n.* to shudder, to shiver, to crack, to rattle.
Hari, } *n. prop.* a name of Vishnu.
Harí, }
Haribhajan, *s. m.* adoration of Vishnu.
Haribhakt, *s. m.* a worshipper of [Vishnu.
Haridás, *s. m.* a servant of Vishnu.
Haridwár, *n. prop.* a famous place of pilgrimage.
Haríf, *adj.* clever, cunning: *s. m.* a rival, an enemy, an adversary.
Harilá, *adj.* verdant, green, grassy.
Harír, *s. m.* silk-cloth.
Haríra, *s. m.* a kind of pap, a caudle given to lying-in women.
Harís, *adj.* covetous, greedy, gluttonous.
Hariyálá, *adj.* verdant, green, grassy.
Hariyáná, *v. n.* to become green, to wax green.
Harj, *s. m.* hindrance, interruption.
Harjái, *adj.* vagabond, stroller; a strumpet.
Hárjít, *s. m.* gambling, hazard.
Hárjít karná, to gamble.
Harj marj, *s. m.* trouble, affliction.
Hárjoṛá, } *s. m.* name of a medicinal
Haṛjoṛá, } plant.
Harjotá, *s. m.* a ploughman.
Har kahíṇ, everywhere.
Harkáná, *v. a.* to frighten away.
Harkára, *s. m.* a running footman, a courier, a messenger.
Har koí, every one, whoever.
Har lahza, *adv.* momentarily, every moment.
Hár mán lená, } to give up a dispute,
Hár mánná, } or in despair to acknowledge all lost.

Harmushṭá, *adj.* stout, robust, strong.
Harmushṭí, *s. f.* robustness, strength.
Hárná, *v. n.* to be overcome, to be unsuccessful; to lose, (in play); to be tired out: *v. a.* to lose.
Harná, *s. m.* a stag, a buck, a male antelope; a pommel of a saddle.
Harnauṭá, *s. m.* a fawn.
Harní, *s. f.* a doe, a hind.
Harpharaurí, } name of a sour fruit.
Harpharewrí, }
Harráf, *adj.* ingenious, clever; wicked; abandoned.
Har roz, *adv.* every day, daily.
Har sál, *adv.* yearly, every year, annual.
Hársingár, } *s. m.* name of a tree
Harsingár, } which bears a flower the stem of which is used in dyeing.
Hartál, *s. f.* orpiment.
Har taraf, *adv.* every side.
Hárú, *s. m.* a loser.
Hárún, *n. prop.* Aaron, the brother of Moses.
Harwáhá, *s. m.* a ploughman.
Har waqt, *adv.* always, at all times.
Haṛwáṛ, *s. m.* a family burial-place.
Haryá, *adj.* green.
Har yak, every one, each, apiece.
Haryá kaddú, green pumpkin or bottle gourd.
Has, *s. m.* a consonant.
Hasab o nasab, *s. m.* pedigree, lineage.
Hasad, *s. f.* envy, malice, emulation, ambition.
Hasáí, *s. f.* see Hansáí.
Hasan, *s. m.* a proper name, a son of Ạlí.
Hasáná, *v. a.* to make or cause to laugh.
Hasb, *adv.* agreeably, according to, in conformity with.
Hasb i dilḳhwáh, agreeably to one's desire.
Hasb i hál, agreeably to circumstances, as exigency may require.
Hasb ul amr, } agreeably to or-
Hasb ul hukm, } ders.
Hasb ul imkán, as far as possible.
Hasb ul irshád, agreeably to orders.
Hasb ul mạmúl, agreeably to custom.
Háshá lilláh, *interj.* God forbid! by no means.
Hasharát, *s. f.* the buzzing noise of a crowd.
Hasharát ul arz, reptiles, insects, animalcules.
Háshiya, *s. m.* a margin, hem, border.
Hashmat, *s. f.* state, dignity, equipage, retinue.
Hashr, *s. f.* the resurrection.
Hashshásh bashshásh, *adj.* joyful.
Hásid, *s. m.* an enemy.
Hásil, *s. m.* produce, profit; result, inference, acquiring; revenue.
Hásil honá, *v. n.* to be acquired, to accrue.
Hásil i kalám, } in short, briefly.
Hásil kalám }
Hásil karná, to acquire, to gain; to produce, to collect, to learn.
Hasín, *adj.* beautiful.
Hasiyá, *s. m.* a reaping-hook.
Haslí, *s. m.* the collar-bone; an ornament worn round the neck.
Hasná, *v. n.* to laugh, to deride.
Hasrat, *s. f.* regret, grief.
Hast, *s. f.* being, existent.
Hat, *interj.* be gone! fye!
Haṭ, *s. f.* insisting upon, obstinacy, perverseness.
Hát, *s. m.* the hand.
Háṭ, *s. f.* a market, a moveable market or fair.
Háta, *s. f. prop.* Iháta, a surrounding, an enclosure, a fence, a compound.
Hatak. *s. m.* affront, disrespect.
Haṭákaṭá, *adj.* stout and active, robust.
Haṭáná, *v. a.* to repel, to drive backwards, to back, to worst.

Hatberí, *s. f.* handcuffs, manacles.
Hath, contraction of Háth.
Háth, *s. m.* the hand; a cubit; possession, power.
Haṭh, *s. m. f.* see Haṭ.
Háṭh, *s. f.* see Háṭ.
Háthá, báṇhí karná, to scuffle or struggle together.
Háth ána, to come into one's possession or power, to be obtained.
Hathauṛá, *s. m.* a sledge hammer.
Hathauṛí, *s. f.* a small hammer.
Hathauṭí, *s. f.* dexterity, art, skill.
Háth baiṭhná, to acquire perfection in any art by practice.
Háth band honá, to be much engaged in business, to have no leisure.
Háth bándhná, to supplicate, to entreat earnestly.
Háth baṛháná, to endeavour to get anything, to gain possession of the property of others.
Háṭh bázár, *s. m.* see Háṭ.
Háṭh bázár karná, to market.
Háth bajhná, to have the hands full of work.
Háth bhar, a full cubit.
Háth chálákí, *s. f.* expertness.
Háth chaṭná, to relish food much.
Hathchhúṭ, *s. m.* a beater, a striker.
Háth ḍálná, to meddle, to interfere (in.)
Háth dená, to concern one's self in or about.
Háth dho baiṭhná, to give up in despair.
Háth dhoná, to be disappointed, to be hopeless, to relinquish.
Hathelí, *s. f.* the palm of the hand.
Hathí, *s. f.* a hair glove for rubbing down horses, a rubber.
Haṭhí *adj.* peevish, obstinate, perverse.
Háthí, *s. m.* an elephant.
Háthídánt, *s. m.* ivory.
Háthí háth karná, to act in concord, to pull together.
Haṭhílá, *adj.* perverse, obstinate, contumacious.
Háthíwán, *s. m.* an elephant-driver.
Hathiyá, *s. m.* the thirteenth mansion of the moon.
Hathiyáná, *v. a.* to seize.
Hathiyár, *s. f.* see Hathyár.
Háth jhúṭhá honá, to have the hands defiled, to miss (as with a sword.)
Háth joṛná, to supplicate, to entreat earnestly.
Háth kamar par rakhná, to be very feeble.
Háth kánoṇ par rakhná, to be astonished, to deny vehemently.
Hathkaṛá, *s. m.* } a handcuff, fetter,
Hathkaṛi, *s. m.* } manacle.
Háth karná, to subdue.
Haṭh karná, see Haṭ karná.
Háth khainchná, to refrain, to desist, to abstain.
Hathkhanḍá, *s. m.* dexterity, art, knack, style.
Háth lagáná, to be employed in any business.
Háth lagná, to be employed, to be got, obtained, acquired.
Hath lapak, *s. m.* a thief, a pilferer.
Háth malná, *v. n.* to regret, to repent, to lament.
Háth márná, to plunder, to wound.
Háth meṇ áná, see Háth áná.
Háth meṇ rakhná, to possess, to hold in subjection.
Háth miláná, to claim equality, to prepare to wrestle.
Hathní, *s. f.* a female elephant.
Háthoṇ háth, quickly, expeditious, out of hand.
Háthoṇ háth lejáná, to carry away quickly.
Háth pahunchná, see Háth áná.
Háth pakṛe lejáná, to hand or lead a person.
Haṭhpaná, *s. m.* obstinacy, perverseness.
Háth páṇw phailáná, to extend one's business or schemes.

Háth paṛná, to come into one's possession.
Háth pasárná, to ask, to beg.
Háth patthar tale dabná, to be helpless, to be unable to act.
Háth phenkná, to fence, to be restless.
Hathpher, borrowing.
Hathpher lená, to borrow.
Háth pherná, to stroke, to caress, to coax.
Háthphúl, a kind of firework.
Háth rokná, to prevent.
Háth sáf karná, to learn, practise, or exercise any art; to slay.
Háth sameṭná, to refrain from giving, &c.
Háth uṭháná, to leave off, to refrain from; to salute by raising the hand to the head; to beat.
Hathyár, *s. m.* a tool, arms, implements.
Hathyárband, armed.
Hathyár bándhná, to arm.
Hátí, *s. m.* an elephant.
Hátídánt, *s. m.* ivory.
Hátim, *adj.* liberal, generous, bountiful.
Haṭiyá, *s. f.* a market.
Haṭ jáná, *v. n.* see Haṭná.
Haṭ karná, to resist or disobey obstinately, to insist upon, to be perverse or peevish.
Hatná, *v. a.* to kill.
Haṭná, *v. n.* to go back, to be driven back, to retire; to budge, to flinch, to be defeated.
Hatní, *s. f.* a female elephant.
Hattal maqdúr, Hattal wusa, *adv.* to the best of one's ability, to one's utmost.
Hatthá, *s. m.* a shovel, a baker's peel.
Hatyá, *s. f.* murder, slaughter.
Hatyárá, *s. m.* a murderer, assassin, villain.
Hatyárí, *s. f.* a female murderer.
Hatyárpaná, *s. m.* wickedness.
Hauda, Haudaj, *s. m.* a litter carried by elephants or camels.
Hauj, *prop.* Hauz, which see.
Hauká, Haukhá, *s. m.* greediness, covetousness.
Haul, *s. m.* terror, horror.
Haulá, *adj.* see Halká.
Hauldil, terrified; hypochondriac, affection, melancholy.
Haule, Haule haule, *adj.* gently, softly.
Haul hojáná, to become flurried.
Haulnak, *adj.* frightful, terrible, dreadful, dismal, dreary.
Haulzada, terrified, aghast.
Haunhár, *adj.* see Honhár.
Haunkná, *v. a.* to blow or fan (the fire, &c.)
Hauns, *s. f.* desire, wish, ambition, lust.
Hauns karná, to desire.
Hauṛáhauṛí, *s. f.* striving to the best of one's power.
Hausila, *s. m.* the stomach, maw; capacity, ambition, resolution.
Hausilamand, *adj.* ambitious, aspiring.
Hauwá, *s. m.* a bugbear, a hobgoblin.
Hauwáná, *v. n.* to itch.
Hauz, *s. m.* a reservoir, a pond, a cistern, a vat.
Havildár, see Hawáldár.
Hawá, *s. f.* wind, air, atmosphere.
Hawá batáná, to disappoint.
Hawá chhoṛná, to break wind.
Hawádár, *adj.* airy: *s.* a lover.
Hawá dená, to air.
Hawáhirs, covetousness, greediness, envy.
Hawá hojáná, to scamper off, to vanish, to disappear.
Hawáí, *s. f.* a sky-rocket.
Hawá karná, to fan.
Hawá kháná, to take the air, to walk about idly.
Hawála, *s. m.* custody, charge, care, possession.
Hawála karná, to deliver in charge.
Hawáldár, *s. m.* a military officer of inferior rank, havildar.
Hawále, *adv.* in the charge, care, &c.

Hawále karná, to give in charge or possession, to intrust, to deliver.

Háwan, *s. m.* a mortar for pounding in.

Háwan dasta, mortar and pestle.

Hawá o hawas, lust, concupiscence, sensuality, vanity.

Hawárí, *s. m.* a disciple or apostle of Jesus Christ.

Hawas, *s. f.* desire, lust, ambition; inordinate desire.

Hawasdár, *adj.* desirous.

Hawá se bát karná, to rival the wind in speed.

Hawasnák, *adj.* full of desire.

Hawáss, *s. m. plur.* the senses.

Hawáss bákhta, *adj.* out of one's senses, crazy.

Hawáss i khamsa, the five senses.

Hawázadugí, *s. f.* the cholera.

Hawelí, *s. f.* house, dwelling, habitation, mansion.

Hawwá, *n. prop.* Eve, the mother of mankind.

Haya, *s. f.* modesty, shame.

Hayádár, *adj.* modest.

Hayát, *s. f.* life.

Hazam, *s. m.* see Hazm.

Hazár, *adj.* thousand.

Hazárá, } *s. m.* a kind of double
Hazára, } flower.

Hazár dástán, a kind of nightingale.

Hazárhá, thousands, by thousands.

Hazárí bázárí, high and low, people of sorts.

Hazárpáe, *s. m.* a centipede.

Házima, *s. m.* the digestive powers.

Hazín, *adj.* sorrowful.

Házir, *adj.* present, ready, at hand; willing, content; the second person in grammar.

Házirát, *s. m.* commanding or imprisoning demons, &c.; raising the devil.

Házirbásh, *adj.* attendant.

Házirbáshí, *s. f.* constant attendance.

Házir honá, to be at hand, to be ready, to consent.

Házirí, *s. f.* breakfast, dessert; presence, attendance; muster-roll; an offering made to a saint.

Házirí kháná, to breakfast.

Házirjawáb, *adj.* pert, answering wittingly.

Házirjawábí, *s. f.* repartee.

Házir o názir, *adj.* present and seeing.

Házir rahná, to attend, to wait on.

Házir zámin, *s. m.* bail, security for the appearance of another; a bondsman.

Házir záminí, *s. f.* the act of giving bail for another, a bail-bond,

Hazl, *s. m.* a jest, a joke.

Hazlgo, an idle talker.

Hazliyát, jests, jokes, nonsensical talk.

Hazm, *s. m.* digestion.

Hazm honá, to be digested.

Hazm karná, to digest, to embezzle.

Hazrat, majesty, highness, &c. (a title addressed to superiors.)

Hazrat Ísá, Jesus Christ.

Hazrat salámat, sir; a respectful mode of salutation.

Hazz, *s. m.* enjoyment.

He, a vocative particle, O!

Hech, *adj.* nothing; worthless, good for nothing,

Hekaṛ, *adj* incapable, simpleton.

Helá márná, *v. n.* to launch, to dash through water.

Helná, *v. n.* to swim.

Henbená, *adj.* spoiled, ruined; distressed.

Heṭá, } *adj.* insolent, pusillani-
Heṭhá, } mous, inferior.

Hí, *s. m.* heart, mind, soul: emphatic affix or *adv.* very, exactly, even, indeed, truly.

Hiba, *s. m.* a gift, a bequest.

Hiba karná, to bequeath or devise.

Hibanáma, *s. m.* a deed of gift.

Hichakná, *v. n.* to draw back from, to decline, to waver.

Hichar michar, *s. m.* dispute, cavil, excuse.

Hichkáná, *v. n.* to jolt.
Hichkí, *s. f.* the hiccough.
Hichkicháná, *v. n.* to doubt, to hesitate, to be in suspense.
Hidáyat, *s. f.* guidance, direction in the right way, especially to salvation.
Hifázat, *s. f.* custody, care, guardianship, protection.
Hifázat karná, to preserve, to defend, to take care of.
Hifz, *s. m.* memory.
Hifz karná, to repeat from memory, to keep in memory.
Hijáb, *s. m.* modesty, bashfulness, shame; a veil, a curtain.
Hijáb karná, to cover, to hide, to conceal; to shame.
Hijáb kháná, to blush.
Hijáb uṭhná, to be lost (the sense of shame.)
Hije, *s. m.* spelling.
Hijṛá, } *s. m.* an hermaphrodite, a
Híjṛá, } eunuch, (*met.*) pusillanimous, unmanly.
Hijrí, *adj.* of the Muhammadan era.
Hík, *s. m.* sickness at the stomach, disgust.
Hík áná, to feel sick; to be disgusted.
Hikáyat, *s. f.* a history, story, tale, narration.
Hikláhá, *s. m.* a stammerer.
Hikláná, *v. n.* to stammer, to stutter, to falter.
Hikmat, *s. f.* wisdom, skill, cleverness, knack, contrivance, device; a treatise on medicine.
Hikmatí, *adj.* clever, ingenious skilful.
Hilá, *adj.* domesticated, tame.
Híla, *s. m.* stratagem, deceit, pretence, trick, means.
Hílabáz, *adj.* artful, insidious, wily, deceitful.
Hílabází, *s. f.* artfulness, stratagem, trick, wiliness.
Hílagar, *adj.* see Hílabáz.
Hílagarí, *s. f.* see Hílabází.
Hilá milá, *adj.* amicable, attached.
Hiláná, *v. a.* to move; to tame; to cause to swim.
Hílasáz, *adj.* see Hílabáz.
Hílasází, *s. f.* see Hílabází.
Hilkorá, *s. m.* a wave, a billow, a surge.
Hilmil jáná, *v. n.* to be intimate.
Hilná, *v. n.* to shake, to be moved, to be tamed.
Hilorá, *s. m.* a wave, billow, surge.
Hilorí márná, to heave, to rise (as the sea.)
Hilorná, *v. n.* to billow, to wave.
Hilsá, *s. f.* name of a fish, the tamarind fish.
Himándista, *s.* a mortar and pestle.
Himálaya, *s.* the name of a range of snowy mountains which separate India from Chinese Tartary.
Himáqat, *s. f.* folly, stupidity, boasting, bragging.
Himáyat, *s. f.* countenance, patronage.
Himáyatí, *s. m. f.* defender, patron.
Himáyat karná, to defend, to patronize, to countenance.
Himmat, *s. f.* spirit, resolution, bravery, courage, liberality, magnanimity.
Himmatí, *adj.* bold, daring.
Himmatwálá, *adj.* high-minded, liberal, brave.
Himyání, *s. f.* *prop.* Hamyání, a purse.
Hiṉ, an emphatic particle, very exactly. See Hí.
Hín, } *adj.* deficient, little, abated,
Híná, } left, quitted, void of.
Hiná, *s. f.* *prop.* Hinná, which see.
Hínchna, *v. a.* to pull.
Hind, *s. m.* India, an Indian.
Hindasa, *s. m.* geometry, figures, arithmetic.
Hindasadán, geometrician, arithmetician.
Hindasí, *adj.* geometrical.
Hindí, Indian, relating to India.

Hindiní, *s. f.* an Indian woman. See Hindúí.
Hindolá, *s. m.* a swing, a cradle.
Hindú, *s. m.* an Indian, a Gentoo, a Hindú.
Hindúí, *s. f.* the name of the language spoken by the Hindús of upper Hindústhán.
Hindústán, Hindústhán, } *s. m.* India.
Hindústhání, *adj.* belonging to Hindústhán; the language spoken by the Muhammadans of Hindústhán; an inhabitant of upper Hindústhán.
Hing, Híng, } *s. m.* assafœtida.
Híng hagná, to void by stool involuntarily, (*met.*) to pine.
Hinhináná, *v. n.* to neigh.
Hín i hayát, *s. f.* lifetime.
Hinná, *s. f.* the tree with which the Indians stain their hands and feet.
Hinnáí, *adj.* of the colour of Hinná, stained with Hinná.
Hinsá, *s. m.* geometry, arithmetic; killing.
Hinsá karná, to destroy animal life, especially of a cow.
Hiqárat, *s. f.* contempt, scorn, affront, vileness.
Hír, *s. m.* essence, pith, energy, vigour; heart (of a tree.)
Hírá, *s. m.* a diamond.
Híráman, *s. m.* a kind of paroquet.
Hiran, *s. m.* a deer, an antelope, a hart.
Hirásán, *adj.* frightened, frightening.
Hirásat, *s. f.* care, watching, guarding.
Hirásat karná, to take care of, to guard.
Hiráse hojáná, to be frightened.
Hirdá, Hirdáya, } *s. m.* heart, breast, mind, soul.
Hirní, *s. f.* a doe, hind.
Hirs, *s. f.* greediness, avidity, ambition, avarice.
Hirsáhá, Hirsí, } *adj.* covetous, greedy, gluttonous, ambitious.
Hirs karná, to covet.
Hisáb, *s. m.* computation, calculation, reckoning, accounts.
Hisábdán, *s. m.* an arithmetician.
Hisáb dená, to give an account.
Hisábí, *adj.* accurate, correct (in accounts.)
Hisáb joṛná, Hisáb karná, } to calculate, to make up accounts.
Hisábkitáb, *s. m.* accounts.
Hisábkitáb karná, to keep accounts.
Hisáb lená, to take an account.
Hisábnawíz, *s. m.* an accountant.
Hisáb pák karná, Hisáb rafạ karná, } to clear or settle accounts.
Hisáb rakhná, to keep account of, to register.
Hiská, *s. m.* imitation, copying, contention, rivalry, emulation.
Hiská hiskí, *s. m.* mutual emulation.
Hiská karná, to copy, to imitate, to ape, to vie (with.)
Hissa, *s. m.* share, lot, portion, division.
Hissadár, *s. m.* a sharer, a partner.
Hissa karná, to share, to apportion, to divide.
Hissarasad, an equal share, a proportional part.
Hit, *s. m.* love, friendship, affection.
Hitú, *s. m. f.* a friend.
Hiwáo, *s. m.* courage, bravery.
Hiya, Hiyá, } *s. m.* heart, mind, soul.
Hiyáo, *s. m.* courage, bravery.
Ho áná, *v. n.* to have gone to and returned.
Ho chukná, *v. n.* to be finished.
Ho jáná, *v. n.* to have happened, to become.
Hoke, *adv.* through, by.
Holá, *s. m.* the chickpea; a kind of boat.
Ho lená, *v. n.* to be completed, to [follow.

Holí, *s. f.* a Hindú festival; the song which is sung in the Holí.

Hom, }
Homád, } *s. m.* an oblation, a burnt-offering.

Homná, *v. a.* to perform the sacrifice of the Hom.

Honá, *v. n.* to be, to exist, to become, to belong, to have, to do, to stand; to die.

Honehárá, }
Honewálá, } *adj.* expected, about to be.

Honhár, *adj.* possible, what is to happen.

Hons, *s. m. prop.* Hosh, which see.

Hont, }
Honth, } *s. m.* the lip.

Honthí, *s. m.* the bit of a bridle.

Ho rahná, *v. n.* to be, to become.

Horí, *s. f.* see Holí.

Hos, *s. m. prop.* Hosh, which see.

Ho sakná, *v. n.* to be possible.

Hosh, *s. m.* understanding, sense, intellect, mind, soul.

Hoshdár, }
Hoshmand, } *adj.* intelligent, prudent, wise.

Hoshmandí, *s. f.* intelligence, understanding.

Hosh meṇ áná, to come to one's self, to recover one's senses.

Hosh pakaṛná, to recollect.

Hoshyár, *adj.* intelligent, cautious, alert, watchful, prudent, clever, sensible.

Hoshyárí, *s. f.* sobriety, caution, carefulness, taking care, prudence.

Hoshyár karná, to make acquainted, to caution, to put one on his guard.

Hoṭ, *s. m.* the lip.

Hotá játá, coming and going.

Hote, *adv.* in the being, during, in the presence.

Hote hote, *adv.* gradually.

Hoṭh, *s. m.* the lip.

Ho na ho, it must be.

Ho to ho, it may be.

Hubáb, *s. m.* a bubble.

Hubáb uṭhná, to bubble.

Hubábí, *adj.* bubble-like (weak.)

Hú ba hú, *adv.* quite, perfectly, exactly.

Hub bul watan, love of one's country, patriotism.

Huddá, }
Hudda, } *s. m.* business, office, appointment; *prop.* Uhda.

Huddadár, *adj.* holding an office, a native officer of the army.

Hudhud, *s. m.* name of a bird.

Hujjat, *s. f.* an argument, proof, altercation, disputation.

Hujjatí, *adj.* disputatious, obstinate: *s. m.* a sophist, a wrangler, an obstinate person.

Hujra, *s. m.* a cell, a closet, a chamber.

Hujúm, *s. m.* a crowd, a mob, a throng, an assault, attack.

Hujúm karná, to rush (upon.)

Húk, *s. f.* pain.

Hukam, *s. m. prop.* Hukm, which see.

Hukamá, *s.* (*plur.* of Hakím), philosophers, sages, physicians.

Húk húk kar roná, to weep with sobbing or from much pain.

Hukká, *s. m. prop.* Huqqa, which see.

Hukkábardár, *s. m. prop.* Huqqabardár, which see.

Hukm, *s. m.* a command, an order, a decree, sentence, award, authority, precept, permission.

Hukmbardár, *adj.* obedient, obeying an order.

Hukmbardárí, *s. f.* obedience.

Hukm karná, to command, to order.

Hukm máuná, to obey.

Hukmnáma, *s. m.* written orders.

Hukmrání, *s. f.* sway, authority.

Hukúmat, *s. f.* dominion, sovereignty, government, jurisdiction.

Hukúmat karná, to govern, to rule.

Húl, *s. f.* a thrust, stab; sickness at the stomach, qualm.

Húl áná, to feel sick.

Húlaṛ, *s. m.* tumult, uproar, disturbance, confusion, bustle.

Hulasná, *v. n.* to be pleased, delighted.

Hulkárná, *v. a.* to set on (as a dog or bull), to instigate, to halloo on.

Hullaṛ, *s. m.* see Húlaṛ.

Húlná, *v. a.* to goad, to push.

Hulsáná, *v. a.* to cheer, to delight.

Humakná, *v. n.* to stretch forward.

Hummá, *s. m.* high tide.

Húṇ, *adv.* too, also, yes; (I) am.

Hunar, *s. m.* art, excellence in any art, skill, ingenuity, cleverness.

Hunarmand, *adj.* clever, skilful, ingenious.

Hunarmandí, *s. f.* cleverness.

Hunarwar, *adj.* skilful, clever, ingenious.

Hunḍá bháṛá, *s. m.* contract for transportation of goods, including the payment of duties; settlement for price or hire.

Hunḍár, Húnḍár, *s. m.* a wolf. See Huṇṛár.

Hunḍáwan, *s. m.* exchange, or price paid for a bill of exchange.

Hunḍaví, Hunḍí, *s. f.* a bill of exchange.

Hunḍíwál, an exchange merchant.

Hunḍiyáwan, *s. m.* see Hunḍáwan.

Huṇkár, Huṇkárá, *s. m.* cry, outcry, alarm, uttering the sound húṇ, to terrify, &c.

Húṇ karná, to assent, to consent.

Huṇṛár, *s. m.* a wolf.

Hunúd, *s. plur.* the Hindús.

Huqqa, *s. m.* an apparatus for smoking.

Huqqabardár, *s. m.* the servant who prepares to Huqqa.

Huqqabáz, a great smoker of the Huqqa.

Húr, *s. f.* a virgin of paradise, a black-eyed nymph.

Huṛdangá, *adj.* turbulent.

Huṛdangí, *s, f.* turbulence.

Húrí, *s. f.* see Húr.

Huṛká, *s. m.* a bar for a door or gate, a bolt.

Hurmat. *s. f.* dignity, character, honour, chastity, reputation, reverence, esteem.

Hurmatdár, *adj.* respectable, honourable.

Hurmat dená, to bestow honour, to exalt; to incur disgrace, to lose one's character.

Hurmat karná, to treat honourably and respectfully.

Hurmat lená, to violate, to ravish, to disgrace.

Hurmat toṛná, to disgrace.

Hurmatwálá, *adj.* possessing dignity or reputation.

Húrná, *v. a.* to beat down (as paviers), to strike (a blow.)

Hurúf, *s.* (*plur.* of Harf), letters.

Hurúf tahajjí, the letters of the alphabet.

Huṛukná, *v. n.* to pine away.

Husain, a proper name, a son of Ạlí.

Husainí kabáb, a kind of roast meat.

Hushyár, *adj.* see Hoshyár.

Hushyárí, *s. f.* see Hoshyárí.

Hushyár karná, see Hoshyár karná, to rouse.

Husn, *s. m.* beauty, elegance, goodness.

Husn iḳhláq, Husn ḳhulq, a good disposition.

Husúl, *s. m.* profit, advantage, gain.

Hút, *s. f.* the sign Pisces.

Huzúr, *s. m.* presence; used also respectfully for the second personal pronoun.

Huzúrí, *s. f.* presence.

I.

I, a short vowel, pronounced invariably as *i* in pin.

Í, a long vowel, pronounced invariably as *ee* in reed.

Iádat, *s. f.* visiting the sick.

Ịaráf, *s. m.* purgatory.

Ịạtibár, *s. m.* confidence, faith, belief, reliance.

Iạtibárí, *adj.* of credit, trustworthy.

Iạtibár karná, } to give credit, to
Iạtibár rakhná, } trust, to believe.

Iạtikáf, *s. m.* continuing in the temple or mosque at the end of Ramazán.

Iạtimád, *s. m.* reliance, trust, confidence.

Iạtimád karná, } to rely, to de-
Iạtimád rakhná, } pend (on), to believe, to trust.

Iạtiqád, *s. m.* dependence, belief, confidence, trust.

Iạtiqád rakhná, to rely, to depend (on), to trust.

Iạtiráz, *s. f.* objection, opposition, discussion, criticism.

Iạtiráz karná, to object, to discuss, to criticise.

Ịbádat, *s. f.* divine worship, adoration.

Ịbádatgáh, *s. f.* a place of worship.

Ịbádatí, *s. m.* a devotee, a religious person.

Ịbárat, *s. f.* style, idiom.

Iblís, *s. m.* Satan, the devil.

Ibráhím, *n. prop.* Abraham.

Ịbrání, *adj.* Hebrew.

Ịbrat, *s. f.* warning.

Ibtidá, *s. f.* beginning, commencement.

Ibtidá karná, to begin, to commence.

Ichchhá, *s. f.* wish, desire.

Ịd, *s. f.* festival, holy-day, Easter.

Idhar, } *adv.* here, hither, on this
Ịdhar, } side.

Idhar udhar, about, around, up and down, here and there.

Idhir, *adj.* see Idhar.

Ịdí, *adj.* a customary present on the day of Ịd, or on some holiday.

Idrís, *n. prop.* the patriarch Enoch.

Ịfá. *s. f.* performing (a promise, &c.), fulfilling.

Ifáqa, *s. m.* convalescence, recovery.

Ifáqa honá, to be convalescent.

Iflás, } *s. f.* poverty, penury, indi-
Iflásí, } gence.

Ifrát, *s. m. f.* excess, superfluity, abundance.

Iftár, *s. m.* breaking a fast.

Iftár karná, to break one's fast in the evening after fasting all day.

Igárah, *adj.* eleven.

Igárahán, } *adj.* eleventh.
Igárahwán, }

Iháta, *vulg.* Háta, *s. f.* a surrounding, an inclosure, a fence, a compound.

Ihin, this very (place.)

Ihsán, *s. m.* favour, courtesy, kindness; the conferring of an obligation.

Ihsán karná, to confer a favour or benefit, to oblige.

Ihsánmand, *adj.* obliged, bound (by favour.)

Ihtilám, *s. m.* nocturnal pollution.

Ihtimál, *s. m.* doubt, uncertainty; probability.

Ihtimál honá, to be doubtful, to be probable.

Ihtimál karná, to doubt.

Ihtimám, *s. f. m.* care, diligence.

Ihtiyáj, *s. f.* necessity, want, occasion, need.

Ihtiyát, *s. f.* caution, care.

Ihtiyát karná, to take care.

Ịjá, *s. f. prop.* Ịzá, which see.

Ịjád, *s. m.* invention, contrivance: *adj.* invented.

Ịjá dená, *prop.* Ịzá dená, which see

Ịjád honá, to be invented.

Ịjád karná, to invent, to contrive, to devise.

Ijára, *s. m.* hire, rent, a lease.

Ijáradár, *s. m.* a farmer of land, or of revenue.

Ijázat, *s. f.* permission, leave, sanction commands.

Ijázat dená, to permit, to allow.

Ij'hár, *prop.* Iz'hár, which see.

Ijjat, *s. f. prop.* Ịzzat, which see.

Ijjatdár, see Ịzzatdár.

Ijjat karná, see Izzat karná.
Ijlás, s. f. act of sitting, especially of a court of justice, like the word sessions.
Ijrá, } s. m. circulation.
Ijráe, }
Ijráe karná, to perform.
Ik, a prefix signifying one.
Ikánavwe, adj. ninety-one.
Ikásí, adj. eighty-one.
Ikaṭhá, } adj. collected together,
Ikaṭṭhá, } in one place.
Ikáwan, adj. fifty-one.
Ikbál, s. m. prop. Iqbál, which see.
Ikbálmand, adj. see Iqbálmand.
Ikbár, for Ekbár, one time, once.
Ikchit, adj. of one mind.
Íkh, s. f. a sugar-cane.
Ikhattar, adj. seventy-one.
Ikhlás, s. m. affection, friendship.
Ikhlás karná, to esteem, to act friendly and affectionately.
Ikhlásmand, adj. sincere, friendly.
Ikhlás rakhná, see Ikhlás karná.
Ikhtiláf, s. m. difference (of opinion), disagreement, contradiction, misunderstanding between friends.
Ikhtilát, s. m. intercourse, friendship, conversation.
Ikhtiyár, s. m. choice, will; election, authority, power.
Ikhtiyárí, adj. in one's power, at one's disposal.
Ikhtiyár karná, to approve of, to adopt, to choose.
Ikhtiyár meṉ honá, to be in power of, or dependent on.
Ikká, s. m. a kind of one horse vehicle.
Ikkís, adj. twenty-one.
Iklá, adj. alone, only.
Ikláí, s. f. an article of dress consisting of one breadth.
Iklauntá, } adj. only.
Iklautá, }
Ikrár, s. m. prop. Iqrár, which see.
Ikrárnáma, see Iqrárnáma.
Iksaṭh, adj. sixty-one.
Iksír or aksír, s. f. a powder pretended to be capable of converting other metals to gold; the philosopher's stone.
Ikṭak, s. a fixed look at anything without closing the eyes.
Iktális, adj. forty-one.
Ikṭhán, } adj. see Ikaṭhá.
Ikṭhaurá, }
Iktís, adj. thirty-one.
Ikwál, prop. Iqbál, which see.
Iláchí, } s. f. cardamums.
Iláechí, }
Iláechídána, s. m. comfits in which are cardamums.
Iláhí, adj. divine.
Iláhíyat, s. f. the divinity, godhead.
Iláj, s. m. f. a remedy, medicine, cure.
Iláj karná, to cure, to remedy, to apply a remedy.
Iláqa, s. m. prop. Aláqa, dependence, relation, connexion, interest.
Iláqaband, a gold-lace worker.
Iláqamand, adj. related, connected.
Iláqa rakhná, to concern, to be connected, to belong, to regard, to relate (to.)
Ilhám, s. m. inspiration, revelation.
Ilhán, s. m. note, modulation, tune, an air (in music.)
Illá, s. m. a wart.
Illat, s. f. cause; filth, dirt; a bad habit.
Illatí, adj. filthy.
Ilm, s. m. science, knowledge.
Ilmdár, adj. learned.
Ilm i músiqí, music.
Ilm i riyází, the mathematical science.
Ilmwálá, adj. learned.
Iltifát, s. f. friendship, kindness, courtesy, respect.
Iltifát karná, to attend to, to have regard or respect.
Iltijá, s. f. entreaty, request.
Iltimás, s. m. f. supplication, prayer, request.
Iltimás karná, to beseech, to request, to supplicate.

Ilzám, *s. m. prop.* conviction; but commonly accusation, impeachment.

Ilzám dená, to accuse, to impeach.

Ilzám honá, to be convinced, confuted, &c.

Imám, *s. m.* a leader in prayer.

Imámat, *s. f.* leading in prayers.

Imámbáṛá, *s. m.* } the place where **Imámbáṛí**, *s. f.* } Muhammadans deposit the ṭáziya and where offerings are made to the dead.

Imámdasta, *prop.* Háwandasta, mortar and pestle.

Imámiya, *adj.* name of a Muhammadan sect, who make Ạlí the rightful Imám immediately after Muhammad.

Ỉmán, *s. m.* faith, belief, religion, conscientiousness.

Ỉmándár, *adj.* faithful, honest, trustworthy.

Ỉmándárí, *s. f.* faithfulness, conscientiousness, honesty, fidelity.

Ỉmán láná, to believe.

Ịmárat, *s. f.* a large edifice or building.

Imlá, *s. m.* orthography, writing correctly.

Imlí, *s. m.* tamarind fruit.

Imroz, *adv.* to-day.

Imroz fardá, to-day or to-morrow, *i.e.* soon.

Im sál, *adv.* this year.

Im shab, to-night.

Imtihán, *s. m.* proof, trial, examination, temptation.

Imtihán karná, to try, to test, to tempt.

Imtihán lená, to examine, to test.

Imtiyáz, *s. m.* discrimination, good breeding, politeness.

Imtiyází, *adj.* having the quality of discriminating; a person of distinction.

Imtiyáz karná, to discriminate, to treat with distinction.

In, *pron. plur.* in the oblique case, those, them.

Inạ́m, *s. m.* a present, a gift, a reward.

Inạ́m bakhshish, *s. f.* a gift, a present.

Inạ́m dená, to bestow a gift.

Inạ́m i ikrám, an honourable gift.

Ịnáyat, *s. f.* favour, kindness, bounty.

Ịnáyát, *s. f. plur.* of Ịnáyat.

Ịnáyat karná, to give, to grant.

Ỉnchná, *v. a.* to draw, to attract, to pull.

Indárá, *s. m.* a large well of masonry.

Indhan, } **Ỉndhan**, } *s. m.* firewood.

In dinoṇ, now-a-day.

Ịndiya, *s. m.* opinion, one's own opinion.

Indra, *s. m.* the regent of the visible heavens, and of the inferior divinities.

Indrání, *s. f.* the wife of Indra.

Indráyan, *s. f.* colocynth, wild gourd.

Indrí, *s. f.* an organ of sense, the senses, (internal and external.)

Indrí julláb, a diuretic medicine.

Inḍúá, *s. m.* a round fold or roll used in carrying a burthen on the head.

Infisál, *s. m.* decision (of a cause.)

Infisál karná, to decide, to settle (a cause.)

Ỉngur, *s. m.* red-lead.

Injíl, *s. m.* the New Testament, the Gospel.

Injor, } **Injorá**, } *s. m.* light.

Injoriyá, *s. m.* moonlight.

Inkár, *s. m.* denial, negation, disallowance.

Inkár karná, to deny, to disallow.

Inṛúá, *s. m.* see Inḍúá.

Insáf, *s. m.* decision (of a cause or question), equity, justice.

Insáf karná, to decide (a cause) equitably.

Insán, *s. m.* a man, a human being.

Insání, *adj.* human, relating to man.

Insániyat, *s. f.* humanity, good-breeding, politeness.

In shá allahu taạ́lá, God willing, if God please.

Ĭnṭ,
Ĭnṭá, } *s. f.* brick.
Ĭnṭáwálá, *s. m.* a brick-maker.
Ĭnṭgáṛí, *s. f.* brick-work.
Intifá, *s. m.* profit, advantage.
Intihá, *s. f.* termination, end, extremity, utmost verge, summit.
Intikháb, *s. m.* selection, making extracts from books.
Intikháb karná, to select, to make extracts (from books.)
Intiqál, *s. m.* decease, dying.
Intiqál honá,
Intiqál karná, } to die.
Intizám, *s. m.* arrangement, order, regularity, management, administration.
Intizár, *s. m.*
Intizárí, *s. f.* } expectation, looking out for.
Intizárí karná,
Intizár karná, } to expect, to look out for.
Ĭnṭwálá, *s. m.* a brick-maker.
Iqbál, *s. m.* prosperity, good fortune, auspices.
Iqbálmand, *adj.* prosperous, fortunate.
Iqrár, *s. m.* confession, acknowledgments, avowal, promise, agreement.
Iqrár karná, to confess, to acknowledge, aver, declare ; to promise.
Iqrárnáma, *s. m.* written agreement, bond, contract, &c.
Iqtidár, *s. m.* power, authority.
Iráda, *s. m.* desire, inclination, purpose, design, plan, intention.
Iráda karná, to form a design, to make an attempt, to intend or purpose.
Ĭrán, *n. prop.* Persia.
Ĭrání, *adj.* Persian.
Ĭrkhá, *s. f.* envy, spite, emulation.
Irshád, *s. m.* direction, command, order.
Irshád karná, to direct, to command.
Is, *pron. dem. sing. inflec.* this.
Ĭs, *s. m.* Lord, a name of Shiva.
Ịsá, *n. prop.* Jesus.
Ịsáí, *adj.* Christian.
Is alang, on this side.
Ịsawí, *adj.* belonging to Jesus, of Jesus, Christian.
Is dam, *adv.* this moment, directly.
Ịshá, *s. m.* the first watch of the night, the prayers said when going to rest.
Is'hál, *s. m.* purging, flux, diarrhœa.
Isháq, *n. prop.* Isaac.
Ishára, *s. m.* sign, wink, mark, signal, hint.
Ishára karná, to beckon, to make a sign or signal, to hint.
Ịshq, *s. m.* love.
Ịshqbáz, *s. m.* a gallant, a rake.
Ịshqbází, *s. f.* gallantry, &c.
Ishráq, *s. m.* sun-rising.
Ịshrat, *s. f. vulg.* Ạshrat, pleasure, delight, enjoyment, mirth.
Ishṭ, *s. m.* a god, a deity.
Ishṭ dew, *s. m.* a god, a deity.
Ishtiạ́l, *s. m. f.* lighting a fire or candle, fomenting or instigating a quarrel.
Ishtiạ́l dená, *v. a.* to foment (quarrels), to make a light burn brightly.
Ishtihá, *s. f.* appetite, desire, hunger.
Ishtihár, *s. m.* proclamation, publication, advertisement, fame, renown.
Ishtihár karná, to publish, to make a proclamation, to advertise.
Ishtihárnáma, *s. m.* a written proclamation.
Ishtiyáq, *s. m.* wish, desire, strong inclination.
Ĭshwar, *s. m.* God.
Iskandar, *n. prop.* Alexander.
Isláh, *s. f.* correction, amendment.
Isláh dená,
Isláh karná, } to correct, to amend.
Islám, *s. m.* the Muhammadan religion.
Islámí, *s. m. f.* a Muhammadan.
Is liye, for this reason, hence, because.

Ism, *s. m.* name, a noun.
Ismáíl, *n. prop.* Ishmael, son of Abraham.
Ism bá musammá, a name fitly denoting the qualities of the named.
Is meṉ, in the mean time.
Ispaghol, *s. m.* seed of fleawort or plantain.
Is par, for this reason, hence, on this.
Is par bhí, moreover, nevertheless, yet.
Ispát, *s. m.* steel.
Is qadar, *adv.* thus much, to this degree, so much, thus.
Isráfíl, *s. m.* the name of the angel who, it is said, will sound the last trumpet at the resurrection.
Istabal, *vulg.* Astabal, *s. m.* stable.
Is talak, to this degree.
Isṭám, *Eng. s. m.* a stamp (paper.)
Istámbol, *n. prop.* Constantinople.
Is tarah, Is tarah se, Is taur, Is taur se, } *adv.* in this manner, thus.
Isthir, *adj.* settled, steady, firm, fixed.
Istiạdád, *s. f.* readiness, ability, means.
Istiạmál, *s. m.* custom, daily practice, exercise, use.
Istiạmálí, *adj.* used, usual: *s. m.* fine rice.
Istiạmál karná, to use.
Istibágh, *s. m.* dipping, baptism.
Istífá, *s. m.* resignation, resigning one's office.
Istífá dená, to resign office or service.
Istifsár, *s. m.* inquiry, interrogation.
Istifsár karná, *v. a.* to inquire, to investigate.
Istighfár, *s. m.* begging mercy, craving grace.
Istighfár karná, to crave mercy.
Istiláh, *s. f.* a phrase, idiom, technical term.
Istiláhí, *adj.* idiomatical, phraseological, technical.
Istiláhí mạní, idiomatical meaning or acceptance.
Istinjá, *s. m.* purification after making urine.
Istiqbál, *s. m.* going to meet a visitor.
Istirí, Istrí, } *s. f.* a woman: *s. m.* a smoothing iron.
Istrí karná, *v. a.* to marry; to iron, to smooth with an iron.
Is waqt, this time, now.
Íswar, *s. m.* God.
Íswartá, *s. f.* divinity, godhead.
Is wáste, for this reason, because.
Itá, *adj.* this much, as much as this.
Itáạt, *s. f.* subjection, submission, obedience, loyalty, worshipping.
Itáạt karná, to obey.
Ịtáb, *s. m.* reproof, reprimand, rebuke, anger, displeasure.
Itek, *adj.* so much, thus much.
Itek meṉ, in the mean time.
Iṭhláná, *v. a.* to walk affectedly or coquettishly.
Ití, et cetera.
Itibár, *s. m. prop.* Iạtibár, which see.
Itibárí, *prop.* Iạtibárí, which see.
Itíhás, *s. m.* history, story, fable.
Itmínán, *s. f.* tranquillity, rest, repose, quiet, content.
Itmínán honá, to be tranquil.
Itmínán i ḳhátir, peace of mind.
Itná, *adj.* as much as this, thus much, so much, so many.
Itne meṉ, in the mean time, meanwhile.
Ịtr, *vulg.* Ạtr, perfume, fragrance, essence, ottar (of roses.)
Itráná, *v. a.* to give one's self airs, to assume airs.
Ịtrdán, *s. m.* a perfume-box.
Ittá, *adj.* see Itná.
Ittifáq, *s. m.* agreement, concord, friendship, chance, accident, incident, opportunity.
Ittifáqan, *adv.* accidentally, by chance.

Ittifáq honá, to happen, to be agreed.
Ittifáq karná, to accord, or agree together, to concur, to unite.
Ittihád, *s. m.* amity, friendship.
Ittiláạ, *s. f.* notice, notification, information, knowledge.
Ittiláạ karná, to acquaint, to inform, to apprize.
Itwár, *s. m.* Sunday.
Iwaj, *s. m. prop.* Ịwaz, which see.
Iwají, see Ịwazí.
Ịwaz, *s. m.* reward, return, recompense: *prep.* instead, for.
Ịwazí, *adv.* instead, for: *s. m.* proxy, substitute.
Ịwazí dená, to supply a substitute (as a servant.)
Ịwazí rakhná, to take a substitute.
Ịyádat, *s. f.* visiting of the sick.
Iyál, *prop.* Ayál, *s. f.* horse's mane.
Ịyál, *s. m.* family, children, domestics.
Ịyáldár, having a family.
Ịyál o atfál, see Ịyál.
Ịzá, *s. f.* pain, distress, trouble, oppression.
Ịzá dená, to pain, to trouble, to vex, to distress.
Izáfa, *s. m.* addition, annexation, augmentation.
Izáfat, *s. f.* the *i.* between two Persian nouns, corresponding to the English genitive, *of.*
Izár, *s. f.* drawers, trowsers.
Izárband, *s. m.* the string with which drawers are tied.
Iz'hár, *s. m.* declaration in a court of justice or before police officers.
Iz'hár karná, to disclose, reveal, notify.
Ịzráíl, *n. prop.* the angel of death.
Iztiráb, *s. m.* agitation, perturbation, trouble.
Iztirábí, *s. f.* agitation, impatience.
Ịzzat, *s. f.* grandeur, power, honour, respect, glory.
Ịzzatdár, *adj.* honourable, respectable.
Ịzzat karná, to honour, to dignify.

J.

Já, *s. f.* a place; (in Braj.) *pron. rel. inflect. sing.* whom, that, which, any one.
Jáb, *s. m.* muzzle for large cattle.
Jab, *adv.* when, at the time when, as soon as.
Jabah, *s. f. prop.* Zabh, sacrifice, slaughter.
Jabah honá, see Zabh honá.
Jabah karná, see Zabh karná.
Jábajá, *adv.* everywhere, here and there.
Jabán, *s. f. prop.* Zabán, which see.
Jabán dená, } *prop.* Zabán, &c., to
Jabán hárná, } promise.
Jabar, *adj. prop.* Zabar, which see.
Jabardast, *adj.* see Zabardast.
Jabardastí, *s. f.* see Zabardastí.
Jabardastí karná, see Zabardastí karná.
Jabardastí se, see Zabardastí se.
Jabar honá, see Zabar honá.
Jabat, *s. m. prop.* Zabt, which see.
Jabat honá, see Zabt honá.
Jabat karná, see Zabt karná.
Jabhí, *adv.* at the very time.
Jabhṛá, *s. m.* the jaw.
Jábí, *s. f.* muzzle for small cattle.
Jab jab, }
Jab kabhí, } *adv.* whenever.
Jab kabhú, }
Jab ká tab, *adv.* at the time when, at the proper moment.
Jab ki, *adv.* at the time when, when.
Jab lag, *adv.* till when, whilst, as long as.
Jab na tab, *adv.* perpetually, now and then.
Jabr, *s. m.* oppression, violence, force, power.
Jabṛá, *s. m.* the jaw.
Jabraíl, } the archangel Gabriel.
Jabráíl, }
Jabran, *adv.* by violence, forcibly.
Jabríl, the archangel Gabriel.
Jabr se, *adv.* see Jabran.
Jab se, since.

Jab tab, *adv.* now and then.

Jab tak, }
Jab talak, } *adv.* till when, whilst, as long as.
Jab toṛí, }

Jabún, *adj. prop.* Zabún, which see.

Jabúní, *s. f.* see Zabúní.

Jachá, }
Jachchá, } *s. f.* a woman in child-birth and for forty days after, a lying-in woman.

Jad, *adv.* as, while, whilst, when, as soon as, so soon, at the time when.

Jádád, *s. f.* household and landed property.

Jadapi, *conj.* though, although.

Jadd, *s. m.* a grandfather, ancestor.

Jaddí, *adj.* ancestral, belonging to ancestors.

Jad lag, *adv.* see Jad tak.

Jad na tad, *adv.* constantly.

Jad tak, }
Jad talak, } *adv.* till, until, yet, whilst, as long as, while.

Jádú, *s. m.* magic, enchantment, incantation, juggling.

Jádú chaláná, to practice incantation, to conjure, to enchant.

Jádúgar, *s. m.* an enchanter, magician, sorcerer.

Jádúgarí, *s. f.* the art of sorcery, necromancy.

Jádúgarní, *s. f.* a sorceress.

Jádú karná, see Jádú chaláná.

Jadwal, *s. f.* lines drawn in a book (as ruling, or to separate the margin.)

Jadwalí, *adj.* marked with lines (a book.)

Jadyapi, *conj.* though, although.

Jáe, *s. f.* a place.

Jáedád, }
Jáedát, } *s. f.* household and landed property.

Jáenamáz, *s. f.* a carpet, mat, or cloth on which prayers are said.

Jáephal, *s. m.* a nutmeg.

Jáezarúr, *s. f.* the necessary.

Jáfarí, *s. f.* a sort of screen, lattice-work.

Jag, *s. m.* the world, universe; sacrifice.

Jagadís, *s. m.* lord of the world.

Jagah, }
Jágah, } *s. f.* place, station, room, vacancy, stead.

Jagah chhoṛná, *v. a.* to leave a blank.

Jagah sir kharachná, to expend to advantage.

Jagáná, *v. a.* to awake, to wake, to rouse from sleep.

Jágaran, *s. m.* waking, watchfulness.

Jagat, *s. m.* the world, the universe.

Jagatujágar, enlightening the world.

Jágír, *s. f.* land given by government as a reward of service, or as a fee; pension in land.

Jágírdár, *s. m.* the holder of a jágír.

Já girná, *v. n.* to fall.

Jagjagá, *s. m.* brass-tinsel, very thin plates of brass used in decoration.

Jagjagáhaṭ, *s. f.* splendour, much light, glitter.

Jagmagá, *adj.* glittering, splendid.

Jagmagáhaṭ, *s. f.* see Jagjagáhaṭ.

Jagmagáná, *v. n.* to glitter, to shine.

Jagná, }
Jágná, } *v. n.* to awake, to be awake, to wake, to watch.

Jág paṛná, *v. n.* to awake.

Jágrí, *s. f.* treacle, refuse of sugar.

Jágtíjot, *adj.* possessed of or exerting miraculous powers.

Jág uṭhná, *v. n.* to awake.

Jaháj, *prop.* Jaház, which see.

Jahájí, *prop.* Jahází, which see.

Jahálat, *s. f.* ignorance, brutality.

Jahán, *s. m.* the world.

Jahán, *adv.* where, in which place, which place.

Jahándída, one who has seen the world, a great traveller.

Jahán jahán, }
Jahán kahín, } *adv.* wherever.

Jahán ká tahán, *adv.* everywhere, in the same place as before.

Jahannam, *s. m.* hell.

Jahannamí, *adj.* hellish, belonging to hell.

Jahán panáh, refuge of the world; his majesty, your majesty.
Jaháṇ se, *adv.* whence, from which place, where.
Jaháṇ taháṇ, *adv.* here and there, everywhere.
Jaháṇ taháṇ phirná, to straggle, to wander.
Jaháṇ tak, *adv.* as far as.
Jahar, *s. m. prop.* Zahr, poison.
Jaharmuhrá, *s. m. prop.* Zaharmuhrá, a bezoar.
Jaház, *s. m.* a ship.
Jahází, *s. m.* a sailor: *adj.* naval, nautical.
Jaház par, *adv.* aboard a ship.
Jahez, *s. m.* a bride's portion, dower.
Jáhil, *adj.* ignorant, illiterate.
Jáhil honá, to be ignorant.
Jahíṇ, *adv.* wherever.
Jáhir, *adj. prop.* Záhir, apparent, evident, open.
Jáhir honá, see Záhir honá.
Jáhirí, *adj.* see Záhirí.
Jáhir karná, see Záhir karná.
Jáhir meṇ, see Záhir meṇ.
Ja'í, *s. f.* oats.
Jai, *s. f* triumph, victory, bravo! *adj.* as many as.
Jáí, *s. f.* a daughter.
Jaiber. *adj.* as many times, as often as.
Jaíf, *adj. prop.* Zaíf, which see.
Jaijaikár, *s. m.* rejoicings, exultations, triumph.
Jaimán, *adj.* victorious.
Jaisá, *adj.* in the manner which, as, what like, such as, according as.
Jaisá cháhiye, as may be desired, as it ought.
Jaisá ká taisá, *adv.* precisely the same as before.
Jaisá ki, as, though, as if.
Jaisá taisá, as well as, so so.
Jaise ká taisá, } such as before, the
Jaise ká waisá, } self same, unaltered.
Jait, *s. m.* name of a plant.
Jáiz, *adj.* lawful, permitted, right, proper, allowable.
Jájak, *s. m.* an officiating priest.
Jájam, *s. f.* a cloth thrown over the carpet to sit on, a floor-cloth.
Jaját, *prop.* Jádád, which see.
Jajmán, *s. m.* a customer, a person to whose custom bráhmans, barbers, and some other persons, have a legal claim.
Jajmání, *s. f.* the stipend paid by a Jajmán; wife of a Jajmán.
Jakam, *s. m. f. prop.* Zakhm, which see.
Jakamí, *adj.* see Zakhmí.
Jakam kháná, see Zakhm kháná.
Jákar, *s. m.* goods taken away by pedlars for sale, but returned if not sold.
Jakaṛband, *adj.* tight.
Jákaṛ bechná, to sell on commission.
Jákaṛ lejáná, to take away goods to sell on commission.
Jakaṛná, *v. a.* to tighten, to draw tight, to bind, to pinion.
Jakát, *s. f. prop.* Zakát, alms.
Jal, *adj.* forged, counterfeit: *s. f.* forgery.
Jál, *s. m.* a net, a snare; a cobweb; a sash.
Jal, *s. m.* water.
Jálá, *s. m.* a cobweb; a jar; a speck on the eye.
Jalá, *s. m.* a lake.
Jalá balá, *adj.* fretful, passionate; scorched.
Jalá bhuná, *adj.* passionate, hot-tempered.
Jalá dená, *v. a.* to burn.
Jalag, *adv.* till when, as long.
Já lagná, *v. a.* to arrive at.
Jala'í, *s. f.* a kind of nail used for seaming the boards of boats, &c.
Jalál, *s. m.* dignity, majesty, splendour, grandeur, power, glory.
Jalamai, *s. m.* flood, inundation.
Jalan, *s. m.* burning, heat, passion.

Jaláná, *v. a.* to burn, to kindle, to inflame, to light; to make jealous.

Jalandar, } *s. m.* the dropsy.
Jalandhar, }

Jalápá, *s. m.* envy, anger.

Jaláwan, *s. f.* firewood, fuel.

Jalbal, burnt up, consumed with fire.

Jal bujhná, to burn to ashes.

Jalchar, *adj.* aquatic (as birds, but not fish), moving or going in water.

Jald, *adj.* quick, nimble, speedy, expeditious, alert: *adv.* quickly.

Jaldbáz, *adj.* expeditious, fleet, hasty.

Jaldbází, *s. f.* haste, quickness, briskness.

Jáldár, *adj.* reticulated.

Jaldí, *s. f.* quickness, haste, hurry, celerity, rashness, impetuosity: *adv.* quickly, soon.

Jaldi karná, to make haste, to hurry; to be precipitate or rash.

Jald jáná, to go quickly.

Jaldmizáj, *adj.* passionate, hasty.

Jald qadam, *adj.* fleet.

Jalebí, *s. f.* a kind of sweetmeat.

Jale par non lagáná, to triumph over, to insult.

Jạlí, *adj.* counterfeited, forged.

Jálí, *s. f.* network, a web; a caul; lattice, grate; a net bag for chaff.

Jálim, *s. m. prop.* Zálim, which see.

Jálí paṛná, to become hard (the stone of a mangoe.)

Jạliyá, *s. m.* a forger.

Jaliyá, *s. m.* a fisherman.

Jalíl, *adj. prop.* Zalíl, which see.

Jalíl honá, see Zalíl honá.

Jalíl karná, see Zalíl karná.

Jal jal, *adj.* full of water.

Jaljalá, *adj.* indignant, excessively hot (the weather.)

Jaljaláná, *v. n.* to be indignant.

Jaljantu, *s. m.* an aquatic animal (as porpoise, shark, &c.)

Jallá, *s. m.* a lake.

Jallád, *s. m.* an executioner, a hangman: *adj.* cruel, hard-hearted.

Jalládí, *s. f.* the office of an executioner; cruelty, villany.

Jalná, *v. n.* to burn, to be kindled, to get into a passion, to be enraged.

Jalpachchhí, *s. f.* water-fowl.

Jalpáí, *s. f.* an olive.

Jalpán, *s. m*, eating, taking a little food between meals, a luncheon, repast.

Jalsa, *s. m.* meeting, assembly.

Jálsáz, *s. m.* a forger.

Jálsází, *s. f.* forgery.

Jal thal, *s. m.* ground half covered with water, marshy ground.

Jal uṭhná, to break out (as fire.)

Jalwáná, *v. a.* to cause to burn.

Jáma, *s. m.* a garment, robe; neat.

Jamạ, *s. f.* collection, sum total, amount, plural number.

Jamáạt, *s. f.* a crowd, an assembly, meeting, congregation.

Jamạbandí, *s. f.* accounts of the revenues, settlement of the revenue.

Jamạdár, *s. m.* a native officer of the army so called, the head of any body of people.

Jamạdárí, *s. f.* the business of a Jamạdár.

Jamáhi, *s. f.* gaping, yawning.

Jamạ honá, to be collected, to assemble, to flock.

Jamáí, *s. m.* a son-in-law.

Jamạ karná, to collect, to amass, to add together, to assemble, to heap.

Jamálgoṭá, *s. m.* the name of a purgative nut, croton seed.

Jáman, *s. f.* a fruit and tree so called.

Jamáná, *v. a.* to collect, to sum up, to coagulate, to congeal; also for Zamána, which see.

Jamáo, *s. m.* a crowd, a collection, coagulation.

Jamạ o ḳharch, *s. m.* account of receipt and disbursement, account current.

Jamạ o ḳharch karná, to make up, or balance an account.
Jamáoṛá, s. m. a collection, a crowd.
Jámawár, s. m. a kind of chintz in which the flowers are woven.
Jamạ wásil báqí, an account stating payment periodically due, with the amount received and the arrears.
Jambhírí, s. f. a fruit of the lime kind.
Jámdání, s. f. a kind of cloth with flowers interwoven : *adj.* flowered, embossed.
Jamghāṭ, s. m. crowd, multitude.
Jamhái, s. f. gaping, yawning.
Jamhái lená, v. n. to gape, to yawn.
Jamí, *adj.* all, universal.
Jamídár, *prop.* Zamíṇdár, which see.
Jámin, s. f. *prop.* Zámin, which see.
Jamín, s. f. *prop.* Zamín, which see.
Jámiṇdár, s. m. *prop.* Zámindár, surety.
Jámíṇdár, s. m. *prop.* Zamíṇdár, which see.
Jámindárí, s. f. *prop.* Zámindárí, suretyship.
Jamíṇdárí, s. f. see Zamíṇdárí.
Jamíṇdární, s. f. see Zamíṇdární.
Jáminí, s. f. *prop.* Záminí, surety, bail.
Jáminí kabúl karná, *prop.* Záminí qabúl karná, to admit as bail.
Jamjam, *adv.* always, constantly, perpetually.
Jamná, v. n. to germinate, to grow; to be coagulated, to be collected; to adhere, to stick.
Jamuná, n. *prop.* f. name of a river.
Ján, s. f. life, soul, spirit, mind; a sweetheart.
Jan, s. m. man, a person, an individual.
Jáná, v. n. to go, to be, to pass, to continue.
Janáb, majesty, highness, excellency.
Janáb i ạlí, your majesty, your or his excellency.

Janáí, } s. f. a midwife.
Janáí dáí, }
Janak, n. *prop.* the father of Sítá.
Janakpur, s. m. the name of a city, the metropolis of Rájá Janak.
Janam, s. m. birth, life.
Janambhúm, s. f. birthplace.
Janamdin, s. m. birthday.
Janamná, v. n. to be born.
Janampatrí, s. f. horoscope, nativity.
Janamswárth, a fortunate, or well-spent life.
Janáná, v. a. to deliver, to bring to bed; to inform, to remind, to tell, to point out, to seem.
Janána, *prop.* Zanána, which see.
Janáwar, s. m. an animal, a bird.
Janáza, s. m. a bier, a funeral.
Jan bachche, offspring, family.
Jánbaḳshí, s. f. pardon of a capital crime.
Ján balab, *adj.* at the point of expiring.
Ján balab honá, to be at the point of death.
Jánbáz, *adj.* risking life, venturesome, daring.
Jánbází, s. f. risking life (in battle), working at any thing as if life depended on success.
Ján bújhke, *adv.* wilfully, purposely.
Jánch, s. m. trial, examination, test, proof.
Jánchná, v. a. to examine, to inquire into, to ascertain, to approve, to assay.
Jándár, having life, active, spirited, lively (as a horse.)
Jáne anjáne, wittingly or unwittingly.
Jáne dená, v. a. to liberate, to let go; to excuse, to pass over (as a fault.)
Jáne do, never mind, let alone, don't.
Janerá, s. a tall species of the millet kind.
Janeu, s. m. the bráhmanical thread; a flaw in a diamond.
Jánfishání, s. f. very hard labour, extreme diligence, devotion.

Jánfishání karná, to strain every nerve.

Jang, *s. f.* battle, war, combat, fight: *s. m. prop.* Zang, rust.

Jangál, *s. m.* verdigris, canker (of copper). See Zangál.

Jangal, *s. m.* a forest, a wood, a wilderness, weeds, any bushy place.

Jangalá, *s. m.* palings.

Jangal jáná, } *v. n.* to go into the
Jangal phirná, } fields to ease nature.

Jangal ṭangal, *s. m.* weeds and bushes.

Jangámushtí, *s. f.* boxing.

Jángar, *s. m.* the thigh and leg.

Jángar toṛná, to labour hard for one's living.

Jángh, } *s. f.* the thigh.
Janghá, }

Jánghiyá, } *s. m.* a kind of short
Janghiyá, } drawers or breeches.

Jánghiyal, *s. m.* a kind of heron.

Jangí, *s. m.* a combatant: *adj.* warlike, hostile, quarrelsome.

Jang karná, to fight.

Janglá, *s. m.* palings.

Jang lagná, *prop.* Zang lagná, which see.

Janglí, *adj.* wild, savage, clown, boor.

Janglí billí, *s. f.* a wild cat.

Janglí kauwá, *s. m.* a raven.

Jang o jadal, *s. m.* brawl, squabble, altercation.

Jánhár, *adj.* going, passing away, precarious.

Jání, *adj.* of the heart, dear, beloved: *s. m.* a lover.

Jánib, *s. f.* part, side.

Jání dushman, an enemy desirous of one's life, a mortal enemy.

Janjál, *s. m.* trouble, difficulty, embarrassment, perplexity.

Jan jánwar, *s. m.* man and beast.

Janjír, *s. f. prop.* Zanjír, a chain.

Jánkandaní, *s. f.* the agonies of death.

Ján kisí par dená, to love excessively; to die, to fall a sacrifice.

Ján lená, to get a knowledge of, to understand.

Janma, *s. m.* birth.

Janmáná, *v. a.* to beget, to make vegetate.

Ján márná, to overcome, to oppress, to vex, to perplex.

Ján meṇ ján áná, to be satisfied, to be comforted.

Jánná, *v. a.* to know, to understand, to comprehend, to suppose, to believe.

Janná, *v. n.* to produce young, to be delivered of a child, to be born.

Jannat, *s. f.* paradise.

Jannatí, *adv.* of paradise, heavenly.

Janoṇ, *adv.* perhaps.

Ján pahchán, *s. m.* an acquaintance, an intimate friend.

Ján par áná, to be exposed to imminent danger.

Ján par khelná, to run the hazard, to risk one's life.

Ján paṛná, to be refreshed.

Ján par naubat áná, to be in imminent danger of life.

Ján par paṛná, to be exposed to imminent danger.

Ján se márná, to kill.

Jánt, *s. f.* a kind of basket for raising [water.

Jántá, *s. f.* a stone-mill for grinding corn, a hand-mill of two stones one over the other.

Jantáná, *v. n.* to be squeezed, to be pressed.

Jantr, *s. m.* an engine; an amulet; juggling.

Jantrí, *s. m.* an instrument for drawing wire; a conjuror, a juggler.

Jantr mantr, *s. m.* juggling, conjuring, incantation.

Jantu, *s. m.* an animal, a creature.

Janúb, *s. m.* south.

Janúbí, *adj.* southern.

Jánwar, *s. m.* an animal, a bird.

Janwásá, *s. m.* the place at the bride's house where the bridegroom and his train are received.

Jáo, (*imper.* of jáná), go.
Jap, } *s. m.* repetition of the name of
Jáp, } God, counting one's beads, muttering prayers.
Jápak, } *s. m.* one who counts his
Jápí, } beads, &c.
Japmál, } *s. f.* a rosary, a string of
Japmálá, } beads for counting, &c.
Japná, *v. a.* to count one's beads, to recite the bead-roll, to make mention.
Jap tap, *s. m.* devotion, adoration.
Jur, *s. f.* a root: *s. m.* a fever.
Jaṛ, *s. f.* a root, origin: *s. m.* an inanimate body, an idiot.
Jáṛá, *s. m.* cold, coldness, the winter.
Jaṛáí, *s. f.* price or act of setting jewels.
Jaṛaiyá, *s. f.* ague after fever.
Jaran, *s. f.* burning.
Jaṛáná, *v. n.* to be cold: *v. a.* to cause to stud or set jewels.
Jaráná, *v. a.* to burn, to kindle.
Jaṛáo, *s. m.* setting of jewels.
Jaṛáwal, *s. f.* warm clothes, winter dress.
Jaráwan *s. m.* firewood, fuel.
Jaṛáwar, *s. f.* see Jaṛáwal.
Jard, *prop.* Zard, which see.
Jardí, *s. f.* see Zardí.
Jard rang, *adj. prop.* Zard rang, yellow.
Jáṛe ká din, the cold weather.
Járí, *adj.* running, flowing, proceeding, current, in use, usual.
Jaṛí, *s. f.* the root of a medicinal herb.
Jaṛí búṭí, *s. m.* medicinal herbs, drugs.
Járí honá, to flow, to pass current, to be in force, to proceed (as business), to circulate.
Járí karná, to begin, to set on foot or a-going, to introduce (a custom), to issue or put in force (an order.)
Jarímána, *s. m.* penalty, forfeit, fine.
Jaṛiyá, *s. m.* a jeweller, a setter of jewels.

Jarná, *v. n.* to burn: *s. m.* firewood, fuel.
Járná, *s. m.* firewood, fuel; to burn.
Jaṛná, *v. a.* to stud, to set jewels, to fix, enchase.
Jaṛpeṛ, *s. f.* root and branch.
Jaṛpeṛ se ukháṛná, *v. a.* to exterminate.
Jarra, *prop.* Zarra, which see.
Jarráh, *s. m.* a surgeon.
Jarráhí, *s. f.* surgery.
Jarúr, *adj. prop.* Zarúr, which see.
Jarúrat, *s. f.* see Zarúrat.
Jarúr honá, to be necessary.
Jarúrí, *adj. prop.* Zarúrí, necessary.
Jaṛwáná, *v. a.* to cause to set with jewels.
Jas, *s. m.* name, character, fame, reputation, renown.
Jashn, *s. m.* a feast, a festival.
Jast, } *s. m.* pewter.
Jastá, }
Jástí, *prop.* Ziyáda, which see.
Jasudhá, *s. m.* a perpendicular post in a boat to which the mast is secured.
Jásús, *s. m.* a spy, an emissary.
Jásúsí, *s. f.* the action of a spy, spying.
Jásúsí karná, to act the spy.
Ját, *s. f.* caste, sect, tribe, class, kind, birth, production. See Zát.
Ját, *s. m.* the name of a tribe among Rájpúts.
Jaṭ, } *s. f.* matted hair of a devotee.
Jaṭá, }
Jaṭádhárí, *adj.* wearing a head of matted hair: *s. f.* the cockscomb flower.
Jaṭal, *s. f.* see Zaṭal.
Jaṭámánsí, } *s. f.* spikenard.
Jaṭámásí, }
Játá rahná, to be lost, to be missing, to disappear, to go away, to die.
Ját bháí, persons of the same caste.
Ját dená, *v. a.* to give up one's caste.
Jaṭh, *s. m.* the cylinder of an oil mill.
Jathá, *s. m.* a company, band, party, class.

Jathá bándhná, to form a party.
Jathárth, *adv.* in fact, exactly, truly.
Jatí, *s. m.* a religious mendicant.
Ját jáná, *v. n.* to lose caste.
Ját lená, see Zát lená.
Ját márná, *v. a.* to destroy one's caste.
Játpánt, *s. f.* pedigree.
Játrá, *s. f.* a pilgrimage, a journey, march; a festival, a procession.
Játrá karná, *v. a.* to go on pilgrimage, to march.
Játrí, *s. m.* a pilgrim.
Jau, *s. m.* barley: *adv.* when, what time.
Jauhar, *s. m. f.* a gem, jewel, pearl, essence, substance: *adj.* well-tempered.
Jauharát, *s. pl.* jewels.
Jauharí, *s. m.* a jeweller.
Jau jau hisáb lená, to take a strict account.
Jaukob, *adj.* half-pounded, bruised.
Jau lag, Jau laun, } *adv.* until, as long as.
Jaun, *pron. rel.* who, what, which.
Jaun, *adv.* as, when.
Jaunár, *s. f.* a feast.
Jaushan, *s. m.* ornament.
Jautarí, Jautrí, } *s. f.* mace, the spice so called.
Jautuk, *s. m.* dower, nuptial present.
Jawá, *s. m.* a clove of garlic, a kind of stitch in needlework.
Jawáb, *s. m.* an answer, a reply, anything answering to another.
Jawáb dená, to be accountable for, to reply, to answer, to discharge from office.
Jawábí, *s. m.* respondent.
Jawáb milná, to be dismissed or discharged.
Jawáb sawál, *s. m.* altercation, conversation.
Jawáhir, *s. m.* a jewel, a gem, &c.
Jawáhirát, essences, substances.
Jawáí, *s. m.* a son-in-law.
Jáwán, *adj.* twin (children.)
Jawán, *adj.* young: *s. m.* a youth, lad, man, adult: *s. f.* a young woman.
Jawánámarg, *s. f.* death in the bloom of youth, untimely death.
Jawánámarg marná, to die prematurely.
Jawání, *s. f.* youth.
Jawání maut, *s. f.* untimely death.
Jawání maut marná, to die prematurely.
Jawánmard, *adj.* brave, manly, generous: *s. m.* a fine young fellow, a hero.
Jawánmardí, *s. f.* manliness, courage, bravery, generosity, magnanimity.
Jawánpan, Jawánpaná, } *s. m.* youth.
Jawár, *s. m.* flood-tide.
Jáwatrí, *s. f.* mace, the spice so called.
Jawedár, *adj.* sewed in a particular manner.
Jazá, *s. f.* retaliation, requital, reward, compensation.
Jázam, *s. f.* see Jájam.
Jazb, *s. m.* allurement, altercation, absorption, drawing (as of a plaster.)
Jazba, *s. m.* passion, rage, fury.
Jazb honá, to be absorbed.
Jazb karná, to attract, absorb, imbibe, to draw (as a plaster.)
Jazíra, *s. m.* an island.
Jeb, *s. f.* a pocket.
Jebkatra, *s. m.* a pickpocket.
Jehalkhána, *s. m. Eng.* jail.
Jehar, *s. f.* two pots filled with water and placed one over the other.
Jelkhána, *s. m. Eng.* jail.
Jeoná, *v. a.* to eat.
Jeonár, *s. f.* a treat, feast, entertainment.
Jerband, *s. m. prop.* Zerband, a martingal.
Jerbár honá, see Zerbár honá.
Jerdast, *adj.* see Zerdast.
Jer karná, *prop.* Zer karná, which see.
Jetá, *adj.* as much as, so much.
Jetá ki, *adv.* though, although.
Jeṭh, *s. m.* husband's elder brother, name of the second Hindú month.
Jeṭhá, *adj.* elder, firstborn; the first

and strongest tint obtained from the flower kusum.

Jeṭhání, *s. f.* the wife of a husband's elder brother.

Jeṭhí madh, *s. m.* liquorice root.

Jetik, *adj.* see Jetá.

Jewar, *s. m. prop.* Zewar, jewels, ornaments.

Jewar pahinná, to put on jewels, to adorn.

Jewná, *v. a.* to eat.

Jewnár, *s. f.* a feast, entertainment.

Jhabbá, *s. m.* a tassel.

Jhabiyá, *s. m.* the name of an ornament.

Jhabṛá, *adj.* long-haired, shaggy.

Jhagaṛná, *v. n.* to wrangle, to quarrel, to dispute, to cavil, to contend, to squabble.

Jhagṛá, *s. m.* wrangling, quarrelling, contention, squabble, strife.

Jhagṛá karná, *v. a.* to quarrel.

Jhagṛálin, } *adj.* quarrelsome, contentious.
Jhagṛálú, }

Jhagṛáná, *v. a.* to set a wrangling.

Jhagṛá ragṛá, *s. m.* squabbling and wrangling, squabble.

Jháin, *s. f.* freckles on the skin.

Jhajhá, *s. m.* see Jhanjhaṭ.

Jhajhakná, *v. n.* see Jhijhakná.

Jhajhkárná, *v. a.* to browbeat, to speak snappishly.

Jhajjhar, *s. m.* a goglet.

Jhak, *s. f.* passion, nonsense, rant.

Jhakájhak, *adj.* shining, glittering with gold and silver.

Jhakí, *adj.* passionate, raver, ranter.

Jhakjhorí, *s. f.* scrambling and wrangling, snatching.

Jhakhná, *v. n.* to lament, to grieve.

Jhakkaṛ, *s. m.* a squall, a storm, a tempest.

Jhakná, *v. n.* to lament, to grieve.

Jhakmargí, *s. f.* the acting fruitlessly or absurdly, nonsense.

Jhak márná, to act fruitlessly or absurdly, to talk nonsensically, to rant.

Jhakolá, *s. m.* see Jhakorá.

Jhakolná, *v. a.* to shake.

Jhakorá, *s. m.* a squall, a gust, a shaking.

Jhakorná, *v. a.* to shake.

Jhál. *s. m.* sharpness, fieriness (as of pepper), hot (as with spices.)

Jhal, *s. f.* passion, anger, jealousy; the heat from fire.

Jhalábor, *adj.* shining, splendid, covered with jewels and ornaments.

Jhalájhal, *adj.* luminous, resplendent, embroidered.

Jhalak, *s. f.* brightness, glitter, glare, reflection of light.

Jhalakná, *v. n.* to shine, to glare.

Jhálar, *s. f.* fringe, frill.

Jhálardár, *adj.* fringed.

Jhaljhal, *s. m.* glitter.

Jhaljhaláhaṭ, *s. f.* glitter, splendour.

Jhaljhaláná, *v. n.* to glitter, to glare.

Jhalkáná, *v. a.* to cause to shine.

Jhalkí, *s. f.* a glance.

Jhálná, *v. a.* to polish, to clean (plate); to solder.

Jhalná, *v. a.* to fan, to move to and fro (as a fan): *v. n.* to be soldered or repaired.

Jhalwáná, *v. a.* to cause to fan; to cause to be soldered or repaired.

Jháma, *s. m.* pumice-stone, bricks burnt to cinder.

Jhamájham, *adv.* incessantly (as rain.)

Jhamáká, *s. m.* a heavy shower; haste.

Jhamakná, *v. n.* to glitter; to dance.

Jhamakṛá, *s. m.* splendour.

Jhamar jhamar, *adv.* drop by drop (rain.)

Jhamjham, *adv.* incessantly (as rain.)

Jhámp, *s. m.* a matted shutter or door.

Jhámpná, *v. a.* to cover, to shut.

Jhan, *s. m.* used to express the clanking of metallic bodies.

Jhanak, *s. f.* ringing, tinkling, jingle, clinking.
Jhaṇḍá, *s. m.* a banner, flag, ensign.
Jhaṇḍúlá, *adj.* with a fine head of hair (a child.)
Jhangá, *s. m.* an upper garment or vest.
Jhánjh, *s. m.* cymbals; horse-bells.
Jhanjhanáná, *v. n.* to tinkle, to clink, to tingle, to ring, to rattle.
Jhanjhar, *adj.* thin (as cloth.)
Jhanjhaṭ, *s. m.* wrangling, perplexity.
Jhanjhaṭí, *adj.* perplexing, difficult, vexatious.
Jhanjhkár, *s. f.* clinking, tinkling, ringing.
Jhanjhrí, *s. f.* a lattice; a kind of play with a boat by twirling it round.
Jhánk, *s. m.* bough of a tree, underwood; a herd of deer, flock of birds, &c.
Jhánká jhonkí, *s. f.* peeping.
Jhánkaṛ, *s. m.* bushes, brambles, underwood.
Jhankár, *s. f.* clinking, tinkling, ringing, clank, jingle, rattle.
Jhankháṛá, } **Jhankhaṛá**, } *s. m.* a tree without leaves.
Jhankhná, *v. n.* see Jhakná.
Jhánkná, *v. a.* to spy, to peep.
Jháṉsá, *s. m.* deceit, trick, deception.
Jháṉsná, *v. a.* to drink anything intoxicating; to deceive.
Jhánṭ, *s. f.* the hair of the private parts, pubes.
Jháṉwáṉ, *s. m.* bricks burnt to cinder.
Jháṉwlá, *adj.* sunburnt, faded.
Jháṉwlí, *s. f.* a wink, coquetry.
Jháṉwlíbáz, a coquette.
Jháṉwrá, *adj.* see Jháṉwlá.
Jhap, } **Jhapájhap**, } *adv.* quickly.
Jhapájhapí, *s. f.* haste, hurry.
Jhapak, *s. f.* a doze.
Jhapakná, *v. a.* to spring (as a tiger), to snatch.
Jhapaṭ, *s. f.* a match, a spring (as of a tiger), rush, snap.
Jhapaṭ lená, *v. n.* to snatch, to spring or pounce upon.
Jhapaṭná, same as Jhapaṭ lená; also, to make haste in travelling.
Jhapaṭṭá, *s. m.* the spring of a tiger; a snatch.
Japaṭṭá márná, to snatch, to dart (as a kite on its prey.)
Jhapeṭ meṉ áná, to become possessed or bewitched.
Jhap jhap, *adv.* hastily, quickly.
Jhapkí, *s. f.* a spring (as of a tiger); drowsiness, doze.
Jhapsá, *s. f.* rainy weather.
Jhap se, *adv.* quickly, in a trice.
Jhaṛ, *s. f.* heavy rain, a storm, a tempest; a kind of lock.
Jháṛ, *s. m.* bushes, brambles, underwood; a lustre or chandelier.
Jháṛá, *s. m.* a stool, a purge; search.
Jháṛá dená, to submit to search.
Jháṛá lená, to search.
Jháṛá jhapṭe jáná, to go to the necessary.
Jhaṛájhaṛ, *adv.* hastily, rapidly.
Jháṛá jhaṭká phirná, to go to the necessary.
Jhaṛák, } **Jhaṛáká**, } *s. m.* speed, haste, hurry.
Jháṛan, *s. f.* sweepings; a coarse cloth for wiping furniture, &c.
Jhaṛáná, *v. a.* to get swept, to cause to be exorcised.
Jháṛá phirná, to go to the necessary.
Jháṛ bándhná, to rain without ceasing.
Jhaṛbatás, *s. f.* a hurricane, a storm of wind and rain.
Jhaṛber, *s. m.* } **Jhaṛberí**, *s. f.* } a wild ber-tree.
Jháṛ ḍálná, } **Jháṛ dená**, } *v. a.* to sweep, to brush, to clear away.
Jhárí, *s. f.* a water vessel, with a spout.
Jháṛí, *s. f.* forest, wood, brushwood, copse.

Jhaṛí, *s. f.* continued rain, wet weather, showers.

Jháṛ jhankhár, *s. m.* brambles, large dry bushes.

Jhaṛjhaṛáná, *v. n.* to shake, to jerk.

Jháṛ jhaṭak, *s. f.* sweeping.

Jháṛ jhúṛ, *s. f.* sweepings; thicket.

Jhaṛkájhaṛkí, *s. f.* mutual, wrangling.

Jháṛkhanḍ, *s. m.* the forest of Baijnáth.

Jharná, *s. m.* a skimmer; a spring, a cascade; *v. n.* to flow.

Jhaṛná, *v. n.* to fall off (as fruit from a tree), to drop, to shake, to fall, to pour, to be sounded (the naubat.)

Jháṛná, *v. a.* to sweep, to brush, to clean, to knock off, to strike fire (as with a flint), to exorcise.

Jháṛná phúnkná, to exorcise, to repeat spells or charms.

Jharokhá, *s. m.* a lattice, a window.

Jháṛ pahár, digression.

Jhaṛpájharpí, *s. f.* fighting (as of birds), sparring, contention.

Jháṛ phúnk, *s. f.* juggling, conjuring, hocus pocus (particularly to cure the bite of a snake or a disease.)

Jhaṛ túfán, *s. m.* a hurricane, a tempest.

Jháṛú, *s. m.* a broom, a besom; a comet.

Jháṛúbardár, *s. m.* a sweeper.

Jhaṛwáná, *v. a.* to cause others to sweep.

Jhaṭ, *adv.* quickly, instantly.

Jhaṭak, *s. f.* twitch.

Jhaṭakná, *v. a.* to twitch, to jerk: *v. n.* to become lean, to shake, to stride out in walking.

Jhaṭás, *s. f.* driving rain, wind and rain.

Jhaṭ jhaṭ, *adv.* quickly, hastily.

Jhaṭká, *adj.* slaughtered by cutting off the head, broken asunder or torn by a sudden jerk; a squall of wind.

Jhaṭ paṭ, Jhaṭ se, *adv.* quickly, hastily.

Jháú, *s. m.* name of a tree similar to fir.

Jhauṛ, *s. f.* squabbling.

Jhauwá, *s. m.* see Jháú.

Jhijhak, *s. f.* start.

Jhijhakná, *v. n.* to start or boggle.

Jhíkhná, Jhíkná, *v. n.* to grieve, to lament, to think of anything with sorrow.

Jhíl, *s. f.* a lake.

Jhilam, *s. f.* armour, a coat of mail.

Jhilam ká ṭop, an iron helmet.

Jhilangá, Jhilgá, *s. m.* the netted bottom of a bed or couch when worn out and separated.

Jhillí, *s. f.* a thin skin, the caul.

Jhilmilá, *adj.* sparkling.

Jhilmiláná, *v. n.* to undulate as the flame of a candle or as water, to twinkle, to scintillate.

Jhilmilí, *s. f.* a venetian blind, a shutter.

Jhíná, *adj.* fine, subtile, thin.

Jhíngá, *s. f.* a shrimp, a prawn.

Jhíngur, *s. m.* a cricket.

Jhinjhoṛná, *v. n.* to shake, to break or tear or worry with the teeth.

Jhinjhrí, *s. f.* see Jhanjhrí.

Jhinká, *s.* the quantity of grain put at once into a hand-mill.

Jhínkná, *v. n.* see Jhíkná.

Jhiṛak, *s. f.* threat, jerk.

Jhiṛakná, *v. n.* to browbeat, to threaten, to speak snappishly, to jerk.

Jhirjhir, *adj.* running in a slender stream (water, &c.)

Jhirjhiráná, *v. n.* to trickle, to rill.

Jhiṛkí, *s. f.* rebuff, snappishness, frowning, jerk.

Jhísí, *s. m.* mizzling rain.

Jhojh, *s. m.* a pendulous belly.

Jhok, *s. f.* a jolt, a puff or gust.

Jhoká, *s. m.* a contact, collision; a gust, a blast, breeze or current (of wind.)

Jhokná, *v. a.* see Jhonkná.
Jhol, *s. m.* puckering or wrinkling (as of new-made clothes); cobweb, soot; a litter, brood, farrow, hatch, a birth.
Jholá, *s. m.* a stroke of the sun; the palsy; a wallet; a knapsack.
Jholí, *s. f.* a wallet.
Jholjhál, *s. m.* soot and filth.
Jhompṛá, *s. m.* } a cottage, a shed,
Jhompṛí, *s. f.* } a hut.
Jhonk, *s. f.* a shove or push in swinging, the impulse of a squall or sudden blast of wind, a jolt, a jerk.
Jhonk dená, to throw dust, &c.; to throw away (the lives of men uselessly.)
Jhonkná, *v. a.* to push; to throw; to cast fuel into an oven or fireplace.
Jhonṭá *s. m.* } the hair of the back
Jhonṭí, *s. f.* } part of the neck.
Jhopṛá, *s. m.* } a cottage, a hut, a
Jhopṛí, *s. f.* } shed.
Jhuká dená, } *v. a.* to bend.
Jhuká lená, }
Jhukáná, *v. a.* to cause to stoop, to bend forwards; to make to nod.
Jhuk jáná, } *v. n.* to nod, to bow, to
Jhukná, } stoop, to be bent downwards, (as the bough of a tree.)
Jhúl, *s. f.* body clothes of cattle, housings.
Jhúlá, *s. m.* a swing; a kind of garment.
Jhuláná, *v. a.* to swing, to shove a swing, to rock (a cradle), to dangle, to hang, to make another (as a dun) dance after one.
Jhulas dená, *v. a.* to sear, to singe.
Jhulas jáná, } *v. n.* to be seared,
Jhulasná, } singed or scorched.
Jhulná, } *v. n.* to swing (for exer-
Jhúlná, } cise), to swing, to dangle, to oscillate; *s. m.* a kind of poem.
Jhulsáná, *v. a.* to cause to singe, to singe, to sear, to scorch.

Jhúmak, *s. f.* } the bell-shaped pen-
Jhumká, *s. m.* } dant of an ear-
Jhúmká, *s. m.* } ring; a bunch of flowers or fruit; name of a flower.
Jhúmkí, *s. f.* a kind of ear-ring.
Jhúmná, *v. n.* to wave, to move the head up and down, to slumber, to gather (the clouds.)
Jhúná *s. m.* a kind of muslin.
Jhunḍ, *s. m.* a crowd, swarm, flock, troop, a clump (of trees.)
Jhunjhláhaṭ, *s. f.* peevishness, raging, storming.
Jhunjhláná, *v. n.* to be peevish or fretful, to be petulant or irritable, to rage, to storm.
Jhunjhuná, *s. m.* a child's rattle.
Jhunjhuní, *s. f.* little bells worn on the feet; the tingling sensation felt when a limb is asleep.
Jhúṉmná, *v. n.* see Jhúmná.
Jhúṉsná jháṉsná, *v. a.* to deceive.
Jhúṉṭhá, see Jhúṭhá.
Jhúṉṭhan jháṉṭhan, *s. m.* leavings.
Jhúpṛí, *s. f.* see Jhopṛí.
Jhúṛ, *s. m.* bramble.
Jhúrá, *adj.* withered.
Jhurí, *s. f.* wrinkle.
Jhurmaṭ, *s. m.* a multitude, a crowd; a row, a conflict.
Jhurná, *v. n.* to wither, to fade (from grief), to pine.
Jhúrná, *v. a.* to shake fruit from the tree: *v. n.* to pine.
Jhúṭ, *adj.* false: *s. m.* a lie, falsehood.
Jhúṭálná, *v. n.* to prove to be false, to prove one in the wrong, to pollute victuals by touching them, &c.
Jhúṭh, *adj.* see Jhúṭ.
Jhúṭhá, *adj.* liar, false; (among Hindús) that which has touched food and therefore is defiled; offal, refuse, left (food): *s. m.* leavings of food.
Jhúṭhá chāṭná, to eat leavings, to be very wretched.
Jhúṭhá jháṭá, *s. m.* offals, left food.
Jhúṭh bolná, to lie, to tell a lie, to speak falsehood.

Jhuṭhláná, *v. a.* to belie, to falsify.
Jhúṭh múṭh, lie, lying, falsehood; deception, falsely.
Jí, yes, sir, master, madam: *s. m.* life, soul, spirit, mind.
Jí á jáná, to have the mind suddenly fixed (on anything.)
Jíb, *s. f.* the tongue.
Jí bahláná, to amuse one's self, to dissipate reflection.
Jí baṛháná, to be moderately desirous.
Jíbh, *s. f.* the tongue.
Jí bhar jáná, to be at ease or contented.
Jíbh baṛháná, to be loquacious and abusive; to pursue pleasures beyond one's reach.
Jíbh dábke bát kahná, to speak with reserve.
Jíbhí, *s. m.* an instrument for cleaning the tongue; a bit of a bridle.
Jíbh káṭná, to forbid by signs.
Jíbh nikalná, to be extremely fatigued or thirsty.
Jí burá karná, to vomit, to have a nausea,
Jí cháhná, } to desire.
Jí chalná, }
Jí chhipáná, } to do a work carelessly and lazily; to neglect.
Jí churáná, }
Jidd, *prop.* Zidd, which see.
Jiddí, *adj. prop.* Ziddí, which see.
Jidd karná, see Zidd karná.
Jidhar, } *adv.* where, wherever, whither, there.
Jídhar, }
Jí dhaṛakná, to have a palpitation of the heart.
Jidhar tidhar, *adv.* hither and thither, here and there, everywhere.
Jí ḍúb jáná, to faint.
Jigar, *s. m.* the liver, vitals, heart, mind, courage.
Jigar chák, *adj.* heartbroken.
Jigarí, *adj.* belonging to the liver or heart.
Jigarí dágh, *s. m.* indelible stain or mark, inconsolable grief.
Jihád, *s. m.* war (especially against infidels.)
Jihálat, *s. f.* ignorance, barbarism.
Jihan, *s. m. prop.* Zihn, which see.
Jí hárná, to be discouraged, to be spiritless.
Jihat, *s. f.* cause, reason, account.
Jí haṭ jáná, to detest.
Jí jaláná, to befriend; to plague, to perplex.
Jí jalná, to be vexed or troubled in mind.
Jikar, *s. m. prop.* Zikr, which see.
Jikar karná, see Zikr karná.
Jí ke badal jí dená, to take up the cause of another.
Jí kholke kuchh karná, to do with pleasure or cheerfully.
Jíl, *s. f.* a high note or tone in music, the treble. See Zíl.
Jilá, *s. f.* splendour, lustre, brightness; scouring, polishing: *s. m.* for Zilạ, a district, a division.
Jiládár, *s. m.* a person who superintends the fulfilment of engagements of agriculturists.
Jí lagáná, to place or fix the mind.
Jí lagná, to contract affection for any person or thing; to love; to hanker after.
Jiláná, *v. a.* to give life to, to vivify, to recover any thing almost dead; to foster, to patronize.
Jiláwatan, *s. m.* emigration, leaving one's country.
Jiláwatan honá, to emigrate or abandon one's country, to be exiled.
Jiláwatan karná, to abandon one's country, to exile.
Jild, *s. f.* the binding of a book, a volume, a book.
Jildband, *adj.* bound (a book.)
Jildbandí, *s. f.* bookbinding.
Jildgar, *s. m.* a bookbinder.
Jildgarí, *s. f.* bookbinding.
Jí lená, to kill.
Jilwá, *s. m.* the meeting of the bride and bridegroom (in presence of the relations.)

Jimá, *s. f.* copulation.
Jimáná, *v. a.* to feed, to entertain.
Jímár, *adj.* mortifying one's desires.
Jí márná, to mortify one's desires.
Jí meṉ áná, to come into the mind, to occur to the recollection.
Jí meṉ jal jáná, to be tormented with envy and jealousy.
Jí meṉ jí áná, to be comforted.
Jí miláná, to contract friendship.
Jimma, *s. m. prop.* Zimma, which see.
Jimme karná, } see Zimme karná.
Jimme lená, }
Jímná, *v. a.* to eat.
Jin, *pron. rel. plur. inflect.* whom, [what.
Jín, *s. m. prop.* Zín, a saddle.
Jíná, *v. n.* to live ; *s. m.* living.
Jiná, *s. f. prop.* Ziná, which see.
Jinákár, *s. m.* see Zinákár.
Jinákárí, *s. f.* see Zinákárí.
Jín bándhná, *prop.* Zín bándhná, to saddle.
Jinda, *adj. prop.* Zinda, alive, living.
Jindagání, *s. f.* see Zindagání.
Jindagí, *s. f.* see Zindagí.
Jí nikalná, to die; to fear exceedingly.
Jinis, *s. f. prop.* Jins, which see.
Jinn, *s. m.* a genius, demon, one of the genii.
Jinnát, *s.* (*plur.* of Jinn), genii.
Jínposh, *s. m. prop.* Zínposh, which see.
Jins, *s. f.* genus, kind, sort, species; family ; goods ; corn.
Jí páná, to understand one's temper; to revive.
Jí pání karná, to harass, to tear, to perplex.
Jí par khelná, to risk one's life.
Jí pasíjná, to compassionate, to feel affection.
Jí phaṭ jáná, to be broken-hearted, to be offended.
Jí phir jáná, to be satiated or disgusted.
Jí pighal jáná, } to be compassionate,
Jí pighalná, } to feel affection.

Jírá, *s. m.* cummin-seed.
Jis, *pron. rel. sing. inflect.* of Jo, that, what, who, whom, which.
Jis dam, *adv.* when, while, whilst, any one.
Jí se márná, to kill.
Jí se utar jáná, to sink in the opinion of another.
Jis jagah, *adv.* where, wherever.
Jis jis, whichever, each of which.
Jis ká, *pron. rel. sing.* whose, of whom.
Jis kisí ká, of whomever.
Jis kisí ko, to whomever.
Jis ko, to whom.
Jism, *s. m.* body of any being.
Jismání, *adj.* belonging to body, corporeal, material.
Jismániyat, } *s. f.* materiality.
Jismiyat, }
Jis qadr, *adv.* to what degree, as, as much as, whatever, whatsoever.
Jis taraf, *adv.* where, even.
Jis tarah, *adv.* according to, as; what manner or fashion, (in) what manner.
Jis taur, *adv.* in what mode.
Jis tis, whomever, whatever, some or other.
Jis waqt, when, since, what time, at what time, wherever.
Jít, *s. f.* winning, victory.
Jítá, *adj.* alive, living ; over, above, [more.
Jítab, *s. m.* life, existence.
Jítá honá, to be over, to exceed.
Jitáñá, *v. a.* to cause to win or conquer.
Jíte jí, *adj.* alive, living, lifetime.
Jitek, *adj.* as much as, as many as.
Jiṭhání, *s. f.* husband's elder brother's wife.
Jítiyá, *s. f.* name of a Hindú fast.
Jítná, *v. a.* to win, to conquer, to overcome.
Jitná, *m.* } *adj.* how much, so much,
Jitní, *f.* } as much as, as many.
Jitne meṉ in as much (time), as.
Jittá, *adj.* see Jitná.

Jítwaiyá, } s. m. a winner.
Jítwant, }

Jíú, s. m. see Jíw.

Jíúgar, *adj.* resolute, bold.

Jí uṭháná, to raise to life; to cure.

Jíviká, s. f. pension, livelihood.

Jíw, s. m. life, soul; animal; a sweetheart: *interj.* bravo!

Jíwan, s. m. livelihood, living.

Jiwáná, v. a. to feed, to entertain.

Jiwár, s. m. neighbourhood, vicinity.

Jíwaṭ, *adj.* brave, courageous, resolute.

Jíwgar, *adj.* resolute, bold.

Jíwná, v. n. to live.

Jíwṛá, s. m. life, soul.

Jiyáda, s. m. *prop.* Ziyáda, which see.

Jiyáda honá, see Ziyáda honá.

Jiyáda karná, see Ziyáda karná.

Jiyáfat, s. f. *prop.* Ziyáfat, which see.

Jiyán, s. m. *prop.* Ziyán, which see.

Jiyáná, v. n. to cause to live.

Jiyará, s. m. life, soul.

Jiyárat, s. f. *prop.* Ziyárat, which see.

Jiyúṛá, s. m. life, soul.

Jo, in *compos.* seeking, seeker: *pron. rel.* who, what, which: *conj.* if, that.

Joár, s. f. the name of a grain, Indian corn, maize.

Joban, s. m. puberty, prime, youth, breast.

Jo chíz, what thing, whatever.

Jodhá, s. m. a hero, a warrior, a brave fellow.

Jog, s. m. junction, fitting; intense devotion: *adj.* possible, capable, fit; in *compos.* able, worthy.

Jogí, s. m. a Hindú faqír, a devotee.

Jogin, s. f. female of Jogí.

Jogní, s. f. a class of female deities attendant on the goddess Debí; spirits governing periods of good and ill luck.

Jogya, *adj.* accomplished, fit, capable.

Johná, v. a. to expect, to look out for.

Jojan, s. m. a measure of four kos.

Jo jo, whoever, whatever.

Jok, s. f. a leech.

Jokh, s. f. weight.

Jokhim, s. f. risk, venture, danger, injury; easily broken or injured.

Jokhim uṭháná, to run the hazard, to risk, to suffer loss.

Jokhimí, s. m. one who risks.

Jokhná, v. a. to weigh.

Jokhoṇ, s. f. see Jokhim.

Jo koí, whoever.

Jo ki, though, although.

Jo kuchh, whatever.

Jolá, s. m. fraud, deceit.

Jolá dená, to deceive.

Joláh, s. m. a weaver.

Joṇ, *adv.* as, when.

Jonhíṇ, *adv.* as soon as, exactly when.

Joṇk, s. f. a leech.

Joṇ ká toṇ, in the same way as it was, as before, unaltered.

Joṇk lagáná, to apply leeches.

Joṇ toṇ, *adv.* in some way.

Joṇ toṇkar, } *adv.* in any way, by
Joṇ toṇkarke, } some means, somehow or other, as it could be done.

Jor, s. m. *prop.* Zor, which see.

Joṛ, s. m. junction, joint, joining, connexion; a patch, a seam.

Joṛá, s. m. a joining, a pair, a couple, a pair of shoes; a suit (of clothes.)

Joṛan, s. m. solder; runnet.

Jorávar, *adj.* see Zorávar.

Jorávarí, s. f. see Zorávarí.

Joṛ dená, to cast up, to add the sum.

Joṛí, s. f. a pair, a couple.

Joṛiyáná, to put together in order.

Joṛ jáṛ, s. m. savings, scrapings together.

Jor karná, } see under Zor.
Jor márná, }

Joṛná, } v. a. to join, to mend, to add
Jorná, } together, to reckon, to cast or sum or add up; to solder, to cement, to set (a bone, &c.)

Joṛtí, s. f. calculation, reckoning.

Joṛ toṛ, s. m. contrivance, arrangement.

Jorú, s. f. a wife.

Jorú laṛká, wife and children, family.

Josh, *s. m.* ebullition, effervescence, heat, passion, lust.

Joshánda, *s. m.* a decoction.

Josh dená, to cause to boil, to boil.

Josh kháná, to boil or bubble up.

Jot, *s. f.* cultivation, cultivated land, tillage; brilliancy, light, lustre; the sunbeams, the flame of a candle or lamp; vision.

Jotí, *s. f.* the string which suspends the scale of a balance.

Jotik, } *s. m.* astrology, astronomy.
Jotikh, }

Jotikhí } *s. m.* an astrologer, an astronomer.
Jotikí, }

Jotish, *s. m.* see Jotikh.

Jotíswarúp, self-resplendent; an epithet of God.

Jotná, *v. a.* to yoke; to plough, to till.

Júá, *s. m.* a yoke; playing with dice, &c., gambling.

Júá khelná, to gamble.

Juárí, *s. m.* a gambler.

Jubán, *s. f. prop.* Zubán, which see.

Jubba, a kind of long vest resembling a shirt.

Judá, *adj.* separate, distinct, away, apart, aside, asunder, different.

Judá honá, to be separated.

Judáí, *s. f.* separation.

Judá judá, *adj.* various, one by one, severally, separately.

Judá judá kahná, to particularize.

Judá karná, to separate, to disjoin, to part, to disengage, to part with, to dispose of, to sell.

Judh, *s. m.* battle, war, fight.

Júebáz, *s. m.* a gambler.

Júeḳhána, *s. m.* a gaming-house.

Juft, *s. m.* evenness; a party; a couple, a match.

Juftí kháná, *v. a.* to pair (as birds.)

Jug, *s. m.* a period, an age, one of the four great Hindú periods.

Jugálí, *s. f.* the cud.

Jugálná, *v. a.* to chew the cud.

Jugáná, *v. a.* to be careful of, to keep with care.

Jugat, *s. f.* contrivance, dexterity.

Júgat, *s. f.* a pun or double meaning.

Júgatbáz, a punster, one who is fond of uttering double meanings.

Jugatí, *adj.* artful, clever, cunning, facetious.

Jughráfiya, *s. m.* geography.

Jug jug, *adv.* constantly, eternally.

Jug jug jíná, to live for ever.

Jugní, *s. f.* a glowworm.

Jugnú, *s. m.* the firefly; a jewel worn about the neck.

Jugtáná, *v. a.* to procure, to get.

Juhár, *s. f.* Hindú salutation, obeisance.

Júhí, *s. f.* jasmine, a kind of firework.

Jújh marná, } *v. n.* to die fighting, to be killed in battle.
Júj́hná, }

Jul, *s. m.* deceit, cheating, a trick.

Julaf, *s. f. prop.* Zulf, which see.

Juláh, } *s. m.* a Muhammadan weaver.
Juláhá, }

Julam, *s. m. prop.* Zulm, which see.

Julamáná *s. m. prop.* Jarímána, a fine, penalty.

Julam honá, see Zulm honá.

Julamí, *adj.* see Zulmí.

Julam karná, see Zulm karná.

Julláb, *s. m.* a purgative medicine, a purge.

Julús, *s. m.* the accession (to a throne); pomp.

Juma, *s. m.* Friday.

Jumád ul áḳhir, name of the sixth Arabian month.

Jumád ul auwal, name of the fifth Muhammadan month.

Jumád us sání, name of the sixth Muhammadan month.

Jumagí, *s. f.* a present given on a Friday by schoolboys to their preceptor.

Jumarát, *s. f.* Thursday.

Jumbish, *s. f.* motion, agitation,

Jumerát, *s. f.* Thursday.

Jumlagí, *s. f.* universality, totality.

Jun, } *s. m.* time.
Jún, }

Júṇí, *s. f.* a louse.
Junún, *s. m.* madness, insanity.
Junúní, *adj.* mad, insane, passionate.
Júṛá, *s. m.* the hair done up in a knot behind; the hinder part of a turban.
Jura dená, } *v. a.* to procure.
Juráná, }
Juṛáná, *v. a.* to cause to join, to couple, to get mended.
Jurat, *s. f.* courage, boldness, bravery, temerity, valour.
Júṛí, *s. f.* an ague.
Jurímána, *s. m.* see Jarímána.
Jurná, *v. n.* to be procured or obtained, to come to hand.
Juṛná, *v. n.* to be joined.
Jurráb, *s. m.* a sock, stocking.
Juruá, *s. f.* a woman.
Justjú, } *s. f.* searching, seeking,
Justojú, } search, inquiry.
Justojú karná, to seek.
Juṭ, *s. m.* a fellow, a mate, a match.
Jútá, *s. m.* a shoe, a slipper.
Jutáná, *v. n.* to be joined, to yoke; to be tilled.
Jútí, *s. f.* a shoe, a slipper.
Jútíkárí, *s. f.* act of beating with slippers.
Jútíḳhor, } *adj.* beaten with slip-
Jútíḳhora, } pers.
Jútí márná, *v. a.* to beat with a shoe or slippers.
Jútí paizár karná, to kick.
Jútí paizár kháná, to be kicked.
Jutiyáná, *v. a.* to beat with a shoe or slippers.
Juṭná, *v. n.* to close with, to engage in close fight, to unite, to close, to join (as the edges of a wound.)
Juṭwáná, *v. a.* to cause to join or yoke.
Juvá, *adj.* young.
Juwár, *s. f.* flood-tide.
Juz, *s. m.* a part, portion; a division of a book consisting of eight leaves.
Juzbandí, *s. f.* arrangement of the parts of a book for binding.
Juzdán, *s. m.* a cloth in which books are wrapped up, a portfolio.
Juz o kull, *adj.* totally, entirely, great and small.
Jwálá, *s. f.* flame.
Jwar, *s. m.* fever.
Jyauṇ, } *adv.* how much the more, so,
Jyúṇ, } when as, as if.
Jyún, }
Jyúṇ jyúṇ, at what time.
Jyúṇkar, as.
Jyúṇ ká tyúṇ, *adv.* precisely the same.
Jyúṇ tyúṇ, somehow or other.

K.

Ká, *postpos.* of, belonging to; in *Braj. pron. inflect. sing.* of Kaun, whom, what, which.
Kab, *adv.* when?
Kạba, *s. m.* the temple of Mecca.
Kabáb, *s. m.* roasted meat, a roast, roasted.
Kabábchíní, *s. f.* cubebs.
Kabáb honá, *v. n.* to burn, to be roasted, to be enraged.
Kabábí, *adj.* fit to be roasted, roasting fowl.
Kabáb karná, *v. a.* to burn, to roast.
Kabaḍḍí, *s. f.* a game among boys.
Kabáhat, *s. f. prop.* Qabáhat, perplexity, inconvenience.
Kabáil, *s. m. prop.* Qabáil, which see.
Kabaj, *s. f. prop.* Qabz, costiveness, gripes.
Kabaj karná, see Qabz karná.
Kabalsúrat, *adj. prop.* Qabúlsúrat, handsome.
Kabalsúratí, *s. f.* see Qabúlsúratí.
Kabar, *s. f. prop.* Qabr, a grave, a tomb.
Kabargáh, *s. f. prop.* Qabrgáh, a burying-ground.
Kabaristán, *s. f. prop.* Qabristán, a burying-ground.
Kabhí, *adv.* ever, sometime or other, sometime.

Kabhí kabhí, *adv.* sometimes, now and then, at times.
Kabhí ke, of sometime.
Kabhíṉ, *adv.* see Kabhí.
Kabhí nahíṉ, *adv.* never.
Kabhí na kabhí, sometime or other, first or last.
Kabhú, Kabhúṉ, } *adv.* even, sometime or other, sometime.
Kabhúṉ nahíṉ, *adv.* never.
Kabi, *s. m.* a poet.
Kabí, *adv.* see Kabhí.
Kábil, *adj. prop.* Qábil, which see.
Kabílá, *s. f. prop.* Qabíla, wife.
Kábil honá, *prop.* Qábil honá, to deserve, to merit.
Kabír, *n. prop.* name of a faqír.
Kabírpanthí, *s. m.* a follower of Kabír.
Kabíswar, *s. m.* an eminent poet.
Kabit, *s. m.* poetry, verse.
Kabitá, *s. m.* a poet.
Kabja, *s. m. prop.* Qabza, which see.
Kabja karná, Kabje meṉ karná, Kabje meṉ láná, } *prop.* Qabza, &c., to seize, to take possession of.
Kabjíyat, *s. f. prop.* Qabzíyat, which see.
Kab ká, *adv.* since when? of what time?
Kab kab, when.
Kab ke, Kab kí, } *adv.* since when? of what time?
Kab lag, Kab loṉ, } till when? how long?
Kabrá, *adj.* gray, dirty white.
Kab se, since when?
Kabsúrat, *prop.* Ḳhúbsúrat, which see.
Kab taiṉ, Kab tak, Kab talak, } *adv.* till when? how long?
Kabú, *adv.* see Kabhú.
Kábú, *s. m. prop.* Qábú, which see.
Kábú chaláná, see Qábú chaláná.
Kábúchí, *adj. prop.* Qábúchí, despotic, tyrannical.
Kábúchípaná, *s. m.* tyranny.
Kábuk, *s. f.* a pigeon-house, a box for pigeons.
Kábul, *n. prop.* name of a country and city, Cabool.
Kabúl, *s. m. prop.* Qabúl, which see.
Kábúlí, *s. f.* a kind of pea.
Kabúliyat, *s. f. prop.* Qabúliyat, a written agreement.
Kabúl karná, see Qabúl karná.
Kábúpaná, *prop.* Qábúpaná, which see.
Kabútar, *s. m.* a pigeon.
Kabútarbáz, one who rears pigeons.
Kabútarḳhána, *s. m.* a dove-cot, a pigeon-house.
Kách, *s. m.* glass.
Káchá, *adj.* see Kachchá.
Kachahrí, *s. f.* a hall of justice, court, an office for transacting business.
Kacháí, *s. f.* rawness.
Kachak, *s. f.* pain from sprain, &c., sprain.
Kachakná, *v. n.* to strain, to sprain, to twist, to limp, to pain.
Kacharí, *s. m.* name of a fruit.
Kachar kachar, *s.* supping sound in eating.
Kachaurí, *s. f.* a kind of cake.
Kachbach, *s. m. plur.* infants, brats, children, family.
Kachbachiyá, the pleiades.
Kachchá, *adj.* unripe, crude, raw; built of unbaked earth; silly, unexperienced; false; beneath a certain standard of weights and measures.
Kachchá khání, to get into a rage.
Kachchápaná, *s. m.* rawness, crudity.
Kachchhap, *s. m.* a tortoise, a turtle.
Kachchhí, a kind of horse (with a hollow back.)
Kachchhú, *s. m.* a tortoise, a turtle.
Kachchí ser, a ser which is beneath the standard of eighty rupees weight.
Kachchí taul, beneath the standard weight.

Kachchú, *s. m.* name of a plant with an esculent root.

Kacherí, *s. f.* see Kachahrí.

Kachh, *s. m.* a tortoise, a turtle.

Káchh, Káchhá, } *s. m.* a cloth worn round the hips passing between the legs and tucked in behind the upper part of the thigh.

Kachhárná, *v. a.* to wash, to rinse.

Kachhauṭí, *s. f.* a cloth worn between the legs to conceal the privities.

Kachhlampaṭ, *adj.* incontinent, lecherous, libertine.

Káchhná, *v. a.* to bind on or tie up the Káchh; to skim up, to wipe up anything that is spilled with the hand; to half wash or rinse (cloth.)

Kachhná, Kachhní, Káchhní, } *s. f.* a cloth worn between the legs to conceal the privities.

Kachhúá, *s. m.* a tortoise, a turtle.

Kachhúáḍáhar, *adj.* deep and shallow alternately.

Kachhwáhá, *s. m.* a tribe of Rájpúts.

Kachiyá, *s. m.* a reaping-hook or sickle.

Kachiyáná, *v. n.* to be frightened, to draw back.

Kachkach, *s. m.* debate, altercation.

Kachkacháhaṭ, *s. f.* the act of debating, &c.

Kachkáná, *v. n.* to strain, to sprain, to twist.

Kachkaṛá, *s. m.* whalebone.

Kachkelá, *s. m.* a kind of plantain dressed as a vegetable.

Kachko, *adj.* not well-burnt, as tiles, bricks, &c.

Kachlohí, Kachlohiyá, } *s. f.* untempered iron.

Kachnál, Kachnár, } *s. f.* a tree whose buds are a delicate vegetable.

Kachpach, *adj.* close, thick, stuffed together.

Kachpachiyá, the pleiades.

Kachpan, *s. m.* rawness, simplicity.

Kachrá, *s. m.* a kind of melon; a rope used in boats, a tethering rope.

Kachúr, *s. m.* the name of a poisonous plant or drug.

Kad, *adv.* when? also for Qadd, which see.

Kádá, *s. m.* slime, mud, mire, soft clay.

Kadáchit, *adv.* should, sometimes, perhaps.

Kadalí, *s. f.* a plantain tree.

Kadam, *s. m.* the name of a tree; also for Qadam, which see.

Kadápi, *adv.* see Kadáchit.

Kadar, *s. f. prop.* Qadr., which see.

Kadáwar, *adj. prop.* Qaddáwar, tall.

Kaddá, *s. m. prop.* Qadah, which see.

Kadhí, Kadhiṉ, Kadhú, Kadhúṉ, } *adj.* ever, sometime or other.

Kadím, *adj. prop.* Qadím, ancient, old.

Kadíma, *s. m.* a kind of pumpkin.

Kádir, *adj. prop.* Qádir, which see.

Kadjawáb, a rejoinder.

Kádo, *s. m.* slime, mud, mire.

Kadú, *s. m.* a pumpkin, a pumpion, a gourd.

Kadúdána, *s. m.* the name of a disease, tape-worms.

Káephal, *s. m.* name of a medicine.

Kaf, *s. f.* foam, froth, spittle, phlegm.

Kafan, *s. m.* a winding-sheet, a shroud.

Kafanchor, a shroud-stealer; caitiff, miscreant.

Kafaní, *s. f.* a garment worn by Muhammadan mendicants.

Kafára, *s. m.* atonement, expiation for sin.

Káfí, *s. m. Eng.* coffee.

Kafgír, *s. m.* a skimmer.

Kafíl, security.

Káfila, *s. m. prop.* Qáfila, a body of travellers, a caravan.

Káfir, *adj.* infidel, impious: *s. m.* an infidel, one who is not a Muhammadan.

Káfirí, *n. prop.* a Caffre, a native of a part of Africa.

Kafnáná, *v. a.* to shroud, to dress for the grave.

Kafní, *s. f.* a dress worn by Faqírs.

Káfúr, *s. m.* camphor.

Káfúr hojáná, } to run away, to
Káfúr honá, } disappear, to scamper off, to vanish.

Káfúrí, *adj.* camphorated, made of camphor.

Káfúrí battí, a camphor-wick candle.

Kág, } *s. m.* a crow.
Kágá, }

Kágad, } *s. m.* paper.
Kágaj, }

Kágají, see Kághazí.

Kágur, *s. m.* edge, border, architrave.

Kághaz, *s. m.* paper.

Kághazí, a kind of lime; a stationer, a paper-maker: *adj.* delicate, soft, thin.

Kághazí lembú, } *s. m.* a lime with
Kághazí nembú, } a very thin rind.

Kághazpatr, *s. m.* a written document, a deed.

Kah, *imper. sing.* (of Kahná), speak, tell.

Kahá, *s. m.* order, saying, word.

Kahákahí, *s. f.* altercation, expostulation.

Kahálat, *s. f.* indolence, sloth, inactivity.

Kahálatí, *adj.* lazy, slothful.

Kaháŋ, *adv.* where?

Kaháná, *v. a.* to cause to speak, to cause to tell; to be called.

Kahání, *s. f.* a tale, story, fable.

Kaháŋ ká kaháŋ, to what degree, extremely, immensely.

Kaháŋ se, *adv.* where?

Kaháŋ tak, } how far? how
Kaháŋ talak, } long? to what degree?

Kahár, *s. m.* a palanquin-bearer; name of a caste.

Kahárin, *s. f.* the feminine of Kahár.

Kaharná, *v. n.* to groan.

Kahásuní, *s. f.* repetition of what one has heard.

Kaháwat, *s. f.* a proverb, an adage, a saying.

Kah dená, to tell, bid, order, &c.

Káhe, *pron. inflect.* what? which? why? wherefore?

Káhe ko, for what? why? wherefore?

Kahgil, *s. f.* mud plaster for walls.

Kahí, *s. f.* a foraging party.

Káhí ká gosht, grass-fed meat.

Káhil, *adj.* slow, indolent, lazy, languid, sick, tardy.

Káhilí, *s. f.* indolence, sloth, tardiness.

Káhil mizáj, *adj.* indolent.

Kahíŋ, *adv.* somewhere, anywhere, wherever.

Kahíŋ aur, elsewhere.

Kahíŋ nahíŋ, nowhere.

Kahíŋ na kahíŋ, somewhere or other.

Kahlá bhejná, *v. n.* to send a message, to send and tell, to inform.

Kahláná, *v. a.* to cause to say; to be called.

Kahná, *v. a.* to tell, to say, recount, state, bid, order, affirm, assert, aver, advise, speak; *s. m.* saying, advice, order, command.

Kahúŋ, *adv.* somewhere, anywhere.

Kahwá, *s. m. prop.* Qahwa, coffee.

Kahwádán, *s. m. prop.* Qahwadán, a coffee-pot.

Kahwáná, *v. a.* to cause to speak.

Kai, *s. f. prop.* Qai, vomiting.

Káí, *s. f.* the green mould that sticks to walls and pavements; scum, fur; the green scum on the surface of stagnant water.

Kai, } *pron.* how many? *adj.* se-
Kaí, } veral, some.

Kaid, *s. f. prop.* Qaid, which see.

Káida, *s. m. prop.* Qáida, which see.
Kaid honá, see Qaid honá.
Kaidí, *s. m.* see Qaidí.
Kaid karná, see Qaid karná.
Kaidkháná, *s. m.* a prison.
Kaid meṉ rakhná, see Qaid, &c.
Kaid rahná, see Qaid, &c.
Kai ek, } some, some few, a few.
Kaí ek, }
Kaifiyat, *s. f.* relation, statement.
Kai karná, *prop.* Qai karná, to vomit.
Káil, *prop.* Qáil, which see.
Káil honá, see Qáil honá.
Káil karná, see Qáil karná.
Káim, } *adj. prop.* Qaím, which
Káimí, } see.
Káim mizáj, see Qáim mizáj.
Káim karná, *prop.* Qáim karná, to establish.
Kainchí, *s. f. prop.* Qainchí, scissors, shears; an oblique cross.
Kainchlí, *s. f.* the slough of a snake.
Kairí, *s. f.* a small unripe mango.
Kairiánkh, a wall-eye, an eye the pupil of which is grey.
Kaisá, *pron. adj.* how? in what manner? what sort of? what like?
Kaisá hí, howsoever.
Kaiseṉ, *adv.* how?
Kait, } *s. m.* name of a tree.
Kaithá, }
Kaiyá, *s. m.* a tool for soldering.
Kaiyál, *s. m.* a weigher of grain.
Kaj, *s. m.* crooked, curved, awry.
Káj, *s. m.* business, occupation, an action, affair; by reason (of), for the sake (of); a button-hole.
Kajá, *s. f. prop.* Qazá, death.
Kajaí, *s. f. prop.* Qáiza, the short rein of a harness; the bridle used when the horse is curried.
Kaják, *s. m. prop.* Qazzák, a robber.
Kájal, *s. m.* lampblack (applied to the eyes.)
Kájaldán, *s. m.* a box for holding lampblack.
Kajáwa, *s. m.* a camel's saddle; a pannier; a kind of box for keeping vessels, &c., in.
Kájáyá, *prop.* Qazáyá, which see.
Kájí, *s. m. prop.* Qází, a Muhammadan judge.
Kají, *s. f.* crookedness, crossness.
Kajiyá, *s. m. prop.* Qaziya, which see.
Kajiyá karná, see Qaziya karná.
Kajjal, } *s. m.* see Kájal.
Kajlá, }
Kajlauṭí, *s. f.* an iron instrument like snuffers, used to receive smoke for preparing lampblack.
Káká, *s. m.* a paternal uncle.
Kakahrá, *s. m.* the alphabet.
Kákátúá, a cockatoo-parrot.
Kakhaurí, *s. f.* a painful suppurating tumor in the armpit.
Kakhoṛná, *v. a.* see Kakorná.
Kákí, *s. f.* a paternal aunt.
Kakná, *s. m.* } a ring worn on the
Kakní, *s. f.* } wrist, a bracelet.
Kakorná, *v. a.* to scratch; to scrape (the earth as fowls), to hollow, to excavate.
Kákreza, *s. m.* name of a colour approaching to purple.
Kákrezí, *adj.* purple-coloured.
Kakṛí, *s. f.* a kind of cucumber.
Kal, *s. m.* to-morrow, yesterday: *s. f.* ease, tranquillity, quiet, rest; a trap, a machine.
Kál, *s. m.* death; (*met.*) a snake; time, season, dearth, famine, calamity; to-morrow.
Kálá, *adj.* black, dark: *s. m.* name of a snake.
Kalába, *s. m.* see Kaláwa.
Kálábál, *s. m.* the lower part of the belly.
Kalábattú, } *s. m.* twisted silver
Kalábattún, } and silk thread.
Kalábází, *s. f.* turning over head and heels, tumbling, juggling.
Káládána, *s.* name of a purgative seed.
Kalah, *s. m.* quarrel.
Kalahí, *s. f.* a scold, a termagant, a vixen.

Kalahkár, *s. m.* a quarrelsome man.
Kalahkáriní, *s. f.* a quarrelsome woman.
Kaláí, *s. f.* wrist; a kind of pulse.
Kalaí, *s. f. prop.* Qalaí, which see.
Kalaígar, *prop.* Qalaígar, which see.
Kalaí karná, to tin (vessels.)
Kálájíra, *s. m.* black cummin-seed.
Kálá kos, a great distance.
Kalál, *s. m.* see Kalár.
Kalálin, *s. f.* see Kalárin.
Kalam, *s. f. prop.* Qalam, which see.
Kalám, *s. m.* a word, speech, talk, conversation.
Kalamdán, *s. m. prop.* Qalamdán, which see.
Kalamí, *adj. prop.* Qalamí, which see.
Kalamtarásh, *s. m. prop.* Qalamtarásh, a penknife.
Kálá munh karná, to disgrace, to expel.
Kalám 'ul láh, the word of God; the Qurán is so called.
Kalá na lagná, not to have an advantage, not to avail.
Kálá namak, *s. m.* a kind of rock salt; black salt.
Kalank, *s. m.* calumny, suspicion, scandal, brand, stigma, obloquy, defamation, a moral stain or taint, guilt.
Kalankí, *adj.* liable to reproach, blemished.
Kalap, *s. m.* starch.
Kálápan, *s. m.* blackness.
Kalapát, Kálápát, Kálápátí, *s. m.* a calker.
Kalapná, *v. n.* to be grieved, to grieve.
Kalár, *s. m.* a distiller; a seller of spirituous liquors.
Kalárin, *s. f.* female of Kalár.
Kalas, *s. m.* the spire or ornament on the top of a dome or pillar, a spire.
Kálásámp, Kálásarp, *s. m.* a very venomous black snake.
Kalaú, *s. m.* name of the fourth age.
Kalaunjí, *s. f.* the name of a medicinal seed.
Kaláwa, many colours worn round the neck in the Muharram.
Kál bas honá, to be in the hands of death.
Kál bitáná, to waste one's time, to spend time.
Kálbud, Kalbút, *s. m.* last, a mould for shoes; the human body; a figure, form.
Kálebaran, of the colour of a snake.
Kaleja, *s. m.* the liver, courage, spirit, magnanimity.
Kaleja kámpná, to be afraid, to suffer cold.
Kaleja men ḍál rakhná, to love or esteem exceedingly.
Kaleja phaṭná, to be disturbed with grief.
Kaleja par sámp phirná, to suffer jealousy or envy.
Kaleja ṭhanḍhá karná, to obtain one's wishes, to get ease.
Kaleja ulaṭná, to be fatigued with excessive vomiting.
Kaleje se lagá lená, to caress, to embrace, to love exceedingly.
Kaleje se lagá rakhná, to take great care of.
Kále kos, a great distance.
Kales, *s. m.* sickness, pain, trouble, torment.
Kaleú, Kalewá, *s. m.* stale victuals, a luncheon, a breakfast.
Kál ganwáná, to waste one's time, to spend time.
Kalghí, *s. f.* an ornament worn on the turban, a plume; the comb of a cock.
Kálí, *adj. f.* black: *s. f.* a Hindú goddess; ink, blacking; name of a fabulous snake with one hundred and ten hoods.
Kalí, *s. f.* a bud, an unblown flower; quicklime, wet lime.
Kalijug, *s. m.* the fourth or present Hindú age.

Kálik, *s. f.* blackness, soot.

Káliká, *n. prop. f.* name of the Hindú goddess.

Kálikh, *s. f.* stain, spot, soot, disgrace, stigma.

Kalima, *s. m.* the Muhammadan confession of faith.

Kalima paṛhná, to make the Muhammadan confession of faith.

Kálí mirch, *s. f.* black pepper.

Kálí miṭṭí, *s. f.* a black earth.

Kalím ul láh, the speaker with God, Moses.

Kalísa, } *s. m.* a Christian church.
Kalísiyá, }

Kálítulsí, *s. f.* the name of a plant.

Káliyá, *adj.* black (complexioned.)

Kaliyáná, *v. n.* to blossom, to bloom, to bud.

Kaliyug, *s. m.* see Kalijug.

Kálízírí, *s. f.* name of a medicine.

Kaljibhá, *adj.* malignant; whose curses prevail.

Kal ká ádmí, a puppet.

Kalkal, *s. m.* wrangling.

Kál káṭná, to waste one's time, to spend time.

Kal kí bát, news of yesterday, something that happened very lately.

Kalla } *s. m.* the head, cheek, the
Kallá, } gills (of a fish.)

Kallákár, *adj.* noisy, tumultuous.

Kalláḳhushk, lantern-jawed.

Kallápáya, the head and feet.

Kalledaráz, *adj.* talkative.

Kalledarází, *s. f.* talkativeness, loquacity.

Kalma, *s. m.* see Kalima.

Kalmakal, *s. f.* uneasiness, disquiet, distraction, trouble.

Kalmaláná, *v. n.* to fidget, to writhe.

Kalme kí unglí, *s. f.* the forefinger.

Kalmí, *s. f.* name of a creeper.

Kalol, *s. f.* wantonness, friskiness, frolic, gambol, play, sport.

Kalor. *s. f.* a heifer.

Kál paṛná, to happen a famine.

Kalsá, *s. m.* a kind of water-pot.

Kalsí, *s. f.* a water-pot. See also Kalas.

Kalwár, *s. m.* a distiller, a vender of spirituous liquors.

Kalyán. *s. m.* welfare, happiness, prosperity.

Kam, *adj.* deficient, less, little, abated, scanty, rarely, seldom.

Kám, *s. m.* business, action, act, deed, affair, occupation, work, use, employment; lust.

Kamáí, *s. f.* earnings, gains, savings, work.

Kamál, *s. m.* perfection, excellence: *adj.* complete, entire, perfect.

Kamal, *s. m.* a blanket.

Kamalwálá, *s. m.* a wearer or seller of blankets.

Kamán, *s. f.* a bow; *Eng.* command; a cannon.

Kám áná, to come into use, to be of use, to avail, to stand in stead.

Kamáná, *v. a.* to earn; to work, to perform; to clean (leather, or a privy.)

Kamán daghná, to fire (the gun.)

Kamání, *adj.* bowed, bent: *s. f.* a spring; the sticks of a paper kite; a carpenter's bow for boring.

Kamán jáná, to go on command (as soldiers.)

Kamán ke taṛke, early, morning gunfire.

Kamaql, *adj.* stupid, ignorant.

Kamaqlí, *s. f.* want of understanding, stupidity.

Kamar, *s. f.* the loins, waist.

Kamará, *s. m.* a chamber, a room, an apartment, a European's residence.

Kamar baiṭhná, to become weak.

Kamarband, *s. m.* a girdle, a zone, a waistband, a long piece of cloth girt round the loins.

Kamar bándhná, to begird, to get ready, to resolve, to be intent, to arm.

Kamarbasta, *adj.* having the loins girt, ready.

Kamar khol baiṭhná, to sit at ease.

Kamar kholná, to quit service.

Kamar mazbút karná, to undertake a work of expense.

Kamar pakaṛke uṭhná, to be weak.

Kamar rah jáná, to have a pain in the loins (from long standing, &c.)

Kámárthí, } a person who carries
Kámárthú, } baskets filled with the water of the Ganges.

Kamar ṭúṭná, to be hopeless, to be deserted by one's friends.

Kamasl, *adj.* low-bred, vile.

Kamásut, *s. m.* a journeyman, a workman, an earner.

Kámátur, *adj.* distracted with lust, libidinous, lustful.

Kamáú, *adj.* laborious.

Kambaḵht, *adj.* unfortunate, unhappy, wretch.

Kambaḵhtí, *s. f.* unfortunateness, adversity, misfortune, wretchedness, misery.

Kambal, *s. m.* a blanket.

Kam besh, more or less, thereabout.

Kám chaláná, to carry on business.

Kámchor, } a skulker.
Kamchor, }

Kám dekhná, to come into use.

Kámdew, *n. prop.* Cupid; lust.

Kam faham, *adj.* stupid.

Kam fursat, } *s. f.* want of oppor-
Kam fursatí, } tunity, leisure or ease.

Kam gher, *adj.* scanty, not full (a robe.)

Kam himmat, *adj.* spiritless, mean-spirited.

Kam honá, *v. n.* to lessen, to decrease, to abate, to fail.

Kámí, *adj.* libidinous, lustful; busy.

Kamí, *s. f.* deficiency, loss, paucity, abatement, diminution, decrease.

Kámij, *s. m. prop.* Qamíz, a shirt or shift.

Kámil, *m.* } *adj.* perfect, complete,
Kámila, *f.* } accomplished, learned.

Kamíla, *s. m.* name of a drug.

Kámin, *s. f.* a beautiful woman.

Kamína, *adj.* mean, base, ignoble, wicked, vile, of low condition, vulgar or common (person.)

Káminí, *s. f.* a beautiful woman.

Kámkáj, business, occupation.

Kámkájí, *adj.* laborious, active, alert.

Kam kam, a little, little by little.

Kam karná, *v. n.* to diminish, to lessen; to depreciate.

Kám karná, to labour, to work, to accomplish a business.

Kámkeli, amorous dalliance, coition.

Kamḵharch, *adj.* parsimonious, moderate expenditure.

Kamḵharchí, *s. f.* parsimony.

Kamḵhorák, abstemious, eating little.

Kamḵhwáb, *s. m.* silk worked with gold and silver flowers, brocade.

Kamlí, *s. f.* a small blanket.

Kammal, *s. m.* a blanket.

Kám meṉ láná, to employ, to use.

Kámná, *s. f.* desire, wish, inclination.

Kam nasíb, *adj.* unfortunate.

Kam nasíbí, *s. f.* misfortune, bad luck.

Kám nikálná, to make answer one's purpose, to accomplish one's desires.

Kam o ziyád, more or less.

Kámp, *s. f.* bamboos split very fine for making birdcages, &c.

Kampá, *s. m.* a trap to catch birds.

Kampáhá, *adj.* tremulous, fearful.

Kampáná, *v. a.* to cause to tremble, to shake, to agitate.

Kampás, a pair of compasses; a shaft for one horse.

Kampáswálá, *s. m.* a land-surveyor.

Kamphná, } *v. n.* to shiver, to
Kampná, } tremble, to quake,
Kámpná, } to shake.

Kam qadam, *adj.* slow-paced.

Kam qadr, *adj.* worthless.
Kam qímat, *adj.* low-priced, of little value.
Kam qúwat, *adj.* feeble, powerless, weak.
Kamrakh, *s. m.* the name of a fruit.
Kám rakhná, to be difficult to be done.
Kamrí, *s. f.* a small blanket: *adj.* weak in the loins (a horse.)
Kam se kam, very little, least.
Kam shauq, *adj.* indifferent.
Kam sinn, *adj.* young, prime (of life.)
Kam sukhan, *adj.* taciturn, speaking little.
Kam talásh, *adj.* scarce.
Kám tamám honá, to be finished, killed or made away with.
Kám tamám karná, to accomplish, to finish; to kill, to make away.
Kamtar, *adj.* less, least.
Kamtarín, *adj.* least, meanest.
Kamṭhá, *s. m.* a bow.
Kamtí, *s. f.* deficiency, scarcity, abatement.
Kamtí karná, to lessen, to decrease.
Kamwáná, *v. a.* to cause to work; to make one pay his debt by labour.
Kam zarf, *adj.* ignoble, vile.
Kam zát, low-bred, of low caste.
Kam zihn, forgetful, without abilities.
Kam ziyád, more or less.
Kamzor, *adj.* weak, powerless, infirm.
Kamzorí, *s. f.* weakness, infirmity, debility.
Kan, in *compos.* digging, digger: *s. m.* rice-dust; appraisment of a crop on the field, valuation.
Kán, *s. m.* the ear.
Káná, *adj.* blind of one eye, one-eyed; rotten in part (fruit, nuts, &c.)
Kanaiṭhí, Kanaiṭí, } *s. f.* pulling the ears.
Káná kanauṛá, *adj.* favoured, standing in awe of or afraid to meet another.
Kán ameṭná, to pull the ears, to chastise.
Kanán, *n. prop.* Canaan.
Káná phúsí, *s. f.* whispering.
Kanát, *s. f. prop.* Qanát, which see.
Kanauṛá. *adj.* weak, delicate. See also Káná kanauṛá.
Kanauṛá karná, to gain ascendancy over another, or to make him stand in awe.
Kanauṭhá, *s. m.* any situation in an apartment close to an angle of a wall.
Kán buchiyáná, see Kán dabáná.
Kán bhar dená, Kán bharná, } to excite dissension by tale bearing.
Kánch, *s. m.* glass; a disorder in which the intestinum rectum is prolapsed.
Kanchan, *s. m.* gold.
Khachaní, *s. f.* a dancing girl.
Kand, *s. m.* an esculent root, loaf-sugar.
Kánd, *s. m.* a section, part, division.
Kanḍá, *s. m.* dry cow-dung used for fuel.
Kán dabáná, to turn back the ears as a horse does when about to bite, to turn a deaf ear.
Kán dená, to hear, to be attentive.
Kán de sunná, to hear attentively.
Kandhá, Kándhá, } *s. m.* the shoulder.
Kándhá dená, to assist, to carry away the dead.
Kán dharná, to hear, to listen, to attend, to be attentive.
Kándú, *s. m.* a caste whose business it is to parch corn.
Kane, *postpos. m.* near, to, with, at, &c.
Kanel, *s. f.* the name of a tree.
Kanen, see Kane.
Kaneṭí, *s. f.* pulling the ears.

Kangál, *adj.* poor, friendless, needy, indigent.

Kangál bánká, } poor and proud.
Kangál bánkṛá, }

Kangálí, *adj.* see Kangál.

Kangálpaná, *s. m.* want, indigence, poverty, penury.

Ḳangan, *s. m.* an ornament for the wrist.

Kanghí, *s. f.* a comb.

Kanghí karná, to comb.

Kangná, *s. m.* a thread tied round the bridegroom's wrist.

Kangní, *s. f.* a small grain, millet; a small bracelet.

Kangojar, *s. m.* a centipede.

Kangura, } *s. m.* a pinnacle, a turret.
Kangúra, }

Kanguradár, *adj.* spired.

Kánh, }
Kanhái, } *n. prop.* the name of Krishna.
Kanhaiyá, }

Kán hiláná, to acquiesce.

Kán honá, to understand, to be warned or take example.

Kaní, *s. f.* a spark of a diamond or other gem.

Kání, *adj.* a woman blind of one eye.

Kání kauṛí, a kauṛí or shell with a hole in it; a bit of money of the lowest value (*fig.*) a farthing.

Kaniyá, *s. f.* see Kanyá.

Kaniyáná, *v. a.* to go one side, to avoid one, to dodge, to shun.

Kanjar, *s. m.* name of a caste generally employed in selling strings, making ropes, &c.

Kán jhukáná, to desire to hear.

Kánjí, *s. f.* starch, rice-water, rice-gruel, congee.

Kánjí haus, a congee-house; a pound for cattle.

Kanjús. *s. m.* a miser, a niggard.

Kanjúsí, *s. f.* } stinginess, mean-
Kanjúspaná, *s. m.* } ness, penuriousness, niggardliness.

Kankan, *s. m.* a bracelet.

Kankaní, *s. f.* piercing cold.

Kankar, *s. m.* a nodule of limestone, stone, gravel.

Kankarí, *s. f.* a small stone or pebble.

Kan karná, to appraise (a crop.)

Kankar patthar, precious stones.

Kankaṭá, *adj.* ear-cropt, earless.

Kán káṭná, to get the better of, to surpass, to outwit.

Kánkh, *s. f.* the armpit.

Kankhajúrá, *s. m.* centipede.

Kán khaṛe honá, to be alarmed.

Kankhí, *s. f.* a side glance, ogle, squint, wink.

Kankhí márná, to wink, to ogle.

Kánkhná, *v. n.* to scream (a pig.)

Kankí, *s. f.* broken rice, the scraps that fly off in pounding rice.

Kán khol dená, } to inform, to warn,
Kán kholná, } to caution.

Kankrelá, *adj.* gravelly.

Kán lagná, to get into one's confidence.

Kánmail, *s. m.* ear-wax.

Kánmailwálá, a person who picks or cleans the ears.

Kán malná, to punish, to chastise.

Kán meṉ ḍálná, } to whisper, to tell.
Kán meṉ kahná, }

Kán meṉ paṛná, to be heard (a speech.)

Kán meṉ tel ḍálke so rahná, to sleep soundly.

Kán meṉ tel ḍálná, to pretend not to hear.

Kán meṉ unglí de rahná, to stop one's ears, to turn a deaf ear to what is said.

Kanná, *s. m.* the part of a paper kite to which the string is tied.

Kán par háth dharná, to deny.

Kanpaṭí, *s. f.* the temple.

Kanphaṭá, *s. m.* a kind of Jogí or Hindú faqír with split ears.

Kán phoṛná, to make a noise.

Kán phúnkná, to tell tales; to disciple.

Káṇs, *s. f.* a kind of grass.

Kans, *n. prop.* the tyrant whom Krishna was born to destroy.

Káṇsá, *s. m.* bell-metal or white brass.

Kánsaláí, } *s. f.* name of an insect
Kansaláí, } said to get into the ear.

Káṇṭá, *s. m.* a thorn, a large nail; spur (of a cock); a fork, a pitch-fork; small goldsmith's scales; the tongue of a balance; a fish bone; pricker (of a gun); an instrument with hooks to catch hold of things under water, a drag; an enemy.

Káṇṭá boná, to prepare distress or misfortune for one's self or another.

Kanṭh, *s. m.* the windpipe, throat, voice: *adj.* by heart, by rote, committed to memory.

Kanṭhá, *s. m.* a necklace made of silver or crystal, &c., a collar.

Kanthá, *s. m.* a garment of shreds or rags worn by beggars called Gudaṛdás.

Kanṭhí, *s. f.* a short necklace of small wooden beads.

Kanṭh karná, to get by heart.

Kanṭhmálá, *s. m.* a kind of necklace of gold and jewels.

Kanṭh phúṭná, *v. n.* to be broken (the voice of a boy becoming hoarse as he approaches to puberty.)

Káṇṭí, *s. f.* a nail.

Káṇṭoṇ par ghasíṭná, to drag upon thorns, to extol or exalt one above his merits.

Kánún, *s. m prop.* Qánún, which see.

Kánúngo, *s. m.* see Qánúngo.

Kaṇwal, *s. m.* the lotus.

Kanyá, *s. f.* a girl not above ten years of age, a virgin, a daughter.

Kanyádán, the gift of a daughter or virgin in marriage.

Kapál, *s. m.* the forehead, the top of the head, the skull; fate, luck, destiny.

Kapál khulná, to have a favourable turn of fortune.

Kapál phúṭná, to be unfortunate.

Kapár, *s. m.* see Kapál.

Kapaṛ chhán karná, to strain.

Kapardhúl, *s. m.* a kind of gauze.

Kaparkúṭ, clay pounded up with rags, cotton, &c., for making crucibles, &c.

Kapás, *s. f.* cotton (undressed); the cotton plant.

Kapaṭ, *adj.* deceitful, designing, hypocritical: *s. f.* deceit, subterfuge, trick.

Kapaṭbhek, an assumed character.

Kapaṭí, *adj.* insincere, false, acting an assumed part.

Kapaṭ rúpdhárí, a hypocrite.

Kapkapí, *s. f.* shivering, trembling, quaking.

Kapná, } *s. m.* to shiver, to tremble,
Kápná, } to quake, to quiver.

Kapṛá, *s. m.* cloth, clothes, dress, habit.

Kapṛá oṛhná, } to put on clothes,
Kapṛá pahanná, } to clothe.

Kapṛe, *plur.* dress, apparel.

Kapṛe wapṛe, clothes.

Kapṛoṇ se honá, to have the menses.

Kapúr, } *s. m.* camphor.
Kápúr, }

Kapúrí, *adj.* a kind of betel leaf so called.

Kapút, *s. m.* a degenerate or villanous son.

Kapútí, *s. f.* degeneracy, villany.

Kaputr, *s. m.* see Kapút.

Kar, *s. m.* the hand; tribute, duty, custom, tax.

Kár, *s. m.* business, affair, work, labour.

Kárá, *adj.* black: *s. m.* a black snake.

Kaṛá, *adj.* stiff, hard; austere, severe, harsh, cruel: *s. m.* a ring worn on the wrists, ancles, &c.; the handle of a door, anything in the form of a ring; a link (of a chain.)

Káṛá, *s. m.* a young buffalo.

Karába, *s. m. prop.* Qarába, which see.

Karábín, *s. f. prop.* Qarábín, a carbine.

Kaṛáh, *s. m.* a shallow iron boiler (in which sugar, &c., is boiled), caldron.

Karáhí, } *s. f.* a frying-pan.
Kaṛáhí, }

Karáhná, *v. n.* to sigh and utter ah! from pain, to groan, to moan.

Karait, } *s. m.* a very venomous
Karaitá, } kind of snake.

Káraj, *s. m.* business, affair, work, profession.

Karaj, *s. m. prop.* Qarz, which see.

Karajdár, *prop.* Qarzdár, which see.

Karajdárí, *prop.* Qarzdárí, which see.

Karaj dená, *prop.* Qarz dená, to lend.

Karaj lená, } *prop.* Qarz, &c., to
Karaj mángná, } borrow.

Karaj rakhná, *prop.* Qarz rakhná, to owe.

Kárak, *s. m.* case (in grammar.)

Kaṛak, *s. f.* a crash, a crack, forked lightning.

Kaṛáká, *s. m.* the crash made by breaking anything; a rigid fast (from poverty.)

Kaṛákaṛ, *s. m.* successive crashes.

Kaṛakná, *v. n.* to lighten (forked.)

Karaknáth, *s.* name of a species of fowl whose bones are black.

Karákul, *s. m.* name of bird, a kind of heron or curlew.

Karam, *s. m.* see Karm.

Karámat, *s. f.* a miracle.

Karámát, *s. plur.* of Karámat, miracles.

Karambhog, *s. m.* fulfilling of destiny; the suffering or enjoyment of the consequences of evil or good actions.

Karamkallá, *s. m.* a cabbage.

Karamkartá, *s. m.* the superintendent of any business, a manager.

Karan, *s. m.* making, doing, cause; lace, gold or silver lace used for ornamenting caps, shoes, &c.

Káran, *s. m.* account, cause, reason.

Karáná, *v. a.* to cause to be done or made, to actuate, to effect.

Karanáe, *s f.* a kind of trumpet or clarion.

Karanhár, *s. m.* doer, maker.

Karanphúl, *s. m.* a kind of ear-ring.

Karár, *prop.* Qarár, which see.

Karárá, *adj.* hard, stiff. See Karáṛá.

Karáṛá, } *s. m.* the perpendicular
Kaṛáṛá, } bank of a river, &c.

Karár dená, *prop.* Qarár dená, which see.

Karárí, see Qarárí.

Karárnáma, see Qarárnáma.

Karaundá, *s. m.* name of a fruit.

Karbalá, *s. f.* the place where Husain son of Ạlí was killed and buried, the place where the tạziya is buried, any place where water is not procurable, a desert.

Kárbár, *s. m.* business, trade.

Kárbárí, *adj.* fit for business, active, industrious, engaged in business.

Karchhá, *s. m.* a large spoon, a ladle.

Karchhál, *s. m.* a riddle or coarse sieve.

Karchhí, *s. f.* a spoon.

Karchhul, *s. f.* an iron spoon.

Kárchob, *s. m.* embroidery.

Kárchobí, *adj.* embroidered.

Kardhaní, *s. f.* a gold or silver girdle.

Kaṛelá, *s. m.* the name of a bitter vegetable.

Karerá, *adj.* hard, stiff, vehement.

Kargah, *s. m.* a weaver's shop; the hole in the ground in which a weaver's feet play.

Káṛhá, *s. m.* a decoction, drink-diet.

Kaṛhí, *s. f.* a dish consisting of the meal of pulse dressed with sour milk.

Káṛhná, *v. a.* to draw forth (as a sword); to draw, to draw off, to skin, to take out; to delineate, to draw, to paint; to work flowers on cloth, &c.

Kaṛhúá, *s. m.* a loan, a debt.
Káṛí, *s. f.* a young buffalo.
Kárí, in *compos.* making, maker, doer: *adj.* effectual, operating, penetrating; the dish called curry.
Kaṛí, *s. f.* a rafter, a long piece of timber generally about three or four inches square; a link (of a chain), a ring used to manacle or to fetter with.
Karíb, *adv. prop.* Qaríb, which see.
Kárígar, *s. m.* an artisan, mechanic, artificer, a workman, a good expert workman.
Kárígarí, *s. f.* masterly work, good workmanship, manufacture.
Karíl, *s. m.* the name of a plant.
Karím, *adj.* bountiful, gracious, liberal; an epithet of God.
Karímí, *s. f.* grace, bounty, liberality.
Kárinda, *s. m.* a workman, a mechanic, a manager, an agent.
Káristání, *s. f.* cleverness.
Kariyá, *adj.* black.
Karjí, *adj. prop.* Qarzí, which see.
Karkaráhaṭ, *s. f.* cracking.
Kaṛkaṛáná, *v. n.* to give such a sound as oil or butter when boiling; to make a noise like the roof of a house when falling.
Kárkarda, experienced in business.
Karkas, *adj.* harsh, violent, sharp.
Karkasá, *s. f.* a termagant, a scold.
Karkhá, *s. m.* stigma, stain, blame.
Kárḳhána, *s. m.* a workshop, manufactory, arsenal, any place where public works are carried on; a great work.
Karḳhaniyá, *s. m.* a manufacturer, one who superintends a business.
Kar láná, to effect, to settle.
Karm, *s. m.* action, act, business, fortune, fate, destiny.
Kaṛmaṛ, *s. m.* a grating or cracking sound, the noise arising from a dog's gnawing a bone.
Kaṛmaṛáná, to gnaw (as a dog does a bone.)
Karmí, *adj.* doing works, a person who turns his hand to anything, ingenious.
Karm kárak, *s. m.* the accusative case.
Karná, *v. a.* to do, to make, to form, to perform, to execute, to effect, to act: *s. m.* making, doing, &c., a kind of trumpet or clarion.
Karnewálá, a maker, doer.
Karní, *s. f.* action, business; a mason's trowel.
Kárnis, *s. Eng.* a cornice.
Károbár, *s. m.* transaction, negotiation, business, concern.
Karondá, *s. m.* name of a fruit, the corinda.
Karor, Karoṛ, Kaṛoṛ, } *adj.* ten millions.
Kaṛoṛá, *s. m.* an inspector, an overseer.
Karoṛpatí, possessor of a karoṛ.
Kárpardáz, a transactor or manager, one who superintends a business.
Kárrawáí, *s. f.* carrying on of a business; temporary arrangement or work.
Kársáz, *adj.* adroit, dexterous: *s. m.* the Deity.
Kársází, *s. f.* cleverness dexterity; artifice, trick.
Karsí, *s. f.* small lumps of cow-dung.
Kartá, *s. m.* maker, author, creator; nominative (in grammar.)
Kartab, *s. m.* action, business, deed.
Kartál, *s. f.* a kind of small cymbal.
Kartár, *s. m.* the creator, maker, an author, doer.
Kártik, *s. m.* name of a Hindú month.
Kártikí, *adj.* of or relating to the month of Kártik.
Kártús, *s. m.* a cartridge.
Kartút, *s. f.* action, business.
Karúá, *s. m.* a pot with a spout.
Kaṛúá, *adj.* see Kaṛwá.
Kaṛúá kaselá, *adj.* astringent; bitter.
Karwá, Kaṛwá, } *adj.* bitter, acrid; strong virulent; churlish, snappish.

Kaṛwáhaṭ, *s. f.* bitterness.
Kaṛwá honá, to be enraged.
Kaṛwá kháná, the food that is sent for three days from relations to a family in which one of the members has died.
Kárwán, *s. m.* a caravan.
Karwáná, *v. a.* to cause to make or do.
Kárwánsará, *s. f.* a caravansera.
Kaṛwás, *s.* bitterness.
Karwaṭ, *s. f.* sideways, sleeping on the side, turning from side to side.
Kaṛwá tel, mustard-oil.
Karwaṭ karná, to turn over.
Karwaṭ lená, to turn (in bed.)
Kaṛwe kasele din, hard and cruel times.
Kás, *s. f.* a kind of grass of which rope is made.
Kasab, *s. m.* see Kasb.
Kasab karná, to play the whore.
Kasad, *s. m. prop.* Qasd, which see.
Kasáí, *s. m. prop.* Qasáí, which see.
Kasá kasáyá, *adj.* ready, prepared, tied up.
Kasála, *s. m.* affliction, distress.
Kasam, *s. f. prop.* Qasam, an oath.
Kasam dená, to adjure.
Kasam diláná, to administer an oath.
Kasam kháná, to take an oath, to swear.
Kasam khiláná, to administer an oath.
Kasáná, *v. a.* to cause to try, prove, or assay; to cause to be tightened: *v. n.* to be spoiled by standing in a metal vessel.
Kasáo, *s. m.* see Kasáwaṭ.
Kasár, *s. m.* a kind of sweetmeat.
Kasar, *s. m. prop.* Qasr, which see.
Kasar honá, see Qasr honá.
Kasar karná, see Qasr karná.
Kasar nikálná, see Qasr nikálná.
Kasar rakhná, see Qasr rakhná.
Kasaundí, *s. f.* a kind of pickle; name of a plant.
Kasauṭí, *s. f.* a touchstone.
Kasáwá, *s.* a handkerchief tied round the head on going to bed, &c.
Kasáwaṭ, *s. f.* tightness, compactness; an astringent; bad taste.
Kasáyá, *adj.* ready tied up.
Kasb, *s. m.* trade, profession, employment.
Kasbá, *s. m. prop.* Qasba, a small town.
Kasbí, *s. f.* a prostitute, a common strumpet.
Kasbíbáz, *s. m.* a whoremonger.
Kasbíbází, *s. f.* whoredom.
Kasbin, *s. f.* a prostitute, a common strumpet.
Kase kasáe, *adj.* tied up, prepared, ready.
Kaserá, *s. m.* a brazier or pewterer.
Kaserú, *s. m.* a kind of vegetable root.
Kásh, *adv.* would to God, God grant.
Káshí, *s. f.* the city of Benares.
Káshke, may it happen! God send! would!
Kashmír, Káshmír, } *n. prop.* Cashmere.
Kashmírí, Káshmírí, } *s. m.* a Cashmerian: *adj.* produced in Cashmere.
Kashmírní, Káshmírní, } *s. f.* a woman of Cashmere.
Kashṭ, *s. m.* want, penury, distress, difficulty, agony.
Káshta, cultivation.
Káshta karná, to cultivate the earth, to plough, to sow.
Kásí, *s. f.* the city of Benares.
Kásid, *s. m. prop.* Qásid, a messenger, a courier.
Kasís, *s. m.* martial vitriol, copperas or green vitriol.
Kaskut, *s. m.* bell-metal.
Kasmasáná, *v. n.* to become fatigued; to move (the body.)
Kasná, *v. a.* to tighten, to tie, to brace; to try, to assay, to prove, examine; to fry in melted butter.
Kásní, *s. f.* endive herb.
Kasrat, *s. f.* abundance, excess, the being much or many, practice, usage.

Kastúrá, s. f. an oyster.
Kastúrí, s. f. musk.
Kasúr, s. m. *prop*. Qasúr, which see.
Kaswáná, v. n. to cause to tighten, tie, bind, &c.
Káṭ, s. f. a cut, incision; sediment.
Kátá, s. m. a ḍom's knife for cutting bamboos.
Kaṭahá, *adj*. snapping, inclined to bite, snappish.
Katáí, s. f. spinning, the price paid for spinning.
Katáí karná, to spin.
Katal, s. m. *prop*. Qatl, which see.
Katal honá, *prop*. Qatl honá, which see.
Katal karná, *prop*. Qatl karná, which see.
Katáná v. a. to get spun, to cause to spin.
Kaṭáná, v. a. to cut or cause to cut.
Katanaí, s. f. spinning.
Káṭan kúṭan, parings, clippings, chips.
Kaṭáo, s. m. a kind of flowering on cloths.
Katár, s. f. *prop*. Qatár, which see.
Kaṭar, *Eng*. a cutter.
Kaṭár, s. m. a dagger, a dirk.
Katárá, s. m. a kind of sugar-cane.
Katarbyont, s. m. cutting out.
Kaṭárí, s. f. a dagger.
Katárí, s. f. sugar-cane.
Kaṭariyá, s. m. a kind of cloth with stripes in form of daggers.
Kaṭar kaṭar, s. m. the sound occasioned by eating hard substances.
Katarná, v. a. to clip, to cut, to cut out, to pare; to cut up.
Katarní, s. f. scissors.
Kaṭás, s. m. a polecat.
Kaṭásá, *adj*. inclined to bite.
Káṭ ḍálná, to cut off, to amputate.
Káṭh, s. m. wood, timber, block; a pair of stocks.
Kath, s. m. an astringent vegetable extract, which the natives eat with betel-leaf.
Kaṭh, s. m. *contract*. of Káṭh.
Kathá, s. f. a story, tale, fable, narrative.
Kaṭ'hal, Kaṭ'har, } s. m. name of a fruit and tree, the jack tree and fruit.
Káṭ'hará, s. m. a wooden cage, a railing, a palisade.
Kaṭhaut, s. m. Kaṭhautí, s. f. } a tub, a plate, a trencher, a platter.
Kaṭhbelá, s. m. name of a flower.
Kaṭhghará, s. m. a wooden cage.
Kaṭhguláb, s. m. a kind of rose.
Káṭh honá, to be petrified with astonishment; to become callous.
Káṭhí, s. f. body; scabbard; wood; a saddle.
Kaṭhin, *adj*. difficult, abstruse, hard, rigid, harsh, severe, cruel, austere.
Kaṭhin samai, s. m. a time of difficulty or distress, hard times.
Kaṭhin subháo, *adj*. cruel, inflexible, hard, severe.
Kaṭhin waqt, s. m. see Kaṭhin samai.
Káṭh kabáṛ, wooden articles.
Káṭh ká ullú, s. m. a blockhead.
Kaṭhmastá, *adj*. very stout and lusty.
Káṭh meṉ páṉw dená, to be imprisoned, to be in the stocks.
Kathná, v. a. to tell, to say, to relate, &c.
Kaṭhor, *adj*. hard, severe, relentless, cruel, callous.
Kaṭhortá, s. f. relentlessness, cruelty.
Kaṭhphoṛá, s. m. a woodpecker.
Kaṭhputlí, s. f. a puppet, a toy.
Kaṭhrá, s. m. a tub, a trough.
Kaṭhrí, s. f. a small tub, a trough.
Kaṭi, s. f. the loins, the waist.
Kátib, s. m. a writer, scribe, clerk, amanuensis.
Kátik, s. m. the name of a month.
Kátil, *prop*. Qátil, which see.
Kaṭílá, *adj*. thorny: s. m. name of a plant; land covered with underwood.
Katílá, Katírá, } s. m. a medicinal gum.

Kaṭit honá, to be cut, to be taken away (as sin.)

Kaṭiyá, s. f. an earthen milk pot, a small earthen vessel.

Kaṭkalejí, s. f. the febrifuge nut.

Káṭ karná, v. a. to wound, to cut.

Kaṭkarnj, s. f. see Kaṭkalejí.

Káṭ kháná, } v. a. to bite.
Kaṭkháná, }

Kaṭkhaná, adj. inclined to bite.

Kaṭkinádár, an under-tenant.

Káṭkúṭ, s. m. a stopping of wages or part of a demand.

Káṭkúṭ karná, to clip, to cut out, to deduct.

Kaṭmastá, adj. very stout and lusty.

Katná, v. n. to be spun.

Kátná, v. a. to spin.

Kaṭná, v. n. to be cut, to be clipped or cut off, to be spent or passed (time, life, &c.); to be abashed.

Káṭná, v. a. to cut, to clip; to bite, to corrode; to saw; to reap; to waste, to spend (the time); to pass, to travel (a road); to interrupt, to intercept.

Kaṭní, s. f. the season for cutting the grain, harvest.

Kaṭorá, } s. m. a brass bowl, a cup,
Kaṭora, } &c., of metal.

Kaṭorí, s. f. a small bowl or cup of metal.

Katrá, s. f. a kind of boat: s. m. prop. Qatra, a drop.

Kaṭrá, s. m. a street of shops.

Katráí, s. f. price paid for cutting out.

Katráke chalná, to desert one's companion, to cut the society of any one.

Katran, s. f. parings, clippings.

Katráná, v. a. to cause to clip, to cut out, to leave the high road, stealing away by by-paths, to slink away from.

Kattal, s f. a lump or chip of stone, brick, &c.

Kaṭṭar, adj. inclined or addicted to bite (a horse.)

Kaṭṭhá, s. m. a measure of capacity which differs in different places; a land measure, the twentieth part of a bíghá.

Katthá, s. m. see Kath.

Katthak, s. m. a kind of singer and dancer.

Kaṭwáná, v. a. to cause to cut.

Kaudan, adj. weak in mind, dull, stupid.

Kaul, s. m. prop. Qaul, which see.

Kaulá, s. m. a kind of orange.

Kaul karár, s. m. prop. Qaul qarár, which see.

Kaul karár karná, see Qaul qarár karná.

Kaum, s. f. prop. Qaum, which see.

Kaun, pron. who? which? what?

Kaundhá, s. m. lightning.

Kauṇlá, s. m. see Kaulá.

Kaun sá, which? what? what sort of.

Kauṇsal, Eng. council, the sitting of a court of inquiry.

Kauṇsal karná, to sit (a court of inquiry.)

Kaur, s. m. a mouthful.

Kauṛa, s. m. a shell.

Kauṛí, s. m. a small shell used as coin; money, fare, hire.

Kauṛíálá, s. m. a kind of snake.

Kauṛíwálá, s. m. a rich man.

Kausal, Eng. council. See Kauṇsal.

Kauwá, s. m. a crow.

Kauwá ṭhenṭhí, s. f. name of a flower.

Kawá, s. f. prop. Qabá, which see.

Káwá dená, v. a. to trick, to sham.

Kawáid, prop. Qawáid, which see.

Kawálá, s. m. prop. Qabála, which see.

Káwar, s. f. the baskets in which the Hindús carry about the Ganges water.

Káwarwálá, s. m. one who carries the Káwar.

Káyá, s. f. the body, appearance, person.

Káyar, *adj.* coward.

Káyasth, } *s. m.* name of a tribe of
Káyath, } Hindús, a person of the writer class.

Ke, *postpos.* of, belonging to.

Kechwá, *s. m.* an earthworm, a worm.

Kedalí, *s. f.* a plantain tree.

Keharí, *s. m.* a lion.

Kekṛá, *s. m.* a crab.

Kel, *s. f.* amorous dalliance, coition.

Kelá, *s. m.* a plantain, banana.

Keli, *s. f.* see Kel.

Kenchlí, } *s. f.* the slough or skin of
Kenchul, } a snake.

Keṇchwá, *s. m.* an earthworm, a worm.

Kendúábágh, *s. m.* a species of tiger.

Kenkṛá, *s. m.* a crab.

Keoṛá, *s. m.* the name of a flower.

Ke pás, near.

Ker, *s. m.* penis.

Keṛá, *s. m.* a sapling.

Keráyá, *s. m. prop.* Kiráya, which see.

Keráyádár, see Kiráyadár.

Kes, *s. f.* the hair of the head, a cock's comb.

Kesar, *s. f.* saffron.

Kesariyábáná, yellow or saffron-coloured dress.

Ketá, *adj.* how much? how many?

Ketáb, *s. f. prop.* Kitáb, a book

Ke taiṇ, } *postpos.* to, up to, for, on,
Ke taíṇ, } at, or denoting the objective case.

Ketakí, *s. f.* name of a flower.

Ketik, *adj.* some, a few, a little; how much? how many?

Kewal, *adv.* only, solely, peculiarly.

Kewáṇch, *s. f.* name of a creeper.

Kewár, } *s. m.* a wooden door
Kewáṛ, } which turns on a
Kewárá, } wooden pivot.

Khábar, *adj.* uneven, rugged.

Ḳhabar, *s. f.* news, information, intelligence, care.

Ḳhabardár, *adj.* careful, cautious, active, attentive; taking care, on (one's) guard; informed, acquainted: *interj.* have a care!

Ḳhabardár honá, to be on (one's) guard, to take care.

Ḳhabardárí, *s. f.* caution, care, attention, taking care, carefulness.

Ḳhabardár karná, to put on (one's) guard, to guard, to alarm.

Ḳhabar dená, *v. a.* to apprize, to inform, to acquaint, to report.

Ḳhabargír, *s.* a protector, a patron.

Ḳhabargírí, *s. f.* aid, care, protection, the taking care of a person.

Ḳhabar honá, to be informed.

Ḳhabar karná, to apprize, to inform, to acquaint, to report.

Ḳhabar lená, to accommodate, to give, to take care or notice (of), to guard, to look after, to inquire into.

Ḳhabar rakhná, *v. n.* to be informed, or acquainted.

Ḳhabís, *adj.* wicked, malignant, impure: *s. m.* an evil spirit.

Ḳhachchar, *s. m. f.* a mule: *adj.* stupid.

Khachṛá, *adj.* mongrel.

Khád, *s. f.* dung, manure: *s. m.* a pit.

Khadbadáná, *v. n.* to simmer, to make a boiling noise.

Khaḍḍá, *s. m.* pit, dimple, nick.

Khadeṛná, *v. a.* to pursue, to hunt.

Ḳhádim, *s. m.* a servant.

Khadkhadáná, *v. n.* to simmer, to make a boiling noise.

Ḳhafa, } *adj.* angry, wrathful, en-
Ḳhafá, } raged.

Ḳhafagí, *s. f.* displeasure, anger, pet.

Ḳhafaqán, *s. m.* palpitation, (a disease of the heart especially.)

Ḳhafaqání, *adj.* subject to palpitation.

Ḳhafgí, *s. f.* see Ḳhafagí.

Ḳhafíf, *adj.* light, of no weight or consequence, of light character.

Ḳhafíf honá, to be vilified, to be spoken ill of, to be put to shame, to be ashamed.

Khág, *s. m.* the horn of a rhinoceros.
Khag, *s. m.* a bird.
Khages, *s. m.* the adjutant bird.
Ḳhagína, *s. m.* a kind of dish made of eggs, an omelet.
Kháí, *s. f.* a ditch, a trench, a moat.
Khaichná, *v. a.* to pull, to draw, to tighten; to strip off, to flay; to delineate, to paint; to endure, to suffer.
Khainch, *s. f.* pulling, drawing; scarcity; a cross for lifting beams, ridge poles, &c.
Khainchákhainch, Khainchákhainchí, } *s. f.* pulling and hauling, struggle, scuffle; partiality.
Khainchátání, *s. f.* hauling, pulling and hauling; disputation, contention.
Khainch karná, to have one's own way (in argument, &c.); to stick to one's price.
Khainch khameṭ, *s. f.* struggle.
Khainch lená, to pull or draw out, to draw (as a plaster), to extract, to extort.
Khainchná, *v. a.* see Khaichná.
Khainchwáná, *v. a.* to cause to pull, draw, tighten, &c.
Ḳhair, *adj.* good, best, well: *s. f.* goodness, health, happiness.
Khairá, *s. m.* a fish like a sprat: *adj.* brown.
Ḳhairáfiyat, *s. f.* health, welfare.
Ḳhairát, *s. f.* alms, charity.
Ḳhairátí, *adj.* intended for charitable purposes, given (or to be given) or received in charity.
Ḳhairiyat, *s. f.* welfare.
Ḳhair ḳhabar, *s. f.* news.
Ḳhairḳhwáh, a friend, a well-wisher.
Ḳhairḳhwáhí, *s. f.* good-will, wishing well, friendship.
Ḳhair o áfiyat, *s. f.* health, welfare.
Ḳhaiyát, *s. m.* a tailor.
Kháj, *s. f.* the itch.
Khájá, *s. m.* name of a sweetmeat like pie-crust.
Khajáná, *s. m. prop.* Ḳhazána, which see.
Khajánchí, *s. m. prop.* Ḳhazánchí, a treasurer.
Khájlá, *s. m.* Khajlá, *s. m.* Khajlí, *s. f.* } name of a sweetmeat like pie-crust.
Khajúr, *s. m.* a date, or date tree, wild date, a kind of sweetmeat.
Khajúriyá, *s. m.* a date.
Ḳhák, *s. f.* dust, earth, ashes.
Khakár, *s. m.* phlegm.
Khakárna, *v. n.* to hawk (spit up), to hem.
Ḳhák chhánná, to labour or to exert one's self to no purpose.
Ḳhák ḍálná, to conceal a thing from which disgrace may be expected.
Khakheṛná, *v. a.* to scatter about (as fowls in search of food.)
Ḳhák hojáná, to moulder or pine away.
Khakhorná, *v. a.* to scrape, to scratch.
Ḳhákí, *adj.* earthy, earthly.
Ḳhákí anḍá, *s. m.* a wind-egg.
Ḳhák karná, *v. a.* to waste, to ruin, to demolish; to burn to ashes, to calcine.
Ḳhák meṉ miláná, to destroy, to spoil, to demolish.
Ḳhák meṉ milná, to die, to perish, to be ruined or demolished.
Ḳhák phánkná, to wander, to stray.
Ḳhákrob, *s. m.* sweeper.
Ḳháksár, *adj.* humble.
Ḳháksárí, *s. f.* humility.
Ḳhák sir par uṛáná, to lament.
Ḳhák siyáh karná, to plunder and lay waste a country, to spoil.
Khal, *s. m.* a worthless person, a malicious person; a stone mortar for grinding medicines.
Khál, *s. f.* skin, hide, bellows; rivulet.
Khálá, Khála, } *s. f.* maternal aunt, mother's sister.
Ḳhaláiq, *s. f. plur.* of Ḳhalq, men, people, creatures, the creation.
Ḳhalal, *s. m.* disturbance, confusion,

disorder, damage, injury, defect, ruin.

Ḳhalal i dimágh, *adj.* mad, hare-brained, hot-headed, brainsick.

Khalás, *adj.* free, liberated, redeemed.

Ḳhalás honá, *v. n.* to be freed, or set at liberty, to be released or discharged, to emit.

Ḳhalásí, *s. m.* a native artilleryman; a tent pitcher.

Ḳhalás karná, *v. a.* to release, to liberate, to free.

Ḳhálátí, *adj.* descended from or related to a maternal aunt.

Ḳhálátí bahin, *s. f.* a first cousin, daughter of a maternal aunt.

Ḳhálátí bhái, *s. m.* a first cousin or son of a maternal aunt.

Khalbal, *s. f.* hurry, bustle, agitation, alarm, tumult.

Khalbaláná, *v. n.* to boil, to bubble; to be agitated or tossed up and down.

Khalbalí, *s. f.* see Khalbal.

Ḳhalerá, *adj.* see Ḳhálátí.

Ḳhalerá bahin, *s. f.* see Ḳhálátí bahin.

Ḳhalerá bhái, *s. m.* see Ḳhálátí bhái.

Khalí, *s. f.* the dregs of mustard-seed, &c., after the oil is pressed out, oil-cakes.

Ḳhálí, *adj.* empty, vacant, void; pure, mere, only, unmixed; unoccupied, unemployed, without effect.

Ḳhalífa, *s. m.* a fencing master, a master wrestler; cooks, tailors, &c., are so called.

Khalíhán, *s. m.* threshing-floor.

Ḳhálí háth, *adj.* empty-handed.

Ḳhálí karná, to empty, to evacuate.

Ḳháliq, *s. m.* the Creator.

Ḳhális, *adj.* pure, genuine, unadulterated.

Ḳhálisa, *s. m.* land held immediately under government.

Khaliyán, *s. m.* a threshing-floor.

Khaliyáná, } *v. a.* to skin, to
Khál khainchná, } flay, to take the skin off.

Ḳhalḳhál, *adj.* loose (as a garment.)

Khalkhaláná, *v. n.* to boil; to rumble, to grumble (the bowels.)

Khalḷí, *s. f.* oil-cakes. See Khalí.

Khallí miṭṭí, *s. f.* chalk.

Ḳhalq, *s. f.* the creation, the world, creature, people.

Ḳhalq ul láh, God's creatures.

Khalṛá, *s. m.* skin, hide.

Khalṛí, *s. f.* skin, hide; the prepuce, foreskin.

Ḳhálú, *s. m.* husband of mother's sister.

Kham, *s. m.* a pillar, a post.

Ḳham, *adj.* twisted, crooked, coiled: *s. m.* a coil, curve, crook, crookedness.

Khamáchí, *s. f.* a bamboo lathe.

Ḳhámaqlí, folly, weak understanding.

Khambá, *s. m.* a post, a pillar.

Ḳham bajáná, *v. a.* to strike the arms previously to wrestling, &c., to challenge (as wrestlers do.)

Khambh, } *s. m.* a pillar, a post.
Khambhá, }

Ḳhamdár, *adj.* twisted, curled, bent, crooked, curved.

Ḳhámí, *s. f.* defect, fault, loss.

Khámind, *s. m. prop.* Ḳháwind, lord, master, husband.

Khámindági, } *s. f.* dominion, mas-
Khámindí, } tership, authority; kindness.

Ḳhamír, } *s. m.* leaven, whatever is
Ḳhamíra, } used to ferment.

Ḳhamírí, *adj.* leavened.

Ḳham karná, *v. a.* to curl, to coil, to crook.

Ḳham márná, *v. a.* see Ḳham bajáná.

Khamná, *v. n.* to bow, to bend.

Ḳhamosh, } *adj.* silent, dumb, si-
Ḳhámosh, } lence!

Ḳhámso, *adj. prop.* Ḳhámshob, half-washed, rinsed.

Kham ṭhokná } *v. a.* see Ḳham ba-
Ḳham ṭhonkná, } jáná.

Ḳhán, *s. m.* lord, prince, a title principally used by Paṭháns.
Khán, *s. f.* a mine; a heap, abundance.
Khan, *s. m.* story, flight of rooms.
Kháná, *v. a.* to eat, to embezzle; to suffer; to get, to hold, to contain: *s. m.* food, dinner, eating.
Ḳhána, *s. m.* house, dwelling, chamber, a drawer, partition, compartment.
Ḳhána ábád, (a benediction, meaning) may your house flourish.
Ḳhánadámád, *s. m.* a son-in-law who lives in the house of his wife's father.
Khánadárí, *s. f.* housekeeping.
Ḳhánajang, *s.* a breeder of disturbances.
Ḳhánajangí, *s. f.* intestine broils, bickering, family strife.
Ḳhánaḳharáb, *adj.* ruined.
Ḳhánaḳharábí, *s. f.* ruin.
Ḳhánaḳhudá, a mosque.
Ḳhánam, *s. f.* lady, princess.
Kháná píná, *s. m.* meat and drink, food, board, fare.
Ḳhánazád, the child of a slave.
Khánchá, *s. m.* a tray, a basket, a pannier; a hen-coop.
Khánḍ, *s. m.* part, portion, division of a house, apartment, division of the earth.
Khánḍ, *s. m.* coarse sugar.
Khánḍá, *s. m.* a sword, cutlass, a cleaver.
Khanḍá, *s. m.* piece, part, portion.
Ḳhándán, *s. m.* family, race, household.
Khanḍan, *s. m.* the refuting of an argument, confutation.
Khanḍan karná, to refute, to confute.
Ḳhandaq, *s. m.* a ditch, a trench, moat.
Khanḍar, *s. m.* a ruinous or broken-down building.
Ḳhándárí, *s. f.* housekeeping.
Khanḍ'har, *s. m.* see Khanḍar.
Khanḍit karná, to prevent, to interrupt, to refute.
Khanḍlá, *s. m.* a slice (especially of fish.)
Khánḍná, *v. a.* to excavate, to pound.
Khánehárá, *s. m.* eater, devourer.
Khangál ḍálná, } *v. a.* to wash, to rinse.
Khangálná, }
Khangar, *s. m.* semi-vitrified brick.
Ḳhángí, *s. f.* a prostitute.
Khánhárá, *s. m.* eater, devourer.
Ḳhanjar, *s. m.* a dagger.
Ḳhanjarí, *s. f.* a mode of staining silk.
Khanjarí, *s. f.* a small tambourin, a timbrel.
Khank, *adj.* weak, feeble.
Khankárná, *v. n.* to hem, to hawk, to expectorate.
Khankhanáná, *v. n.* to sound crazy (as cracked vessels.)
Khankhaṛ, *adj.* dry and crackling (as a tree); decrepit.
Khánkhar, } *s. m.* anything very dry; not well filled (as grain.)
Khankhar, }
Kháṇkhar, *s. m.* anything very dry; a skeleton.
Khankhárná, see Khankárná.
Ḳhánqáh, *s. f.* a monastery.
Kháṇṛ, *s. m.* coarse sugar.
Kháṇṛá, *s. m.* see Khánḍá.
Ḳhánsámáṇ, } *s. m.* a house steward, butler.
Ḳhansámáṇ, }
Ḳhánsámin, } *s. f.* the wife of a Ḳhánsámáṇ.
Ḳhansámin, }
Kháṇsí, *s. f.* cough.
Kháṇsná, *v. n.* to cough.
Khantí, *s. f.* a paddle for making holes in the ground.
Khapách, *s. f.* a splinter.
Khapáná, *v. a.* to destroy, to make away with; to mix things of a bad quality with better.
Khapná, *v. n.* to sell, to go off, to be expended or made away with; to mix with; to die.
Khappar, *s. m.* an earthen cup used by Jogís, the vessel in which the

blood of a victim is offered; a chafing-dish.

Khaprá, } s. m. a tile.
Khaprail, }

Khaprí, s. f. an earthern frying-pan, the bottom of a water-pot used as a frying-pan.

Khapṭá, s. m. a broken tile; a slice of mango; bones of fish.

Khaptí, adj. insane, mad.

Khar, s. f. coarse grass for thatching, straw.

Khár, s. m. saltness, barrenness (of soil); alkali, potash.

Khar, s. m. an ass.

Ḳhár, s. m. a thorn, a thistle, bramble; a spur, a cock's spur.

Khárá, adj. salt, brackish.

Khará, adj. pure, prime, best sort, genuine, honest, candid, sincere.

Khaṛá, adj. erect, upright, standing up, standing, steep, perpendicular.

Ḳharáb, adj. bad, evil, depraved, wicked; ruined, depopulated, deserted, abandoned, lost, miserable, spoiled, waste.

Ḳharáb ahwál, see Ḳharáb hál.

Ḳharábátí, s. m. a rake, a debauchee.

Ḳharáb hál, down (in circumstances), wretched, distressed.

Ḳharábí, s. f. badness, depravity, destruction, mischief, an ill or evil, wickedness, ruin, desolation, evil.

Ḳharáb karná, v. a. to deprave, spoil, corrupt, vitiate, mar, ruin, waste, depopulate, to lay waste, to desolate.

Kharábḳhasta, adj. ruined, desolated.

Ḳharach, s. m. see Ḳharch.

Ḳharachná, v. n. to expend, to spend, to sell.

Ḳharád, s. f. a lathe.

Ḳharádí, s. m. a turner.

Ḳharádná, v. a. to turn in a lathe, to turn.

Kharáhind, s. f. stink (of urine, &c.)

Khaṛá honá, to stand up, to be erect, to rise, to stand.

Kharahrá, s. m. a currycomb.

Kharáí, s. f. probity, rectitude, trustiness, honesty, candour.

Kharak, s. a cow-house or cow-shed; a pound for cattle.

Kharáká, s. m. a crashing noise.

Khaṛá karná, to raise, to station, to place, to stay or stop, to stick up, to place erect, to erect, to procure a fictitious person for some purpose.

Khaṛak jáná, to become dry (as a river); to become dear (as grain); to take warning, to be apprised.

Khaṛakná, v. n. to rustle, to rattle, to clank.

Kharanjá, s. m. masonry in which bricks are placed on their sides or ends (as in pavements, floors, arches, &c.)

Ḳhár ánkhoṉ ká, an eyesore, disagreeable.

Khaṛáṉw, s. m. pattens (wooden.)

Khaṛáṉwdár, a kind of shoes fastened to pattens.

Kharal, s. m. a stone for grinding medicine, a mortar.

Kharápan, s. m. honesty, candour, sincerity.

Khaṛá rahná, v. n. to stand, to stay, to remain standing.

Khaṛáúṉ, s. m. pattens (wooden.)

Kharb, adj. a million million.

Kharbar, s. f. sound of a horse's feet in galloping.

Khaṛbaṛáhaṭ, } s. f. tumult, uproar,
Khaṛbaṛí, } noise of horses' feet; griping on going to stool.

Kharbújá, } s. m. a musk-melon.
Kharbúza, }

Ḳharch, s. m. expenditure, spending, disbursement, outgoing.

Ḳharcha, s. m. expense, costs of lawsuits.

Ḳharchbardár, s. a servant whose office is to supply the household expenses.

Ḳharch honá, to be expended.

Ḳharchí, *s. f.* price of stupration, provision for a journey, daily expenses.

Ḳharchí murghí, a young fowl.

Ḳharch karná, to expend, disburse, spend.

Khaṛe khaṛe, *adv.* soon, immediately, presently, quickly.

Kharerá, *s. m.* an iron instrument to rub horses with, a currycomb.

Kharg, *s. f.* a sword.

Ḳhargosh, } *s. m.* a hare, a rabbit.
Ḳharhá, }

Khárí, *adj.* salt, brackish: *s. f.* oil-cake, chalk.

Kháṛí, *s. f.* a creek, a gulf.

Ḳharíd, bought: *s. f.* purchase.

Ḳharída, *adj.* purchased, bought.

Ḳharídár, *s. m. f.* a purchaser, a buyer.

Ḳharídárí, *s. f.* buying, purchasing.

Ḳharíd faroḳht, buying and selling, trade.

Ḳharíd ká mol, *s. m.* prime cost.

Ḳharídná. *v. a.* to purchase.

Ḳharíf, *s. f.* autumn, the autumnal harvest.

Ḳhárij, *adj.* being out, external, out, without, outcast.

Ḳhárij karná, to exclude, to expel, dispossess.

Kharí miṭṭí, *s. f.* chalk, pipe-clay.

Ḳhárish, } *s. f.* the itch, scab,
Ḳhárisht, } mange. [scabby.

Ḳhárishtí, *adj.* mangy, itchy,

Khariyá, *s. f.* chalk.

Kharj, *s. f.* the bass (in music.)

Khaṛká, *s. m.* doubt, apprehension; a toothpick.

Khaṛká ḍálná, *v. a.* to sell.

Kkaṛkáná, } *v. a.* to sell, to frighten
Kharkáná, } away, to put to flight.

Ḳharḳhar, purring (of a cat.)

Kharkhará, *s. m.* a currycomb; *adj.* rough.

Khaṛkhaṛáhaṭ, *s. f.* creaking, rattling, jarring (as of a door.)

Kharḳharáná, *v. n.* to snore.

Khaṛkhaṛáná, *v. a.* to rattle, to creak; to grind the teeth; to snore.

Khaṛkhaṛiyá, *s. f.* a palanquin, a litter.

Ḳharḳhar karná, to purr.

Ḳharḳhasha, *s. m.* riot, quarrelling.

Ḳharḳháwind, *s. m.* master, owner, possessor.

Khaṛmanḍal, *s. m.* wrangling.

Ḳharmast, *adj.* stupid: *s. m.* a rake, a debauchee.

Ḳharmastí, *s. f.* baseness, wickedness, viciousness.

Kharochná, } *v. a.* to scrape, to
Kharonchná, } scratch, to claw.

Kharonṭ, *s. f.* a scratch with the nail.

Kharpá, *s. m.* a sandal; a kind of sewing under the armpit.

Kharpák, *adj.* well-burnt (as tiles, bricks, &c.)

Kharrá, *s. m.* the rough draft of a letter or anything written; a sketch.

Ḳharrát, *s. f.* a turner's lathe: *s. m.* a turner.

Ḳharráṭá, *s. m.* snoring.

Ḳharráṭá márná, to snore.

Kharrátí, *s. m.* a turner: *adj.* turned.

Khaṛtal, *adj.* bad, depraved.

Kháruá, *s. m.* a coarse kind of red cloth.

Ḳhas, *s. f.* the name of a grass of the roots of which ṭaṭṭís are made.

Ḳhasam, *s. m.* a husband.

Ḳhasamwálí. *adj. f.* a woman whose husband is alive.

Ḳhashḳhash, } *s. m.* poppy-seed.
Ḳhashḳhásh, }

Ḳhásí, *s. f.* cough.

Khasí, *s. m.* a castrated goat.

Ḳhasís, *adj.* penurious, sordid, avaricious.

Khaskáná, *v. a.* to remove, to shove, to shift out of the way, to slide away, to draw back.

Khaskanṭ, *s. f.* running away.

Khaskhas, s. f. the poppy-head.
Ḳhaskhas, s. f. see Ḳhas.
Khaskhasáná, to have a tickling or itching sensation in the throat.
Khaskhas ká dána, poppy-seed.
Ḳhaslat, s. f. habit, custom; quality, mode, disposition, nature.
Khásná, v. n. to cough.
Khasoṭná, v. a. to pull the hair; to scratch.
Khasrá, s. m. a day-book, waste-book.
Ḳháss, adv. especially, peculiarly.
Ḳhássá, } adj. excellent, noble, pure,
Ḳhássa, } good, charming, delightful, pretty, nice, fine, virtuous.
Ḳhássagí, s. f. excellence.
Ḳhássbardár, s. m. a servant who in a great man's retinue carries a firelock.
Ḳhássdán, s. m. a box for keeping spices, &c., in.
Ḳhássí, adj. f. see Ḳhássá.
Ḳhássiyat, s. f. quality, innate property, attribute, natural disposition.
Ḳhássmahal, s. m. private apartment, the wife's apartment.
Ḳhássmahál, a resumption-court.
Ḳháss o ámm, noble and plebeian.
Khasta, s. m. anything fried in ghí, &c.
Kháṭ, s. f. a bedstead, a couch.
Khát, s. f. manure, dung: s. m. a pit, a subterraneous granary.
Khátá, s. m. daily account, waste-book.
Ḳhatá, s. f. a mistake, error, fault, crime.
Khaṭáí, s. f. accidity, sourness; an acid.
Khaṭáká, s. m. a crash.
Ḳhatá karná, to err, to miss, to blunder.
Khaṭakná, v. n. to rankle, to pierce (as a thorn), to pain.
Khaṭápatí, s. f. wrangling.
Ḳhatar, s. m. danger, risk.
Ḳhatarnák, adj. frightful, dangerous.
Khaṭás, s. m. a polecat; sourness, acidity. [is fastened.
Khaṭáw, s. m. a pin to which a boat
Ḳhátir, s. f. the heart, mind; account, sake, behalf.
Ḳhátirdár, adj. comforter, encourager.
Ḳhátirdárí, s. f. encouragement, comfort.
Ḳhátirdárí karná, v. a. to comfort, to encourage, to treat hospitably.
Ḳhátirjamạ, adj. collected, comforted, contented, tranquil, at ease: s. f. encouragement, confidence, content, collectedness or peace of mind.
Ḳhátirjamí, s. f. comfort, confidence, composure or ease of mind.
Ḳhátir karná, to be desirous of pleasing, to study the interest (of any one.)
Ḳhátir ḳhwáh, agreeable to one's wishes, satisfactory, the desire of one's heart.
Ḳhátir meṉ guzarná, to come into the mind, or head (an idea.)
Ḳhátir meṉ láná, to regard, to mind, to care for, to attend to.
Ḳhátir meṉ rakhná, to remember.
Ḳhátir rakhná, to agree to.
Khaṭiyá, s. f. a bedstead, a bier.
Khaṭká, s. m. apprehension, suspicion, doubt, suspense, sound of footsteps.
Khaṭkáná, v. n. to knock, to rap, to rattle (a door, &c.): s. m. rapping, thumping, rattling, (of a door, &c.)
Khaṭkhaṭ, s. f. noise, sound: adj. difficult, perplexing.
Ḳhaṭkhaṭáná, v. a. to knock, to tap, to pat, to rap.
Ḳhatm, s. m. conclusion, end: adj. done, finished.
Khaṭmal, s. m. a bug.
Ḳhatm honá, to be concluded or finished.
Khaṭmiṭhá, } s. m. a mixed taste of
Khaṭmíṭhá, } sour and sweet.

Ḳhatm karná, to conclude, finish, complete.
Ḳhatna, s. m. circumcision.
Khaṭná, v. n. to last; to sell.
Ḳhatna karná, to circumcise.
Khaṭolá, s. m. a small bedstead.
Khaṭolná, s. a cradle.
Khaṭpaṭ, s. f. jangling, wrangling, contention, quarrel.
Ḳhatra, s. m. danger, fear, risk, venture.
Khaṭrág, s. m. unnecessary work.
Ḳhatra na karná, to make no difficulty, not to fear or anticipate danger.
Khatrání, s. f. the female of Khatrí.
Ḳhatre men ḍálná, to endanger, to risk, to venture, to expose, to hazard.
Khatrí, s. m. one of the four Hindú castes, a man of the military tribe.
Ḳhatt, s. m. a letter, epistle, writing, handwriting; beard.
Khattá, s. m. a cavity in which grain is kept; a hole or pit dug for burying anything.
Khaṭṭá, adj. acid, sour.
Ḳhatt áná, to appear (the beard.)
Khaṭṭásá, adj. sourish, acid.
Khaṭṭá ság, s. m. the herb sorrel.
Ḳhatt banáná, to shave the beard.
Ḳhatt banwáná, to cause to shave the beard.
Khattí, adj. short (a beard.)
Khaṭṭik, s. m. a person who sells vegetables, fruit, &c.
Ḳhatt i kitábat, s. f. correspondence.
Ḳhatt ḳhatút, letters.
Khaṭúá, adj. stale (cooked rice.)
Khaṭwá, s. f. a bedstead.
Kháú, s. a glutton.
Ḳhauf, s. m. fear.
Ḳhauf karná, s. m. to fear.
Ḳhaufnák, adj. frightful, terrifying; frightened, afraid, terrified.
Khaulná, v. n. to boil, to be agitated by heat.
Kháúmít, adj. greedy.
Khaundálná, Khaundh ḍálná, Khaundná, } v. a. to trample, to tread, to work with the feet.
Khauṛ, s. f. the marks which Hindús make on their foreheads with sandal-wood, &c.
Khaurá, s. m. the rot (among sheep), the falling off of the hair.
Ḳháwind, Ḳháwinda, } s. m. lord, master, husband.
Ḳháwindagí, Ḳháwindí, } s. f. dominion, mastership, authority, kindness.
Kháya, s. m. testicle.
Ḳháya bardárí karná, to cringe, to fawn.
Ḳháya sahláná, to curry favour.
Ḳhazán, s. f. autumn, the falling of the leaves.
Ḳhazána, s. m. a treasury, a magazine, granary, reservoir; treasure.
Khazánchí, s. m. a treasurer, cashier.
Ḳhazánchígarí, s. f. treasureship, cash-keeping.
Khedná, v. a. to run after, to pursue, to chase, to persecute.
Kheksá, s. m. see Khiksá.
Khel, s. m. play, game, sport, fun, pastime, frolic.
Khelná, v. a. to play, to sport.
Khemkusal, s. f. health.
Khenchná, v. a. see Khaichná.
Kheoná, v. a. to row, to paddle.
Khep, s. f. a trip, a voyage.
Khep hárná, to sustain a loss on a voyage.
Khepná, v. a. to pass the time.
Kheṛí, s. f. a kind of iron or steel.
Kherí, s. f. afterbirth.
Khes, s. m. a kind of cloth; a sheet or wrapper of such cloth.
Khet, s. m. a field, a field of battle; ground.
Khet áná, to be killed.
Khet chhoṛná, v. a. to flee from the battle.
Khetí, s. f. husbandry: adj. arable.
Khetíbáṛí, s. f. husbandry, agriculture.

Khetwálá, *s. m.* a husbandman.
Khewá, *s. m.* fare, ferry-money; price of passage in a boat, passage-money.
Khewak, *s. m.* a rower, a boatman.
Khewaṭ, } *s. m.* a caste of boat-
Khewaṭiyá, } men.
Khicháw, *s. m.* drag, pull, draught, tenseness, tightness.
Khichchá, *adj.* unripe (grain.)
Khichná, *v. n.* to be pulled, to be drawn, to be extracted; to be endured.
Khíchná, *v. a.* see Khaichná.
Khichṛá, *s. m.* name of a dish made from rice, wheat and various sorts of pulse.
Khichṛí, *s. f.* the same as Khichṛá; earnest money given to dancing women when they are engaged for entertainments; a mixed heap of gold and silver coin; a barbarous mixture of two languages.
Khichwáná, *v. a.* to cause to draw, &c.
Khiḍar dená, *v. a.* to drive.
Khiḍarná, *v. a.* to pursue.
Ḳhidmat, *s. f.* service, attendance, employment, ministry, office, duty, use.
Ḳhidmatgár, *s. m.* a butler, a servant, a table servant.
Ḳhidmatgárí, *s. f.* attendance, ministry, service.
Ḳhidmatí, *s.* servant, attendant: *adj.* employed, in use.
Ḳhidmat karná, to serve, to attend, to wait on.
Khíj, *s. f.* anger, vexation, teasing.
Khijáná, *v. a.* to vex, to tease, to irritate.
Khijháná, *v. n.* to fret, to be vexed.
Khijláná, *v. a.* to vex, to tease, to irritate, to trouble: *v. n.* to get angry.
Khíjná, *v. n.* to be angry, to be vexed.
Khíkorná, } *v. a.* to scrape, to
Khikorná, } scratch, to scratch up earth, (as fowls, dogs,&c.), to scoop.
Khiksá, *s. m.* a dish made with beistings, or the milk of a cow just calved.
Khíl, *s. f.* parched rice puffed out by heat so as to appear like froth.
Ḳhiláf, *s. m.* opposition, contrariety, contrary to; falsehood, lie.
Ḳhiláf-i-ạql, contrary to reason.
Ḳhiláf-i-mizáj, not agreeing with the habit of the body (medicine.)
Ḳhiláf-i-qiyás, improbable, absurd.
Ḳhiláf-i-sharạ, illegal, unlawful.
Ḳhiláf wạda, promise-breaker.
Khiláí, } *s. f.* charge of main-
Khiláípiláí, } tenance.
Khilál, *s. m.* a toothpick.
Khiláná, *v. a.* to feed; to cause to suffer, to cause to take (an oath); to cause to play, to amuse, to play with.
Khiláṛ, *adj.* playsome; an unchaste (woman), an adulteress.
Khiláṛí, *adj.* playsome.
Ḳhilat, *s. m. f.* a dress, a robe of honour.
Ḳhilat dená, } to invest with a
Ḳhilat pahráná, } robe of honour.
Khilauná, *s. m.* a plaything, a toy, a bauble.
Khílí, *s. f.* betel-leaf made up with different ingredients.
Khil jáná, *v. n.* to blossom, to bloom, to laugh, to be delighted.
Khilkhil, *s. m.* laughter, titter, giggle.
Khilkhiláná, *v. n.* to laugh heartily; to giggle, to titter.
Khillí, *s. f.* jest, joke, humour.
Khillíbáz, *adj.* humorous, playsome, funny.
Khillíbází, *s. f.* humour, fun, play.
Khilná, *v. n.* to blow (as a flower), to bloom; to burst (as grain when parched); to be delighted; to laugh.
Khílná, *v. a.* to tack, to stitch together.
Khiloná, *s. m.* see Khilauná.
Ḳhilqat, *s. f.* the creation, people, populace, the world.
Khilwáṛ, *adj.* humorous, playful.

Ḳhilwat, *s. f.* retirement, solitude, a closet, a private conference.
Ḳhilwatḳhána, *s. m.* a place of retirement, a private apartment, closet.
Ḳhíma, *s. m.* a tent, a pavilion.
Ḳhímadoz. *s. m.* a tent-maker.
Ḳhímagáh, *s. f.* a camp.
Khinchháná, *v. a.* to cause to draw or pull; to draw, to tighten,
Khinchná, *v. n.* to be drawn, tightened; to be drawn or delineated (a picture, &c.); to be borne or suffered.
Khínchná, *v. a.* see Khaichná.
Khinchwáná, *v. a.* to cause to draw, pull or tighten, &c.; to relieve pain (by cupping, &c.)
Khinḍáná, *v. a.* to scatter.
Khinḍná, *v. n.* to be scattered.
Khindṛá, *s. m.* } a pallet, a beggar's
Khindṛí, *s. f.* } bedding.
Khingná, *s. m.* an athletic clown: *adj.* able-bodied.
Khír, *s. f.* rice-milk.
Khírá, *s. m.* a cucumber.
Ḳhiráj, *s. m.* tax, duty, revenue, tribute.
Ḳhiráj lagáná, to tax, to assess.
Khírí, *s. f.* udder-flesh.
Khiṛkí, *s.* a window, casement, wicket, back door.
Khirní, *s. f.* name of a tree and its fruit.
Khirsá, *s. m.* a dish made with beistings, or the milk of a cow just calved.
Khis, *s. m.* of inferior quality.
Khís, *s. f.* loss; grin, shrug.
Khísá, *s. m.* a pocket.
Khisak jáná, *v. n.* to slip away, to steal away, to slide.
Khisakná, *v. n.* to stir, to slip, to sheer off, to slip away.
Khisalná, *v. n.* to slip, to be inclined to a thing: *adj.* slippery.
Ḳhisára, *s. m.* } loss, damage.
Ḳhisárat, *s. f.* }
Khisárí, *s. f.* a kind of pulse.
Khisiyáhaṭ, *s. f.* vexation, fretfulness.
Khisiyáná, *v. n.* to become displeased or vexed, to be angry.
Khisiyánpat, *s. f.* vexation, fretfulness.
Khiskáná, *v. a.* to remove, to shove away.
Khiskat, *s. f. prop.* Ḳhistak, drawers, trowsers.
Khiskhisáná, *v. n.* to grind the teeth.
Khisná, *v. n.* to become old, to decline in years.
Khísná, *v. n.* to grin: *v. a.* to rule (lines.)
Khís nikálná, to grin.
Ḳhistak, *s. f.* drawers, trowsers.
Ḳhitáb, *s. m.* a title.
Ḳhiyál, *s. m.* imagination, thought, apprehension; phantom, delusion, vision, whim, chimera.
Ḳhiyálí, *adj.* fanciful, capricious, fantastical.
Ḳhiyál karná, to imagine, to fancy, to think.
Ḳhiyál paṛná, to pursue an object.
Khiyáná, *v. n.* to be worn away, to be abraded.
Ḳhiyánat, *s. f.* perfidy, treachery, knavery, embezzlement.
Ḳhizáb, *s. m.* a black tincture for the hair, beard, &c.
Ḳhizán, *s. f.* autumn, the falling of the leaves.
Ḳhizr, *n. prop.* a companion of Moses, Phineas.
Ḳho, *s. f.* habit, custom, disposition, nature.
Khoá, *s. m.* a cement for roofs of houses; milk inspissated by boiling.
Khoáná, *v. a.* to cause to lose.
Khobár, *s. m.* a pigsty.
Ḳho ḍálná, to habituate, to adopt a habit, to introduce a custom, to accustom.
Khodáná, *v. a.* to cause to dig, to cause to engrave.
Khodaniyá, *s. m.* a gardener who sells flowers, a florist.
Khodará, *adj.* pock-marked, pitted.
Khodná, *v. a.* to dig, to delve, to

hollow, to engrave, to carve, to inoculate, to vaccinate.

Ḳhogír, s. m. a saddle on which the shafts of an Ikká rest.

Ḳhogírdoz, s. m. a saddlemaker for an Ikká horse.

Khoh, s. m. a cavern, abyss, a pit.

Khoí, s. f. swollen parched rice.

Khoiyá, s. f. the dry part of sugarcane after expressing the juice, husk, skin, rind; refuse.

Khoj, s. m. search, inquiry, quest.

Ḳhoja, s. m. a eunuch.

Kho jáná, v. n. to be lost.

Khojiyá, adj. a searcher, inquirer, investigator, inquisitive.

Khoj kháj, s. f. inquiry, search.

Khoj kháj karná, } v. a. to search for,
Khojná, } to inquire after, to seek.

Khokhí, s. f. a cough.

Khokhlá, adj. hollow, excavated (as a tooth, or a tree, &c.)

Khol, s. m. a case, a sheath; hollow (as of a tree, &c.), a cavity; the body or hull of a boat or ship.

Kholáná, v. a. to cause to open, &c.

Kholanhár, s. m. opener, loosener.

Kholaṛ, s. m. hollow of a tree.

Kholná, v. a. to open, to loose, to shine, to untie, to disclose, to reveal, to uncover; to explain; to unfold, to solve, to unravel; to set sail or unmoor (a ship, &c.)

Kholṛá, s. m. hollow of a tree.

Khompá, s. m. the hair of the head braided or tied up on the top of the head.

Khoná, v. a. to loose, to part with, to waste, to squander.

Khonch, s. f. a cut or rent in cloth, &c.

Khonchá, s. m. a thrust; the clothes of women so arranged in front as to make a pocket for holding grain, &c., for food.

Khonchá khánchí, s. f. mutual wrangling or quarrelling.

Khonchá márná, to stab, to spear; to gore.

Khonchí, s. f. a present given to a barber when he goes to invite guests; part of grain which is to be parched taken as pay by the person who parches it; a small round tray.

Khonchná, v. a. to stuff in, to tuck in, to cram.

Khonḍlá, adj. toothless.

Khoṇkar, see Kholaṛ.

Khoṇkhí, s. f. cough.

Khoṇkhí áná, } v. n. to cough.
Khoṇkhná, }

Khoṇsná, v. n. to stuff, to tuck in, to thrust in, to cram.

Khoṇṭ, blemish, defect; flaw, deception.

Khoṇṭá, adj. deficient, adulterated, bad (as coin); false, deceitful: s. m. a bird's nest.

Khoṇṭá aisá bál, thick, long, dirty and uncombed hair.

Khoprá, s. m. the kernel of a cocoanut.

Khoprí, s. f. the skull, pate.

Khoprí khá jáná, v. a. to spend another's property, to weary by overmuch talk.

Ḳhosha, s. m. a cluster, bunch, an ear (of corn.)

Khosná, v. a. to tuck in, to push in, to cram.

Khoṭ, s. f. a blunder, vice, blemish, defect, fault.

Khoṭá, adj. perfidious, counterfeit, base (as coin), false, defective.

Khoṭái, s. f. } perfidy, falseness.
Khoṭápan, s. m. }

Ḳhúb, adj. good, excellent, well, beautiful, pleasant, amiable.

Ḳhúbání, s. f. an apricot.

Ḳhubar khábar, see Khábar.

Khubhná, v. a. to affect, to penetrate, to stick into; to adorn.

Ḳhúbí, s. f. beauty, goodness, excellence, pleasantness.

Khubná, *v. a.* see Khubhná.
Khúbsúrat, *adj.* beautiful, handsome.
Ḳhúbsúratí, *s. f.* beauty, handsomeness.
Ḳhud, *pron.* self.
Ḳhudá, *s. m.* God.
Ḳhúdá e taạlá, the most high God.
Ḳhudá háfiz, God (is) the protector; adieu, farewell.
Ḳhudáí, *s. f.* godhead, divinity: *adj.* divine.
Ḳhudá ká nám lená, to administer justice, to decide.
Ḳhudá kare, would to God.
Ḳhudá ḳhudá karke, with difficulty, by hook or by crook.
Khudáná, *v. a.* to cause to dig.
Ḳhudá na ḳhwásta, God forbid.
Ḳhudáparast, *adj.* God-worshipper.
Ḳhudáparastí, *s. f.* the worship of God.
Ḳhudátars, *adj.* fearing God, virtuous.
Ḳhudáwand, *s. m.* possessor, lord, master, husband.
Ḳhudáwandí, *s. f.* sovereignty, lordship, providence.
Ḳhudáwand i niạmat, a form of address to superiors; beneficent master or lord.
Ḳhud ba daulat, you, your worship, sir; ,his majesty, your majesty, your honour, &c.
Ḳhud ba ḳhud, of thine, his, &c., own accord, of itself, voluntarily.
Khuḍḍí, *s. f.* the spaces in a necessary between the little brick partitions; the space from which a tooth has fallen out or been extracted; the top of the head when the hair is shaven off.
Khuddí, *s. f.* broken rice.
Ḳhudgharaz, *adj.* selfish, self-interested, designing.
Ḳhudgharazí, *s. f.* selfishness.
Khudná, *v. n.* to be dug, to be engraved, to be carved.
Ḳhudparast, *adj.* self-conceited.
Ḳhudparastí, *s. f.* self-sufficiency, self-conceit.
Ḳhudpasand, *adj.* self-complacent, self-conceited.
Ḳhudrá, *adj.* self-conceited.
Ḳhudráí, *s. f.* self-conceit.
Khudwáná, *v. a.* to cause to delve, dig, engrave or carve.
Khujáná, *v. a.* to scratch, to rub gently with the nails, to itch.
Khujláhaṭ, *s. f.* itching, titillation.
Khujláná, *v. n.* to itch, to tickle, to scratch.
Khujlí, *s. f.* the itch.
Ḳhúk, *s. m.* a hog, swine.
Khukh, *adj.* poor.
Khuláná, *v. a.* to open or to cause to open, &c.
Ḳhulása, *s. m.* conclusion, inference, moral sum: *adj.* spacious, roomy.
Ḳhulása honá, to be manifested, to become known.
Ḳhulfa, *s. m. prop.* Ḳhurfa, purslain.
Khuliyá, *s. f.* a small earthen pot.
Khul jáná, to be opened, to become manifest, to be brought to light.
Khul khelná, to practise vice openly.
Khullá, *adj.* open.
Khulná, *v. n.* to open, to be opened, to be revealed, to be untied or unfolded, to be disclosed or uncovered, to be let loose or be loose; to be dispersed (the clouds), to clear up (the sky or rain); to blow or open (a flower.)
Ḳhulq, *s. m.* nature, quality, good disposition, civility, politeness.
Khulwáná, *v. a.* to cause to be opened.
Ḳhumár, *s. m.* sickness, headache, &c.; the effects of drinking.
Ḳhumárí, *adj.* drunken, languishing.
Ḳhumrá, *s. m.* an habitual drunkard.
Ḳhún, *s. m.* blood; murder, killing.
Ḳhúnáḳharábí, see Ḳhúnḳharába.
Ḳhúnálúda, *adj.* stained with blood, bloody.
Ḳhúncha, *s. m. a* small tray.

Khundalná, *v. a.* to trample, to tread, to beat or work with the feet.

Khundhlá, } *s. m.* hollow of a tree.
Khundlá, }

Khúndná, *v. a.* see Khaundná.

Ḳhún honá, to be assassinated or murdered, to be committed (a murder.)

Ḳhúní, *s. m. f.* a murderer: *adj.* sanguinary, bloody.

Ḳhún i jigar píná, see Ḳhún píná.

Ḳhún karná, *v. a.* to assassinate, to kill, to murder.

Khún khána, see Ḳhún píná.

Ḳhúnḳharába, *s. m.* bloody work, deeds of death.

Ḳhún píná, to forbear, to restrain one's anger.

Khuns, *s. m.* animosity, spite, rancour.

Khunsáná, *v. n.* to be angry.

Ḳhún sir chaṛhná, to be distracted by assassinating a person.

Khún sufaid karná, to be unkind.

Khúnṭ, *s. m.* a corner, an angle.

Khúnṭá, *s. m.* a tent-pin, a pin, a peg.

Khúnṭí, *s. f.* a peg, a pin; the root ends of the stalks of grain.

Ḳhunukí, *s. f.* coldness, coolness.

Khur, *s. m.* a (cloven) hoof, a hoof (in general.)

Khurachná, *v. a.* to scrape.

Ḳhúrák, } *s. f.* food, victuals, daily
Ḳhurák, } food, eatables, one meal, one dose (of medicine.)

Ḳhúrákí, } *s. f.* daily allowance of
Ḳhurákí, } food or of money to purchase it, subsistence-money.

Khuránṭ, *adj.* very old.

Ḳhurásan, *n. prop.* name of a country.

Khurchan, *s. f.* pot-scrapings.

Ḳhurda karná, to change money.

Ḳhurdaní, *s. f.* the fee given to carters besides hire.

Khurfa, *s. m.* purslain.

Khurí, *s. f.* a cloven (foot.)

Khuriyá, *s. f.* a kind of bodice in which the breast is made to protuberate.

Ḳhurjí, *s. f.* a wallet, a sack.

Khurkhurá, *adj.* rough.

Khuṛlá, *s. m.* a hole (snake's, &c.); a hen-house.

Ḳhurma, } *s. m.* a date.
Ḳhurmá, }

Khurnáṭ, *adj.* very old.

Khurpá, *s. m.* an instrument for cutting grass for horses.

Khurpí, *s. f.* a scraper, a weeding-knife, the tool with which grass is cut for horses; a shovel for cleaning out a bird cage.

Khurrá, *s. m.* a bedstead without mattress, bedding, &c.

Khusar phusar, *s.* whispering.

Ḳhúsh, *adj.* pleased, delighted, pleasant, good, willing, cheerful, guy, glad, happy, content, merry.

Ḳhúshámad, *s. f.* flattery.

Ḳhúshámadí, *s. f.* flattery: *s.* a flatterer.

Ḳhúshámadí karná, to flatter, to compliment.

Ḳhúsh áná, to be agreeable or pleasing (to); to be acceptable (to); to be delightful.

Ḳhúsháwáz, with a sweet voice.

Ḳhúshbo, *adj.* fragrant, sweet-smelling, odoriferous: *s. f.* perfume, odour.

Ḳhúshbodár, *adj.* aromatic, odoriferous, fragrant.

Ḳhúshboí, *s. f.* perfume, fragrance.

Ḳhúshbú, see Ḳhúshbo.

Ḳhúshdáman, *s. f.* mother-in-law.

Ḳhúshdil, *adj.* happy, pleased, delighted, cheerful.

Ḳhúshhál, *adj.* happy, in pleasant circumstances.

Khúsh honá, to be pleased, to rejoice.

Ḳhúshí, *s. f.* delight, pleasure, mirth, joy, gaiety, happiness, gladness; will, choice.

Khúshí ḳhúshí, } *adv.* with pleasure,
Ḳhúshí se, } cheerfully, gladly, joyfully.

Ḳhushk, *adj.* dry, withered.

Ḳhushka, *s. m.* boiled rice.
Ḳhúsh karná, to gratify, to please, to delight, to amuse, to gladden, to rejoice.
Ḳhúshḳhabarí, *s. f.* glad tidings, good news.
Ḳhúsh ḳharíd, *s. f.* paying ready money, purchasing in private sale.
Ḳhúsh ḳhatt, elegant writing.
Ḳhushkí, *s. f.* dry land; the flour sprinkled on the board, &c., on which dough is kneaded, to prevent its adhering to it.
Ḳhúshlibás, *adj.* well clad.
Ḳhúshmazá, *adj.* delicious.
Ḳhúshnawís, *adj.* writing an elegant hand, a fine penman.
Ḳhúshnumá, *adj.* pleasant to the sight; beautiful, neat, pretty.
Ḳhúsh o ḳhurram, *adj.* cheerful, gay.
Ḳhúshqitạ, *adj.* well-shaped, well arranged.
Ḳhúshrang, *adj.* pleasant in colour.
Ḳhúshrú, *adj.* beautiful.
Ḳhúshtabạ, *adj.* jocular, merry.
Ḳhúshtabạí, *s. f.* jocularity, mirth, merriment.
Ḳhúshtaqrír, *adj.* eloquent.
Ḳhúshtarásh, *adj.* well-made, elegantly cut or shaped.
Ḳhúshwaqt, *adj.* happy, pleased, delighted.
Ḳhúshwaqtí, *s. f.* happiness.
Ḳhúshzáiqa, *adj.* high-flavoured, savoury, delicious.
Khuskhusáná, to pound or bruise slightly.
Ḳhusús, } *adv.* particularly, espe-
Ḳhusúsan, } cially.
Ḳhusya, *s. m.* testicle.
Ḳhuṭái, *s. m.* perfidy, falseness.
Khuṭakná, *v. a.* to nibble.
Khuṭápá, *s. m.* perfidy, falseness.
Khuṭká, *s. m.* see Khaṭká.
Khuṭná, *v. a.* to pluck, to pick the leaves, &c., of vegetables.
Khuṭṭhí, } *s. f.* the scab of a healing
Khuṭṭí } sore.
Khuttí, *s. f.* a purse.
Ḳhwáb, *s. m.* sleep, a dream.
Ḳhwáb dekhná, to dream.
Ḳhwábḳhiyál, *s. m.* a spectre, phantom, delusion.
Ḳhwáh, in *compos.* wishing, desiring: *conj.* either, or, whether.
Ḳhwáhish, *s. f.* desire, wish, will, inclination.
Ḳhwáhish karná, to wish, to desire.
Ḳhwáhishmand, *adj.* desirous.
Ḳhwáhish rakhná, to wish, to desire.
Ḳhwáh ma ḳhwáh, } *adv.* willing or
Ḳhwáh na ḳhwáh, } not willing; nolens volens; certainly, positively, absolutely, at all events.
Ḳhwája, *s. m.* a man of distinction, a gentleman.
Ḳhwája ḳhizr, *n. prop.* a supposed prophet to whom the Muhammadans offer oblations of lamps, flowers, &c., placed on rafts and launched on the river.
Khwájasará, *s. m.* a eunuch.
Ḳhwáncha, *s. m.* a tray.
Ḳhwánda, *adj.* having the knowledge of reading and writing; read, learned.
Khwánposh, *s. m.* a cloth covering of a tray.
Ḳhwánsámán, *s. m.* a butler, a house-steward.
Ḳhwásta, *adj.* desired, wished for, having willed or wished.
Ḳhwesh, *s. m.* a kinsman, a son-in-law.
Ḳhwesh qarábát, kinsmen, relations.
Ḳhyál, *s. m.* play, sport.
Ki, *conj.* that, as, because.
Kí, *postpos. f.* of, belonging to.
Kiámat, *s. f. prop.* Qiyámat, which see.
Kích, *s. f.* dirt, mud, slime, mire.
Kíchaṛ, *s. f.* dirt, mud, slime, mire; the same also as Kichṛá.
Kichar pichar honá, to be very wet (the ground.)
Kichkicháná, *v. n.* to grind or gnash (the teeth.)

Kichṛá, *s. m.* the gummy substance that oozes from the eye.

Kichṛáná, *v. n.* to have a gummy running at the eyes; to be blear-eyed.

Kidar, } *adv.* where? whither?
Kidhar,
Kídhar,

Kidhar se, whence? from where?

Kifáyat, *s. f.* gain, profit, gain on trade; sufficiency, abundance: *adj.* cheap.

Kifáyatí, *adj.* cheap, purchased for less than its value, saving, profitable, gainful, economical.

Kifáyat karná, to save, to lower the price, to come down in price.

Kíkaṛ, *s. m.* the acacia tree.

Kikiyáná, *v. n.* to shriek, to scream.

Kíl, *s. f.* a small nail, peg, tack, wedge, a bolt, the core of a boil; the axis on which a hand-mill turns.

Kílá, *s. m. prop.* Qila, a fort.

Kíládar, see Qiladár.

Kiláf, *s. m. prop.* Khiláf, which see.

Kíl kánṭá, tools, apparatus, accoutrements.

Kilkiláná, *v. n.* to be fretful, to snap, to snarl, to be peevish.

Killí, *s. f.* a bolt.

Kílná, *v. a.* to charm a snake, so as to prevent its biting.

Kilní, *s. f.* a tick (insect that infests dogs, &c.), dog louse.

Kímá, *s. m. prop.* Qíma, minced meat.

Kímat, *s. f. prop.* Qímat, price, value.

Kímatí, *adj. prop.* Qímatí, which see.

Kímiyá, *s. m.* alchemy, chemistry.

Kímiyágar, *s. m.* a chemist, an alchemist.

Kímiyá karná, *v. a.* to work miracles; to adulterate.

Kimkwáb, } *s. m.* silk worked with
Kímkhwáb, } gold and silver flowers.

Kímukht, *s. m.* the leather of a horse or ass, shagreen.

Kímukhtí, *adj.* made of Kímukht.

Kin, *pron. interrog. plur. inflect.* whom? what?

Kína, *s. m.* malice, spite, rancour, hatred, grudge, animosity.

Kinár, *s. f.* side, margin, edge, aside.

Kinára, } *s. m.* margin, shore, coast,
Kinárá, } beach, boundary, edge, brim, hem, border.

Kinára karná, *v. a.* to abstain, to refrain, to lay aside, to keep aloof.

Kinára khainchná, to give up, to quit, to leave.

Kináre, aside, ashore.

Kináre ho jáná, to retire, to withdraw.

Kináre par, ashore.

Kinárí, *s. f.* (gold or silver) lace.

Kinchlí, *s. f.* the slough of a snake, &c.

Kingrí, *s. f.* a sort of fiddle.

Kinkiní, *s. f.* bells or tinkling ornaments.

Kinná, *v. a.* to purchase, to buy.

Kinwaiyá, *adj.* a purchaser.

Kíṛá, *s. m.* a worm, an insect, a maggot, a reptile, a snake.

Kiráe karná, to let, to hire.

Kíṛahá, *adj.* wormy, worm-eaten.

Kiran, *s. f.* the sunbeams, the rays of the sun, moon, &c.

Kiráná, } *s. m.* grocery, &c.
Kiráná chíz, }

Kiráni, *s. m.* a clerk, a writer, a person not in the first society.

Kírat, *s. f.* fame, renown.

Kiráw, *s. m.* a small pea.

Kiráya, *s. m.* hire, fare, rent.

Kiráya chaláná, to let out on hire.

Kiráyadár, a tenant, one who hires anything.

Kiráya karná, to hire, to rent.

Kiráya lená, to rent, to hire, to take on hire.

Kirch, *s. f.* a splinter.

Kíṛhá, *adj.* wormy, worm-eaten.

Kirich, *s. f.* a kind of sword.

Kiriyá, *s. f.* see Kriyá.

Kiriyá karm, see Kriyá karm.

Kiriyá kháná, *v. n.* to swear.

Kiriyá khiláná, *v. a.* to swear a person.

Kirkirá, *adj.* gritty, sandy.
Kirkiráhaṭ, *s. f.* grittiness.
Kirkiráná, *v. n.* to be gritty, to grate.
Kiṛkiṛáná, to gnash the teeth from rage.
Kirm, *s. m.* a worm.
Kirmich, *s. m.* a kind of canvas.
Kirpá, *s. f.* see Kripá.
Kirpál, *adj.* compassionate, benevolent, kind.
Kis, *pron. interrog. inflect.* whom? which? what?
Kísa, *s. m.* a purse.
Kisam, *s. f. prop.* Qism, which see.
Kisán, *s. m.* a husbandman, ploughman, peasant, farmer.
Kisárí, a kind of pulse.
Kisbat, *s. f.* the case (or bag) barbers, surgeons, &c., keep their instruments in; a piece of leather worn by a bihistí or waterman on which he rests the bag containing water.
Kisbí, *s. m.* a dyer.
Kise, *prog. interrog. sing.* to whom? to what? to which?
Kishan, *n. prop.* a name of Krishna.
Kishmish, *s. f.* currants, small dried grapes without stones.
Kishtí, *s. f.* a vessel, boat, a tray; a beggar's plate or pot.
Kishtíkárí, *s. f.* husbandry, agriculture.
Kisí, *inflect. of* Koí, some any.
Kisí ạnuwán se, | Kisí ạnwán se, | Kisí na kisí tarah se, } somehow, some way or other, some manner.
Kisí tarah, | Kisí tarah se, | Kisí taur, | Kisí taur se, } somehow, in some manner.
Kis liye, why? wherefore?
Kismat, *prop.* Qismat, *s. f.* fate, fortune.
Kismatbází, *s. f.* see Qismatbází.
Kis qadr, how much? to what degree?
Kissá, *s. m. prop.* Qissa, which see.
Kissá kahání, see Qissa kahání.
Kist, *prop.* Qist, which see.
Kis tarah, | Kis taur, } in what manner? how?
Kistbandí, *s. f.* an agreement to pay by instalments.
Kistí, *s. f.* see Kishtí.
Kistkiláf, *s. f.* see Qistk̤hiláf.
Kisú, *pron. indef.* some, any.
Kis wáste, why? wherefore? on what account? for what reason?
Kíṭ, *s. m.* an insect; the dregs of oil in a lamp, or that collected in a huqqa.
Kitá, *s. m. prop.* Qitạ, which see.
Kitáb, *s. m.* a book.
Kitábí, *adj.* of a book.
Kitábí chihrá, a long or oval face.
Kitabiyá, *s. f.* a book.
Kitábk̤hána, *s. m.* a library.
Ki taíṉ, *postpos*, to. See Ke taín.
Kitak, *adj.* see Kitek.
Kitá kitá, see Qitạ qitạ.
Kitek, | Kití, } *adj.* how much? how many?
Kitná, how many? how much? some, several.
Kitná hí, howsoever, howsoever much or many.
Kitne ek, some, some few.
Kittá, see Kitná.
Kiwánch, *s. m.* name of a plant.
Kiwáṛ, | Kiwáṛá, } *s. m.* a door which turns on a pivot.
Kiyá, *part. past.* or *s. m.* done, made, deed, act, doing.
Kiyárí, *s. f.* a bed of a garden made to facilitate irrigation.
Ko, *pron.* who? *postpos.* to, for.
Koá, *s. m.* angle or corner (of the eye); slice, division of the jack fruit; cocoon (of the silk worm.)
Kobí, *s. f.* a cabbage.
Kochná, *v. a.* to stuff, to cram, to tuck in.
Kodo, *s. m.* name of small grain.
Koelá, *s. m.* charcoal.

Koerí, } s. m. a husbandman, name
Koeṛí, } of a Hindú caste whose profession is husbandry.

Kofta, *adj*. pounded, beaten (meat), name of a dish.

Koh, *s. m.* a mountain, hill.

Kohaní, *s. f.* the elbow.

Kohistán, *s. m.* a mountainous country.

Kohní, *s. f.* the elbow.

Koí, any, anyone, anybody, someone, or, somebody.

Koí dam meṉ, soon, shortly, immediately.

Koí nahíṉ, nobody.

Koí na koí, somebody or other, some or other.

Koka'í, *s. f.* a small nail, tack.

Kokh, } *s. f.* the womb, the abdo-
Kokhá, } men.

Kokil, } *s. f.* the name of a bird, a
Kokilá, } black cuckoo.

Kol, *s. m.* a creek, a bay, a haven, a harbour, any long narrow passage; name of a tribe of mountaineers.

Kolhú, *s. m.* an oil press.

Kolhú meṉ phirwá dená, to macerate (anything) in a press, &c.

Kolú, see Kolhú.

Komal, *adj*. soft, placid, tender, mild.

Komaltá, *s. f.* softness, placidity, mildness, tenderness.

Komaltáí, *s. f.* softness.

Kompal, *s. f.* a young shoot, a bud.

Kon, }
Koná, } *s. m.* corner, angle.
Kona, }

Konadár, *adj*. cornered, angled.

Koná koní, *adv*. cornerwise, diagonally.

Konákuthrá, *s. m.* hole and corner, every corner.

Konchná, *v. a.* see Kochná.

Koṉpal, *s. f.* see Kompal.

Kop, *s. m.* rage, passion, anger.

Kopí, *adj*. passionate, rageful.

Kopin, *s. f.* a piece of cloth worn between the legs, fastened before and behind to a string tied round the waist.

Kor, *s. f.* edge, border, margin, side.

Koṛ, *s. m.* the leprosy.

Korá, *adj*. new, unused, fresh (applied chiefly to earthen vessels or paper); unbleached (cloth.)

Koṛá, *s. m.* a whip.

Koṛá karná, to whip; to reduce to obedience.

Koṛá márná, to lash.

Korán, *s. m. prop.* Qurán, the Koran.

Korbán, *prop.* Qurbán, which see.

Koṛh, *s. m.* the leprosy.

Koṛhí, *adj*. a leper; lazy.

Koṛí, *s. f.* a score, a corge, twenty: *adj*. leprous, leper; lazy.

Kormá, *s. m.* see Qorma.

Koṛná, *v. a.* to dig out, to scoop, to excavate.

Koro, *s. m.* a rafter.

Kos, *s. f.* a measure of about two miles; a piece added to the end of a sleeve, a cuff.

Kosh, *s. m.* a dictionary.

Koshish, *s. f.* endeavour, effort, attempt, application.

Koshish karná, to endeavour, to attempt, to make effort or exertion, to strive.

Kosná, *v. a.* to curse.

Koṭ, *s. m.* a fort.

Kotá, }
Kotah, } *adj*. short, little, small, brief; mean.
Kotáh, }

Kotah gardan, short-necked.

Kotáhí, *s. f.* deficiency, neglect.

Kotahqadd, *adj*. of short stature.

Kotal, *s. m.* a spare horse or pálkí which goes with a marriage company, &c.

Koṭhá, *s. m.* an upper story; a house having two stories: *adj*. on edge (the teeth.)

Koṭ hávildár, *s. m.* a pay-sergeant.

Koṭhí, *s. f.* a small (pakká) house; a small granary; dwelling, a warehouse, factory; a banking house; the chamber of a gun; the womb.

Koṭhíwál, *s. m.* a banker; a wholesale merchant.

Kothmír, *s. m.* coriander.

Koṭhrí, Koṭhṛí, } *s. f.* a room, a chamber, a closet.

Kotmír, *s. f.* a kind of greens; coriander.

Kotwál, *s. m.* the chief officer of the police (in military cantonments); a village watchman.

Kotwálí, *s. f.* the office of a Kotwál.

Kotwálí chabútara, *s. m.* a place or hall for the office of a Kotwál.

Koyal, see Kokil.

Kránί, *s. m.* see Kiránί.

Kripá, *s. f.* favour, kindness, pity, mercy, compassion, affection, bounty.

Kripánidhán, mansion of kindness, abode of mercy.

Kripásindhu, ocean of grace or mercy.

Kríṛá, *s. f.* sport, play, pastime.

Krishn, Krishna, } *n. prop.* name of a Hindú incarnation.

Krishnávatar, the incarnation of the god Vishnu, in the form of Krishna.

Krishnpachh, Krishnpakh, Krishnpaksh, } *s. m.* the dark half of a month, the fortnight during which the moon is in the wane.

Krit, *adj.* made, done, performed.

Kriyá, *s. f.* deed, an act; a verb; an oath; obsequies.

Kriyá karm, performance of obsequies.

Krodh, *s. m.* anger, passion, rage.

Krodhí, Krodhwán, } *adj.* angry, wrathful, passionate, choleric.

Krúr, *adj.* cruel, pitiless, hard-hearted, severe, harsh.

Ku, *a prepositive particle,* implying bad, ill, vile, little, mean.

Kúá, Kúáṉ, } *s. m.* a well.

Kúár, *s. m.* name of the sixth Hindú month.

Kúárá, *s. m.* an unmarried person, a bachelor.

Kúárí, Kúárí kanyá, } *s. f.* a maid, a virgin.

Kúat, *s. f. prop.* Quwat, which see.

Kub, *s. m.* a hump.

Kubachan, *s. m.* indecent or scurrilous language, obscenity.

Kubaṛ, *s. m.* a hump.

Kuber, *adj.* late.

Kubhárjá, *s. f.* a bad wife.

Kubichár, *s. m.* an unfair judgment, a wrong decision.

Kubja, Kubrá, Kubṛá, } *adj.* hump-backed.

Kúch, *s. m.* marching, march, decampment, departure.

Kuchál, *s. f.* misbehaviour, misconduct.

Kuchal ḍálná, Kuchal dená, } *v. a.* to bruise, to crush, to overlay.

Kuchálí, *adj.* ill-behaved.

Kuchalná, *v. a.* to bruise, to crush.

Kuchh, any, anything, aught, some, something, somewhat, a little.

Kuchh aur gáná, to give a false explanation, to tell a different story.

Kuchh ek, some little, some few.

Kuchh ho, whatever may happen, what may come.

Kuchh ká kuchh honá, to be entirely changed.

Kuchh nahíṉ, nothing, none.

Kuchh na kuchh, some at least.

Kuchh se kuchh honá, to be entirely changed.

Kuchh tum ne paṛá páyá, have you found a treasure?

Kúchí, *s. f.* a mason's brush, a brush for whitewashing, a brush made of the outer rind of the cocoa-nut.

Kúch karná, to march, to decamp, to depart; to die.

Kuchlá, *s. m.* a vomic nut, nux vomica.
Kúd, *s. f.* spring, jump, leap, bound.
Kudakná, *v. n.* to frisk.
Kudál, *s. m.* a hoe or kind of spade, a pickaxe or mattock.
Kudálí, *s. f.* a small mattock.
Kudáná, *v. a.* to dandle; to cause to leap.
Kudár, *s. m.* see Kudál.
Kudáyá, *s. m.* a kind of dove.
Kuḍhab, *adj.* ill-shaped, ill-mannered, ugly, rude.
Kuḍhang, *adj.* unmannerly, ill-bred, rude.
Kudin, *s. m.* an evil or unlucky day, a day of calamity.
Kudná, *v. n.* to leap, to bound, to jump, to rejoice.
Kúdná phándná, to jump about, to leap about (as for joy.)
Kúd phánd, *s. m.* see Kúd.
Kudrat, *s. f. prop.* Qudrat, which see.
Kudratí, *adj.* see Qudratí.
Kudratwálá, *s. m.* one who has power, an able man.
Kudwáná, *v. a.* to cause to dandle or [leap.
Kufr, *s. m.* infidelity.
Kufr bakná, to talk irreligiously, or in opposition to religion.
Kufristán, the land of infidelity.
Kuhásá, Kuhesá, } *s. f.* a fog, a mist.
Kuhní, *s. f.* the elbow.
Kuhrám, *s. m.* lamentation, grief.
Kuhuk, *s. f.* the notes of the kokil.
Kuhukná, *v. n.* to sound as the koyals do.
Kuját, *adj.* base, of mean extraction or bad caste, one who has lost his caste, an outcast.
Kúkar, *s. m.* a dog.
Kukarm, *s. m.* an evil action, wickedness, sin.
Kukarmí, *adj.* wicked, vicious.
Kukarmútá, *s. m.* a mushroom, a toadstool.
Kúk márná, to cry, to sob.
Kúkrí, *s. f.* a spindle of thread; Indian corn.
Kukrondá, *s. m.* name of a plant.
Kúkú, *s. m.* cooing (a dove.)
Kúkur, *s. m.* a dog.
Kul, *s. m.* family pedigree, race, household.
Kúlá, *s. m.* the joint of the hip.
Kulachhan, *s. m.* misconduct, bad temper.
Kulaf, *s. m. corrupt.* of Qulf, a padlock.
Kulang, *s. m.* a fowl of a large breed.
Kulawant, *adj.* of a good or noble family, of noble descent.
Kulawantí, *adj. f.* of pure or noble descent, a gentlewoman.
Kulboṛ, *adj.* one who disgraces his family.
Kul boṛná, *v. a.* to disgrace one's [family.
Kulbuláhaṭ, *s. f.* vermicular motion.
Kulbuláná, *v. n.* to itch, to fidget, to writhe (as a worm or snake), to grumble or rumble (the bowels.)
Kulchá, *s. m.* a kind of bread, biscuit.
Kulfat, *s. f.* trouble, vexation, distress.
Kulháṛá, *s. m.*, Kulháṛí, *s. f.* } an axe, hatchet.
Kulhiyá, *s. f.* a cup, a small round vessel.
Kúlí, *s. m. prop.* Qulí, which see.
Kulícha, *s. m.* a kind of bread, biscuit.
Kulíjan, *s. m.* name of a drug.
Kulín, *adj.* noble, of respectable descent, of good family.
Kulínái, *s. f.* nobility, gentility, respectability of descent.
Kull, *adj.* all, universal: *s. m.* sum.
Kullí, *s. f.* gargling or rinsing the mouth, washing the mouth.
Kull jama, sum total.
Kulmá, *s. m.* a sausage.
Kulpúj, the object of worship of a family, family priest.
Kultáran, *s. m.* a youth who is a credit to his family.
Kulúkh, *s. m.* a clod of earth used by Muhammadans after making urine.

Kumait, *s. m.* a bay-coloured horse.
Kumak, *s. f.* aid, assistance.
Kumbá, *s. m.* tribe, caste, family, brotherhood.
Kumhár, *s. m.* a potter.
Kumhárí, *s. f.* an insect resembling a wasp which builds its house of clay.
Kumhární, *s. f.* a potter's wife, a female potter.
Kumhláná, *v. n.* to wither, to droop, to fade, to dry up, to be blighted.
Kún, *s. f.* podex.
Kúnch, *s. m.* see Kúch.
Kúnchí, *s. f.* a mason's brush, the outer rind of a cocoa-nut used as a brush.
Kund, *adj.* blunt; stupid, slow.
Kuṇḍ, *s. m.* a pool, a well, a spring, or basin of water, especially consecrated to some holy purpose.
Kúṇḍá, *s. m.* a vessel (earthen) for kneading bread in.
Kunda, *s. m.* a block, a gunstock, a billet of wood.
Kunda chaṛháná, } to stock a gun.
Kunda lagáná, }
Kundan, *s. m.* pure gold.
Kúṇḍí, *s. f.* a stone mortar for grinding snuff, bhang, &c.
Kundí, *s. f.* the act of calendering (cloth.)
Kundí karná, to calender (cloth.)
Kuṇḍlí, *s. f.* a coil, ring, curl, hoop.
Kungṛá, *adj.* able-bodied, robust, athletic, stout.
Kunj, *s. m.* a confined place.
Kúnj, *adj.* narrow (as a lane.)
Kunjí, } *s. f.* a key.
Kúnjí, }
Kunjṛá, *s. m.* } name of a caste
Kunjṛin, *s. f.* } whose business is to sell vegetables.
Kunní, *s. f.* sawdust, small chips.
Kúnṛhá, *s. m.* name of a gourd, a pumpkin.
Kúnṛí, *s. f.* an iron bucket for drawing water; a kind of hanging lamp.

Kuṇwáṇ, *s. m.* a well.
Kuṇwár, *s. m.* the son of a rájá, a prince.
Kuṇwárá, *s. m.* an unmarried boy.
Kunwárí, *s. f.* a maiden, a virgin, a young lady fit for marriage.
Kúpairá, *adj.* unlucky.
Kuppá, *s. m.* a large leathern vessel for holding oil, ghí, &c.
Kuppá honá, to become very fat.
Kuppí, *s. f.* a small leathern bottle.
Kúṛá, *s. m.* sweepings, dirt, rubbish.
Kura, *s. m.* a globe, anything spherical.
Kurá, *s. m. prop.* Quṛa, which see.
Kurá ḍálná, see Quṛa ḍálná.
Kúṛh, *adj.* foolish, stupid, simpleton.
Kuṛhan, *s. f.* grief, sorrow, lamentation.
Kuṛháná, *v. a.* to vex, to afflict, to grieve, to displease.
Kuṛhná, *v. n.* to grieve, to mourn, to lament, to pine, to repine, to be afflicted.
Kurít, *s. f.* misconduct, bad behaviour.
Kuríz, *s. f.* moulting (of birds.)
Kuríz karná, to moult (birds.)
Kurk, *s. m. prop.* Qurq, which see.
Kurkí, *adj.* see Qurqí.
Kuṛkuṛáná, *v. n.* to cluck, to cackle (as a hen); to speak angrily, to murmur, to grumble.
Kurkuṭ, *s. f.* sweepings, rubbish.
Kuṛmá, *s. m.* tribe, caste, family, race.
Kurmí, *s. m.* a tribe of husbandmen.
Kúrní, *s. f.* a scoop.
Kursí, *s. f.* a chair, a stool, a seat, a throne; a raised foundation; the base or foot of a pillar.
Kurta, } *s. m.* a kind of tunic, a
Kurtá, } waistcoat, a jacket.
Kurthá, } *s. m.* the thrush.
Kurthan }
Kurthí, *s. f.* a kind of vetch.
Kurtí, *s. f.* a waistcoat or shirt for women, a jacket for soldiers, a coat.
Kuṛuk, *adj.* broody (a hen.)
Kurúp, *adj.* ill-formed, ugly, deformed.

Kús, *s. m.* name of a grass, the sacred grass of the Hindús.

Kusal, Kusalchhem, Kusalkhem, } *s. f.* welfare, well-being, health, prosperity, safety.

Kúsh, *s. m.* see Kús; also *improp.* for Khúsh.

Kusháda, *adj.* expansive, wide, spacious.

Kushal, *s. f.* see Kusal.

Kushtí, *s. f.* wrestling.

Kushtíbáz, a wrestler.

Kushtíbází, *s. f.* wrestling.

Kushtígír, *s. m.* a wrestler.

Kushtí karná, to wrestle, to struggle.

Kusum, *s. m.* name of a flower; safflower.

Kusúr, *s. m. prop.* Qusúr, which see.

Kusúr karná, see Qusúr karná.

Kút, *s. m.* survey, guess, appraisement, measurement (of boats), boat-toll.

Kúṭ, *s. m.* paper used to make pasteboard.

Kuṭ, *s. m.* name of a medicine.

Kutarná, *v. a.* to cut with the teeth.

Kuṭí, *s. f.* a hut.

Kuṭil, *adj.* perverse, untoward, cruel.

Kutiyá, *s. f.* a bitch.

Kutká, *s. m.* a short stick, a cudgel.

Kút karná, *v. a.* to appraise, to guess the weight or capacity of things; to measure (the tonnage of boats.)

Kuṭkí, *s. f.* see Kuṭ; also a gnat.

Kútná, *v. a.* see Kút karná.

Kúṭná, *v. a.* to pound, to beat, to bray, to macerate, to cudgel.

Kuṭná, *s. m.* a pimp.

Kuṭnáí, *s. f.* the wages of a pimp.

Kuṭnáná, *v. a.* to entice, to seduce, to inveigle, to wheedle, to coax.

Kuṭnápá, *s. m.* pimping.

Kuṭní, *s. f.* a bawd, a procuress.

Kutran, that which is gnawed or bitten off with the teeth.

Kuttá, *s. m.* a dog.

Kuṭṭan, *s. m.* a pimp.

Kuṭṭaní, *s. f.* a procuress, a go-between.

Kuṭṭan pesha, *s. m.* pimping.

Kuṭṭí, *s. f.* stalks of grain cut for fodder for cattle.

Kuttí, *s. f.* a bitch.

Kútúbkhána, *s. m.* a library.

Kuṭum, Kuṭumb, } *s. m.* kin, family, tribe, caste, relative.

Kutwál, *s. m.* see Kotwál.

Kúwat, *s. f. prop.* Qúwat, which see.

Kyá, what? how? why? whether, or.

Kyá khúb, brave, well done, how excellent!

Kyárí, *s. f.* a bed (of a garden or field) made for irrigating.

Kyúṉ, Kyoṉ, } *adv.* why? wherefore? how? well? then, because.

Kyúṉkar, Kyúṉkarke, Kyúṉke, } why? how? how, because.

Kyúṉki, *conj.* because, that.

Kyúṉ nahín, why not? certainly, surely.

Kyúṉ na ho, why not?

Kúza, *s. m.* a goglet, an earthen pot for water; a lump of sugar which has been crystallized in an earthen pot.

L

Lá, a negative or privative particle, no, by no means, without, un, ir, in, im, il.

Láb, *s. m.* see Lábh.

Lab, *s. m.* lip, brim, edge, verge, margin, shore, coast, brow (of a hill.)

Labáda, *s. m.* a kind of cloak or great coat.

Labálab, *adj.* brimful, running over.

Labár, *s. m.* a liar, a talker.

Labarkhandá, *m.* Labarkhandí, *f.* } nonsensical, mischievous, foolish, jester.

Labarsabar, Labaṛsabaṛ, } *s. m.* tittle-tattle, nonsense.

Labbá, *s. m.* kernels in fat of meat.

Labedá, *s. m.* a club or short stick.

Labeṉ lená, to shave or prune the beard of the upper lip.

Lábh, *s. m.* gain, profit, advantage, benefit, an acquisition.
Lábh karná, } to attain, to gain, to
Lábh uṭháná, } make profit.
Lab i daryá, the sea-shore, river-side.
Lablaba, *s. m.* sweetbread.
Lab lená, to shave or prune the beard of the upper lip.
Labná, *s. m.* } the pot in which táṛí
Labní, *s. f.* } is collected from the tree.
Labrá, } *s. m.* a liar, a tattler.
Labṛá, }
Labrez, *adj.* brimful, overflowing.
Lachak, *s. f.* spring, elasticity, bending.
Lachakná, *v. n.* to spring, to bend.
Lacháná, *v. a.* to bend, to bow, to crook.
Láchár, *adj.* without remedy, helpless, destitute, forlorn, poor.
Lácháragí, } *s. f.* forlornness, help-
Láchárí, } lessness.
Lachchhá, *s. m.* a bundle (of thread), a ball or skein of thread, &c.
Lachchhan, } *s. m.* sign, mark, symp-
Lachhan, } tom, feature.
Lachhman, *s. m.* name of the half-brother of Rámachandra.
Lachhmí, *s. f.* the goddess of abundance and wife of Vishnu; wealth, riches.
Lachká, *s. m.* a kind of boat; (gold or silver) lace.
Lachkáná, *v. a.* to jolt, to strain.
Lachkhháná, } *v. n.* to bend, to bow.
Lachná, }
Lád, *s. f.* a load, burden; bowels; the contents of the bowels.
Ladáná, *v. a.* to load.
Ladáo, *s. f.* a load.
Lá daʼwá, without claim or demand.
Lá dawá, remediless, incurable.
Laḍḍú, *s. m.* a kind of sweetmeat.
Ládiyá, *s. m.* a loader.
Láḍlá, *adj.* darling, dear.
Ladná, *v. n.* to be loaded, to be laden.
Ládná, *v. a.* to load, to lade, to freight.
Lád phánd, *s. f.* lading and packing.
Ládú, *adj.* accustomed to carry a load (as a bullock.)
Ladwáná, *v. a.* to cause to load or lade.
Láf, *s. f.* boasting, brag, vanity, self-praise, a lie, falsehood: *adj.* false.
Lafaj, *s. m. prop.* Lafz, a word, a saying.
Láfgo, *s.* a liar.
Láfgoí, *s. f.* telling lies.
Láf kahná, to tell a lie, to lie.
Láf márná, to boast, to bluster, to brag.
Lafz, *s. m.* a word, a saying.
Láfzan, a boaster, bragger, blusterer.
Láfzaní, *s. f.* boasting, bragging.
Lag, to, as far as, near, till, until, up to, close to, whilst, during.
Lág, *s. f.* fixing, hitching, defect, obstacle; enmity, rancour, spite, grudge; affection, love; approach.
Lagálag, *adv.* close together.
Lagá lená, to attach to one's self.
Lagám, *s. f.* a bridle, a bit.
Lagá márná, to calumniate.
Lagám dená, to bridle.
Lagán, *s. m.* stopping or making fast (a boat, &c.)
Lagan, *s. m.* affection, friendship; appointing the day of marriage; a kind of large flat dish.
Lagáná, *v. a.* to apply, to close, to attach, to join, to fix, to affix, to ascribe, to impose, to add, to plant, to set, to inflict, to shut, to spread, to fasten, to connect, to plaster, to put to work, to employ, to engage, to use, to impute, to report anything in the way of scandal or malice.
Lagáná bujháná, to excite quarrels.
Lagáo, *s. m.* relation, connexion, adherence, intercourse.
Lagá rahná, to be occupied or busy (in.)
Lagaṛná, *v. a.* to rub.
Lagat, } *s. f.* expense, costs.
Lágat, }

Lagátár, *adj.* successive, incessant.

Lagáwaṭ, *s. f.* connexion, application.

Lagbhag, *adj.* close, near, about, almost, by, thereabout, hard by.

Lag chalná, to follow closely, to court friendship.

Laggá, *s. m.* affection, attachment; a pole with which a boat is impelled.

Laggá na kháná, to be not comparable (with.)

Laggí, *s. f.* a staff, a pole with which a boat is impelled.

Lagham, *s. f.* see Lagám.

Lághar, *adj.* lean, thin, meagre.

Lághari, *s. f.* leanness, meagreness.

Lagho. *adj.* preposterous, contemptible, absurd, false.

Laghú, *adj.* short.

Laghzish, *s. f.* a slip, slipping, tumbling.

Lágit, *s. f.* expense, costs.

Láglágí, *s. f.* affection, love.

Lág lagná, to fall in love.

Lagná, *v. n.* to be applied, to apply, to begin, to be fixed, to be attached, to be close (to), to adjoin, to touch, to be employed, to be imputed, to reach, to suit, to join, to close, to be, to become, to happen, to befall, to seem, to taste, to be connected (with.)

Lag rahná, to continue without interruption, to continue fixed.

Lágú, } **Lagú**, } *adj.* desirous, adhering to.

Lagúá, *s. m.* a paramour, a tradesman with whom one always deals.

Lagwaná, *v. n.* to apply, to fix, to cause to apply, to cause to put or plant, &c.

Láh, *s. m.* lac.

Lahad, *s. f.* a place where the dead are washed.

Lahak, *s. f.* glitter, flash, glare.

Lahakná, *v. n.* to glitter, to shine; to be kindled or lighted; to burn up into a flame; to wave (as herbage before the wind.)

Lá hall, *adj.* not to be solved, abstruse, difficult, indissoluble.

Lahangá, *s. m.* a petticoat or mere skirt which is tied round the loins and extends to the feet or ground.

Lahar, *s. f.* a wave; the effect of the poison of a snake; great heat (in the bowels); a waving pattern in embroidery; emotion.

Lahásí, *s. f.* a cable-rope; a rope for fastening a boat to the shore, &c.

Lá hásil, *adj.* unproductive, profitless, abortive.

Lá haul wa lá qúwata illá bi-l-láh, there is no power or virtue but in God; *i.e.*, there is no striving against fate. It is said also to drive away evil spirits.

Lahbar, *s. m.* a kind of paroquet.

Lahesná, *v. a.* to plaster.

Láhí, *s. f.* name of a plant; a fine sort of cloth; mildew; fowls' dung.

Lahja, *prop.* Lahza, which see.

Lahkáná, *v. a.* to cause to shine or glitter; to blow up a fire.

Lahlaháná, *v. n.* to bloom, to be verdant, to flourish.

Lahná, *s. m.* outstanding debts.

Lahsan, *s. m.* garlic; a freckle.

Lahsoṛá, *s. m.* name of a fruit.

Lahú, *s. m.* blood.

Lahú luhán, *adj.* covered or besmeared with blood.

Lahza, *s. m.* moment, the twinkling of an eye; *improp.* Lajá.

Lai, absorbed (as in the Deity.)

Láí, *s. f.* parched rice mixed with coarse sugar; blight, mildew.

Lai honá, *v. n.* see Lín honá.

Lá ịláj, *adj.* incurable, without remedy.

Lạín, *adj.* accursed.

Láiq, } **Láiqa**, } *adj.* worthy, deserving, adapted, proper, fit, apposite, becoming, expedient, suitable, able, capable, qualified, decent.

Láiq honá, to deserve, to merit.

Lais, *adj.* ready, finished.

Láj, *s.f.* bashfulness, modesty, shame.
Lajálú. *s. m.* the name of a kind of sensitive plant.
Lajáná, *v. n.* to be ashamed or abashed, to blush.
Lá jawáb, *adv.* incapable of answering, silenced, speechless, disconcerted, confuted.
Lájhá, *s. m.* viscosity, glutinousness.
Lajiyáná, *v. n.* to be abashed, to be ashamed, to blush.
Lajjá, *s. f.* bashfulness, modesty, shame.
Lajjámán, *adj.* ashamed, abashed.
Lajjat, *prop.* Lazzat, which see.
Lajjit, *adj.* ashamed, abashed.
Lájubán, *prop.* Lázabán, which see.
Lajwáná, *v. a.* to shame, to cause to blush, to put to shame.
Lajwant, *adj.* modest, bashful, chaste, decent.
Lák, *adj.* a hundred thousand: *s. m.* sealing-wax.
Lak, *adj.* a hundred thousand.
Lá kalám, *adj.* doubtless, unquestionably: *adv.* necessarily, certainly.
Lakaṛ, *s. m.* wood; a large piece of timber, a cudgel.
Lakaṛbáz, a cudgel-player.
Lakaṛbází, *s. f.* cudgel playing, fencing.
Lakaṛhárá, *s. m.* a wood-cutter, a seller of wood, wood-monger.
Lákh, *s. m.* gum lac, sealing-wax: *adj.* a hundred thousand.
Lakhá, *s. plur.* of Lák, hundreds of thousands.
Lákhá, *s. m.* lac, a red dye.
Lakhái dená, *v. n.* to appear, to be in sight.
Laḳharáj, *adj.* exempt from assessment, rent free.
Lakhat, *prop.* Laḳht, which see.
Lakhauṭá, *adj.* besmeared with lac of pán.
Lakhauṭá karná, to smear with lac; to glaze (earthen vessels.)
Lákhí, *s. f.* a red colour procured from lac.
Lákh kí battí, a stick of sealing-wax.
Lákh lagáná, *v. a.* to shut up or conceal.
Lakhlakháná, *v. n.* to gasp or pant from heat or thirst (as birds.)
Lakhná, *v. a.* to see, to look at, to behold, to appear.
Lakhnau, *n. prop.* a city in Oude.
Lakhpatí, *adj.* rich; a millionaire.
Laḳht, *s. m.* a piece, bit, plank.
Lákin, *conj.* but, yet, however.
Lakír, *s. f.* a line, lineament, streak.
Lak lak karná, *v. n.* to glitter, to shine.
Lakpatí, *adj.* rich; a millionaire.
Lakṛá, *s. m.* a large piece of wood; a hyena.
Lakṛí, *s. f.* wood, timber; a staff, stick: *adj.* stiff, emaciated.
Lakshmí, *s. f.* the goddess of abundance and the wife of Vishnu; fortune, &c.
Laḷ, *s. m.* a ruby.
Lál, *adj.* red; inflamed; red hot (as iron); darling, dear: *s. m.* an infant boy, a son; the name of a small bird; a ruby.
Lálá, *s. m.* a schoolmaster; the name of a herb; a head servant, a major-domo.
Lalá, *s. m.* a boy.
Lála, *s. m.* a tulip.
Lálach, *s. m.* covetousness, greediness, longing, avarice.
Lálach karná, to covet, to long for.
Lála paṛná, to be scanty (water, food, &c.)
Laláṛ, *s.m.* the forehead; fate, destiny.
Lála rang, *adj.* tulip-coloured.
Laláṭ, see Laláṛ.
Lálbujhakkaṛ, a prognosticator.
Lalcháná, *v. a.* to excite desire, covet: *v. n.* to be tantalized, long.
Lálchí, *adj.* covetous, interested, selfish, greedy, avaricious.

Lále paṛná, to be scanty (water, food, &c.)
Lalgaṇḍá, *s. m.* a monkey.
Lalí, *s. f.* a girl.
Lálí, *s. f.* redness, ruddiness.
Lál kaddú, *s. m.* a kind of pumpion.
Lalkáná, *v. a.* to excite quarrels, to set on to fight.
Lalkár, *s. f.* call, bawl, challenge.
Lalkárná, *v. a.* to call, to bawl after, to challenge, to set up the war whoop, to bawl out insultingly.
Lallo patí, *s. f.* } wheedling, coaxing,
Lallo patto, *s. m.* } flattering, &c.
Lál mirch, *s. f.* capsicum or red pepper.
Lálṛí, *s. f.* a kind of ruby; a false stone resembling a ruby.
Lalsá, } *s. f.* ardent desire.
Lálsá, }
Lál ság, *s. m.* a kind of greens.
Lám, *s. m.* a division of an army, a brigade.
Lambá, *adj.* long, tall.
Lambáí, *s. f.* length, height.
Lambáí chauṛáí, *s. f.* size, length and breadth; pomp, glory, pride.
Lambá karná, *v. a.* to lengthen, to extend.
Lambán, *s. m. f.* length, tallness.
Lambar, *s. m.* *Eng.* number; an English yard.
Lambí, *adj. f.* long, tall; a kind of bounding pace in a horse.
Lambí sáṇs bharní, to regret, to lament.
Lamboṭ, *s. m.* a longboat, ship's boat.
Lamchhaṛ, } *adj.* tall, long.
Lamchhaṛá. }
Lamḍor, *s. f.* a fishing line.
Lamha, *s. m.* a moment, minute, a glance or twinkling of an eye.
Lamha lamha, every moment, constantly, perpetually.
Lám káf kahná, to abuse, to give abuse.
Lamkáná, *v. n.* to stretch out the hands to take anything.

Lampaṭ, *adj.* false, lying, adulterous, dissolute, libertine.
Lạn, *s. f.* cursing, imprecating.
Láná, *v. n.* to bring; to adduce, to introduce, to persuade; to breed, to produce.
Lạnat, *s. f.* an imprecation, curse, anathema, execration.
Lạnatí, *adj.* cursed, execrable.
Lạnat karná, to curse, to imprecate.
Lanḍ, *s. m.* penis.
Lanḍúrá, *adj.* tailless, docked; (a person) without friends, forlorn.
Lang, *s. m.* lameness: *adj.* lame.
Langar, *s. m.* an anchor; an almshouse; victuals given to the poor; tacking (in sewing.)
Langar ḍálná, } to cast anchor.
Langar karná, }
Langarḳhána, *s. m.* an almshouse, a house were the poor are provided with food.
Langaṛná, *v. n.* to limp, to walk lame.
Langar par honá, to be at anchor.
Langar uṭháná, to weigh anchor.
Langhan paṛná, to catch (as a disorder.)
Langhná, *v. n.* to be jumped over, to pass: *v. a.* to jump or leap over.
Lánghná, *v. a.* to leap or jump over.
Lang kháná, } *v. n.* to halt, to limp,
Lang márná, } to be lame.
Langoṭ, } *s. m.* a cloth worn be-
Langoṭá, } tween the legs to conceal the privities.
Langoṭband, a bandage to which the langoṭ is fastened.
Langoṭí, *s. f.* see Langoṭ.
Langoṭiyá yár, *s. m.* an old friend (from childhood), a very intimate friend.
Langṛá, *adj.* lame, cripple.
Langṛáí, *s. f.* lameness.
Langṛáná, *v. n.* to limp.
Langúr, *s. m.* a baboon, a monkey.
Lanká, *n. prop.* Ceylon.
Lạn tạn, *s. f.* cursing and taunting.
Lantaráni, *s. f.* boasting, airs, conceitedness.

Láo, *imper. plur.* of Láná, bring.
Láo lashkar, *s. m.* an army.
Lap, *s. f.* handful, the space in the palm of the hand closed so as to hold water.
Lapak, *s. f.* a flash (of lightning, &c.); the spring (of a tiger, &c.), bound, a snatch.
Lapakná, *v. n.* to flash (as lightning, &c.), to attack, to spring or rush forth or upon, to make haste, to run, to snatch.
Lapaṭ, *s. f.* odour.
Lapáṭí, *s. f.* lying, tattling.
Lapáṭiyá, *s. m.* a tattler, a liar.
Lapaṭná, *v. n.* to cling; to stick, to adhere together, to cleave to.
Lapeṭ, *s. f.* a fold; girt, circumference, deception.
Lapeṭná, *v. a.* to wrap up, to fold, to enclose, to roll, to pack.
Lapeṭwán, *adj.* ornamented with gold or silver thread wound round it.
Lapjhap, *adj.* nimble, quick, fast.
Lapkáná, *v. a.* to stretch out the hands to take anything.
Lap lap, *adj.* nimble, quick.
Lap lap kháná, to eat quickly.
Lappá, *s. m.* brocade, gold or silver cloth.
Lapsí, *s. f.* a glutinous kind of food, pottage, pap, spoonmeat.
Lapṭáná, *v. n.* see Lapaṭná.
Laqab, *s. m.* a title, surname, nickname.
Laqlaqa, *s. m.* pronunciation.
Laqqá, *s. m.* a kind of pigeon.
Laqwa, *s. m.* a spasmodic distortion of the face.
Laṛ, *s. f.* a string (of pearls, &c.), a thread, a row; a strand of a rope or cord; a party.
Lár, *s. m.* slaver, spittle.
Láṛ, *s. m.* lovingness, coaxing, caress, playfulness of a child.
Laṛá, *s. m.* see Laṛ.
Laṛáí, *s. f.* battle, quarrel, war, fight, fighting.
Laṛáí karná, to war, to fight, to quarrel, to wrangle.
Laṛák, Laṛáká, } *adj.* quarrelsome, fighter.
Laṛakbuddhi, *s. f.* childishness, the wisdom of a child.
Laṛakpan, *s. m.* childhood, childishness.
Laṛálaṛí, *s. f.* mutual quarrelling.
Laṛáná, *v. a.* to make fight, to fight.
Laṛánká, *adj.* quarrelsome, fighter.
Laṛant, *s. f.* fighting, contending.
Larazná, *v. n.* to shake, to quiver, to tremble, quake, totter.
Laṛbaṛáná, *v. n.* to stutter, to stammer, to stagger, to reel.
Larchhá, *s. m.* a skein.
Laṛhá, *s. m.* a cart.
Laṛhí, Laṛhiyá, } *s. f.* a small cart.
Laṛí, *s. f.* a string (of pearls, &c.)
Laṛiyáná, *v. a.* to thread, to string.
Laṛká, *s. m.* a boy, child, infant, babe.
Laṛká bálá, *s. m.* a child, children.
Laṛkáí, *s. f.* childhood, boyhood.
Laṛká laṛkí, *s.* boys and girls, children.
Laṛkápan, Laṛkápaná, } *s. m.* childhood, boyhood.
Laṛkharáná, Larkhaṛáná, } *v. n.* to stagger, to trip, to stutter, to stammer.
Laṛkí, *s. f.* a girl.
Láṛlá, *adj.* darling, dear.
Laṛ meṉ rahná, to be in one's party.
Laṛná, *v. n.* to fight, to quarrel, to contend, to battle, to war.
Laṛwaiyá, *adj.* fond of fighting: *s. m.* a fighter.
Larza, *s. m.* shaking, shivering, tremor; an earthquake.
Larzáná, *v. a.* to shake, to cause to shake, quiver, tremble, &c.
Las, *s. m.* tenacity, glutinousness. clamminess.
Lásá, *s. m.* anything clammy or glutinous, the milk of plants; birdlime.
Lásání, *adj.* incomparable.

Lasdár, *adj*. viscous, glutinous, clammy.

Lásh, *s. f.* a dead body, corpse, carcass.

Lashkar, *s. m.* an army.

Lashkarí, *adj*. belonging to an army, military : *s. m.* a soldier.

Lashṭam pashṭam, *adj*. with difficulty ; with much ado.

Lasiyáná, *v. n.* to be viscous, to be clammy.

Laslasá, *adj*. viscous, clammy, glutinous, adhesive.

Laslasáná, *v. n.* to be clammy or glutinous, to agglutinate.

Lasoṛá, *s. m.* name of a glutinous fruit.

Lassán, *adj*. eloquent.

Lassí, *s. f.* a running sore.

Lásukhan, *s. m.* abuse, improper talk.

Lasún, *s. m.* garlic.

Lat, *s. f.* bad habits, whim ; in *compos. contract.* of Lát, a kick : *s. f.* the hanging branch of a creeper.

Lát, *s. f.* a kick.

Laṭ, *s. f.* tangled hair, a clotted lock.

Láṭ, *s. f.* an obelisk, a pillar.

Látá, *s. m.* a kind of cheap food.

Latá, *s. f.* a creeper, a vine.

Latáfat, *s. f.* deliciousness, pleasantness, facetiousness, wit.

Laṭáí, *s. f.* a kind of roller on which the string of a kite is wound.

Lataif, *pl.* pleasantries.

Laṭakná, *v. n.* to hang, to dangle.

Laṭár, *s. m.* a kick.

Latar, *s. f.* a creeper, a vine.

Laṭárná, *v. a.* to tread down, to affront, to insult.

Láṭh, *s. f.* an obelisk, a club or staff; the vertical part of an oil mill, a machine for drawing water.

Laṭh, *s. m.* a stick, club, cudgel.

Láṭhá, *s. m.* a machine for drawing water ; a large club or stick.

Laṭhá, *s. m.* a beam, a post.

Laṭhálaṭham, *s. m.*
Laṭhálaṭhí, *s. f.*
Láṭháláṭhí, *s. f.*
} mutual beating with cudgels.

Latharná, *v. n.* to be draggled.

Lathárná, *v. a.* to draggle or besmear with dirt.

Laṭhbáz, *s. m.* a cudgeller, a person who thrashes people with a stick.

Laṭhbází, *s. f.* cudgelling.

Latheṛná, *v. a.* see Lathárná.

Láṭhí, *s. f.* a staff, club, stick, crutch.

Láṭhípáṭhí, *s. f.* beating with sticks, a club or stick.

Laṭhiyáná, *v. a.* to belabour, to cudgel.

Laṭhmár, see Laṭhbáz.

Laṭhpaṭh, *adj*. wet, soaked.

Latíf, *adj*. elegant, agreeable, kind, courteous, minute, subtile, fine, delicious, exquisite, witty, facetious.

Latífa, *s. m.* a pleasantry, jest, joke, raillery, elegance.

Latífago, a facetious person, a jester : *adj*. witty.

Latiyá, *adj*. a person of bad habits.

Latiyáná, *v. a.* to kick, to beat.

Laṭ jáná, to become entangled.

Laṭká, *s. m.* incantation : *adj*. hung, suspended.

Laṭkan, *s. m.* anything hanging, a hanging lamp; drops worn in the ears, a pendant; the drops of a crystal lustre; clapper (of a bell.)

Laṭkáná, *v. a.* to hang, to dangle, to append, to suspend.

Laṭkáo, *s. m.* suspension, hanging.

Latkhor, *adj*. kicked, beaten.

Latmardan karná, *v. a.* to trample, to tread on.

Latmardan meṉ paṛná, to be trampled under foot or disgraced.

Lát márná, *v. a.* to kick.

Laṭpaṭ, *adj*. staggering, tripping, tangled; folded, tangled.

Laṭpaṭáná, *v. n.* to stagger, to trip.

Latráhá, *adj*. kicking (a horse.)

Lattá, *s. m.* a rag, a scrap of cloth.

Laṭṭhá, *s. m.* a beam, timber.

Lattí, *s. f.* a skein; a kick when swimming.

Laṭṭú, *s. m.* a child's top.

Laṭṭúdár pagṛí, a kind of turban.
Laṭṭú honá, *v. n.* to fall in love.
Latzada, *adj.* of bad habits.
Lau, *s. f.* the flame of a candle, any pointed flame; desire, wish.
Lauh, *s. m.* a plank, a table; a board or table on which anything is written.
Lau honá, see Lín honá.
Lauká, *s. m.* } a kind of pompion.
Laukí, *s. f.* }
Laukik, *adj.* ceremonial, ceremonious; mundane, worldly.
Lauknä, *v. n.* to shine, glitter, lighten, to become visible, to be seen from a distance.
Lau lagáná, to be constant in prayer, [devotion, &c.
Lau lagná, to have a constant desire or craving (for anything.)
Lauṇ, till, to, up to; a hot wind.
Launá, *v. a.* to reap.
Laund, *s. m.* an intercalary month.
Launḍá, *s. m.* a boy, a slave boy, lad, brat.
Launḍábáz, *s. m.* a sodomite.
Launḍábází, *s. f.* sodomy.
Launḍbáz, *s. m.* a sodomite.
Launḍbází, *s. f.* sodomy.
Launḍí, } *s. f.* a girl, a slave girl,
Launḍiyá, } a servant girl.
Laung, *s. f.* a clove.
Launí, *s. f.* wages in kind to reapers in harvest time.
Lauṛá, *s. m.* membrum verile.
Laus, *s. m. Eng.* gold or silver lace.
Lauṭ, *s. m.* turning over, inverting, returning.
Lauṭáná, *v. a.* to turn over, invert, to turn back, to return, to give back.
Lauṭhá, *s. m.* a young man; an acquaintance.
Lauṭ jáná, to return.
Lauṭná, *v. n.* to turn over; to turn back, to return.
Láw, *s. m.* a rope, the cable of a boat.
Láwá, *s. m.* parched and puffed grain.
Láwalad, *adj.* without offspring, childless.
Láwaná, *v. a.* to bring.
Láwáris, *adj.* friendless, one whose friends are all dead; without an owner or heirs.
Láwárisí, *adj.* without an owner.
Láwáris mál, property to which there is no heir.
Lawázim, } *s. m.* necessary things,
Lawázima, } requisites, baggage.
Lázabán, *adj.* abusive, improper talk; silent, speechless.
Lázim, *adj.* incumbent (on), necessary, requisite, urgent, suitable, proper, expedient, indispensable, meet, fit.
Lazíz, *adj.* delicious, luscious, savoury, nice.
Lázubán, see Lázabán.
Lazzat, *s. f.* pleasure, enjoyment, delight, flavour, taste, savour, deliciousness.
Le, having taken, taking; till, to,
Le áná, *v. n.* to bring, to fetch.
Le bhágná, to run away with.
Le chalná, to take away or along, to carry, to conduct, to lead.
Leí, *s. f.* paste.
Le jáná, *v. n.* to take away, to carry, to run away with, to win.
Lekhá, *s. m.* account, reckoning.
Lekhak, *s. m.* a writer, an accountant.
Lekhakí, *s. f.* the business of a writer.
Lekin, *conj.* but, yet, however.
Le lená, *v. a.* to take, to receive, to accept of, to take before, to extort, to bereave.
Le márná, *v. n.* to calumniate.
Lemú, *s. m.* a line.
Lená, *v. a.* to take, to accept, to assume, to receive, to buy,
Lená dená, } *s. m.* traffic, trade,
Len den, } barter, buying and selling; borrowing and lending.
Lenḍí, *s. f.* goat's dung; a cur, a country dog.
Lep, *s. m.* plastering; ointment.
Lepálak, *s. m.* an adopted child, adopted.

Le pálná, *v. a.* to adopt, to rear, to bring up.
Le paṛná, *v. a.* to lie with; to involve another in one's disgrace.
Lepná, *v. a.* to plaster, or smear over.
Le rahná, *v. n.* to cheat, to pilfer.
Le rakhná, *v. a.* to provide, to keep ready, to procure, to reserve.
Lerú, } *s. m.* a calf.
Lerúá, }
Lesná, *v. a.* to plaster, to spread, to daub.
Leṭná, *v. n.* to repose, to lie down, to lie, to rest.
Lewá, *s. m.* one who takes; that which is spread on the outside of a new pot.
Lewádeí, *s. f.* traffic, trade.
Lewár, *s. m.* mud to plaster a wall with.
Lezam, *s. f.* a kind of bow with an iron chain instead of a string, with which the natives exercise their bodies.
Líbaṛ, *s. m.* rheum (of the eyes.)
Libás, *s. m.* apparel, clothes, dress, attire, robe.
Libásí, *adj.* false (a witness.)
Libás poshák, *s. m.* see Libás.
Lichar, *adj.* obstinate, determined to have something given (as beggars.)
Líchaṛ, *adj.* stingy, niggardly.
Líchí, *s. f.* name of a fruit.
Lichik, *s. m.* a sprain, a bruise.
Líd, *s. f.* the dung of horses or elephants.
Li'e, for, on account of.
Lifáfa, *s. m.* the cover of a letter, an envelope, a wrapper, outward case; outward show.
Lifáfa karná, to wrap up, to enclose.
Liháf, *s. m.* a coverlet, a quilt; a quilted upper garment.
Liháṛá, *adj.* vile, base, mean, contemptible.
Liház, *s. m.* a look, view, respect; regard, observing attentively; shame.
Liház karná, to observe, to behold, to look (to or at), to advert (to), to regard, mind, observe, notice.
Lijáná, see Le jáná.
Lijhṛí, *s. f.* afterbirth, placenta.
Lík, *s. f.* the marks of a carriage-wheel, track, rut; ignominy, stain.
Likanhárá, *s. m.* a writer.
Líkh, } *s. f.* a nit, the egg of a louse.
Likh, }
Likhá, *s. m.* fate, predestination, destiny, writing: *adj.* written.
Likháí, *s. f.* the wages or labour of writing.
Likháná, *v. a.* to cause or teach to write, to get written.
Likhant, *s. m.* writing; fate.
Likháo, *s. m.* } the act of writing, writing.
Likháwaṭ, *s. f.* }
Likh deuá, } *v. n.* to copy, to write.
Likh lená, }
Likhná, *v. a.* to write; to paint.
Likhní, *s. f.* a pen.
Likhtang, *s. m.* a writer.
Likhwáná, *v. a.* to cause to be delineated or written out.
Likná, *v. a.* to write.
Líl, *s. f.* indigo: *adj.* blue.
Lílá, *adj.* blue, of indigo colour: *s. f.* play, sport, diversion.
Liláná, *v. n.* to long for.
Lilár, } *s. m.* the forehead; fate, destiny, fortune.
Liláṭ, }
Lílkanṭh, *s. m.* name of a bird.
Li-l-láh, to God.
Lílná, *v. a.* to swallow, to gulp.
Límbú, } *s. m.* a lime, a lemon.
Límú, }
Lín, *adj.* immersed, absorbed.
Ling, } *s. m.* membrum verile, the emblem of Mahádeva.
Linga, }
Lín honá, to be immersed, to be absorbed (in meditation, &c.)
Lipáná, *v. a.* to cause to smear or plaster.
Lipaṭná, *v. n.* see Lapaṭná.
Lipná, *v. n.* to be plastered, smeared, or washed over.

Lípná, *v. n.* to wash with cow-dung and water, to plaster.
Lipṛí, *s. f.* an old ragged turban, the rags in a turban.
Lipṭáná, *v. n.* see Lapaṭná.
Lipwáná, *v. a.* to cause to plaster, smear, or wash over.
Liṛáná, to cast their young (as animals), to miscarry.
Liṭáná, *v. a.* to cause to lie or repose, to lay : *v. n.* to become besmeared.
Lithaṛná, *v. a.* to draggle.
Lithaṛná, *v. n.* to be draggled.
Liṭṭí, *s. f.* thick cakes baked on coals.
Liwaiyá, *s. m.* a taker.
Liwá láná, *v. a.* to bring, to procure.
Liwáná, *v. n.* to cause to take.
Liyáqat, *s. f.* merit, worth, skill, abilities, dignity.
Liye, for, on account of.
Lo, *imper. of* Lená, take, hold: *interj.* lo! look, see, there now.
Lobán, *s. m.* a kind of gum, incense, benzoin.
Lobh, *s. m.* avarice, covetousness, greediness.
Lobhí, *adj.* covetous, avaricious.
Lobhná, *v. n.* to be enamoured.
Lobiyá, *s. m.* a kind of bean.
Lochan, *s. m.* iron filings; the eye.
Lodhá, *s. m.* name of a tribe of husbandmen.
Log, *s. m.* people, folk, mankind.
Logáí, *s. f.* woman.
Lohá, *s. m.* iron.
Lohán, *adj.* bloody.
Loháni, *s. m.* name of a caste among Paṭháns.
Lohár, *s. m.* a blacksmith.
Lohárin, *s. f.* a blacksmith's wife.
Lohárkhána, *s. m.* a blacksmith's shop.
Lohbandá, *s. m.* a stick hooped with iron, used as a weapon.
Lohchun, } *s. m.* iron filings.
Lohchúr, }
Lohiyá, *adj.* made of iron.
Lohsár, *s. f.* an iron mine.
Lohú, *s. m.* blood.
Lohúluhán, *adj.* covered with blood, bloody.
Lohú phaṭná, to have leprosy.
Loí, *s. f.* blanket, flannel.
Lok, *s. m.* people, a world, region.
Lokáchárí, *s. f.* way of the world.
Lokhar, *s. m.* cobbler's tools, hardware.
Lokná, *v. a.* to catch.
Lom, *s. m.* hair.
Lomṛí, *s. f.* a fox.
Loṇ, *adv.* till, to, up to.
Lon, *s. m.* salt.
Loná, *adj.* salt, brackish; barren or salt (land); the salt that effloresces from walls, &c.
Lonár, *s. m.* salt lands; a place where salt is produced.
Londá, *s. m.* a lump of clay, clod.
Lor, *s. m.* a tear; an earring, drop.
Loṛhá, *s. m.* a stone pestle with which materials are triturated on a stone, a muller.
Loṭ, *s. f.* wallowing, rolling; *Eng.* a bank-note.
Loṭá, *s. m.* a small metal pot, generally of brass.
Loṭan, *s. m.* a tumbler pigeon.
Loth, *s. f.* a corpse, dead body.
Lothṛá, *s. m.* } a lump of flesh.
Lothṛí, *s. f.* }
Loṭná, *v. n.* to wallow, to roll about, to sprawl.
Loṭná poṭná, *v. n.* to wallow, to roll or turn over.
Loṭpoṭ, *adj.* wallowing, tumbling and tossing, rolling about, restless.
Luáb, *s. m.* viscosity, sliminess, spittle, mucus, saliva.
Lubán, *s. n.* frankincense, benzoin.
Lubháná, *v. n.* to excite desire, to allure, to entice.
Luchchá, *s. m.* a vagabond, a libertine, a rake, a profligate.
Luchchápaná, } *s. m.* libertinism, rakishness, lascivi-
Luchpan, } ousness.
Lughat, *s. f.* a dictionary.
Lughawí, *adj.* literal, verbal.
Lughawí maṇí, literal or verbal meaning.

Lúh, *s. f.* a hot wind.
Luhán, *adj.* bloody.
Luhaṇḍá, *s. m.* an earthen vessel for keeping salt in, an iron bucket for drawing water.
Luhár, *s. m.* a blacksmith.
Luhárin, *s. f.* the wife of a blacksmith.
Luhú, *s. m.* blood.
Luhú luhán, *adj.* covered with blood, bloody.
Lúí, *s. f.* a round lump of dough prepared for making into bread or cakes.
Lujlujá, *adj.* weak, frail.
Luk, } *s. m.* a falling star.
Lúk, }
Lúká, *s. m.* pieces of burning matter thrown out from a conflagration.
Lúká lagáná, to inflame or excite quarrels.
Lukáná, } *v. a.* to hide, to conceal.
Lukáwaná, }
Lúkh, *s. f.* a flame.
Lúkhṭí, *s. f.* see Lúkṭí.
Luk luk karná, *v. n.* to glitter.
Lukná, *v. n.* to lie hid, to be concealed.
Luknat, *s. f.* stuttering, lisp, stammering.
Luksán, *s. m.* injury, defect, detriment, damage; also *improp.* for Nuqsán, which see.
Lúkṭí, *s. f.* a wooden poker, or stake burnt at one end, a firebrand.
Lúlá, *adj.* lame-handed, maimed.
Lunḍá, *adj.* tailless, tail-cropt, docked.
Lunḍá munḍá, *adj.* tailless and bald.
Lunḍhná, *v. n.* to roll.
Lunḍí, *s. f.* a ball or spindle of cord.
Lunḍiyáná, to wind (cord.)
Lunḍ munḍ, *adj.* tailless and bald.
Lung, *s. m.* } a cloth worn round the
Lungí, *s. f.* } loins with the end passed between the thighs and tucked in behind, or a cloth worn between the legs.
Lúní, *s. f.* that salt which effloresces from walls, &c.
Lúniyá, *adj.* salt, brackish: *s. m.* a salt-maker.
Lunj, } *adj.* having lost the
Lunj munj, } use of hands and feet.
Luqandrá, *s. m.* a rake, a profligate.
Luqma, *s. m.* a mouthful, a morsel.
Luqmán, *n. prop.* a famous eastern fabulist.
Luṛakhná, } *v. n.* to roll, to fall or
Luṛakná, } roll off, to slip, to slide.
Luṛhakná, *v. n.* to roll; to be spilt, to be upset.
Luṛháná, *v. a.* to cause to roll, to spill, to upset.
Luṛhiyá, *s. f.* see Loṛhá.
Luṛhiyáná, *v. a.* to double hem a garment.
Luṛh jáná, *v. n.* to die.
Luṛhná, *v. n.* to roll; to be spilt.
Lúṭ, *s. f.* plunder, pillage, prize.
Luṭáí, *s. f.* plunder, pillage, booty.
Lúṭálúṭ, *s. f.* plundering.
Luṭá luṭá kar márná, to beat severely.
Luṭáná, *v a.* to squander, to spend or expend, to cause to plunder or be plundered; to cause to wallow or roll about.
Luṭas, *s. f.* plundering, ruin, devastation.
Lúṭbáz, *s. m.* a plunderer.
Luṭerá, *s. m.* a squanderer, a prodigal, a spendthrift, a plunderer.
Lutf, *s. m.* courtesy, favour, kindness, gentleness; pleasantry, wit; the beauty or best (of a thing.)
Luṭiyá, *s. f.* a small pot.
Luṭná, *v. n.* to be sacked or plundered, to be squandered.
Lúṭná, *v. a.* to plunder, to pillage, to spoil, to squander.
Lúṭpáṭ, *s. f.* plunder and sacking.
Lutrá, *s. m.* tell-tale, babbler, a tattler, a backbiter.
Luṭwaiyá, *s. m.* a plunderer, a spendthrift.
Luṭwáná, *v. a.* to cause to be plundered.

M.

Má, *s. f.* mother; it is often used as an affectionate or respectful address to aged women and elder relatives, also to Gangá, and other goddesses, or to a cow; when a man calls his wife by this appellation it is considered as relinquishing her society as a wife.

Mạ, *prep.* with, together, along with.

Maạsh, *s. f.* landed property, subsistence.

Maạshdár, *adj.* possessed of landed property.

Maạsh milkíyat, *s. f.* landed property.

Maạz alláh, God be the refuge! God forbid!

Mabádá, be it not; by no means, God forbid! lest.

Má báp, *s. m.* parents, mother and father.

Mạbúd, *adj.* adored: *s. m.* God, deity.

Machalná, *v. n.* to be perverse, refractory, disobedient, cross, obstinate.

Machámach, *adj.* filled up, stuffed full.

Machán, *s. m.* a shelf, a stage, a platform, a raised seat, a frame or stage on which they sit to drive away birds, &c., from corn-fields.

Macháná, *v. a.* to make, to cause, to stir up, to excite, to perpetrate.

Machar machar, *s. m.* creaking (as of new shoes, bedstead, &c.)

Machchha, *s. m.* a fish; the name of the Hindú first incarnation.

Machchhar, *s. m.* a musquito, a gnat.

Machchhí, *s. f.* a fish; a kiss.

Machh, *s. m.* see Machchha.

Machhandar, *n. prop.* name of a Jogí: *adj.* stupid.

Máchhar, *s. m.* a musquito.

Machhlí, *s. f.* a fish; a kiss.

Machhrí, *s. f.* a fish.

Machhúá, } *s. m.* a fisherman.
Machhwá, }

Machhwáyin, } *s. f.* a fish-woman.
Machhwin, }

Machiyá, *s. m.* a stool, a footstool.

Machkáná, *v. a.* to wink.

Machlá, *adj.* perverse, cross, obstinate.

Machláí, *s. f.* } perverseness, obstinacy, crossness.
Machlápan, *s. m.* }

Machlána, *v. n.* to feel nausea, to be sick at the stomach.

Machmach, an imitative sound.

Machmacháná, *v. n.* to creak (as a bedstead, or anything heavily laden.)

Machná, *v. n.* to be made, to be stirred up.

Machwáná, *v. a.* to cause to make, &c.

Mad, *s. m.* wine, spirits.

Mạda, *s. m.* the stomach; *prop.* Mịda.

Máda, } *adj.* female: *s. f.* a female animal.
Mádá, }

Madad, *s. f.* assistance, help, aid, succour; betel-leaf mixed with opium and used for smoking.

Madadgár, an assister, protector, aider, ally, helper.

Madadgárí, *s. f.* assistance, help.

Madad karná, to assist, to aid, to help, to succour.

Madadḳhwáh, one who asks assistance.

Madak, *s. f.* betel-leaf mixed with opium and used for smoking.

Madár, *s. f.* name of a plant.

Mádar, *s. f.* a mother.

Mádarí, *adj.* maternal, motherly.

Madárí, *s. m.* a juggler.

Mádarzád, *adj.* as born of the mother, naked.

Madd, *s. f.* the mark placed sometimes over alif, thus, آ when the letter is pronounced long and broad.

Maddh, *adv.* amidst, amid; centre, middle: *s. m.* honey.

Maddham, *adj.* middling, temperate, middle: *adv.* dimly burning (as a candle.)

Maderá, *s. f.* spirituous liquor.
Madfan, *s. m.* a burying-place.
Madfún, *adj.* buried, interred.
Madhu, *s. m.* honey.
Madhumákhí, } *s. f.* a honey bee.
Madhumakhí, }
Mádín, *s. f.* a female.
Madína, *s. m.* name of a city in Arabia.
Madírá, *s. f.* spirits, wine.
Madḳhúla, *s. f.* a concubine.
Madrasa, *s. m.* a college, a public school for Muhammadan learning.
Mádwán, *s. f.* a mare.
Máe, *s. f.* mother.
Máf, *prop.* Muạf, which see.
Máfik, *prop.* Muwáfiq, which see.
Maflúj, *adj.* paralytic.
Mafụl, accusative case, the participle passive.
Mag, *s. m.* name of a people.
Magadh, *s. m.* name of a country, including Paṭná, Gyá, &c.
Magaj, *s. m. prop.* Maghz, which see.
Magan, *adj.* delighted, pleased, glad, happy, cheerful, joyful.
Magáná, *v. a.* to send for.
Magar, *conj.* unless, perhaps, except, but: *s. m.* an alligator.
Magarmachh, *s. m.* an alligator.
Magdúr, *s. m. prop.* Maqdúr, which see.
Mágh, *s. m.* name of the tenth Hindú month.
Maghá, *s. m.* name of the tenth mansion of the moon.
Mag'haiyá, *s. m.* an inhabitant of Magadh.
Maghfirat, *s. f.* absolution, remission, pardon.
Maghfúr, pardoned; *met.* applied, to one who is dead, in the sense of the late, the deceased, &c.
Maghí, *adj.* anything belonging to Magadh (a thing.)
Maghlúb, *adj.* conquered, overcome, discomfited, subdued.
Maghmúm, *adj.* grieved, mournful, sorrowful, sad.

Maghrab, } *s. m.* the west, the western regions.
Maghrib, }
Maghribí, *adj.* western, occidental.
Maghrúr, *adj.* proud, arrogant, self-important, haughty, fastidious.
Maghrúrí, *s. f.* pride, arrogance, self-importance.
Maghz, *s. m.* the brain, marrow, kernel, pith.
Maghz bhinnáná, to have a buzzing in the ears.
Maghzí, *s. f.* edging, border, hem.
Maghz ḳhálí karná, to distract, to talk much and foolishly.
Maghz kháná, } to tease, to distract.
Maghz phiráná, }
Magjí, *s. f. prop.* Maghzí, which see.
Magrá, *adj.* proud, haughty, cross, obstinate, headstrong, stubborn, refractory.
Magráhí, *s. f.* arrogance.
Magráí, } *s. f.* haughtiness, obstinacy, refractoriness, insolence.
Magrápan, }
Magrelá, *s. m.* a small black seed of a very pungent smell.
Magrí, *adj.* see Magrá.
Magrúr, *adj. prop.* Maghrúr, which see.
Magrúrí, *s. f. prop.* Maghrúrí, which see.
Máh, *s. m.* the moon; a month.
Mahá, *adj.* great, illustrious; very, extremely.
Mahabbat, *s. f.* friendship, love.
Mahábhárat, *s. f.* the great war of the descendants of Bharat; the name of an epic poem.
Mahábír, *s. m.* a great hero.
Mahádev, *s. m.* name of one of the principal Hindú divinities.
Mahájál, *s. m.* a net used in fishing, a seine.
Mahájan, *s. m.* a banker, money dealer, merchant, a creditor.
Mahájaní, *s. f.* the business of a Mahájan; interest on money lent.
Mahak, *s. f.* odour, perfume, fragrance.

Mahakná, *v. n.* to exhale agreeable smells, to emit odour, to perfume.
Mahákoṛh, *s. m.* a species of leprosy.
Mahalá, *s. m.* the story of a building.
Mahaldár, *s. m.* the watchman of a divsion.
Mahaldárin, *s. f.* the midwife of a Mahall or division.
Mahall, *s. m.* a place, house, mansion, seraglio, residence; time, opportunity.
Maháll, *s.m. plur. of* Mahall, streets, courts, houses, &c.
Mahalla, *s. m.* a quarter (or part of a town), district, division.
Mahallí, *adj.* belonging to the seraglio, a eunuch.
Mahallsará, seraglio, female apartments.
Mahámáí, *s. f.* Dúrgá, the small-pox.
Mahámárí, *s. f.* the plague, pestilence.
Mahangá, *adj.* dear, high-priced, expensive.
Mahangí, *adj.* dear: *s. f.* a dearth, scarcity, famine.
Mahant, *s. m.* a religious superior, a chief of the faqírs, a kind of monk.
Mahápáp, *s. m.* atrocity, great sin.
Mahápápí, *adj.* atrocious, great sinner.
Mahápraśád, *s. m.* meat offered to Jagannáth, and afterwards distributed.
Mahápurush, *s. m.* a holy man.
Mahar, *s. f.* a wife, a woman.
Maháráj, *s. m.* a great king; sir, your honour, your majesty, excellency.
Mahárájá, *s. m.* a Hindú emperor.
Mahárájdhiráj, a great king.
Mahárání, *s. f.* an empress, a queen.
Mahátam, *s. m.* greatness, grandeur, rank; fame, celebrity; the benefit derived from any good work.
Maháwar, *s. m.* lac, the red animal dye so called, extracted from lac insects.
Maháwat, **Maháwath**, } *s. m.* an elephant-driver or keeper.
Máh ba máh, *adv.* monthly.
Mahbúb, *m.* **Mahbúba**, *f.* } *adj.* beloved, lovely: *s.* a sweetheart.
Mahelá, *s. f.* a kind of food given to horses.
Maher, *s. m.* **Maherí**, *s. f.* } the name of a dish consisting of rice or other grain boiled in sour milk.
Mahes, *s. m.* a name of Mahádeva.
Mahfil, *s. f.* the place of meeting, an assembly.
Mahfúz, *adj.* guarded, preserved, protected.
Mahimá, *s. f.* greatness, glory.
Mahín, *adj.* see Mihín.
Mahíná, *s. m.* a month; monthly pay.
Mahíná chaṛhná, to be in arrears.
Mahínádár, *s.* a monthly servant.
Mahkama, *s. m.* a tribunal, court of justice.
Mahkáná, *v. a.* to exhale (agreeable scent), to perfume.
Mahkílá, *adj.* odoriferous, spicy, aromatic.
Máhmáh, *adv.* monthly.
Mahmúdí, *s. f.* a fine sort of muslin.
Mahná, *v. a.* to churn.
Mahr, *s. m.* a marriage portion or gift settled upon the wife before marriage, jointure.
Mahrá, *s. m.* a pálkí bearer.
Mahram, *s. f.* bodice, the part of a woman's dress in which the breasts are confined: *adj.* confidential.
Mahram i ráz, a confidant, a confidential person.
Mahrúm, *adj.* unfortunate, wretched, disappointed.
Mahshar, *s. f.* the last judgment.
Mahsúl, *s. m.* tax, duty, excise, custom, postage.
Máhtáb, **Mahtáb**, } *s. m.* the moon.
Mahtábí, *s. f.* belonging to the moon, like the moon; a kind of firework.
Máhtábí, *s. f.* a kind of firework, blue light; a large kind of lime.

Mahtárí, s. f. a mother.
Mahto, s. m. a person employed by the landholder to collect the rent from a village, a title given to the Koerí caste.
Mahúá, s. m. name of a tree of whose flowers a spirituous liquor is distilled.
Máhur, s. m. poison.
Máhwárí, adv. monthly.
Mahz, adv. in vain.
Mahzúz, adj. glad, cheerful, delighted, pleased, happy.
Máí, s. f. mother.
Maibhá, s. f. a step-mother.
Maidá, } s. m. flour twice sifted.
Maida, }
Maidán, s. m. a plain, open field, area; a field of battle.
Maiká, s. m. parents, family.
Máil, adj. inclined, inclined towards.
Mail, s. m. Eng. mile: s. f. dirt, filth, rust, scum.
Mailá, adj. dirty, defiled, nasty, foul.
Mailá hojáná, to become turbid, to be dirty.
Mailá karná, to dirty, to tarnish, to foul.
Mailá kuchailá, adj. dirty.
Mail baiṭhná, to gather a crust.
Mail chhánṭná, to fine, strain, purify, clarify.
Máil honá, v. n. to incline.
Máil karná, to incline, to bend, to bias.
Mail káṭná, to refine, to purify.
Mailkhora, an apron; a garment which from its colour hides the dirt.
Mail rakhná, to associate with.
Maiṇ, pron. I.
Mainá, s. f. name of a bird.
Main phal, s. m. name of a fruit used in medicine.
Maíshat, s. f. property (of all kinds), subsistence, livelihood.
Maiyá, s. f. mother.
Majá, s. m. prop. Mazá, which see.
Majádár, adj. prop. Mazadár, which see.
Májáí, adj. born of the same mother.
Majál, s. f. power, ability, strength.
Májará, s. m. state, condition, circumstance, incident, occurrence, an event, adventure, accident.
Májáyá, adj. see Májáí.
Majbúr, adj. constrained, forced, helpless, oppressed.
Majbúrí, s. f. constraint, compulsion, subjection.
Majbút, adj. prop. Mazbút, which see.
Majbútí, s. f. see Mazbútí.
Majdúr, prop. Mazdúr, which see.
Majdúrí, s. f. see Mazdúrí.
Maj'hab, } s. m. prop. Maz'hab, which see.
Maj'ham, }
Majhár, s. m. the middle, centre; in the middle.
Májhdhár, s. f. the mid-stream, mid-sea.
Majhlá, } adj. middling, middle, middlemost.
Majholá, }
Majholí, adj. see Majholá: s. f. a small cart.
Maj'húl, adj. unknown, little known; indolent, lazy, idle: subst. passive voice.
Majírá, s. m. small cymbals.
Majíṭh, s. f. name of a drug used for dying red.
Majkúr, see Mazkúr.
Majlis. s. f. an assembly, a company, congregation, convention.
Majlúm, adj see Mazlúm.
Majmạ, s. m. an assembly, a collection; rendezvous, assemblage.
Majmúạ, s. m. a compound perfume: adj. collected, assembled.
Majmún, prop. Mazmún, which see.
Majnún, adj, insane, in love; the name of a celebrated lover.
Majrúh, adj. wounded.
Majún, s. f. an electuary medicine.
Májúphal, s. m. a galnut.
Majúr, } s. m. prop. Mazúr, which see.
Majúrá, }

Majúrí, *s. f.* see Mazúrí.
Majús, *s. m.* the religion of the magi, the magi.
Majúsí, *adj.* relating to the Majús. one of the magi.
Makám, *s.m. prop.* Maqám, which see.
Makán, *s. m.* a place, station, dwelling, abode, home, a country.
Makándár, owner of a place.
Makar, *s. m.* see Makr.
Mákhan, *s. m.* butter.
Makháná, *s. m.* name of a plant.
Makhdúm, *adj.* served, obeyed: *s. m.* lord, master.
Makhlasí, *s. f.* deliverance, liberation, liberty, release.
Makhlúq, *adj.* created, formed: *s.* creature.
Makhlúqát, things created; creation.
Makhmal, *s. m.* velvet.
Makhmalí, *adj.* of velvet.
Makhná, *s. m.* a kind of elephant without tusks.
Makhrí, *s. f.* a spider.
Makhsús, *adj.* peculiar, especial, particular.
Makka, *s. m.* Mecca.
Makkár, *s. m.* / **Makkára**, *s. f.* } a cheat, impostor, a knave: *adj.* deceitful, insidious.
Makkárí, *s. f.* fraud, imposture, cheating, roguery, artifice.
Makkhan, *s. m.* butter.
Makkhaniyá, *s. m.* a butterman.
Makkhí, *s. f.* a fly; the sight of a gun.
Makkhíchús, a miser, a niggard.
Makkhí jhalná, see Makkhí uṛáná.
Makkhí márná, to be idle, to be unemployed, to trifle, to fool.
Makkhí uṛáná, to have ulcers on the body, so as to be constantly employed in driving away the flies from them.
Makoe, / **Mako**, } *s. m.* the Indian gooseberry.
Makoṛá, *s. m.* a large ant.
Makr, *s. m.* fraud, deceit, evasion, imposture, avarice.
Makṛá, *s. m.* a spider.
Makrchakar, *s. m.* fraud and subterfuge.
Makrhá'í, / **Makrhá'iyá**, } *adj.* deceitful.
Makṛí, *s. f.* a spider.
Makṛí ká jálá, a spider's web.
Makrúh, *adj.* hated, odious, detestable, disgusting, abominable.
Makrúhát, disgusting, abominable things.
Maktab, / **Maktabkhána**, } *s. m.* a school, academy.
Maktúb, *adj.* written: *s. m.* a letter.
Mal, *s. m.* dirt, excrement.
Mál, *s. m.* property, wealth, merchandise, goods, effects; garland, &c.
Málá, *s. f.* a Hindú rosary; a necklace, a garland,
Malágír, *s. m.* sandal-wood.
Malágírí, *s. m.* the colour of sandal-wood.
Maláhat, *s. f.* polish (on cloth.)
Maláí, *s. f.* cream.
Maláik, / **Maláika**, } *s. plur.* of Malak, angels.
Malak, *s. m.* an angel.
Malak ul maut, the angel of death, Izráíl.
Malál, *s. m.* sadness, grief, dejection (of mind.)
Malam, *s. m. prop.* Malham, salve, plaster, an ointment.
Málámál, *adj.* full, replete, brimful, abundant.
Malámat, *s. f.* reproach, rebuke, blame.
Malámat karná, to reproach, to blame, to censure, to rebuke.
Maláná, *v. a.* to cause to rub, grind, or scour.
Malang, *s. m.* a kind of dervis.
Malár, *s. f.* name of a musical mode.
Malat, *s.m.* a worn rupee or other coin.
Maldal, rubbing, grinding.
Máldár, *adj.* wealthy, rich.
Malechh, *adj.* an unclean race.

Malepanj, *adj.* aged, above five years (a horse.)
Malfúf, *adj.* wrapped up, enclosed; the enclosure in a letter, &c.
Malghobá, *s. m.* name of a dish.
Málguzár, *s. m.* a tenant, a landholder, one paying rent or taxes.
Málguzárí, *s. f.* land revenue, ground rent.
Malham, *s. m.* salve, plaster, an ointment.
Málí, *s. m.* a gardener, a florist.
Malichh, *adj.* an unclean race.
Malídá, *s. m.* bread or cakes made with flour, milk, butter, sugar, &c.
Málída, *s. m.* a kind of woollen cloth.
Málik, *s. m.* master, lord, possessor, proprietor, owner.
Malik, *s. m.* a king.
Malika, *s. f.* a queen.
Málikána, *s. m.* an annual or monthly allowance paid to a Zamíndár by the person who occupies his lands, whether state or a Jágírdár.
Málin, *s. f.* a gardener's wife, female gardener.
Malín, *adj.* filthy; sad, vexed, troubled.
Málish, *s. f.* rubbing, friction, polishing, furnishing.
Málish karná, to rub, &c.
Maliyá, *s. m.* a small vessel of wood, or of the shell of a cocoa-nut.
Máliyat, *s. f.* price, value.
Málkháwind, a proprietor.
Mall, *s. m.* a hero.
Malláh, *s. m.* a boatman, a sailor, mariner, name of a caste who are boatmen.
Malláhí, *s. f.* the business of a Malláh.
Malláhin, *s. f.* a boatman's wife.
Malljuddh, *s. m.* wrestling.
Malmal, *s. f.* muslin.
Málmast, *adj.* purse-proud.
Mál matá, *s. f.* merchandise, goods, chattels, furniture, &c.
Malmeṭ, *adj.* ruined.
Malmeṭ honá, to be ruined, to perish.
Malmeṭ karná, to destroy, to raze.
Malná, to rub, tread on, to anoint.
Malolá, *s. m.* vexation, grief, affliction, sadness.
Málpúá, *s. m.* a kind of sweet cake, a pancake.
Mạlúm, *adj.* known, notorious, evident, apparent, obvious, acquainted with: *s.* the active voice of a verb.
Mạlúm honá, to appear, to seem.
Mạlúm karná, to find out, discover, understand, know, deem, suppose.
Malụ́n, *adj.* cursed, execrated, excommunicated.
Malwáí, *s. f.* price of scouring, rubbing, &c.
Malwáná, *v. a.* to cause to rub.
Málwar, *adj.* wealthy.
Málzádí, *s. f.* a bawd, a whore.
Málzámin, a security, for property or money.
Málzáminí, *s. f.* suretyship for property.
Mámá, *s. m.* a maternal uncle.
Mamerá, *adj.* relating to the paternal uncle.
Mamerá bháí, mother's brother's son, first cousin, (male.)
Mamerí bahin, mother's brother's daughter, first cousin, (female.)
Mámí, *s. f.* an aunt, maternal uncle's wife.
Mámí píná, *v. a.* to show partiality.
Mamiyá sás, husband's or wife's maternal aunt.
Mamiyá susur, husband's or wife's maternal uncle.
Mámlá, *s. m. prop.* Muạmala, which see.
Mámlat, *s. f. prop.* Muạmalat, which see; *Eng.* omelet.
Mámlatí, *adj.* see Muạmalatí.
Mamoṛá, *s. m.* twist, ache, pain (particularly the bowels), gripes.
Mámú, *s. m.* an uncle, mother's brother; a snake; phrase used at night when it is deemed unlucky to call a serpent by its proper name.
Mạmúl, *adj.* customary, established:

s. m. custom, practice, fixed allowance or gratuity.

Mámúlí, *adj.* customary, practised.

Mámúr, *adj.* in full, complete, replete.

Máṇ, *s. f.* mother.

Mán, *s. m.* character, dignity, honour, respect, haughtiness, pride.

Man, *s. m.* mind, heart, soul, spirit, inclination; the name of a weight (forty ser); a gem, a jewel.

Manạ, *s. m.* prohibition, forbidding, refusal, hindrance.

Manádí, *s. f.* proclamation.

Manáfi, *s.* profit, advantage, gain.

Manáhí, *s. f.* prohibited things; prohibition.

Manạ karná, to forbid, to prohibit.

Manáná, } *v. a.* to persuade,
Manáná danáná, } to cause to agree (to anything), to conciliate, to propitiate, to assuage, to soothe, to appease.

Mánand, *s. f. m.* like, resembling, resemblance.

Manár, } *s. m.* a minaret, a turret,
Manára, } a steeple.

Manárth, *s. m.* intention, desire, purpose.

Manásib, *adj. prop.* Munásib, which see.

Manautí, *s. f.* bail, security, bondsman, surety.

Manáwná, *v. a.* see Manáná.

Man bháná, *v. n.* to be agreeable to the mind.

Manbháwan, } *adj.* acceptable, agree-
Manbháwná, } able, pleasant, amusing.

Manbhog, a delicious kind of plantain.

Mand, a particle, which, added to nouns, implies endowed with, or having; faded, a dull colour.

Mánd, *s. f.* the den of a wild beast.

Mánḍ, *s. m.* rice-gruel, starch.

Manda, } *adj.* gentle, mild, affable,
Mandá, } cheap, abated, slow, tardy.

Mándá, } *adj.* tired, weary, fatigued,
Mánda, } ailing, indisposed, languid.

Mánḍá, *s. m.* film, speck (on the eye); a kind of sweetmeat.

Manḍá, *s. m.* name of a sweetmeat.

Manḍaf, *s. m.* see Manḍap.

Mándagí, *s. f.* fatigue, lassitude.

Manḍal, *s. m.* a circle, orb, sphere, disk, halo of the moon.

Manḍalí, *s. f.* an assembly, a society, a body of people, a congregation.

Manḍap, *s. m.* a temple.

Manḍhná, *v. a.* see Maṛhná.

Mandhir, *s. m.* a temple.

Manḍhwáná, *v. a.* to cause to cover (a book, drum, &c., with parchment.)

Manḍí, *s. f.* a market, a particular market for any one thing.

Mandil, } *s. m.* a temple.
Mandir, }

Manḍiyáná, *v. a.* to starch.

Manḍláná, *v. n.* to make a circuit, to hover (as birds, &c.)

Mạne, *s. m.* meaning, sense, signification.

Manfaạt, *s. f.* profit, gain, advantage.

Máng, *s. f.* a line on the top of the head where the hair is parted.

Mangá bhejná, to send for.

Mangal, *s. m.* health, pleasure; Tuesday, the planet Mars.

Mangal samáchár, *s. m.* good news, the Gospel.

Mangáná, *v. a.* to send for, to ask for, to call for.

Máng dená, *v. a.* to borrow for another, to ask for and give.

Mangetar, *s. m. f.* one to whom a woman is betrothed.

Máng lená, *v. n.* to borrow.

Mangná, } *v. a.* to ask for, to require,
Mángná, } to demand, to beg, to pray, crave, solicit, to want, to desire, to betroth.

Mangní, *s. f.* betrothing, asking in marriage; a loan: *adv.* gratuitously, for nothing.

Mangní dená, to lend.

Máng nikálná, to divide the hair in a straight line on the top of the head.

Mangní mángná, to borrow.

Mangrá, *s. m.* ridge tiles.

Mangtá, *s. m.* a beggar.

Máng táng karná, to ask for.

Mángumán, *s. m.* dignity, state, honour.

Mangwáná, *v. a.* to send for, to cause to ask for.

Máṇh, *adv.* in.

Manháí, *s. f.* forbidding, prohibition.

Máhiṇ, } *adv.* in.
Máhíṇ, }

Man híṇ man, in the very soul.

Manhús, *adj.* unfortunate, unlucky; abominable; bad.

Máni, *s. f. prop.* Maṇí.

Maṇí, *s. f.* meaning, sense, signification, acceptation.

Maní, *s. f.* sperma genitale viri aut mulieris.

Mani, } *s. f.* a gem, a jewel.
Maní, }

Manihár, *s. m.* a person who makes or sells the glass bracelets which the women wear on their wrists.

Manihári, *s. f.* the trade in glass bracelets.

Mánind, *s. m. f.* like, resembling, resemblance.

Manjan, *s. m.* tooth-powder, dentifrice.

Manjar, *s. f.* the blossom (of a tree.)

Mánjh, *s. m.* the middle, in the middle, in.

Mánjhá, *s. m.* a paste mixed with pounded glass and applied to the string of a kite to cut that of another with; present of clothes sent by relations to the bride or bridegroom.

Mánjhdhár, *s. f.* the middle of the stream.

Mánjhí, *s. m.* master of a vessel, a helmsman, a steersman.

Manjhlá, *adj.* middle, second.

Manjhná, *v.* see Manjná or Mánjná.

Manjholá, *adj.* middle, middlemost, middling.

Manjholí, *s. f.* a small car or carriage on two wheels.

Manjil, *s. f. prop.* Manzil, which see.

Manjírá, *s. m.* name of a musical instrument, a kind of cymbal.

Manjíṭ, *s. f.* see Majíṭh.

Manjná, *v. n.* to be polished, cleaned, scoured.

Mánjná, *v. a.* to scour, to scrub, to clean.

Manjúr, *adj. prop.* Manzúr, which see.

Manká, *s. m.* the vertebra of the neck.

Manká ḍhalakná, to be at the point of death.

Mankámná, *s. f.* desire, wish.

Mankúbá, *s. f.* a lawful wife, a married woman.

Manlagan, mind-attachment, heart-engaging.

Man láná, to fix the mind upon, to be attentive, to apply to.

Manmán, } *adj.* agreeable, pleasing, to one's heart's wish or content.
Manmáná, }
Manmántá, }

Man márná, to resist one's own inclinations, to be grieved or troubled in mind.

Man már rahná, to suffer pain or grief with patience.

Manmatá, *s. m.* human opinion.

Manmaují, *adj.* self-conceited.

Manmohan, *s. m.* a sweetheart, a name of Krishna.

Mann, *s. m.* manna.

Manná, *v. n.* to be soothed, to be propitiated.

Mánná, *v. a.* to respect, regard, mind, attend, to observe, obey, heed, believe, accept, acknowledge, agree, allow, accede, assent, confess, consent, grant, admit, trust, yield, submit, suppose, own.

Mannat, *s. f.* a vow, a promise.

Manorath, *s. m.* desire, wish, intention.

Máṇp, *s. m.* measure.

Máṇṛ, *s. m.* rice-water, rice-gruel, starch.

Máṇṛá, *s. m.* film, speck (on the eye.)

Máṇṛí, *s. f.* starch, rice-water, rice-gruel.

Maṇṛúá, *s. m.* / **Maṇṛwí**, *s. f.* name of a grain.

Máṇs, *s. m.* flesh, meat.

Mansá, *s. f.* wish, desire, intention.

Mansab, *s. m.* dignity, office,

Mansabdár, *s. m.* a magistrate, a man of rank.

Mansúb, *adj.* related, belonging to, allied, betrothed.

Mansúba, *s. m.* contrivance, design, project, scheme, plan.

Mansúba bándhná, to contrive, to conspire.

Mansúbabáz, *adj.* considerate, prudent, sagacious, ingenious; contriver, schemer.

Mansúḳh, *adj.* cancelled, obliterated, abolished, annulled.

Mantá, *s. f.* vow, promise.

Mantar, / **Mantar jantar**, *s. m.* a charm, spell, incantation.

Mantiq, *s. f.* logic, reasoning.

Mantiqí, *adj.* logical, logician.

Mantra, *s. m.* see Mantar.

Mantrí, *s. m.* an enchanter.

Manúá, *s. m.* mind, soul, life.

Manukh, / **Mánukh**, / **Mánus**, / **Mánush**, *s. m.* a man.

Manzil, *s. f.* a day's journey; a stage.

Manzil káṭná, to finish a journey.

Manzúr, *adj.* agreeable, admired, chosen, acceptable, approved of, acquiesced in.

Manzúrí, *s. f.* approbation, consent, choice.

Manzúr i nazar, chosen, agreeable to the sight.

Máp, *s. m.* measure.

Mapáná, *v. a.* to cause to be measured.

Mapná, *v. n.* to be measured.

Mápná, *v. a.* to measure,

Mapwáná, *v. a.* to cause to measure.

Maqaḍ, *s. f.* the anus, podex.

Maqám, *s. m.* station, place, a place of residence or encamping, halting of an army.

Maqámí, *adj.* residing, resident.

Maqbara, *s. m.* a tomb, a mausoleum.

Maqbúl, *adj.* accepted, acceptable, agreeable, taken in good part, agreed on.

Maqdúr, *s. m.* power, strength, ability, influence.

Maqdúr bhar, to the best of one's power, with all one's might.

Maqnạ, *s. m.* a bride's veil.

Maqsad, *s. m.* intention, design, meaning, purpose, object, desire; aim, scope, wish.

Maqsúm, *s. m.* fate, destiny.

Máqúl, *adj.* reasonable, just, pertinent, proper.

Már, *s. f.* beating; a battle; a blow.

Márá, *adj.* beaten, slain; foundered, or overturned (a boat, &c.)

Mará, *part. past.* of Marná, dead.

Marad, *s. m.* male, a man, a hero.

Márafat, see Máṛifat.

Márag, *s. m.* a road, path, a way.

Maraiṭhá, *adj.* bound round.

Maraj, *s. m.* *prop.* Maraz, sickness, disease.

Márá jáná, *v. n.* to be slain; to be overcome; to be overturned or sunk (as a boat, &c.), to be cut off (a caravan, detachment.)

Mạraka, *s. m.* a field of battle, fight.

Mạraka karná, to fight.

Maram, *s. m.* a secret, secret meaning or purpose.

Márá mára phirná, to wander.

Márámár chalná, to push on without delay.

Márámárí, *s. f.* mutual beating, scuffle, fray.

Marammat, *s. f.* mending, repairing, repair.
Marammatí, *adj.* requiring repair.
Marammat karná, *v. a.* to mend, to repair.
Marammat karwáná, *v. a.* to cause to mend, or repair.
Marammat talab, *adj.* out of repair, requiring repair.
Maran, *s. m.* death.
Maranhárá, *s. m.* smiter, slayer.
Márá paṛná, to be killed or slain.
Maraz, *s. m.* sickness, disease.
Marbhukkhá, *adj.* starved to death, greedy, voracious, ravenous.
Mard, *s. m.* a male, a man, a hero.
Mardak, *s. m.* a low fellow, a puppy, a rascal.
Már ḍálná, to kill, to smite.
Mardan, *s.* rubbing, anointing, trampling, treading down.
Mardána, *adv.* manly, manlike, brave: *adj.* male.
Mardánagí, *s. f.* manliness, bravery.
Mardání, *s. f.* a masculine (woman): *adj.* used or worn by women.
Mard bachcha, the son of a brave man.
Mard e ádmí, *s. m.* a gentleman.
Már dená, to smite, to beat, to kill.
Márdhár, *s. f.* thumping and beating severely. [rility.
Mardí, *s. f.* manhood, manliness, virility.
Mard i ádmí, *s. m.* a gentleman.
Mardúá, *s. m.* (used by way of contempt), man. [cluded.
Mardúd, *adj.* repulsed, rejected, excluded.
Mardumí, *s. f.* manliness, bravery.
Máre, *s. m.* (by) reason, (on) account, (for) the sake, for.
Marfá, *s. m.* a kind of drum.
Marg, *s. f.* death.
Marghaṭ, *s. m.* the place where Hindús burn their dead.
Marghúb, } *adj.* desirable, desired, amiable.
Marghúb tabạ, }
Margí, *s. f.* the plague, pestilence.
Marg i mufáját, sudden death.
Már giráná, to knock down, to win (the battle.)
Maṛhá, *adj.* lined, headed, covered or topped (as a drum with parchment.)
Marhabá, *interj.* hail! welcome! bravo!
Maṛhaiyá, *s. f.* a small cottage or hut.
Marham, *s. m.* a plaster, salve.
Maṛhan, *s. f.* lining, heading (of a drum, &c.)
Marhaṭá, *s. m.* a Maharatta.
Már haṭáná, to overcome, to beat and drive back.
Marhaṭṭa, *s. m.* a Maharatta.
Maṛhí, *s. f.* a cottage, a temple.
Maṛhná, *v. a.* to cover (as a book with leather or a drum with parchment), to gild, to case.
Marhúm, *adj.* who has found mercy, *i.e*, deceased.
Marí, *s. f.* plague, pestilence; carrion.
Mạrifat, *s. f.* knowledge; account, cause, (by) reason, (by) means, (through) the means, by.
Mariyal, *adj.* lean, emaciated, much reduced by sickness.
Maríz, *adj.* sick, diseased.
Marjá, *s. m.* loss. [respect.
Marjád, *s. f.* station, rank, dignity, respect.
Mar jáná, *v. n.* to die
Marjí, *s. f. prop.* Marzí, which see.
Markar, *adv.* with difficulty.
Markaz, *s. m.* the upper stroke of the letter káf.
Markháhá, *adj.* addicted to beating, striking, or butting (a man or animal.)
Már kháni, to get a drubbing.
Mar khapná, *v. n.* to die.
Már kuṭái, *s. f.* beating and bruising.
Már láná, to rob, to take by robbery.
Már lená, to smite, to conquer.
Marmar, *s. m.* marble.
Maṛmaṛáná, *v. n.* to crack (as anything going to break.)
Már marná, to fall in battle after killing some of the enemy.

Marná, *v. n.* to die, to expire; to desire vehemently, to set one's heart upon anything.

Márná, *v. a.* to smite, to strike, to hit, kill, slay, beat, bang, drive, shoot, punish, mortify, blight, blast, spoil, ruin, conquer, crack, destroy, stamp, sting, stop, calm, quench, run.

Maroṛ, Maṛoṛ, *s. f.* twist, flexion, turn, writhe, convolution, contortion.

Maroṛá, Maṛoṛá, *s. m.* a twisting of the bowels, pain in the bowels, gripes.

Maroṛí, Maṛoṛí, *s. m.* the worm of a ram-rod.

Maroṛná, Maṛoṛná, *v. a.* to twist, to writhe, to contort, to distort, to gripe.

Maroṛphalí, *s. m.* name of a plant the fruit of which is used in medicine.

Már paṛná, to be beaten.

Márpech, *s. f.* intricacies (in law or accounts), a difficulty, quibble.

Márpech kí ráh, a crooked or winding path.

Marpeṇch, *s.* see Márpech.

Márpíṭ, *s. f.* beating and bruising, drubbing.

Már sakná, to be able to beat.

Marsiya, *s. m.* an elegy, a dirge, a funeral eulogium.

Marsiyaḳhwán, a repeater of an elegy or the Marsiya.

Marsiyaḳhwání, repeating or singing an elegy or the Marsiya.

Martaba, *s. m.* step, degree, dignity, office, rank of honour, time. turn.

Martabán, *s. m.* a jar for keeping preserves in.

Mártaul, Martaul, *s. m.* a hammer.

Mártol, *s. m.* a hammer.

Maṛúá, *s.m.* name of a grain of which bread is made.

Mạrúf, *adj.* known, celebrated; the active voice of a verb.

Mạrúz, *adj.* presented. offered, submitted: *s. m.* a representation, a petition.

Marwáná, *v. a.* to cause to be beaten, to cause to be killed.

Máṛwáṛ, *n. prop.* name of a country.

Máṛwáṛí, *s. m.*, **Máṛwáṛin,** *s. f.* an inhabitant of Máṛwáṛ.

Marz, *s. m.* sickness, disease.

Marzí, *s. f.* will, assent, consent, pleasure.

Más, *s. m.* a month; flesh, meat.

Masáfir, *s. m. prop.* Musáfir, which see.

Masahará, *s. m. prop.* Musháhara, which see.

Masaharí, *s. f.* curtains (of a bed), musquito curtains.

Masáil, *s. plur.* of Maslá, the precepts of Muhammad.

Masak, *s. f. prop.* Mashk, which see.

Masakat, *s. f. prop.* Mashaqqat, which see.

Masakná, *v. n.* to be torn, split, rent, [burst.

Masal, *s. f.* a fable, allegory, parable, simile, proverb; an example.

Masál, *s. f. prop.* Mashạl, a torch, a flambeau.

Masálá, *s. m. prop.* Masálih, which see.

Masálá ḍálná, Masálá dená, *v. a.* to season.

Masálchí, *s. m. prop.* Mashạlchí.

Masálih, *s. f.* drugs, spices, seasoning; the materials for any work.

Masalná, *v. a.* to bruise, to crush, to break with the hand.

Masán, *s. m.* a place where a dead body is burnt; an evil spirit.

Masauwir, *s. m.* a painter, limner, drawer.

Masauwirí, *s. f.* drawing, &c.

Masdar, *s. m.* source, origin; infinitive or noun of action (in grammar.)

Maseṇ, *s. f.* down, small hairs on the lips before the beard grows.

Másh, *s. m.* a vetch: *s. f. prop.* Maąsh, landed property.
Másha, *s. m.* name of a small weight consisting of eight rattís.
Masháikh, *s. plur.* of Shaikh, old men; holy persons, dervises.
Mashąl, } **Mashál**, } *s. f.* a torch, flambeau.
Mashąlchí, } **Mashálchí**, } *s. m.* a torch-bearer; a servant who cleans knives, forks, and plates, &c.; a scullion.
Mashaqqat, *s. f.* trouble, labour, toil, assiduity, distress.
Máshdár, *adj. prop.* Maąshdár, which see.
Mashghúl, *adj.* employed, occupied, busy.
Mash'húr, *adj.* celebrated, published, famous, well-known, noted, notorious.
Mash'húr karná, to publish, to proclaim.
Mashk, *s. f.* a leather bag, especially for carrying water, a water-bag.
Mashkíra, *s. m.* a small leather bottle.
Másh milkíyat, *s. f. prop.* Maąsh milkíyat, landed property.
Mashq, *s. f.* exercise, practice, usage, use.
Mashriq, *s. m.* the east.
Mashrú, *s. m.* a kind of cloth made of silk and cotton mixed.
Mashsháqí, *s. f.* practice, constant or great practice.
Masht, } **Mashtí**, } *s. f.* silence.
Mashtí márná, } **Masht márná**, } to remain silent.
Máshúq, *s. m.* } **Máshúqa**, *s. f.* } a beloved object, a sweetheart, a mistress.
Mashwara, *s. m.* } **Mashwarat**, *s. f.* } counsel, consultation, advice.
Mashwarat karná, to consult, to advise (with.)
Masíh, } **Masíhá**, } *n. prop.* Messiah, Christ.
Masíhái, *adj.* Christ-like: *s. f.* office or works of the Messiah.
Masín, } **Masíná**, } **Masína**, } *s. m.* a quicksand.
Masjid, *s. f.* a mosque.
Máskabár, the last day of the month.
Maskan, *s. m.* an abode, a dwelling, a habitation.
Maskáná, *v. a.* to tear, to rend.
Maskhara, *s. m.* a droll, a jester, a buffoon.
Maskharagí, *s. f.* } **Maskharapan**, *s. m.* } **Maskhargí**, *s. f.* } buffoonery, drollery, jesting, jest.
Masla, *s. m.* a precept of Muhammad.
Maslahat, *s. f.* counsel, advice.
Maslahatan, *adv.* advisedly.
Maslahat karná, to consult, to advise, to conspire, to combine.
Maslan, *adv.* for example, *e.g.* namely.
Maslúb, *adj.* crucified.
Masnad, *s. f.* a cushion of state.
Masnaví, *s. f.* the sort of verse in which the couplets rhyme regularly, as in English heroic verse; a poem in that verse.
Masosá, *s. m.* affliction, remorse, regret.
Masosná, *v. a.* to regret, to grieve.
Masraf, *s. m.* expenditure, expense, disbursement.
Masrúf, *adj.* expended, employed, engaged, occupied, busy.
Masrúr, *adj.* glad, cheerful, gay, delighted, pleased.
Massá, *s. m.* a wart, a fleshy excresence.
Mast, *adj.* drunk, intoxicated; libidinous, lustful, lascivious, proud.
Mastak, *s. m.* the forehead of an elephant.
Mastakí, *s. f.* mastic.
Mastána, *adv.* like one intoxicated: *adj.* drunken.
Mastání, *adj.* intoxicated, lustful, lecherous, salacious (woman.)
Mastí, *s. f.* drunkenness; intoxication, lust, wantonness.

Mastúl, *s. m.* mast of a ship.
Mastúra, *s. f.* a chaste woman.
Mastúrát, *s. plur.* women (of the Haram.)
Másúk, *s. m. prop.* Mạshúq, which see.
Másúl, *s. m. prop.* Mahsúl, which see.
Mạsúm, *adj.* innocent, simple: *s.* an infant.
Mạsúmíyat, *s. f.* innocence, simplicity.
Masúr, *s. m.* a kind of pulse.
Masúṛá, *s. m.* the gums of the teeth.
Mat, *s. f.* system, opinion, counsel, advice, a particular sentiment; understanding, intellect: *neg. particle,* not, do not.
Mát, *adj.* outdone, confounded.
Máṭ, *s. m.* a vat or boiler; a large vessel or jar.
Matá, *s. m.* council, advice.
Mátá, *s. f.* mother; the small pox: *adj.* drunk, intoxicated.
Mátabar, *adj.* see Muạtabar.
Mátabarí, *s. f.* see Muạtabarí.
Maṭakná, *v. n.* to wink, to ogle, to coquet.
Matálib, *s. plur.* of Talab, wishes, desires.
Mátam, *s. m.* grief, mourning.
Mátamdár, *s.* a mourner.
Mátamdárí, *s. f.* mourning, observance of mourning.
Mátamí, *adj.* of or relating to mourning.
Mátamí libás, mourning dress.
Mátam karná, to mourn, to lament.
Mátamḳhána, *s. m.* house of mourning.
Mátampursí, oblations, condolence.
Mátamzadá, *adj.* mourning, affected with grief on account of the death of some relative.
Maṭar, *s. m.* a pea.
Maṭh, *s. m.* a convent for the ascetics, a pagan temple.
Máṭhá, *s. m.* buttermilk.
Mathá, } *s. m.* the forehead, prow;
Máthá, } the ridge of a roof.
Mathan, *s. m.* churning.
Mathaniyá, *s. f.* a churn.
Máthá ragaṛná, to implore humbly.
Máthá ṭhanakná, implies a presentiment of a conclusion from certain marks observed in the commencement.
Mat hín, void of understanding.
Maṭhiyá, *s. m.* name of an ornament.
Mathná, *v. a.* to churn; to knead, to work: *s. m.* a churning staff.
Mathní, *s. f.* a churning-staff.
Máṭhú, *s. m.* a buffoon, (a term of reproach.)
Mathurá, *s. f.* name of a city, the birth-place of Krishna.
Mathuriyá, *s. m.* name of a caste of Bráhmans of Mathurá.
Máṭí, *s. f.* earth.
Mati, *s. f.* see Mat.
Maṭiyáná, *v. n.* to grumble, to do a thing unwillingly.
Maṭiyárá, *s. m.* arable land, rich soil.
Mat jáo, don't go.
Maṭká, *s. m.* a large earthen jar.
Maṭkáná, *v. a.* to wink, to ogle, to twinkle.
Mát karná, to win, to outdo, to beat (at chess.)
Maṭkí, *s. f.* a small jar; a wink, a twinkle.
Matlab, *s. m.* intention, wish, desire, object, aim, purpose, purport, meaning.
Matlabbáz. *adj.* having an object in view.
Matláná (jí ká), *v. n.* to be sick at the stomach, to feel nausea.
Matn, *s. m.* the text.
Mátná, *v. n.* to be intoxicated.
Mátrá, *s. f.* a vowel; a dose.
Maṭrá, *s. m.* a he-goat.
Maṭṭhá, *s. m.* buttermilk: *adj.* slow, lazy.
Maṭṭí, *s. f.* earth.
Maṭṭí ḍálná, to conceal the crime or fault of another.
Maṭṭí dená, to bury.
Maṭṭí honá, to become weak or faint, to be ruined.

Maṭṭí karná, to ruin or destroy.
Maṭṭí meṉ milná, to be ruined or disgraced.
Maṭṭí parná, to be buried.
Matwálá, } adj. intoxicated, drunken,
Matwárá, } drunk,
Mauj, s. f. a wave, a surge, billows.
Maujá, s. m. prop. Mauza, which see.
Mauj márná, v. a. to billow, to wave; (met.) is applied to express self-enjoyment without restraint.
Maujúd, adj. existing, present, at hand, existent, standing before, ready.
Maulaví, s. m. a learned man.
Maulná, v. n. to bloom, to blossom, to bud (the mango tree.)
Maulsarí, s. f. name of a tree.
Maun, s. m. silence, taciturnity.
Mauní, s. f. a small round basket.
Maun sádhná, to remain silent.
Mauqa, adj. proper, fit, suitable: s. m. a fit place or time.
Mauqúf, adj. stopped, deferred, delayed, postponed, fixed or dependent (on.)
Mauqúf honá, to depend or rest (on), to be stopped, to cease.
Mauqúf karná, to cease, to leave off, to lay aside, to abolish, to abrogate, to annul.
Maur, s. m. a kind of high turban worn by the bridegroom at the time of marriage.
Mauráná, v. n. to blossom (as the mango tree.)
Maurí, s. f. see Maur.
Mausá, s. m. an uncle, mother's sister's husband.
Mauserá, adj. mas. belonging or related to the mother's sister's husband.
Mauserá bhái, a cousin, son of a mother's sister.
Mauserí bahin, daughter of a mother's sister.
Mausí, s. f. an aunt, mother's sister.
Mausim, s. m. season, time.
Mausimí, adj. seasonable.
Mausim i bahár, the season of spring.
Mausúf, adj. described, celebrated, praised, before-mentioned; a noun substantive qualified by an adjective.
Maut, s. f. death.
Mautá, a calamity.
Mautád, s. f. quantity.
Mauwat, s. f. prop. Maut, death.
Mauza, s. m. a village.
Máwá, s. f. substance, essence, leaven, milk inspissated with boiling.
Mawáshí, s. pl. quadrupeds, cattle.
Maya, in compos. composed of; chiefly consisting or made of.
Mayá, } s. f. kindness, compassion,
Máyá, } mercy, affection; illusion, idealism, a deception, depending on the power of the deity, whereby mankind believe in the existence of external objects, which are in fact nothing but idea.
Mayúb, adj. wicked, vicious, infamous, reprehensible.
Maza, } s. m. taste, flavour, relish,
Mazá, } delight, pleasure, enjoyment, anything agreeable to the palate or mind, &c.; a delicacy.
Mazadár, adj. delicious, relishing, tasteful, palatable, well-tasted, savoury.
Mazákh, s. m. a jest, a joke, pleasantry.
Mazákheṉ karná, to make jokes, to jest.
Mazallat, s. f. baseneness, contempt, abjectness.
Mazámín, s. plur. of Mazmún, the contents.
Mazár, s. f. sepulchre, tomb, or shrine of a saint.
Mazarat, s. f. apology, excuse.
Mazbah, s. m. an altar for sacrifice.
Mazbút, adj. strong, firm, fixed, fast.
Mazbútí, s. f. strength, durability, firmness.
Mazdúr, s. m. a labourer, a carrier, a porter; improp. Majdúr.

Mazdúrí, *s. f.* the price of labour, wages; labour, labouring.
Mazedár, *adj.* see Mazadár.
Maz'hab, *s. m.* religion, sect.
Maz'haka, *s.m.* humour, fun, drollery.
Mází, *s. m.* preterite tense: *adj.* past time.
Mazkúr, *adj.* forementioned, aforesaid, mentioned: *s. m.* mention, discourse; *improp.* Majkúr.
Mazkúr karná, to mention.
Mazlúm, *adj.* injured, oppressed.
Mazmún, *s. m.* sense, signification, meaning, tenour, contents (of a letter, &c.); *improp.* Majmún.
Mazúl, *adj.* deposed, displaced, dismissed, degraded, removed from office.
Mazúl karná, to discharge, dismiss, remove (from office.)
Mazúr, *s. m.* a labourer, a carrier, a porter; *improp.* Majúr.
Mázúr, *adj.* excused, excusable.
Mazúrí, *s. f.* see Mazdúrí.
Megh, *s. m.* a cloud.
Meghbaran, *adj.* of the colour of the clouds.
Meh, *s. m.* rain.
Mehmán, *s. m.* a guest.
Mej, *s. f. prop.* Mez, a table.
Meḳh, *s. f.* a nail, a wedge, a tent-pin, a peg.
Meḳhí rupaiyá, a rupee which has been hollowed and then filled with lead, copper, &c., adulterated.
Meḳh ṭhonkná, to nail.
Mel, *s. m.* connexion, agreement, combination, concord, reconciliation, union, mixture, mixing.
Melá, *s.m.* a fair, an assembly, a crowd, a concourse of people for religious or commercial purposes: *adj.* friendly.
Melá ṭhelá, *s. m.* a crowd, a concourse of people.
Melí, *adj.* friendly, sociable.
Memná, *s. m.* a kid.
Meṇ, *postpos.* in, among, between, at.
Meṇḍ, *s. f.* a bank (raised to separate fields), a border (of a pond, tank, &c.)
Meṇḍak, *s. m.* a frog.
Meṇḍhá, *s. m.* a ram.
Meṇḍkí, *s. f.* a frog.
Mengní, *s. f.* the dung of goats, sheep, camels, &c.
Meṇh, *s. m.* rain.
Meṇh barasná, to rain.
Meṇh barsáná, *v. a.* to cause to rain.
Meṇhdí, *s. f.* the name of the plant with which the natives stain their hands and feet.
Meṇḳh, *s. f.* see Meḳh.
Meṇṛ, *s. f.* see Meṇḍ.
Meṇ se, from within, out of.
Merá, *pron. 1st pers. poss. mas.* my, mine.
Meṛhá, *s. m.* a ram.
Metar, *s. m. prop.* Mihtar, a sweeper.
Metarání, *s. f. prop.* Mihtarání, a female sweeper.
Methí, *s. f.* the plant fenugreek.
Meṭná, *v. a.* to efface, to blot out, to erase, to wipe out, to annihilate, to annul, to cancel, to atone for.
Mewa, *s. m.* fruit.
Mewadár, *adj.* fruit-bearing, fruitful.
Mewafarosh, *s. m.* a fruiterer.
Mewaját, fruits.
Mewátí, *s. m.* a tribe inhabiting the mountainous province of Mewát.
Mez, *s. f.* a table.
Mezbán, *s. m.* an entertainer, a host.
Mezbání, *s. f.* hospitality, entertainment.
Mez baṛháná, to remove the tablecloth.
Mez bichháná, to lay the cloth.
Mezmán, *s. m.* a son-in-law.
Miád, *s. m.* the time of promise or imprisonment.
Michar michar, eating without an appetite.
Míchhná, } *v. a.* to close the eyes, to
Míchná, } shut, to wink.
Michná, *v. n.* to shut, to close.

Michráná, *v. a.* to eat without an appetite.

Mida, *s. m.* the stomach.

Mighnatís, *s. m.* the magnet or loadstone.

Mihdí, *s. f.* name of a plant. See Meṇhdí.

Mihín, *adj.* thin, subtile, fine (not coarse.)

Mihmán, *s. m. f.* a stranger, a guest.

Mihmándár, *s. m.* an entertainer, host.

Mihmándárí, *s. f.* entertainment, hospitality.

Mihmándost, *adj.* hospitable.

Mihmání, *s. f.* see Mihmándárí.

Mihmání karná, to entertain.

Mihnat, *s. f.* labour, toil, industry, trouble, difficulty, calamity, affliction, trial, perplexity, sorrow.

Mihnatána, *s. m.* hire, wages.

Mihnatí, *adj.* laborious, labouring, industrious, labouring person.

Mihnat karná, to labour, to toil.

Mihṇdí, *s. f.* see Meṇhdí.

Mihr, *s. f.* love, friendship, kindness.

Mihráb, *s. f.* a bower, an arch.

Mihrábdár, *adj.* arched (as a doorway.)

Mihrárú, *s. f.* a woman.

Mihrbán, *adj.* kind, friendly, indulgent, gracious.

Mihrbánagí, **Mihrbángí**, **Mihrbání**, } *s. f.* friendliness, kindness, favour.

Mihrbání karná, to favour, to confer favour (on), to befriend.

Mihrí, **Mihriyá**, } *s. f.* a woman, a wife.

Mihtar, *s. m.* a sweeper.

Mihtarání, *s. f.* female of Mihtar; a female innkeeper.

Mijáj, *s. m. prop.* Mizáj, which see.

Míjná, *v. a.* to rub with the hands.

Mijráb, *s. f. prop.* Mizráb, which see.

Mikhiyáná, *v. a.* to beat, to subdue.

Milán, *s.* comparison, collection; the making of things agree with one another.

Miláná, *v. a.* to mix, to blend, to cause to meet, to join, to attach, to connect, to unite, to cement, to close, to compare, to reconcile.

Milansár, *adj.* civil, affable, sociable, friendly, familiar.

Milansárí, *s. f.* sociableness, friendliness, affability, civility.

Miláo, *s. m.* mixture, mixing: *adj.* adulterated.

Miláp, *s. f.* agreement, reconciliation, union, concord, adjustment.

Mile jule rahná, to live together in harmony.

Milk, *s. f.* possession, property, right.

Milkí, *s. m.* a (large) farmer.

Milkíyat, *s. f.* property, possession.

Milná, *v. a.* to be mixed or confounded, to blend, to meet, to join, to be met with, to attain, to be got, to agree, to accord, to tally, to be united, to become connected (with), to coalesce, to correspond.

Milná julná, to meet cordially, to have unrestricted intercourse.

Miloní, *s. f.* admixture.

Milwáná, *v. a.* to cause to mix, &c.

Mimbar, *s. m.* a pulpit.

Mimiyáná, **Mímiyáná**, } *v. n.* to bleat (a kid.)

Mínakárí, *s. f.* the embellishing of things with green colours, enamelling.

Minár, **Mínár**, **Minára**, } *s. m.* minaret, obelisk, steeple.

Minguí, *s. f.* goat or sheep's dung.

Miṇh, *s. m.* rain.

Minhá, *s. m.* deduction, subtraction; remission of revenue, &c.

Minhái, *s. f.* land released from assessments: *adj.* subtracted.

Miṇhdí, *s. f.* see Meṇhdí.

Mínjná, *v. a.* to rub, to scour.

Minjumla, *adv.* out of or upon the whole; universally.

Minnat, *s. m.* entreaty, humble and earnest supplication.

Minnat karná, to entreat, to make earnest supplication.
Mintí, *s. f.* an apology, submission, solicitation.
Miqnátís, *s. m.* the magnet, the loadstone.
Miqráz, *s. f.* scissors, shears.
Mír, *s. m.* a chief, a leader; a title by which Saiyids are called; a winner at play; among schoolboys he that says his lesson first.
Mirá, *pron.* my, mine.
Miráj, *s. f.* ascent, ascension.
Mírán, *s. m.* a portion paid to the head of a department out of the fees received by the inferior officers.
Mirás, *s. f.* heritage, patrimony, hereditary estate.
Mírásan, *s. f.* a woman who plays and sings.
Mirásí, *adj.* hereditary, inherited: *s. f.* a kind of musician.
Mírásin, *s. f.* see Mírásan.
Mirch, *s. f.* pepper.
Mirchá, Mirchái, } *s. m.* chili-pepper, capsicum.
Mirdang, *s. f.* a kind of drum.
Mirdangí, *s. m.* a beater of the Mirdang; an Indian shade to protect the lamp or candle from the wind.
Mirdangiyá, *s. m.* a beater of the Mirdang.
Mirg, *s. m.* a deer.
Mirgchhálá, the skin of a deer, worn and used as a bed by devotees.
Mirgí, *s. f.* the epilepsy.
Mirgíhá, *s. m.* one afflicted with the epilepsy.
Mír i majlis, the master of the ceremonies.
Mirjái, *s. f.* *prop.* Mirzái, a kind of jacket.
Mírshikár, a bird-catcher, a huntsman.
Mirt, *s. f.* death.
Mirthá, *adj.* false, lying, untrue.
Mirzá, Mírzá, } *s. m.* a title of Musalmáns.
Mirzái, *s. f.* a kind of jacket.
Misal, *s. f.* simile, likeness, similitude, parable.
Misar, *s. m.* Egypt. See Mishar.
Mishar, *s. m.* a title of Bráhmins; a Hindú physician.
Misí, *s. f.* a black powder with which the teeth are tinged.
Misir, *s. m.* see Mishar.
Miskín, *adj.* poor, miserable, humble, wretched, indigent.
Miskíní, *s. f.* poverty, indigence, humility.
Misl, *s. f.* similitude, likeness, like.
Mislan, *adv.* for example, *e.g.* namely.
Mismár honá, to be levelled.
Mismár karná, to level.
Misná, *v. n.* to be ground, to be pulverized.
Misná, *v. a.* to grind, to pulverize, to crumble.
Misr, *s. m.* Egypt.
Misrá, *s. m.* a hemistich, a single line in poetry.
Misrí, *s. f.* sugarcandy.
Misrit, *adj.* mixed.
Missí, *s. f.* see Misí.
Mistar, *s. f.* lines for writing, a ruler.
Miswák, *s. f.* a toothbrush; a stick used as a dentifrice.
Mít, *s. m.* a friend, a lover.
Mítá, *s. m.* a namestick; a large cup.
Mítan, *s. f.* a female namesake.
Miṭáná, *v. a.* to efface, to erase, to obliterate, to blot out, to abrogate, to abolish.
Míṭhá, *adj.* sweet; slow: *s. m.* a very active vegetable poison.
Miṭhái, *s. f.* a sweetmeat; sweetness.
Miṭháíwálá, *s. m.* a maker of sweetmeats, a confectioner.
Miṭhás, Miṭhás, Míṭhás, } *s. m.* sweetness.
Miṭhí, *s. f.* a kiss.
Míṭhí roṭí, a kind of bread.
Miṭhiyá, *s. m.* a kiss.
Mithyá, *adv.* falsely: *adj.* false, counterfeit.

Mití, *s. f.* date; interest.
Mítin, *s. f.* a female namesake.
Miṭná, *v. n.* to expire, to be effaced.
Mitr, } *s. m.* a friend.
Mitra, }
Mitrtá, *s. f.* friendship.
Miṭṭhá, *adj.* sweet; slow.
Miṭṭí, *s. f.* earth. See Maṭṭí.
Miyán, *s. f.* a scabbard.
Miyáṉ, *s. m.* sir, an address expressive of kindness; husband, master.
Miyána, *adj.* middling, moderate: *s. m.* a kind of sedan or pálkí.
Miyáṉ ádmí, a respectable person.
Miyána qadd, of middle stature.
Miyání, *s. f.* a cod-piece.
Miyáṉ jí, *s. m.* a mediator, a schoolmaster.
Miyáṉ tahí, *s. f.* the middle fold of any garment which consists of three.
Mizáj, *s. m.* temperament, habit of body; temper, humour, disposition.
Mizájí, *adj* constitutional, habitual.
Mízán, *s. f.* a balance, a pair of scales; the sign Libra; addition in arithmetic.
Mízán dená, } to add, to cast up.
Mízán lagáná, }
Mizráb, *s. f.* the quill with which a stringed musical instrument is struck.
Mo, *pron.* (in *Braj*) me.
Moáfakat, *s. f. prop.* Muwáfaqat, which see.
Moáfik, *adj. prop.* Muwáfiq, which see.
Moch, *s. m.* strain, sprain, twist.
Mochan, *s. m.* see Mochh.
Mochh, *s. m.* release, deliverance, salvation, final and eternal happiness; mustaches.
Mochí, *s. m.* a saddler, a shoemaker, a cobbler.
Mochin, *s. f.* a saddler's or shoemaker's wife.
Mochná, *s. m.* pincers, tweezers.
Mochras, *s. m.* gum of the silk-cotton tree.
Modí, *s. m.* a retail shopkeeper, a grain merchant, a grocer.
Modíḵhána, *s. m.* a pantry.
Mogal, *s. m. prop.* Mughal, a Moghul.
Mográ, *s. m.* a mallet, a rammer; name of a flower.
Moh, *s. f.* fainting; pity, compassion, allurement, sympathy, kindness, love.
Mohanbhog, *s. m.* a kind of sweetmeat.
Mohaní, *s. f.* fascination, a charm.
Mohanmálá, *s. f.* a necklace composed of gold beads and coral.
Mohar, *s. f. prop.* Muhr, which see.
Moháverá, *s. m. prop.* Muháwara, which see.
Moh lená, to attach, to allure, to captivate.
Moh meṉ áná, to be in love.
Mohná, *v. a.* to fascinate, to enchant, to charm, to allure.
Mojá, *prop.* Moza, which see.
Mokaddamá, *s. m. prop.* Muqaddama, which see.
Mokám, *s. m. prop.* Maqám, which see.
Mo kauṉ, to me, me.
Mokhá, *s. m.* a small hole in a wall for admitting light and air, an air hole; a bamboo or grass tied lengthways on the eaves of a house, &c.
Mokhtár, *prop.* Muḵhtár, which see.
Mo ko, } to me, me.
Mo koṉ, }
Mol, *s. m.* purchase, price.
Moláhejá, *s. m. prop.* Muláhaza, which see.
Moláim, *adj. prop.* Muláim, which see.
Mol baṛháná, *v. a.* to enhance.
Mol lená, *v. a.* to buy, to purchase.
Mol ṭhaharáná, *v. a.* to appraise, to estimate, to value.
Moltol, *s. m.* fixing a price, purchasing.
Mom, *s. m.* wax.

Mombattí, *s. f.* a wax candle.
Momdil, *adj.* tender-hearted.
Momí, *adj.* waxen.
Momiyáí, *s. f.* name of a medicine.
Momjáma, *s. m.* wax-cloth.
Mom kí battí, a wax candle.
Mom kí nák, a person of a fickle disposition.
Mom raughan, } *s. m.* wax and oil
Mom roghan, } mixed together.
Moṉ, see Meṉ.
Moná, *v. a.* to steep.
Monḍhá, *s. m.* the shoulder ; a stool, a footstool.
Moṉhrí, *s. f.* see Morí.
Mor, } *s. m.* twist, turn, writhe,
Moṛ, } sprain.
Mor, *s. m.* a peacock : *pron.* my, mine.
Morá, *pron.* my, mine. [see.
Morabbá, *s. m. prop.* Murabbá, which
Morcha, *s. m.* rust ; a battery.
Morchang, *s. f.* a jew's-harp.
Morchhal, *s. m.* a fan for driving away flies (especially of peacock's feathers) ; a brush.
Moṛhá, *s. m.* a footstool ; the shoulder.
Morí, *s. f.* a pipe or drain, a subterraneous passage (for water.)
Mormukuṭ, a crown or crest like that of the peacock.
Morná, } *v. a.* to twist, to turn, to
Moṛná, } bend, to screw.
Morní, *s. f.* a pea-hen.
Morpankhí, *s. f.* a kind of pleasure-boat, a barge.
Moṭ, *s. f.* see Moṭh.
Moṭá, *adj.* fat, corpulent, coarse, thick, large, big, great, bulky.
Moṭáí, *s. f.* fatness, corpulency, thickness, coarseness, bigness, bulk, bulkiness.
Moṭáná, *v. a.* to fatten, to feed.
Moṭápá, } *s. m.* see Moṭáí.
Moṭápan, }
Moṭá táza, *adj.* fat, well-conditioned.
Moṭh, *s. f.* a bundle, package, bale, a load ; amount, total ; a leather bucket for raising water.

Mothá, *s. m.* a kind of grass.
Mothrá, *s. m.* name of a disease in horses, splint, spavin.
Motí, *s. m.* a pearl.
Motíchúr, *s. m.* a kind of sweetmeat.
Motí kí sí áb utarní, to be disgraced.
Moṭiyá, *s. m.* a porter.
Motiyá, *s. m.* name of a flower.
Motiyábind, *s. m.* the name of a kind of blindness.
Moṭkí, *s. f.* a fat woman.
Motrá, *s. m.* see Mothrá.
Moṭrá, *s. m.* a bundle.
Moṭrí, *s. f.* a small bundle, a parcel.
Moza, *s. m.* a sock, a stocking.
Mozawálá, *s. m.* a stocking maker or seller.
Mrig, *s. m.* a deer.
Mrit, *s. f.* death.
Mritak, *s. m.* a dead body, a corpse.
Mritya, *s. f.* death.
Mú, *s. m.* hair.
Múá, *adj.* dead, lifeless, dull.
Muạf, *adj.* absolved, dispensed with, forgiven, pardoned, exempted, excused : *s. m.* forgiveness, exemption.
Muạf honá, to be forgiven, to be pardoned.
Muạfí, *adj.* exempt from rent and tax : *s. f.* a grant of land from a sovereign free of tax ; exemption, remission, pardon.
Muạf karná, *v. a.* to forgive, to pardon, to excuse.
Muạiyan, *adj.* established, fixed, appointed.
Muạiyan karná, to fix, to establish, to appoint, to constitute.
Muạjiza, *s. m.* a miracle.
Muạlaja, *s. m.* curing, healing, treatment, a remedy.
Muạlaja karná, to heal, cure, attend (as a physician.)
Muạllaq, *adj.* suspended, hanging, hung up.
Muạllim, *s. m.* an instructor, a teacher, a preceptor.
Muạmala, *s. m.* treaty, affair, busi-

ness, negotiation, behaviour, procedure, cause or suit (in law.)
Muámaladán, *adj.* see Muámalatí.
Muámala karná, to deal with, treat with, to negotiate.
Muámala muqaddama, *s. m.* cause or suit (in law.)
Muámalat, *s. f.* see Muámala.
Muámalatí, *adj.* fit for business, active, able to manage business; acquainted with the law.
Muammá, *s. m.* an enigma, a riddle.
Muannas, *adj.* feminine.
Muassir, *adj.* penetrating, making an impression, effecting, efficacious.
Muatabar, *adj.* confidential, respectable, reputable, worthy of confidence, creditable, trustworthy.
Muatabarí, *s. f.* confidence, reliance.
Muatád, *s. f.* quantity, or measure, dose. [moderate.
Muatadil, *adj.* temperate, tolerable,
Muataqid, *s. m.* a believer, an adherent.
Muattal, *adj.* unemployed.
Muattar, *adj.* perfumed, fragrant.
Muazzaz, *adj.* honoured, revered.
Muazzin, *s. m.* a public crier to prayers.
Mubaddal, *adj.* changed, exchanged, altered.
Múbáf, *s. m.* a fillet or riband for the hair.
Mú ba mú, hair by hair.
Mubárak, *adj.* happy, fortunate, blessed; blessing, congratulation; welcome! hail! all hail!
Mubárakbád, may it be fortunate! hail! congratulation.
Mubárakbádí, *s. f.* congratulation, benediction, welcome.
Mubárakbádí dená, } to congratulate, to give
Mubárakbádí kahná, } joy, to hail, to compliment.
Mubárakí, *s. f.* auspiciousness, happiness, congratulation, benediction.
Mublagh, *s. m.* ready money: *adj.* much, many.
Mubtadí, *s. m.* a young scholar, tyro, a beginner.
Muchalká, } *s. m.* a bond, a note of
Muchalka, } hand, an agreement, a written obligation.
Muchchá, *s. m.* a large lump of flesh or meat.
Muchh, } *s. f.* the hair of the upper
Múchh, } lip, mustaches.
Múchhail, *adj.* having much hair on the upper lip.
Múchkaná, *v. a.* to sprain.
Mudám, *adv.* or *adj.* eternally, always, perpetual, lasting, eternal.
Mudámí, *adj.* eternal.
Muddaá, *s. m.* desire, wish, meaning, view, object, scope.
Muddaí, *s. m. f.* a plaintiff, suitor, prosecutor, an accuser, an enemy.
Muddaí alaihi, a defendant (in law.)
Muddat, *s. f.* a space or length of time, a long time, antiquity.
Muddat guzarná, *v. n.* to be spent (time.)
Muddatí, *adj.* of old standing, bearing authority for a time.
Muddat i madíd, a long space of time.
Mudrí, *s. f.* a ring, a finger-ring.
Mufáraqat, *s. f.* separation, alienation, absence. [terval.
Mufásala, *s. m.* distance, space, in-
Mufassal, *adj.* distinct, full, ample, detailed: *adv.* particularly, distinctly, in detail, fully: *s. m.* the country in opposition to the town.
Mufat, *prep.* Muft, which see.
Mufíd, *adj.* profitable, useful, salutary, beneficial.
Muflis, *adj* poor, wretched, indigent; unmarried (a man.)
Muflisí, *s. f.* poverty, indigence.
Mufrad, *adj.* solitary, alone, single, simple.
Mufradát, *s. plur.* of Mufrad, simples, uncompounded (medicines.)
Mufsid, a seditious person, author of evil, mischief-maker.

Muft, *adv.* gratuitously, for nothing, gratis, acquired without cost or labour, given away without return or benefit.

Muftarí, *s. m.* a slanderer, a calumniator, false accuser.

Muftí, *s. m.* a superior Muhammadan law officer.

Muftkhora, *adj.* living at free cost.

Muft men, gratis, for nothing.

Mugdar, *s. m.* a club used to exercise with in the manner of dumb-bells.

Mughaiyar, *adj.* changed, altered.

Mughal, *s. m.* a Moghul.

Mughalí, *adj.* of the Moghuls: *s. f.* tying the neck and toes as a punishment.

Mughlání, *s. f.* the female of a Moghul; a needle-woman.

Múgrí, *s. f.* a mallet for beating clothes with.

Muh, *s. m.* see Munh.

Muhabbat, *s. f.* friendship, love, affection.

Muháfa, *s. m.* a kind of pálkí, a litter in which women travel.

Muháfazat, *s. f.* preservation, protection, guardianship, custody, care.

Muháfiz dafter, *s. m.* a record-keeper.

Muhaiyá, *adj.* prepared, ready, arranged.

Muhaiyá karná, } to prepare, to make
Muhaiyá rakhná, } ready.

Muhál, *adj.* impossible, absurd.

Muhammad, *n. prop.* name of the Arabian prophet.

Muhammadí, *adj.* Muhammadan.

Muháná, *s. m.* the mouth of a river, &c., inlet, outlet.

Muhar, *s. f.* see Muhr.

Muharram, *s. m.* the first Muhammadan month—held sacred in honour of Husain.

Muharrir, *s. m.* a writer, a clerk.

Muhásá, *s. m.* a pimple (on the face in youth.)

Muhásaba, *s. m.* computation, account, settlement or audit of accounts.

Muhásaba lená, to settle or audit (accounts.)

Muhassil, *s. m.* a bailiff.

Muháwara, *s. m.* idiom, usage, phraseology.

Muhchang, *s. f.* a jew's-harp.

Muhibb, *s. m.* a friend, a lover.

Muhimm, *adj.* important, serious: *s. f.* urgent, momentous business, important affair, affair of consequence.

Muhlat, *s. f.* respite, time, leisure.

Muhr, *s. f.* a seal; a gold coin.

Muhrá, *s. m.* van, vanguard.

Muhra, *s. m.* a rubber, the instrument with which native paper, &c., is polished.

Muhredár, *adj.* smoothed, polished, glazed (as paper, cloth, &c.)

Muhrí, *s. f.* a drain, a gutter: *adj.* sealed; the cuff of the sleeve of a jacket, or the extremity of the leg of a pair of trowsers.

Muhrkan, *s. m.* a seal-engraver.

Muhr karná, to seal.

Muhtáj, *adj.* necessitous, indigent, in want.

Muhtájagí, } *s. f.* indigence, poverty.
Muhtájí, }

Muj, *pron.* me.

Mujáka, *s. m. prop.* Muzáyaqa, which see.

Mujallad, *adj.* bound (a volume.)

Mujarrab, *adj.* tried, proved; experienced.

Mujarrad, *adj.* solitary, alone, only, single, unmarried.

Mujassam, *adj.* having body, imbodied, corpulent, incarnate.

Mujáwir, *s. m.* a sweeper of, or one attached to, a temple.

Mujáwirí, *s. f.* constant attendance at a mosque.

Muje, *pron.* me, to me.

Mujh, *pron.* me.

Mujhe, *pron.* me, to me.

Mújib, s. m. cause, reason, motive, account.
Mujrá, s. m. obeisance, respects, visit; allowance, deduction.
Mujrá karná, to visit, to pay respects, to make obeisance.
Mujrá lená, to deduct, to subtract.
Mujrim, *adj.* criminal: s. m. a sinner.
Múká, s. m. the fist; a thump, a blow. See Mokhá.
Mukábalá, s. m. see Muqábala.
Mukábalá karná, see Muqábala karná.
Mukaddamá, see Muqaddama.
Mukaddar, *adj.* muddy, troubled, disturbed, vexed.
Mukar. *prop.* Muqarrar, which see.
Mukarná, v. a. to deny.
Mukarrar, *adj.* repeated again.
Mukarrar karná, to repeat.
Mukarrar sakarrar, *adv.* repeatedly.
Mukh, s. m. the mouth, the face.
Muḳhaivar, *adj.* bountiful, charitable, liberal.
Muḳhálafat, s. f. opposition, variance, enmity.
Muḳhálafat karná, to oppose, to envy.
Muḳhálif, *adj.* opposite, contrary; an opponent, adversary, an enemy.
Muḳhammas, s. m. a kind of verse containing five lines.
Muḳhannas, *adj.* effeminate: s. an hermaphrodite, a eunuch.
Muḳhátab, s. m. the person spoken to or addressed; the second person in grammar.
Muḳhátib, s. m. the speaker, the person who addresses another.
Muḳhátib honá, to turn towards in speaking, to address.
Mukh bhiṛ, *adj.* opposite, in front.
Múkhí, s. f. a thump; a kind of pigeon.
Muḳhlis, s. m. a sincere friend.
Muḳhlisána, *adv.* friendly, sincerely.
Mukhṛá, s. m. the mouth, the face.
Muḳhtálif, *adj.* diverse, discordant, different.
Muḳhtár, *adj.* invested with authority: s. m. an agent, an attorney.
Muḳhtárí, s. f. power, authority, attorneyship.
Muḳhtárkár, s. m. an attorney.
Muḳhtárkárí, s. f. attorneyship.
Muḳhtárnáma, s. m. a written authority, a power of attorney.
Muḳhtasar, *adj.* abbreviated, abridged: s. m. a compendium, epitome, abridgment.
Múkí, s. f. a thump, a blow of the fist.
Mukká, s. m. } a thump, a blow with
Mukkí, s. f. } the fist, the fist.
Mukt, *adj.* released, absolved, freed from corporal existence: s. m. pardon, salvation, absolution from sin.
Muktá, s. m. a pearl.
Mukti, s. m. see Mukt.
Mukuṭ, s. m. a crown, a diadem, a crest.
Múl, s. m. origin, root, generation, principal or capital sum of money.
Mulabbab, *adj.* brimful.
Muláhaza, s. m. looking at, contemplation, perusal, view, regard, notice.
Muláí, s. f. appraisement, valuation, asking above its value (for anything.)
Muláim, *adj.* soft, tender, gentle, mild, affable.
Muláim honá, v. n. to become soft, to soften.
Muláim karná, v. a. to soften, to mollify.
Mulamma, *adj.* plated, covered with gold or silver.
Mulána, v. a. to appraise, to inquire the price of anything.
Muláqát, s. f. a meeting, interview, visit.
Muláqát karná, to visit, to meet, to have an interview with.
Mulátafa, s. m. roll of letters.
Muláyamat, s. f. softness, tenderness, gentleness.
Mulázamat, s. f. paying respects to a superior.
Mulázim, s. a servant, attendant.

Mulhaṭṭí, *s. f.* name of a medicinal root, liquorice.
Múlí, *s. f.* a radish.
Muljam, *prop.* Mulzam, which see.
Mulk, *s. m.* a country, kingdom, realm, dominion.
Mulkdárí, *s. f.* dominion, government, ruling.
Mulkgírí, *s. f.* political affairs; going the circuit.
Mulkí, *adj.* belonging to a country.
Mullá, *s. m.* a schoolmaster, doctor.
Multán, *s. m.* Mooltan, name of a country.
Multání, *adj.* of Multán.
Multání maṭṭí, *s. f.* Armenian bole.
Multaví, *adj.* delayed, postponed, spun out, protracted.
Muluk, *s. m. prop.* Mulk, which see.
Mulzam, *adj.* convicted, convinced, confuted, blameable.
Mumání, *s. f.* an aunt, mother's brother's wife.
Múmin, *s. m.* a Musalman weaver.
Mumkin, *adj.* possible.
Mumkin honá, to be possible.
Múṇ, *s. m.* see Muṇh.
Múná, *v. n.* to die.
Munádí, *s. f.* proclamation.
Munáfạ, *s. m.* profit, advantage, gain.
Munáfiq, *s. m.* a hypocrite, infidel, atheist.
Munáját, *s. f.* prayer, supplication.
Munajjim, *s. m.* an astronomer, astrologer.
Munaqqa, *s. m.* a species of raisins.
Munásib, *adj.* proper, pertinent, fit, suitable, meet, becoming, expedient, apposite.
Munázara, *s. m.* a disputation, discussion, argument.
Múṇchh, *s. f.* see Múchh.
Munḍ, *s. m.* the head; a headman, a ring-leader.
Múnḍ, *s. m.* the head.
Munḍá, *s. m.* the head; the head of a paper kite: *adj.* shaven, bald, uncovered.
Munḍáuá, *v. a.* to shave.
Mundaraj, } *adj.* contained, inserted,
Mundarij, } included, comprised.
Munḍásá, *s. m.* a kind of small turban.
Munḍer, *s. f.* coping of a wall.
Múndhná, *v. a.* see Múndná.
Munḍí, *s. f.* name of a medicinal plant.
Múnḍí, *s. f.* the head.
Munḍlá, *adj.* shaved.
Munḍmál, *s. f.* a necklace of heads.
Munḍná, *v. n.* to be shaved.
Múnḍná, *v. a* to shave; to instruct, to convert or make a disciple.
Mundná, *v. n.* to be shut, closed, contracted: *v. a.* to close.
Múndná, *v. a.* to shut, to cover, to close, to imprison.
Munḍpaná, *s. m.* disobedience, insolence, arrogance, refractoriness.
Mundrá, *s. m.* } a ring, a collar, a
Mundrí, *s. f.* } finger-ring.
Munḍwáná, *v. a.* to cause to be shaved.
Múng, *s. f.* name of a kind of pulse.
Múngá, *s. m.* coral.
Muṇh, } *s. m.* mouth, face, counte-
Múṇh, } nance, orifice.
Muṇhámuṇh, *adj.* brimful.
Muṇháná, *s. m.* soreness in the mouth, thrush; salivation.
Muṇh andherá, } twilight, evening.
Muṇh andhiyárá, }
Munhaní, *adj.* lean, thin, decrepit.
Múṇhánmúṇh, tête-à-tête, face to face, brimful, topful.
Múṇhánmúṇhí, *s. f.* altercation, squabble, wrangle.
Muṇh báná, to open the mouth, to gape.
Muṇh banáná, to make faces or mouths.
Muṇh band karná, to hold one's tongue.
Muṇh bárná, to refrain.
Muṇh bigáṛná, to frown, to make faces; to punish.
Muṇh bigaṛná, to have the taste blunted or depraved.
Muṇhbolá bhái, } an intimate friend.
Muṇhbolí bahin, }

Muṇh chaláná, to bite (as a horse); to eat.
Muṇhchang, a jew's-harp.
Muṇh chaṛhná, to become too familiar, to be saucy, to presume.
Muṇh chhipáná, to hide one's face (from bashfulness.)
Muṇh chiṛáná, to make mouths.
Muṇhchor, shame-faced, bashful, timid.
Muṇhchorí, bashfulness.
Muṇh ḍálná, to beg.
Muṇh dekhkar bát karná, to flatter, to speak what one supposes will be agreeable to one's hearers.
Muṇh dekhná, to look up to (for aid, &c.); to be astonished or helpless; to be partial.
Muṇh dekh rahná, to stare at with surprise.
Muṇh dená, to familiarize, to favour, to countenance.
Muṇhdikhái, s. f. a present given by the friends of the family and the women of the neighbourhood on their first visit to a bride.
Muṇh dikháná, to show one's face.
Muṇh jhuṭálná, to eat something.
Muṇh kálá karná, to incur disgrace; to punish, to disgrace.
Muṇh ká phuhar, abusive.
Muṇh karná, to turn one's face or direct one's steps towards any particular object or place.
Muṇh kholná, to abuse.
Muṇh lagáná, to familiarize, to be intimate with inferiors.
Muṇh lagná, to become too familiar, to presume, to be saucy.
Muṇh laṭkáná, to be down in the mouth, to make a long face.
Muṇh leke rah jáná, to be silent from shame.
Muṇhmángá, requested or asked for by word of mouth.
Muṇh moṛná, to turn away, to abstain or desist from anything.
Muṇhnál, s. m. the mouthpiece of a huqqa.
Muṇh páná, to get into one's good graces.
Muṇh par fákhta uṛ jáná, to change colour.
Muṇh par láná, to tell, to relate.
Muṇh pasárná, to gape (with surprise, &c.)
Muṇh phailáná, to presume, to desire much.
Muṇh pherná, to abstain from.
Muṇh phirná, to turn away from, to be displeased with, to be disgusted.
Muṇh sukaṛná, to change colour from cold or shame.
Muṇh ṭeṛhá karná, to make wry faces.
Muṇh toṛná, to punish.
Muṇh utar jáná, to have the face shrunk or withered by weakness or emaciation.
Muṇhzor, adj. headstrong, obstinate.
Muṇhzorí, s. f. headstrongness, obstinacy.
Muṇhzubání, adj. verbal (message or evidence.)
Muni, } s. m. a holy man, a sage, a
Muní, } devotee.
Muníb, s. m. a master, a client, a patron.
Muníbí, s. f. mastership, lordship.
Munim, s. m. a benefactor.
Munís, s. m. a saint, a chief of the saints.
Muniyá, s. f. the female of the little bird called amadavats.
Múnj, s. f. the name of a grass of which ropes are made.
Munje, pron. me, to me.
Munjh, pron. me.
Múṇ ká saggá, a flatterer.
Muṇkh, s. m. the face.
Múṇkí, s. f. a blow with the fist.
Munkir, adj. denying, rejecting; one who denies, denier.
Munkir honá, to deny.
Munkir Nakír, the names of two angels, who, agreeably to the Muhammadan creed, examine the spirits of the departed in the tomb.

Múṉkiyáná, *v. a.* to beat or knock with the fist.
Múṉ par muhr karná, to be silent.
Munqaṭi, *adj.* broken off, terminated, finished.
Munqaṭi honá, to be cut off, to be finished, to be settled, terminated.
Múṉṛ, *s. m.* the head.
Muṉṛáná, *v. a.* to shave.
Múṉṛí, *s. f.* the head.
Múṉṛlá, *adj.* head-shaven.
Múṉṛná, *v. a.* to shave.
Muṉṛwáná, *v. a.* to cause to be [shaved.
Múṉsal, *s. m.* see Músal.
Munshí, *s. m.* a writer, a secretary; a tutor, a teacher.
Munshígarí, *s. f.* the business of a munshí, secretaryship.
Munsí, *s. m. prop.* Munshí, which see.
Munsif, *adj.* just, equitable: *s. m.* a judge, an arbitrator.
Munsifí, *s. f.* decision, justice, judgment.
Munsif mizáj, just in temperament, a person of propriety and taste.
Múṉ síná, to be silent.
Múṉslá, *s. m.* see Musal.
Muntashar karná, *v. a.* to scatter, to disperse.
Muntazir, *adj.* expecting with impatience, waiting, tarrying for, looking out for.
Múṉzor, *adj.* headstrong, obstinate.
Muqába, } *s. m.* a dressing-box or
Muqábá, } case.
Muqábala, *s. m.* comparison, collation, opposition, confronting, contest, contending, comparing, presence.
Mukábala karná, to contend, to confront, to oppose, to emulate, to compare, to collate.
Muqábil, *adj.* opposite, confronting, matching, resembling.
Muqaddam, *adj.* antecedent, prior, preceding.
Muqaddama, *s. m.* lawsuit, business, an affair, a matter.
Muqaddamát, *s. plur.* of Muqaddama.
Muqaddam honá, to precede.
Muqaddam jánná, to prefer, to consider preferable (over.)
Muqaddar, *adj.* predestinated: *s. m.* fate, destiny.
Muqaddas, *adj.* holy, sanctified.
Muqaffal, *adj.* locked.
Muqaiyad, *adj.* bound, fettered, in chains, imprisoned.
Muqám, *s. m.* see Maqám.
Maqámí, *adj.* see Maqámí.
Muqarrar, *adj.* established, fixed, certain, infallible, unquestionable, appointed, employed: *adv.* certainly, assuredly, positively.
Muqarrar hojáná, } to be certain or
Muqarrar honá, } fixed or appointed,
Muqarrarí, *adj.* fixed, appointed: *s. f.* a fixed stipend.
Muqarrar karná, to fix, to settle, to establish, to appoint, to employ, to assign.
Muqbara, *s. m.* a tomb, a mausoleum.
Muqirr, *adj.* confessing, confession, asserter, avower.
Maqirr honá, to confess, to avow.
Muqqaish, *s. m.* brocade (gold or silver thread.)
Muqqaishí, *adj.* brocaded.
Muqtadí, *s.* follower, imitator.
Muqúm, *s. m.* a resident, an inhabitant.
Múṛ, *s. m.* the head.
Murabbá, *s. m.* a preserve, jam, confection.
Murabbạ, *adj.* square, quadrangular.
Murabbạ karná, to square.
Murabbí, *s. m.* a tutor, guardian, patron, father.
Murád, *s. f.* desire, wish, intention, design, purport.
Muraí, *s. f.* radish.
Múrak, } *adj.* ignorant, foolish,
Múrakh, } stupid, idiot, fool.
Muraḵhḵhas, *adj.* permitted, allowed (to depart.)

Múrakhpaná, s. m. | barbarism, folly,
Múrakhtá, s. f. | ignorance, stu-
Murakhtái, s. f. | pidity.

Murakkab, *adj.* compounded, composed, combined, mixed.

Murakkabát, s. *plur.* of Murakkab, compounds (in medicine), not simple.

Murakná, *v. n.* to be twisted, to be sprained.

Muranḍá karná, to tie.

Muráqaba, *s. m.* contemplation.

Múrat, *s. f.* a statue, an image, an idol, a person (term used by Bairágís.)

Murattab, *adj.* arranged, regulated, prepared.

Murauwaj, *adj.* current, saleable, usual.

Murchang, *s. f.* jew's-harp.

Murchhá, | s. f. a swoon, stupefac-
Múrchhá, | tion.

Múrchhá jáná, to swoon, to faint.

Múrchhit, *adj.* fainted, in a swoon, entranced,

Murda, *adj.* dead: *s. m.* a corpse, a dead body.

Murdafarosh, name of a caste whose business it is to carry the dead.

Murdaní, *adj.* fit to die, having the symptoms of death.

Murdár, *adj.* polluted, impure; dried or dead (skin): *s. m.* carrion.

Murdársang, |
Murdásang, | s. m. litharge.
Murdasang, |

Murdasho, one who washes the dead.

Murde ghaṭí, *s. f.* see Marghaṭ.

Murgh, *s. m.* fowl, bird, cock, (particularly house-fowl.)

Murghá, *s. m.* a cock.

Murghábí, *s. f.* a water-fowl.

Murghbáz, *s. m.* a cock-fighter.

Murghí, *s. f.* a hen.

Murgh i ḳhángí, the domestic cock or hen.

Murghíwálá, s. m. | a poulterer.
Murghíwálí, s. f. |

Múṛh, *adj.* foolish, stupid, ignorant.

Murhá, *s. m.* a squib.

Múrí, *s. f.* a radish.

Muríd, *s. m.* a disciple, a scholar, a follower.

Murídí, *s. f.* tuition, instruction.

Murjháná, *v. n.* to wither, to fade, to pine, to droop, to be dejected or dispirited.

Murkáná, *v. a.* to twist, to writhe.

Murkí, *s. f.* an ornament worn in the ear.

Murlí, *s. f.* a fife, flute, pipe.

Muṛná, *v. n.* to be turned back, bent, twisted, turned; to turn.

Murrá, *s. m.* a squib.

Murshid, *s. m.* an instructor, a spiritual guide.

Murúwat, *s. f.* manliness, virility, fortitude, affection, generosity, urbanity, affability.

Murúwatdár, *adj.* generous, affable, affectionate.

Murúwat toṛná, to cease behaving affectionately.

Músá, *s. m.* a mouse, a rat: *n. prop.* Moses.

Musabbar, *s. f.* aloes.

Musabbib, *s. m.* the causer, the first [cause.

Musabbib i haqíqí, God.

Musabbib ul asbáb, the causer of causes, *i.e.*, God.

Musáfaha, *s. m.* shaking hands.

Musáfarat, *s. f.* travelling, travel, journey.

Musaffá, *adj.* clean, clear, clarified.

Musáfir, *s. m.* a traveller, passenger, stranger.

Musáfirána, *adv.* traveller-like.

Musáfirat, *s. f.* travelling, journeying.

Musáfirí, *s. f.* travelling.

Musáhabat, *s. f.* companionship, society.

Musáhib, *s. m. f.* a companion, friend; aide-de-camp, associate.

Musal, | s. m. a wooden pestle used
Músal, | in cleaning rice from the husk, &c.

Musaláṇ súṇ ḍhol bajáná, to feast, to make merry.

Musaldhár barasná, v. n. to rain very heavily.

Musallá, s. m. a carpet to pray on.

Musallah, adj. armed for war, in armour.

Musallí, adj. one who prays.

Musalmán, s. m. a believer in Muhammad.

Musalmání, s. f. circumcision; a female Musalmán.

Musalmín, Muhammadans or a Muhammadan.

Musammá, adj. named, denominated, entitled, called.

Musammam, adj. fixed, concluded, determined.

Musáná, v. n. to cause to steal.

Musannaf, adj. composed.

Musannif, s. m. composer, an author.

Musauwada, s. m. a sketch or rough draught of a letter, &c.

Musauwir, s. m. a limner, a drawer.

Musauwirí, s. f. drawing, figuring.

Musáwát, s. f. equation, evenness, equality.

Musáwí, adj. equal, all one, suitable, convenient.

Músh, s. m. a mouse.

Mushábaha, s. m. } similitude, re-
Mushábahat, s. f. } semblance.

Mushábih, adj. like, resembling: s. m. resemblance, similitude.

Mus'haf, s. m. the Qurán.

Musháhara, s. m. monthly salary, pay, wages.

Mushajjar, s. m. a kind of brocade.

Musháta, s. f. a woman who makes or concerts marriages, a go-between.

Mushátagarí, } s. f. the making or
Mushátagí, } concerting of a
Mushátagirí, } marriage.

Mus'hil, adj. a purgative.

Mushír, s. m. a counsellor, a senator.

Mushk, s. m. musk.

Mushkeṇ bándhná, } v. a. to pinion,
Mushkeṇ chaṛháná, } to tie the hands behind the back.

Mushkí, adj. dark bay, approaching to black (colour of a horse.)

Mushkil, adj. difficult, intricate, hard, painful: s. f. difficulty.

Mushrik, s. m. an idolator, a polytheist.

Mushtáq, adj. full of desire, desirous, wishing, longing.

Mushtari, s. f. the planet Jupiter.

Musíbat, s. f. a misfortune, disaster, affliction, calamity, adversity, evil, misery, ill.

Musíbatzada, adj. unfortunate.

Muskán, s. f. a smile, a grin.

Muskáná, v. n. to smile, to grin, to smirk.

Muskuráhat, } s. f. smiling, grinning,
Muskurái, } smirk, laughing.

Muskuráná, v. n. to smile, to grin, to smirk.

Múslá, s. m. see Musal.

Músládhár, s. m. raining.

Músládhár barasná, to rain very heavily.

Músná, v. a. to pilfer, to steal, to filch, to defraud.

Músrá, s. m. the axis of a hand mill; the screw of a machine or vice; the core of the jack fruit, &c.

Musrif, adj. prodigal, extravagant.

Mustafá, s. m. one of the titles of Muhammad.

Mustafíd, adj. gaining, profiting, acquiring.

Mustahiqq, adj. worthy, deserving, having a right, rightful.

Mustaịd, adj. prepared, ready, fit, capable, able, worthy, adept.

Mustájir, s. m. a renter, a farmer.

Mustạmal, adj. used, applied, accustomed.

Mustaqbil, s. m. future, the future tense.

Mustaradd, adj. returned, restored.

Mút, s. m. urine.

Mutạ, s. m. taking a wife for a time, a temporary marriage of the Shiạs.

Mutạddid, adj. many, various.

Mutaạiyin, *adj.* appointed, fixed, constituted, deputed.
Mutaạiyin karná, to appoint, to depute, &c.
Mutaạjjib, *adj.* wonderful, astonished, amazed, admiring.
Mutaạjjib honá, *v. n.* to be astonished.
Mutaạlliq, *adj.* connected with, attached to, occupied or engaged (in.)
Mutaạlliq honá, to depend.
Mutábaqat, *s. f.* conformity, equality, analogy.
Mutabarrak, *adj.* fortunate, blessed, holy.
Mutábiq, *adj.* conformable, suitable, answering, correspondent, agreeable to.
Mutafakkir, *adj.* contemplative, thinking, reflecting, thoughtful, serious, pensive, grave.
Mutafanní, *adj.* vicious.
Mutafarriq, *adj.* separate, distinct, dispersed.
Mutafarriqát, *plur.* of Mutafarriq, various and scattered things.
Mutaghaiyir, *adj.* changed, altered.
Muṭáí, *s. f.* see Moṭáí.
Mutakallim, *s. m.* a speaker; the first person in grammar.
Mutálaạ, *s. m.* reading, study, perusal.
Mutálaạ karná, to study, to read, to peruse.
Mutaláshí, *s. m.* an inquirer, searcher.
Mutanaffis, *adj.* solitary, single.
Mutanjan puláo, *s. m.* a kind of dish.
Muṭápá, *s. m.* fatness, plumpness, bigness.
Mutaraddid, *adj.* irresolute, perplexed, hesitating, wavering.
Mutárí, *s. f.* see Mutihrí.
Mutarjim, *s. m.* an interpreter, a translator.
Mutás, *s. f.* desire or inclination to make urine.
Mutássá, *adj.* desirous of making urine.
Mutasaddí, *s. m.* an accountant, a clerk, a writer.
Mutasaddígarí, *s. f.* office of a clerk.
Mutawajjih, *adj.* turning or looking towards, attentive, favouring, countenancing, intent on.
Mutawajjih honá, to turn the face (towards), to attend (to), to look (towards), to regard, to be intent (on.)
Mutawátir, *adj.* successive, successively.
Mutawattin, *s.* inhabitant, a native of any country.
Muṭh, *s. m.* the fist.
Múṭh, *s. f.* handle, hilt; fist; name of a game.
Múṭhí, *s. f.* the fist.
Muṭhí, *s. f.* fist, handful.
Muṭhiyá, name of a sweetmeat.
Mutihrí, *s. f.* a hole in a stable in which the urine collects.
Muṭiyá, *s. m.* bearer of burdens, a porter.
Mutlaq, *adv.* wholly, not in the least, never, entirely.
Mutlaqan, *adv.* absolutely (not) at all.
Mutná, *adj.* one who makes much urine, a piss-a-bed,
Mútná, *v. n.* to make urine, to make water.
Muttafiq, *adj.* agreeing, concurring, united: *s.* an accomplice, co-operator.
Muttafiq honá, to agree together, to accord, to concur, to co-operate.
Muttaqí, *adj.* abstinent, abstemious, temperate, pious.
Muttasil, *adj.* joined, near, contiguous, adjoining.
Muṭṭhí, *s. f.* fist, a handful.
Muṭṭhí bhar, a handful.
Muwáfaqat, *s. f.* conformity, analogy, agreement, acquaintance, friendship.
Muwáfaqat karná, to enter into friendship, to conform, &c.
Muwáfiq, *adj.* conformable, like, suiting, analogous, fit, agreeing, according to, congruous, favourable.

Muwakkal, *s. m.* a vicegerent, a superintendent.
Muyassar, *adj.* attainable, attained, procurable obtainable.
Muyassar ho jáná, } *v. n.* to be attained or got.
Muyassar honá, }
Muzabzab, *adj.* doubtful, ambiguous : *s.* doubt, suspense,
Muzáhamat, *s. f.* prevention, impediment, hindrance.
Muzáhim, *s. m.* a preventer.
Muzakkar, *adj*, masculine (in gender.)
Muzári, *s. m.* the aorist (in grammar.)
Muzáyaqa, *s. m.* moment, consequence, significance.
Muzhda, *s. m.* joyful tidings, good news.
Múzí, *adj.* hurter, vexer, tormentor, pesterer, troubler.
Muzirr, *adj.* pernicious, hurtful, baleful, injurious, noxious.
Muztarib, *adj.* agitated, disturbed, distracted, afflicted.
Myán, *s. m.* see Miyán.

N.

Na, a negative or prohibitive particle, no, not, nay, neither, nor.
Ná, no, not, a negative prefix to nouns having the same meaning as the English prefixes in, un, im, il, dis, non, &c., or the affix less.
Náb, *s. m.* the middle of a tree.
Nabaj, *s. f. prop.* Nabz, the pulse.
Ná báligh, a child not arrived at the age of maturity, a minor,
Nábar, *adj.* denying.
Nabát, *s. f.* vegetation: a herb, vegetable, plant, grass.
Nabátát, *s. plur.* of Nabát, vegetables.
Nabawí, *adj.* prophetical.
Nábdán, *s. m.* a gutter.
Nábhi, *s. f.* the navel ; the nave of a wheel ; a centre.
Nabí, *s. m.* a prophet.
Nábíná, *adj.* blind.
Nábúd, annihilated, vanished : *s.* non-existence.
Nabúwat, *s. f.* prophecy.
Nabz, *s. f.* the pulse.
Nabz dekhná, to feel the pulse.
Nách, *s. m.* a dance, the act of dancing.
Nacháná, *v. a.* to make to dance.
Náchár, *adj.* remediless, helpless, forlorn, distressed, without resource.
Náchárí, *s. f.* helplessness, impotence, necessity.
Náchghar, *s. m.* a dancing-room, a ball-room.
Nachhattar, *s. m.* a mansion of the moon.
Náchíz, *adj.* of no consequence, insignificant, worthless, contemptible; a bauble, a trifle.
Náchízí, *s. f.* insignificance.
Náchná, *v. n.* to dance.
Nách nacháná, *v. a.* to make to dance, to tease.
Nachwaiyá, *s. m.* a dancer.
Nachwáná, *v. a.* to make to dance.
Nad, *s. m.* a river (commonly Nadí.
Nád, *s. m.* a kind of large earthen pan.
Nadámat, *s. f.* repentance, contrition, regret, penitence.
Nádán, *adj.* ignorant, simple, silly.
Nádání, *s. f.* ignorance, simplicity, folly, foolishness, stupidity.
Nádánista, *adj.* unwittingly, ignorantly.
Nádhná, *v. a.* to begin ; to yoke.
Nadí, *s. f.* a river.
Nádihand, *adj.* not paying what is due ; stingy, close-fisted.
Nádir, *adj.* rare, wonderful, choice.
Nadiyá, *s. f.* a river, a small stream.
Nádná, *v. a.* to begin.
Nádurust, *adj.* crooked, untrue, false, improper, imperfect, incorrect.
Nádurustí, *s. f.* injustice.
Náf, *s. f.* the navel, the middle.
Náfa, *s. m*, a pod of musk,
Nafa, *s. m.* profit, gain, advantage, interest.

Nafa honá, to be benefitted.
Nafa karná, to profit, to benefit.
Nafa nuqsán, profit and loss.
Nafar, s. m. a servant; an individual or person.
Náfarmán, adj. disobedient; name of a flower; name of a beautiful purple colour.
Náfarmán bardár, adj. disobedient.
Náfarmán bardárí, s. f. disobedience.
Náfarmání, s. f. disobedience: adj. of the colour of the Náfarmán.
Nafas, see Nafs.
Nafís, adj. precious, delicate, exquisite.
Nafl, s. m. a work of supererogation.
Nafrat, s. f. abomination, aversion, abhorrence, disgust.
Nafs, s. m. the soul, spirit; concupiscence, sensuality; penis.
Nafsání, adj. sensual, carnal, lustful.
Nafsáníyat, s. f. sensuality, carnality.
Nafsí, adj. of the soul, carnal, sensual, animal or beastly.
Nafskashí, s. f. temperance, self-restraint.
Nag, s. m. the stone of a ring, or a stone on which a name, &c., is cut, a jewel.
Nág, s. m. a snake, a serpent.
Nágá, s. m. a class of Hindú faqírs; prop. Nágha, which see.
Nagad, s. m. prop. Naqd, which see.
Nagadá nagadí, see Naqdánaqd.
Nagadí, adj. see Naqdí.
Nágáh, } adv. suddenly, unawares,
Nágah, } unexpectedly, all at once.
Nágahán, } adj. sudden, unexpect-
Nágahání, } ed, accidental: adv. suddenly.
Náganí, s. f. a serpent (female.)
Nagar, s. m. a city, a town.
Nagarí, s. f. a town, a village: adj. of or belonging to a city.
Nágarí, the most common Hindí character of writing; called also Deva-nágarí.
Nágarmothá, s. m. name of a sweet-smelling grass.
Nágaur, s. m. name of a country near Márwár.
Nágaurá, adj. a fine breed of bullocks so called.
Nágawár, adj. unpleasant, unacceptable, unpalatable.
Nagcháná, v. n. to approach.
Nagdá, s. m. prop. Naqd, which see.
Nágesar, s. f. name of a flower.
Nágha, adj. vacant, void, unemployed, absent: s. m. adjournment,
Nagích, prop. Nazdík, which see.
Nágin, s. f. a serpent (female.)
Nagín, } s. m. the stone of a ring,
Nagína, } &c.
Náginí, s. f. a serpent (female.)
Náhak, prop. Náhaqq, which see.
Nahalwáná, v. a. to cause to be bathed or washed.
Nahán, s. m. bathing, ablution.
Naháná, v. n. to bathe, to wash.
Nahaní, s. f. an instrument for cutting nails; a kind of chisel.
Náhaqq, adj. unjust, improper, wrong, undeserved: adv. unjustly, improperly.
Nahárí, s. f. breakfast.
Nahármunh, adj. without eating.
Naharní, s. f. an instrument with which the nails are pared.
Nahí, }
Nahin, }
Náhin, } adv. no, not, nay, no indeed.
Náhín, }
Nahín, }
Nahín nihín, not at all.
Nahín to, conj. otherwise, else.
Nahiyar. s. f. wife's family.
Nahláná, v. a. to cause to bathe.
Naho, s. f. syntax, grammar.
Nahr, s. f. a stream, a rivulet, a canal (of running water.)
Nahúrná, v. n. see Nihúrná.
Náí, s. m. a barber.
Na'í, adj. f. new, produced in the present year.
Nai, s. f. a reed.
Náib, s. m. a deputy, a superintendent, substitute.

Náibdíwán, *s. m.* the deputy-treasurer or accountant.
Náibí, *s. f.* deputyship.
Naicha, *s. m.* a huqqa-snake or tube.
Naichaband, *s.* the person who makes huqqa-snakes.
Naihar, *s. f.* a wife's mother's family.
Náin, *s. f.* a barber's wife.
Nain, *s. m.* the eye.
Náinsáf, *adj.* unjust.
Náinsáfí, *s. f.* injustice.
Nainsukh, *s. m.* a fine sort of muslin.
Nai shakar, *s. m.* sugar-cane.
Naiyá, *s. m.* a boatman, ferryman.
Nájáis, *adj.* unsuitable, unlawful.
Najar, *s. f. prop.* Nazr and Nazar, which see.
Najarána, *s. m. prop.* Nazarána, which see.
Najarband, *s. m.* see Názarband.
Najarbandí, *s. f.* see Nazarbandí.
Naját, *s. f.* freedom, liberation, deliverance, pardon, salvation.
Najdík, Najík, } *prop.* Nazdík, which see.
Nájins, strange in kind, of another sort or species.
Najis, *adj.* dirty, filthy, unclean.
Najm, *s. m.* a star, a horoscope.
Nájúk, *adj. prop.* Názuk, which see.
Nak, *s. f.* the nose.
Nák, in *compos.* (as an affix), full, affected with, &c. : *s. f.* the nose.
Náká, *s. m.* the extremity of a road; the eye of a needle.
Nakal, *s. m. prop.* Naql, which see.
Nakaliyá, *adj.* mimicing, imitating, copying.
Nakalnavís, *s. m.* a copyist.
Nakár, *s. m.* refusal, denial.
Nákára, Nakára, } *adj.* useless, worthless, fit for nothing, invalid.
Nakárá, *s. m. prop.* Naqára, a kettle-drum.
Nakárná, *v. a.* to refuse, to deny.
Nakchaṛhá, *adj.* angry, fretful, warm, passionate, fastidious.
Nák chaṛháná, to be angry or displeased.
Nákebandí, shutting up a road.
Nakel, *s. f.* the wooden or iron instrument fixed to a camel's nose, and to which the string by which he is led is fastened.
Nakghisní, *s. f.* rubbing the nose on the ground in prostration or by way of humility.
Nakh, *s. m.* a finger or toe nail; the string of a paper kite.
Ná ḳhalaf, *adj.* degenerate, wicked, undutiful (son.)
Nákhándá, *prop.* Náḳhwánda, which see.
Naḳhḳhás, *s. m.* a market for slaves or cattle.
Nákhodá, *prop.* Náḳhudá, which see.
Naḳhrá, Naḳhra, } *s. m.* trick, artifice, joke, waggery, sham, pretence, coquetry.
Naḳhrábáz, *adj.* waggish, shaming, coquettish.
Naḳhrábází, *s. f.* affectation, coquetry.
Naḳhrátillá, coquetry, blandishments.
Nakh se sikh talak, Nakh sikh talak, } from top to toe, entirely; (*lit.*) from the (toe) nails to the hair on the crown of the head.
Náḳhudá, *s. m.* master or commander of a ship, captain or supercargo.
Náḳhudátars, not fearing God.
Náḳhun, *s. m.* nail (of the finger, toe, &c.), talon, claw.
Náḳhun lená, to pare the nails; to trip or stumble (a horse.)
Náḳhuntarásh, *s. m.* an instrument for cutting the nails with.
Náḳhúsh, *adj.* displeased, not pleased, not joyful, unhappy, indisposed.
Náḳhúshí, *s. f.* displeasure, the want of pleasure or joy.
Náḳhúsh karná, *v. a.* to displease.
Náḳhwánda, *adj.* unread, unlearned, illiterate, one who cannot read.
Nákí, *adj.* nasal.
Nakír, *s. m.* name of an angel; a line.
Nákis, *adj. prop.* Náqis, which see.
Nák ká bál, *adj.* respected, honoured.

Nakkáduá, a kind of game at dice.
Nák kátná, to dishonour.
Nakkí, *s. f.* speaking through the nose, nasal sound.
Nakkí múnṭh, *s. f.* the name of a game.
Nákoat, *adj. prop.* Náqúwat, which see.
Nakrá, Nakṛá, Nákṛá, } *s. m.* an inflammation in the nose.
Nák rakhná, to preserve one's honour.
Naksán, *s. m. prop.* Nuqsán, which see.
Nakshá, *s. m. prop.* Naqsha, which see.
Nakṭá, *adj.* nose-clipt, noseless.
Nakṭorá, *adj.* droll, waggish.
Nal, *s. m.* a tube, spout, joint of bamboo, &c.; large tiles.
Nál, *s. m.* a tube, barrel or tube of a gun; the navel string.
Naʻl, *s. m.* a horse-shoe, a hoof.
Nálá, *s. m.* a rivulet, a brook, a ravine (dry but in the rainy season.)
Nála, *s. m.* lamentation, moan.
Náláiq, *adj.* unworthy, unfit, improper.
Náláiqí, *s. f.* unworthiness, impropriety.
Náláiqpaná, *s. m.* unworthiness, impropriety, wickedness.
Nála karná, to lament, to complain, to moan.
Nál áṇwal, *s. f.* navel-string and afterbirth.
Naʻlband, *s. m.* a farrier, a shoeing smith.
Naʻlbandí, *s. f.* shoeing, giving a horse new shoes; a light tribute.
Nalí, *s. f.* a tube, spout; a gun-barrel; the bone of the leg.
Nálí, *s. f.* a drain, a gutter, a sluice.
Nális, *s. f. prop.* Nálish, a complaint.
Nálish, *s. f.* a complaint, accusation in a law court.
Nálishí, *adj.* a complainant, a plaintiff.
Nálish karná, to complain against.
Nálish karnewálá. *s. m.* a complainer, plaintiff.
Nálkí, *s. f.* a sort of sedan or litter.
Nál puren, *s. f.* navel-string and afterbirth.

Nam, *adj.* moist, damp, wet.
Nám, *s. m.* name, character, fame, reputation, honour.
Náma, *s. m.* a letter, writing, treatise; in *compos.* a book, history, account.
Námahram, not a confidant.
Námaʻlúm, *adj.* unknown.
Namáj, *s. f. prop.* Namáz, which see.
Namak, *s. m.* salt; bread, subsistence; (*met.*) spirit, animation.
Namakdán, *s. m.* a saltcellar.
Namak'halál, *adj.* loyal, faithful, grateful, submissive.
Namak'halálí, *s. f.* loyalty, fidelity, gratitude.
Namak'harám, *adj.* disloyal, wicked, disobedient, perfidious, ungrateful.
Namak'harámí, *s. f.* perfidy, unfaithfulness, disloyalty, treachery, ingratitude.
Namak ká tezáb, muriatic acid.
Namak maháll, revenue derived from salt.
Námanzúr, *adj.* unwilling, unapproved, null, void, not agreed, not accepted.
Námaʻqúl, *adj.* irrational, absurd, unreasonable, improper.
Námard, *adj.* unmanly, a coward; impotent.
Námardí, *s. f.* cowardice, impotence, unmanliness.
Namaskár. *s. m.* salutation, adoration.
Námáwar, *adj.* famous, renowned.
Namáz, *s. f.* prayer; the Musalmán repetition of prayers.
Namázgáh, the place in a mosque where prayers are read.
Namází, *s. m.* a person who prays: *adj.* devout.
Namáz karná, to pray.
Namdá, *s. m.* felt, or a coarse woollen cloth used as coverings for horses, &c.
Námdár, *adj.* famous, celebrated.
Nám dharná, to name, to fix a name on.
Nám dharwáná, to give a name to a child; to be defamed.

Nám ḍuboná, to lose one's reputation, to disgrace.

Nameṭ, *adj.* Malmeṭ, ruined.

Namgíra, *s. m.* a canopy, an awning.

Nám honá, to be famous or renowned, to be conspicuous.

Námí, *adj.* illustrious, celebrated.

Namí, *s. f.* coolness, moistness.

Námí honá, to be celebrated.

Námihrbán, *adj.* unkind, unfriendly.

Námihrbánagí, Námihrbání, *s. f.* unkindness.

Nám i Ḳhudá, in God's name.

Nám karná, to make famous, to establish a name.

Namkín, *adj.* salt, salted, corned, savoury, saline, brackish; handsome.

Namkíní, *s. f.* saltness, agreeableness, sweetness.

Namkín pání, brine, pickle.

Nám lekar máng kháná, to beg alms in the name of another.

Nám lená, to praise, to repeat the name of God.

Nám nikálná, to become celebrated, to investigate, the perpetrator of any crime.

Nám nishán rahná, to be or continue renowned.

Nám o nishán, name and vestige, or address.

Nám rakhná, to name.

Námubárak, *adj.* unfortunate.

Namúd, *s. f.* show, appearance: *adj.* apparent, public, famous, conspicuous, noted.

Namúd honá, to be celebrated, to appear.

Namúd karná, to exhibit, to display, to expose, to show.

Námuláim, *adj.* hard.

Námumkín, *adj.* impossible.

Namúna, *s. m.* a model, a pattern, a sample, muster, specimen, type.

Námunásib, *adj.* improper, unsuitable, unfit, unbecoming.

Námurád, *adj.* disappointed.

Námuwáfiq, *adj.* contrary, adverse, disagreeing.

Námwar, *adj.* celebrated, renowned.

Námwarí, *s. f.* celebrity, renown.

Náṇ, *adv.* no, not.

Nán, *s. f.* a kind of bread.

Náná, *s. m.* maternal grandfather: *adj.* various, many: *v. a.* to put one thing into another; to bend, to bow down.

Nanad, *s. f.* a sister-in-law, husband's sister.

Nának, *n. prop.* name of a faqír, founder of the sect of Sikhs.

Nánakpanthí, Nánakshàhí, *s. m.* a Sikh, or follower of Nának.

Náná prakár, *adj.* of various kinds.

Nánbáí, *s. m.* a baker.

Nánd, *s. f.* a large earthen pan.

Nándhná, *v. a.* to begin.

Nandoí, Nandosí, *s. m.* husband's sister's husband.

Nang, Nangá, *adj.* naked, shameless.

Nangá jháṛí, *s. f.* searching, examining (as a people leaving a workshop to prevent pilfering.)

Nangá karná, to bare, to uncover.

Nangá mádarzád, stark naked.

Nangá munangá, Nanga mungá, *adj.* utterly naked.

Nangar, *s. m.* an anchor.

Nangá sir, bare-headed.

Nang dhaṛang, Nang dhaṛangá, *adj.* stark naked.

Nange pairoṇ, Nange páoṇ, bare-footed.

Nánghná, *v. a.* to step across, to jump over, to leap over.

Nangí talwár, a drawn sword.

Nangtá, *adj.* naked.

Náṇh, *adv.* no, nay.

Nanihál, Nánhiyál, *s. f.* maternal grandfather's family.

Nání, *s. f.* maternal grandmother.

Náṇ i nahárí, breakfast.

Nanká, *s. m.* a little child, a son.

Nánḳhatáí, *s. f.* a kind of sweetmeat.

Nannháṇ, *adj.* small, neat, natty, tiny.
Náṇw, *s. m.* a name.
Náo, *s. f.* a boat, ship, vessel : *s. m.* a barber. See Nám.
Náoṇ, *s. m.* see Nám.
Náoná, *v. a.* to bend downwards, to bow, to cause to stoop.
Náp, *s. f.* measure.
Nápáedár, *adj.* unstable, frail, fickle, unsteady, transitory, inconstant.
Nápaid, } lost, not to be found, miss-
Nápaidá, } ing.
Nápák, *adj.* polluted, dirty, filthy, impure, unclean, defiled.
Nápákí, *s. f.* impurity, uncleanness, defilement.
Nápák karná, to pollute, to defile.
Nápasand, unacceptable, disapproved of.
Naped, *adj.* see Nápaid.
Nápigár, } *adj.* filthy, vile.
Nápikár, }
Nápjokh, measuring and weighing.
Nápná, *v. a.* to measure, to weigh.
Napunsak, *adj.* neuter (gender) : *s. m.* an hermaphrodite.
Naqáb, *s. m.* a veil.
Náqábil, *adj.* unfit, incapable, worthless.
Náqabúl, *adj.* unacceptable, rejecting, refusing.
Náqabúl karná, to reject, to deny.
Naqára, *s. m.* a kettle-drum.
Naqára bajáte phirná, to publish, to make celebrated.
Naqárchí, } *s. m.* one who beats the
Naqárí, } kettle-drum.
Naqárḳhána, *s. m.* the place at the porch of a palace where drums are beaten at stated intervals.
Naqb, *s.* a hole dug in a wall by thieves.
Naqd, } *s. m.* ready money, cash.
Naqda, }
Naqdánaqd, } prompt payment,
Naqdánaqdí, } ready money.
Naqdí, *adj.* relating to cash (paid, &c.); in cash, possessing ready money.
Naqíb, *s. m.* a servant whose business it is to proclaim the titles of his master, and to introduce those who pay their respects to him.
Náqis, *adj.* bad, vile, worthless, defected, deficient, mutilated, imperfect.
Náqis i ạkl, *adj.* deficient in understanding, foolish, ignorant.
Náqis honá, to be spoiled, to want.
Náqis karná, to mutilate, to spoil.
Naql, *s. m.* a tale, narration ; a transcript, a copy ; copying, counterpart, mimicing.
Naqlí, *adj.* artificial, copied, fictitious, traditional : *s. m.* a buffoon.
Naqliyá, *adj.* mimicing, imitating, copying.
Naqliyát, *s. plur.* stories, tales.
Naql karná, to relate, to narrate, to copy, to act ; to represent (a character.)
Naqlnavís, *s. m.* a copyist.
Naqlnavísí, *s. f.* copying.
Naqsh, *s. m.* a picture, portrait, map, drawing, painting, delineation.
Naqsha, *s. m.* feature, visage ; map, plan, pattern, model, chart ; a portrait.
Naqsh karná, to imprint, to impress.
Náqúwat, *adj.* weak, impotent, infirm.
Náqúwatí, *s. f.* weakness, impotency.
Nar, *s. m.* a man, a male : *adj.* masculine.
Nár, *s. m.* the navel string.
Naṛa, *s. m.* clamour, noise, shout.
Nárá, *s. m.* red thread.
Náráj, *adj. prop.* Náráz, which see.
Náráji, *s. f.* see Nárází.
Narak, *s. m.* hell.
Narakgámí, *adj.* going to hell.
Narakí, *adj.* hellish.
Narakkuṇḍ, a well or pit in hell.
Nárangí, *s. f.* an orange.
Náranjí, *adj.* orange-coloured.
Nárawá, *adj.* unworthy, inadmissible, "no go."
Naráyan, *s. m.* a Hindú name for the deity.

Náráyaní, *s. f.* the wife of Náráyan: *adj.* of or relating to Náráyan.
Náráz, *adj.* dissatisfied, displeased, discontented, unwilling; not pleased or satisfied.
Nárázagí, } *s. f.* displeasure, dissatis-
Nárází, } faction.
Nareṭá, *s. m.* } throat, windpipe.
Nareṭí, *s. f.* }
Nareṭí dabáná, to throttle.
Nargis, *s. f.* a narcissus.
Narí, *s. f.* a weaver's shuttle, a kind of leather, skin.
Nárí, *s. f.* a woman in general; the pulse, an artery.
Nárí dekhná, to feel the pulse.
Nariyá, *s. f.* a tile.
Náriyal, *s. m.* a cocoa-nut, a huqqa made of a cocoa-nut.
Náriyalí, *s. f.* a huqqa made of cocoa-nut.
Náriyar, *s. m.* see Náriyal.
Narkaṭ, *s. m.* a reed of which mats are made.
Narkí, *adj.* hellish, infernal.
Narlok, *s. m.* the earth, the world inhabited by man.
Narm, *adj.* soft, tender, mild, gentle, humble, supple, pliant, easy; defective (coin), inferior (quality.)
Narma, *adj.* soft.
Narmái, *s. f.* softness, tenderness.
Narmáná, *v. a.* to soften.
Narmí, *s. f.* softness, tenderness, mildness.
Narmíyat, *s. f.* softness.
Narm mizáj, *adj.* gentle, meek, yielding.
Narra, *s. m.* a kind of firework.
Narrúp, *s. m.* the human form.
Narsingá, *s. m.* a horn, a wind instrument.
Narsingh, *s. m.* the name of the fourth incarnation of Vishnu.
Narsoṇ, *adv.* the fourth day past or to come.
Nas, *s. f.* a sinew, a vein.
Nás, *s. f.* snuff: *s. m.* annihilation, destruction, ruin, perdition.

Nasab, *s. m.* genealogy, lineage.
Nasabnáma, *s. m.* pedigree, account of descent, genealogical tree.
Násabr, } *adj.* impatient.
Násabúr, }
Nasal, *s. f.* see Nasl.
Násamajh, *adj.* unintelligent.
Násamajhí, *s. f.* ignorance.
Nasáná, *v. a.* to spoil, to destroy.
Nasárá, *s. m.* Nazarine, a Christian.
Násáz, *adj.* indisposed.
Násdán, *s. m.* a snuff-box.
Násh, *s. m.* annihilation, destruction, ruin, perdition.
Nashá, } *s. m.* intoxication, intoxica-
Nasha, } ting liquor; stupefaction (from gluttony or drunkenness.)
Nashábáz, a person who takes intoxicating drugs, &c., a drunkard.
Nashábází, *s. f.* drunkenness, &c.
Nasháḳhor, see Nashábáz.
Nashe meṇ chúr honá, to be intoxicated.
Nashílá, *adj.* intoxicating.
Náshpátí, *s. f.* a pear.
Nashṭ, *adj.* lost, destroyed, perished, spoiled, ruined, debauched.
Náshtá, *s. m.* breakfast, repast.
Náshtá karná, to breakfast.
Nashtar, *s. f.* a lancet, a fleam.
Nashtar lagáná, } to bleed, to phle-
Nashtar márná, } botomize.
Nashṭ karná, to spoil, to ruin, to destroy, to debauch, to deflower, to taint.
Náshukr, *adj.* ungrateful.
Náshukrí karná, to act ungratefully.
Nasíb, *s. m.* fortune, fate, destiny, luck, chance.
Nasíba, *s. m.* lot, fortune.
Nasíbawar, *adj.* fortunate.
Nasíb jagná, to be fortunate.
Nasíb laṛná, to be greatly favoured by fortune (after adversity.)
Nasíhat, *s. f.* advice, counsel, exhortation, admonition.
Nasíhat dená, } to advise, to counsel,
Nasíhat karná, } to admonish, to exhort, to chastise.

Násná, *v. a.* to destroy.

Nasl, *s.f.* race, progeny, family, breed, caste, offspring.

Nasl ba nasl, } generation after ge-
Nasl dar nasl, } neration.

Nasr, *s. f.* prose.

Nasrání, *s. m.* a Christian.

Nást, nonentity, annihilation.

Nastạlíq, *s. m.* a kind of Persian writing.

Nástik, } *s. m.* an atheist, an infidel.
Nástikí, }

Nástik mat, *s.f.* the tenets of atheism.

Násúr, *s. m.* a fistula, an ulcer.

Naṭ, *s. m.* the name of a tribe who are generally jugglers, rope-dancers, &c.

Nátá, *s.m.* relationship, kin, alliance.

Náṭá, *adj.* dwarf, dapper, short.

Natait, *s. m.* a relative, kinsman.

Nátamám, *adj.* unfinished, imperfect, incomplete, deficient.

Nátáqat, *adj.* weak, infirm.

Nátáqatí, *s. f.* weakness, inability.

Nátawán, *adj.* powerless, weak, infirm, impotent.

Nátawání, *s. f.* impotence, weakness.

Nátedár, *adj.* akin: *s. m. f.* relation, relative.

Náth, *s. m.* a master, husband, lord; often used as an affix to the names of jogís: *s. f.* the string in a bullock's nose.

Nath, *s. f. m.* a ring for the nose worn by women.

Nathná, *s. f.* a nostril, a ring for the nose: *v. n.* to have the nose pierced (a bullock.)

Náthná, *v. a.* to bore a bullock's nose and put a string in it to guide him by.

Nathní, *s. f.* a small ring worn in the nose.

Nathí, *s. f.* a file or bundle of official papers tied up together.

Nátí, *s. m.* grandson, daughter's son.

Nátídár, *s. m. f.* relation, relative.

Natíjá, *s. m.* result, consequence, what necessarily follows, retribution.

Nátin, } *s. f.* granddaughter, daugh-
Natiní, } ter's daughter.

Naṭin, *s. f.* the female of Naṭ.

Naṭkhaṭ, *adj.* roguish, waggish, artful, trickish, wicked, troublesome, vexatious.

Naṭkhaṭí, *s. f.* trick, roguery, artifice; wickedness.

Naṭní, *s. f.* the female of Naṭ.

Natní, *s. f.* granddaughter, daughter's daughter.

Naṭúá, } *s. m.* a juggler, rope-
Naṭuwá, } dancer, &c.

Nau, *adj.* new, young, fresh; nine: *s. f.* a ship, a boat.

Náu, *s. f.* a ship, a boat.

Nauábád, *adj.* newly-settled, colonized, cultivated.

Naubat, *s. f.* time, turn; instruments of music sounding at the gate of a great man at certain intervals.

Naubat bajná, } *v. n.* to be sounded
Naubat jhaṛná, } (the Naubat.)

Naubatḳhána, *s. m.* a platform for musicians who play the Naubat.

Nauchháwar, *s. f.* a propitiatory offering, sacrifice, victim.

Nauchí, *s. f.* young girls kept by bawds.

Nauha, *s. m.* the name of a book; lamentation, moaning.

Naujawán, *s. m.* a lad, youth, young man; in the prime of life, in the bloom of youth.

Naujawání, *s. f.* prime of life, bloom or flower of youth.

Nauká, *s. f.* a boat.

Naukar, *s. m.* a servant.

Naukar chákar, servants.

Naukarí, *s. f.* service, attendance.

Naukarí pesha, one who lives on employments.

Naumáṣá, *s. m.* name of a feast given in the ninth month of pregnancy.

Náumed, *adj.* hopeless, despairing.

Naumí, } *s. f.* ninth day of a lunar
Naumín, } fortnight.

Náummaid, *adj.* hopeless, despairing.
Náummaidí, *s.f.* hopelessness, despair.
Náummed, *adj.* hopeless, despairing.
Nauná, *v. n.* to bend, to bow, to incline downwards.
Nauṉtná, *v. a.* to invite.
Nauratan, a bracelet consisting of nine jewels.
Nauṛháná, *v. a.* to bow, to bend.
Nausádar, *s. m.* sal ammoniac.
Naushah, *s. m.* a bridegroom.
Nausikh, *s. m.* a novice, a student.
Nautá, *s. m.* invitation.
Nautná, *v. a.* to invite.
Nauwá, *s. m.* a barber.
Nauwáb, *s. m.* a nabob, a governor of a town or district.
Nauwábí, *s. f.* deputyship; *adj.* relating to a Nabob.
Nauwáṉ, *adj.* ninth.
Nauwásí, *adj.* eighty-nine.
Nauwe, *adj.* ninety.
Naved, *s. m.* invitation.
Navís, in *compos.* writing, writer.
Navishta, *adj.* written: *s. m.* writing.
Navísí, *s. f.* in *compos.* writing.
Navve, *adj.* ninety.
Náw, *s. f.* a boat, a vessel.
Nawáh, *s. f.* district, environs, vicinity.
Nawála, *s. m.* a morsel, a mouthful.
Nawálí, *s. f.* a titbit, a small morsel.
Nawáṉ, *adj.* ninth.
Nawáná, *v. a.* to bend downward, to bow, to cause to submit to, to cause to stoop.
Náwáqif, *adj.* unskilled, unacquainted with, ignorant, unexperienced.
Náwaqt, *adj.* out of time, unseasonable.
Nawásá, Nawása, } *s. m.* a grandson, a daughter's son.
Nawásí, *s. f.* a granddaughter, a daughter's daughter.
Nawáz, in *compos.* cherishing, caressing, soothing; playing.
Nawází, *s. f.* in *compos.* cherishing.
Nawázish, *s. f.* caresses, kindness, favour, patronage.
Nawázish karná, to caress, to favour, to patronize.
Nawázná, *v. a.* to cherish, to caress, to favour.
Náwná, *v. a.* to put one thing into another.
Nawwáb, *s. m.* see Nauwáb.
Nawwábí, see Nauwábí.
Nawwásí, *adj.* eighty-nine.
Nawwe, *adj.* ninety.
Nayá, *adj.* new, novel.
Náyáb, *adj.* scarce, rare, difficult to be found or got.
Náyak, *s.m.* a corporal in native corps.
Nayan, *s. m.* the eye.
Naye panj, *s. m.* a horse under five years old.
Naye sir se, anew, afresh.
Náyiká, *s. f.* mistress of a brothel.
Náz, *s. m.* blandishments, coquetry, playfulness, amorous playfulness.
Náza, *s. m.* the urethra.
Nazákat, *s. f.* delicacy, delicateness, softness.
Nazar, *s. f.* a look, sight, glance, observation, regard. See also Nazr.
Nazára, *s. m.* sight, view.
Nazar áná, to come to sight, to appear, to come in sight.
Nazarána, *s. m.* see Nazrána.
Nazar bacháná, to avoid the sight.
Nazarband, *s. m.* fascination (of conjurors): *adj.* fascinated, strictly watched (without being imprisoned.)
Nazarbandí, fascination, confinement, arrest, imprisonment.
Nazarbáz, *s. m.* an ogler, a juggler.
Nazarbází, *s. f.* ogling, juggling, imposing upon the sight.
Nazar karná, to look, to see, to behold, &c.
Nazar miláná, to look in the face.
Nazaroṉ se girná, to be disgraced.
Nazar se girá dená, to disgrace.
Náz bardár, one who bears the whims of another.
Názbo, *s. m.* name of a herb.

Nazdík, *adj.* near, hard by, with, close to, in the vicinity, contiguous, neighbouring.

Nazdíkí, *s. f.* propinquity, vicinity, proximity, approximation.

Názil, descending, dismounting.

Názil honá, to descend.

Nazír, *s.m.* example, instance, parallel.

Názir, *s. m.* an officer in a court of justice superior to the bailiffs and peons, a sheriff.

Nazirí, *s. f.* the business of a Názir.

Nazla, *s. m.* a defluxion of humours, rheum, a catarrh.

Nazm, *s. f.* poetry, verse.

Názní, } *adj.* delicate, lovely : *s. f.*
Náznín, } a delicate woman.

Náz nakhrá, *s. m* coquetry, dalliance.

Nazr, *s. f.* a present, a gift (offered to a superior), an offering.

Nazrána, *s.m.* present, presents given and received when persons of rank meet or pay their respects to a prince; a kind of tribute.

Názuk, *adj.* thin, light, subtle, delicate, brittle, fragile, nice, tender, elegant.

Názukbadan, *adj.* delicate.

Názukbadaní, *s. f.* delicacy of form or body.

Názukmizáj, *adj.* delicate in constitution or complexion.

Náz uṭháná, to bear with the airs or whims of another.

Nazzám, a governor, a ruler; the title of the prince of Hyderabad.

Ne, a particle affixed to the name of the agent with a transitive verb in a past tense: *adv.* no, not, neither, nor; nay.

Nebú, *s. m.* lime or lemon.

Nefá, *s. m.* a breeches belt, the part of the drawers through which the string runs to tie them round the loins with.

Neg, } *s. f.* presents at marriages
Neg jog, } and on other festive occasions made to relations and particular servants, and considered by them as perquisites which they are entitled to.

Neh, *s. f.* affection, love, friendship.

Nek, *adj.* good, lucky, pure.

Nekbakht, *adj.* fortunate, virtuous, happy.

Nekbakhtí, *s. f.* virtue, good fortune, felicity.

Nekí, *s. f.* goodness, piety, purity, virtue, probity.

Nekkhaslat, }
Nekkho, } of good dispositions or habits, good-natured.
Nekkhulq, }

Nekmard, a good man.

Neknám, a good name, of good character or repute, renowned.

Neknámí, *s. f.* good character, renown, praise.

Neknazar, sharp or clear sight.

Nekníyat, well-meaning.

Nekníyati, *s. f.* goodness of intention.

Nekokár, of good actions, a beneficent person, benefactor.

Nekokárí, *s. f.* beneficence, doing good.

Nekpák, *adj.* virtuous.

Nekzát, of good disposition.

Nem, *s. m.* a vow, resolution, devotion, piety.

Nemdharm, *s. m.* abstinence, good conduct.

Nemí, *adj.* conscientious, continent, abstemious.

Neotá, *s. m.* an invitation.

Nepál, *n. prop.* name of a country.

Nere, beside, near, close by.

Nesh, *s. m.* sting (of a venomous reptile.)

Neshá, *s. m. prop.* Nashá, which see.

Neshábáz, *s. m.* a drunkard.

Neshábází, *s. f.* drunkenness, inebriety intoxication.

Neshtar, *s. m.* a lancet.

Nest, naught, non-existence.

Nest honá, to perish.

Nest karná, to annihilate, ruin, destroy.

Nest nábúd honá, to perish, to be annihilated, to be ruined.

Nest nábúd karná, } to demolish,
Nest o nábúd karná, } to annihilate, to ruin.

Neṭá, *s. m.* snot, snivel.

Netr, *s. m.* the eye.

New, *s. f.* the foundation of a house, &c.

Newal, } *s. m.* a weasel, a ferret, a
Newalá, } mongoose.

Newáná, *v. a.* to bend, to bow down.

Newár, *s. f.* tape.

Newárná, to smear with a wash of red earth (a wall, &c.)

New ḍálná, to found, to lay (a foundation.)

Newná, *v. n.* to stoop, to bow.

Neza, *s. n.* a spear, lance, javelin, dart, pike; a piece of reed from which pens are made.

Nezebardár, } a spearman.
Nezedár, }

Nhanná, *adj.* small, little.

Ni, a prefix to words to denote negation, contraction of Nir.

Niạmat, *s. f.* favour, graciousness, benefit.

Nibáh, *s. m.* accomplishment, performance, supply, maintenance, performing an engagement.

Nibáhná, *v. a.* to accomplish, to perfect, to perform; to protect, to take care of; to keep one's faith.

Nibal, *adj.* weak, powerless.

Nibaṛná, *v. n.* to be spent, to be ended, to be accomplished.

Nibáṛná, *v. a.* to accomplish, to perform, to end, to spend.

Nibháná, *v. a.* to perform, &c. See Nibáhná.

Nibháṛná, *v. a.* see Nibáṛná.

Nibhná, *v. n.* to serve, succeed, pass, live; to be accomplished, perfected or performed.

Níbú, *s. m.* a lemon, a lime-tree.

Ních, *adj.* low, base, vile, mean, vulgar; below, beneath, under.

Níchá, *adj.* below, down, low.

Níchái, *s. f.* lowness.

Nichán, *s. m.* a cavity, bottom, valley.

Nichant, *adj.* see Níchint.

Níchá únchá, up and down; uneven ground,

Níche, *adv.* below, beneath, under, down.

Níche giráná, to knock a person down.

Niche jáná, to descend, to subside.

Níche úpar, upside down.

Nichakká, *adj.* pure, genuine.

Nichháwar, *s. f.* a propitiatory offering, sacrifice, victim.

Nichint, *adj.* free from thought, anxiety, or care; unconcerned, careless, at leisure.

Nichint honá, to be at leisure, to be disenganged, to have finished.

Nichoṛná, *v. a.* to wring, to squeeze, to press, to strain, to extort.

Nichoṛwáná, to cause to wring, &c.

Níchú, *adv.* below, beneath, down.

Ních únch. *s. f.* inequality; the ups and downs of life.

Níd, *s. f.* sleep, slumber, repose.

Nidágh, *adj.* spotless, immaculate.

Nidam, *adj.* breathless, lifeless.

Nidán, *adv.* at last, at length, lastly, after all; an end.

Niḍar, *adj.* fearless, dauntless: *adv.* without fear, fearlessy.

Niḍarí, *s. f.* fearlessness.

Nidhán, *s. m.* a place, house, mansion, abode.

Nidhaṛak, *adv.* or *adj.* without fear, fearlessly, abruptly.

Nidrá, *s. f.* sleep, sleepiness.

Nigáh, } *s. f*, a look, sight; watch-
Nigah, } ing, custody, care.

Nigáhbán, } *s. m.* a guard, a keeper,
Nigahbán, } a watch, a protector, an overseer.

Nigáhbání, } *s. f.* watching, guard-
Nigahbání, } ing, superintendence, taking care of, custody.

Nigahdár, *s. m.* a watchman, an overseer, a guardian.

Nigahdárí, *s. f.* watching, superintendence; observation.
Nigáh karná, to observe, look, regard, view, oversee.
Nigáh rakhná, to take care of, to lay by, to guard.
Nigálí, *s. f.* the wooden pipe of a huqqá-snake.
Nigalná, *v. a.* to swallow, to gulp down.
Nigoṛá, *s. m.* wretch.
Nihái, *s. f.* an anvil.
Nihál, *s. m.* a young plant, a sucker, a shoot: *adj.* exalted, pleased, happy.
Nihálí, *s. f.* a kind of quilt.
Nihán, *s. m.* bathing, ablution.
Niháná, *v. a.* to bathe, to wash.
Nihárná, *v. a.* to look at, to watch, to look after, to spy, to see.
Nihatthá, *adj.* unarmed.
Niháyat, *adj.* very, exceeding, much, excessive, remarkable: *adv.* at the utmost, extremely.
Niháyat kahná, to ask a fair price.
Nihchai, *s. m.* see Nischai.
Nihorá, *s. m.* begging, requesting humbly, coaxing.
Nihuráná, *v. a.* to cause to crook, to bend, to bow.
Nihurná, } *v. n.* to condescend, to
Nihuṛná, } incline or bend downwards, to stoop, to bow.
Nihúrná, } *v. a.* to bend downwards,
Nihúṛná, } to bow down, to incline, to stoop. [personal.
Nij, *adj.* own, particular, individual,
Nijgut, *adj.* true, correct (as information.)
Nijjot, lands cultivated by the proprietors. [belonging to self.
Nijká, *adj.* own, peculiar, personal,
Niká, *s. m. prop.* Nikáh.
Nikáh, *s. m.* a kind of marriage.
Nikáhí, *adj.* married (a woman.)
Nikái, *s. f.* the price paid for weeding a field, the act of weeding.
Nikál, *s. m.* outlet, issue, vent.
Nikálá jáná, to be put out, or away.
Nikal bhágná, to run away, to get off, to be off.
Nikal chalná, to escape; (*met.*) to surpass another.
Nikál ḍálná, to deduct, to strike out.
Nikál dená, to expel, to eject, to discard, to drive or turn out, to exclude, to cashier.
Nikal jáná, to escape, to go away.
Nikál láná, to bring off.
Nikál lená, to dig up, to take out, to extract.
Nikalná, *v. n.* to issue, to go forth or out, to be extracted, drawn, pulled, or taken out, to come or get out, secede, depart, to be performed or accomplished, to exceed, to be uttered, to be produced, to result, to prove, to turn out, to escape.
Nikálná, *v. a.* to cause to issue, to take out, to turn out, to expel, to cause to exceed, to utter, to discover or find out, to invent, to take off, to exclude, to extract, to protrude, to deduce, to extricate, to exhibit, to produce, to hatch, to pull, to do, to accomplish, to pick.
Nikal paṛná, *v. n.* to come out, to be drawn forth.
Nikalwá dená, to expel, to banish.
Nikalwáná, *v. a.* to cause to issue, to cause to go out or come out, to expel, &c.
Nikammá, *adj.* useless, good for nothing, base, worthless.
Nikáná, *v. a.* to weed.
Nikapaṭ, *adj.* without deceit or fraud, sincere, candid.
Nikarná, *v. n.* see Nikalná.
Nikás, *s. m.* skirts, suburbs, issue, outgoing, discharge, outlet, vent; adjustment of accounts.
Nikásí, *s. f.* taxes collected on goods passing out of a town.
Nikás karná, *v. a.* to liberate, to set free. [Nikalná.
Nikasná, *v. n.* to issue, &c. See

Nikásná, *v. a.* see Nikálná.
Nikaswáná, see Nikalwáná.
Nikaṭ, *adv.* near, proximate, about, with, close by.
Nikauní, *s. f.* weeding, the act of weeding.
Nikhális, *adj. prop.* Khális, pure, genuine, unadulterated.
Nikharach, without discount or deduction.
Nikhárná, *v. a.* to strain, to bleach.
Nikhaṭar, *adj.* implacable.
Nikhráná, *v. a.* to settle, to purify, to clear.
Nikosná, *v. a.* to grin.
Niktí, *s. f.* small scales, a balance.
Níl, *s. m.* indigo, blue; the indigo plant: *n. prop.* the river Nile.
Nílá, *adj.* blue, dark blue.
Nilajjá, *adj.* shameless, barefaced, bold, rude, impudent.
Nílám, *s. m.* auction.
Nílám ghar, *s. m.* an auction-room.
Nílá pílá, black and blue.
Nílá thothá, *s. m.* blue vitriol.
Nílbaṛí, *s. f.* a ball or square of indigo.
Nílgáw, *s. f.* name of an animal, Nylghau.
Nílkanṭh, *s. m.* name of a bird.
Nílwálá, *s. m.* an indigo planter.
Ním, *s. m.* name of a tree: *adj.* half, the middle.
Níma ástín, half-sleeved, a particular kind of jacket.
Nimáj, *s. f. prop.* Namáz, which see.
Nimak, *s. m.* salt.
Nimakdán, *s. m.* a saltcellar.
Nimak'halál, *adj.* see Namak'halál.
Nimak'halálí, *s. f.* see Namak'halálí,
Nimak'harám, *adj.* see Namak'harám.
Nimak'harámí, *s. f.* see Namak'harámí.
Niman, } *adj.* strong, solid, stout,
Níman, } tight, good.
Nímasham, *s.* evening, early in the evening.
Nímbú, *s.* lemon, lime.
Nímcha, *s. m.* a dagger, a hanger.
Nímján, half dead (with fear, &c.)
Nimkí, *adj.* salt, salted, corned.
Nímrází, *adj.* somewhat satisfied, half-pleased.
Nímshab, *s. f.* midnight.
Ninánawe, *adj.* ninety-nine.
Ninánwáṇ, *s. m.* the thrush.
Nínd, *s. f.* sleep.
Nindá, *s. f.* censure, scorn, defamation, reviling language.
Nindás, *s. f.* drowsiness.
Nindásá, *adj.* drowsy, sleepy.
Nínd bhar soná, to sleep soundly, to be at ease.
Níndí, *s. f.* sleepiness, drowsiness.
Níndná, *v. a.* to deny: *v. n.* to sleep.
Nínd uchát honá, to be unable to sleep, to have sleep broken.
Ningalná, *v. a.* to swallow, to gulp down.
Ningláná, *v. a.* to cause to swallow.
Nipaṭ, *adv.* very, exceedingly.
Nipaṭná, *v. n.* to terminate, to be finished, to be settled.
Nipṭáná, *v. a.* to settle, to decide, to conclude, to terminate.
Niput, } *adj.* childless, having no
Nipútá, } son.
Nir, a preposition, only used in composition; it gives the idea of privation, absence, or negation.
Nír, *s. m.* tears.
Nirá, *adj.* mere; pure, unalloyed, single, simple, unadulterated.
Nirádar, *adj.* disrespectful, without respect, unpolite.
Nirákár, *adj.* incorporeal, without form or figure.
Nirakhná, *v. a.* to look at.
Nirálá, *adj.* retired, lonely; pure, unmixed, unalloyed.
Niràle, } apart, aside, in private.
Niràle meṇ, }
Níranjan, *adj.* pure, free from stain, holy; the Supreme Being.
Nirankál, } *adj.* incorporeal, with-
Nirankár, } out form, (the Deity.)
Niras, *adj.* dry, tasteless, insipid.

Nirás, } *adj.* hopeless, despairing,
Nirásá, } desperate.
Nirásí, *s. f.* despair.
Nirbal, *adj.* weak, strengthless.
Nirbaltá, *s. f.* weakness, impotence.
Nirbans, *adj.* childless, without offspring, extinct (a family.)
Nirbas, *adj.* powerless, enfeebled.
Nirbhai, *adj.* fearless, undaunted.
Nirdaya, } *adj.* pitiless, merciless,
Nirdayí, } hard-hearted, unfeeling, inhuman, cruel, relentless.
Nirdhan, *adj.* poor, needy.
Nirdokh, } *adj.* blameless, free from
Nirdosh, } fault, innocent, with-
Nirdoshí, } out defect or blemish.
Nirgun, *adj.* without passions or human qualities (an epithet of God); worthless, useless.
Nirḳh, *s. m.* price current; price (fixed by the officers of the police); tariff.
Nirḳhnáma, *s. m.* an account of current market prices.
Nirlajj, *adj.* shameless, impudent.
Nirlajjá, *s. m.* want of shame, immodesty.
Nirlobhí, *adj.* not covetous, void of avarice, contented.
Nirmal, } *adj.* pure, clear, clean,
Nirmalá, } transparent, limpid.
Nirmalí, *s. f.* name of a seed with which water is cleared.
Nirmúl, *adv.* wholly, entirely: *adj.* destitute of a root or origin.
Nirog, } *adj.* free from disease, in
Nirogí, } high health and spirits, healthy.
Nirphal, *adj.* fruitless, unprofitable.
Nirúp, *adj.* without form, incorporeal.
Nirúpan, *s. m.* the establishing of a rule, the appointing of any circumstance or thing, determining.
Niruttar, *adj.* without answer, unable to answer.
Nis, a privative particle used in *compos.* without, &c.: *s. f.* night.
Nisandeh, *adj.* free from doubt: *adv.* undoubtedly.
Nisár honá, to be sacrificed.
Nisár karná, to scatter, strew or throw (as a public donation, &c.); to sacrifice.
Nisbat, *s. f.* relation, affinity, reference; espousal: *postpos.* respecting, regarding.
Nisbatí, *adj.* related, having reference to: *s. m.* a brother-in-law.
Nischai, *s. m.* certainty, clear knowledge of a thing: *adj.* indubitable, certain: *adv.* certainly, indubitably.
Nischar, *s. m.* man or animal that prowls about at night; a demon.
Nisf, *adj.* half.
Nisf á nisf, halved, in halves, half and half.
Nisf á nisfí, *adv.* half and half, in halves.
Nisfí, *adj.* halved, half.
Nishá, *s. m.* see Nashá.
Nishábáz, see Nashábáz.
Nishábází, *s. f.* drunkenness, &c.
Nishá karná, *v. a.* to be responsible.
Nishán, *s. m.* a mark, sign, an ensign, flag, standard, colours.
Nishána, *s. m.* a mark, a butt.
Nishánbardár, *s. m.* a standard bearer, one who carries the colours.
Nishán dená, to point out.
Nishání, *s. f.* a token of remembrance, a keepsake, a mark.
Nishast, *s. f.* sitting.
Nishásta, *s. m.* a kind of paste.
Nishastbarḳhást, *s. f.* manners, good breeding, etiquette.
Nishastgáh, *s. f.* a place where people meet to sit and talk.
Nishast karná, to sit.
Nishchai, see Nischai.
Nishchar, *s. m.* a prowler.
Nishe meṉ honá, to be drunk or intoxicated.
Nishín, in *compos.* sitting, seated on, dwelling in, &c.
Niskalank, *adj.* spotless, unstained, immaculate.

Nispáp, Nispápí, } *adj.* sinless.
Nisphal, *adj.* see Nirphal.
Nistár, *s. m.* release, acquittal, salvation.
Nistí, *s. f.* a catalogue, a list.
Nisyán, *s. m.* forgetfulness, oblivion.
Nít, *s. f.* conduct, morality, manners.
Nit, *adj.* or *adv.* always, continually, ever, constantly.
Nithárná, *v. a.* to purify water or other liquid by letting the feculent matter subside and pouring off the clear.
Nithrá, *adj.* clear (water whose impurity has subsided.)
Niṭhur, *adj.* hard, relentless, cruel.
Nití, *s. f.* small scales, such as goldsmiths use.
Nit nit, Nituṭh, Nituṭhke, } *adv.* perpetually, constantly, always.
Níw, *s. f.* the foundation of a house, &c.
Niwálá, *s. m.* a morsel.
Niwáná, Niwáoná, } *v. a.* to bend downwards, to bow; to cause to submit, to cause to stoop.
Niwár, *s. f.* tape (of a coarse kind.)
Niwárá, Niwáṛá, } *s. m.* a boat, a particular kind of boat.
Niwárbáf, a tape-weaver.
Niwárí, Niwáṛí, } *s. f.* straw.
Niwárná, *v. a.* to smear or wash over with a wash of earth or cow-dung, &c.
Niwaṛná, *v. n.* to bend, to stoop.
Niyáe, *s. m.* justice, equity.
Niyar, *adv.* near, beside, close by.
Niyárá, *adj.* see Nyárá.
Niyáre, *adv.* apart, separately.
Níyat, *s. f.* intention, design, purpose, desire.
Níyatí, *adj.* intentional.
Níyat karná, *v. a.* to design, to purpose.
Niyáya, *s. m.* justice, equity.
Niyáz, *s. f.* a thing dedicated, an offering.
Niyáz karná, to dedicate, to devote.
Nizám, *s. m.* a ruler.
Nizámat, *s. f.* the administration of criminal justice, government.
Noch, *s. m.* a pinch, a scratch.
Nochná, *v. a.* to pinch, to scratch, to claw.
Nok, *s. f.* a bill, a beak, nib; end, point, tip; angle.
Nokdár, *adj.* pointed.
Nokílá, *adj.* sharp-pointed.
Nok jhok, *s. f.* pulling and hauling.
Non, *s. m.* salt.
Noná, *adj.* salt, brackish.
Noní, *s. f.* efflorescence of salt on a wall.
Noniyá, *s. m.* a maker of or dealer in salt, a saltpetre-maker.
Noniyár, *s. m.* name of a caste.
Noniyá ság, *s. m.* a kind of greens.
Nosh, *s. m.* a drink, a draught.
Nosh farmáná, Nosh i ján farmáná, Nosh i ján karná, Nosh karná, } to eat, to drink.
Nuchná, *v. n.* to be pinched or scratched.
Nuchwáná, *v. a.* to cause to pinch or pluck out, &c.
Núh, *n. prop.* Noah.
Nuh, *s. m.* nail (of the finger, toe, &c.), talon.
Nuh lená, to trip, to stumble.
Nujúm, *s. plur.* of Najm, stars.
Nujúmí, *s. m.* an astrologer, an astronomer.
Nukílá, *adj.* see Nokílá.
Nuktachín, a caviller, a critic.
Nuktachíní, *s. f.* cavil, criticism.
Numá, in *compos.* showing, exhibiting, appearing; an index.
Numáí, in *compos. s. f.* display, showing.
Nuniyá, *s. m.* see Noniyá.
Nuql, *s. m.* a sort of sweetmeat.
Nuqra, *s. m.* a white colour in horses; silver.

Nuqra'í, *adj.* made of silver.
Nuqsán, *s. m.* loss, defect, detriment, blemish, damage, mischief.
Nuqsání, *s. f.* defect, injury, damage, &c.
Nuqta, *s. m.* a point, a dot, a stain; centre (of a circle), geometrical point.
Nuqtachín, a caviller.
Núr, *s. m.* light, splendour.
Núrání, *adj.* serene, bright, clear.
Nuskha, *s. m.* recipe.
Nutfa, *s. m.* seed, sperma hominis.
Nyáe, *s. m.* justice, equity, reason.
Nyáe karná, to judge, to administer justice.
Nyáeshástr, *s. m.* logic.
Nyáí, *s. m.* a distributor of justice.
Nyárá, *adj.* apart, aloof, separate, distinct, different.
Nyáre, *adv.* apart, separately.
Nyautná, *v. a.* to invite.
Nyáw, *s. m.* justice, equity, decision.
Nyáw karná, to judge, to administer justice, to decide.
Nyoṛáná, *v. a.* to bend, to bow.
Nyoṛhná, } *v. n.* to bend, to bow, to
Nyoṛná, } stoop.
Nyotá, *s. m.* an invitation.
Nyotná, *v. a.* to invite.

O.

O, the vocative interjection O! *conj.* and, too, also: *pron.* he, she, it, that; a vowel pronounced as *o* in *no.*
Ochhá, *adj.* tight (as clothes); light, of little consequence, trifling, absurd, silly; mean.
Ochhá honá, *v. n.* to want, to be deficient (in size or measure.)
Odá, *adj.* wet, moist, damp.
Odá cháwal, *s. m.* moist rice.
Ogairah, *prop.* Waghaira, which see.
Oghrá, *s. m.* a kind of food (for sick persons.)
Oho, *interj.* heigh! ho!
Ojan, *s. m. prop.* Wazn, which see.
Ojar, *s. m. prop.* Ụzr, which see.
Ojhá, *s. m.* a snake-catcher, one who pretends to cure the bite of snakes and to cast out evil spirits by means of charms.
Ojháí, *s. f.* the profession of an Ojhá.
Ojhal, *s. f.* privacy, retirement. See also Oṭ.
Ojhal honá, to be concealed.
Ojhal karná, to conceal, to screen.
Ok, *s. f.* sickness at stomach, inclination to vomit.
Okálat, *s. f. prop.* Wakálat, which see.
Okálatnáma, *s. m. prop.* Wakálatnáma, a power of attorney.
Okhlí, *s. f.* a wooden mortar.
Okná, *v. n.* to vomit.
Ol, *s. m.* name of a vegetable the root of which is eaten.
Olá, *s. m.* hail.
Olá hojáná, to become cold.
Olák, *s. f. prop.* Uláq, a kind of boat.
Olkobí, *s. f.* knolcole.
Oltí, *s. f.* the eaves of a roof.
Omar, *s. f. prop.* Ụmr, which see.
Onḍá, *adj.* deep.
Ondhá, *adj.* upside down.
Onṭh, *s. m.* the lip.
Opár, *s.* the opposite bank of a river or pond, the further side of anything.
Or, *s. f.* way, side (ward.)
Oṛá, *s. m.* a kind of basket.
Orak, *s. m. prop.* Waraq, which see.
Oṛhná, *v. a.* to put on (dress): *s. m.* a sheet, cloak or mantle.
Oṛhní, *s. f.* a small sheet, a cloth used by Hindú women to hide their faces.
Orí, *s. f.* the eaves of a house.
Oṛiyá, *s. f.* a kind of basket.
Or nibáhná, to be constant to, to protect (for ever.)
Os, *s. f.* dew.
Osar, *s. f.* a heifer.
Ostád, *s. m. prop.* Ustád, which see.
Ostádí, *s. f. prop.* Ustádí, which see.

Oṭ, *s. f.* screen, shelter, partition, protection.
Oṭá, *s. m.* a raised entrance to a house.
Otá, *adj.* so much, so many.
Ote meṉ, in the mean time.
Oṭ honá, to be concealed, &c.
Otik, *adj.* that much, so much.
Oṭ karná, to conceal, screen, &c.
Oṭná, *v. a.* to separate the seed from cotton.
Otná, that much, or many.

P.

Pa, *conj. adv.* or *postpos. contract.* of Par, but, yet, on, at, &c.
Pá, *s. m.* the leg, foot; a termination affixed to nouns to denote the abstract quality.
Pá andáz, *s. m.* a carpet spread at the entrance of a room for cleaning the feet on.
Páband, *adj.* engaged, employed, occupied.
Páband honá, *v. n.* to be married.
Pá ba zanjír, *adj.* fettered, in chains.
Pabitr, *adj.* pure, holy, undefiled.
Pabitrtá, *s. m.* holiness, purity.
Pachá ḍálná, *v. a.* to digest, to embezzle.
Páchak, *s. m.* a digestive, a stomachic, a tonic, a solvent.
Pacháliyá, *adj.* talking in an obscene manner.
Pacháná, *v. a.* to digest, to ferment.
Pachánauwe, *adj.* ninety-five.
Pachánná, *v. a.* see Pachhánná.
Pachás, *adj.* fifty.
Pachási, *adj.* eighty-five.
Pachauní, *s. f.* the stomach, the entrails, the guts.
Pachchar, *s. f.* a wedge.
Pachchar márná, to tease, to harass, to distress.
Pachchham, *s. m.* west.
Pachchhawá, *s. f.* a westerly wind.
Pachchhí, *s. m.* a bird.
Pachchhim, *s. m.* west.
Pachh, *s. m.* partiality; the half of a lunar month; a fortnight comprising fifteen days.
Páchh, *s. m.* scarification; the incision made in the poppy head for the opium to ooze out.
Pachháṉ, *s. m.* west.
Pachhán, see Pahchán.
Pachhánná, *v. a.* to know, to be acquainted with, to recognize.
Pachháṛ, *s. f.* a fall or throwing down.
Pachhaṛ jáná, *v. n.* to lag behind.
Pachháṛ kháná, to fall down.
Pachhaṛná, *v. n.* to fall, to tumble down.
Pachháṛná, *v. a.* to throw down, to dash down, to abase, to conquer.
Pachhattar, *adj.* seventy-five.
Páchhe, Páchheṉ, } *adv.* behind, after, afterwards, in the absence, subsequently.
Pachhiyá, *s. f.* a westerly wind.
Páchhná, *v. a.* to inoculate, to scarify.
Pachhná, *s. m.* the act of scarifying, tattooing; inoculation, vaccination.
Pachhní, *s. f.* the scarifying of the poppy head to procure opium.
Pachhtáná, *v. a.* to regret, to repent, to rue, to grieve.
Pachhtáwá, *s. m.* regret, repentance, grief, concern, contrition, compunction, remorse.
Pachhwá, *s. f.* westerly wind.
Pachís, *adj.* twenty-five.
Pachísí, *s. f.* a game played with [kauṛís.
Pachlaṛá, *adj.* consisting of five strings (a necklace, &c.)
Pachlaṛí, *s. f.* a necklace consisting of five rows or strings.
Pachmaballá, Pachmahlá, } *adj.* of five stories (a house.)
Pachmel, *adj.* mixed, confused.
Pachná, *v. n.* to be digested.
Pachpach, *s. m.* the noise made by walking in damp places.
Pachpan, *adj.* fifty-five.
Pachtáná, *v. n.* to regret, to repent, to rue, to grieve.

Pachtáo, } s. m. repentance.
Pachtáwá, }

Pad, s. m. the foot, footstep.

Pád, s. m. wind expelled from behind, a fart.

Padáná, v. a. to cause to break wind.

Pádá non, s. m. a kind of black salt.

Padar, s. m. father.

Padárth, s. m. a rarity, delicacy, a good, a blessing; the meaning of a word.

Padás, s. f. inclination to expel wind, flatulency.

Padásá, *adj*. inclined to expel wind, flatulent.

Padawí, } s. f. rank, character, dignity, name, surname.
Padbí, }

Pádghábrá, *adj*. frightened out of one's wits.

Padmaní, s. f. a description of women.

Pád márná, } v. n. to expel wind backwards, to fart.
Pádná, }

Pádná, } *adj*. see Padásá.
Padoṛá, }

Pádsháh, s. m. a king, a sovereign.

Pádsháhána, *adj*. royal, imperial: *adv*. like a king, kingly.

Pádsháhat, s. f. royalty, empire, kingdom, government.

Pádsháhí, *adj*. royal: s. f. royalty, sovereignty.

Pádsháhzáda, s. m. a prince.

Padví, see Padawí.

Páe, s. m. the foot, the stand of a table, chair, &c.

Páeband, *adj*. fettered, tied by the leg; encumbered with a family.

Páedár, *adj*. firm, steady, permanent, durable, lasting, perpetual.

Páedárí, s. f. permanence, durability, stability, firmness.

Páejáma, s. m. drawers, long drawers or loose trowsers very wide in the legs.

Páeḵhána, s. m. a necessary.

Páemál, *adj*. trampled on, ruined.

Páemálí, s. f. destruction, ravage, ruin.

Páemál karná, to trample on, to destroy, to lay waste, to ravage.

Páemardí, s. f. courage, resolution.

Páemoz, s. m. a kind of pigeon.

Páetába, s. m. a sock, short stocking.

Páezanjír, *adj*. chained by the leg.

Páezeb, s. f. anklets.

Pág, s. f. a thick syrup.

Pag, s. m. the foot.

Pagá, s. m. a rope fastened round the neck of a bullock, a tether.

Págal, *adj*. insane, mad: s. m. a fool, idiot, madman.

Págalḵhána, s. m. an insane hospital.

Pagár, s. m. a bank raised to separate fields; a path.

Pagḍanḍí, s. f. a by-path, a by-way, footpath.

Paghá, s. m. see Pagá.

Pagiyá, s. f. a turban.

Paglá, *adj*. foolish, silly.

Pagṛí, s. f. a turban.

Págur, s. m. act of chewing the cud, rumination.

Páguráná, } v. n. to ruminate, to chew the cud.
Págur karná, }

Pah, s. f. dawn.

Pahal, s. m. a flock of cotton; beginning.

Pahanáná, v. a. to cause to dress or put on.

Pahanáwá, s. m. clothing, dress.

Pahanná, v. a. to put on, to wear, to dress.

Pahar, s. m. a division of time consisting of eight ghaṛís, a watch of three hours.

Paháṛ, s. m. a mountain, a hill.

Paháṛá, s. m. the multiplication table.

Paharewálá, s. m. a sentinel, a sentry, a guard.

Paháṛí, s. f. a hill, a small mountain.

Paháṛiyá, *adj*. belonging to or of a mountain: s. m. a mountaineer.

Paharná, v. a. to put on clothes, to dress, to wear.

Paháṛ sí ráten, long nights (especially of sorrow.)

Pahár talí, the foot of a hill or mountain.
Pahchán, *s. f.* acquaintance, knowledge, recognisance.
Pahchánná, *v. a.* to know, to recognise, to discriminate, to distinguish.
Pahelí, *s. f.* a riddle, an enigma.
Pahichánná, *v. a.* see Pahchánná.
Pahilá, *adj.* first: *adv.* before, rather.
Pahilauṭá, *adj.* firstborn.
Pahile, *adv.* see Pahle.
Pahináná, *v. a.* to dress, to cause to put on,
Pahinná, *v. a.* to put on, to wear, to dress.
Pahiráná, *v. a.* to cause to dress, to clothe, to invest.
Pahiráwan, *s. m.* dress, clothing, &c.
Pahirná, *v. a.* to put on clothes, to dress, to wear.
Pahiyá. *s. m.* a wheel.
Pahlá, *adj.* first: *adv.* rather, before, soon.
Pahlaunṭhá, *adj.* firstborn.
Pahlawán, *s. m.* a hero, a champion, a stout fellow, a wrestler.
Pahlawání, *s. f.* heroism.
Pahle, *adv.* at first, in the first place, first, sooner, rather, before, chiefly.
Pahlú, *s. m.* the side.
Pahnáná, *v. a.* to dress, to cause to put on.
Pah phaṭná, *v. n.* to dawn.
Pahrá, *s. m.* a watch, a sentinel; tour of watch.
Pahrá dená, to watch.
Pahráná, *v. a.* to cause to dress, to clothe, to invest, to dress.
Pahráwa, *s. f.* dress.
Pahre meṉ ḍálná, to give in charge to a guard.
Pahre meṉ paṛná, to be given in charge to a guard.
Páhun, } *s. m.* a guest.
Páhuná, }
Pahuna'í, *s. f.* hospitality, entertainment.
Pahunch, *s. f.* arrival, reach, access, admittance; sagacity, penetration.
Pahunchá, *s. m.* the wrist.
Pahuncháná, *v. a.* to cause to arrive, to convey, to transmit, to bring, to conduct.
Pahunchí, *s. f.* an ornament worn on the wrist. [to extend.
Pahunchná, *v. n.* to arrive, to reach,
Pahunchwáná, *v. a.* to cause to arrive, convey, or conduct.
Páhuní, *s. f.* a female guest.
Páí, *s. f.* a coin, the fourth part of an áná, in accounts twelve páí are reckoned an áná; pins used by weavers to wind off the warp from.
Pai, *s. f.* a fault.
Paidá, *adj.* born, created, produced.
Paidá honá, to be born or created; to be earned, to be produced.
Paidáish, *s. f.* birth, creation, production, earnings, profit.
Paidá karná, *v. a.* to produce, to create, to get, to earn, to gain, to invent, to procure.
Paidal, *adv.* on foot: *s. m.* infantry.
Pai dar pai, *adv.* one after another, successively.
Paidáwár, *s. m.* produce of a field; profit of trade, &c.
Paighám, *s. m.* a message.
Paighámá paighámí, *s. f.* mutual messages, correspondence.
Paighámbar, } *s. m.* a messenger, a
Paighambar, } prophet.
Paighámbarí, } *s. f.* mission (especi-
Paighambarí, } ally as a prophet.)
Paikár, *s. m.* a pedlar.
Paikaṛí, *s. f.* iron chains on a culprit's legs; a kind of anklets.
Paimáish, *s. f.* measure.
Paimán, *s. m.* a promise, treaty, agreement, compact.
Paimána, *s. m.* a measure, a cup.
Painá, *s. m.* a stick.
Painálá, *s. m.* a gutter, a spout.
Painchá, *s. m.* a loan; one leg of a pair of trowsers.

Painchná, *v. a.* to winnow, to sift.
Paiṇsaṭh, *adj.* sixty-five.
Paiṇtális, *adj.* forty-five.
Paiṇtáná, *s. m.* } the foot of a bed,
Páintí, *s. f.* } the side towards the feet.
Paiṇtís, *adj.* thirty-five.
Pair, *s. m.* the foot.
Pairáhan, } *s. m.* a long robe, or
Pairahan, } shirt or shift.
Pairák, *s. m.* a swimmer.
Pairákí, *s. f.* act or art of swimming.
Pairáná, *v. a.* to cause to swim.
Pairáo, *adj.* beyond man's depth, where it is necessary to swim.
Pairau, *adj.* following, follower.
Pairau'í, *s. f.* following, imitation.
Pairí, *s. f.* an ornament worn on the legs.
Pairná, *v. n.* to swim.
Paisá, *s. m.* the name of a copper coin; money, cash.
Paisá ḍúbná, to be sunk (money.)
Paisá ḍuboná, to sink money, to lay out money without return.
Paisá kháná, to spend extravagantly, to waste; to take bribes.
Paisá lagáná, to lay out or expend money.
Paisá pher phár karná, to turn the penny.
Paisá uṛáná, to spend extravagantly.
Paisewálá, *adj.* moneyed.
Paisna, *v. n.* see Paiṭhná.
Paitará, *s. m.* flourishing about before cudgelling, &c.
Paiṭh, *s. m.* entrance, ingress, admission, access.
Paiṭhálná, *v. a.* to force in, to make, to penetrate, to thrust, to run in, to introduce.
Paiṭhná, *v. n.* to penetrate, to rush or run into, to enter, to pervade.
Paiwand, *adj.* joining, joined, connected: *s. m.* conjunction, joint, a patch, graft.
Paiwandí, *adj.* ingrafted.
Paiwand lagáná, to patch, to graft, to inoculate (a tree.)

Paiwast, *s. f.* junction, connexion: *adj.* joined, penetrated.
Paiyá, *s. m.* a wheel.
Paizár, *s. f.* a slipper, a shoe.
Paizárápaizárí, *s. f.* fighting or mutual beating with slippers.
Paizár kháná, to be beaten with slippers.
Pájáma, *s. m.* trowsers, long drawers.
Pajauṛá, *adj.* mean-spirited, low.
Pajáwá, *s. m. prop.* Pazáwa, a brick-kiln.
Pájí, *adj.* mean, contemptible, base, abject.
Pájímizáj, *adj.* mean-spirited, low.
Pájípaná, *s. m.* meanness.
Pajoṛá, *adj.* low, mean, shabby.
Pák, *s. f.* sirup: *adj.* pure, clean, holy, innocent, spotless, immaculate.
Pakáí, *s. f.* the price paid for cooking, baking, &c.
Pakáná, *v. a.* to ripen, to dress victuals, to cook, to bake.
Paká pakáyá, ready cooked.
Pakaṛ, *s. f.* seizure, capture, catch, hold, objection, difficulty.
Pákaṛ, *s. m.* the citron-leaved Indian fig-tree.
Pakaṛná, *v. a.* to catch, to lay hold of, to seize, to apprehend, to take, capture, to gripe, to handle; to object.
Pakaṛwáná, *v. a.* to cause to seize, &c.
Pákbáz, *adj.* undefiled, honest, candid, sincere.
Pákbází, *s. f.* purity, honesty, candour.
Pákdáman, *adj.* chaste, pure, modest (woman.)
Pakh, *s. m.* the first or second half of a lunar month.
Pákhá, *s. m.* see Pakhwá.
Pakhál, *s. f.* a leather bag for holding water, generally carried on bullocks.
Pakhán, *s. m.* a kind of fowl-house.
Pákhanḍ, *s. m.* wickedness, deceit, hypocrisy.
Pákhanḍí, } *adj.* hypocritical, deceit-
Pakhanḍí, } ful, heretical.

Pakháwaj, *s. f.* a kind of drum, a timbrel.

Pakháwají, *s. m.* one who beats the pakháwaj, a drummer.

Pakherú, *s. m.* a bird.

Pakhrauṭá, *s. m.* a bit of gold or silver leaf covering a bíṛá or mouthful of betel.

Pakhṛí, *s. f.* a nosegay.

Pakhwá, *s. m.* } side, flank, gable
Pakhwái, *s. f.* } end (of a house.)

Pákí, *s. f.* purity, cleansing.

Pákí lená, *v. a.* to shave the hairs of the privities.

Pákíza, *adj.* clean, pure, neat, chaste.

Pákízagí, *s. f.* cleanness, neatness, purity, chastity.

Pákíza ḳhaslat, of chaste habits or dispositions.

Pakká, *adj.* ripe, mature, matured; boiled, dressed (opposite to raw), cooked, baked (as bricks), made of brick; cunning, knowing, instructed, firm, strong, proved expert, adept.

Pakká karná, to establish a claim, agreement, or proposition, so that no doubt or subject of dispute can remain.

Pakká poṛhá karná, see Pakká karná.

Pakná, *v. n.* to be dressed or cooked, to ripen; to suppurate (as an inflammation, boil, &c.); to turn grey (hairs.)

Pákná, *v. n.* to boil in syrup.

Pakṛáná, *v. a.* to cause to be caught, seized or laid hold of; to give in charge, to deliver over.

Páksáf, *adj.* pure, clean, unpolluted, undefiled.

Pakwáí, *s. f.* price paid for cooking.

Pakwán, *s. m.* sweetmeats, victuals fried in butter or oil.

Pakwáná, *v. a.* to cause to be dressed or cooked, to cause to ripen.

Pal, *s. m.* a moment.

Pál, *s. m.* a sail; small tent, layers of straw, leaves, &c., between which unripe mangos are ripened; the copulation of beasts.

Pálá, *s. m.* frost, hoarfrost, snow; a heap of earth made by children to separate the two parties in a game called Kabaḍḍí.

Pálak, *s. m.* a kind of greens; cherisher, protector, keeper.

Palak, *s. f.* the eyelid, eyelash; a moment.

Pálakbeṭá, an adopted son.

Palak daryá, *s. m.* clouds.

Pálakjúhí, } *s. f.* name of a medi-
Palakjúhí, } cinal plant.

Palak ke márte, in the twinkling of an eye.

Palak lagná, closing of the eyes.

Palak márná, } *v. a.* to wink.
Palak maṭkáná, }

Palak men, in the twinkling of an eye.

Pálak putr, an adopted son.

Pálan, *s. m.* bringing up, cherishing, rearing, breeding, nourishing.

Palán, } *s. m.* packsaddle.
Pálán, }

Palang, *s. m.* a bed, a bedstead, a couch, a cot (to sleep on.)

Palangposh, *s.m.* a coverlet, a counterpane.

Palangṛí, *s. f.* a small bedstead.

Palánná, *v. a.* to saddle a bullock or ass.

Pálá paṛná, *v. n.* to freeze, to snow.

Palás, *s. m.* name of a tree on which the lac insects feed (Butea frondosa.)

Palás pápṛa, *s. m.* the seeds of the Butea frondosa used in medicine.

Pálaṭ lená, *v.a.* to hire from a washerman the clothes of another person.

Palaṭná, *v. n.* to return, to change, to turn over.

Palauṭhá, *adj.* first-born.

Pál chaṛháná, to hoist a sail.

Pale paṛná, *v. a.* to fall within the power of another.

Palethan, *s. m.* dried flour laid over and under bread when it is rolled.

Paleṭná, *v. a.* to fold, to wind.

Palí, *s. f.* a ladle used to take out oil with.

Palisht, *adj.* polluted, impure, unclean.

Palít, *adj.* unclean, polluted, impure, nasty.

Palítá, *s.m.* a match, a match of a gun.

Pálkí, *s. f.* a litter, a sedan, palanquin.

Pálkínishín, } one who rides in a
Pálkísawár, } Pálkí.

Palla, } *s. m.* one scale (or side of a
Pallá, } pair of scales.)

Pallá, *s. m.* space, distance; a sheet (generally applied to chintz or a shawl); one shutter or fold of a door.

Pallákash, *s. m.* a kind of hook for drawing the strings of the top of a tent through the holes in a wall of a tent.

Palledár, a porter who has bags to carry burthens.

Palledárí, *s. f.* the business of a porter.

Pal márná, *v. a.* to wink.

Pal márte, *adv.* in the twinkling of an eye.

Palná, *v. n.* to be reared, nourished, or fattened.

Pálná, *v. a.* to preserve, protect, to rear, to bring up, to cherish, to nourish, to breed: *s. m.* a cradle.

Palṛá, *s. m.* a scale, *i.e.*, one side of a pair of scales.

Palṭá, *s. m.* recompense, revenge.

Palṭá lená, to take revenge.

Palṭan, *s. f.* a regiment, a corps or body of troops, an army.

Palṭáná, *v. a.* to turn, to cause to turn, to return.

Palṭaniyá, *adj.* belonging to a regiment or army.

Pálú, *s. m.* a yoke (for oxen.)

Pálúda, } *s. m.* a kind of flummery.
Palúda, }

Pál uṛáná, to carry sail (a boat.)

Palwal, *s. m.* the name of a vegetable and its plant.

Palwal latí, *s. f.* the palwal plant.

Palwáná, *v. a.* to cause to nourish, to bring up, &c.

Palwár, *s. m.* a kind of boat.

Pámál, *adj.* trodden on, ruined, destroyed.

Pámálí, *s. f.* devastation, ruin, the being beaten down by treading.

Pámardí, *s. f.* resolution, valour.

Pámrí, *s. f.* a kind of silk or woollen cloth used as a loose garment.

Pán, *s. m.* betel-leaf; drinking in general.

Pan, } a termination affixed to
Paná, } nouns to denote the abstract quality, and answering to the English terminations, *ship*, *hood*, *ness*, &c.

Páná, *v. a.* to get, to acquire, to find, to obtain, to enjoy, to suffer, overtake, to reach, accept, attain.

Panáh, *s. f.* shade, shelter, protection; asylum, refuge.

Panáh dená, to protect, to harbour, to give shelter.

Panáhí, *s. f.* in *compos.* protection, or the being the protector of.

Panáh kisí se mángná, to seek protection; to avoid.

Panálá, *s. m.* } a pipe or drain fixed
Panálí, *s. f.* } under the eaves of a house to catch the water that falls from the roof and conducts it away.

Panapná, *v. n.* to commence increasing in bulk (a man, tree, &c.); to become fat; to prosper, to flourish, to thrive.

Panárí, *s. f.* see Panálá.

Panbaṭṭá, *s. m.* a betel-box.

Panbhará, *s. m.* see Panhárá.

Panbharin, *s. f.* see Panhárin.

Pánch, *adj.* five.

Panch, *s. m.* a council, an assembly, a meeting; arbitrators.

Panchakkí, *s. f.* a water-mill.

Panchamí, } s. f. the fifth day of
Panchamíṇ, } the lunar fortnight.
Pancháwan, *adj.* fifty-five.
Pancháyat, } s. f. a meeting of any
Pancháyatí, } particular society (generally as a court of inquiry); a jury, an inquest, a council.
Panchhí, s. m. a bird.
Panchlaṛá, *adj.* of five rows or strings (a necklace, &c.)
Panchoṇ, associates.
Panchpiriyá, any person, Hindú or other, who worships the five Pírs or saints of the Musalmáns.
Pánchsát, s. m. perplexity.
Panchtatwa, s. m. the five elements, or principles according to the Hindús, viz., fire, earth, air, water, and ether or space.
Pánchwáṇ, *adj.* the fifth.
Pánchwíṇ, s. f. the fifth day of the moon or of the half month.
Pand, s. m. advice, admonition.
Paṇḍá, s. m. a Bráhman who presides at the temple of an idol.
Pándán, s. m. a box for holding betel and its apparatus.
Páṇḍav, descendant of Rájá Páṇḍú.
Páṇḍe, s. m. see Páṇṛe.
Paṇḍit, *adj.* wise, learned: s. m. a learned Bráhman.
Paṇḍitáí, s. f. the learning of a Bráhman, learning.
Paṇḍitkhána, s. m. a prison, a lock-up house.
Paṇḍiyáyan, s. f. the wife of a Páṇṛe.
Pandrah, *adj.* fifteen.
Pandrahwáṇ, *adj.* fifteenth.
Pandrawárá, s. m. a fortnight.
Paṇḍúbá, s. m. a ghost said to haunt the river-side.
Paṇḍubbí, } s. f. a water-fowl, the
Paṇḍubí, } coot, the diver.
Paṇḍuk, s. m. a turtle-dove.
Pángá, s. m. culinary salt.
Panghaṭ, s. m. a passage to a river, a stair or quay (for drawing water.)
Pangrí, } *adj.* cripple,
Pangú, }
Panhá, s. m. width, breadth.
Panhárá, s. m. a man who carries water in pots on his head.
Panhárí, } s. f. a woman who car-
Panhárin, } ries water on her head.
Panhí, } s. f. a slipper.
Panhíṇ, }
Pání, s. m. water; sperm; lustre.
Paníhá, s. m. an aquatic animal.
Pání karná, *v. a.* to abash, to facilitate.
Pání na mángná, to be so wounded as to die instantly.
Pání paṛná, *v. n.* to rain.
Pání pí pí kosná, to curse excessively.
Panír, s. m. cheese.
Panírmáya, s. m. runnet.
Pání se patlá karná, to abash, to put to shame.
Pání ṭorná, to draw (water, a ship, &c.)
Paniyá, s. m. water. See Paníhá.
Paniyálá, s. m. name of a fruit and its tree.
Paniyáná, *v. a.* to irrigate, to water; to temper (steel, &c.)
Panj, *adj.* five; of seven years old (a horse.)
Panja, s. m. a hand with the five fingers extended, claw, clutch, paw, grasp; a hand of ivory, &c., to scratch the back with; a sort of torch resembling the five fingers.
Panjáb, s. m. name of a country.
Panjábí, *adj.* an inhabitant of the Panjáb.
Panja karná, } to lock the fingers to-
Panja laṛná, } gether (two persons to try their strength.)
Panjar, } s. m. the ribs, the side; a
Pánjar, } side or quarter.
Panjarí, s. f. a rib.
Panjáyat, the five chapters of the Qurán, which are read during the mourning of a Musalmán.
Panjírí, s. f. a caudle.

Panj roza, the space of five days.
Panjsál, s. m. five years.
Panjsálá, *adj.* of five years.
Panjsháḳha, s. m. a sort or torch resembling the five fingers.
Panjshamba, s. m. Thursday.
Pánk, } s. m. a bog, mire, mud, slough, quagmire.
Pánká, }
Pankh, s.m. a feather, a wing; quicklime.
Pankhá, s. m. a feather; a fan.
Pankhí, s. f. a small fan; a bird.
Pankhrí, } s. f. a petal, a flower-leaf.
Pankhṛí, }
Panná, s.m. a beverage; embroidery; the upper part of a shoe; an emerald; a leaf.
Panní, s. f. tinfoil.
Páṉoṉ, s. m. foot, leg, feet.
Páṉoṉ páṉoṉ, } *adj.* on foot.
Páṉoṉ piyáda, }
Páṉp, sin, fault, crime.
Páṉṛe, s. m. a title of Bráhmans, a schoolmaster.
Páṉsá, s. m. a die.
Pán sai, five hundred.
Pansál, } s. m. a stand where water is provided for passengers.
Pansálá, }
Pansallá, }
Pansár haṭṭá, s. m. a quarter where are many druggists' shops.
Pansárí, s. m. a druggist; a grocer.
Pán sau, five hundred.
Panserí, s. f. a weight or measure of five sers.
Pansoí, s. f. a small boat so called.
Pánsú, s. f. a rib, the rib bones.
Pánt, s. f. a row, a line; a rank of soldiers.
Pant, s. m. a sect, a religious order.
Pántar, s. m. a desert field.
Panth, s. m. see Pant, a road.
Panthí, s. m. a sectary, a follower.
Pántí, s. f. see Pánt.
Pántí pántí, in rows.
Páṉw, s. m. leg, foot.
Paṉwárá, } s. m. a story, tale, fable.
Paṉwáṛá, }
Panwárí, s. f. a betel garden.
Paṉwáriyá, } s. m. a bard, a story-teller.
Paṉwáṛiyá, }
Páṉw bhar jáná, numbness of the feet, sleeping of the feet.
Pánw ḍálná, to prepare for and commence an undertaking.
Paṉw soná, to sleep (the foot.)
Paṉw ḍigná, to slip.
Páṉw jamáná, to stand firmly.
Páṉw ká angúṭhá, the great toe.
Páṉw kí unglí, a toe.
Páṉw lagná, to make obeisance by embracing the feet.
Páṉw paidal, *adj.* a foot, on foot.
Páṉw pakaṛná, to beseech submissively; to prevent one from going.
Páṉw páṉw, *adj.* a foot, on foot.
Paṉw paṛná, to entreat submissively.
Páṉw par páṉw rakhná, to sit at ease, to sit cross-legged.
Páṉw phúk phúk rakhná, to do anything carefully.
Páṉw pújná, to honour another, to avoid another.
Páṉwroṭí, s. f. a loaf of bread.
Páṉw se páṉw bhiṛáná, to be near.
Páṉw tale malná, to give any one pain, to annoy,
Páṉw toṛná, to be tired.
Páṉw utarná, to be dislocated (the foot.)
Páṉw uṭháná, to go quickly.
Páṉyatí, s. f. the foot of a bed.
Páo, s. m. a quarter, a fourth part.
Páoṉ, s. m. leg, foot, feet.
Páp, s. m. sin, fault, crime, guilt.
Papaiyá, s. m. a sort of child's whistle; name of a tree and its fruit.
Pápaṛ, s. m. a thin crisp cake made of any grain of the pea kind.
Pápaṛ belná, to undergo great labour or pain.
Pápátmá, *adj.* sinful, wicked; a sinner.
Pápbhog, s. m. suffering the consequences or punishment of sin.
Pápí, *adj.* m. a sinner, a criminal.
Papíhá, s. m. a sparrow-hawk.

Pápin, Pápiní, *adj. f.* a sinner, a criminal, wicked (woman.)
Pápishta, very wicked.
Papítá, *s. m.* name of a tree and its fruit.
Pápiyáda, *adv.* on foot, walking.
Pápkarm, *s. m.* a sinful action.
Páp karná, to commit sin.
Páp káṭná, to atone for sin.
Papní, *s. f.* the eyelash.
Páposh, *s. f.* a slipper, a shoe.
Papoṭá, *s. m.* the maw.
Papṛá, *s. m.* crust.
Papṛí, *s. f.* scales formed by the drying up of moist earth; thin cakes of bread.
Papṛiyákath, *s. f.* a kind of white-coloured kath.
Par, *adj.* distant, remote, other, another, strange, foreign: *adv.* and *conj.* but, yet, however: *prep.* on, upon, at, notwithstanding: *s. m.* a feather, a quill, a wing; a fin.
Pár, *s. m.* the opposite bank or shore: *adv.* across, over, on or to the other side, through, beyond.
Páṛá, *s. m.* a small buffalo calf.
Párá, *s. m.* quicksilver, mercury; a sentinel, sentry.
Pára, *s. m.* quicksilver, mercury.
Pará, *s. m.* a company, a body (of troops); a rank, a file.
Parab, *s. m.* a festival, holiday, feast, a sacred day.
Parachhná, *v. a.* to move a lamp or candle over the heads of a bride and bridegroom, to drive away evil spirits, propitiate good ones, &c.
Paráchín, *adj.* old, ancient.
Paráchit, *s. m.* atonement, expiation.
Parádhín, *adj.* dependent.
Párápár, *s. m.* the two banks of a river.
Paráeistrígaman, *s. m.* adultery.
Paráeistrígámí, *s. f.* an adulterer.
Parág, *s. m.* the ancient name of Allahabad.
Parágauda, *adj.* dispersed, scattered, distracted.
Parakh, *s. f.* inspection, examination, experiment, trial, proof.
Parakhaiyá, Parakhdár, *s. m.* an inspector, an examiner, prover, assayer.
Parakhdárí, *s. f.* the bringing of things to the test, the making of experiments.
Parakhná, *v. a.* to inspect, to examine, to prove, to try, to assay.
Parakhwaiyá, *s. m.* see Parakhaiyá.
Parakná, *v. n.* to be habituated, to acquire a habit.
Parákram, *s. m.* great power, ability, force, strength, prowess, [strong.
Parákramí, *adj.* bold, powerful,
Parálabh, *s. f.* fate, predestination.
Param, *adj.* first, supreme, best, excellent; used in *compos.*
Parámarsh, *s. m.* advice, counsel.
Parameshwar, *s. m.* the Almighty, the Chief or Supreme God.
Paramhans, *s. m.* an ascetic; a very religious man.
Paṛáná, *v. a.* to lay down, to put to sleep, to cause to repose.
Parand, Paranda, *adj.* flying, winged; a bird.
Paráṇṭhá, *s. m.* a kind of cake, paste.
Parantu, *conj.* but, afterwards, also.
Paṛáo, *s. m.* a halting place.
Paṛá páná, *v. a.* to find, to get easily.
Paṛápaṛ, *adj.* with reiterated strokes.
Parápat, Parápta, *s. m.* gain, income, produce, benefit: *adj.* acquired, attained.
Paras, *s. m.* act of touching, a touch.
Parás, *s. m.* name of a tree; oakum made of the bark of that tree.
Páras, *s. m.* the philosopher's stone; Persian.
Parasná, *v. a.* to touch.
Paraspar, mutually, reciprocally.
Páras patthal, Páras patthar, *s. m.* the philosopher's stone, a stone supposed to have the property of turning whatsoever it touches into gold.

Parast, in *compos.* adorer, worshipper, devoted to.
Parastí, in *compos.* worship, adoration.
Parastish, *s. f.* worship, devotion, adoration.
Parastishgáh, *s. f.* a place of worship.
Parastrígaman, *s. m.* adultery.
Parastrígámí, *s. m.* an adulterer.
Parat, *s. m.* a fold, plait, ply, layer, crust, a stratum.
Parát, *s. f.* a large plate.
Paráṭhá, *s. m.* bread made of butter or ghí, and like pie-crust.
Parátí, *s. f.* a small plate.
Paṛáw, *s. m.* a halting place.
Paráyá, *adj.* strange, foreign, belonging to another.
Parbá, *s. m.* the full and change of [the moon.
Par badalná, to change (clothes.)
Parbas, *adj.* depending on the will of another, dependent.
Parbasí, *s f.* the being subject to the will of another, dependence.
Parbat, *s. m.* a mountain, a hill.
Parbatí, Parbatiyá, } *s. m.* a mountaineer; a production of the hills.
Parbat paháṛ, a long distance.
Parbhú, *s. m.* lord, master.
Parbrahm, *s. m.* the Supreme God.
Parchá, *s. m.* proof, trial, experiment; a bit, scrap.
Párcha, *s. m.* a piece of cloth, a fragment, a scrap; cloth, clothing.
Parchháná, *v. a.* to introduce to a person.
Parchár, *s. m.* publication, disclosure.
Parchháíṉ, *s. f.* image, shadow, shade.
Parchháíṉ ápne se bhágná, to be frightened at one's own shadow.
Parchhatí, *s. f.* the roof of mud walls.
Parchháwáṉ, *s. f.* image, shadow, shade.
Parchúniyá, *s. m.* a general merchant.
Parda, Pardá, } *s. m.* a curtain, a screen, film; secrecy, privacy, modesty, partition.
Pardádá, *s. m.* a great-grandfather by the father's side.
Pardádí, *s. f.* a great-grandmother by the mother's side.
Pardafásh, betraying secrets.
Parda karná, to conceal.
Pardákht, *s. f.* patronising, supporting.
Parda kisí ká kholná, to reveal the faults of another.
Pardanishín, remaining behind the curtain, modest.
Parda parda karná, to do a thing secretly or privately.
Pardaposh, keeping a secret, a veil over faults.
Pardaposhí, *s. f.* the throwing a veil over a person's faults.
Parda rakhná, to give obscure hints, or to relate a matter in such terms as to be understood by part only of the hearers.
Parde meṉ surákh karná, spoken of women who secretly indulge in licentious practices.
Pardes, *s. m.* a remote or foreign country: *adj.* in another country, abroad.
Pardesí, *s. m.* foreigner, stranger: *adj.* foreign.
Pardhán, *s. m.* a president, leader, chief.
Pardhan, *s. m.* another's wealth.
Pare, *adv.* beyond, yonder, at a distance.
Pare rahná, to remain at a distance.
Paṛe rahná, *v. n.* to be in a hopeless or desperate state.
Pareshán, *adj.* perplexed, confused, troubled, afflicted, distracted, distressed, ruined.
Pareshándil, *adj.* troubled in mind.
Pareshánhál, distressed in condition.
Pareshání, *s. f.* distress; perplexity, distraction, trouble, destruction.
Pareshán karná, to perplex, to confound, to trouble, to distract.
Pareshánkhátir, *adj.* troubled in mind.
Paretá, *s. m.* a reel (for winding yarn.)
Paretná, *v. a.* to reel (thread or yarn.)
Pargana, *s. m.* an inferior division of a country, a district.

Parganát, *s. m. plur.* of Pargana.
Pargaṭ, *adj.* see Pragaṭ.
Pargaṭ honá, *v.a.* to become manifest, to appear.
Pargaṭ karná, *v. a.* to make known.
Parghaṭ, see Pragaṭ.
Par giráná, to get new feathers after moulting.
Paṛhá, *part. pass.* read, learned, of much reading.
Paṛhágunáá, *adj.* a learned experienced man.
Paṛhan, *s. f.* the act of reading.
Paṛháná, *v. a.* to cause or teach to read, to instruct, to teach, to teach to sing or speak (as birds.)
Paṛhant, *s. f.* magic, a spell; study.
Parhez, *s. m.* abstinence, forbearance, continence, control of the passions.
Parhezgár, *adj.* continent, chaste: *s. m.* one who controls his passions.
Parhezgárí, *s. f.* abstinence, control of the passions.
Parhezí, *s. m.* one who controls his passions: *adj.* fit for a person under a regimen.
Parhez karná, *v. a.* to control one's passions; to abstain from; to observe a regimen.
Páṛhí, *s. f.* crossing a river; a young buffalo, a buffalo calf.
Pár hojáná, to go away, to be off, to escape, to be stolen.
Paṛhná, *v. a.* to read, to repeat, to say.
Paṛhnewálá, *s. m.* a reader.
Paṛhwáná, to cause to be taught reading, to teach to read.
Párí, *s. f.* time, tour, turn.
Parí, *s. f.* a fairy.
Parichchhá, } *s. f.* ordeal, examination, trial, proof.
Paríkshá, }
Parikrimá, *s. f.* act of going round to the right by way of adoration.
Parimán, *s. m.* quantity, dose, proportion.
Parishram, } *s.m.* fatigue, labour, toil.
Parisram, }
Parisramí, *adj.* active, laborious.
Paristán, *s. m.* fairy-land.
Pariwá, *s. f.* the first day of the moon's increase or wane.
Pariwár, *s. m.* family, dependents.
Paṛiyá, *s. f.* a female buffalo.
Parizád, *adj.* a fairy, a beauty.
Parjá, *s.m.* a subject, a tenant, renter.
Par jalná, to be without power or ability.
Paṛ jáná, *v. n.* to lie down, to repose, to abate; to cease (as the wind.)
Par jhalná, see Par giráná.
Parkáj, *s. m.* the business or affairs of another.
Parkájí, *adj.* attentive to the business or interest of others, serving others, beneficent.
Parkála, } *s. m.* window glass, a pane of glass.
Parkala, }
Parkáná, *v. a.* to accustom, to habituate.
Par ká qalam, a pen made of a quill.
Parkár, *s. f.* a pair of compasses.
Parkárí, *s. f.* work done with compasses.
Pár karná, to ferry over; to finish; to perforate; to transfix; to carry off.
Parkás, *adj.* apparent, conspicuous, clear: *s. m.* light, daylight.
Parkháí, *s. f.* the act of examining; the price paid for examination; trial, proof.
Parkhaiyá, *s. m.* examiner, prover, (especially of coins.)
Parkháná, *v. a.* to cause to inspect, examine, try, or to prove.
Parlai, *s. f.* a general destruction (as at the deluge.)
Parlok, *s. m.* another world, a future state.
Parmal, *s. m.* parched grain of joár or bájrá.
Parmán, *s. m.* quantity; proof, attestation, limit; cause.
Parmat, *s. m.* a different opinion.
Paṛná, *v. n.* to fall, to lie down, to repose, to encamp, to drop; to

happen, to befall, to be confined to bed by sickness.

Parnálá, *s. m.* } a gutter, a drain, a
Parnálí, *s. f.* } conduit.

Parnám, *s. m.* salutation, bow, obeisance.

Parnáná, *s. m.* a great-grandfather by the mother's side.

Parnání, *s. f.* maternal great-grandmother.

Par nikálná, *v. a.* to invent.

Parojan, *s. m.* purpose, use, exigence, necessity.

Paroná, *v. a.* see Pironá.

Paropakár, *s. m.* the helping of others.

Paropakárí, *s. f.* aiding others.

Paros, } *s.m.* neighbourhood, vicinity.
Paṛos, }

Parosaiyá, *s. m.* a distributor of victuals to guests, a waiter.

Parosí, } *s. m.* a male neighbour.
Paṛosí, }

Paṛosin, *s. f.* a female neighbour.

Paṛosiyá, *s. m.* a neighbour.

Parosná, *v. a.* to serve up dinner, to distribute food to guests.

Parpanch, *s. m.* delusion, fraud, imposition, treachery, deceit.

Parpanchí, *adj.* insidious, fraudulent, artful.

Parparáhaṭ, *s. f.* acrimony, smart.

Parparáná, *v. n.* to smart.

Paṛpaṛáná, *v. n.* to prattle, to chatter; to throb (with pain.)

Parpaṭ maidán, a clean level field or plain.

Parpotá, *s. m.* great-grandson.

Parpotí, *s. f.* great-granddaughter.

Párs, *s. m.* Persia.

Pársá, *adj.* abstemious, chaste.

Parsád, *s. m.* viands, victuals, food that has been offered to the deities.

Pársáí, *s. f.* chastity, abstinence, continence.

Parsál, } *adv.* last year, the year be-
Pársál, } fore last.

Pársí, *s. m.* a Persian, the Persian language.

Parsoṉ, *adv.* the day before yesterday; the day after to-morrow.

Parsúrám, *n. prop.* the sixth incarnation of Vishnu.

Parsút, *s. m.* the whites, flour albus.

Partal, *s. f.* the baggage of a horseman carried all on one bullock or ṭaṭṭú.

Partalá, *s. m.* a sword belt, shoulder belt.

Partal ká ṭaṭṭú, a pack-horse.

Partí, *s f.* waste or uncultivated land.

Partít, *s. f.* faith, confidence, trust.

Partít karná, to believe, to trust.

Par ṭúṭná, see Par jalná.

Parvat, *s. m.* a mountain, a hill.

Párvatí, *s. f.* Durgá, the wife of Siva.

Parwá, } *s. f.* care, concern, anxiety,
Parwáh, } inclination.

Parwáí, *adj.* necessitated, having occasion for, wanting.

Parwána, *s. m.* an order, a pass, a command, a warrant; a moth.

Parwánagí, *s. f.* command, order, permission.

Parwánaját, *s. m.* orders, licences, passes.

Parwána kisí ká honá, to be desperately in love with any one.

Parwán chaṛhná, to grow up.

Pár wár, *adv.* on both sides of a river; quite through, through and through.

Parwar, *s. m.* name of a kind of gourd; in *compos.* a patron, protector, nourisher, cherisher.

Parwarda, brought up, nourished.

Parwardigár, *s. m.* an epithet of the Deity.

Parwarí, *s. f.* in *compos.* fostering, nourishing, cherishing.

Parwarish, *s. f.* fostering, nourishment, maintenance, support, sustenance, rearing, protection.

Parwarish karná, to foster, to nourish, to maintain, to bring up, rear, support, &c.

Parwarish páná, to obtain a livelihood.
Parwastí, s. f. see Parwarish.
Párwatí, s. f. Durgá, the wife of Siva.
Pás, postpos. at the side, near, beside, about, at, in the possession of.
Pas, adv. after, behind, then, therefore, consequently, finally.
Pásá, s. m. a die, a throw of dice.
Pasáná, v. a. to skim, to pour off superfluous water.
Pasand, s. f. choice, approbation: adj. approved, grateful, approving, choosing, pleasing.
Pasand áná, to be approved or chosen, to please.
Pasandáz, s. m. savings.
Pasandída, adj. chosen, approved of, liked.
Pasand honá, to be pleased.
Pasand karná, to approve, to choose, to accede to, to like.
Pásang, Pasangá, s. m. something placed in one scale to balance the other, a make-weight.
Pasárí, s. m. one who sells spices; a druggist.
Pasarná, v. n. to be spread, stretched out, expanded.
Pasárná, v. a. to spread, distend, stretch out, open, expand.
Pásbán, s. m. f. a watchman; a shepherd.
Pásbání, s. f. watch, guard, protection, keeping.
Pascháttáp, s. m. regret, repentance, remorse.
Pásdárí, s. f. watching, guardianship.
Paseo, s. m. perspiration, sweat.
Paserí, s. f. a weight of five ser.
Pasghaibat, adv. in one's absence, behind one's back.
Pashemán, adj. penitent, sorry, ashamed, abashed.
Pashemán honá, to be ashamed.
Pashemání, s. f. regret, shame.
Pashm, s. f. wool, hair, fur; the hair on the privities.
Pashmí, Pashmín, Pashmína, adj. woollen, woollen goods, made of wool.
Pashm na ukhaṛná, to suffer nothing from the enmity of another.
Pashm par márná, Pashm samajhná, to despise, to disregard.
Páshoya, s. m. washing of the feet.
Pásh pásh, shivered in pieces.
Pashtáná, v. n. to repent, to regret.
Pashtáwá, s. m. regret, remorse.
Pashu, s. m. an animal, a beast,
Pásí, s. m. one who extracts palm juice: adv. near, next, close by.
Pasíjná, v. n. to perspire, to sweat, to melt; to compassionate.
Pasíná, s. m. perspiration, sweat.
Pasíná chhúṭná, to sweat.
Paslí, s. f. a rib, the præcordia.
Paslí phaṛakní, a thrilling over the ribs.
Pasmánda, s. m. savings.
Pas o pesh, s. m. evasion, prevarication, hesitation.
Pasqadd, low of stature, a dwarf.
Past, adj. low, abject, mean, below.
Pastáná, v. n. to regret, to repent.
Pastáwá, s. m. see Pachhtáwá.
Past himmat, adj. low-minded, mean-spirited.
Pastí, s. f. lowness, inferiority.
Past qadd, low of stature.
Pasú, Pasu, s. m. a beast, an animal.
Pasújná, v. a. to stitch; to swell.
Pat, s. f. honour, character: s. m. lord, husband; a leaf.
Paṭ, s. m. the sound of falling or beating; a shutter, the valve of a folding door: adj. upside down, overturned.
Pát, s. m. a leaf; an ornament worn in the upper part of the ear.
Páṭ, s. m. a millstone; a plank on which washermen beat clothes; breadth (of cloth or of a river.)
Patá, s. m. sign, mark, direction, address or place to which one is directed.
Paṭá, s. m. a foil, a wooden scimitar for cudgelling with.
Pátába, s. m. a very short sock.

Paṭailá, *s. m.* a flat-bottomed boat.
Pátak, *s. m.* sin, crime, vice.
Paṭáká, } *s. m.* a cracker, a squib:
Paṭákhá, } *s. f.* a flag, a banner.
Pátakí, *adj.* sinner, criminal, wicked.
Paṭakná, *v. a.* to dash against anything, to throw on the ground with violence.
Pátál, *s. m.* in Hindú mythology the infernal regions, hell.
Páṭambar, *s. m.* silk, cloth, a silk [garment.
Páṭan, } *s. m.* roofing, flooring, &c.
Paṭan, } (with planks or boards.)
Paṭáná, *v. a.* to irrigate, to water; to place the beams on the roof of a house; to pay money; to besmear with a wash of clay.
Patá na lagná, not to be found.
Patang, *s. m.* a moth; a child's kite.
Patangá, *s. m.* a moth; a spark.
Patang uṛáná, to fly a paper kite.
Paṭaniyá, *adj.* made at Paṭná: *s. m.* an inhabitant of Paṭná.
Paṭáo, *s. m.* irrigating.
Paṭápaṭ, *s. m.* the sound of beating or of the falling of drops of rain.
Pátar, *adj.* weak, lean.
Patariyá, *s. f.* a prostitute.
Patariyábáz, a whoremonger.
Paṭebáz, a fencer, a cudgeller.
Paṭelá, *s. m.* } a kind of flat-bottomed
Paṭelí, *s. f.* } boat.
Páṭh, *s. m.* a reading, lecture, lesson.
Path, *s. m.* road, path, highway.
Páṭhá, *s. m.* a young animal full grown (generally a goat or elephant); a youth or young wrestler.
Paṭhán, *n. prop.* an Afghán.
Paṭháná, *v. a.* to send, to despatch.
Páthar, *s. m.* a stone.
Paṭhauná, *v. a.* to send, to despatch.
Páṭhí, *s. f.* a young she-goat.
Paṭhingá, *s. m.* shelter, refuge.
Paṭhiyá, *s. f.* a young full-grown animal (applied to kids, &c.)
Páthná, *v. a.* to make up cow-dung into cakes for fuel.
Pathráná, *v. n.* to be petrified.
Pathrí, *s. f.* the flint of a musket; a gizzard; gravel; stone in the bladder.
Pathrílá, *adj.* stony (as soil.)
Páṭhsálá, *s. f.* a school, a college.
Pati, *s. m.* a lord, master, husband; a leaf.
Páṭí, *s. f.* the side pieces of a bedstead; a kind of mat; a board on which children learn to write.
Pátí, *s. f.* a letter, a note; a leaf.
Patibratá, *adj. f.* chaste (woman.)
Patidin, *adv.* daily, always, constantly.
Patíl, *adj.* thin, fine: *s. m.* a wick.
Patílá, *s. m.* a pan, a pot.
Patílsoz, *s. f.* the stand or support of a lamp.
Patit, *adj.* abject, fallen, guilty.
Patit páwan, purifying the guilty (an epithet of the Deity.)
Patiyáná, *v. a.* to confide in, to trust, to believe, to depend on.
Patiyárá, *s. m.* trust, confidence, belief, dependence.
Patjhaṛ, *adj.* without leaves; the fall of the leaves; autumn.
Patjhaṛ honá, to lose its leaves in autumn (a tree); (*met.*) to decay (a person from old age.)
Patjhaṛí, *s. f.* autumn.
Paṭká, *s. m.* a girdle, a sash.
Paṭká jáná, *v. n.* to be dashed or thrown on the ground.
Paṭkan, *s. f.* a knock, a fall.
Paṭkáná, *v. a.* to dash against anything, to throw on the ground with violence.
Paṭkaní dená, *v. a.* to dash on the ground, to throw against anything with violence.
Paṭkan kháná, to fall down.
Paṭkárná, *v. a.* see Paṭkáná.
Paṭkí dená, *v. a.* to dash on the ground with violence.
Patlá, *adj.* fine, thin (cloth or liquids); lean, delicate, weak.
Patláí, *s. f.* thinness, fineness, meagreness, weakness.

Paṭná, *v. n.* to be paid; to be watered; to be covered, to be roofed: *s. m.* name of a city.
Páṭná, *v. a.* to roof; to cover, to fill, to fill up; to irrigate, to water.
Patní, *s. f.* a wife.
Patoh, *s. f.* son's wife.
Paṭotan, *s. m.* roofing, &c.; flooring with planks or boards, &c. [plain.
Paṭpar maidán, a clean level field or
Paṭpaṭ, the sound of beating.
Pátr, Pátra, } *s. m.* a vessel in general, a plate; a leaf.
Patrá, *s. m.* an almanac.
Paṭrá, *s. m.* a plank, a plank to sit on; a bench, a stool; a board on which dough is kneaded, &c.: *adj.* trampled under foot or destroyed by locusts, hail, &c. (as a field of corn.)
Paṭrá kar dená, *v. n.* to deprive one of his power or strength; to shake or pelt the fruit off a tree.
Paṭrí, *s. f.* a plank to write on, a narrow slip or plank of wood.
Patrí, *s. f.* see Pattal.
Paṭsál, *s. m.* a school, schoolhouse.
Pattá, *s. m.* a leaf; a trinket.
Paṭṭá, *s. m.* a lock of hair; a dog's collar; a blind halter; a deed, particularly a title deed to land or a deed of lease.
Paṭṭádár, *s. m.* a leaseholder.
Pattál, *s. m.* the infernal regions, or a place under the earth.
Pattal, *s. f.* a plate or trencher formed of leaves.
Pattar, *s. m.* a leaf; plate or clamp of metal; a deed, document.
Paṭṭá salámí, *s. f.* a present given to obtain a lease.
Paṭṭh, Paṭṭhá, } *s. m.* a young full grown animal; a youth, a wrestler.
Patthar, *s. m.* a stone.
Pattharchúr, *s. m.* name of a plant.
Patthar honá, to be heavy; to stand still; to be unmerciful.
Pattharkalá, *s. m.* cock (of a gun.)
Patthar pasíjná, to be softened or melted (a stony heart.) [gizzard.
Patthrí, *s. f.* the flint of a musket; a
Patthrílá, *adj.* stony.
Paṭṭí, *s. f.* felly of a wheel; assessment; a board to write on; the side pieces of the frame of a bedstead; a bandage, a fillet; a plaster; a row (of houses); deception, deceit.
Pattí, *s. f.* a leaf; hemp, of which an intoxicating potion is made.
Pattiyá, *s. m.* a small leaf.
Paṭṭú, *s. m.* a kind of woollen cloth; a cloth to cover with from rain, &c.
Paṭúá, *s. m.* a man who strings pearls; a kind of hemp for making ropes; the sorrel plant and flower.
Paṭúká, *s. m.* a cloth worn round the waist, a girdle.
Paturiyá, *s. f.* a prostitute.
Patwál, *s. f.* a rudder, a helm.
Paṭwáná, *v. a.* to roof, to floor; to water.
Patwáṛ, *s. f.* a rudder, a helm.
Paṭwárí, *s. m.* one who keeps account of lands, a land steward.
Patyáná, *v. a.* see Patiyáná.
Paudhá, *s. m.* a young tree or plant, for transplantation.
Paulád, *s. m.* see Polád.
Paun, *adj.* three-quarters, a quarter less than any given number.
Paunchná, *v. n.* see Pahunchná.
Paunḍá, *s. m.* a kind of sugar-cane.
Paune, *adj.* one quarter less (either of one, or of the aggregate number which may follow.)
Pau phaṭná, to dawn.
Pauwá, *s. m.* a quarter, a weight or measure of a quarter of a ser.
Pavitra, *adj.* see Pabitr.
Pawáj, *s. plur.* of Pájí, mean people.
Pawan, *s. f.* air, wind.
Páwná, *v. a.* see Páná.
Páyá, Páya, } *s. m.* the foot of a table, chair, &c.

Páyal, *s. f.* an ornament for the foot or ankle.
Payám, *s. m.* a message, news, intelligence.
Payambar, *s. m.* see Paighambar.
Payambarí, *s. f.* see Paighambarí.
Pazáwá, *s. f.* a brick-kiln.
Pazhmurda, *adj.* withered, pallid, decayed, blighted, faded.
Pech, *s. f.* a screw; twist, a coil, a plait; difficulty, perplexity, trouble; an intricate scheme, deceit, complication.
Pechá, *s. m.* an owl.
Pechak, *s. f.* a ball, a skein of thread.
Pechish, *s. f.* pain in the bowels, tenesmus, gripes.
Pech chunná, to bind the twists of a turban with care.
Pech ḍálná, to throw obstacles in the way; (in playing with paper kites) to entangle the string of an adversary's kite.
Pechdár, *adj.* twisted, coiled, intricate.
Pech dar pech, coil within coil, entangled, complex, intricate.
Pech dená, to circumvent, to deceive, to twist, to screw, &c.
Pech karná, to deceive, to trick, to grapple.
Pechkas, } *s. f.* a turnscrew, a corkscrew.
Pechkash, }
Pech kháná, to coil; to be perplexed; to sustain a loss.
Pech kholná, to untwist, to unscrew.
Pech khulná, to be untwisted or unscrewed.
Pechpách, } *s. m.* see Pech.
Pechpánch, }
Pech paṛná, to become difficult or intricate, to occur (as an obstacle), to be entangled.
Pech uṭháná, to suffer loss or distress.
Pechwán, *adj.* twisted (generally applied to huqqas or huqqa-snakes.)
Pekhná, } *s. m.* the artifices and pretences of a woman.
Peḳhná, }
Pel, *s. m.* a shove, push, thrust.
Pelaṛ, *s. m.* a testicle.
Pel márná, *v. n.* to shove, to push.
Pelná, *v. a.* to shove, to push; to stuff, to cram.
Pem, *s. m.* love, friendship.
Peṉch, *s. m.* see Pech.
Penchá, *s. m.* an owl.
Pendá, *s. m.* } the bottom (of a vessel, box, pot, &c.)
Pendí, *s. f.* }
Peng, *s. f.* the exertion made by people in a swing, when two persons keep the swing in motion without assistance from bystanders.
Penná, *v. a.* see Pahinná.
Penṭh, } *s. f.* a market, mart.
Penṭhiyá, }
Peoṛí, *s. f.* a yellow colour.
Peṛ, *s. f.* a tree, a plant.
Peṛá, *s. m.* a kind of sweetmeat made with curds; an unbaked loaf.
Peṛ lagáná, to plant trees.
Peṛná, *v. a.* to press (oil by means of a mill), to squeeze, to rack.
Perú, *s.* a turkey.
Peṛú, *s. m.* the stomach below the navel, the pubes.
Pesh, *s. m.* before, in front, forward; the vowel point ُ.
Pesha, *s. m.* trade, profession, business.
Pesháb, *s. m.* urine.
Peshábband, *s. m.* strangury.
Peshagí, *s. f.* an advance (of money.)
Peshámad, *s. f.* access, admittance.
Pesh áná, to treat, to behave, to negotiate, to come before, to occur, to happen, to present (itself.)
Pesháni, *s. f.* the forehead, the brow.
Peshaur, *n. prop.* name of a city.
Peshaurí, *s. f.* a kind of shoe.
Pesháwar, *n. prop.* name of a city.
Peshbandí, *s. f.* foresight, timely preparation.
Peshgí, *s. f.* an advance (of money.)
Peshkár, *s. m.* a manager, agent, deputy.
Peshkárí, *s. f.* deputyship, agency.
Peshkash, *s. m.* a present, a tribute.

Pesh khaima, *s. m.* a tent or baggage sent on before.
Peshqabz, *s. m.* a kind of dagger.
Peshtar, *adv.* before, prior, sooner, formerly, heretofore, ago.
Peshwá, *s. m.* a leader, a guide.
Peshwáí, *s. f.* guidance.
Peshwáz, *s. f.* a gown, a female dress.
Peṭ, *s. m.* the belly, the womb, pregnancy, cavity, capacity.
Peṭá, *s. f.* a large basket.
Peṭárthú, *adj.* gluttonous, epicurean.
Peṭ bándhná, to eat less than one's appetite demands.
Peṭ baṛháná, to eat voraciously; to encroach on the share or rights of another.
Peṭ bathná, to be pained or griped (the bowels.)
Peṭbhar, *adv.* bellyful.
Peṭ bharná, to fill one's belly; to be satisfied.
Peṭ chalná, **Peṭ chhúṭná**, } to be purged, to have a diarrhœa.
Peṭ dikháná, to complain of poverty and hunger.
Peṭ gargaṛáná, to have boborygmi.
Peṭ giráná, to cause an abortion.
Peṭ girná, to miscarry (a female.)
Peṭhá, *s. m.* a kind of gourd.
Peṭ harbaṛáná, to have a griping or inclination to stool.
Peṭhiyá, *s. f.* a market, a bazaar.
Peṭí, *s. f.* a belly-band, a girth; a box, a tumbril.
Peṭ jalná, to be very hungry.
Peṭ jári honá, to be fluxed, to be purged.
Peṭ ká dukh dená, to starve.
Peṭ káṭná, to pinch one's belly, to starve one's self.
Peṭká parda, *s. m.* the omentum.
Peṭ kí ág, *s. f.* maternal affection; hunger.
Peṭ kí báteṇ, *s. f.* bosom secrets.
Peṭ lag jáná, to be starving with hunger.
Peṭ lag rahná, to be very hungry.
Peṭ márná, to show partiality.
Peṭ meṇ lená, to bear or put up with, to endure.
Peṭ meṇ paiṭhná, to worm one's self into the secrets of another, to become intimate.
Peṭ pálná, to get a livelihood.
Peṭ phúlná, to burst with laughter.
Peṭ píṭh ek honá, to be greatly emaciated.
Peṭponchhan, the last child of a woman.
Peṭposú, **Peṭposúá**, } *adj.* glutton.
Peṭ rahná, to be pregnant.
Peṭ rakháná, to get with child.
Peṭ se, *adj.* pregnant.
Peṭ se honá, to be pregnant.
Peṭú, *adj.* gluttonous, epicurean.
Peṭwálí, *adj.* pregnant.
Pewakkaṛ, *s. m.* a tippler, a drinker.
Pewṛí, *s. f.* see Peoṛí.
Phabakná, *v. n.* to shoot forth (as a plant); to grow, sprout.
Phabná, *v. n.* to become, to befit.
Phabtá, *adj.* pertinent, fitting.
Phabtí, *s. f.* conjecturing what a person is by his dress.
Phabtí kahná, *v. a.* to say what is conjectured by one's dress.
Phadphadáná, *v. n.* to spread (as a sore); to ferment (as sour milk, &c.)
Phág, *s. m.* the gambols of the Holí.
Phágan, *s. m.* see Phágun.
Phaguá, *s. m.* the same as Holí.
Phágun, *s. m.* the name of the eleventh Hindú month.
Pháhá, *s. m.* a flock of cotton; a flock of cotton wetted with ạtr or scented water.
Phailáná, *v. a.* to spread, to expand, to widen, to stretch out, to extend, to distend, to publish, to proclaim, to branch out.
Phailáo, *s. m.* expansion, extension.
Phailná, *v. n.* to be spread, to spread, to be expanded, to be diffused, to become public.
Phaináná, *v. n.* to foam, to froth.

Phainṭá, *s. f.* a small turban.
Phák, *s. m.* a chasm, an aperture.
Phakkaṛ, *s. m.* wrangling, mutual abuse; raillery.
Phakkaṛbáz, an abuser, an indecent chatterer.
Phakṛí, *s. f.* the act of treating with rudeness. [betel-nut.
Phál, *s. f.* a plough-share; a lump of
Phal, *s. m.* fruit, effect, advantage; reward; children, progeny; the punishment of a crime; the blade of a knife or other instrument; a plough-share.
Phaláná, *v. n.* to cause to produce, to fructify.
Phaláng, *s. f.* a stride, leap, bound.
Phaldár. *adj.* fruitful, bearing fruit.
Phaldáyak, *adj.* giving fruit, fruitful.
Phalí, *s. f.* a cod, a pod of any leguminous plant, but particularly of peas; a loop; the head of a spear or arrow; a plough-share.
Phalíkash, *s. m.* a hook for drawing the strings through the holes by which the walls of a tent are laced to the top.
Phaliyáná, *v. n.* to bear fruit.
Phalná, *v. n.* to bear fruit; to produce; to be fortunate.
Phal páná, to reap the reward of (good or bad actions.)
Phal phalárí, fruits of various kinds.
Phálsá, *s. m.* name of a fruit.
Phaltáṛ, *s. m.* the fruit bearing táṛ.
Phalwant, *adj.* fruitful, advantageous.
Phámphaṛ, *s. m.* a hole, an orifice.
Phan, *s. m.* the hood of a snake, his expanded neck. [Phándá.
Phánd, *s. m.* circumference. See also
Phándá, } *s. m.* a noose, a net; per-
Phandá, } plexity, difficulty.
Phanda, *s. m.* the place in the string of a pellet-bow on which the pellet is placed to fire it off.
Phandáná, *v. a.* to cause to jump or leap over. [trap.
Phandláná, *v. a.* to ensnare, to en-
Phándná, *v. a.* to bound, to spring, to jump or leap over; to ensnare.
Phangá, *s. m.* } a grasshopper.
Phangí, *s. f.* }
Phaní, *s. m.* a wedge.
Phánk, *s. f.* a slice, a piece of fruit; a part, a division.
Phanká, *s. m.* a handful of anything eaten by being chucked into the mouth.
Phanká márná, to eat by chucking into the mouth, to chuck food into the mouth.
Phánkí, *s. f.* a slice or piece of fruit.
Phánkná, *v. a.* to chuck into the mouth from the palm of the hand.
Phanphanáná, *v. n.* to hiss (as a snake.)
Pháṇs, *s. m.* a noose, a slip-knot.
Phaṇsáná, *v. a.* to cause to be ensnared, caught or involved in, &c., to entrap.
Phaṇsáo, } *s. m.* entanglement, stick-
Phaṇsáw, } ing.
Pháṇsí, *s. f.* a noose, a loop; strangulation.
Pháṇsí dená, *v. a.* to hang, to strangle.
Pháṇsígar, *s. m.* see Phaṇsíyárá.
Pháṇsí lagáná, *v. a.* to kill one's self by hanging.
Pháṇsí paṛná, *v. n.* to be hanged.
Phaṇsiyárá, *s. m.* a foot-pad who strangles passengers or travellers.
Pháṇsná, *v. a.* to noose, to ensnare, to entrap.
Phaṇsná, *v. n.* to be entangled, to stick, to be involved (in calamity, &c.), to be ensnared, noosed, or entrapped, to be caught.
Phaṇswáná, *v. a.* to cause to noose, strangle, &c.
Phan uṭháná, *v. a.* to spread the hood (a snake.)
Pháo, *s. m.* a small quantity given above the quantity purchased, to boot.
Pháoṛá, *s. m.* a mattock, a hoe.
Pháoṛí, *s. f.* an instrument like a

small rake or hoe for removing filth, &c,

Phapholá, *s. m.* a blister.

Phaphole phúṭná, to break (a blister.)

Phaphsá, *adj.* insipid; swelled.

Phaphundí, Phaphúndí, } *s. f.* mouldiness; mould (on fruit, bread, &c., from dampness.)

Phapolá, *s. m.* a blister.

Phaṛ, *s. f.* a gaming-table, a particular game; the pole of a carriage.

Pháṛá, *part. pass.* torn, broken, split, rent.

Pharahrá, *s. m.* a vane, a pennant.

Pharahrí, *adj.* half-dried (as the ground after rain.)

Phaṛakná, *v. n.* to vibrate with convulsive involuntary motion, as the eyelids and other muscles.

Phaṛáná, *v. a.* to cause to be torn, split, or cleaved.

Phaṛbáz, *s. m.* a gamester, a player at dice.

Phaṛbází, *s. f.* gambling, playing at dice.

Pharchá, *s. m.* clearing away or dispersion (of clouds, &c.); fair weather; decision, definitive sentence (of a judge.)

Pharcháná, *v. a.* to settle, to decide.

Pharchhá, *adj.* fair (not cloudy.)

Pharchhá honá, *v. n.* to clear up, to become fair (the weather.)

Pharchhá karná, *v. a.* to settle.

Pharí, *s. f.* a shield, a target.

Phaṛiyá, *s. m.* a person who sells grain, &c., on comission.

Pháṛ kháná, *v. a.* to worry, to bite and gnaw.

Pháṛná, *v. a.* to tear, to lacerate, to rend, to split, to break, to cleave (wood, &c.), to tear open, to burst, to rip.

Pharphand, *s. m.* trick, deceit, wickedness.

Pharphandiyá, *adj.* deceitful, treacherous, wicked.

Phaṛphaṛáhaṭ, *s. f.* disquietude, agitation, flutter.

Phaṛphaṛáná, *v. n.* to boast, to flutter.

Phaṛphaṛiyá, *s. m.* a boaster.

Pharráná, *v. n.* to fly (as a flag.)

Pharráṭá, *s. m.* a piece of bamboo; a sound made by the flying of a flag or the breathing of a horse.

Pharsá, *s. m.* an axe, a hatchet.

Phasáná, *v. a.* to cause to stick (as in mud, &c.), to entangle; to cause to be imprisoned.

Phasáo, *s. m.* sticking, entanglement.

Phaskan, Phaskaṛ, } *s. m.* sitting on the ground with extended legs.

Phasná, *v. n.* to be stuck (as in mud, &c.), to be caught, ensnared, imprisoned, entangled or involved (in calamity, &c.)

Phasphasá, *adj.* loose (as shoes.)

Phaṭá, *s. m.* a crack, a rent.

Pháṭak, *s. m.* a gate, a large door; stocks, arrest.

Phaṭákhá, *s. m.* a cracker (firework.)

Phaṭakná, *v. n.* to winnow, to dust, to shake or knock off any light thing: *v. n.* to be separated.

Phaṭe meṇ páṇw dená, to interfere in anything.

Phaṭkarí, *s. f.* alum.

Phaṭná, *v. n.* to be torn, split, rent, broken, cracked, torn asunder, to burst.

Phaṭ paṛná, *v. n.* to be produced plentifully.

Phaṭphaṭáná, *v. n.* to shake or flap the wings (as birds just going to fly); to give a sound (as the shoes of a person walking.)

Phattar, *s. m.* a stone.

Phauṛá, *s. m.* a mattock, a hoe.

Pháw, *s. m.* see Pháo.

Pháyá, *s. m.* a flock of cotton.

Phen, *s. m.* foam, froth.

Phenáná, *v. n.* to foam, to froth.

Phenk dená, to throw away.

Phenkná, *v. a.* to throw, to fling, to dart, to let fly: to set off (a horse at full speed), to gallop.

Phenk phánk karná, to throw away.

Pheṇpṛá, *s. m.* the lungs.

Phenṭá, *s. f.* a small turban; a waistband.
Phenṭí, *s. f.* a skein (of thread, &c.)
Phenṭná, *v.a.* to mix, to beat (as eggs, &c.), to triturate.
Phenus, *s. m.* biestings, the milk of a cow, &c., for some days after calving.
Phephṛá, *s. m.* the lights or lungs.
Pher, *s. m.* turning, meander, twisting, circumference; difficulty, distance; equivocation, ambiguity: *adv.* again, back.
Pherá pherí, *s. f.* alternating, alternation.
Pher dená, to return, restore, refund.
Pherí, *s. f.* hawking, going about (with commodities for sale.)
Pheríwálá, *s. m.* a pedlar.
Pher kháná, to wind (as a river), to meander; to go round about; to meet with perplexities.
Pherná, *v. a.* to turn, to turn back, to return, to invert, to reverse, to turn away; to walk backwards and forwards; to carry or bring back; to plaster; to stroke.
Pher paṛná, to differ.
Pherphár, *adj.* alternate.
Pherphár karná, to alternate.
Pheṭá, *s. m.* a small turban; a waistband.
Pheṭná, *v. a.* to beat up and mix, to froth, to mix by trituration.
Phík, *s. f.* the point of a whip, &c.
Phíká, *adj.* weak, vapid, tasteless, insipid, pale, sallow, light (in colour), saltless, weak (as tobacco, &c.)
Phikait, *s. m.* a thrower (of a spear, &c.)
Phikáná, *v. a.* to cause to throw.
Phikká, *adj.* see Phíká.
Phillí, *s. f.* the leg.
Phínch ḍálná, } *v. a.* to wash cloth, to
Phínchná, } rinse, to squeeze.
Phinkná, *v. n.* to be thrown.
Phinkwáná, *v. n.* to cause to fling or throw.

Phir, *adv.* again, then.
Phiráná, *v. a.* to cause to turn, to whirl, to wheel, to make to go about, to roll, to return, to wander.
Phirat, *s. m.* rejected things; money paid by a lewd woman to her paramour.
Phir jáná, *v. n.* to return, to revolt; to be distorted; to go from one's word.
Phirkí, *s. f.* whirligig, anything turned as on an axis.
Phirná, *v. n.* to turn, to return, to walk about, to go round, to whirl, to wheel, to wander, to travel, to ramble, to change, to revolt.
Phirtábhaṛá, *s. m.* return hire.
Phirtá rahná, *v. n.* to wander, to perambulate, to walk about.
Phirtí, *s. f.* returning, return, homeward-bound.
Phirtí ká bhaṛá, the hire of a return boat, carriage, &c.
Phirwáná, *v. a.* to cause to be returned.
Phisalná, *v. n.* to slip, to slide; to err: *adj.* slippery.
Phislahá, *adj.* slippery.
Phisláná, *v. a.* to cause to slip, slide, or err.
Phisphisáná, *v. n.* to be terrified.
Phiṭ, *s. m.* curse, malediction: *adv.* fie!
Phiṭáná, *v. a.* to beat up and mix, to froth.
Phiṭkár, *s. f.* curse, malediction.
Phiṭkárná, *v. a.* to curse.
Phiṭkirí, *s. f.* alum.
Phok, *adj.* hollow.
Phokná, *s. m.* the bladder.
Pholá, *s. m.* a blister, a gall.
Phonk, *adj.* hollow, not solid (particularly jewels.)
Phoṇpar, *adj.* hollow.
Phoṇphí, *s. f.* a pipe, a tube; anything perforated or hollow.
Phoṇprá, *adj.* hollow.
Phoṛá, *s. m.* a boil, a sore, an ulcer.
Phoṛná, *v. a.* to break, to burst, to disclose, to divulge (a secret.)

Phúá, *s. f.* paternal aunt.
Phudakná, *v. n.* to jump, to leap, to hop, to dance about in token of delight.
Phudkí, *s. f.* the name of a bird.
Phúhá, *s. m.* an artificial teat or pap, formed of cotton or other substance, by which milk is given to a young animal, when unable to suck its mother.
Phúhaṛ, *adj.* stupid, foolish; a bad housewife, a slattern.
Phúhaṛpan, } **Phúhaṛpaná**, } *s. m.* stupidity, folly, silliness.
Phúhí, *s. f.* small rain.
Phukná, *s. m.* the bladder: *v. n.* to be blown, to be blown up (a fire.)
Phúkná, *v. a.* to blow, to inflate.
Phukní, *s. f.* a blow-pipe.
Phúl, } **Phul**, } *s. m.* a flower, a blossom; a bunch of ribands, or a cockade; a swelling; a kind of bell metal; menses; a ceremony performed in honour of a deceased person on the third or fourth day after his death.
Phúlá, *adj.* swelled; blossomed.
Phuláná, *v. a.* to cause to swell, to distend; to fatten.
Phúlá na samáná, not to be able to contain one's self from delight, to be overjoyed, to exult.
Phuláo, *s. m.* swelling.
Phulaurí, *s. f.* bread or cake made of fruit and pulse, and fried in ghí or oil.
Phúl baiṭhná, *v. n.* to be glad.
Phulel, *s. m.* oil impregnated with the essence of flowers by steeping them in it; sweet-scented oil.
Phúlí, *s. f.* a disorder in the eye, the albugo.
Phúl jáná, *v. n.* to swell; to be delighted, to be pleased; to become fat.
Phúljhaṛí, } **Phuljhaṛí**, } *s. f.* a kind of firework like a fountain.
Phúl jhaṛná, *v.n.* to speak eloquently.
Phulká, *adj.* inflated, puffed up. *s. m.* a kind of cake or small loaf; a blister.
Phulkárí, *s. m.* flowered cloth.
Phulkí, *s. f.* a cake of raised bread, fritters.
Phúlkobí, *s. f.* a cauliflower.
Phullá, *s. m.* } **Phullí**, *s. f.* } a disease of the eye, cataract.
Phulná, } **Phúlná**, } *v. n.* to blossom, to blow, to flower; to be pleased, to flourish; to swell, to be puffed up (with pride, &c.)
Phúl uṭhná, *v. n.* to be performed (a ceremony in honour of the dead.)
Phulwárí, } **Phulwáṛí**, } *s. f.* a flower-garden.
Phunang, *s. f.* the topmost branch of a tree; summit.
Phundná, *s. m.* a tassel.
Phungí, *s. f.* a sprout, bud, the point of an ear of corn, &c.
Phuṇhár, *s. f.* small drops of rain.
Phuṇhárá, *s. m.* a fountain, a jet d'eau.
Phúṇhí, *s. f.* small drizzling rain.
Phuniyá, *s. f.* penis puerilis.
Phúnk, *s. f.* act of blowing; a puff, a blast, blowing up (fire, &c.)
Phunkár, } **Phunkárí**, } *s. f.* hiss (of a snake.)
Phunkárí márná, } **Phunkárná**, } *v. n.* to hiss (a snake.)
Phúnk dená, to set on fire; to charm; to blow.
Phúnkná, *v. a.* to blow with the breath, to blow up (a fire, &c.), to set on fire, to kindle; to blow (a horn, &c).
Phunkná, *v. n.* to be blown (with the breath): *s. m.* the bladder.
Phúnk phúnkke páṇw dharná, to act or walk carefully and cautiously.
Phunkwáná, *v. a.* to cause to blow, to cause to set on fire.
Phunni, } **Phunno**, } *s. f.* penis puerilis.
Phunsí, *s. f.* a pimple.
Phúphá, *s. m.* father's sister's husband.

Phupherá, *adj.* related through a paternal aunt.
Phupherá bháí, the son of a paternal aunt, cousin (male.)
Phupherí bahin, daughter of a paternal aunt, cousin (female.)
Phuphí, } *s. f.* father's sister, a pater-
Phúphí, } nal aunt.
Phuphiyá sás, *s. f.* the sister of a father-in-law.
Phuphiyá susur, *s. m.* the husband of a father-in-law's sister.
Phuphkár márná, } *v. n.* to hiss (a
Phuphkárná, } snake.)
Phuphú, } *s. m. f.* father's sister's hus-
Phúphú, } band, or father's sister.
Phupphá, *s. m.* see Phúphá.
Phuṛiyá, *s. f.* a sore, a pimple, a boil.
Phurr, *s. m.* the noise of a bird, as a partridge or quail, suddenly taking wing, or of a small quantity of gunpowder exploding.
Phurt, } *s. f.* activity, quickness,
Phurtí, } alertness, agility.
Phurtílá, *adj.* quick, nimble, active, smart, alert, expert.
Phus, *s.* sound, &c. See Awáz.
Phús, *s. m.* old dry grass or straw.
Phusáhindá, *adj.* disgusting, stinking.
Phusarphusar, *s. m.* whispering.
Phusláhaṭ, *s. f.* cajolery, seduction.
Phuslání, *v. a.* to coax, to wheedle, to cajole, to flatter, to decoy, to entice, to seduce.
Phusláú, } *s. m.* a coaxer, a
Phuslauniyá, } wheedler, instigator.
Phusphusáná, *v. n.* to whisper.
Phusphusáwaṭ, *s. f.* whispering.
Phuṭ, *adj.* odd, unpaired, separated.
Phúṭ, *s. f.* a kind of melon; odd, unpaired; difference of opinion; separation.
Phúṭá, *adj.* broken, cracked (as a rupee.)
Phúṭá pání, *s. m.* boiling water.
Phúṭ honá, to be divided in opinion.
Phuṭkar, *adj.* odd, unpaired.
Phuṭkí, *s. f.* a blot, spot, stain.
Phúṭná, *v. n.* to be broken; to be dispersed, to be separated; to burst; to arise (as a smell), to burst forth; to sink (ink on paper); to boil (as water); to burst forth.
Phúṭ paṛná, to arise (dissension.)
Phúṭ pháṭ honá, to become separated (from dissension, &c.)
Phúṭ phúṭ kar roná, } to weep exces-
Phúṭ phúṭ roná, } sively, to burst into tears.
Phúṭ rahná, to be unpaired.
Pí, see Piyá.
Píáj, *s. f. prop.* Piyáz, an onion.
Píák, *s. m.* a tippler, a toper.
Píás, *s. f. prop.* Piyás, thirst.
Píásá, *adj. prop.* Piyásá, thirsty.
Píb, *s. f.* pus, matter, corruption, purulent running.
Píbiyáná, *v. n.* to suppurate.
Pichakná, *v. n.* to be squeezed, to be shrivelled.
Pichchí, *adj.* adhering, sticking, joined.
Pichchí honá, to be stuck together (as with glue.)
Píchh, *s. f.* rice-water, rice-gruel.
Píchhá, *s. m.* the hinder part, the rear; pursuit, following, persecution, absence.
Píchhá karná, to pursue, to chase, to follow; to recoil (a gun, &c.)
Píchhá lená, to pursue, to importune, to be obstinately persevering.
Pichhalná, *v. n.* to slip, to slide.
Pichhánná, *v. a.* to know, to be acquainted with, to recognize.
Pichháṛí, *s. f.* the rear; the ropes by which a horse's hind legs are tied: *adv.* in the rear, behind.
Pichhe, } *adv.* in the rear, after, be-
Píchhe, } hind, afterwards, astern, in the absence.
Píchhe lagná, to pursue, to follow.
Píchheṇ, } *adv.* see Píchhe.
Pichheṇ, }
Píchhe paṛná, to run after, to importune, to dun, to persecute.

Pichhlá, *adj.* hindermost, hinder, latter, last, modern, recent.
Pichhláná, *v. a.* to cause to slip,
Píchhú, see Píchhá.
Pichhút, *s. m.* back of a house: *adv.* behind.
Píchhwá, *s. m.* the hinder part (of a saddle particularly.)
Pichhwáṛá, *s. m.* } the rear, the back
Pichhwáṛí, *s. f.* } part: *adj.* hindermost, abaft, hinder, in the rear.
Pichkáná, *v. a.* to squeeze, to press together, to shrivel.
Pichkárí, *s. f.* a squirt, a syringe.
Pichpichá, *adj.* flabby, watery, clammy.
Pidar. *s. m.* father.
Piddá, *s. m.* name of a bird,
Pidṛí, } *s. f.* a tomtit.
Pídṛí, }
Pigalná, } *v. n.* to melt or be melted,
Pighalná, } to be in fusion,
Pighláná, *v. a.* to melt, to fuse, to soften (an angry or hard person), to assuage, to mollify.
Pí jáná, *v. a.* to drink or be drunk, to stifle one's passions, to refrain from answering.
Pík, *s. f.* the juice of the betel-leaf chewed and spit out.
Píkdán, *s. m.* a spitting pot.
Píkdání, *s. f.* a small spitting pot.
Píl, *s. m.* an elephant.
Pílá, *adj.* yellow.
Píláí, *s. f.* yellowness.
Pila'í, *s. f.* the spleen, a disease from enlargement or inflammation of the spleen.
Pílám, *s. m.* a coarse calico.
Piláná, *v. a.* to give or cause to drink, to suckle, to nurse.
Pílbán, *s. m.* an elephant-driver, one who has charge of elephants.
Pílbání, *s. f.* the business of taking care of elephants.
Píldandán, *s. m.* ivory.
Pílí, *s. f.* yellowness; the blight.
Pilindá, *s. m.* } a bundle.
Pilindí, *s. f.* }
Pillá, *s. m.* a pup, a whelp, a cub.
Pillú, *s. m.* a worm.
Pilná, *v. a.* to attack, to assault.
Pílpá, *adj.* afflicted with elephantiasis.
Pílpáya, *s. m.* a pillar, a column.
Pilpilá, *adj.* soft, flabby, flaccid.
Pilpiláhaṭ, *s. f.* softness.
Pilpiláná, *v. a.* to soften.
Pílú, *s. m.* the name of a tree.
Pilúá, *s. m.* a worm.
Píná, *v. a.* to drink, to smoke (tobacco): *subst.* drinking, &c.: *s. m.* the dregs or refuse (of linseed, &c.); the oil-cake of the poppy-seed.
Pínak, *s. f.* intoxication and drowsiness from opium; drowsiness.
Pínas, *s. m.* a disease in the nose, cold, catarrh; a kind of boat or barge, a pinnace.
Pinḍ, *s. m.* body, person; balls made of flour or rice and offered to the manes at a religious ceremony of the Hindús.
Pinḍá, *s. m.* balls made of flour, &c. See Pinḍ.
Pinḍárá, *s. m.* a plunderer, or pillager among Maharattas.
Pinḍ chhuṛáná, to avoid, to escape.
Pinḍí, *s. f.* a lump of anything that may be contained in the fist; a ball of tobacco; a small clue or ball of string.
Pinḍlí, *s. f.* the calf of the leg.
Pinḍ paṛná, to follow, to pursue, to be intent on.
Pinháná, *v. a.* to clothe, to put on (clothes), to adorn, to dress.
Píní, *s. f.* tobacco (for smoking.)
Pinjrá, *s. m.* a cage, a trap.
Pinjrá honá, to be or grow lean.
Pinkí, *s. f.* see Pínak.
Pinná, *s. m.* a cake of mustard-seed remaining after the expression of the oil, and given to cows, &c., for food.
Pinpináná, *v. n.* to twang, to whiz,

Pío, *s. m.* husband, lover, sweetheart.
Pípá, *s. m.* a pipe, a barrel, a cask.
Pípal, *s. m.* a species of fig-tree: *s. f.* long pepper.
Píplá, *s. m.* the point of a sword, &c.
Píplámúl, Píplámúr, } *s. m.* the root of the long pepper-tree.
Pír, *s. m.* a saint a spiritual guide; an old man; Monday: *s. f.* pain, pity, feeling, compassion.
Pírá, *adj.* yellow.
Píṛá, *s. f.* pain, sickness, anguish.
Piráná, *v. n.* to have pain, to be painful, to pain, to ache.
Píṛhá, *s. m.* a stool, a chair, a seat.
Píṛhí, *s. f.* a stool, a chair; a generation of progenitors.
Pírí, *s. f.* the act of making proselytes; old age, decrepitude.
Pirich, *s.* a saucer.
Pironá, *v. a.* to thread (as a needle); to string (as pearls), to spit.
Pirthamí, Pirthí, } *s. f.* the earth, the ground.
Piṛwáná, *v. a.* to cause to press, to squeeze or pound.
Pisáb, *s. m.* the act of making urine; urine.
Pisách, *s. m.* an evil spirit of a particular class, a demon, a spectre.
Pisáchní, *s. f.* a female pisách.
Pisáí, *s. f.* price paid for grinding.
Pisán, *s. m.* meal, flour, bottledust.
Pisáná, *v. a.* to reduce to meal, to grind.
Pisar, *s. m.* a boy, a son, a child.
Pisháb, *s. m.* urine.
Pishách, *s. m.* see Pisách.
Pishwáz, *s. f.* a gown or female dress.
Pisláná, *v. a.* to cause to grind.
Písná, *v. a.* to grind, to triturate; to bruise to powder; to gnash (the teeth.)
Pisná, *v. n.* to be reduced to meal, to be ground, to be bruised or broken to powder; to be ruined or distressed.
Pissú, *s. m.* a flea.
Pista, *s. m.* a pistachio-nut.
Pista'í rang, *s. m.* pea-green.
Pistaul, Pistol, } *s. m.* a pistol.
Pít, *s. f.* love, affection, kindness.
Pitá, *s. m.* a father.
Pítal, *s. m.* brass.
Pítam, *s. m.* a lover, a sweetheart; a husband.
Pitámbar, Pitámbar, } *s. m.* a silk cloth of yellow colour.
Pítambar, a silk cloth.
Piṭáná, *v. a.* to cause to beat, thrash, pound, &c.
Piṭárá, *s. m.* a large basket, a portmanteau; a kind of balloon.
Piṭárí, *s. f.* a small basket, a portmanteau.
Pitarpakh, *s. m.* the first or dark fortnight of the lunar ásin month.
Piṭárú, *s.* a glutton, a gormandizer.
Píṭh, *s. f.* the back.
Píṭhá, *s. m.* a kind of food made of rice and flour.
Piṭháná, Piṭhauná, } *v.a.* to send, to despatch.
Píṭh deuá, to run away, to flee; to turn, to shrink from.
Piṭhiyá, *s. f.* a market.
Piṭhiyá ṭhonk, *adv.* closely.
Píṭh lagná, to have a sore on the back (a horse.)
Píṭh par háth pherná, to pat on the back, to encourage.
Píṭh pherná, to turn one's back, to depart, to flee, to withdraw.
Píṭh ṭhonkná, to animate, to encourage, to pat on the back.
Pitiyá, *s. m.* a paternal uncle, a father's brother.
Pitiyáwat bháí, a first cousin (male).
Pitlá, *adj.* brazen, made of brass.
Pitláná, *v. n.* to be contaminated with verdigris (as food kept in copper vessels.)
Piṭná, *v. a.* to beat, thrash, dash, strike, knock, pound.
Piṭná, *v. n.* to be beaten.

Pitt, *s. m.* bile, gall.
Pittá, *s. m.* bile, the gall-bladder; anger; emotion of the mind.
Pittá márná, to subside (anger.)
Pittá nikálná, to chastise.
Pittjwar, *s. m.* a bilious fever.
Piṭwáná, *v. a.* to cause to be beaten or thrashed.
Pi'u, } *s. m.* husband, lover, sweet-
Píw, } heart: *adv.* dear.
Píwakkaṛ, *s. m.* a tippler, a toper.
Piya, } *adj.* beloved, dear: *s. m.* hus-
Piyá, } band, a lover, a sweetheart.
Piyáda, *s. m.* a footman, a messenger.
Piyádagírí, *s. f.* the business of a footman.
Piyádapá, *adv.* on foot.
Piyáj, *s. f. prop.* Piyáz, an onion.
Piyála, *s. m.* a glass, a cup; priming pan (of a musket.)
Piyálí, *s. f.* a small glass or cup.
Piyáná, *v. a.* to give to or cause to drink water; to water, to irrigate.
Piyár, *s. m. f.* love, affection, fondness.
Piyárá, *adj.* beloved, a sweetheart.
Piyárá jánná, to esteem.
Piyárí, *adj.* beloved: *s. f.* a sweetheart.
Piyár karná, to fondle, to caress.
Piyás, *s. f.* thirst.
Piyásá, *adj.* thirsty.
Piyás bujháná, to quench thirst.
Piyás lagná, to be thirsty.
Piyáwaná, *v. a.* see Piyáná.
Piyáz, *s. f.* an onion.
Piyází rang, *s. m.* a reddish colour.
Poá, *s. m.* a very young serpent; a nursling of any animal.
Poál, } *s. f.* straw.
Poár, }
Pochhná, *v. a.* to wipe, to clean.
Poddár, *s. m.* a cash-keeper; a person whose business is to reckon and examine money.
Podína, *s. m.* mint.
Poe, *s. f.* a kind of vegetable.
Pohdá, *s. m.* see Paudhá.
Pohná, *v. a.* to make bread.
Poís, *interj.* ho! holla! have a care.
Pokhar, } *s. m.* a pond, a lake, a
Pokhará, } tank.
Polá, *adj.* soft, hollow.
Polád, *s. m.* the finest Damascus steel.
Poná, *v. a.* to make bread, to string (pearls.)
Ponchhan, *s. m.* wipings.
Ponchhná, } *v. a.* to wipe, to clean,
Ponchná, } to expunge.
Ponká, *s. m.* the ship-worm.
Ponṭá, *s. m.* snot.
Poplá, *adj.* one whose teeth are fallen out, toothless.
Por, *s. f.* the space or interval between two joints or articulations (of the body, or of a bamboo, sugar-cane, &c.)
Porí, *s. f.* a joint of bamboo, sugar-cane, &c.
Por por, *adv.* every joint.
Posh, in *compos.* covering, wearing.
Poshák, *s. f.* vestments, dress, garments, clothes, raiment.
Poshákí, *adj.* fit for making garments (cloth.)
Poshída, *adj.* concealed, hidden, secret, secretly.
Poshídagí, *s. f.* concealment.
Poshída karná, to conceal.
Poshná, } *v. a.* to breed, to rear, to
Posná, } nourish, to bring up, to tame.
Post, *s. m.* crust, shell, skin, bark, hide, rind; poppy-head or capsule.
Postá, *s. m.* poppy-head.
Postí, *s. m.* one who intoxicates himself with infusion of poppy-heads; a lazy indolent person, a sot.
Postín, *adj.* leathern (garment.)
Pot, *s. m.* glass beads, beads.
Poṭ, *s. f.* a clove of garlic.
Pota, *s. m.* the scrotum, the testicles.
Potá, *s. m.* grandson, son's son; the scrotum, the testicles; rent (of land.)
Poṭá, *s. m.* the eyelid; the crop or craw (of birds); stomach.

Poth, *s. m.* a small glass bead.
Pothá, *s. m.* a large book.
Pothí, *s. f.* a book; a clove of garlic.
Potí, *s. f.* granddaughter, son's daughter.
Poṭlá, *s. m.* a large bundle.
Poṭlí, *s. f.* a bundle, packet.
Potná, *v. a.* to besmear, to plaster: *s. m.* the cloth with which walls or floors, &c., are besmeared with a wash of cow-dung and clay.
Potrá, Potṛá, } *s. m.* baby cloths, clouts.
Poyá, *s. m.* a kind of vegetable.
Pra, *prep.* in *compos.* forth, forward, off, abroad, away.
Prabes, *s. m.* admittance, access.
Prabhú, *s. m.* lord, master, principal.
Prabhutá, Prabhutáí, } *s. f.* government, superiority, influence.
Prág, *s. m.* the ancient name of Ilábábád.
Pragaṭ, *adj.* obvious, notorious, apparent, manifest, public.
Pragaṭ honá, to become public or manifest.
Pragaṭ karná, to publish, to show, to disclose, to reveal, to manifest.
Prajá, *s. m.* a subject, a tenant, a renter.
Prakár, *s. m.* manner, method, kind, sort.
Prakás, *adj.* apparent, conspicuous, clear: *s. m.* light, daylight.
Prálabdh, *s. f.* fate, lot, destiny, predestination.
Pramán, *s. m.* quantity; proof, verification, example.
Prán, *s. m.* breath; soul, life; sweetheart.
Pran, *s. m.* promise, vow, resolution.
Pranám, *s. m.* salutation, bow, obeisance.
Pránì, *adj.* having life, an animated being, a human being.
Prápta, *s. m.* Prápti, *s. f.* } see Parápat.
Prasád, *s. m.* see Parsád.
Prasádí, *adj.* offered to deities, &c.
Prasann, *adj.* rejoiced, pleased.
Prasann honá, to acquiesce; to like.
Prasann karná, to be pleased with, to like.
Prasautí, *s. f.* a puerperal woman.
Práschit, *s. m.* atonement, expiation.
Prashn, *s. m.* question.
Prasiddh, *adj.* notorious, famous.
Prasút, *s. m.* the whites, fluor albus.
Prasútí, *s. f.* see Prasautí.
Prát, *s. m.* morning, dawn of day.
Pratáp, *s. m.* auspices; splendour, glory.
Pratápí, Pratápwán, } *adj.* glorious, potent.
Pratham, *adj.* first, before.
Prathmí, *s. f.* the earth, ground.
Prati, *prep.* again, against, back again, for, in exchange, instead, each, every.
Pratidin, each day, every day, day by day, daily.
Pratimá, *s. f.* likeness, image.
Pratipál, *s. m.* patronising, rearing, breeding, cherishing.
Pratipálak, *s. m.* cherisher, patron.
Pratipálan, *s. m.* see Pratipál.
Pratipálná, *v. a.* to preserve, to keep, to cherish, to rear.
Pratishṭhá, *s. f.* celebrity, renown; consecration of a heathen temple or god.
Prátkál, Prátsamai, } *s. m.* morning, dawn of day
Pratyachh, *adj.* perceptible, obvious, evident, apparent, public: *adv.* in the presence of, before, evidently, openly.
Práyashchit, *s. m.* see Práschit.
Prayág, *s. m.* see Prág.
Preg, Prek, } *s. m.* a nail.
Prem, *s. m.* love, affection, friendship, kindness.
Premí, *adj.* affectionate; a lover.
Preran, *s. m* the act of sending.
Prerit, sent, despatched.

Pret, *s. m.* a spirit of the dead, ghost, evil spirit, fiend.
Pretní, *s. f.* a female ghost, ghostess.
Prít, *s. f.* love, friendship, affection.
Prítam, *s. m.* a favourite lover, a sweetheart.
Prithí, *s. f.* the earth, ground.
Prithínáth, *s. m.* lord of the earth; sovereign, a king.
Prithwí, *s. f.* the earth, ground.
Príti, *s. f.* see Prít.
Priyá, *adj.* beloved, dear: *s. m.* a lover.
Púá, *s. m.* a kind of pancake.
Púáṛá, *s. m.* explanation of a story.
Puchárá, *s. m.* whitewash, a thin coat of clay for laying on a wall or floor; the sponge of a gun; a brush for white-washing.
Puchárá dená, } **Puchárá pherná**, } to lay a thin coat of clay, &c., on the walls or floor, &c.; to whitewash a wall; to flatter.
Púchh, *s. f.* } **Puchhár**, *s. m.* } inquiry, investigation.
Púchhí, *s. f.* the tail of a fish.
Púchhná, } **Puchhná**, } *v. a.* to ask, to inquire, to question, to interrogate.
Púchhná puchhárná, see Puchhná.
Púchh páchh, } **Púchh puchhár**, } *s. f.* inquiry, interrogation.
Puchhwaiyá, *s. m.* an inquirer.
Puchhwáná, *v. a.* to cause to ask.
Pújá, *s. f.* worshipping, adoration, devotion, idolatry.
Pujáná, *v. a.* to cause to worship; to fill, to complete.
Pajárí, *s. m.* a worshipper; a priest having charge of an idol temple.
Pújná, *v. a.* to worship, to adore, to venerate; to idolatrize: *v. n.* to be filled, completed, accomplished, fulfilled, perfected.
Pujná, *v. n.* to be filled or completed.
Pujwáná, *v. a.* to cause to worship; to cause to fill or complete.
Pukár, } **Pukárá**, } *s. f.* a bawl, cry, call, shout, calling out.
Pukár dená, *v. a.* to proclaim publicly, to call.
Pukárná, *v. a.* to call aloud, to bawl, to cry out, to shout, to exclaim.
Pukhráj, *s. m.* a topaz.
Puḳhta, *adj.* dressed (as victuals); baked (as bricks); of brick or stone; ripe; sly, shrewd, knowing, expert, strong, solid.
Puḳhta karná, to make strong; to make shrewd; to ripen.
Puḳhta paz karná, see Pakká karná.
Pul, *s. m.* a bridge.
Púlá, *s. m.* a bundle of grass or straw.
Pulád, *s. m.* steel in general.
Puláo, *s. m.* a kind of dish made of flesh, &c., and rice boiled together.
Pul bándhná, *v. a.* to abound; to limit.
Púlí, *s. f.* a small bundle of any grass or straw, &c.
Pulindá, *s. m.* a bundle.
Puling, *adj.* the masculine gender.
Pulpuláhaṭ, *s. f.* fear.
Pulpuláná, *v. n.* to fear, to dread.
Pul sirát, *s. m.* a bridge over which, in the belief of Muhammadans, the righteous will pass to heaven, and from which the wicked will fall into hell, on the day of judgment.
Pun, *s. m.* virtue, virtuous action, moral or religious merit: *adv.* again.
Púṉ, *s. f.* a sound of farting.
Puna, } **Punar**, } again.
Púnchh, *s. f.* a tail.
Punchhná, *v. a.* see Púchhná.
Puni, again.
Púní, *s. f.* rolls of cotton prepared for spinning.
Púnjí, *s. f.* a capital in trade, stock, principle, sum.
Punya, *s. m.* virtue, moral or religious merit: *adj.* pure, holy.
Punyátmá, } **Punyawán**, } *adj.* charitable, virtuous, religious.

Pur, *adj.* full, complete.
Púr, Pura, } *s. m.* a city, a town; much used in composition.
Púrá, *adj.* entire, complete, full, perfect; sufficient, just. [&c.)
Puṛá, *s. m.* a large parcel (of physic,
Púrab, *s. m.* east: *adj.* eastern; former, prior, preceding.
Púrá karná, *v. a.* to fill, to fulfil, to reimburse, to accomplish.
Purán, *s. m.* Hindú mythological books.
Púran, *adj.* full, filled, complete, perfect, accomplished.
Puráná, *v. a.* to fill, to make full: *adj.* old, ancient.
Puraniyá, *s. m.* an old man, an elder; name of a district and town.
Púran karná, *v. a.* to fulfil, to accomplish, to perfect, to complete.
Púranmásí, Púranwásí, } *s. f.* the day of the full moon.
Púrá paṛná, *v. n.* to be successful.
Purátam, Purátan, } *adj.* old, ancient.
Púrbí, *adj.* eastern, from the east.
Puren, *s. f.* afterbirth.
Púrí, *s. f.* a kind of cake fried in butter or ghí.
Purí, a city, a town.
Puṛiyá, *s. f.* a dose; a parcel (of physic, &c.)
Purkár, *adj.* thick, coarse, stout (as paper, &c.)
Purkárí, *s. f.* thickness, coarseness.
Purkhá, *s. m.* an old man, an elder, an ancestor.
Purkhe, *s. m.* ancestors, ancestry.
Púrná, *v. n.* to be filled.
Purohit, *s. m.* a priest, a family priest.
Purs, in *compos.* asking, inquiring.
Pursa, *s. m* condolence, kind inquiry.
Pursá, *s. m.* condolence: *adj.* of man's height; the extent of a man's reach in height, when extending the arms and fingers; a fathom.
Pursish, *s. f.* inquiry (generally after health, &c.), questioning.
Purukh, Purus, Purush, } *s. m.* a man, a male, human being.
Purva, *s. m.* the east.
Purví, *adj.* oriental.
Purwá, Purwaiyá, } *s. f.* an easterly wind.
Purwáná, *v. a.* to cause to be filled.
Purza, *s. m.* a scrap (generally applied to paper), piece, bit, rag.
Purzarúr, very necessary, most essential.
Pús, *s. m.* name of the ninth Hindú month. [ancestry.
Pusht, *s. f.* the back; progenitors,
Pushṭ, *adj.* nourished, fat.
Pushta, *s. m.* a buttress, prop, bank, glacis, dike.
Pshtabandí, *s. f.* embankment.
Pushṭa'í, *adj. f.* restorative, provocative.
Pushtak, *s. m.* a vice in horses, plunging and kicking up behind.
Pushtánga, *adj.* fat.
Pusht ba pusht, generation by generation.
Pushtk͟hár, *s. m.* an instrument for scratching the back.
Pushtpanáh, *s. m.* an ally, a protector.
Pushtú, *s.* the Afghán language.
Puspút, *s. m.* adopted son.
Puspút karná, to adopt (as a son.)
Pustak, *s. f.* a book, a volume.
Pút, *s. m.* a son.
Puṭ, *s. m.* a menstruum, solvent, flux.
Putáí, *s. f.* price paid for besmearing walls, &c.
Púṭhá, *s. m.* the paper or pasteboard cover of a book.
Púṭkí, *s. f.* a term of abuse; the anus.
Putlá, Pútlá, } *s. m.* a puppet, an idol, an image, effigy.
Putlí, Pútlí, } *s. f.* a small puppet or image; the pupil of the eye.
Putr, Putra, } *s. m.* a son.
Putrí, *s. f.* a daughter.

Pútrí, *s. f.* a puppet, an image.
Puṭṭhá, *s. m.* the buttock, the hip of an animal.
Puṭṭí, *s. f.* felly of a wheel.
Puwál, *s. f.* straw.
Púzí, *s. f.* part of the ornamental accoutrements of a horse.
Pyála, *s. m.* see Piyála.
Pyáná, *v. a.* see Piyáná.
Pyár, *s. m.* love, affection, fondness.
Pyárá, *adj. m.* beloved, pleasant.
Pyárá jánná, to esteem.
Pyárí, *adj. f.* beloved; sweetheart.
Pyár karná, to fondle, to love, to caress.
Pyás, *s. f.* thirst.
Pyásá, *s. m.* thirst: *adj.* thirsty.
Pyás bujháná, to quench thirst.
Pyáse marná, to be very thirsty.
Pyásí, *adj. f.* thirsty.
Pyás lagná, to be thirsty.
Pyás márná, to suffer thirst.
Pyás marná, applied to thirst which vanishes without drinking.

Q.

Qáb, *s. f.* a large dish used for serving rice, &c., in at a meal, or for kneading dough in, &c.
Qabá, *s. f.* a peculiar kind of vest or upper garment.
Qabáhat, *s. f.* perplexity, inconvenience.
Qabáil, *s. m.* family (wife and children, &c.)
Qabal, *adv.* before.
Qabála, *s. m.* a deed, writing, a deed of sale.
Qábil, *adj.* skilful, capable, able, clever, worthy.
Qabíla, *s. f.* a wife.
Qábil honá, to deserve, to merit.
Qábilíyat, *adj.* skill, capability, ability.
Qabl, *adv.* before.
Qabr, *s. f.* a grave, a tomb.
Qabrgáh, **Qabristán**, } *s. f.* a burying-ground.
Qábú, *s. m.* power, opportunity, possession: *adj.* within the power or under the control of another.
Qábú chaláná, to take advantage of, to exercise one's power.
Qábúchí, *adj.* despotic, tyrannical.
Qábúchípaná, *s. m.* tyranny.
Qabúl, *s. m.* consent, favourable reception, acceptance, approbation, assent: *adj.* accepted, approved, consented.
Qabúlí, *s. f.* a kind of food; rice and pulse boiled together.
Qabúlíyat, *s. f.* a written agreement.
Qabúl karná, **Qabúlná**, } *v. a.* to agree to accept, to allow, to confess, to consent, to assent, to comply with, to receive, to agree to, to promise, to make choice of.
Qabúlsúrat, *adj.* handsome.
Qabúlsúratí, *s. f.* handsomeness.
Qábú páná, to get advantage or power over.
Qabz, *s. f.* costiveness.
Qabza, *s. m.* gripe, possession, wrist; handle, hilt, a hinge.
Qabza karná, **Qabze meṉ karná**, **Qabze meṉ láná**, } to seize, to take possession of.
Qabzíyat, *s. f.* costiveness, astringency.
Qabz karná, to be costive, to gripe.
Qadah, *s. m.* a goblet glass, bowl, cup.
Qadam, *s. m.* a space, a step, a footstep; the foot.
Qadam ba qadam, step by step, gently.
Qadambáz, *adj.* fleet.
Qadambos, *adj.* kissing the feet, paying respects.
Qadambosí, *s. f.* kissing the feet, respects.
Qadam chhúná, to touch or embrace one's feet.
Qadam chúmná, to kiss the feet, to bid adieu.
Qadam lagná, to take protection; to walk well (a horse.)

Qadam ranja farmáná or karná, to take the trouble of going or coming (spoken respectfully.)

Qadar, *s. f.* price, value, importance, dignity, quantity, size, measure, degree.

Qadd, *s. m.* stature.

Qaddáwar, *adj.* tall.

Qadd o qámat, *s. m.* stature, figure (of a person.)

Qadím, *adj.* ancient, old.

Qadímí, *adj.* old, ancient, aged.

Qadím se, of old, of former times, from ancient times.

Qádir, *adj.* potent, powerful, capable, skilful.

Qadr, *s. f.* see Qadar.

Qadrdán, a just appreciator, one who knows the worth of a person or thing.

Qadrdání, *s. f.* due regard to the worth of any one, patronage.

Qadre, } *adj.* somewhat, a little.
Qadre qalíl, }

Qáfila, *s. m.* a body of travellers, a caravan.

Qahar, *s. m.* see Qahr.

Qahba, *s. f.* an adulteress, a whore.

Qahqah, } *s.m.* loud laughter, horse laugh.
Qahqahá, }
Qahqaha, }

Qahr, *s. m.* rage, fury, vengeance, indignation, calamity.

Qaht, *s. m.* famine, dearth.

Qahwa, *s. m.* coffee.

Qahwadán, *s. m.* a coffee-pot.

Qai, *s. f.* vomiting, sick at stomach.

Qaid, *s. f.* imprisonment, an obstacle: *adj.* imprisoned.

Qáida, *s. m.* rule, custom, principle, manner; the rules of grammar.

Qaid honá, to be imprisoned, bound or fettered, &c.

Qaidí, *s. m.* a prisoner, a captive.

Qaid karná, to imprison, bind, fetter, captivate.

Qaidkhána, *s. m.* a prison.

Qaid meṉ rakhná, to take great care [of.

Qaid rahná, to remain in bonds, prison, &c.

Qai karná, to vomit.

Qáil, agreeing, acknowledging, giving up a point: *adj.* subdued, confuted.

Qáil honá, to acquiesce, to acknowledge, assent, consent, yield.

Qáil karná, to confute, convince, convict.

Qáim, } *adj.* firm, fixed, durable, lasting, continuing.
Qáimí, }

Qáim karná, to establish.

Qáim maqám, a vicegerent, locum tenens.

Qáim mizáj, of a settled temper.

Qainchí, *s. f.* scissors, shears; an oblique cross.

Qáiza karná, *v. a.* to tie up a horse's head by passing the bridle to his tail to prevent his kicking, &c., while rubbing down.

Qalaí, *s. f.* the tinning of vessels.

Qalaígar, a tinner of pots.

Qalaígarí, *s. f.* the business of tinning pots.

Qalaí khulná, the removing of the disguise of any one so that his real qualities appear.

Qalam, *s. f.* a reed, a pen, cuttings of trees, &c., for planting; a set, a slip.

Qalamdán, *s. m.* a box for holding pen, inkstand and paper, &c., a pen-case.

Qalamí, *adj.* of the pen, written; crystallized (saltpetre, &c.)

Qalamkárí, *s. f.* drawing.

Qalam karná, to cut.

Qalam lagáná, to plant slips or cuttings.

Qalamtarásh, *s. m.* a penknife.

Qalaq, *s. m.* perturbation, anxiety, trouble.

Qalb, *s. m.* the heart, mind, soul.

Qalíb, *s. m.* a mould, model, form (used in masonry for making arches, &c.), the body.

Qálícha, *s. m.* a small carpet.

Qaliya, s.m. the name of a dish, a stew.
Qamchí, s. f. a twig, a thin lath.
Qamíz, s. m. a shirt or shift.
Qanáạt, s. f. content, tranquillity.
Qanáạt karná, to be content (on.)
Qanát, s. f. the walls of a tent, or canvas enclosure.
Qand, s. m. loaf-sugar.
Qandhár, n. prop. name of a city, Candahar.
Qandíl, s. f. a kind of paper lantern.
Qannauj, n. prop. name of a city.
Qánún, s. m. rule, regulation, statute, canon.
Qánúngo, s. m. an officer in each district acquainted with its customs, &c.
Qáqá karná, to croak (as a raven.)
Qarába, s. m. a flagon (generally for rose-water.)
Qarábat, s.f. kin, affinity, relationship.
Qarábatí, adj. related, relative, akin; (substantively) a relation, a relative.
Qarábín, s. f. a carbine.
Qarár, s.m. rest, tranquillity, firmness, stability, agreement, engagement, promise, patience.
Qarár dená, to fix, to establish, to promise.
Qarárí, adj. firm, stable, ratified, agreed to, engaged for, promised.
Qarár i wáqiʿ, effectively, effectually, efficaciously.
Qarárnáma, s.m. a written agreement, treaty, &c.
Qaraulí, s. f. name of a weapon.
Qaríb, adv. near, nigh, almost, about.
Qarnáe, } s. f. a trumpet, a horn, a
Qarnáí, } clarion.
Qárúra, s. m. an urinal; bottle (sent to physicians, &c.)
Qarz, s. m. a loan, debt, money borrowed at interest.
Qarzdár, s. a debtor, one who borrows money or other articles.
Qarzdárí, s. f. being in debt.
Qarz dená, to lend.
Qarzí, adj. borrowed, being in debt.
Qarz i hasana, money lent without interest.
Qarz lená, } to borrow.
Qarz mángná, }
Qarz rakhná, to owe.
Qasába, s. m. a handkerchief tied round the head.
Qasáí, s. m. a butcher who kills only bullocks: adj. cruel, hard-hearted.
Qasam, s. f. an oath.
Qasam dená, to adjure.
Qasam diláná, to administer an oath.
Qasam kháná, to take an oath, to swear.
Qasam khiláná, to administer an oath.
Qasba, s. m. a small town.
Qasd, s. m. desire, design, intention purpose, attempt.
Qasdan, adv. voluntarily, intentionally, purposely, expressly.
Qasd karná, to design, intend, propose to one's self to make an attempt, to make one's object or aim.
Qásid, s. m. a courier, an express, a messenger, a postman.
Qasída, s. m. a poem, a long ode.
Qasr, s. m. diminution, defect, reduction, deficiency; retaliation, revenge.
Qasr honá, to be deficient.
Qasr karná, to decrease, to deduct.
Qasr nikálná, to take revenge.
Qasr rakhná, to be at enmity.
Qassáb, s. m. a butcher who kills only bullocks.
Qasúr, s. m. fault, defect, omission, a coming short, failing, flame.
Qatạ, s. f. cutting, form, cut (of a coat, &c.)
Qatạí, s. f. a tailor's measure.
Qatạ karná, to cut, to cut out or off.
Qatár, s. f. a line, a string (of animals), rank, order, row.
Qátil, s. m. a murderer, an assassin: adj. mortal, deadly, strong (as spirits or vinegar.)
Qatl, s.m. slaughter, carnage, murder, killing, assassination.

Qatlá, *s. m.* a slice.
Qatlgáh, *s. f.* place of murder.
Qatl honá, to be killed; to be ruined.
Qatl i ạmm, a general massacre.
Qatl karná, to kill, to murder, to execute, to ruin one.
Qatra, *s. m.* a drop.
Qatt, *s. m.* making a pen, cutting transversely.
Qatt lagáná, to mend a pen.
Qattzan, *s. m.* a pin or peg on which pens are cut.
Qaul, *s. m.* agreement, promise, contract, a word, saying, assertion.
Qaul bándhná, *v. a.* to promise, to make an agreement.
Qaulnáma, *s. m.* a written agreement.
Qaul o fiạl, *s. m.* word and deed.
Qaul o qarár, } *s. m.* agreement, compact.
Qaulqarár, }
Qaulqarár karná, to covenant, to stipulate.
Qaum. *s. f.* tribe, sect, caste, a people, nation, family.
Qaumíyat, *s. f.* connexion, being of the same tribe, &c.
Qawáịd, *s. pl.* of Qáịda, rules, customs; military evolution or exercise, drill, review.
Qauwál, *s. m.* a kind of musician, singer.
Qawí, *adj.* strong, robust, powerful.
Qazá, *s. f.* fate, destiny; death; saying a prayer after the time appointed for it is passed.
Qazákár, by chance.
Quzalbáshí, *s. m.* a kind of Mughal soldier.
Qazáyá, *s. pl.* of Qaziya, quarrels, &c.
Qází, *s. m.* a judge, a justice.
Qaziya, *s. m.* a quarrel, wrangle, contention, broil.
Qaziya karná, to quarrel, to wrangle.
Qaziya mol lená, to take on one's self the quarrel of another, to interfere without cause in the disputes of others.
Qazzák, } *s. m.* a robber.
Qazzúq, }
Qazzáqí, *s. f.* pillage, brigandage.
Qibla, *s. m.* that part to which Muhammadans direct their face in prayer, Mecca; (and by way of respectful address,) worship! father! &c.
Qibla e ạlam, his majesty, your majesty.
Qiblagáh, a superior, father.
Qiblanumá, the mariner's compass.
Qilạ, *s. m.* a fort.
Qilạdár, commandant of a garrison.
Qilạdárí, *s. f.* the command of a garrison.
Qíma, *s. m.* minced meat.
Qíma karná, to mince, to cut up meat very fine, to bruise much by beating.
Qimám, *s. m. prop.* Qiwám, thick syrup.
Qímapuláo, a kind of dish.
Qímat, *s. f.* price, value.
Qímatí, *adj.* valuable, high-priced.
Qirmiz, *s. m.* crimson.
Qism, *s. f.* kind, species, sort.
Qismat, *s. f.* fate, fortune, lot.
Qismatbází, *s. f.* trying one's fortune or luck.
Qissa, *s. m.* a tale, a story, a narration; a quarrel, a dispute.
Qissa kahání, *s. f.* a tale, a story, a narration.
Qissa kotáh, in short, in one word.
Qissa kotáh karná, to settle a dispute.
Qissa mukhtasar, in short.
Qist, *s. f.* instalment.
Qistbandí, *s. f.* a settlement by instalment.
Qistkhiláf, *s. f.* failure in the payment of an instalment.
Qitạ, *s. m.* a share, a division, spot or parcel of land, portion.
Qitạ qitạ, by shares, by lots or parts.
Qitạ qitạ karná, to divide by shares, to distribute, to parcel out.
Qiwám, *s. m.* thick syrup.
Qiyám, *s. m.* standing erect, stability, reṣidence.
Qiyámat, *s. f.* the general resurrection, the last day, calamity.

Qiyámat karná, to oppress; to do anything wonderful.
Qiyámí, *s. f.* stability, steadiness.
Qiyás, *s. m.* judgment, opinion, opposition, guess.
Qiyás karná, to guess, think, suppose.
Qorma, }
Qormá, } *s. m.* a kind of dish.
Qubúl, *s. m.* see Qabúl.
Quddús, *adj.* pure, holy.
Qudrat, *s. f.* power, authority, omnipotence.
Qudratí, *adj.* of omnipotence, not made or produced by man.
Qudratí rang, natural colour.
Quds, *adj.* holy, pure.
Qufl, *s. m.* a lock,
Qulába, *s. m.* a staple.
Qulfí, *s. f.* a tin pot for moulding ice, &c., *prop.* Qufli, a copper pipe for the curve of a huqqa-snake.
Qulfídár, huqqa-snake having the Qulfí or copper pipe.
Qulí, *s. m.* a slave, a labourer, porter, a cooly.
Qulma, *s. m.* a sausage.
Qulma kasná, to stuff, to be a tight fit.
Qulqul, *s. f. m.* the noise made by water in the neck of a bottle when pouring out, guggling.
Qumquma, a vessel in which the red mixture is put and thrown on persons in the Holí.
Qumrí, *s f.* a turtle-dove, a ring-dove.
Quṛa, *s. m.* a wager, wagering, drawing lots.
Quṛa ḍálná, to draw lots.
Qurán, *s. m.* the Koran.
Qurán ká jáma pahinná, to swear excessively.
Qurán par háth dharná, } to swear, to
Qurán uṭháná, } take an oath.
Qurb, *s. m* propinquity, proximity, vicinity; kindred, relationship.
Qurbán, *s. m.* a sacrifice, victim, oblation.
Qurbángáh, *s. f.* an altar.
Qurbán honá, to be sacrificed or devoted.
Qurbání, *adj.* devoted, sacrificed.
Qurbán karná, to sacrifice, to devote.
Qurbat, *s. f.* nearness, relationship.
Qurq, *s. m.* confiscation, seizure, the distraining of goods.
Qurqí, *adj.* confiscated.
Qurqí parwána, a warrant issued to sequester a property.
Qusúr, *s. m.* fault, defect, omission, failing, blame.
Qusúr karná, to fail; to do amiss.
Qutb, *s. m.* the polar star, the north pole; a title or degree among religious mendicants.
Qúwat, *s. f.* power, virtue, authority, strength, vigour, energy.

R.

Raạiyat, *s. f.* a subject, or the subjects, a tenant.
Raạiyatí, *s. f.* subjection, tenancy.
Raạiyatḳhána, *s. m.* a collection of houses for hire.
Raạiyatnawáz, cherisher of subjects.
Raạiyatparwar, protector of subjects.
Ráb, *s. f.* the liquid juice of the sugar-cane.
Rabaṛ, *s. f.* fatigue, fruitless labour, trudging.
Rabaṛná, *v. n.* to fatigue one's self, to run about fruitlessly.
Rabat, *s. m. prop.* Rabt, practice, habit, use.
Rabb, *s. m.* lord, preserver; a name of God.
Rabí, *s. f. prop.* Rabíạ, which see.
Rabíạ, *s. f.* the spring; the spring harvest, or grain cut in the spring.
Rabibár, *s. m.* Sunday.
Rabíị, *adj.* produced in the spring, vernal.
Rabị ul ákhir, the fourth month of the Muhammadan year.
Rabị ul auwál, the third month of the Muhammadan year.

Rabí us sání, the fourth month of the Muhammadan year.
Rabṛáná, *v. a.* to fatigue, to cause to run about uselessly.
Rabṛí, } **Rábṛí,** } *s. f.* a kind of food like pap.
Rabt, *s. m.* practice, habit, use.
Rachak, *s. m.* a maker, a composer.
Racháná, *v. a.* to set to work, to set a-going, to make, to do; to make merry, to celebrate.
Rachaná, *s. f.* forming, creating, invention, created thing, workmanship.
Rachchhá, *s. m.* protection, guarding, keeping, preservation, safety.
Rachchhak, *s. m.* a protector, a keeper.
Ráchhas, *s. m.* a demon, fiend, an evil spirit.
Ráchhasaní, *s. f.* a female of Ráchhas.
Ráchhasí, *adj.* of or relating to a Ráchhas, demoniacal: *s. f.* a female Ráchhas.
Rachit, done, made or written by.
Rachná, *v. n.* to be made, to be created, to be employed, to be about (a business), to penetrate: *v. a.* to make, to form, to invent, to compose.
Radd, *s. m.* rejection, repulsion, refutation; vomiting.
Raddá, *s. m.* a layer of a wall, a row.
Radd badal, *s. f.* argument, discussion, altercation, controversy.
Raddí, *adj.* rejected: *s. m.* rejected things, refuse.
Radd i jawáb, a reply, a rejoinder, retort.
Radd karná, to reject, to confute, to refute; to vomit.
Rádhánagarí, *s. m.* a kind of silk cloth made at Rádhánagar.
Ráe, a Hindú title, a chief; wisdom.
Ráegáṇ, *adv.* in vain.
Rafạ, *s. m.* finishing, decision; repulsion.
Rafạ dafạ, deciding, settling, finishing.
Rafạ honá, to be decided (a suit.)
Rafạ karná, to decide, to settle.
Rafíq, *s. m.* a friend, ally, companion, comrade, associate.
Ráfizí, *s. m.* a heretic, particularly a Shíạ.
Raft, in *compos.* going, motion.
Raftagí, *s. f.* departure.
Rafta rafta, *adv.* by degrees, gradually, in process of time.
Raft guzasht, } **Raft o guzasht,** } past and gone.
Rafú, *s. m.* darning, a darn.
Rafú chakkar, making one's escape, stealing off.
Rafúgar, *s. m.* a darner.
Rafúgarí, *s. f.* the employment of darning.
Rafú karná, to darn.
Rág, *s. m.* a mode in music, music.
Rag, *s. f.* a vein, sinew, nerve, a fibre.
Ragaṛ, *s. f.* attrition, friction, rubbing, abrasion.
Ragaṛá, *s. m.* quarrelling; rubbing, polishing.
Ragaṛá ragaṛí, *s. f.* a rubbing together.
Ragaṛná, *v. a.* to rub, scour, grate, to fret, to abrade, to excoriate.
Rag chaṛhná, to be obstinate, pettish, or proud.
Ragedná, *v. a.* to pursue, to chase.
Rág gáná, to sing a song.
Raghbat, *s. f.* strong desire, avidity, wish, curiosity; pleasure.
Raghbat karná, to desire to covet.
Rághib, *adj.* desirous, desiring, wishing.
Rágí, *s. m.* a singer; a lover.
Rágini, *s. f.* a mode in music.
Rag marná, *v. n.* to lose virility; to become impotent.
Ragṛá, *s. m.* see Ragaṛá.
Ragṛá jhagṛá, *s. m.* quarrel, discussion.
Rágrang, *s. m.* music, gaiety.
Rag resha, *s. m.* veins and fibres; everything, all.

Rag utarná, *v. n.* to have a rupture.
Ráh, *s. f.* road, way; manner.
Rah, *s. f.* a road, path, way.
Raháí, *s. f.* see Riháí.
Raháish, *s. f.* stay, delay, halt.
Raham, *s. m.* see Rahm.
Rahan, *s. f.* method, manner.
Rahanṭ, *s. m.* a wheel for drawing water with.
Rahar, *s. m.* name of a pulse.
Ráhat, *s. f.* quiet, repose, ease, tranquillity.
Rahaṭ, *s. m.* see Rahanṭ.
Ráh bándhná, to establish a custom.
Ráhbar, Rahbar, } *s. m.* a guide, a conductor.
Ráhbarí, Rahbarí, } *s. f.* guidance, direction, showing the road.
Ráh batáná, to discharge, dismiss; to guide.
Ráh chalná, to traverse the road.
Ráhdárí, *s. f.* a passport, a permit.
Ráh dekhná, to expect, to await.
Ráh dená, to give place or way.
Ráh ḍhúnḍhná, to search for the way.
Ráh dikháná, to make one wait for.
Ráhgír, Rahgír, } *s. m.* a traveller, a wayfarer.
Ráhguzar, Rahguzar, } *s. m.* road, way.
Ráhí, *s. m.* a traveller, wayfarer.
Rahím, *adj.* merciful (God.)
Rahit, *adj.* destitute, void of.
Rah jáná, *v. n.* to wait, stay, delay, desist, give up; remain (undone.)
Ráh kāṭná, to travel a road.
Ráh ḳharch, *s. m.* way-charges, travelling expenses.
Ráh khoṭí karní, to linger on the road.
Ráh lená, to go, to depart.
Rahm, *s. m.* mercy, compassion, kindness, pity; a sort of sweet cake of a white colour.
Rahmán, *adj.* merciful, forgiving (God.)
Rahmání, *adj.* divine.
Rahmár, *s. m.* robber, highwayman.
Ráh márná, to waylay, to rob, to ruin one's prospects in life.
Rahmat, *s. f.* mercy, kindness, pity.
Rahmatulláh i ąlaihi, the mercy of God (be) upon him.
Rahmdil, *adj.* tender-hearted, merciful.
Rahm karná, to pity.
Rahm kháná, to feel pity, to pity.
Rahná, *v. a.* to stay, stop, remain, be, exist, last, stand, continue, lie, live, inhabit, dwell, reside.
Ráhnáma, *s. m.* a road book.
Ráh nápná, to employ one's self unprofitably.
Rahne dená, to give permission to stay.
Rahne lagná, to begin to stay.
Rahne páná, to obtain permission to stay.
Rahnewálá, an inhabitant.
Ráh nikálná, to devise a new mode of conduct.
Ráhnumá, Rahnumá, } *s. m.* a conductor, guide, pilot, leader.
Ráhnumáí, Rahnumáí, } *s. f.* guiding, guidance.
Ráh par áná, to mend one's manners.
Ráh rakhná, to keep up an intercourse.
Ráh rást, right way.
Ráh rawish, *s. f.* manners, habits, customs.
Ráh takná, to expect, to wait for.
Rahte, (in the) remaining; in the presence of, during the existence of, notwithstanding.
Ráhú, Ráhu, } *s. m.* the dragon that is supposed to devour the sun or moon during an eclipse.
Rahwaiyá, *s. m.* an inhabitant, dweller.
Ráhzan, Rahzan, } *s. m.* a highwayman, footpad, robber.
Ráhzaní, Rahzaní, } *s. f.* highway robbery, act of plundering.
Ra'í, *s. f.* a churning-staff; bran.
Ráí, *s. f.* a kind of mustard seed.

Ráíchhái, broken to small pieces or atoms.

Rá'ij, *adj*. customary, usual, fashionable, common, current.

Rá'ij ul waqt, present currency.

Rain, *s. f.* night.

Ra'ís, *s. m.* a prince, a chief, principal, head, citizen, inhabitant, dweller.

Raiṭhá, *s. m.* name of the tree of a kind of vetch (rahar.)

Raiyat, *s. f. prop.* Raạiyat, which see.

Ráj, *s. m.* government, sovereignty, reign, royalty, kingdom, empire, realm; a mason, bricklayer.

Raj, *s. f.* dust; the farina of flowers; menses; the quality of sensuality.

Rajá, *s. f. prop.* Razá, which see.

Rájá, } *s. m.* a king, a prince, a king
Rája, } at chess.

Rajab, *s. m.* the seventh month of the Muhammadan year.

Rajáí, *s. f. prop.* Razáí, a quilt.

Rájdharm, *s. m.* royal duty.

Rájgádí, *s. f.* king's cushion, throne.

Ráj'hans, } *s. m.* a goose, the flamin-
Ráj'háṇs, } go.

Ráji, *prop.* Rází, which see.

Rájí honá, see Rází honá.

Rájí karná, see Rází karná.

Rájínáma, see Rázínáma.

Rájkanyá, *s. f.* a princess.

Rájkárj, *s. m.* state affairs.

Rájkul, *s. m.* a royal family.

Rájkumár, } *s. m.* a king's son, a
Rájkuṇwar, } prince.

Rájmandir, *s. m.* a palace, a royal residence.

Ráj mistrí, *s. m.* a head mason.

Rájníti, *s. f.* political science, politics.

Rájpáṭ, *s. m.* sovereignty, reign; a royal throne.

Rájpatní, *s. f.* a queen.

Rajpút, } *s. m.* the name of a tribe.
Rájpút, }

Rájpútána, *s. m.* the province of Ajmeer is so called.

Rájsabhá, *s. f.* the king's court or assembly.

Rájṭíká, } *s. f.* the royal mark in the
Rájtilak, } forehead, the coronation of a king.

Rajwáṛá, *s. m.* a king, a country under the control of a Rájá.

Rákas, *s. m.* a demon, an evil spirit.

Rakat, *s. m.* blood: *adj.* red.

Rakạt, *s. f.* bowing the body in prayer.

Rákh, *s. f.* ashes.

Rakhá lená, to take in charge.

Rakháná, *v. a.* to give in charge, to cause to keep, put, place.

Rakh chhoṛná, to place, to keep, to have, to give in charge.

Rakh dená, to put down, to place, to keep, to put by.

Rákhí, *s. f.* an amulet or string which Hindús tie round their arms on a certain festival.

Rakh lená, to take in charge, to take into keeping or service, to engage.

Rakhná, *v. a.* to keep, put, place, have, hold, possess, preserve, reserve, save, lay, set, station, apply, ascribe, impute, esteem, consider, leave, own, stop.

Rákhná, *v. a.* to keep, to put.

Raḳht, *s. m.* goods and chattels, property, apparatus, furniture, apparel.

Raḳht bándhná, to pack up.

Rakhwáí, *s. f.* the price paid for keeping, &c.

Rakhwál, } *s. m.* a keeper, guard,
Rakhwálá, } shepherd, cowherd, goatherd.

Rakhwá lená, to take in charge.

Rakhwálí, *s. f.* keeping, guarding, custody, grazing cattle.

Rakhwáná, *v. a.* to cause to keep, place, &c.

Rakhwáṛá, *s. m.* see Rakhwál.

Rakkas, } *s. m.* a demon, an evil
Rákshas, } spirit.

Rakt, *s. m.* blood; *adj.* red.

Raktálú, *s. m.* a sort of yam.

Raktchandan, *s. m.* red sandal-wood.

Rál, s. f. resin, rosin, pitch; saliva.

Rám, } s. m. the seventh Hindú
Ráma, } incarnation; God.

Ramal, s. m. geomancy, foretelling by figures.

Rámánandí, s. m. a sect of Hindú faqírs, believers in Ráma.

Rámávatár, s. m. the incarnation of of Vishnu in the person of Ráma.

Rámáwat, s. m. system of a sect of Hindú faqírs.

Rámáyan, s. f. the great epic poem of the Hindús which treats of the birth and actions of Ráma.

Ramazán, s. m. name of the ninth Muhammadan month.

Rámchandra, n. prop. son of Dasaratha, and conqueror of Lanká or Ceylon; the seventh avatár.

Rámcherá, } s. m. a common appel-
Ramcherá, } lation of a slave.

Rámduhái, s. f. an asseveration, by Ráma, by God.

Rámjaní, s. f. a Hindú dancing-girl, a prostitute.

Rámkahání, the Rámáyan; a long story.

Rammál, s. m. a soothsayer, a fortune-teller, a conjuror.

Ramná, v. n. to roam, to go, to range, to wander: s. m. a park.

Ramna, s. m. a park.

Rámpí, s. f. a knife for paring leather.

Ram rahná, to remain concealed.

Rám rám, s. m. a Hindú form of salutation.

Rámtura'í, s. f. the name of a vegetable.

Rán, s. f. the thigh.

Ran, s. m battle, war.

Ráná, s. m. a Hindú title of a prince or Rájá.

Ranbhúmi, s. f. field of battle.

Rand, s, m. the castor-oil plant.

Ránd, s. f. a widow, a woman.

Randa, } s. m. a plane (for smooth-
Randá, } ing wood.)

Ránda, adj. driven, driven out, rejected, expelled.

Randa karná, v. a. to plane a board, &c.

Rándápá, }
Randápá, } s. m. widowhood.
Randápan, }

Randí, s. f. a woman; a prostitute.

Randíbáz, s. m. a whoremonger.

Randíbází, s. f. whoring, fornication.

Randiyá, s. f. a widow.

Ránd ká sánd, son of a widow, a spoilt child.

Rándná, v. a. to expel.

Rándparos, s. m. neighbourhood.

Randsálá, } s. m. a widow's dress,
Randsála, } widow's weeds.

Randúá, s. m. a widower.

Rang, s. m. dye (colour), colour; manner, method, sort; paint; amusement, pleasure.

Rángá, s. m. tin, solder.

Rangái, s. f. the price paid for dyeing.

Rangáná, v. a. to colour, to tinge.

Rangat, s. f. colour, dye, tint.

Rangáwat, s. f. colour, colouring.

Rang ba rang, s. m. various colours or sorts: adj. various.

Rangdár, adj. coloured, showy, fine.

Rang dekhná, to look at or examine the state, condition, result, conclusion, or consequence of anything.

Rangdhalúá, s. m. a person who makes ornaments, &c., of Rángá, or tin.

Rang fak hojáná, to grow pale (from fear or astonishment.)

Rangílá, s. m. a rake: adj. gaudy, fine, showy.

Rangín, adj. coloured, painted; figurative, fine, showy, gaudy.

Rangíní, s. f. colouring.

Rang karná, to enjoy, to lead a life of pleasure.

Rang lagáná, v. a. to colour, to paint.

Rang márná, to win (in gaming.)

Rangná, v. a. to colour, to dye.

Rang raliyán, s. f. plur. merriment, pleasure, mirth.

Rangras, delight, melody, pleasure.
Rangrez, *s. m.* a dyer.
Rangrezí, *s. f.* dying, tinging.
Rangrúp, *s. m.* colour, form, appearance.
Rangtará, *s. m.* a kind of orange.
Rang uṛ jáná, to change colour, to be afraid.
Rang utarná, to become pale; to be grieved.
Rangwáí, *s. f.* the price paid for colouring, dying, &c.
Rangwaiyá, *s. m.* a dyer.
Ráni, *s. f.* a queen or princess.
Ranj, *s. m.* grief, affliction, trouble, pain, anguish of mind, offence.
Ranjak, *s. f.* priming-powder.
Ranjakdán, *s. m.* priming-pan.
Ranjak piláná, *v. a.* to prime.
Ranjak uṛáná, *v. a.* to burn priming, to flash in the pan.
Ranjak uṛná, *v. n.* to flash in the pan (priming.)
Ranj dená, to give pain.
Ranjída, *adj.* afflicted, offended, displeased, grieved, vexed.
Ranjídagí, *s. f.* affliction, vexation.
Ranjída karná, to afflict, to offend, displease, grieve.
Ranjídakḳhátir, afflicted in mind.
Ranjish, *s. f.* grief, affliction. See Ranj.
Ranj uṭháná, to endure grief.
Ráṇṛ, *s. f.* a widow.
Ránsawárí, *s. f.* riding on horseback.
Ranthí, *s. f.* a bier.
Ranwás, *s. m.* the seraglio of a Rájá.
Ráorá, *pron.* yours, of you.
Rapaṭ, *s. m.* fatigue, hard labour; *prop.* Rabt, which see.
Rapaṭná, *v. n.* to become tired.
Rápí, *s. f.* a shoemaker's knife.
Raqam, *s. f.* handwriting: character, manner, kind, sort; grain.
Ráqim, *s. m.* a writer.
Rás, *s. f.* reins of a bridle: *s. m.* a head of cattle, (*i.e.*, one ox, or one horse, &c.)
Ras, *s. m.* the savour of a thing; juice, humour, essence, relish, enjoyment; the pith or marrow of a discourse.
Rasad, *s. f.* store of grain laid in for an army, &c., grain, provision.
Rasáí, *s. f.* access, entrance.
Rasam, *s. f.* see Rasm.
Rasaut, *s. f.* see Raswat.
Rasáyan, *s. m.* slowness, mildness; alchymy, chemistry.
Rasáyaní, *s. m.* a chemist.
Rase, *adv.* softly, gently.
Raṣha, *s. m.* a tremour, shaking, the shaking palsy.
Rashk, *s. m.* malice, spite, jealousy.
Rasíd, *s. f.* acknowledgment of receiving or arrival; a receipt.
Rasída, *n. compos.* arrived.
Rasílá, *adj.* juicy, luscious.
Rasiyáná, *v. n.* to be moist; to ooze.
Raskapúr, *s. m.* corrosive sublimate.
Ráslílá, *s. m.* a festival in honour of the lewd gambols of Krishna and the milk-maids.
Rasm, *s. f.* custom; law; model, plan.
Rasmasá, wet with perfumed essences or perspiration.
Rasmí, *adj.* customary.
Rasná, *v. n.* to leak, to ooze.
Ras nikálná, *v. a.* to extract the juices of a thing.
Rasoí, *s. f.* victuals; a kitchen.
Rasoíghar, *s. m.* a cook-room.
Rasoiyá, *s. m.* a cook.
Rasoṇt, *s. f.* see Raswat.
Rasrá, *s. m.* rope, a cable.
Rasrí, *s. f.* string, cord.
Rassá, *s. m.* rope, a cable.
Rassí, *s. f.* string, cord, rope; a serpent.
Rást, *adj.* right, true, just.
Rástá, Rastá, Rasta, } *s. m.* a road, a way, a path, a street.
Rástá katráná, to slink away.
Rást áná, to be set to rights.
Rástbáz, *adj.* faithful, honest, righteous, to be depended on.
Rástbází, *s. f.* fidelity, fair play.

Rástgo, *adj.* a speaker of truth.
Rástgoí, *s. f.* speaking truth.
Rástí, *s. f.* sincerity, fidelity.
Rást muámala, *adj.* just, of good actions, of upright conduct.
Rasúl, *s.m.* a messenger, Muhammad.
Rasúm, *prop.* Rusúm, which see.
Raswat, *s. f.* a kind of collyrium, a kind of root which is pounded and used for calking boats.
Rat, *s. f.* *contraction* of Rát.
Rát, *s. f.* night.
Rátal, *s. m.* a large beam (for scales.)
Ratálú, *s. m.* a yam.
Ratan, *s. m.* a jewel, gem, a precious stone; the pupil of the eye.
Ratáná, *v. n.* to rut, to be lewd.
Ratanjot, *s. f.* name of a plant, name of a medicine said to be good for the eyes.
Ratanmálá, *s. f.* a necklace of precious stones.
Rátárátí, *adv.* in the night, by night.
Rataundhá, *s. m.* } blindness at night.
Rataundhí, *s. f.* } blindness at night.
Rataundhiyá, *adj.* blind at night.
Rath, *s. f.* a four-wheeled carriage, a coach; the car of Jagannáth.
Rathbán, *s. m.* a coachman.
Rathjátrá, *s. m.* the festival of the procession of Jagannáth's car.
Rathwán, *s. m.* a coachman.
Rati, *s. f.* venery, coition; a little, a trifling quantity.
Ratí, *s. f.* a weight or measure equal to eight barleycorns; fortune.
Rátib, *s. m.* a daily allowance of food (to animals), allowance.
Ratí chamakná, to begin, to prosper, to flourish.
Ratjagá, watching all night on religious occasions.
Raṭná, *v. a.* to repeat, to iterate, to order or demand repeatedly.
Ráton rát, in the middle of the night.
Rátri, *s. f.* the night.
Rattí, *s. f.* a weight.
Ratúbat, *s. f.* humidity, moisture, freshness.

Rau, in *compos.* going.
Raud, *s.* solar heat, sunshine.
Raughan, *s. m.* grease, oil, boiled butter; varnish, lacker.
Raughaní, *adj.* greasy, oily; buttery.
Raughan i talkh, *s. m.* mustard oil.
Raughan i zard, *s. m.* melted butter, ghí.
Raulá, *s. m.* noise, tumult, alarm.
Raunaq, *s. f.* beauty, elegance, splendour, ornament, symmetry.
Raunaqdár, *adj.* brilliant, splendid.
Raundan, *s. m.* trampling, treading under foot.
Raundhná, } *v. a.* to trample on, to tread down, to ride over.
Raundná, } *v. a.* to trample on, to tread down, to ride over.
Raus, *s. f.* a passage, an avenue.
Raushan, *adj.* see Roshan.
Rauza, *s. m.* a mausoleum.
Rávan, } *n. prop.* the sovereign of Lanká, the great enemy of Ráma.
Rávana, } *n. prop.* the sovereign of Lanká, the great enemy of Ráma.
Ravish, *s. f.* custom, law, institution, rule; avenue, walk, passage.
Raw, in *compos.* going.
Rawá, *adj.* right, proper, lawful, allowable: *s. m.* gold or silver filings; a grain or particle of sand, gunpowder, &c.
Rawádár, an approver, chooser.
Rawádárí, *s. f.* approbation.
Rawáj, *s. m.* usage, custom: *adj.* customary, current, vendible.
Rawán, *adj.* going, moving, flowing, running.
Rawána, *s. m.* a pass, a passport: *adj.* despatched, departed.
Rawánagí, *s. f.* passing, going, departure, travelling.
Rawána honá, *v. n.* to be despatched, to go, to pass; to flow.
Rawána karná, to set a going, to despatch, to send.
Rawanna, *s. m.* a pass, a permit.
Rawárau, } *s. f.* going, proceeding, travelling.
Rawárauí, } *s. f.* going, proceeding, travelling.
Ráwat, *s. m.* a caste of sweepers.
Ráwí, *s. m.* an historian, a narrator.

Rawíya, *s.m.* custom, fashion, manner.
Ráwtí, *s. f.* a kind of tent.
Ráz, *s. m.* a secret, a mystery.
Razá, *s. f.* acquiescence, consent, good pleasure; permission, leave,
Razáí, *s. f.* a quilt.
Razá lená, to take leave, to go on leave.
Razámand, *adj.* acquiescing, consenting, permitting.
Razámandí, *s. f.* consent, acquiescence, permission.
Rázdár, *adj.* trusty, faithful, confidant.
Rázdárí, *s. f.* keeping of secrets, secrecy.
Rází, *adj.* satisfied, contented, agreed, pleased, willing: *s.f.* good pleasure.
Rází ba rizá, resigned to the will of God.
Rází honá, to consent, to acquiesce, assent, accede, agree, to be content, to be satisfied.
Rází karná, to content, to satisfy, please, gratify.
Rázínáma, *s. m.* an acknowledgment, of a cause being finally settled, given by the plaintiff.
Ráziq, *s. m.* sustainer; affording sustenance, a title of the Deity.
Rázposhí, *s. f.* keeping or concealing secrets.
Razzáq, *adj.* an epithet of the Deity; provider of daily food.
Re, *m.* a vocative used by way of disrespect or admiration: holla! bravo! O!
Reh, } *s. f.* fossil alkali, used for
Rehí, } washing and making soap.
Rekh, } *s. f.* stripe, line, mark, fate,
Rekhá, } destiny.
Reḳhta, *s. m.* the Urdú language is so called, being a mixed dialect; mortar, plaster.
Rel, *s. m.* abundance, plenty,
Relá, *s. m.* a flood; rushing, shove; a line or string of animals, &c.
Relná, *v. a.* to shove, push, rush.
Relpel, *s. f.* abundance, plenty.
Rend, } *s. f.* palma christi.
Reṇḍí, }
Reṇḍí ká tel, *s. m.* castor oil.
Rengná, *v. n.* to creep, to crawl; to bray.
Rengní, *s.f.* name of a medicinal herb.
Renkná, *v. n.* to bray (as an ass.)
Reṛ, *s. m.* } palma christi; the
Reṛí, *s. f.* } castor oil tree.
Reṛí ká tel, *s. m.* castor oil.
Reṇṭá, *s. m.* snot, snivel.
Resha, *s. m.* fibre, stringiness of a mango.
Reshadár, *adj.* fibrous, stringy.
Resham, *s. m.* silk.
Reshmí, } *adj.* silken, woven or
Reshmína, } made of silk.
Ret, *s f.* sand; filings.
Retáí, *s. f.* price paid for polishing or filing.
Retal, *adj.* sandy: *s.f.* sandy ground.
Retí, *s. f.* sandy ground on the shore of a river; a file.
Retílá, *adj.* sandy, gritty.
Retiyáná, } *v. a.* to file, to polish.
Retná, }
Rewand chíní, *s. f.* rhubarb.
Rewṛí, *s. f.* a kind of sweetmeat.
Rez, in *compos.* pouring, scattering, dropping, shedding, &c.
Reza, *s. m.* a scrap, piece, bit; children employed on mason work, &c.; boys who carry brick, mortar, &c.; small silver coin.
Reza reza, *s. m.* scraps, pieces: *adj.* in pieces, broken in pieces.
Rezgí, small silver coin; a scrap, a bit, a piece.
Rez karná, to begin to speak or talk (as young birds.)
Rí, *f.* a vocative particle used by way of disrespect or admiration: holla! bravo! O!
Riạ̈yá, *s. plur.* of Raạiyat, subjects, tenants, peasantry.
Riạ̈yat, *s. f.* kindness, favour, guarding, protecting, taking care (of), paying attention; remission, indulgence.

Riáyat karná, to take off something from the price asked; to guard; to show kindness.
Riáyatí, s. m. a favoured person.
Ríchh, s. m. a bear. [friendship.
Rifáqat, s. f. society, companionship,
Rifáqat karná, to associate with.
Riháí, s. f. liberation, escape, deliverance, discharged, release.
Riháí bakhshná, to deliver.
Riháí dená, s. m. to release, to acquit.
Riham, s. m. the womb.
Rihl, s. f. a support for a book.
Rihlat, s. f. marching (particularly to the other world); death.
Rihlat karná, v. n. to die.
Rihm, s. m. the womb.
Rihn, s. m. a pledge, a pawn.
Rijálá, adj. mean, vulgar, vile, base.
Ríjh, s. f. choice, approbation, desire; pleasing, satisfying.
Rijháná, v. a. to please.
Ríjhná, v. n. to be pleased, to be gratified, to be delighted.
Rikáb, s. f. a dish, a plate; a stirrup; equipage, train.
Rikábdár, keeper of the dishes.
Rikábdoál, s. f. a stirrup-leather.
Rikábí, s. f. a dish, a plate.
Rikábí mazhab, adj. parasitical,
Rikebí, s. f. a dish, a plate.
Rikh, Rikhí, } s. m. a sage, a saint.
Rím, s. f. matter, pus.
Rímí, adj. purulent.
Rin, s. f. borrowing, debt.
Rínchh, s. f. a bear,
Rind, Rindá, } s. m. a reprobate, a drunkard, a debauchee, a blackguard,
Ríndhná, v. a. to dress (victuals), to cook.
Rindí, s. f. trick, fraud, debauchery.
Ríngná, v. n. to creep, to crawl.
Riní, adj. indebted: s. m. a debtor.
Riniyá, s. m. f. a debtor.
Ríṛh, s. f. the backbone.
Ríriyáná, v. n. to cry (as a child); to importune, to beg earnestly.

Rís, s. f. anger, wrath, passion.
Risála, s. m. a book, a treatise, a small tract; a troop of horse,
Risáladár, the commander of a troop of horse.
Risáladárí, s. f. the command of a troop of horse.
Risálat, s. f. mission, apostleship.
Risálatpanáh, asylum of prophecy, i.e., Muhammad.
Risáná, v. n. to be displeased, to be angry, to be vexed.
Rísh, s. f. beard.
Ris'há, adj. passionate, wrathful.
Rishi, s. m. a sage, a saint.
Rishta, s. m. relationship, connexion, kin.
Rishtadár, s. m. a relation, a kinsman.
Rishtadárí, s. f. relationship, affinity.
Rishwat, s. f. a bribe.
Rishwat dená, to bribe.
Rishwatí, adj. a taker of bribes.
Rishwat kháná, to take bribes.
Rishwatkhor, adj. a taker of bribes.
Rishwat lená, to take bribes.
Risiyáná, v. n. to be vexed, to be angry, to be provoked.
Risná, v. n. to drop slowly; to be angry.
Rít, s. f. custom, usage, habit, rule.
Rítá, adj. empty, void.
Ríṭhá, s. m. the name of a fish; the name of a fruit; soap-nut.
Ríti, s. f. custom, usage, habit, rule.
Ritu, s. f. season; the Hindús divide the year into six seasons.
Riwáj, s. f. custom, usage, fashion: adj. customary, current.
Riwáyat, s. f. a history, narrative, tale, fable, fiction.
Riwáyát, plur. histories, narrations.
Riyá, s. m. hypocrisy, dissimulation, evasion, affectation.
Riyákár, s. m. a hypocrite, dissembler.
Riyákárí, s. f. hypocrisy, dissimulation.
Riyásat, s. f. government, command, dominion, sway.

Riyásat karná, to govern.
Riyází, *s.m.* mathematics.
Rizál, } *adj.* mean, worthless, vile,
Rizála, } base.
Rizálpan, } *s. m.* meanness, baseness,
Rizálpaná, } worthlessness.
Rizq, *s. m.* food, wealth, subsistence, daily bread, support.
Rizq dená, } to give food, to
Rizq pahunchána, } support.
Roáb, *s.m. prop.* Ruạb, which see.
Roáí, *s. f.* lamentation.
Roáṉ, *s. m.* hair of the body, down, wool.
Roáná, *v. a.* to make cry, to vex, to displease.
Roás, *s. f.* inclination to cry.
Rob, in *compos.* sweeping.
Rodá, } *s. m.* (a sinew used as) a
Roda, } bowstring; a gut, catgut.
Rodan, *s. m.* weeping, crying; a tear.
Ro dená, to cry, to weep.
Roeṉ, *s. f.* the hair on the arms, &c., bristle, nap, down.
Roeṉ badalná, to become sleek and fat (a horse), to change his coat.
Rog, *s. m.* sickness, disease.
Roghan, *s. m.* see Raughan.
Rogí, }
Rogílá, } *adj.* sick, ailing; an in-
Rogiyá, } valid.
Rohaní, *s. f.* see Rohiní.
Rohaṭ, *s. f.* weeping, crying, tears.
Rohiní, *s. f.* name of the fourth mansion of the moon.
Rohú, *s. f.* the name of a fish.
Roj, *s. m. prop.* Roz, day.
Rok, *s. f.* prevention, hindrance.
Rokaṛ, *s. f.* ready money, cash.
Rokaṛbahí, *s. f.* a cash-book.
Rokaṛiyá, *s. m.* a cash-keeper, a treasurer.
Rokná, *v. a.* to enclose, surround, stop, prevent, restrain, hinder, detain, interrupt, prohibit.
Rok ṭok, let, hindrance, opposition, resistance.
Roláná, *v. a.* to cause to weep.
Rom, *s. m.* down, small hair of the body.
Rompná, *v. a.* to plant, to transplant.
Roná, *v. n.* to cry, to weep: *s. m.* lamentation, grief: *adj.* addicted to crying.
Roná dhoná, to be bathed in tears.
Roní súrat, *adj.* of a sad countenance: *s. m.* a melancholy or rueful countenance.
Ronṭiyá, *adj.* treacherous.
Ronṭná, *v. a.* to deny.
Ropná, *v. a.* to plant, to transplant.
Roṛá, *s. m.* a stone, a fragment of stone or brick, a brickbat.
Rorokar, *adj.* with difficulty, with labour and pain.
Roshan, *adj.* light, luminous, manifest, conspicuous.
Roshanckaukí, *s. f.* name of a musical instrument.
Roshandán, *s. m.* a small hole for admitting light.
Roshandil, *adj.* of an enlightened mind.
Roshangar, *s. m.* an oilman.
Roshaní, *s. f.* light, splendour.
Roshan karná, to light, to illuminate, to kindle.
Roshnáí, *s. f.* ink; light, splendour.
Roshní, *s. f.* light, splendour, brightness.
Rosná, *v. n.* see Rúsná.
Roṭ, } *s. m.* thick bread; sweet-
Roṭá, } meats offered to Hanúmán.
Roṭí, *s. f.* bread; an unleavened cake.
Roṭíwálá, *s. m.* a baker.
Royá karná, *v. n.* to be ever crying.
Roz, *s. m.* a day.
Roza, *s. m.* fast, fasting; Lent.
Rozadár, *s. m.* one who fasts.
Roza i jazá, day of judgment.
Roza kholná, to break a fast.
Rozána, *s. m.* daily allowance; daily.
Roza rakhná, to keep a fast, to fast.
Roz ba roz, *adv.* daily, constantly.
Rozgár, *s. m.* service, earning.

Rozgárí, *adj.* one who earns.
Rozgár karná, to serve to earn.
Rozí, *s. f.* daily food, employment.
Rozína, *s. m.* daily food.
Rozínadár, *s. m.* one who receives daily wages.
Roz i shumár, the day of judgment.
Roz marra, *adv.* always, daily.
Roznáma, } *s. m.* a daily account-
Roznámcha, } book, a journal.
Roz o shab, day and night, always, constantly.
Roz roz, *adv.* daily, every day.
Rú, *s. m.* face, surface; cause, reason.
Ruạb, *s. m.* fear, terror, awe; dignity.
Rubậí, *s. f.* a stanza of four lines.
Rúbakár, *adj.* under consideration (a cause.)
Rúbakárát, causes, &c., brought to court.
Rúbakárí, *s. f.* proceedings (of a cause.)
Rúbarú, *s. m.* presence: *adv.* face to face, before, over against.
Ruch, *s. f.* desire, wish.
Ruchná, *v. n.* to be agreeable to the mind or palate, to be approved, to be relished.
Rudhir, *s. m.* blood.
Rúe, face, surface.
Rúezamín, *s. f.* face of the earth.
Rúh, *s. f.* soul, spirit.
Ruhání, *adj.* spiritual.
Rúháníyat, *s. f.* spirituality.
Rúh ul láh, the Spirit of God, Jesus Christ.
Rúh ul quds, the Holy Spirit.
Rúí, *s. f.* cotton.
Rúídár, *adj.* quilted or stuffed with cotton.
Rujụ, *s. m.* turning towards, bias.
Rujụ honá, to be inclined or turned to.
Rujụ karná, to have recourse to a higher authority, to repair to.
Rujụ láná, to turn towards, to side with, to submit, to yield.
Rukáná, *v. a.* to cause to enclose, to surround, to stop, to hinder.
Rukáo, *s. m.* } hindrance, deten-
Rukáwat, *s. f.* } tion, prevention.
Rukh, *s. m.* the cheek; face, side, point, quarter.
Rúkh, *s. m.* a tree.
Rúkhá, *adj.* dry, plain, rough, harsh, unkind; unseasoned.
Rukhái, } *s. f.* plainness, dryness (of
Rúkhái, } bread), unkind looks, unfriendliness.
Rukhání, *s. f.* a carpenter's chisel.
Rúkhá súkhá, *adj.* plain, blunt, harsh (words.)
Rukh badalná, to turn away from (words, &c.), to be angry, to be displeased.
Rúkhí, *s. f.* a squirrel.
Rukh karná, to turn the face (towards), to proceed (towards), to attend to, to accede to.
Rukh pherná, to turn away from, to be angry.
Rúkhṛá, *adj.* rough uneven.
Rukhsár, } *s. m.* the cheek, face,
Rukhsára, } mien, complexion.
Rukhsat, *s. f.* leave, licence, permission, dismissal.
Rukhsat dená, to permit, to dismiss, to give leave to go.
Rukhsat honá, to depart, to have leave to depart.
Rukhsatí, *s. f.* departure, anything given at parting.
Rukhsat karná, to permit, to give leave, to dismiss.
Rukhsat lená, to take one's leave, to depart.
Rukná, *v. n.* to stop, to be hindered or prohibited; to be enclosed.
Rukṛá, *adj.* rough, uneven.
Rukụ, *s.m.* bowing the body in prayer, &c.
Rukwaiyá, *s. m.* a preventer.
Ruláná, *v. a.* to cause to cry, to vex, to displease, to afflict.
Rúm, *n. prop.* Rome; Constantinople, the Turkish empire.
Rúmál, } *s. m.* a handkerchief, a
Rumál, } towel.

Rúmálí, *s. f.* a mode of exercising the arms by turning the mugdars over the head.

Rúmí, *s. m.* a Grecian.

Rundná, *v. n.* to be trod or trampled on.

Rúnghaṭ, *s. f.* dirt, filth.

Rúngṭá, *s. m.* the short hairs of the body.

Rúngṭe khaṛe honá, *v. n.* the standing of the hairs on end (from cold, fear, &c.)

Rúp, *s. m.* countenance, form, shape, appearance, face; beauty.

Rúpá, *s. m.* silver.

Rúpahlá, **Rúpahrá**, **Rupahrá**, } *adj.* silvered, made of silver.

Rupaiyá, **Rúpí**, **Rúpíyá**, **Rúpiya**, } *s. m.* a coin so called, a rupee.

Rúpjast, *s. m.* pewter.

Rúposh, *adj.* hiding the face, concealed.

Rúposh honá, *v. n.* to be concealed, to hide one's face, to abscond.

Rúposhí, *s. f.* concealment, hiding.

Rúpwán, **Rúpwant**, } *adj.* well-shaped, handsome, beautiful.

Rupyá, *s.m.* a coin so called, a rupee.

Ruqa, *s. m.* a note, a letter.

Ruqaát, *s. plur.* of Ruqa, notes.

Rusáná, *v. n.* to be displeased.

Rúsí, *s. f.* scurf.

Rúsiyáh, *adj.* disgraced, criminal, unfortunate.

Rúsiyáhí, *s. f.* disgrace, criminality.

Rúsná, **Rusná**, } *v. n.* to be angry, to be displeased, to have a misunderstanding with a friend.

Rustam, *n. prop.* one of the twelve champions of Persia; a hero.

Rustamí, *s. f.* valour, heroism.

Rusúm, *s. f. plur.* of Rasm, customs, fees, taxes, duties, postage.

Ruswá, *adj.* infamous, dishonoured, disgraced: *s. m.* disgrace, infamy.

Ruswáí, *s. f.* ignominy, infamy, dishonour, disgrace, &c.

Rutba, *s. m.* rank, degree, dignity, step, stair.

Rutba baṛhná, to advance in dignity.

Rúṭhá rúṭhí, *s. f.* mutual coolness, misunderstanding.

Rúṭhná, *v. n.* to have a misunderstanding with a friend, to be cool, to be angry or displeased.

Rúṭhní, *adj.* quarrelsome: *s. f.* the name of a species of sensitive plant.

Rutúbat, *s. f.* humidity, freshness.

S.

Sa, a prepositive particle, signifying with, possessed of, or related to.

Sá, like, resembling; an adjunct, the meaning of which is at times scarcely perceptible, though often it seems to give intensity to the preceding word, as Baṛá, large; Baṛásá, largish; Kálásá, blackish.

Saądat, *s. f.* felicity, happiness, good fortune.

Saądatmand, *adj.* prosperous, fortunate, happy.

Saądatmandí, *s. f.* prosperity.

Sáąt, *s. f.* a moment, minute, hour.

Sab, *adj.* all, every, the whole, total (in the inflection of the plural this word generally becomes sabhon.)

Sabá, *s. f.* a gentle breeze, morning breeze.

Sabab, *s. m.* cause, reason, motive: *postpos.* on account of, by reason of.

Sabad, *s. m.* see Sabd.

Sábadhán, *adj.* see Sávadhán.

Sabaj, *adj. prop.* Sabz, which see.

Sabal, *adj.* powerful, forcible.

Sabaláí, *s. f.* power, force, strength.

Saban, *adj. plur*, all.

Sában, *s. m.* soap.

Sabaq, *s.m.* a lesson, lecture, learning.

Sabaq lená, to take a lesson.

Sabaq paṛhná, to read a lesson.

Sabar, *s. f.* see Sabr.

Sábar, *s. m.* a leather of elk's or any

kind of deer's hide for bedding; an elk.

Sábásh, *prop.* Shábásh, which see.

Sábáshí, see Shábáshí.

Sabd, *s.m.* sound in general, a sound, a word.

Saber, *adj.* early, soon, in good time.

Saberá, *s. m.* morning dawn.

Sabere,*adv.* in the morning, early, soon.

Sabhá, *s. m.* an assembly, meeting, company.

Sabhápati, *s. m.* chief or president of an assembly.

Sabhí, all.

Sabhoṉ, *adj. plur. inflect.* of Sab, all, the whole.

Sabíl, *s. f.* water distributed to thirsty travellers during the ten first days of Muharram.

Sábiq, *adj.* former, preceding, foregoing: *adv.* formerly, of yore, heretofore, ago, before time.

Sábiqa, *s. m.* former friendship, previous intimacy.

Sábiqan, } **Sábiq dastúr**, } according to ancient or former custom; as before.

Sábiq meṉ, *adv.* formerly, of yore, heretofore, ago, before time.

Sábir, *adj.* patient.

Sábit, *adj.* firm, constant, durable, stable, fixed, proved, ascertained, established, confirmed.

Sábit honá, to be proved or confirmed, to be firm.

Sábit karná, to confirm, establish, verify, prove by witness.

Sabjí, *s. f. prop.* Sabzí, which see.

Sab kahiṉ, *adv.* everywhere.

Sab ká sab, } **Sab ke sab**, } all, every one, everything, the whole.

Sab khauwá, *adj.* omnivorous, one who eats all kinds of food without exception.

Sab koí, every one, every body, all.

Sab kuchh, everything, all.

Sabotar, *adj.* everywhere.

Sabr, *s. f.* patience, endurance.

Sabr honá, to be satisfied (from eating.)

Sabr karná, to wait, have patience, endure.

Sabúj, *adj. prop.* Sabz, which see.

Sábún, } **Sábun**, } *s. m.* soap.

Sábúngar, *s. m.* a soap-boiler.

Sabúr, *adj.* patient, mild, enduring.

Sabúrí, *s. f.* patience, forbearance.

Sabút, *s. f.* firmness, stability, confirmation by evidence.

Sábút, *adj.* whole, entire.

Sabút honá, to be firm.

Sabz, *adj.* green, verdant, fresh, flourishing; grey-coloured (a horse.)

Sabza, *s. m.* an incipient beard; a green stone worn in the ear as an ornament; verdure.

Sabz honá, to flourish.

Sabzí, *s. f.* greenness, verdure; greens, culinary vegetables, a pot herb; an intoxicating potion made of bhang.

Sabzímaṇḍí, *s. f.* a place where vegetables are sold.

Sabzqadam, *adj.* unfortunate, unlucky.

Sach, } **Sách**, } *adj.* true, real, correct: *s. m.* truth: *adv.* indeed, in earnest, actually, truly.

Sachábat, } **Sachái**, } *s.f.* truth, veracity, honesty, probity, authenticity.

Sáchaq, *s. m.* wedding gifts.

Sachauṭí, *s. f.* see Sachái,

Sachchá, *adj.* true, genuine, real, honest, faithful, just, sincere, sure: *s. m.* a truth-teller.

Sachet, *adj.* with circumspection, with caution; attentive, cautious.

Sach honá, to be true.

Sachidánand, *s. m.* the Supreme Spirit.

Sach kahná, to speak truly.

Sach karná, to act truly.

Sachmuch, *adj.* or *adv.* truly, true.

Sad, *adj.* hundred.

Sád, *s. f.* the fourteenth letter of the Arabic alphabet.

Sadá, *s. f.* sound, tone, echo, noise, voice: *adv.* always, perpetually.

Sáda, *adj.* plain, white, unadorned, humble; artless, open, sincere.

Sadábart, *s. m.* alms or food distributed daily to the poor, travellers, &c.

Sádadil, *adj.* artless, simple, stupid.

Sádagí, *s. f.* plainness; simplicity, sincerity, artlessness.

Sáda kághaz, *s. m.* writing paper which has not been written on.

Sadákál, *adv.* continually, always.

Sádakár, *s. m.* a (kind of) goldsmith.

Sádakárí, *s. f.* the business of a goldsmith.

Sádalauh, *adj.* artless, stupid, simple.

Sadán, *adv.* always.

Sadánand, always happy.

Sadáqat, *s.f.* sincerity, candour, truth.

Sadar, see Sadr.

Sadásiva, a name of Mahádeva.

Sadásuhágan, *s. f.* a kind of faqír dressed like a woman.

Sádát, *s. plur.* of Saiyid.

Sádataur, a plain manner.

Sádataurí, *s. f.* gentleness, affability; simplicity, stupidity.

Sadeh, bodily, in the body.

Sádh, *adj.* virtuous, holy: *s. m.* a religious person; a faqír.

Sádhan, *s. m.* } practice, accomplishment.
Sádhaná, *s. f.* }

Sadháná, *v. a.* to train animals.

Sadhná, *v. n.* to be fully instructed or disciplined.

Sádhná, *v. a.* to familiarize gradually to any habit, to teach, learn, habituate, accustom, use, practise, regulate, to accomplish.

Sádhú, *adj.* pious, honest; a religious person, a mendicant.

Sádí, *s. f. prop.* Shádí, marriage.

Sádiq, *adj.* true, just, sincere.

Sádiq ul qaul, speaking truth.

Sadma, *s. m.* a blow, a stroke of fortune, adversity, accident, calamity.

Sadqa, *s. m.* alms, propitiatory offerings, sacrifice.

Sadqa dená, } to sacrifice for the welfare, &c., of another.
Sadqa karná. }

Sadqe honá, } to become a sacrifice for the welfare, &c., of another.
Sadqe jáná, }

Sadqe karná, to sacrifice for the welfare, &c., of another.

Sadr, *adj*, chief, principal, supreme: *s. f.* government, the place where government is administered.

Sadr ạdálat, *s. f.* the chief court of justice.

Sadrạlá, *n. prop.* principal umpire, investigator or arbitrator; an officer in the civil courts superior to a Sadr Amín.

Sadramín, *n. prop.* an umpire, investigator, arbitrator, an officer in the civil courts superior to an Amín.

Sadrbázár, *s. m.* the chief bázár in a military station.

Sadr díwání ạdálat, *s. f.* the chief civil court.

Sadr i sudúr, the chief judge.

Sadr rastá, *s. m.* the highway.

Sáf, *adj.* clean, clear, transparent, pure, candid, innocent.

Sáfá, } *s. f.* purity, cleanness, clearness: *adj.* pure, clean.
Safá, }

Safáí, *s. f.* purity, cleanness, clearness, perspicuity.

Safáí batáná, to refuse flatly.

Safáí karná, to make clean work of it, to accomplish fully.

Safar, *s. m.* journey, voyage, travel, travelling, journeying: *s. m.* the second month of the Muhammadan year.

Safarí, *s. m. f.* a traveller: *adj.* of or relating to travelling.

Safaríám, *s. m.* a guava.

Safárish, *s. f.* recommendation, intercession.

Safárish karná, to recommend, to intercede.

Safar karná, to travel; to go, to depart, to die.

Safar ul muzaffar, *s. m.* the second month of the Muhammadan year.

Safát, *f. plur.* of Sifat, praises, qualities, attributes.

Sáfdil, *adj*. of a pure heart, candid, frank.
Safed, *adj*. white.
Safedá, *s. m*. white lead.
Saff, *s. f*. series, order, rank, file; a mat.
Saff bándhná, to form a line or row.
Sáfgo, *adj*. speaking truth.
Safha, *s. m*. a page (of a book.)
Sáfí, *s. f*. a filter or cloth through which drinks, medicines, &c., are strained, a strainer; a duster, a dishclout or cloth for wiping with.
Safína, *s. m*. a blank book, a common-place book.
Sáfínáma, *s. m*. a general release, discharge from obligation.
Safrá, *s. f*. bile, gall: *adj*. yellow.
Safráí, *adj*. bilious.
Safríám, *s. m*. a guava.
Saftálú, *s. m. prop*. Shaftálú, a peach.
Safúf, *s. m*. a medicine taken dry and unmixed, a powder (in opposition to an electuary.)
Sag, *s. m*. a dog.
Ság, *s. m*. greens, edible vegetables, culinary herbs, potherbs.
Sagá, *adj*. related, full, own.
Sagábhái, own brother.
Sagáí, *s. f*. betrothing for marriage, second marriage of a woman of low tribe. [to betroth.
Sagáí karná, to engage for marriage,
Sagal, *adj*. all, every, the whole.
Sagaṛ, *s. m*. a kind of cart.
Ságar, *s. m*. the sea, the ocean.
Sagautí, **Ságautí**, } *s. f*. animal food, meat, flesh.
Sagbán, *s. m*. a dog-keeper.
Saggaṛ, *s. m*. a kind of cart.
Saghír, *adj*. small, slender, junior.
Saghír sinn, *adj*. of tender age.
Ságird, *s. m. prop*. Shágird, which see.
Ságpát, *s. m*. greens.
Sagrá, *adj*. all, every, the whole.
Sagun, *s. m*. augury, omen; endowed with properties, qualities, &c.

Ságwán, *s. f*. teak-wood or tree.
Sagyán, *adj*. with knowledge, knowing, intelligent, wise.
Sagyání, *adj*. wise, intelligent.
Sáh, *s. m*. a merchant, a shopkeeper: *s. f*. a season.
Sahad, *s. m. prop*. Shahd, honey.
Saháe, **Saháí**, } *s. m*. an aider, assistant, helper: *s. f*. aid, help, assistance.
Sahaj, *adj*. easy, not difficult, facile: *adv*. easily.
Sahajná, *s. m*. a tree the root of which supplies the place of horse-radish.
Sahákár, *s. m*. assistance.
Sáhan, *s. f*. female of Sáh.
Sahan, *s. m*. a court-yard, an area; a kind of cloth.
Sahána, *adj*. coloured (as cloth.)
Sahanhár, *adj*. sufferable, bearable, tolerable.
Saháo, bearing, endurance.
Sahar, *s. m. prop*. Shahr, a city.
Sahárá, *s. m*. assistance, aid, help.
Sahárá dená, *v. a*. to help, to assist.
Sahárá karná, to abet.
Sahargáhí, *s. f*. food taken at early dawn or a little sooner, as among Muhammadans in time of fasting.
Sáhas, *s. m*. courage, spirit, valour.
Sáhasí, *adj*. resolute, brave, bold.
Sahasr, *adj*. a thousand.
Saháyatá, *s. f*. aid, help, assistance.
Sahelí, *s. f*. female companions in a seraglio, handmaid, concubine.
Sáhí, *s. f*. a porcupine.
Sahí, an emphatical particle; (it is) true or correct, truly, indeed, certainly; straight.
Sáhib, *s. m*. lord, master; (in *compos*.) possessor, possessed of, endowed with.
Sáhiba, *s. f*. a lady, mistress, &c.
Sáhibán, masters, gentlemen.
Sáhibí, *s. f*. rule, command, lordship.
Sáhib i ikhtiyár, possessed of free election or option.

Sáhib i jamál, *adj*. beautiful.
Sáhibí karná, to rule, lord, govern.
Sáhib i ḳhána, master of the house.
Sáhib iqbál, *adj*. fortunate, prosperous.
Sáhib kamál, *adj*. perfect, excellent, a saint.
Sáhib salíqa, endowed with taste, a man of taste.
Sáhibzáda, genteelly born; a young gentleman; a son.
Sahífa, *s. m.* a book, a leaf, a page.
Sahíh, *adj*. accurate, just, perfect, entire, right, certain, authentic, correct, genuine; a plumb-line.
Sahíh karná, to sign, to correct, to rectify.
Sáhil, *s. m.* a porcupine.
Sáhir, *s. m.* an enchanter, a magician, a necromancer.
Sahiráná, *v. n.* to thrill, to have the hair stand on end: *v. a.* to rub gently, to stroke.
Sahirí, *s. f.* enchantment, magic, necromancy, conjuration.
Sahit, *prep*. with, together with, along with.
Sahiyárná, *v. a.* to arrange.
Sahjaná, *s. m.* see Sahajná.
Sahl, *adj*. easy, not difficult, simple: *adv*. easily.
Sahláná, *v. a.* to stroke, to rub gently, to tickle.
Sahmáná, *v. a.* to frighten, to terrify.
Sahmná, *v. n.* to fear, to be afraid.
Sahn. *s. m.* a court-yard, area; a kind of cloth.
Sahná, *v. n.* to bear, endure. support.
Sahnak, *s. f.* a plate, dish, &c.
Sahodar, *adj*. descended from one mother.
Sahodar bháí, *s. m.* full brother,
Sahrá. *s. m.* a desert, a plain.
Sahráná, *v. n.* see Sahiráná.
Sahú, *s. f.* an error, mistake, blunder, inadvertency.
Sáhú, *adj*. honest: *s. m.* a merchant.
Sáhúkár, *s. m.* a great merchant, banker.
Sáhúkárí, *s. f.* traffic, trade, commerce, exchange of money.
Sáhúl, *s. m.* a plummet.
Sahw, *s. f.* see Sahú.
Sahwaiyá, *s. m.* a sufferer.
Sahwan, *adv*. erroneously, inadvertently.
Saʻí, *s. f.* endeavour, attempt, effort, enterprise.
Sai, *adj*. hundred.
Saif, *s. f.* a sword.
Saihún, Mount Sion.
Saikaṛá, *adv*. a hundred per cent.
Saʻí karná, to endeavour, attempt, strive.
Saikṛá, *adv*. a hundred per cent.
Sáil, *s. m.* an interrogator, asker.
Sail, *s. f.* walking or going about for amusement.
Sailáb, *adj*. abounding with water: *s. f. m.* a flood, a torrent, a deluge.
Sailání, *adj*. fond of going about for amusement.
Sailsapáṭá, *s. m.* walking or going about for amusement.
Sáín, *s. m.* lord, master; a faqír, the Deity.
Sain, *s. f.* a wink, sign, token, hint, a signal; sleep, repose.
Sáínjí, *s. m.* a religious mendicant.
Sain karná, to beckon.
Sainkṛá, *adv*. hundred.
Sainsaṭh, *adj*. sixty-seven.
Saintális, *adj*. forty-seven.
Saintís, *adj*. thirty-seven.
Saintná, *v. a.* to adjust, to put to rights.
Saiqal, *s. m.* polish, lustre, furbishing; the polishing instrument.
Saiqalgar, a polisher, furbisher, burnisher.
Saiqal honá, to be burnished or polished.
Saiqal karná, to polish, furbish, burnish.
Sair, *s. f.* perambulation, excursion, tour, taking the air, recreation, amusement, moving about; perusal.

Sáir, *s. m.* tax, duty levied on personal property.
Sairgáh, *s. f.* place for walking.
Sair karná, to take the air, to perambulate, to travel; to read, to peruse.
Saís, } *s. m.* a groom, a horsekeeper.
Sáís, }
Sáísí, *s. f.* the business of a groom.
Saitán, *s. m. prop.* Shaitán, the devil, Satan.
Saitná, *v. a.* to take care of, to husband; to kill.
Saiyáh, *s. m.* a traveller, a pilgrim.
Saiyáhí, *s. f.* travelling, voyage.
Saiyára, *s. m.* a planet.
Saiyid, *s. m.* a lord, a prince; a descendant of Husain.
Saj, *s. f.* shape, ornament, appearance, preparation.
Sáj, *s. m.* harness, accoutrements; preparation.
Sajáí, *s. f.* the price paid for making belts or scabbards; preparation.
Sajan, *s. m. f.* a person of respectability.
Sájan, *s. m.* a sweetheart, a lover.
Sajáná, *v. a.* to cause to prepare.
Sajáo, *s. m.* preparation, ornament.
Sajáwaṭ, *s. f.* preparation; contrivance.
Sajdár, *adj.* well-shaped, handsome.
Saj dhaj, *s. f.* preparation and appearance.
Sájhá, *s. m.* partnership, association.
Sájhí, *s. m.* a partner, an associate.
Sajílá, *adj.* well-shaped, handsome, graceful, beautiful.
Sajíw, } *adj.* alive, living, endowed with life.
Sajív, }
Sajjí, } *s. f.* a kind of mineral alkali, impure carbonate of soda.
Sajjímaṭṭí, }
Sájlá, *s. m.* third brother of four or more.
Sajná, *v. n.* to be prepared; to fit, to become, to beseem.
Sájná, *v. a.* to prepare, to dress, to decorate, to bedeck, to regulate.

Sajwáná, *v. a.* to cause to prepare.
Sak, *s. m. prop.* Shakk, which see.
Sakal, *adj.* all, the whole, every: *s. f. prop.* Shakl, which see.
Sakárná, *v. a.* to accept (a bill of exchange, &c.)
Sakas, *s. m. prop.* Shaḳhs, which see.
Sakat, *s. f.* ability, strength, power. See also Saḳht.
Sakelá, *s. m.* a kind of iron.
Saket, *adj.* narrow, strait: *s. m.* want, distress.
Sákh, *s. f.* trust, credit, reputation.
Sakhá, *s. m.* a friend, a companion.
Sákhá, *s. f.* a branch of a tree.
Saḳháwat, *s. f.* liberality, generosity.
Saḳháwat karná, to show liberality.
Sákhí, *s. m.* an evidence, a witness.
Sakhí, *s. f.* a kind of faqír who dresses like a woman; a friend, a companion.
Saḳhí, *adj.* liberal, generous.
Sáḳht, *s. f.* make, fabrication, fashion, construction.
Saḳht, *adj.* hard, strong, tough, difficult, obdurate; stingy; very cruel, austere, severe, harsh (to the ear.)
Saḳhtí, *s. f.* hardness, harshness; severity, stinginess; hardship; obduracy; distress, difficulty.
Saḳhun, *s. m.* speech, language, a word.
Sákin, *s. m.* an inhabitant: *adj.* quiescent (letter), *i.e.*, a consonant not followed by a vowel,
Sakná, *v. n.* to be able.
Sakoṛná, *v. n.* to shrink, shrivel, wrinkle: *v. a.* to contract, draw up.
Sakrá, *adj.* small (not having room enough), narrow, strait.
Sakráí, *s. f.* smallness, want of room.
Sakráná, *v. a.* to cause to accept (bill, &c.); to straiten, to deprive of necessary room.
Sakránt, *s. f.* the entering of the sun into a new sign,
Sakrántí, *adj.* relating to the Sakránt.

Sákshí, *s. m.* an eye-witness, an evidence.
Sakti, *s. f.* ability, strength, power.
Saktimán, *adj.* powerful, mighty.
Sákú, } *s.* name of a timber.
Sakúá, }
Sakucháná, *v. a.* to abash.
Sakuchná, *v. n.* to fear, to be abashed.
Sakúnat, *s. f.* residence, dwelling, habitation.
Sál, *s. m.* name of a timber tree; a hole made by driving a pin into the ground, &c.; a year; in *compos.* house, place, school.
Sála, in *compos.* a termination affixed to numbers to denote as many years old.
Sálá, *s. m.* a wife's brother, brother-in-law; in *compos.* house, place.
Salábat kúncha, *s. m.* an intrenchment.
Salabmisrí, *s. m.* Salep.
Salag, *adj.* the whole.
Sálagrám, *s. m.* a particular stone worshipped as an emblem of Vishnu.
Saláh, *s. f.* peace, concord, treaty; advice, counsel.
Saláhíyat, *s. f.* morning report (of police.)
Saláh karná, to consult, advise, to take counsel together.
Salái, *s. f.* a knitting needle; a piece of wire for tinging the eyelids with a collyrium; a match; the wires or bars of a cage.
Salám, *s. m.* salutation, peace, safety.
Salám ạlaikum, for Salámun ạlaikum.
Salám ạlek, for Salámun ạlaika,
Salámat, *s. f.* safety, health, peace: *adj.* safe, well, in safety.
Salámatí, *s. f.* health, safety; in health or safety.
Salámí, *s. f.* salute; a present given to a landlord for granting a lease, &c.
Salám karná, to salute, hail, accost; to give up, refrain, bid adieu.
Salám lená, to return the salutation.
Salámun ạlaika, peace be upon thee.
Salámun ạlaikum, peace be upon you.
Sálan, *s. m.* flesh, meat.
Sálána, yearly, annual, annually.
Sálár, *s. m.* a chief, head, leader, general or commander (of an army.)
Sálár i qáfila, the chief of a caravan, leader of a troop.
Salás, *adj.* three.
Salátín, *s. plur.* of Sultán, kings, sultans.
Sál ba sál, year by year, annually.
Salesale, *adv.* by slow degrees, indolently, lazily.
Salgam, *s.m.prop.* Shalgham, a turnip.
Sál girih, *s. f.* birthday, on the anniversary of which a knot is annually added on a string kept for this purpose.
Sálhá, *plur.* of Sál, years, for years.
Sálhá sál, for years, annually.
Sál hásil, yearly produce.
Sálí, *s. f.* sister-in-law, wife's sister.
Sál i áyanda, next year.
Salíb, *s. m.* a crucifix, a cross.
Sál i guzashta, last year.
Sálih, *s. m.* a man of probity and honour.
Salím, *adj.* pacific, mild, affable.
Salím ut tabạ, *adj.* affable, mild, gentle, pacific.
Salína, *s. m.* see Sáliyána.
Salínadár, an annuitant.
Salíqa, *s. m* method, knack, knowledge, skill; nature, genius, taste, good disposition.
Salís, *adj.* easy, not abstruse, simple.
Salíta, *s. m. prop.* Shalíta, which see.
Sáliyána, *s. m.* an annual stipend, an annuity: *adj.* annual.
Sáliyánadár, an annuitant.
Sall ạlá, blessed, very fine.
Sallam, *s. m.* a kind of coarse cloth.
Sallú, *s. m.* thongs, narrow slips of leather for stitching shoes.
Sálná, *v. a.* to perforate, bore, pierce; *v. n.* to ache, be in pain, to smart.

Salná, *v. n.* to pierce, to perforate.
Sálsá, *s. m.* sarsaparilla.
Salsaláná, *v. n.* to creep (as a snake, &c.), to pierce (a thorn), to rankle.
Saltanat, *s. f.* empire, sovereignty, reign, dominion.
Sálú, *s. m.* a kind of red cloth.
Salúno, *s. f.* the time the rákhí is tied round the wrist.
Sálwár, *adj.* by or according to the year.
Salwát, *s.* prayers, benediction; abuse.
Sam, *adj.* like, alike, similar.
Sám, *s. f.* a ferrule: *prop.* Shám, evening.
Sámá, *s. f.* provisions.
Samá, *s. m.* time, season; concord, harmony, unison.
Samá bandhná, *v. n.* to be in concert.
Samáchár, *s. m.* news, tidings, information; account of circumstances or health.
Sámadán, *s. m. prop.* Shamadán, a candlestick.
Samadán, *adj.* everlasting, eternal.
Samádh, *s. f.* tomb of a Jogí, particularly where Hindús, from religious motives, submit to be buried alive.
Samadí, *adj.* everlasting, eternal.
Sámagrí, *s. f.* furniture, tools, apparatus, articles.
Samai, *s. f.* time, season.
Samái, *s. f.* endurance, patience, capability, room, space.
Samáj, *s. m.* society: multitude.
Samájat, *s. f.* adulation, entreaty, solicitation.
Samajh, *s. f.* comprehension, understanding, opinion, knowledge, conception, thought.
Samajhná, *v. a.* to comprehend, to understand, suppose, think, conceive, consider, deem, fancy, perceive, apprehend, know, come to an understanding (with.)
Samájí, *s. f.* musicians that attend dancers.
Samálú, *s. m.* the name of a plant.
Sámán, *s. m.* furniture, apparatus, necessaries, tools.
Samán, *adj.* equal, adequate, similar, alike, akin, one, uniform: *s. f.* equality, level.
Samán, *s. m.* time, season.
Samáná, *v. n.* to be contained in, to go into.
Samánatá, *s. f.* likeness, resemblance, equality.
Samán i jang, *s. m.* warlike apparatus, ammunition.
Samántá, *s. f.* see Samánatá.
Samánya, *adj.* common, general.
Samáo, *s. m.* room, space.
Samápan, *s. m.* conclusion, completion.
Samápit, **Samápt**, *adj.* accomplished, finished, perfected.
Samápti, *s. m.* end, accomplishment, conclusion, finis.
Sámar, *s. m.* a kind of salt.
Samar, **Samara**, *s. m.* fruit, produce, profit, offspring.
Samarth, **Sámarth**, **Samarthatá**, *s. f.* ability, power.
Samarthí, **Sámarthí**, *adj.* powerful, mighty, able, capable.
Samast or **Samasta**, all, the whole.
Sambád, *s. m.* communication (of news or intelligence.)
Sambandh, *s. m.* connexion, affinity, relation.
Sambandhí, *s. m.* relation; son or daughter's father-in-law.
Sambat, *s. m.* a year, an era.
Sambat bándhná, to establish an era.
Sambhalná, *v. n.* to be supported, to stand, to be firm; to recover one's self from a fall, &c.
Sambhálná, *v. a.* to support, prop, sustain, hold up, assist, help, shield, protect, check.
Sámbhar, *s. m.* a kind of rock salt.
Sambhárná, *v. a.* see Sambhálná.
Sambodhan, *s. m.* vocative case.
Sambosa, *s. m.* see Samosa.
Samdhí, *s. m.* child's father-in-law;

the relationship between two persons whose children are married to each other.
Samdhin, *s. f.* child's mother-in-law.
Samdhiyáná, *s. m.* the family of a child's father-in-law.
Same, } *s. m.* time, season; fit or
Sameṇ, } proper time.
Samet, *adv.* with, along with, together with.
Sameṭná, *v. a.* to collect together, to amass; to fold up (a carpet.)
Samhálná, *v. a.* see Sambhálná.
Sámhná, *s. m.* encountering, front, confronting, facing, opposition.
Sámhná karná, to confront, oppose, encounter.
Sámhne, *postpos.* or *adv.* in front, fronting, before, confronting, opposite.
Sámí, *s. f.* a ferrule.
Sámil, *adv.* and *adj. prop.* Shámil, which see.
Samíp, *adj.* proximate, at hand: *postpos. mas.* near.
Samípí, *s. f.* proximity, nearness.
Samiyáná, *s. m. prop.* Shamiyána, a canopy, an awning.
Samjháná, *v.a.* to make comprehend, explain, account for, convince, describe, inform, warn, admonish, instruct, apologize.
Samjhautí, } *s. f.* act of explaining,
Samjháwá, } convincing or giving confidence.
Sammat, *s. m.* a year, an era.
Sámná, *s. m.* see Sámhná.
Sámne, *postpos.* or *adv.* see Sámhne.
Samosá, *s. m.* pastry of minced meat.
Sámp, *s. m.* a snake, a serpent.
Sampat, *s. f.* affluence, wealth, riches.
Samperá, *s. m.* a snake-keeper.
Sampolá, } *s. m.* a young snake.
Sampoliyá, }
Sampúran, } *adj.* perfect, full, com-
Sampúrna, } pleted, all, the whole.
Samshán, *s. m.* a cemetery, a place where dead bodies are burnt, &c.

Samt, *s. f.* see Simt.
Samúchá, } *adj.* entire, whole, full,
Samuchá, } complete.
Samudr, } *s. m.* sea, ocean.
Samudra, }
Samudrphen, *s. m.* the dorsal scale or bone of the cuttle-fish.
Samudrsokh, *s. m.* name of a medicine.
Samúh, *s. m.* assemblage, heap.
Samulkhár, *s. m.* arsenic.
Samundar, *s. m.* sea, ocean.
Samundarkhár, *s. m.* arsenic.
Samundarphal, *s. m.* name of a medicine.
Samundar phen, *s. m.* foam of the sea.
Sán, *s. f.* a whetstone, a grindstone; the whetting or grinding of a tool.
San, *s. m.* a kind of flax; a year.
Saná, *s. m.* senna: *s. f.* praise, applause.
Sanad, *s. f.* signature, a deed, a document or proof, a warrant; certificate.
Sanadí, *adj.* held by written deeds.
Sanam, *s. m.* a lover.
Sanaṭ, *s. f.* art, make, workmanship, fabrication.
Sanátan, *adj.* eternal, everlasting.
Sáṇch, } *adj.* true, proper, correct,
Sáṇchá, } exact, real.
Sánchá, *s. m.* a mould, a matrix.
Sanchhep, *adj.* abridged, short.
Sánḍ, *s. m.* a bull, a stallion; an impudent extravagant fellow.
Sánḍá, *s. m.* name of an animal resembling a lizard.
Sanḍá, *adj.* strong, fat, stout.
Sandal, *s. m.* sandal-wood.
Sandalauṭá. *s. m.* a stone on which sandal-wood is ground.
Sandalí, *adj.* made of sandal-wood; of the colour of sandal-wood; *s. f.* moveable steps.
Sanḍá musanḍá, *adj.* stout, robust.
Sanḍás, *s. m.* a necessary, a sink.
Sanḍásí, *s. m.* a caste of Hindú faqírs.
Sandeh, *s. m.* suspicion, doubt, apprehension, anxiety.

Sandehí, *adj.* doubtful, scrupulous.
Sán dená, *v. a.* to grind.
Sandes, } *s. m.* a message, news,
Sandesá, } tidings, information.
Sandesí, *s. m.* a messenger.
Sandhán, *s. m.* prying into secrets.
Sandhán páná, *v. a.* to trace to discover.
Sandhyá, *s. f.* twilight.
Sánḍní, *s. f.* a female camel, a dromedary.
Sánḍnísawár, one who rides on a dromedary.
Sanḍsí, *s. f.* small pincers, tongs.
Sandúq, *s. m. f.* a box, a trunk, case, chest, coffer, coffin.
Sandúqcha, *s. m.* a small box, a casket.
Sandúqí, *adj.* like a box.
Saneh, *s. m.* friendship, love, affection.
Sanehí, *s. m.* friend, lover.
Sáng, *s. m.* a spear or javelin; disguise, mimicry, sham.
Sang, *s. m.* a stone; company, union, society: *adv.* along with, in the company of.
Sangam, *s. m.* coition; meeting, conflux, union, company.
Sangat, } *s. f.* collection, company;
Sangati, } a place where the Sikhs celebrate their religious ceremonies.
Sangatí, } *s.* companion, associate,
Sangátí, } comrade.
Sangdil, *adj.* stony-hearted, hard-hearted, cruel.
Sangdilí, *s. f.* hard-heartedness.
Sanghárná, *v. a.* to kill, to make away with.
Sanghátí, *s. m.* a companion, a friend.
Sanghiyá, *s. m.* a companion.
Sangí, *s. m.* a companion, a comrade, an accomplice: *adj.* stony, of stone.
Sángí, *s. f.* a support on which the pole of a cart is propped.
Sang i marmar, *s. m.* marble.
Sang i miqnátís, the loadstone.
Sang i músá, a black stone so called.
Sangín, *adj.* stony, heavy; solid: *s. f.* a bayonet.
Sangíní, *s. f.* solidity.
Sang i sulaimání, *s. m.* agate, onyx.
Sang i sumáq, porphyry.
Sang i yashm, *s. n.* a kind of jasper or agate.
Sáng láná, to imitate, to mimic.
Sangrah, *s. m.* compilation, abridgment; collection.
Sangrám, *s. m.* battle, war.
Sangreza, *s. m.* gravel.
Sangsár, *s. m.* stoning to death.
Sangsár karná, to stone to death.
Sangsí, *s. f.* pincers, forceps.
Sangtara, } *s. m.* a kind of orange.
Sangtará, }
Sangtarásh, *s. m.* a stone-cutter.
Sángumán, understanding and imagination.
Sangyá, *s. f.* a noun.
Sanhak, *s. f. prop.* Sahnak, a dish, plate, &c.
Sání, *s. f.* chaff or straw mixed with grain as food for cattle.
Sáni, *s. m.* artificer, maker, creator.
Saníchar, *s. m.* Saturn, Saturday.
Sanichará, *adj.* unlucky (fellow.)
Sánj, *s. f.* evening.
Sanjáf, *s. f.* edging, border, (tacked to the outer part of a garment.)
Sanjáfí, *adj.* adorned with a border (clothes.)
Sánjh, } *s. f.* evening.
Sanjhá, }
Sanjhákál, } *s. m.* evening.
Sánjhkál. }
Sanjog, *s. m.* accident, event, chance, hap, luck; junction.
Sanjogí, a person who has everything in place and order.
Sanjogná, *v. a.* to prepare.
Sanjukt, *adj.* joined, joined with, compounded.
Sank, } *s. f.* fear, terror, doubt, sus-
Sanká, } picion.

Sánkal, *s. f.* a chain.

Sankalp, *s. m.* a solemn vow or declaration of purpose.

Sankaṭ, *s. m.* vexation, misfortune, pang, anguish, pain.

Sankh, *s. m.* a conch which the Hindús blow; a shell.

Sánkho, *s. m.* a kind of timber.

Sankhiní, *s. f.* a description of a woman.

Sankhyá, *s. f.* a number: *s.m.* arsenic.

Sankoch, *s. m.* shame, bashfulness, reserve, diffidence.

Sankránt, *s. f.* the sun's entering into a new sign.

Sánkrí, *adj.* narrow, close, strait.

Sanmán, *s. m.* respect, esteem, reverence, regard.

Sanmuk, **Sanmukh**, *adv.* opposite, confronting, over against.

Sanná, *v. a.* to be stained, soiled, to be kneaded, mixed up (as flour, dough, earth, &c.)

Sánná, *v. a.* to knead, to mix up (flour, dough, earth, &c.); to stain, to defile; to whet.

Sannáṭá, *s. m.* the roaring of the waves, rumbling noise made by wind and rain at a distance, sound, bluster: *adj.* still, lonely, silent, dreary, dismal.

Sannyás, *s. m.* abandonment of all worldly things.

Sannyási, *s.m.* a religious mendicant.

Sanpát, *s. m.* the name of a disease in which the body is seized with universal chilliness.

Sáṇr, *s. m.* see Sánḍ.

Sáṇṛní, *s. f.* a female camel; a dromedary.

Saṇṛsí, *s. f.* tongs, small pincers.

Sáṇs, *s. f.* breath, sigh.

Sáṇsá, **Sansá**, **Sansai**, *s. m.* doubt, uncertainty; apprehension, fear.

Sansanáná, *v. n.* to sing (as water about to boil); to simmer; to faint.

Sansár, *s. m.* the world.

Sansárí, **Sansárik**, *adj.* worldly, of this world.

Sáṇs bharná, to sigh, to regret.

Sanskár, *s.m.* an essential and purificatory rite among the Hindús.

Sanskrit, the Sanskrit language.

Sáṇsná, *v. a.* to snub, to distress, to threaten.

Sáṇs rokná, *v. a.* to suffocate, to stifle.

Sáṇs rukná, *v. n.* to be smothered or throttled.

Sáṇs ultí lení, to gasp or draw in the breath (as a person in agony.)

Sánt, *adj.* calm, tranquil, pacified.

Sant, *s. m.* a kind of faqír, a saint: *adj.* pious, virtuous.

Sáṇṭ, *s. f.* joining, sticking; confederacy, collusion.

Sáṇṭá, *s. m.* a kind of whip.

Santán, *s. m.* progeny, offspring, children.

Santáp, *s. m.* sorrow, pain, affliction, distress, misery, repentance.

Santápí, *adj.* sad, sorrowful, afflicted.

Sante, *adv.* instead, stead.

Sánt honá, *v. n.* to be appeased or pacified.

Sánt karná, *v. a.* to appease, pacify.

Sáṇṭná, *v. a.* to join thread, to join, to splice, to stick together.

Santokh, *s. m.* content, patience.

Santokhí, *adj.* patient, contented.

Santokh karná, to be patient, to be content.

Santushṭ, *adj.* satisfied, gratified, content, delighted.

Sáṇwá, **Sáṇwáṇ**, *s. m.* the name of a very small grain.

Sáṇwan, *s. m.* the name of the fourth Hindú month.

Saṇwarná, *v. n.* to be prepared or arranged, to be decorated; to become reformed.

Saṇwárná, *v. a.* to prepare, to dress, decorate, adjust, adorn, arrange.

Sáṇwlá, **Sáṇwrá**, *adj.* of a dark or sallow complexion.

Sanyási, *s. m.* see Sannyásí.

Sanyog, *s. m.* see Sanjog.
Sanyogí, see Sanjogí.
Sanyukt, *adj.* see Sanjukt.
Sáp, *s. m.* a snake; a curse.
Sapardá, *s. m.* a musician attending on singing women.
Sapat or Sapath, *s. f.* an oath.
Saped, *adj.* white.
Sapedí, *s. f.* whiteness, whitewash; light of the dawn.
Sápin, **Sápiní**, *s. f.* a female snake.
Sapn, Sapná, *s. m.* a dream.
Sápná, *v. a.* to curse.
Sapolá, Sapoliyá, *s. m.* a young snake just hatched.
Sapúran, *adj.* see Sampúran.
Sapút, **Sapútr**, *s. m.* a tractable or dutiful son.
Sáqí, *s. m.* a cup-bearer, a page.
Saqíl, *adj.* indigestible, heavy, lazy.
Sáqit honá, *v. n.* to be fallen, to be degraded.
Saqilát, *s.* scarlet cloth.
Saqqá, *s. m.* a water-carrier.
Sár, *s. f.* pith or sap of trees, &c.; essence, quintessence: *s. m.* manure; a camel.
Sar, *s. m.* the head, summit, end, point, beginning, chief, principal.
Sará, *s. f.* a caravansary, an inn: *s. m.* an earthen cover of a pot.
Saṛá, *adj.* rotten, musty, stinking.
Sárá, *adj.* all, the whole: *s. m.* wife's brother-in-law.
Saráb, *s. f. prop.* Sharáb, which see.
Sarábí, *s. m. prop.* Sharábí, a tipler, a drunkard.
Sarácha, *s. m.* a tent surrounded with an enclosure.
Sarad, *prop.* Sard, cold, damp.
Saráe, *s. f.* a caravansary, an inn.
Saráecha, *s. m.* see Sarácha.
Sarafráz, *adj.* exalted, promoted.
Saráh, *s. f.* praise, commendation.
Saṛáhaṭ, *s. f.* rottenness, mustiness.
Saṛáhind, *s. f.* a disagreeable smell, smell of putrid meat.

Saráhná, *v. a.* to praise, to commend, to applaud, to celebrate.
Saṛak, *s. f.* the high road.
Sarákat, *s. f. prop.* Sharákat, partnership.
Sarakná, *v. n.* to be moved, to remove, to move, stir, to get out of the way, to budge.
Saram, *s. f. prop.* Sharm, which see.
Saramáná, *v. n. prop.* Sharmáná, which see.
Saṛan, *s. f.* rottenness, putrification.
Saran, *s. f.* an asylum, shelter, protection.
Saráná, *v. a.* see Saráhná.
Saṛáná, *v. a.* to cause to rot, to make ferment; to steep.
Saranágat, *s. m.* a refugee, one who comes for protection or refuge.
Sárang, *s. m.* a chief lascar, a mariner.
Sárangí, *s. f.* a musical instrument like a fiddle.
Sárangiyá, *s. m.* a fiddler.
Saranjám, *s. m.* conclusion, end; apparatus, utensils, goods and chattels, stores, materials, ingredients, requisites.
Saranjám honá, to be concluded.
Saranjám karná, to prepare; finish.
Sarap, *s. m.* a snake, a serpent.
Saráp, *s. m.* cursing, an imprecation.
Sarápá, *adv.* from head to foot, totally: *s. m.* the whole from head to foot.
Saráp dená, Sarápná, *v. a.* to curse, to imprecate.
Saras, *adj.* best, excellent, prime; more, abundant, plenty.
Sáras, *s. m.* a species of heron.
Sarásar, *adj.* all, the whole, entirely, from one end to the other, from beginning to end.
Sarásarí, *adj.* summary.
Saraswatí, *n. prop.* the goddess of speech and wife of Brahmá.
Sarat, *s. f. prop.* Shart, which see.
Sarb, *adj.* all, the whole.

Sarbadá, *adv.* always, continually, perpetually, at all times.
Sarbaggya, *adj.* all-wise, all-knowing, omniscient.
Sárbán, *s. m.* a camel-driver.
Sar ba muhr, *adj.* sealed.
Sarbar, *adj.* equal; *s. m.* a pond.
Sarbaráh, *s. f.* supply, travelling expenses, or cash to pay them.
Sarbaráhí, *s. f.* the act of providing supplies for a journey, direction, management.
Sarbaráhkár, *s. m.* a commissary of supplies; a steward.
Sarbas, *s. m.* everything, the whole property.
Sarbasar, *adj.* all, the whole, entirely, from one end to the other.
Sarbat, *s. m. prop.* Sharbat, which see.
Sarbbyápak, } *adj*, all-pervading.
Sarbbyápí, }
Sarbdarsí, *adj.* omniscient, all-seeing.
Sarbgahan, }
Sarbgrahan, } *s. m.* a total eclipse.
Sarbgrás, }
Sarbsaktimán, *adj.* almighty, all-powerful.
Sarbuland, *adj.* glorious, exalted.
Sarbulandí, *s. f.* exaltation, eminence.
Sarchashma, *s. m.* a spring, a fountain.
Sard, *adj.* cold, damp.
Sardá, *s. m.* a kind of water-melon.
Sardal, *s. m.* timber put on the top of a doorway to support the wall above it.
Sardár, *s. m.* a chief, a head-man, a commander.
Sardard, *s. m.* headache, trouble, perplexity.
Sardardí, *s. f.* vexation, trouble, toil.
Sardárí, *s. f.* chiefship, dominion, lordship, command, authority.
Sardárí karná, to act as chief.
Sard honá, to die.
Sardí, *s. f.* a cold, coldness, dampness; the cold weather.
Sard karná, to cool, to pacify.
Sáṛe, *adj.* see Sáṛhe.
Sare, *a.* or *per.* (as, "sare gaz kai rupai, how many rupees a yard, or per yard?")
Sarepá, } *adv.* all, the whole, from head to foot.
Sarepáo, }
Saresh, *s. m.* glue.
Sarf, *s. m.* expenditure; the orthographical and etymological parts of grammar.
Sarfaráz, *adj.* exalted, eminent, distinguished, promoted.
Sarfaráz honá, to be exalted.
Sarfarází, *s. f.* exaltation, promotion.
Sarfaráz karná, to exalt, dignify, honour, ennoble.
Sarf honá, to be expended.
Sarf karná, to spend, disburse, pass.
Sarfonaho, *s. f.* grammar.
Sarg, } *s. m.* heaven, the firmament, the sky.
Sarga, }
Sargardán, *adj.* distressed, wandering, straying.
Sargardání, *s. f.* distress, confusion, amazement.
Sargarm, *adj.* intent on, earnest, eager, attentive, zealous.
Sargarmí, *s. f.* application, attention, diligence, zeal, earnestness.
Sarglok, *s. m.* see Sarg.
Sargun, *adj.* possessing all good qualities (an epithet of God.)
Sarguroh, *s. m.* the chief of the troops, &c., leader, commander.
Sarguzasht, *s. f.* an event, accident, account of circumstances.
Sarhadd, *s. f.* boundary, extremity, frontier, limits, confines.
Sáṛhe, *adj.* (used with nouns of number denotes) with a half (of one or of the aggregate number, in addition to the number specified), as sáṛhe tín, three and a half.
Sáṛhú, *s. m.* a wife's sister's husband.
Sárí, } *s. f.* a dress consisting of one piece of cloth worn by Hindú women round the body and passing over the head.
Sáṛí, }
Sarífa, *s. m. prop.* Sharífa, a custard-apple.

Saríh, *adj*. apparent, evident, palpable, clear, obvious.
Saríhan, *adv*. clearly, openly, evidently, plainly.
Sarík, *s. m. prop*. Sharík, which see.
Sáriká, *s. f.* name of a bird.
Saríkhá, *adj*. like, resembling, so.
Sar i mú, the point of a hair, a hair's breadth.
Sar i nau, recommencement, renewal; anew, afresh, over again.
Sárinda, *s. m.* a violin, a fiddle.
Sarír, *s. m.* body, constitution.
Sar i ráh, *s. m.* the high road, the higher part of the road.
Sarírí, **Sarírik**, } *adj*. corporeal, material.
Sar i rú, *s. f.* the cephalic vein in the arm.
Sar i sál, commencement of the year.
Sar i shám, evening, early in the evening.
Sarishṭ, *s. f.* the creation, the world.
Sarisht, *s. f.* nature, temperature, constitution, disposition.
Sarishta, *s. m.* custom, usage.
Sarishtadár, *s. m.* the chief under native officer in the courts.
Saṛiyal, *adj*. rotten, stinking.
Sariyáná, *v. a.* to arrange, to pack.
Sarjanhár, *s. m.* creator.
Sarjú, *n. prop. f.* name of a river.
Sarkáná, *v. a.* to remove, to put on one side, to remove out of the way.
Sarkanḍá, *s. m.* a reed.
Sarkár, *s. f.* the king's court; government, a superintendent, a title by way of respect given to a person present or absent.
Sarkárí, *s. f.* superintendence: *adj*. belonging to the state or to the government.
Sar karná, to obtain victory.
Sarkash, *adj*. rearing the head, disobedient, refractory, rebellious, insolent, mutinous.
Sarkashí, *s. f.* disobedience, mutiny, insolence, refractoriness.
Sarkashí karná, to disobey.
Sarḳhatt, *s. m.* an agreement to hire, service; bill of sale.
Sarḳhúsh, *adj*. cheerful, gay, merry.
Sarḳhúshí, *s. f.* gaity, exhilaration.
Sarmá, *s. m.* winter; the cold season.
Sarmáí, *s. f.* winter-clothing.
Sarmashq, *s. f.* copy lines; a copy for writing.
Sarmast, *adj*. intoxicated (with wine, lust, power, &c.), dead drunk.
Sarmastí, *s. f.* intoxication.
Sarmáya, *s. m.* stock in trade, capital, funds, means.
Sarmindá, *adj*. *prop*. Sharminda, [which see.
Sarná, *s. f.* see Saran.
Saṛná, *v. a.* to rot, to ferment.
Sarnáma, *s. m.* title, address, superscription of a letter.
Sární, *s. f.* a she-camel.
Sarnígún, hanging the head, abashed.
Saro, *s. m.* the cypress-tree.
Sarohí, *s. f.* a kind of scimitar.
Sarokár, *s. m.* business, intercourse.
Saropá, *adv*. all, the whole, from head to foot: *s. m.* a vest with which princes honour their subjects.
Sar o sámán, *s. m.* apparatus.
Sarotá, *s. m.* a kind of scissors for cutting betel-nut.
Sarovar, *s. m.* a lake or large pond.
Sarp, *s. m.* a serpent.
Sarpaṭ, *s. f.* galloping.
Sarpaṭ phenkná, to gallop off.
Sarpech, **Sarpesh**, } *s. m.* an ornament worn in the turban.
Sarposh, *s. m.* a cover, lid, pot-lid.
Sarráf, *s. m.* a banker, a money-changer.
Sarráfa, *s. m.* the place where bankers transact their business.
Sarráfí, *s. f.* banking, money-changing.
Sarsá, *adj*. best, excellent, prime.
Sarsabz, *adj*. fresh, verdant, flourishing, prosperous, fortunate, happy.
Sarsabzí, *s. f.* verdure, freshness, vegetation, flourishing state.
Sarsám, *s. m.* delirium, frenzy.

Sarsaráhat, *s. f.* creeping sensation.
Sarsaráná, *v. n.* to creep along (as a snake), to make the noise a snake does when creeping.
Sarshár, *adj.* intoxicated; brimful.
Sarshárí, *s. f.* intoxication; fulness.
Sarsoṇ, *s. f.* a species of mustard.
Sartáj, *s. m.* a chief.
Sarúp, *s. m.* own or natural shape or form, appearance, shape, form, with appearance, with form.
Sarv, *s. m.* the cypress-tree.
Sarwá, *s. m.* wife's brother.
Sárwán, *s. m.* a camel-driver.
Sarwan, *s. m,* the ear; the act of hearing.
Sarwar, *adj.* equal.
Sarwat, *s. f.* wealth.
Sarzad, *adj.* happening.
Sarzad honá, *v. n.* to happen, occur, come out, to come to light.
Sarzamín, *s. f.* the earth; country, region, territory: limits, confines.
Sarzer, *adj.* humbled.
Sarzor, *adj.* mutinous, rebellious, disobedient, headstrong.
Sarzorí, *s. f.* mutiny, rebellion, disobedience.
Sás, *s. f.* a mother-in-law.
Sasarná, *v. n.* see Sarakná.
Sásná, *v. a.* to chastise, to admonish.
Sastá, *adj.* cheap, easy to procure.
Sastái, or Sastágí, *s. f.* cheapness.
Sástar, *s. m. prop.* Shástr, which see.
Sásu, *s. f.* a mother-in-law.
Sasur, *s. m.* father-in-law.
Sat, *s. m.* virtue; truth: *adj.* true, virtuous, right: *adv.* actually.
Sát, *adj.* seven; the same also as Sáth.
Sáṭá, *s. m.* a graft.
Saṭak, *s. f.* a rod.
Saṭakná, *v. n.* to run away, to disappear, to flee, to sheer off.
Satálú, *s. m. prop.* Shaftálú, a peach.
Satáná, *v. a.* to tease, to vex, to fret, annoy, grieve, harass, gall.
Saṭaná, *v. a.* to unite, to stick, to make to adhere.
Satar, *s. f.* a line, row, rank, series: *s. m.* privities.
Sartarbandí, *s. f.* lines for writing on.
Sátárohan, *s. m.* six wolves and a dog who associate together.
Saṭásaṭ, *s. f.* sticking or striking together, adhering, uniting.
Satáú, *s.* vexer, teaser, tormentor.
Satbádí, *adj.* speaker of truth.
Sáṭbáṭ, *s. f.* combination, collusion, confederating.
Sáṭh, *adj.* sixty.
Sáth, *adj.* with, together, along with: *s. m.* society, company.
Sathattar, *adj.* seventy-seven.
Sáth dená, to join, to associate with.
Sáthí, *s. m.* a companion, comrade, accomplice, associate, ally.
Sáṭhí, *s. m.* a kind of rice produced in the rains (so called because it ripens in sixty days from the time of sowing.)
Sáthin, *s. f.* a female companion.
Sáthísáth, together, in one company.
Sáth iske, along with this, besides, moreover.
Saṭhiyáná, *v. n.* to be turned of sixty years, to be decrepit or in one's dotage.
Sáth lená, to take with.
Sáthoṇsáth, together with, along with.
Sáth uske, along with that, although, nothwithstanding.
Sáthwálá, a comrade, a companion.
Satí, *postpos.* from, with: *s. f.* a woman who burns on her husband's funeral pile: *adj.* chaste, virtuous.
Satíchauṇrá, *s. m.* the place where a Satí is burned.
Satíṇ, *postpos.* from, with.
Satír, *s. m. prop.* Shahtír, a beam.
Saṭísaṭí, *adj.* joined, glued, stuck together, crowded.
Satíwáṛá, *s. m.* see Satíchauṇrá.
Satjug, *s. m.* the age of virtue, the golden age.
Saṭká, *s. m.* a rod.
Saṭkáná, *v. a.* to balk, to disappoint, to cause to disappear.
Satkarm, virtuous action, piety.

Satkhaná, *adj.* of seven divisions or stories (a house, &c.)
Satlaṛá, *adj.* seven-fold, of seven strings (a necklace, &c.)
Satlaṛí, *s. f.* necklace of seven strings.
Satmásá, *s. m.* a feast given in the seventh month of pregnancy: *adj.* a child born in the seventh month.
Satmí, *s. f.* the seventh lunar day.
Saṭná, *v. n.* to join, to adhere, to stick, to unite.
Sátpánch karná, to be in doubt, to be unable to decide what to do.
Saṭpaṭáná, *v. n.* to be confounded, to be surprised.
Satrah, *adj.* seventeen.
Satrahwáṉ, *adj.* seventeenth.
Satranj, *s. f. prop.* Shatranj, chess.
Satranjí, *s. f. prop.* Shatranjí, a kind of carpet.
Satsa'í, **Satsaiyá**, *s. f.* the name of a book written by Bihárílál in Brajbhákhá.
Satsang, *s. m.* association with wise men.
Satsaṭh, *adj.* sixty-seven.
Saṭṭábaṭṭá, *s. m.* an amour; combination, collusion, cabal, intrigue.
Sattáis, *adj.* twenty-seven.
Sattánawe, **Sattánwe**, *adj.* ninety-seven.
Sattar, *adj.* seventy.
Sattásí, *adj.* eighty-seven.
Sattáwan, *adj.* fifty-seven.
Sattú, *s. m.* parched grain reduced to meal and made into a paste.
Sattur, *s. m.* an enemy.
Satúá, *s. m.* see Sattú.
Satúásakránt, the entering of the sun into Aries, on which day parched grain is distributed to the Bráhmans.
Satún, *s. m.* a pillar, a column, a [prop.
Satwa, *s. m.* the principle of goodness.
Sátwáṉ, *adj.* the seventh.
Satwáṉsá, *adj.* see Satmásá.
Satwantá, *adj.* virtuous, honest, adhering to truth, truthful.
Sátwíṉ, *s. f.* the seventh day of the lunar month.
Satya, *adj.* true, sincere, honest: *s. m.* truth.
Satyabádí, *adj.* speaker of truth.
Satyánás, *s. m.* depravation, destruction.
Satyánás honá, or **jáná kisí ká**, to be the depravation, destruction, ruin, &c. (of any one or anything), to be destroyed or ruined.
Satyánásí, *adj.* depraved, bad, destroyed, damaged.
Satyánás karná kisí ká, to make the ruin, destruction, or mischief of any one or anything; to blast (reputation.)
Satyatá, *s. f.* truth, integrity, virtue.
Sau, *adj.* a hundred.
Saudá, *s. m.* melancholy, madness; trade, traffic; marketing.
Saudágar, *s. m.* a merchant.
Saudágarí, *s. f.* merchandise, trade.
Saudáí, *adj.* melancholic, insane, mad.
Saudásuluf, *s. m.* traffic, barter.
Saugand, *s. f.* an oath, asseveration.
Saugandh, *s. f.* perfume.
Saugand kháná, to make oath, to swear.
Saughát, *s. f.* a rarity, present, curiosity.
Saughátí, *adj.* given as a present or memorial; fit for a present, rare.
Sauguná, a hundred-fold.
Sauk, *s. m. prop.* Shauq, which see.
Saukín, *a. prop.* Shauqín, which see.
Sauṉf, *s. f.* aniseed.
Sauṉp, *s. f. prop.* Sauṉf, aniseed.
Sauṉpná, *v. a.* to deliver over, commit to charge, give, consign, resign, entrust, deposit.
Sauṉrá, *s. m.* a dark colour.
Saúr, *s. m. prop.* Shuúr, which see.
Saut, *s. f.* rival (wife), contemporary wife, (one wife is saut to another.)
Sautelá, *adj.* of one father by different mothers.

Sautelá bháí, *s. m.* step-brother.
Sautelí bahin, *s. f.* step-sister.
Sautelí má, *s. f.* step-mother.
Sautin. *s. f.* see Saut.
Sautiyáḍáh, *s. f.* malice of a rival wife.
Sávadhán, *adj.* with attention, cautious, cautiously.
Sávadhání, *s. f.* caution, care.
Sawá, *adj.* with a quarter, a quarter more.
Sawáb, *s. m.* the future reward of virtue, a virtuous action, reward.
Sawábí, *adj.* meritorious, virtuous.
Sawád, *s. m.* relish, flavour, taste, sweetness; pleasure.
Sawáí, *s. m.* a quarter more.
Sawain, *s. f.* vermicelli.
Sawaiyá, *adj.* a quarter more.
Sawál, *s. m.* interrogation, question, query, proposition, request.
Sawálí, *s. m.* a questioner.
Sawál karná, to beg, interrogate, question.
Sáwan, *s. m.* the name of the fourth Hindú month.
Sawáng, *s. m.* mimicry acting, imitation, disguise, sham.
Sawángí, *s. m.* an actor, a mimic.
Sawáng láná, to imitate, &c.
Sawár, *s. m.* a rider; mounted or riding (on a ship, horse, or anything else); cavalry, a trooper: *adj.* drunk, tipsy.
Sawár honá, to ride.
Sawárí, *s. f.* riding; equipage, suite, cavalcade.
Sawáyá, *adj.* a quarter added.
Sawer, *adj.* early, soon, in good time.
Sawerá, *s. m.* morning, dawn of day.
Sawere, *adv.* early in the morning, soon.
Sáyá, } *s. m.* shadow, shade, shelter,
Sáya, } protection; an apparition, spectre; a petticoat.
Sáyabán, *s. m.* a canopy; an extension to the fly of a tent.
Sáyad, *adv. prop.* Sháyad, which see.
Sáyadár, *adj.* shady.
Sáya kisí ká parná, to imitate the manner of another.
Sayan, *s. m.* sleep, repose.
Sayána, *adj.* see Syána.
Sayánpan, *s. m.* cunning, art.
Sáya tale áná, to take protection.
Sáz, in *compos.* a maker, making: *s. m.* arms, accoutrements, apparatus; harness; musical instruments.
Sazá, *s. f.* (literally) one's desert; (generally means) correction, punishment, retribution, chastisement, penalty.
Sazá dená, *v. a.* to punish.
Sazá karná, *v. a.* to punish, chastise.
Sazá milná, } to be punished.
Sazá páná, }
Sazáwal, *s. m.* a tax-gatherer, a land steward; bailiff.
Sazáwalí, *s. f.* the business of Sazáwal.
Sazáwar, } *adj.* worthy, deserving,
Sazáwár, } fit, suitable, excellent.
Sazáwár honá, to deserve, to merit.
Sazáwárí, *s. f.* worthiness, suitableness; excellence.
Sáz báz, *s. m.* apparatus, accoutrements, &c. (the word báz being expletive.)
Sází, in *compos. s. f.* making, preparing.
Sázinda, *s. m.* maker; musical performer.
Sázish, *s. f.* combination, collusion, cabal, conspiracy.
Sázwár, *adj.* agreeing, well-arranged.
Se, *postpos.* from, of, out of, by, with, at, through, than; *inflect.* of Sá, like, &c.
Seb, *s. m.* an apple.
Sehí, *s. f.* a porcupine, hedgehog.
Sej, *s. f.* a bed, a couch.
Sejband, *s. m.* a cord for fastening bedding to the bedstead.
Sekh, *s. m. prop.* Shaikh, which see.
Sekhí, *s. f. prop.* Shekhí, boasting, bragging.
Sekná, *v. a.* see Senkná.

Selá, a kind of rice.
Selí, *s. f.* a necklace (of thread) worn by faqírs.
Sem, *s. f.* a kind of flat bean.
Semal, *s. m.* a kind of silky cotton, or the tree producing it.
Sembal, *s. m.* the silk-cotton tree.
Sen (for Se), *postpos.* from, with, by.
Sená, *s. f.* an army.
Senápat, **Senápati**, } *s. m.* the commander of an army.
Sendh, *s. m.* a hole made in a wall by thieves.
Sendhá, *s. m.* rock-salt.
Sendh dená, **Sendh márná**, } to make a hole in a wall to enter by (as thieves.)
Sendhná, *v. a.* to mine.
Sendur, **Sendúr**, } *s. m.* red lead, minium.
Sendúriyá, *s.* a sort of mango; one who sells red lead.
Senkná, *v. a.* to toast, to parch, to warm before, or with, anything hot, to foment, to air (by warming), to apply heat for removing pain.
Senkṛá, *adj.* hundred, per cent.
Senk sánk karná, to toast, to warm.
Sent, *adv.* gratis, free cost.
Senṭhá, *s. m.* **Senṭhí**, *s. f.* } a kind of reed, reed-grass.
Sentná, *v. a.* to adjust, to put to rights.
Ser, *adj.* full, satiated, satisfied: *s. m.* name of a weight; *prop.* Sher, which see.
Seráb, *adj.* full of water, moist, fresh, blooming.
Ser bhar, a full Ser.
Ser honá, to be satisfied.
Serí, *s. f.* satiety, repletion, fulness.
Ser karná, *v. a.* to fill, to satisfy.
Serúá, *s. m.* the head and foot parts of a bed-frame.
Ses, **Sesh**, } *s. m.* remainder, end.
Seshnág, **Sesnág**, } *s. m.* the king of the serpent race of a thousand heads, on one of which he is said to support the world.
Set, *adj.* white: *s. m.* a bridge.
Seṭh, *s. m.* a wholesale merchant, a banker.
Setí, **Setín**, } *postpos.* from, with, &c. See Se.
Sew, *s. m.* a kind of sweetmeat; an apple.
Sewá, *s f.* service, worship, attendance on a superior.
Sewa'ín, *s. m.* vermicelli, macaroni.
Sewak, *s. m.* a servant, a worshipper.
Sewakáí, *s. f.* service.
Sewár, *s. m.* green vegetation at the bottom of pools or other water.
Sewárí, *s. f.* sugar that has been purified with Sewár.
Sewná, *v. a.* to attend on, to serve; to brood, sit, hatch, incubate,
Sewṛá, *s. m.* wizard.
Sewtí, *s. f.* a white rose.
Shab, *s. f.* night.
Shabáb, *s. m.* youth, prime of life.
Shabáhat, *s. f.* similarity, resemblance, likeness.
Shabán, *s. m.* the eighth Arabian month.
Shabána roz, the civil day of twenty-four hours, night and day.
Shabánroz, *adv.* night and day.
Shabároz, *adv.* night and day, *i.e.*, always.
Shábásh, **Shábash**, } *interj.* bravo! excellent! hey!
Shabáshab, *adv.* in the night time, during the night.
Shábáshí, **Shábashí**, } *s. f.* praise, applause.
Shabbásh, one who stays all night; a lodger.
Shabbáshí, *s. f.* staying all night, nightly lodging.
Shabbedár, waking, or watching all night, sleepless.
Shabbedárí, *s. f.* sleeplessness.
Shabd, *s. m.* sound, word, voice,
Shabdeg, *s. f.* a dish composed of

meat and turnips dressed all night on the fire.

Shab i barát, *s. f.* the fourteenth day of the month Shaban, on which the Muhammadans make offerings and oblations in the names (if not to the manes) of deceased relations.

Shabíh, *adj.* like, resembling: *s. f.* a likeness.

Shab i máh, *s. f.* light night, moonlight.

Shabína, *adj.* last night's, stale.

Shab i tár, Shab i tárik, } a dark night.

Shabkhún, *s. m.* a night attack.

Shabkhúní, *s. f.* robbery at night.

Shabkhwábí, *s. f.* night-clothes.

Shabnam, *s. f.* dew: *s. m.* a kind of fine linen.

Shab o roz, night and day.

Shád, *adj.* pleased, delighted, glad, cheerful, exulting.

Sháda, *adj.* joyful, glad.

Shádáb, *adj.* fresh, verdant, moist: *s. m.* fresh herbage.

Shaddá, *s. m.* the banners that are carried with the taziya in the muharram.

Shádil, *adj.* cheerful, delighted, happy.

Shád honá, *v. n.* to be glad.

Shádí, *s. f.* pleasure, delight, joy; marriage, festivity.

Shádí karná, to feast, to marry.

Shádiyána, *adj.* relating to marriage or rejoicings.

Shádiyána bajáná, to triumph.

Shád karná, *v. a.* to gladden, delight, rejoice, exhilarate.

Shádmán, *adj.* pleased, delighted, joyful.

Shádmání, *s. f.* pleasure, delight, joy.

Shafá, *s. f.* cure, remedy, healing, convalescence.

Shafáat, *s. f.* intercession, entreaty, recommendation.

Shafáat karná, to intercede.

Shafá honá, Shafá páná. } to recover.

Shafaq, *s. m.* evening, twilight.

Shafaqat, *s. f.* clemency, compassion, mercy.

Shafaqat karná, *v. a.* to have compassion (on.)

Shaffáf, *adj.* transparent, pellucid.

Shafí, *adj.* advocate, patron.

Sháfí, *s. m.* an intercessor, advocate.

Shafií, *n. prop.* one of the chiefs of the four principal sects of the Muhammadan religion.

Shafíq, *s.* a friend.

Shaftálú, *s. m.* a peach.

Shághil, occupied, employed.

Shágird, *s. m.* a scholar, disciple, apprentice.

Shágirdí, *s. f.* learning, studying, apprenticeship.

Shágird pesha, *s. m.* a servant.

Shagun, Shagún, } *s. m.* augury, omen.

Sháh, *s. m.* a king, a prince; a title assumed by faqírs; the king at chess.

Shaháb, *s. m.* a red colour.

Shahádat, *s. f.* evidence, testimony, witness, martyrdom.

Sháhána, *m.* Shahána, *m.* Shahání, *f.* } *adj.* royal, princely, regal: *s. f.* a nuptial dress.

Sháhanshah, Shahanshah, Shahanshah, } *s. m.* king of kings, an emperor.

Sháhanshahí, Shahanshahí, } *s. f.* empire, sovereignty; *adj.* royal

Shahar, *s. m.* a city.

Shahat, *s. m. prop.* Shahd, honey.

Shahbálá, *s. m.* the companion of a bridegroom.

Shahbáz, *s. m.* a royal falcon.

Shahd, *s. m* honey.

Sháhdará, *s. m.* the highway.

Shahd kí makkhí, Shahdmakkhí, } *s. f.* a honey-bee.

Sháhí, *s. f.* reign, sovereignty, royalty: *adj.* royal, imperial, kingly, regal.

Sháhid, *s. m.* a witness.
Shahíd, *s. m.* a martyr.
Shahíd honá, to be killed.
Sháhidí, *s. f.* evidence, testimony, witness, attestation.
Sháhid i hál, a witness of facts.
Shahnáí, *s. f.* a kind of musical pipe, flute.
Shahnáíchí, *s. m.* a player on the shahnáí.
Shánáma, *s. f.* a celebrated epic poem, containing a history of the kings of Persia.
Shahpar, } *s. m.* strongest feather in
Sháhpar, } a bird's wing.
Shahr, *s. m.* a city.
Shahr ábád karná, to cause to be populous or inhabited.
Shahrag, *s. f.* the great vein in the arm.
Sháhráh, *s. f.* the highway.
Shahr badar, an exile.
Shahr badar karná, to banish.
Shahr basáná, to cause to be populous or inhabited.
Shahrí, *s. m.* a citizen or anything belonging to the city, a townsman.
Shahrkhabrá, *s. m.* news-monger, an intelligencer.
Shahrpanáh, *s. f.* wall, or entrenchments round a town.
Sháhtara, } *s. m.* name of a medicine.
Shahtara, }
Sháhtír, } *s. m.* a beam.
Shahtír, }
Shahtút, *s. m.* a mulberry.
Shahwat, *s. f.* concupiscence, lust, sensuality.
Shahwatangez, *adj.* lust-exciting, lascivious.
Shahwatí, } *adj.* lascivious, lust-
Shahwatparast, } ful, sensual.
Shahwatparastí, *s. f.* sensuality.
Shahzáda, } *s. m.* a prince (generally
Sháhzáda, } means the prince royal.)
Sháhzádagí, *s. f.* the period of the minority of a prince.
Shahzádí, *s. f.* a princess.

Shahzor, *adj.* stout, strong, brave, heroic.
Shahzorí, *s. f.* valour, heroism.
Shai, *s. f.* a thing.
Shaikh, Shekh, *vulg. s. m.* an old man, a venerable old man.
Shár, *s. m.* a poet.
Shárí, *s. f.* poesy, versification, poetry.
Shaitán, *s. m.* the devil, satan.
Shaitání, *adj.* devilish, diabolical.
Shajará, *s. m.* a list of saints or holy predecessors (in the manner of a genealogical tree) given to disciples.
Shakar, *s. f.* sugar.
Shakarqand, *s. m.* sweet potatoes.
Shákh, *s. f.* a bough, branch (of a tree); a horn.
Shákhdár, *adj.* branchy.
Shakhs, *s. m.* a person, body, individual.
Shakhsíyat, *s. f.* nobility, rank, humanity.
Shakíl, } *adj.* well-shaped, hand-
Shakílá, } some.
Shakk, *s. m.* doubt, suspense, hesitation, uncertainty.
Shakkar, *s. f.* sugar.
Shakkí, *adj.* doubtful, perplexing.
Shakkí mizáj, *adj.* undetermined, wavering, hesitating.
Shakl, *s. f.* shape, form, figure, appearance, semblance.
Shakl banáná, to assume a form.
Shaklnavís, *s. m.* a portrait-painter.
Shakti, *s. f.* ability, power; strength.
Shakwá, *s. m.* complaint, upbraiding.
Shakwá karná, *v. a.* to complain.
Shál, *s. f.* a shawl; name of a tree.
Shálbáf, *s. m.* a shawl-weaver.
Shalgham, *s. m.* a turnip.
Shálí, *s. m.* rice, paddy.
Shalíta, *s. m.* a canvas-sack, &c. for baggage or a tent.
Shalkh, *s. f.* a round (of musketry, &c.), a discharge, a volley.
Shall, *adj.* one who can take nothing in his hands (from sickness or cold.)

Shám, *s. f.* evening: *s. m.* Syria.
Shámá, *s. m.* the name of a bird; name of a grain.
Shamạ, *s. f.* a lamp, a candle.
Shamạdán, *s. m.* a candlestick.
Shámat, *s. f.* bad luck, adversity.
Shámatí, *adj.* unfortunate.
Shamba, *s. m.* Saturday.
Shámí, *adj.* Syrian, relating to Syria.
Shámil, *adv.* together; *prep.* with, along with: *adj.* united, blended, confederated, included.
Shámí lagáná, to shoe with iron.
Shámilhál, connected from circumstances, of similar circumstances; general.
Shámil honá, to be blended, to be united, to participate.
Shámil karná, *v. a.* to blend.
Shámil rahná, to live together.
Shámiyána, } **Shamiyána,** } *s. m.* a canopy, awning.
Shamla, *s.m.* the work or embroidered end of a turban or kamarband, sometimes tucked into the folds, and sometimes left flying loose; a narrow kind of shawl for tying round the waist or the head.
Shams, *s. m.* the sun.
Shamshád, *s. m.* the box-tree.
Shamsher, *s. f.* a scimitar, a sword.
Shamsí, *adj.* solar.
Shán, *s. f.* dignity, pomp.
Shána, *s. m.* a comb.
Shándár, *adj.* stately, a man of rank or dignity.
Shangarf, } **Shanjarf,** } *s. m.* vermilion.
Shanká, *s. f.* apprehension, fear; doubt.
Shankh, *s. m.* a conch.
Shaqq, *s. m.* a fissure, crack, rent.
Shaqq honá, to be torn, split, rent.
Sharạ, *s. m.* the precepts of Muhammad, law, equity; a high-road.
Sharáb, *s. f.* wine, spirituous liquor.
Sharában tahúrá, nectar.
Sharábí, *s.m.* a drunkard, wine-bibber.
Sharábḳhána, *s. m.* a tavern.
Sharábḳhwár, drinking wine, wine-drinker.
Sharábḳhwárí, *s. f.* drunkenness, wine-drinking.
Sharábor, *adj.* soused, dripping wet.
Sharaf, *s. m.* nobility, eminence, rank, honour.
Sharáfat, *s. f.* nobility.
Sharah, *s. f.* Sharh.
Sharákat, *s. f.* partnership, participation, fellowship.
Sharárat, *s. f.* wickedness, vice, depravity, villany, atrocity.
Sharbat, *s. m.* sherbet, beverage, drink, sugar and water.
Sharbatí, *s. f.* a kind of lime or lemon.
Sharh, *s. f.* explanation, commentary, annotation, description; allowance, pay, rate.
Sharhwár, *adv.* explicitly.
Sharị, *adj.* conformable to the sharạ, lawful.
Sharíạt, *s. f.* the laws of Muhammad, law, justice, equity.
Sharíf, *adj.* noble, eminent, honourable, illustrious, a shell.
Sharífa, *s. m.* a custard-apple.
Shárị i ạmm, *s. m.* a public road, highway.
Sharík, *s. m.* a partner, an accomplice, associate, comrade.
Sharík honá, to partake, to participate.
Sharír, *adj.* vicious, wicked; also for Sarír.
Sharm, *s. f.* bashfulness, modesty, shame.
Sharmáná, *v. n.* to be ashamed, to feel shame, to be abashed.
Sharmá sharmí, *adv.* modestly.
Sharmáú, } **Sharmílá,** } *adj.* bashful, abashed.
Sharminda, *adj.* blushing, abashed, ashamed, modest.
Sharmindagí, *s. f.* bashfulness, modesty; shame, disgrace.
Sharq, *s. m.* the east; rising.

Sharqí, *adj.* eastern, oriental.
Sharr, *s. f.* wickedness, depravity, malignancy, evil.
Shart, *s. f.* condition, stipulation, agreement; a wager.
Shart bándhná, to stipulate; to bet, to wager.
Shartí, *adj.* conditional.
Shart karná, to stipulate, to agree, to bargain.
Shash, *adj.* six.
Shash o panj, (sixes and fives), confusion, perplexity.
Shash pahal, *adj.* having six sides, hexagonal; a hexagon.
Shástr, } *s. m.* scripture, science, in-
Shástra, } stitutes of religion, law, or letters, especially considered of divine origin.
Sháshtrárth, *s. m.* the object or true intent of the shástra, or sacred writings.
Shástrí, *adj.* skilled in Hindú law or religious books, one skilled in holy science.
Shástrí achchhar, the Debanágarí character.
Shatír, *s. m. prop.* Shahtír, a beam.
Shatranj, *s. f.* chess.
Shatranjbáz, a chess-player.
Shatranjí, *s. f.* a kind of carpet.
Shatranjíbáf, *s. m.* a carpet-weaver.
Shatru, *s. m.* an enemy.
Shatrutá, *s. f.* enmity.
Shattáh, *adj.* meretricious, lascivious, obscene, lewd.
Shauhar, *s. m.* a husband.
Shaukat, *s. f.* state, dignity, magnificence, majesty.
Shauq, *s. m.* desire, inclination, love, eagerness, fondness; gaiety, cheerfulness; curiosity.
Shauqín, *adj.* desirous, intent upon, fond of pleasure or curiosity; gay; lascivious.
Shauq zauq, *s. m.* pleasure, delight, gratification.
Shauwál, *s. m.* the tenth month of the Muhammadan year.
Sháyad, *adv.* possibly, probably; may be so, perchance, perhaps.
Sháyasta, *adj.* well-bred, polite.
Sházz, *adv.* seldom.
Shekh, *s. m. prop.* Shaikh, an old man, a venerable old man.
Shekhí, *s. f.* boasting, bragging.
Sher, *s. m.* a tiger, a lion.
Sherní, *s. f.* a lioness, a t gress.
Shewá, } *s. m.* business, trade, pro-
Shewa, } fession, habit, custom.
Shía, *s. m.* a follower of the sect of Alí.
Shiar, *s. m.* poetry, verse.
Shiarkhwání, *s. f.* reading or studying poetry.
Shiddat, *s. f.* violence, force, vehemence; adversity, affliction, difficulty.
Shifá, *s. f.* cure, remedy, healing, convalescence.
Shifá honá, or páná, to recover.
Shifákhána, *s. m.* a hospital.
Shigáf, *s. m.* split, rent, slit, cleft, fissure, crack, flaw, crevice.
Shíghra, *adj.* expeditious, quick, hasty, fast; *adv.* soon, quick, speedily.
Shíghra karná, to make haste.
Shigufta, *adj.* expanded, blooming, blown (as a flower.)
Shigufta honá, to be blown (a flower), to bloom, to be delighted.
Shikam, *s. m.* the belly.
Shikamparwar, *s.* a glutton.
Shikan, *s. f.* wrinkle, crease.
Shikanja, *s. m.* boards in which binders press books.
Shikár, *s. m.* hunting, chase, prey, game.
Shikárband, *s. m.* cords, &c., for tying game in or to (tied to a horse's saddle.)
Shikárbáz, *s. m.* a sportsman.
Shikárgáh, *s. f.* place for hunting in.
Shikárí, *adj.* of the chase, relating to hunting, &c.: *s. m.* a fowler, hunter, sportsman.

Shikár karná, to hunt, to catch (as prey.)
Shikár khelná, to go a hunting.
Shikast, *s. f.* breaking, fracture, defeat, deficiency, loss; *adj.* broken.
Shikasta, *adj.* broken, dispersed: *s. m.* the Persian running-hand.
Shikastadil, *adj.* distressed, afflicted.
Shikastadilí, *s. f.* distress, affliction.
Shikastagí, *s. f.* breaking, brokenness; defeat; dejection; affliction.
Shikastahál, *adj.* distressed, wretched, ruined.
Shikastahálí, *s. f.* indigence, distress, wretchedness.
Shikastakhátir, *adj.* distressed in mind, afflicted, offended.
Shikáyat, *s. f.* a complaint, accusation.
Shikm, *s. m.* the belly.
Shikoh, *s. f.* dignity, grandeur, pomp.
Shikra, *s. m.* a hawk, a falcon.
Shikwá, } *s. m.* complaint, upbraiding.
Skikwa, }
Shimál, *s. m.* the north; the northwind.
Shimálí, *adj.* northern.
Shimálnumá, *s. m.* the mariner's compass.
Shimar, *adj.* vile, infamous.
Shinákht, *s. f.* knowledge, understanding, acquainted with.
Shinás, *in compos.* knowing, intelligent, intimate with.
Shinásáí, *s. f.* acquaintance, knowledge.
Shinásí, *s. f. in compos.* knowing.
Shinawá, hearing, hearer.
Shír, *s. m.* milk.
Shíra, *s. m.* syrup, juice of fruit.
Shíráza, *s. m.* the worked head-bands in bound books.
Shírázbandí, *s. f.* a style of binding books with worked head-band.
Shírbirinj, *s. m.* rice-milk.
Shírgarm, *adj.* milk-warm, lukewarm.
Shírín, *adj.* sweet, pleasant, gentle, affable.
Shíríní, *s. f.* sweetness, eloquence.
Shiríntabą, *adj.* of gentle manners, of mild disposition.
Shírínzabán, *adj.* eloquent, affable, sweet-spoken.
Shirk, *s. m.* polytheism, paganism; partnership.
Shirkat, *s. f.* partnership.
Shírkhurda, }
Shírkhwár, } a suckling, an infant.
Shírkhwára, }
Shírmál, *s. f.* bread made with milk.
Shírní, *s. f.* sweetmeats, &c. offered in memory of saints, &c.
Shísha, *s. m.* glass, a bottle, a glass.
Shíshabáshá, *adj.* very delicate, tender.
Shíshagar, a glass-maker.
Shíshagarí, *s. f.* glass-making.
Shísham, *s. f.* a kind of wood.
Shíshamahall, a house or palace all hung with glass, a cabinet adorned with mirrors.
Shíshí, *s. f.* a small glass phial.
Shist, *s. f.* aim; a large fishing hook, (not used in angling with the hand, but left attached to a strong line which is fastened to the shore.)
Shishtáchár, *s. m.* see Sistáchár.
Shist bándhná, to aim.
Shitáb, *s. m.* haste, quickness; *adj.* quick, speedy; *adv.* quickly, expeditiously.
Shitábbáz, *adj*, hasty, expeditious.
Shitábí, *adv.* quick, hastily; *s. f.* quickness, haste, speed, despatch.
Shiv, } *s. m.* a name of Mahádeva.
Shivá, }
Shivrát, a night so called by the Hindús.
Shiwálá, *s. m.* a temple of Shiva.
Shlok, *s. m.* a verse, a stanza.
Sho, *in compos.* washing, washer.
Shob, *s. m.* washing.
Shoí, *s. m. f. in compos.* washing.
Shokh, *adj.* mischievous, pert, saucy, playful, wanton, presumptuous, insolent.

Shoḳhí, *s. f.* mischief, playfulness, wantonness, sauciness, coquetry.
Sholá, *s. m.* the name of a plant, the stalks of which, commonly called light-wood, are used as floats for fishing nets, and for making a light kind of hat.
Shola, *s. m.* a dish consisting of rice and pulse boiled together and given to sick persons.
Shor, *s. m.* cry; noise, outcry, clamour, din, renown, uproar, tumult: *adj.* salt, brackish.
Shora, *s. m.* nitre, saltpetre. [petre.
Shoragar, *s.m.* a manufacturer of salt-
Shorba, } *s. m.* broth, soup.
Shorbá, }
Shorbor, *adj.* very wet, drenched.
Shoriyat, *s. f.* saline quality. [hoot.
Shor machāná, to make a noise, to
Shorpusht, *adj.* quarrelsome, noisy.
Shorshár, *s. m.* noise, tumult, disturbance, bustle, clamour.
Shorwa, *s. m.* broth, soup.
Shorzamín, *s. f.* barren land.
Shosha, *s. m.* a particle, a part.
Shráddha, *s. m.* see Sráddha.
Shram, *s. m.* fatigue, toil.
Shresṭh, *adv.* best, most excellent, pre-eminent, senior.
Shuạ́, *s. f.* the rays of the sun, sunshine, radiance.
Shuạla, *s. m.* flame, blaze, light.
Shubha, *s. m.* doubt, suspicion, ambiguity, uncertainty.
Shubha honá, *v. n.* to be in doubt.
Shubha karná, } *v. a.* to doubt, to
Shubha láná, } suspect.
Shudaní, *s. f.* occurrence, coming to pass: *adj.* practicable, possible.
Shudbúd, *adv.* so so. [ment
Shughl. *s. m.* occupation, employ-
Shugúfa láná, to produce something new and wonderful.
Shugufta, *adj.* expanded, blooming, blown (as a flower.)
Shugufta honá, to be blown (a flower), to bloom, to be delighted.

Shuguftaḳhátirí, *s. f.* blooming or expansion of mind.
Shugun, *s. m.* augury, omen.
Shuhadá, *s. plur.* of Shahíd, martyrs.
Shuhdá, *s. m.* a rake, prodigal, debauchee, blackguard, scoundrel, vagabond.
Shuhdápan, *s. m.* raking, rakishness, debauchery, dissoluteness.
Shuhra, *s. m.* } fame, renown, cele-
Shuhrat, *s. f.* } brity, report, rumour, divulging.
Shujáạ, *adj.* brave, intrepid, bold.
Shujáạt, *s. f.* bravery, valour.
Shukr, *s. m.* thanks, gratitude; the planet Venus.
Shukrána, *s. m.* gratitude, acknowledgment of gratitude, thanksgiving.
Shukrguzár, *adj.* grateful, thankful.
Shukrguzárí, *s. f.* gratitude, thanksgiving, thanks.
Shukr karná, to thank, to return thanks, to acknowledge a favour.
Shukrwár, *s. m.* Friday.
Shúm, *adj.* miser, niggard.
Shumá, *pron. plur.* you.
Shumár, *s. m.* counting, numbering, number, account, estimation.
Shumárí, *s. f.* counting.
Shamár karná, to number, reckon, count, compute, regard.
Shúmí, *s. f.* avarice, niggardliness.
Shumṛá, *m.* } *adj.* miserly, avaricious;
Shúmṛá, *m.* } miser.
Shúmṛí, *f.* }
Shuqqa, *s. m.* a letter, a billet.
Shurafá, *s. plur.* of Sharíf, nobles, grandees. [ment.
Shurụ́, *s. m. f.* beginning, commence-
Shurụ́ honá, to be begun or commenced.
Shurụ́ karná, to commence, to begin.
Shushkárí, *s. f.* impelling a dog to the chase.
Shushkárná, *v. n.* to encourage or stimulate a dog to the chase, by the sound shush.

Shutur, *s. m.* a camel.
Shuturbán, a camel-driver (or keeper.)
Shuturmurgh, *s. m.* an ostrich.
Shuturqatár, a string of camels.
Shutursawár, mounted on a camel, rider of a camel.
Shuturwán, a camel-driver (or keeper.)
Shuúr, *s. m.* wisdom, intelligence, knowledge, discernment.
Shyám, *adj.* black, or dark blue.
Si, *adj.* three.
Sí, *adj.* thirty.
Sibandí, *s. m.* a military soldier employed in collecting rents.
Sichchhá, *s. f.* tuition, teaching.
Síchná, *v. a.* to water, to irrigate.
Sidara, *adj.* three-doored (room, &c.)
Siddat, *s. f. prop.* Shiddat, which see.
Siddha, *adj.* ready, completed, accomplished: valid (in law); proved (in logic); *s. f.* success, accomplishment of an object.
Siddhánt, *s. m.* result, consequence; a system of science.
Sidh, see Siddha.
Sídh, *adj.* straight, accurate.
Sídhá, *adj.* straight, right, direct, opposite; simple; fair; candid, upright; *s. m.* provisions, victuals (undressed.)
Sídháí, *s. f.* straightness, simplicity, candour, uprightness.
Sídhá karná, to straighten, to discipline.
Sídhápan, *s. m.* simplicity, candour.
Sidhárná, *v. n.* to go, to depart, to set off.
Sidháwat, *s. f.* candour, simplicity.
Sidq, *s. m.* truth, veracity, sincerity.
Sifálí, *adj.* earthen, earthenware.
Sifárish, *s. f.* recommendation, intercession, introduction.
Sifárishí, *s.* an intercessor.
Sifárish karná, to recommend, to intercede.
Sifárishnáma, *s. m.* a letter of introduction.
Sifat, *s. f.* praise: quality, attribute; a noun adjective.
Sifát, *s. plur.* of Sifat, qualities, &c.
Sifl, *s. m.* sediment.
Sifla *adj.* ignoble, mean, contemptible.
Sighrá, *prop.* Shíghra, which see.
Sígha, *s. m.* a word declinable and derivative, the mood of a verb conjugation, derivation; a form of words used in marriage ceremonies,
Sigosha, *s. m.* a triangle.
Sigrá, *adj.* every, the whole.
Siharná, *v. n.* to shiver, to shake with cold.
Sihhat, *s. f.* health, entireness, soundness, accuracy, correctness.
Sihr, *s. m.* enchantment, magic.
Sihrá, *s. m.* a chaplet, a garland, wreath (worn on the head by a bridegroom and bride at the marriage ceremony.)
Sihráná, *v. n.* see Sahiráná.
Síj. *s. m.* a species of Euphorbia, the milky hedge-plant.
Sijda, *s. m.* bowing so as to touch the ground with the forehead in adoration, especially to God, adoration.
Sijdagáh, *s. f.* the place of performing the Sijda.
Sijháná, *v. a.* to tan; to boil, to seethe, to melt.
Síjná, *v. n.* to exude, to sweat; to seethe, to boil, to dissolve, to become soft by boiling.
Sikáná, *v. a.* see Sikháná.
Sikandar, *n. prop.* Alexander the Great.
Sikandarí, *adj.* of or relating to Alexander; a kind of yard for measuring.
Sikanjabín, *s. f.* lime-juice or other acid mixed with sugar or honey.
Sikár, *s. m. prop.* Shikár, which see.
Sikast, *s. f. prop.* Shikast, which see,
Síkh, *s. f.* a spit, a skewer.

Sikh, *s. m.* a disciple, a scholar, a pupil; a follower of Nának.
Sikhái, *s. f.* teaching, instruction.
Sikháná, *v. a.* to teach, to admonish, to chastise.
Sikhar, *s. m.* three or more strings tied together forming a support to hang anything on; the cords of a bahangí; in which the baskets rest.
Síkháwaná, *v. a.* see Sikháná.
Síkhcha, *s. m.* a skewer, a small spit.
Síkhiyákabáb, *s. m.* meat roasted on a spit.
Síkhláná, } *v. a.* to teach, to admo-
Sikhláná, } nish, to chastise.
Síkhná, *v. a.* to learn, to acquire.
Síkhpá, rearing (a horse.)
Sikka, *s. m.* a coining die, an impression on money; sterling, current; stamped coin.
Sikláná, *v. a.* to teach.
Siklí, *prop.* Saiqal, which see.
Siklígar, *prop.* Saiqalgar, which see.
Siklí honá, see Saiqal honá.
Sikná, *v. a.* see Sikhná.
Sikná, *v. n.* to be toasted or parched: *v. a.* to learn, to acquire.
Síkrí, *s. f.* a wire-chain.
Siktá, *s. m.* a potsherd, shard.
Sikurná, *v. n.* to be shrunk.
Síl, *s. m.* habit, disposition; complaisance, civility, humanity, politeness, generosity.
Sil, *s. f.* a stone on which spices, &c. are ground, or knives sharpened; a stone (in general.)
Silafchí, *s. f.* see Silapchí. [sewing.
Siláí, *s. f.* the price of sewing; seam,
Siláná, *v. a.* to cause to sew, or stitch.
Silapchí, *s. f.* a wash-hand-basin of metal with a cover to it; ewer.
Silbattá, *s. m.* two stones with which spices, paint, &c, are ground.
Silí, *s. f.* a whetstone, a hone; the trunk of a tree when cut down; plank; the heap of grain and chaff on the threshing-floor.

Silpat, *adj.* smooth, even, level.
Silsilá, *s. m.* a chain, series, concatenation, succession, descent of a family, genealogy.
Silsil i baul, *s. m.* a diabetes, a morbid copiousness of urine.
Silwáná, *v. a.* to cause to be sewn.
Sílwant, *adj.* of good or amiable disposition, well-conducted.
Sím, *s. m.* silver.
Símá, *s. f.* limit, restriction, boundary.
Símáb, *s. m.* quicksilver, mercury.
Simat jáná, *v. n.* to shrivel, to shrink.
Simatná, *v. n.* to be concentrated, to shrink, to be contracted or drawn together, to shrivel.
Símbadan, silver-bodied, with a body fair as silver. [towards.
Simt, *s. f.* a way, path, side, quarter,
Símtan, see Simbadan. [griffin.
Símurgh, *s. m.* a fabulous bird, a
Síná, *v. a.* to sew, to stitch.
Sína, *s. m.* breast, bosom.
Sínaband, *s. m.* stays, bodice.
Sinakná, to blow the nose.
Sínazaní, *s. f.* beating the breast.
Sínazor, *adj.* robust, proud of strength.
Sínazorí, *s. f.* strength, robustness, force; pride of power.
Sínchái, *s. f.* the price paid for irrigation or watering.
Sínchná, *v. a.* to irrigate, to water.
Sindh, *s. m.* sea, ocean; the name of a country.
Sindhu, *s. m.* sea, ocean.
Sindúr, *s. m.* red lead, minium.
Sing, } *s. m.* a horn.
Síng, }
Singá, } *s. m.* a horn (musical.)
Síngá, }
Singár. *s. m.* ornament, dress, decoration, embellishment.
Singárdán, *s. m.* a toilet-bag or dressing-case.
Singárhár, *s. m.* the weeping Nyctanthes.
Singármez, *s. f.* a dressing-table.

Singárná, *v. a.* to dress, to decorate, to embellish, to adorn.
Singauṭí, a polishing tool, made of horn; an ornament of metal on the horns of a bullock.
Singh, *s. m.* a lion; the sign Leo; a title used by Hindús.
Singháṛá, *s. m.* a handkerchief folded diagonally; water-chestnut.
Singhásan, *s. m.* a throne.
Singhiní, *s. f.* a lioness.
Síngí, *s. f.* name of a kind of fish; a cup for cupping; a small horn (musical.)
Síngí lagáná, to cup.
Síngiyá, *s. m.* a kind of poison.
Síngṛá, } Singṛá, } *s. m.* a powder horn.
Singṛí, *s. f.* a small powder horn for priming with.
Síní, *s. f.* a salver, tray, trough.
Sínk, *s. f.* the culm of the grass of which brooms are made.
Sínkiyá, *adj.* striped.
Sinn, *s. m.* age, period of life.
Sinn o sál, age, period of life.
Síp, *s. f.* a shell; kind of mango.
Sipáh, *s. f.* (used in the plural,) soldiers, an army.
Sipáhá, *s. m.* a tripod, trivet.
Sipahal, *adj.* trilateral.
Sipahar, *s. m.* } Sipaharí, *s. f.* } afternoon, from midday to three o'clock.
Sipáhgarí, } Sipahgarí, } *s. f.* the miltary profession or art.
Sipáhí, *s. m.* a soldier, military.
Sipáh phir jání (implies) a revolt or treachery in an army.
Sipáhsálár, } Sipahsálár, } *s, m.* a general, a commander of an army.
Sipái, *s. f.* a tripod, trivet, a three-legged stool or table.
Sipar, *s. f.* a shield.
Sipára, *s. m.* one of the thirty sections into which the Qurán is divided.
Sipárish, *s. f.* a recommendation, intercession, introduction.
Sípí. *s. f.* a shell.
Sir, *s. m.* the head, the top.
Siṛá, *adj.* mad, insane.
Sirá, *s. m.* head, extremity, end.
Sirajná, } Sirájná, } *v. a.* to create, to produce, to form.
Siráná, *v. a.* to cool, to make cold: *s. m.* place of the head.
Sírat, *s. f.* way of life, morals, manners, conduct.
Siráyat, *s. f.* penetrating.
Sircharhá, *adj.* proud, haughty.
Sircharháná, to exalt, to assume, to be arrogant; to show respect.
Sirchoṭ, *s. m.* displeasure, disgust.
Sird dawál, *s. f.* headstall; reins of a bridle.
Sir de de márná, to be desperate.
Sir dharná, to be obedient.
Sir dhunná, } Sir ḍuláná, } to shake the head from affliction, &c.
Sirf, *adv.* purely, merely, only, solely, alone: *adj.* pure, mere.
Sírgarm, *adj. prop.* Shírgarm, which see.
Sir ghúmná, to be giddy or dizzy, to swim (the head.)
Sirháná, *s. m.* the head part or side of anything (as of a tomb or bedstead), the place where the head rests or reclines.
Siṛhí, } Síṛhí, } *s. f.* a ladder, stair, step; degree.
Siṛí, *adj.* mad, insane.
Siris, or Sirish, *s. m.* the name of a tree.
Sirisht, *s. f.* nature, temperament, constitution, disposition.
Sirka, or Sirká, *s. m.* vinegar.
Sirkaṭá, beheaded, decapitated.
Sir ke bhal, *adv.* headlong.
Sir ke zor, with all (one's) might.
Sir khujáná, to court punishment.
Sirkí, *s. f.* a kind of reed of which mats are made, reed grass; a sort of mat to keep off rain.
Sir márná, to take great pains, to search diligently.

Sir muṇḍáná, to quit one's connexions and adopt a life of mendicity.

Sir nawáná, to be humble, to be obedient.

Sírní, *s. f. prop.* Shírní, which see.

Sir parastí karná, to protect, to aid.

Sir par chaṛháná, to spoil (as a child, &c.); to raise an inferior above one's self; to show respect.

Sir par ḳhák ḍálná, to lament.

Sir pherná, to revolt from obedience.

Sir píṭná, to lament.

Sirrí, *adj.* mad, insane.

Sir ṭhaṭhauwal, Sir ṭhaṭhauwar, *s. m.* salutation (with displeasure.)

Sir ṭorná, *v. a.* to subdue.

Sir uṭháná, to rebel, to rise up against one.

Sir uṭháte hí pámál honá, to be crushed in the commencement of one's undertaking.

Sís, *s. m.* the head.

Sísá, *s. m.* lead; *prop.* Shísha, which see.

Sisakná, *v. n.* to sob.

Sisála, *adj.* triennial.

Sís charháná, see Sir chaṛháná.

Sishṭáchár, *s. m.* see Sisṭáchár.

Sísí, *s. f. prop.* Shísí, a small glass phial.

Siskí, *s. f.* sobbing; an almost imperceptible hole (in a vessel, &c.)

Siskiyáṉ bharná, to sob.

Síso, *s. m.* a kind of wood or name of a tree.

Sísphúl, *s. m.* an ornament for the head (worn by females.)

Sisṭáchár, *s. m.* politeness, complaisance, good manners.

Sít, *s. f.* dew; cold, wetness, moistness.

Sítá, *n. prop.* the wife of Ráma.

Sitáish, *s. f.* praise, returning thanks.

Sítal, *adj.* cool, cold.

Sítalá, *s. f.* small-pox.

Sítalchíní, *s. f.* allspice.

Sítalpáṭí, *s. f.* a kind of fine cool mat.

Sítaltá, *s. f.* coolness.

Sitam, *s. m.* tyranny, oppression, injury, violence.

Sitamgar, Sitamgár, *s. m.* a tyrant, an oppressor: *adj.* tyrannical.

Sitamgarí, *s. f.* see Sitam.

Sítáphal, *s. m.* the custard-apple.

Sitár, *s. m.* a kind of guitar with three strings.

Sitára, *s. m.* a star; a kind of firework; name of a musical instrument with three strings.

Sitáragán, *plur.* of Sitára, stars.

Sitára peshání, having a star in the forehead.

Sitárashinás, *s. m.* an astrologer.

Sitárbáz, *s. m.* one who plays on the guitar.

Sitárí, *s. f.* a small guitar.

Sitáriyá, *s. f. m.* see Sitárbáz.

Sítbáí, *s. f.* the palsy.

Síṭh, *s. f.* dregs of betel, or of anything that has been chewed.

Síṭhá, *adj.* insipid, tasteless, pithless.

Síṭháí, *s. f.* insipidness, tastelessness.

Síṭhí, *s. f.* whistling; dregs.

Síṭí, *s. f.* whistling.

Síṭí bajáná, to whistle.

Síṭíbáz, a whistler.

Sítjwar, *s. m.* ague.

Sítkál, *s. m.* winter, the dewy season.

Sítlá, *s. f.* small-pox.

Siṭṭhí, *s. f.* dregs, dross, lees.

Siṭṭí, *s. f.* whistling.

Siva, *s. m.* name of an Indian deity.

Sivarát, Sivarátrí, *s. f.* the night of Siva, a Hindú festival.

Siwá, Siwáe, *adj.* more, better: *prep.* or *postpos.* besides, without, except, but; over and above.

Siwálá, *s. m.* a temple of Mahádeva.

Síwan, *s. m.* sewing.

Siwáná, Siwána, *s. m.* verge, limit, boundary,

Siwár, *s. m.* see Sewár.

Siyáh, *adj.* black, unfortunate, bad.

Siyah, *adj.* black.

Siyáhá, *s. m.* an account-book, or written book.
Siyáhá karná, to take an account of.
Siyáhdil, *adj.* black-hearted, malevolent.
Siyáhfám, *adj.* black.
Siyáhgosh, *s. m.* name of an animal.
Siyáhí, *s. f.* blackness; ink; blacking.
Siyáh karná, see Siyáhá karná.
Siyáhposh, *adj.* clad in black.
Siyáhrú, *adj.* black-faced; unlucky; disgraced.
Siyáhtálú, *adj.* whose curses prevail.
Siyál, *s. m.* a jackal.
Siyán, } *adj.* see Syáná.
Siyáná, }
Siyáq, *s. m.* arithmetic by the Arabic alphabet; accounts.
Siyár, *s. m.* a jackal.
Siyásat, *s. f.* punishment, pain, chastisement, pang, agony.
Siyásat karná, to chastise, to punish.
Siyásat meṉ honá, to be in pain.
Slok, *s. m.* see Shlok.
Snán, *s. m.* bathing.
Sneh, *s. m.* love, kindness, affection.
Snehí, *adj.* kind, affectionate.
So, *pron. correl*, that, he, she, it; so: *postpos.* from, &c. See Se.
Soá, *s. m.* fennel.
Sobhá, *s. f*, beauty, splendour, ornament, dress, decoration.
Sobháw, *s. m.* nature, natural state, property or disposition, genius.
Sobhná, *v. n.* to become, to befit.
Soch, *s. m.* consideration, reflection, thought, meditation.
Sochná, *v. a.* to consider, to think, to meditate, to reflect.
Sodh, *s. f.* discharge (of debt); search, inquiry.
Sodhná, *v. a.* to pay, to discharge (a debt), to liquidate; to refine metals.
Sog, *s. m.* affliction, grief, sorrow, lamentation, anguish.
Sogí, *adj.* afflicted, grieved.
Sogwár, *adj.* afflicted, sorrowful.
Sogwárí, *s. f.* affliction, grief, sorrow.
Sohágá, *s. m.* borax.
Sohán, *s. f.* a kind of sweetmeat; a file.
Sohíṉ, *adv.* before, in front of.
Sohná, *v. n.* to become, to beseem; *v. a.* to weed.
Soí, that, very, he himself.
Sojh, *s. f.* straightness, directness.
Sojhá, *adj.* straight, direct.
Sok, *s. m.* affliction, grief, lamentation, sorrow.
Sokh, *adj. prop.* Shoḳh, which see.
Sokhí, *s. f. prop.* Shoḳhí, which see.
Sokhná, *v. a.* to soak up, absorb.
Soḳht, *adj.* burnt: *s. f.* burning.
Soḳhta, *adj.* burnt, scorched: *s. m.* tinder.
Soḳhtagí, *s. f.* vexation, heartburning.
Solah, *adj.* sixteen.
Solahwáṉ, *adj.* the sixteenth.
Som, *s. m.* the moon; Monday.
Sompná, *v. a.* to deliver over, commit to charge, give, consign, resign, intrust, deposit.
Somwár, *s. m.* Monday.
Soṉ, *s. f.* an oath: *postpos.* from, &c. [See Se.
Son, *s. m.* name of a river.
Soná, *v. n.* to sleep; (*met.*) to die; *s. m.* gold.
Sonahlá, *adj.* golden.
Sonahlá pání, *s. m.* gilding.
Sonahrá, *adj.* golden.
Sondhá, *s. m.* smelling like that of a new earthen vessel when wetted, or from parching of pulse.
Sondháhaṭ, *s. f.* fragrance; a smell like that of new earth or anything burnt (as food, &c., from being kept too long on the fire.)
Sondhná, *v. a.* to rub cloth in mud preparatory to washing; to mix, to smear.
Sone ká nawálá, an expensive banquet, a delicious morsel.
Soṉh, *s. f.* an oath.
Soṉh dená, to adjure, to swear.
Sonhín, *adv.* face to face, opposite, before, in front.

Soṇh khiláná, to adjure, to make swear, to administer an oath.
Sonṭ, *s. f.* dry ginger.
Sonṭá, *s. m*, a club, mace; pestle.
Sonṭebardár, a mace-bearer.
Sonṭh, *s. f.* dry-ginger; a miser.
Sorá, *s. m. prop.* Shora, nitre, saltpetre.
Sorah, *adj.* sixteen.
Soraṭh, *s. f.* name of a musical mode.
Sosan, *s. f.* a lily.
Sosní, *s. f.* a bluish colour.
Sot, *s. m. f.* } a spring, a fountain, a
Sotá, *s. m.* } stream, a rivulet.
Sotá, *part. pres.* asleep: *s. m.* asleep, sleeping.
Soú, see Soí.
Soz, *s. m.* a stanza of a marsiya or elegiac poem.
Sozák, *s. m.* a gonorrhœa, a clap.
Sozan, *s. f.* pricker (of a gun.)
Sozish, *s. f.* burning, inflammation, pain, vexation.
Sozní, *s. f.* a kind of quilted coverlet.
Sráddha, *s. m.* funeral obsequies, consisting in the feeding of priests, and other prescribed ceremonies in honour of ancestors.
Sram, *s. m.* fatigue, toil, pains.
Sráp, *s. m.* cursing, an imprecation.
Srawan, *s. m.* the ear, the act of hearing.
Sresh, *s. m.* glue.
Sreshṭh, *adj.* best, most, excellent; pre-eminent.
Srí, *s. f.* a word always written at the beginning of the Hindú proper names of persons, like master or sir.
Srishṭ, } *s. f.* the creation, the
Srishṭi, } world.
Stán, (affixed to certain words, denotes) place, station; as Hindústán, India.
Sthán, *s. m.* place, station, abode, residence.
Sthápan, *s. m.* causing to stand, placing, fixing, founding, erecting.
Sthápaná, *s. f.* ordering, arranging.
Sthápit, *part. pass.* established, placed, fixed, founded, erected.
Sthir, *adj.* settled, steadfast, stable, fixed; mild, calm.
Strí, *s. f.* a woman or female in general; a wife.
Stuti, *s. f.* praise, eulogy.
Su, *prepos.* good, well, easy; (in Braj) *postpos.* from or of whom, by, with, of, &c.
Súá, *s. m.* a parrot; a packing-needle; a needle with which gunny bags are sewed.
Súar, *s. m.* a hog.
Súarí, *s. f.* a sow.
Súar ká gosht, pork.
Súba, *s. m.* a province; a governor.
Súbadár, *s. m.* the chief of a province; a military officer among Indian troops.
Súbadárí, *s. f.* the government of a province; viceroyalty.
Subah, *s. f.* morning dawn.
Subah i kázib, just before daybreak, the false dawn.
Subah i sádiq, dawn of day.
Súbaját, *s. plur.* of Súba, provinces.
Súbaran, } *s. m.* pure gold: *adj.*
Súbarn, } golden.
Subás, } *s. f.* sweet smell, fragrance,
Súbás, } odour, perfume.
Subh, *adj.* good, pleasant, agreeable, fortunate, auspicious.
Súbhá, *s. m. prop.* Shubha, which see.
Sub'han, in the morning, at dawn.
Sub'hán, *s. m.* praising, glorifying (God); a title of the Deity.
Sub'hánalláh, *interj.* O God! O holy God! Good God! Ha!
Subháw, } *s. m.* good disposition, na-
Súbháw, } ture, natural state, property, disposition: *adj.* well-disposed, of good disposition.
Subhítá, } *s. m.* opportunity, conve-
Subítá, } nience, time, leisure.
Subkái, } *s. f.* lightness, levity, fri-
Subka'í, } volousness, indignity,
Subkí, } dishonour, disgrace.

Subuk, *adj.* light (either in weight or character), unsteady.
Subuk mizáj, of a fickle temper.
Subút, *s. m.* firmness, stability, confirmation by evidence, conviction, proof: *adj.* firm, proved.
Suchet, *adj.* attentive, mindful, careful, cautious.
Súchham, *adj.* subtle, thin, slender, minute, small.
Suchit, } Súchit, } *adj.* at leisure, disengaged, at ease, attentive.
Súd, *s. m.* profit, interest, usury.
Suḍaul, *adj.* well-shaped, graceful.
Súdbaṭṭá, profit and loss.
Sudbud, *adj.* see Sudbudh.
Suddháṇ, *adj.* together with.
Sudh, *s. f.* memory, remembrance, consciousness; *adj.* accurate, correct, pure, clear, unpolluted.
Súdhá, *adj.* simple, artless; straight.
Suḍhab, *adj.* well-shaped, elegant.
Súdhái, *s. f.* simplicity, artlessness.
Suḍhál, *adj.* neat, elegant, graceful.
Sudháṇ, together with.
Sudháná, *v. a.* to put in mind, to cause to remember.
Sudharná, *v. n.* to correct, to be mended, to avail, to succeed.
Sudhárná, *v. a.* to adorn, to adjust, to arrange, to rectify, to mend.
Sudhbudh, *s. f.* sense, perception, care, correct knowledge.
Sudh lená, to take care of, to look after, to inquire into.
Súdí, *adj.* (money) borrowed at interest, (money) at interest.
Sudí, *s. f.* the light half of the lunar month, or from the new to the full moon.
Súdḳhor, an usurer.
Súdmand, *adj.* profitable, useful, beneficial, lucrative.
Súdmandí, *s. f.* profitableness.
Súdr, } Súdra, } *s. m.* a person of the fourth or servile tribe among the Hindús. [caste.
Súdrání, *s. f.* a female of the Súdr

Sufaid, *adj.* white.
Sufaida, *s. m.* the dawn; whiteness, white lead.
Sufaidí, *s. f.* whiteness.
Sufed, *adj.* white.
Súfí, *s. m.* a Sofi.
Súfíya, the sect of Súfís.
Sufúf, *s. m.* powder (medicine); the rags put in the bottom of an inkstand to absorb the ink.
Súgá, *s. m.* a paroquet.
Sugan, *s. m.* an omen, an augury.
Sugand, } Sugandh, } Súgandh, } *s. m.* good smell, odour, perfume, fragrance, *adj.* fragrant, odoriferous.
Sughaṛ, *adj.* elegant, accomplished, beautiful, virtuous.
Sughṛáí, *s. m.* } Sughṛápan, *s. f.* } elegancy, accomplishment.
Sugun, *s. m.* see Sugan.
Súhá, *adj.* red, crimson.
Suhág, *s. m.* the red marks in the forehead of a woman whose husband is alive.
Suhágá, *s. m.* borax.
Suhágan, *s. f.* a married woman whose husband is alive.
Suhágpuṛá, *s. m.* a paper of ingredients for painting the head, presented by the bridegroom to the bride.
Suhál or Suhálí, *s. f.* bread (or cakes) fried in butter or oil.
Suháná, *adj.* agreeable, pleasant, charming: *v. n.* to be agreeable, to please, to be liked or approved of.
Súháná, *v. n.* to become, to beseem: *v. a.* to weed; see also Suháná.
Suhátá, *adj.* agreeable, charming.
Suháwan, *adj.* agreeable, pleasant, charming.
Suháwaná, see Suháná.
Suhbat, *s. f.* companionship, society, an assembly, a fair; coition.
Suhbatdárí, *s. f.* associating, acquaintance.
Suhbatí, *s. m.* companion, comrade.
Suhdá, *s. m. prop.* Shuhdá, which see.

Súí, or Súíṉ, *s. f.* a needle.
Suj, *s. f.* swelling, rising.
Sújá, *s. m.* a borer, a gimlet, an awl.
Sújan, *s. f.* swelling, rising.
Sujáná, *v. a.* to cause to swell.
Sujaní, *s. f.* see Sozní.
Sújh, *s. f.* sight, perception.
Sujháná, *v. a.* to show, to make understand.
Sújhná, } Sujhná, } *v. n.* to be visible, to be seen, to appear, to seem, to be able, to be seen.
Sújí, *s. f.* the heart of wheat, as flour.
Sújná, *v n.* to swell, to rise.
Súk, *s. m.* the planet Venus; Friday.
Súká, *adj.* dry: *s. m.* a quarter of a rupee piece.
Sukal, *adj.* white.
Sukalpachchh, *s. m.* the light half of the month, the fifteen days from new to full moon.
Sukar, *s. m. prop.* Shukr, thanks, gratitude.
Sukaṛná, *v. n.* to be shrunk or contracted, to shrink; to draw in, to collect, to shrivel.
Sukh, *s. m.* ease, tranquillity, easy circumstances, content, happiness, pleasure, delight.
Sukhá, } Súkhá, } *adj.* dry: *s. m.* dry tobacco eaten with betel-leaf.
Suḳhan, *s. m.* speech, language; a word.
Sukháná, *v. a.* to dry, to emaciate, to cause to pine away; to evaporate.
Suḳhan ḍálná, *v. a.* to ask, to question, to interrogate.
Suḳhan takiya, *s. m.* a cant word introduced into one's conversation without any meaning, an expletive.
Suḳhanwar, *adj.* eloquent.
Suḳhanwarí, *s. f.* eloquence.
Sukhchain, *s. m.* ease, rest, tranquillity.
Sukhdáí, *adj.* ease-affording, comforter, giver of ease.
Sukhdarsan, *s. m* a shrub, the juice of which is given for the ear-ache.
Sukhdáyak, *adj.* see Sukhdáí.

Sukhí, *adj.* at ease, happy, tranquil, contented, comfortable.
Sukhí ḳhatáí, a very thin person.
Sukhit, *adj.* tranquil.
Sukh karná, to live at ease.
Sukhláná, *v. a.* see Sukháná,
Sukhná, } Súkhná, } *v. n.* to dry, dry up, evaporate, fall away, to pine away, shrivel, wither. &c.
Sukh páná, to get ease, rest, leisure,
Sukhtalá, *s. m.* a piece of leather placed on the sole within the shoe.
Suḳhun, see Suḳhan.
Súkí, *s. f.* a quarter of a rupee piece.
Súkná, *v. n.* to dry, to become dry.
Sukr, *s. m.* the planet Venus; Friday.
Sukrit, *s. f.* virtue, a good action, moral merit.
Sukṭá, *adj.* lean, thin, dry, emaciated.
Sukṭí, *adj.* lean, thin, dry, emaciated: *s. f.* dry fish.
Sukucháná, } Sukuchná, } *v. n.* to be ashamed, to be afraid, to be abashed.
Sukumár, *adj.* soft, delicate, tender.
Sukúnat, *s. f.* residence, dwelling, habitation.
Sukút, *s. f.* silence, quietness, peace.
Sukwár, *adj.* delicate, feeble.
Súl, *s. m. f.* colic; the point of a spear.
Sulachchhan, *s. m.* good distinguishing mark or character.
Sulá dená, to kill, to murder.
Sulagná, *v. n.* to light, to be kindled, to be inflamed.
Sulah, *s. f.* see Sulh.
Sulaimán, *n. prop.* Solomon the son of David.
Sulaimání, *adj.* belonging to Solomon: *s. m.* an onyx.
Sulajhná, *v. n.* to be unravelled or disentangled.
Suláná, *v. a.* to cause to sleep, to kill, to murder.
Sulfa, *s. m.* little balls of tobacco smoked in a huqqa, without the intervention of a tile.

Sulgáná, *v. a.* to light, to inflame, to kindle.

Sulh, *s. f.* peace, reconciliation, treaty, concord, truce.

Sulha, *s. m.* friendship.

Súlí, *s. f*, an impaling stake.

Súlí chaṛháná, } to impale.
Súlí dená, }

Suljháná, *v. a.* to unravel, to disentangle.

Sultán, *s. m.* a prince, a sovereign, an emperor, sultan.

Sultání, *adj.* regal, princely: *s. f.* a kind of broad-cloth.

Sulúk, *s. m.* manner, mode, conduct, intercourse, treatment, civility, kindness, attention.

Sulúk karná, to treat, to proceed with, to treat with kindness.

Sulwáná, *v. a.* to cause to put to sleep.

Sum, *s. m.* a hoof.

Súm, *s. m.* a miser.

Sumár, *s. m. prop.* Shumár, which see.

Sumaran, *s. m.* remembrance: *s. f.* a small rosary, or string of beads.

Súmarin, *s. f.* a niggard, a miser.

Sumaṛná, *v. a.* to remember, to keep in memory; to mention.

Sumbá, *s. m.* a sponge-staff, a ramrod.

Sumbul, *s. m.* spikenard (to which the locks of a mistress are compared.)

Sumiran, *s. m.* see Sumaran.

Sumirná, *s. m.* see Sumarná.

Súmní, *s. f.* a sow.

Sumran, *s. m.* see Sumaran.

Sun, *adj.* insensible, without sensation, palsied; void, dreary, desolate and silent.

Sún, *adj.* silent, dreary, dismal.

Súná, *adj.* empty, deserted, void.

Sunahrá, } *adj.* golden, made of gold.
Sunahrí, }

Sunáná, *v. a.* to cause to hear, to inform, to tell, to warn, to advise.

Sunanhár, *s. m.* hearer.

Sunár, *s. m.* a goldsmith.

Sunárí, *adj.* clever, skilful: *s. f.* the business of a goldsmith.

Sunární, *s. f.* a goldsmith's wife.

Sunbahrí, *s. f.* name of a disease.

Súnḍ, *s. f.* proboscis of an elephant.

Súnḍá, *s. m.* a weevil, or small insect in grain.

Sundar, *adj.* beautiful, handsome, comely, seemly, good, virtuous.

Sundarí, *s. f.* woman; beauty, comeliness; name of an elastic timber tree.

Sundartá, *s. f.* beauty, handsomeness.

Sundháwaṭ, *s. m.* smell, perfume, odour, scent; an earthy smell.

Súnḍkí, *s. m.* a pillow under a saddle.

Sungháná, *v. a.* to cause to smell.

Súnghná, *v. a.* to smell.

Súnghní, *s. f.* snuff.

Súngná, } *v. a.* to smell.
Sungná, }

Sungun lená, *v. a.* to act the spy.

Sunidrá, *s. f.* sound sleep.

Sunná, *v. a.* to hear, to hearken, listen or attend to: *s. m.* hearing; a dot, a cipher.

Sunnat, *s. f.* circumcision; the traditions of Muhammad.

Sunnáṭá, *s. m.* see Sannáṭa.

Sunnat karná, *v. a* to circumcise.

Sunní, *s. m.* an orthodox Muhammadan.

Suṇph, *s. f.* aniseed.

Súṇṛí, *s. m.* a distiller and vender of spirituous liquors.

Súṇs, *s. m.* a porpoise.

Sunsán, *adj.* void, dreary, desolate and silent, still, lonely, dismal.

Súnthná, } *v. a.* to strip leaves off vegetables, &c., to draw (a sword.)
Súntná, }

Súnya, *s. m.* a dot, a cipher.

Súp, *s. m.* a kind of basket for winnowing corn with.

Súpábená, } *s. m.* name of a bird, a swallow.
Súpábení, }

Súpárá, or **Supárá**, *s. m.* glans penis.

Supárí, *s. f.* betel-nut; glans penis.
Supárish, *s. f.* see Sifárish.
Supath, *s. m.* a good road, good conduct.
Suphal, *adj.* bearing good fruit, fruitful, profitable, useful.
Súpiyárí, *s. f.* betel-nut.
Supurd, *s. f.* charge, keeping, care, trust, custody.
Supurd honá, to be consigned to one's care.
Supurdí, *s. f.* the article, &c., given up.
Supurd karná, to give in charge, to recommend to one's care, to consign, to intrust.
Supút, Suputr, } *s. m.* a tractable or dutiful son.
Supyárí, *s. f.* betel-nut.
Sur, *s. m.* a god, a deity; tone, melody, accent, note; a vowel.
Súr, *s. m.* a hero: *s. f.* a kind of musical instrument, a horn, a trumpet.
Súra, *s. m.* a chapter or division of the Qurán.
Súrá, *s. m.* a hero.
Surágh, *s. m.* search, inquiry, spying.
Surágh lená, to search, to seek, to spy, to inquire for.
Suráhí, *s. f.* a goblet, a long-necked flask, a goglet, a jar, a jug.
Suráhídár, *adj.* shaped in form of a Suráhí (a pearl.)
Súraj, *s. m.* the sun.
Súraj gahan, Súraj grahan, } *s. m.* eclipse of the sun.
Súrajmukhí, *s. f.* sunflower.
Súrákh, *s. m.* a hole, orifice, passage.
Surákh, *s. m. prop.* Surágh, which see.
Surang, *s. f.* a mine (particularly dug by thieves), a subterraneous passage: *adj.* light bay (horse.)
Surap, *s. f.* sipping or sucking up (as broth) or the noise made thereby.
Surapná, *v. n.* to sip.
Surat, *s. f.* see Surt.
Súrat, *s. f.* form, figure, face, countenance, portrait, probability; manner; condition, state, circumstances. See also Súra.
Súratan, *adv.* apparently.
Súratáshná, an acquaintance.
Súratáshnáí, *s. f.* acquaintance.
Súrat i hál, *s. f.* a statement of facts, written declaration.
Súrbír, *s. m.* a hero, a champion.
Súrdás, *n. prop.* name of a Hindú poet and singer who was blind; hence a blind man is called Súrdás.
Surkh, *adj.* red.
Surkha, *s. m.* a sort of pigeon of a [red colour.
Surkhá, *adj.* of a white, or gray, or cream colour (a horse.)
Surkháb, *s. m.* name of a bird.
Surkhbádá, *s. m.* the name of a disorder, Anthony's fire, erysipelas.
Surkhí, *s. f.* redness; brickdust.
Surkhposh, *adj.* dressed in red.
Surkhrú, *adj.* honourable, unabashed.
Surkhsufaid, *adj.* fair.
Súrmá, *adj.* bold, brave.
Surma, *s. m.* collyrium.
Surmadán, Surmadání, } a box for holding Surma.
Surma honá, to be reduced to an impalpable powder.
Surma'í, *adj.* of the colour of Surma, greyish.
Surmán, *adj.* brave, bold.
Surmápan, *s. m.* bravery.
Sur miláná, to sing in tune.
Sursuráhat, *s. f.* the noise of a snake in creeping or of a trailed rope, &c.
Sursuráná, *v. n.* to creep along as a snake, to make the noise a snake does when creeping.
Sursurí, *s. f.* titillation.
Surt, *s. f.* recollection, consideration, reflection, memory.
Surtá, Surtílá, } *adj.* mindful, considerate, attentive, prudent.
Surú, *s. m. f. prop.* Shurú, which see.
Surukná, Surukná, } *v. a.* to swallow by gulps, to gulp.

Surúp, *adj.* handsome, beautiful.
Surúr, *s. m.* pleasure, joy, cheerfulness.
Suryání, *adj.* Syriac, the Syriac language.
Sús, *s. m.* a porpoise.
Susandes, *s. m.* good tidings.
Susar, *s. m.* father-in-law.
Súsí, *s. f.* a kind of cloth.
Susíl, *adj.* well-disposed, goodnatured, polite.
Suskárná, *v. n.* to sibilate, to hiss.
Susrá, *s. m.* father-in-law.
Susrál, **Susrár**, *s. f.* father-in-law's house or family.
Sust, *adj.* relaxed, weak, frail, lazy, negligent, slothful, idle, slow, indolent, inactive, languid, feeble.
Sustáná, *v. n.* to rest.
Susthir, *adj.* firm, ready, stable.
Sustí, *s. f.* relaxation, languor, laziness, slothfulness, idleness, slowness, negligence, dilatoriness.
Sust iạtiqád, *adj.* lax in confidence, fickle.
Sust, or Sustí karná, to relax, to work lazily.
Sustípaná, *s. f.* see Sustí.
Sustí ṭorná, to break one's laziness.
Sut, *s. m.* a son, a male child.
Sút, *s. m.* thread, yarn; a tendril, a stamen (in botany.)
Sutá, *s. f.* a daughter.
Sutár, *s. m.* time, opportunity.
Sutárí, *s. f.* an awl, a bodkin.
Suthan, **Súthan**, **Súthná**, *s. m.* drawers, trousers.
Súthní, *s. f.* drawers; an edible root.
Suthrá, *adj.* good, well, excellent, elegant, neat, beautiful, adorned.
Suthráí, *s. f.* neatness, beauty, elegance.
Sútí, *adj.* made of cotton thread.
Sútlí, *s. f.* string, twine.
Sútná, *v. n* to sleep.
Suṭukná, *v. a.* to swallow by gulps with a noise, to become afraid.
Suwaiyá, *s. m.* a sleeper.
Suwál, *s. m.* interrogation, questioning, question, query, proposition, request, begging.
Suwálí, *s. m.* a questioner.
Suwál karná, to ask a question, to interrogate, to beg.
Suwáná, *v. a.* to cause to sleep.
Swád, *s. m.* see Sawád.
Swádit, *adj.* delicious, relishing, of high flavour.
Swámí, *s. m.* a master, owner, lord, a husband, proprietor; the ḍanḍí faqírs are so called.
Swán, *s. m.* a dog, a hound.
Swáng, *s. m.* mimicry, imitation, disguise, sham.
Swángí, *s. m.* an actor, a mimic.
Swáng láná, to imitate, &c.
Swapna, *s. m.* a dream.
Swar, *s. m.* a vowel.
Swarg, *s. m.* heaven; the sky.
Swarga lok, *s. m.* paradise.
Swargí, **Swargiyá**, *adj.* heavenly, celestial.
Swárth, *s. m.* self-interest, selfishness; having one's own object.
Swárthí, *adj.* selfish.
Swarúp, *s. m.* see Sarúp.
Swás, **Swásá**, *s. m.* breath, respiration, breathing: life.
Swáti, *s. f.* the fifteenth mansion of the moon.
Swátibúnd, a drop of rain fallen when the moon is in the fifteenth mansion, which, if into a shell, is believed to become a pearl.
Swayambar, *s. m.* a girl's electing a husband for herself.
Swet, *adj.* white.
Syám, *adj.* black, or dark blue.
Syáná, *adj.* cunning, artful, shrewd, sly, knowing, sagacious, clever, mature (in understanding); grown up.
Syánpan, **Syánpaná**, *s. m.* cunning, art.
Syúnṭhá, *s. m.* tongs.

T.

Tá, *adv.* to, until, as far as, so far, whilst, as long as, even to, in order that, to the end that, in such a manner that.

Taạffun, *s. m.* stink, fetor, fetidness.

Taạiyun, *s. m.* appointing, appointment, establishment, deputing.

Taạjjub, *s. m.* wondering, admiration, astonishment, surprise, amaze.

Taạjjub honá, to be astonished.

Taạjjub karná, to wonder, to admire.

Taạlá, *adj.* most high.

Taạl alláh, *interj.* good God! *s.* the most high God.

Taạlluq, *s. m.* relationship, dependence, connexion, concern, appertaining; a manor, a lordship, an estate.

Taạlluqa, *s. m.* landed property, fee, manor; connexion, relationship.

Taạlluqát, *s. plur.* connexions, concerns.

Taạlluqát i dunyawí, worldly concerns.

Taạlluqdár, *s. m.* the lord of a manor, the owner of an estate, the proprietor of a taạlluq.

Taạlluqdárí, *s. f.* the tenure, office or estate of a taạlluqdár.

Taạlluq rakhná, to appertain, to belong, to depend.

Taạm, *s. m.* victuals, food.

Taammul, *s. m.* meditation, reflection, consideration.

Taammul karná, to collect one's self, to consider, to reflect.

Taạshshuq, *s. m.* falling in love, making love, being in love.

Taassuf, *s. m.* brooding over affliction, pining, lamenting, grief, regret, remorse.

Taassuf karná, to grieve, lament, pine, regret (over.)

Táạt, *s. f.* devotion, obedience.

Taạzzur, *s. m.* apology.

Táb, *s. f.* heat, light; power; endurance; twisting; contortion,

Tab, *adv.* then, at that time, so soon afterwards.

Tabạ, *s. f.* nature, genius, temperament, disposition.

Tabábat, *s. f.* the practice of medicine.

Tabaddul, *s. m.* change, alteration.

Tabáh, } *adj.* bad, wicked, depraved,
Tabah, } ruined, wretched, spoiled.

Tabáhhál, *adj.* ruined.

Tabáh honá, to be depraved.

Tabáhí, *s. f.* wickedness, depravity, ruin, perdition, wreck.

Tabáhí khání, to be afflicted.

Tabáhízada, *adj.* ruined, afflicted, distressed.

Tabáh kar dená, to ruin.

Tabáh karná, to spoil.

Tabal, *s. m.* a kind of axe.

Tabaldár, *s. m.* a man who uses the tabal or axe to cut down trees or to cleave wood.

Tá ba maqdúr, to the utmost of ability, as much as possible.

Tabáncha, *s. m.* a slap, a blow, a box.

Tabancha, *s. m.* a pistol.

Tabaq, *s. m.* gold leaf, tinfoil, &c., a leaf; a layer or stratum; story of a house.

Tabáq, *s. m.* a vessel for kneading dough in.

Tabar, *s. m.* a hatchet, an axe.

Tabarbardár, } *s. m.* an axe-bearer, a
Tabardár, } wood-cutter. See Tabaldár.

Tábarṭoṛ, *adv.* successively, repeatedly.

Tabáshír, *s. f.* the sugar of the bamboo.

Tabạzád, invention, production of genius, produced by the genius.

Tá ba zíst, while life remains.

Ṭabbar, *s. m.* family.

Tábdán, *s. m.* a lattice, a skylight.

Tábdár, *adj.* twisted (as the hair.)

Táb dená, to twist.

Tabdíl, *s. f.* change, alteration, difference.

Tabdíl karná, to change, to alter.

Tabela, *s. m.* a stable, a stall.
Tab'hí, *adv.* at that very time.
Tab'hí to, then, indeed.
Tab'hí se, thence, thenceforth.
Tábi̤, *adj.* dependant, follower, subject.
Tabi̤, *adj.* natural, innate, constitutional.
Tabi̤at, *s. f.* genius, nature, disposition, temperament, constitution.
Tabíb, *s. m.* a physician.
Tabíbí, *s. f.* the business of a physician.
Tábi̤dár, *adj.* dependant, follower.
Tábi̤dárí, *s. f.* allegiance, obedience, fidelity, subjection.
Tábi̤dárí karná, to obey, to serve, to submit.
Tábi̤ honá, to be subject, to be dependent.
Tábi̤ karná, to control, to subject.
Ta̤bír, *s. f.* explanation, interpretation (particularly of dreams.)
Tabi̤yat, *s. f.* nature, genius, disposition, constitution.
Táb kháná, to be twisted.
Tabla, *s. m.* a small tambourin.
Tab lag, *adv.* till then, so long.
Tablak, *s. f*, a little drum.
Táb láná, to be able to bear.
Tablaq, *s. m.* a paper in which a bundle of papers are bound and on which the kind of papers is written.
Tab taiṉ, } *adv.* till then, so long,
Tab tak, } up to that time.
Tábtáqat, *s. f.* power, ability.
Tábtillí, *s. f.* an induration of the spleen attended with or preceded by fever; splenetis.
Tabtoṛí, *adv.* till then, so long.
Tábút, *s. m.* a coffin, a bier; the ark of the covenant.
Tad, *adv.* then, at that time, afterwards, in that case, so soon.
Ta̤dád, *s. f.* number, computation, enumeration.
Tá dam zíst, while life remains.
Tadáruk, *s. m.* remedy, an expedient, precaution, preparation (particularly to obtain justice); chastisement.
Tadáruk karná, to provide against, to make preparation, to take precaution, to chastise.
Tad bhí, *adv.* still, nevertheless, however, notwithstanding.
Tadbír, *s. f.* deliberation, counsel, contrivance, expedient, advice, arrangement, order, management.
Tadbírát, *s. pl.* counsels, deliberations, regulations.
Tadfín, *s. m.* burial, sepulture.
Tad'hí, *adv.* at that very time, in that case only.
Tad se, *adv.* thence, since that time.
Tad to, *adv.* then, in that case.
Tafakhkhur, *s. m.* pride, boasting, arrogance.
Tafakkur, *s. m.* reflection, meditation, cogitation, anxiety.
Tafarqa, *s. m.* separation, dispersion.
Tafarqa karná, to separate.
Tafáwut, *s. m.* distance, difference, disparity: *adj.* distant, separate, far away, remote.
Tafáwut bolná, to prevaricate.
Tafríh, *s. f.* rejoicing, exhilaration, amusement, gratification.
Tafríh i taba̤, ease of mind, cheerfulness, hilarity.
Tafríq, *s. f.* separation, division, misunderstanding.
Tafríq karná, to analyse.
Tafsíl, *s. f.* explanation, analysis, detail or particulars of an account.
Tafsíl karná, to detail, to explain in full length.
Tafsílwár, *adv.* distinctly, in detail.
Tafsír, *s. f.* explanation, commentary, an interpretation of the Qurán.
Tag, *adv.* till, to, up to, while.
Tág, } *s. m.* thread.
Tágá, }
Tagái, *s. f.* the price paid for quilting, &c.: the act of quilting.
Tagáná, *v. a.* to cause to be quilted, to get stitched together.

Tagápú, *s. f.* see Tagdau.
Ṭagaráná, *v. a.* to roll; to spill.
Ṭagarná, *v. n.* to roll, to be spilt.
Tagdau, *s. f.* fatigue, running about on business or in search of employment, great exertion.
Taggí, *s. f.* a kind of fishing line not used with a rod.
Taghaiyur, *s. m.* change, alteration.
Ṭaghalná, *v. n.* to be melted, to rarefy; to roll.
Taghár, *s. m.* a tub, bucket, trough, platter.
Taghárí, *s. f.* a small tub, trough or bucket.
Ṭagharná, *v. n.* to roll, to be spilt.
Taghír, *s. f.* alteration, change: *adj.* changed, discharged, dismissed.
Taghír honá, *v. n.* to be altered, removed or dismissed.
Taghír karná, to remove (from an office), to dismiss, to discharge.
Ṭaghláná, *v. a.* to roll.
Taghma, *s. m.* a medal, device on a shield, &c.
Ṭaghráná, *v. a.* to roll, to spill.
Tagná, *v. a.* to quilt, to stitch together.
Tágná, *v. a.* to stitch, to thread.
Tag o dau, *s. f.* see Tagdau.
Tágtoṛ, *s. m.* lace.
Tah, *s. f.* fold, plait, ply; layer or stratum; the bottom; intent, meaning.
Taháif, *s.* (*plur. of* Tuhfa), rarities, curiosities, presents, choice articles.
Tahaiyá, *s. m.* preparation, provision, putting in order.
Tahaiyur, *s. m.* amazement, wonder, astonishment.
Tahajjí, *s. f.* spelling.
Tahajjí karná, to spell.
Tahajjud, *s. m.* a form of prayer said during the night.
Tá hál, yet, hitherto, till now.
Ṭahal, *s. f.* housewifery, housekeeping; service, duty, work, drudgery.
Ṭahal karná, to serve, to drudge.
Ṭahal lagáná, to dance attendance.
Ṭahalná, *v. n.* to walk backwards and forwards, to take the air, to rove, to ramble.
Ṭahalní, *s. f.* a housewife.
Ṭahal ṭakor, *s. f.* see Ṭahal.
Ṭahal ṭakor karná, to serve, to drudge.
Táham, yet, nevertheless, still.
Tahammul, *s. m.* patience, endurance, forbearance, long-suffering.
Tahammul karná, to endure, bear, forbear, to be patient.
Taháṇ, *adv.* thither, there.
Ṭahaná, *s. m.* a branch or large bough of a tree.
Taháná, *v. a.* to fold, to ply, to wrap.
Tá hanoz, yet, hitherto, till now.
Taháṇ taháṇ, in each place.
Tahárat, *s. f.* purity, cleanliness; ablution, ceremonial purification.
Taháshí, *s. m.* fear.
Tahas nahas, *adj.* ruined, destroyed, dispersed.
Tahattuk, *s. m.* altercation, contention, dispute, wrangle, wrangling.
Tahband, *s. m.* a cloth worn round the waist, and passing between the legs.
Tah ba tah, *adv.* plait by plait, every fold.
Tah ba tah karná, to pile one upon another.
Tahbázárí, *s. f.* ground-rent of a stall in the market.
Tahdarz, *adj.* new.
Tahdegí, *s. f.* the scrapings of a pot, the burnt part of victuals that sticks to the bottom of a pot.
Tah dená, to tinge slightly.
Tahíṇ, *adv.* thither, there, exactly there, in that very direction.
Táhir, *adj.* pure, unsullied, chaste.
Táhirí, *s. f.* a kind of dish.
Tah jamáná, to plait.
Tah karná, to fold.
Tah kar rakho, fold and lay it by, *i.e.*, keep it to yourself (is used to

express the speaker's independence, or his not wanting the thing spoken of.)

Tahḳhána, *s. m.* a cavern, a cellar, a room under ground, a lower story, a vault.

Ṭahláná, *v. a.* to lead about, to cause to walk backwards and forwards (as a horse or child.)

Tahlíl, *s. f.* digestion, solubility.

Tahlíl honá, to waste, to consume.

Tahlíl karnewálá, digestive.

Ṭahlúá, *s. m.* a manager of household concerns, a servant, a drudge.

Ṭahlú'í, *s. f.* a housewife.

Ṭahluka, *s. m.* consternation, alarm, pang, agony.

Ṭahná, *s. m.* or Ṭahní, *s. f.* a branch.

Tah o bálá, topsy-turvy, upside down.

Tah o bálá karná, to subvert, to overthrow.

Ṭahoṇ, *s. m.* the voice of a new-born child.

Tahqíq, *s. f.* ascertaining, ascertainment, investigation, trial, verification; truth, certainty: *adj.* authentic, ascertained, actual, real, indubitable: *adv.* truly, indeed.

Tahqíqát, inquiry, investigation, &c.

Tahqíqát karná, } to ascertain, investigate, inspect.
Tahqíq karná, }

Tahqír, *s. f.* despising, scorn, neglect, disdain.

Tahqír karná, to despise.

Tahrír, *s. f.* written, a writing.

Tahrír honá, to be written, &c.

Tahrír karná, to write, describe, record.

Tahsíl, *s. f.* gain, acquisition, profit; collection (particularly of revenues.)

Tahsílát, *s.* (*plur.* of Tahsíl), collections, acquisitions.

Tahsíldár, *s. m.* a collector, a tax-gatherer.

Tahsíldárí, *s. f.* collectorship, tax-gathering.

Tahsíl karná, to acquire, to gain, to learn; to collect (revenue, &c.)

Tahsílná, *v. a.* to collect, to gather a tax.

Tahsnahs, *adj.* spoilt, broken, dispersed, overthrown, destroyed.

Taht, *s. m.* subjection, possession; below, under, the inferior part.

Taht i tasarruf, *s. m.* subjection, dominion.

Taht lafzí, *adj.* literal: *adv.* verbally, literal translation.

Taht meṇ láná, to conquer, subjugate, bring under, reduce.

Taht us sará, under the earth.

Tahvíl, } *s. f.* trusts, cash; (in) the charge.
Tahwíl, }

Tahwíldár, *s. m.* a cash-keeper, a treasurer.

Tahwíldárí, *s. f.* the office of cash-keeper.

Tai, *s. m.* travelling, passing or crossing over; rolling up, folding, (in Braj.) *adj.* so many.

Taiber, so often, so many times.

Táíd, *s. f.* aid, assistance.

Táídát, *s. plur.* aids, helps, &c.

Táifa, *s. m.* a band (particularly of musicians and dancing women.)

Tai karná, to travel, to pass or cross over; to fold, to roll up.

Taiṇ, *pron.* thou.

Taíṇ, *postpos.* up to, to, at, (or denoting after a genitive form the objective case.)

Taínát, *s. m.* appointments, appointment, business.

Taiṇtís, *adj.* thirty-three.

Tairná, *v. a.* to swim, to cross over.

Taisá, *adj.* such: *adv.* so, in that manner, in like manner, at the same moment.

Taish, *s. f.* anger, passion.

Táit, *s. m.* an amulet, a charm.

Taiyár, *adj.* ready, prepared, finished, complete, alert.

Taiyár honá, to be ready.

Taiyárí, *s. f.* readiness, preparation.

Taiyár karná, to get ready.

Táj, *s. m.* a crown, a diadem; the comb of a bird.

Taj, *s. f.* the bay tree or its bark, woody cassia; abandoning, forsaking.

Tájá, *adj. prop.* Táza, which see.

Tájagí, *s. f. prop.* Tázagí, which see.

Tajammul, *s. m.* dignity, retinue.

Tajassus, *s. m. f.* spying, search, inquiry, exploring, espionage.

Tajassus karná, to pry into, to search diligently, to explore.

Tajáwuz, *s. m.* deviation, departing.

Tajáwuz karná, to deviate, to depart (from), to err.

Taj'híz, *s. f.* burial.

Taj'híz tafkín, shrouding and burial.

Tájí kuttá, *s. m. prop.* Tázíkuttá.

Tájím, *s. f. prop.* Tazím, which see.

Tájiyá, *s. m. prop.* Taziya, which see.

Tájir, *s. m.* a merchant, a trader.

Taj dená, to give up.

Tajná, *v. a.* to abandon, to desert, to quit, to leave.

Tajriba, *s. m.* experiment, proof, experience, assay, probation.

Tajribakár, *adj.* expert, conversant in.

Tajribakárí, *s. f.* experience.

Tajruba, *s. m.* see Tajriba.

Tájúb, *s. m. prop.* Taajjub, which see.

Tajwíz, *s. f.* investigation, inquiring into, scrutiny, contrivance, judgment, justice; determination, trial, scheme, plan.

Tajwíz honá, to be examined, contrived, ascertained, &c.

Tajwíz karná, to examine, investigate, inquire into, contrive, plan, to sentence or pass sentence, prescribe, appoint, to consider.

Tak, *adv.* till, to, up to, while, toward, near to: *s. f.* aim.

Ṭak, *s. f.* temper, nature, disposition; a look, a stare.

Ták, *s. f.* look, fixed regard, glance; the act of aiming, pointing (a dog): *s. m.* for Táq.

Ṭaká, *s. m.* a copper coin equal to two paisá; money (in general.)

Takabbur, *s. m.* arrogance, haughtiness, pride, insolence of office.

Takabburí, *s. f.* haughtiness.

Ṭakáí, *s. f.* a cheap trull.

Takájá, *s. m. prop.* Taqáza, which see.

Takalluf, *s. m. plur.* Takallufát, ceremony, trouble, taking much pains one's self in any matter; extravagance, profusion.

Takalluf karná, to take pains, to be ceremonious (in.)

Takulluf mizáj, *adj.* ceremonious.

Takán, *s. m.* motion, agitation.

Takáná, *v. a.* to aim.

Tákat, *s. f. prop.* Táqat, which see.

Ták bándhná, to covet; to point (a dog.)

Tak or Ṭak bándhná, to gaze, to stare.

Takbír, *s. f.* repeating the Muhammadan creed.

Takfín, *s. f.* putting on the winding-sheet, laying in the coffin, &c., shrouding, sepulture.

Takfín karná, to shroud, to coffin.

Taḳhfíf, *s. f.* alleviation, abatement, relief, abridgment, mitigation, palliation; making light.

Taḳhfíf dená, to alleviate, assuage, &c.

Taḳhfíf karná, to extenuate, to mitigate, to allay, to remit.

Táḳhír, *s. f.* delay, procrastination.

Táḳhír honá, to delay.

Táḳhír karná, to delay, to postpone.

Taḳhmína, guess, appraisement, conjecture, valuation.

Taḳhmínan, *adv.* by guess, by appraisement; nearly, about.

Ṭaḳhná, *s. m.* the ankle or ankle-joint.

Táḳht, *s. f.* assault, attack, inroad, invasion, incursion.

Taḳht, *s. m.* a throne.

Taḳhta, *s. m.* a plank, a board; deck (of a ship); a stool, bench; a sheet of paper; a bed of flowers, &c.

Taḳhtabandí, wainscot, boarding.

Taḳhtabandí karná, to board, to plank, to floor with boards.

Taḳhtanard, *s. m.* backgammon.

Takht chhorná, to abdicate a throne.
Takhtgáh, *s. f.* the royal residence, metropolis.
Takhtí, *s. f.* a small plank, a little board like a slate which children write on.
Takht i rawán, *s. m.* a travelling throne.
Tákht karná, to assault, attack, invade.
Takhtnishín, *s. m.* a king, a sovereign.
Takhtnishíní, *s. f.* reign, reigning.
Tákt o táráj, *s. m.* see Tákhttáráj.
Takht par baiṭhálná, to enthrone.
Takht par baiṭhná, to reign.
Takht se utárná, to dethrone.
Tákhttáráj, *s. m.* assault, plunder, devastation, depredation.
Tákí, *s. f. prop.* Táqí, which see.
Ṭakí, *s. f.* stare, fixed look, aim.
Tá ki, so that, to the end that, until, so long, whither.
Tákíd, *s. f.* confirmation, emphasis, injunction, ascertaining.
Tákíd karná, to enjoin strictly, to urge, to insist.
Takiya, *s. m.* a pillow, bolster, a faqír's stand; reliance.
Takiyadár, a dervis.
Takiya karná, to support, to encourage.
Takiya kisí par karná, to depend upon.
Takiya lagáná, to lean, to bolster.
Ṭakkar, *s. f.* the knocking of head to head, butting; equality.
Ṭakkar márná, to knock against, (*met.* from the suppliants' striking their heads on the ground,) to pray; to curse.
Taklá, *s. m.* a spindle.
Tak lagáná, to gaze, to stare.
Ṭak lagáná, to expect, to long for.
Taklí, *s. f.* a weaver's reel.
Taklíf, *s. f.* ceremony, trouble, difficulty, distress, affliction, inconvenience, annoyance, molestation.
Taklífát, *s. f. pl.* ceremonies, &c.

Taklíf dená, to annoy, to molest, incommode, trouble.
Taklíf karná, to take the trouble.
Takná, *v. n.* to be looked at, to be stared at, to look: *v. a.* to look at, observe, aim at, watch.
Ṭakná, *v. n.* to be stitched, &c.
Tákná, *v. a.* to stare at, to aim, peep, see, spy, watch, view, behold, look for.
Ṭakor, *s. f.* the sound of a drum.
Ṭakorá, *s. m.* a very small unripe mango.
Tak rahná, to gaze, to stare.
Ṭakráná, *v. a.* to knock together the heads of two people, to dash the head on something, to dash together, to butt; *v. n.* to grope in a dark place or passage.
Takrár, *s. f.* altercation, contention, dispute, wrangle, cavil; repetition, tautology.
Takrárí, *adj.* importuning, fond of argument, wrangler, caviller.
Takrár karná, to dispute, debate, wrangle, cavil, repeat.
Takrím, *s. f.* honour, reverence, respect: *s. f.* treating with respect, honouring.
Ṭaksál, *s. m.* a mint.
Ṭaksálbáhar, *adj.* uneducated, unpolished, rude.
Ṭaksál charhná, to be educated.
Ṭaksálí, } *s. m.* officers of the
Ṭaksáliyá, } mint.
Ṭaksál ká khoṭá, *adj.* spoilt in education.
Ṭakṭakí, *s. f.* staring, fixed, look.
Ṭakṭakí bándhná, to regard with a fixed look, to gaze.
Takúá, }
Ṭakúá, } *s. m.* a spindle.
Takwáhí, *s. f.* watching, overseeing, looking sharp after.
Takya, *s. m.* see Takiya.
Tal, *adv.* for Tale, under, beneath.
Tál, *s. m.* time in music; slapping the hands together or against the arms previous to wrestling, &c.

Ṭál, } *s. f.* a heap (of grain, &c.), a
Ṭálá, } stack, a rick; evasion, putting aside, putting off or out of the way, rejecting a request.

Talá, *s. m.* the bottom of anything; the sole of a foot. [High.

Tạlá, *s. m. prop.* Taạlá, the Most

Tálá, *s. m.* a lock.

Táláb, *s. m.* a pond, a reservoir of water, a tank.

Talab, *s. f.* pay, wages, salary; desire, wish; inquiry, search, demand, request, sending for, summons; in *compos.* seeking, searching.

Ṭálá bálá batáná, to put off.

Talabána, *s. m.* daily pay to constables, &c., paid by those they guard, &c.

Talabdár, *adj.* desirous: *part. act.* asking, inquiring: *s. m.* one who receives pay.

Talabgár, *adj.* desirous: *s.* a seeker.

Talabgárí, *s. f.* desirous, wishing, inquiring, seeking.

Talab karná, to demand, seek, ask for, call, summon.

Talabnáma, *s. m.* summons, citation.

Talaf, *s. m.* ruin, destruction, loss, prodigality.

Talaffuz, *s. m.* utterance, expression, pronunciation.

Talaf honá, to meet with a loss, to be destroyed.

Talaf karná, to waste, to consume.

Talaiyá, *s. f.* a small pond.

Talag, } *adv.* till, to, up to, while.
Talak, }

Ṭaláná, *v. a.* to cause to disappear, to cause to give way.

Taláo, } *s. m.* a pond, a reservoir of
Táláo, } water, a tank.

Talapná, *v. a.* to flutter, to palpitate, to be restless.

Taláq, *s. f.* divorce, repudiation.

Taláq dená, to divorce.

Taláqnáma, *s. m.* a bill of divorcement.

Talásh, *s. f. improp.* Talás, search, inquiry.

Taláshí, *s. m. f.* searching, searcher, seeker.

Talásh karná, }
Taláshná, } *v. a.* to seek, to search for.
Talásná, }

Ṭálá ṭolí, } *s. f.* evasion, prevarica-
Ṭál baṭál, } tion, putting off, shuffling.

Ṭál baṭál karná, to put off.

Ṭál dená, to put off, to evade.

Tál dená, to chime. [under.

Tale, *adv.* below, down, beneath,

Tale tale dekhná, to see clandestinely. [fused.

Taleúpar, *adj.* upside down; con-

Talí, *s. f.* the bottom of anything; the sole of a shoe; beneath, under.

Tálí, *s. f.* a key; clapping of the hands.

Ṭálí, *s. f.* a half-rupee piece.

Tálị, *s. m.* fortune, prosperity; destiny (good or bad), rising (the sun.)

Táliázmái, *s. f.* trying one's fortune.

Tálib, *s. m.* an inquirer, seeker, asker.

Tálí bajáná, to clap the hands (generally, by way of censure and ridicule); to hoot.

Tálib i dunyá, worldly-minded.

Tálib i ịlm, } a student searching
Tálib ul ịlm, } after knowledge.

Tálib ul ịlmí, *s. f.* search of knowledge, study.

Tạlím, *s. f.* teaching, instruction, tuition; a copy to write from.

Tálịmand, *adj.* fortunate, wealthy.

Tálí márná, *v. a.* to hoot; to applaud.

Tạlím karná, to teach.

Táliqa, *s. m.* an inventory, catalogue, list.

Tálịwar, *adj.* fortunate, wealthy.

Tálịwarí, *s. f.* good fortune.

Ṭal jáná, *v. n.* to get out of the way, to disappear, to vanish, to pass away.

Ṭál karná, to put off, to heap.
Talḳh, *adj*. bitter, acrimonious, rancid; malicious.
Talḳhdána, *s. m.* darnel, tares.
Talḳhí, *s. f.* bitterness, rancour.
Talḳh karná, to embitter or make bitter, to aggravate.
Talḳhmizáj, ill-tempered.
Talḳhrú, *adj*. morose, surly.
Ṭallenavísí, *s. f.* unprofitable employment, wasting of time.
Tálmakhháná, *s. m.* the name of a medicinal herb.
Ṭalmaláná, *v. n.* to totter.
Tál márná, *v. a.* see Tál ṭhokná.
Ṭál márná, to heap.
Ṭálmaṭál, *s. m.* evasion, putting off, shuffling.
Ṭálmaṭál karná, to put off.
Ṭálmaṭol, *s. m.* see Ṭálmaṭál.
Ṭalná, *v. n.* to give way, to shrink from, to flinch; to disappear, pass away.
Ṭálná, *v. a.* to evade, to prevaricate, to avoid, to put off, to postpone, to defer; to put aside, to move, to remove.
Talpaṭ, *adj*. ruined, destroyed, more especially crops by the trampling of cattle.
Talqín, *s. f.* instructing, informing, religious instruction.
Talqín honá, to be instructed.
Talqín karná, to instruct, to inform, to teach.
Tál ṭhokná, to strike the hands against the arms preparatory to wrestling.
Ṭálṭol, *s. m.* evasion, prevarication, putting off, shuffling.
Tálú, *s. m.* the palate, the ridge or slit in the roof of the mouth; the lampreys.
Ṭalúá, *s. m.* a man who watches over a ṭál and sells wood, &c.
Talúá, *s. m.* the sole of the foot.
Tálúk, *s. m. prop.* Taạlluq, which see.

Talúpar, *adj*. upside down; confused.
Talwá, *s. m.* the sole of the foot.
Ṭálwálá, *s. m.* see Ṭalúá.
Talwáná, *v. n.* to have blistered feet from the heat of the sun.
Talwár, *s. f.* a sword, a scimitar.
Talwariyá, *s. f.* scimitar: *s. m.* swordsman, a sword player.
Talwá sahláná, to rub the soles of the feet; to flatter.
Talwásná, *v. a.* spoken of the feet of an animal which are worn by treading on hard rocky ground.
Talwoṉ se ág lagní, implies excessive anger.
Tam, *s. m.* the quality of darkness, darkness, gloom.
Tamạ, *s. f.* avarice, covetousness, avidity, greediness.
Támá, *s. m.* copper.
Tamácha, } *s. m.* a slap, a blow, box,
Tamáchá, } cuff, thump, &c.
Tamagun, *s. m.* the quality of darkness, whence proceed folly, ignorance, mental blindness, worldly delusion, &c.
Tamạ karná, to covet.
Tamákú, *s. m.* tobacco.
Tamám, *adj*. entire, perfect, the whole, complete.
Tamám honá, to be finished, to die.
Tamámí, *s. f.* completion, totality; brocade, cloth of gold, tissue.
Tamám karná, to perfect, to complete, to finish, to end.
Tamámshud, it is finished.
Tamancha, *s. m.* a pistol.
Tamáncha, *s. m.* a slap, a blow, box, thump, cuff.
Tamáncha lagáná, } to give a slap,
Tamáncha márná, } &c.
Tamanná, *s. f.* request, prayer, supplication, petition.
Tá maqdúr, to the utmost of ability, as much as possible.
Tamáshá, *s. m.* an entertainment, show, exhibition, a spectacle, sight, amusement, fun.

Tamáshábíní, *s. f.* libertinism.
Tamáshágáh, *s. f.* a place of show.
Tamáshágír, *s. m.* a spectator; one who sees shows or sights; a person who exhibits sights.
Tamáshái, *s. m. f.* a spectator.
Tamáshá karná, *v. a.* to exhibit a sight; to make fun; to jeer, to jest.
Tamáshbín, *s. m.* a spectator; a rake, a whoremaster.
Tamáshbíní, *s. f.* raking, whoring.
Tamasḳhur, *s. m.* buffoonery, joking.
Tamassuk, *s. m.* a note of hand, bond, obligation, receipt.
Támbá, *s. m.* copper.
Tambá, *s. m.* a kind of very wide drawers, almost like a petticoat.
Tambákú, *s. m.* tobacco.
Tambán, *s. m.* a kind of trousers.
Tambíh, *s. f.* admonition, correction, punishment, beating.
Tambíh dená, } to chastise, punish,
Tabíh karná, } correct.
Tambol, *s. m.* the betel-leaf.
Tambolí, *s. m.* a caste whose business is to sell betel-leaf.
Tambolin, *s. f.* a woman whose business it is to sell betel-leaf.
Támbṛá, *s. m.* a copper colour (in pigeons); a false stone resembling a ruby.
Tambú, *s. m.* a tent, a pavilion.
Tambúr, *s. m.* a drum.
Tambúra, *s. m.* a guitar with six wires or strings.
Tambúrchí, *s. m.* a drummer.
Tambú tánná, to pitch tents.
Támi, *adj.* covetous, greedy.
Tạmír, *s. f.* building, structure, repairing.
Tạmír honá, to be built.
Tạmír karná, to build,
Tamíz, *s. f.* discernment, judgment, distinction, discretion.
Tamká, *s. m.* a stroke of the sun.
Tamkanat, *s. f.* dignity, pride.
Ṭamkí, *s. f.* a little drum.
Ṭamkí piṭná, to make proclamation.
Támṛá, *s. m.* see Támbṛá.
Tamr i hindí, *s. f.* a tamarind.
Tamsíl, *s. f.* comparison, similitude. allegory, parable, an example.
Tamsílan, *adv.* by way of similitude, allegorically.
Tamsílát, *s. plur.* parables, &c.
Tamsíl láná, to allegorize.
Ṭamṭam (*vulg.* ṭomṭom), a small drum, also the sound of such a drum.
Tamtamáná, *v. a.* to grow red (in the face); to glow, sparkle, twinkle.
Tamṭam honá, to be cried.
Tạn, *s. m.* blame, censure, reproach, chiding, reviling.
Ṭan, *s. m.* twang.
Tan, *s. m.* the body, person.
Tán, *s. f.* a note in music, a tone; stretching, tension.
Táná, *s. m.* the warp, the threads that are extended lengthways upon a loom: *v. a.* to heat, to prove, to assay.
Tạna, *s. m.* taunting, reproach, scoff.
Tanáb, *s. f.* a tent rope.
Tanaffur, *s. m.* aversion, disgust.
Ṭanak, *s. f.* a harsh sound.
Tanak, *adj.* slight, small, a little: *adv.* slightly, in a small degree.
Tạna márná, to cast reproach, to gibe, to twit.
Tanáná, *v. a.* to extend, to stretch.
Tanásub, *s. m. f.* resembling, relation, proportion.
Ṭánáṭání, *s. f.* a reciprocal pulling: a rivalry in a trade.
Tánátaríz, *adj.* unfortunate.
Tanáwul, *s. m.* eating.
Tanáwul karná, to eat.
Tạnazan, *s. m.* a reproacher, a taunter.
Tạnazaní, *s. f.* taunting, jeering, scoffing, reproaching.
Ṭanch, *adj.* miserly, hard, untractable.
Ṭánch, *adj.* perverse, audacious, troublesome.

Tan chhipáná, to hide the body or one's self.

Ṭanchṛá, *adj.* see Ṭánch.

Ṭánḍá, } *s. m.* a venture (of goods);
Tánḍá, } the goods of a banjárá.

Tandih, a person of application.

Tandihí, *s. f.* application, exertion, diligence, attention.

Tandúr, *s. m.* an oven.

Tandurust, *adj.* healthy, vigorous.

Tandurustí, *s. f.* health, vigour.

Tang, *adj.* straight, tight, narrow, confined; scarce; distressed, sad: *s. m.* a horse-belt, a girth.

Ṭáng, or Ṭang, *s. f.* the leg.

Tángá, *s. m.* a small two-wheeled car without covering, and on which one person only can sit.

Tangá, *s. m.* two paisá.

Ṭángan, *s. m.* a kind of horse, a highland pony.

Tang áná, to be distressed, to be exhausted, to be dejected.

Ṭangárí, *s. f.* a small hatchet.

Tangcháí, *s. f.* stinginess, parsimony.

Tangdast, *adj.* poor, distressed, miserly.

Tangdastí, *s. f.* parsimony, poverty, inability.

Ṭáng dená, *v. a.* to hang up, to hang; to be a catamite.

Tangdil, *adj.* narrow-hearted; miserly, niggard.

Tangdilí, *s. f.* stinginess, parsimony, narrow-heartedness,

Tang'hál, *adj.* poor, distressed; straitened in circumstances.

Tang'hálí, *s. f.* poverty, distress, narrow circumstances.

Ṭánghan, *s. m.* see Ṭángan.

Tang'hausila, *adj.* unable to keep anything secret, blab.

Ṭángí, *s. f.* a hatchet.

Tangí, *s. f.* straightness, tightness, narrowness; distress, poverty, want; a bag, a sack.

Ṭang jáná, *v. n.* to be hung, to be suspended.

Tang karná, to straiten, to tighten to distress, to contract.

Ṭangná, *v. n.* to be hung, to be suspended.

Ṭángná, *v. a.* to hang up, to dangle, to hang by a string, &c.

Ṭángṛí, or Ṭangrí, *s. f.* the leg, the foot.

Tanhá, *adj.* alone, solitary; private, apart: *adv.* only, single.

Tanháí, *s. f.* loneliness, solitude.

Tání, *s. f.* the warp of cloth; the price paid for weaving.

Tanik, *adj.* or *adv.* see Tanak.

Tánís, *s. f.* feminine gender.

Tan i tanhá, *adv.* alone, solitary.

Taniyá, *s. m.* a kind of covering for the waist.

Ṭánk, *s. f.* a stitch; an iron pin.

Tanká, *s. f. prop.* Tanḳhwáh, which see.

Ṭanká, *s. m.* the jingle (of plates, &c.)

Ṭáṇká, *s. m.* a stitch; solder.

Táṇká dená, } to stitch, to tack.
Ṭáṇká márná, }

Ṭánke lagáná, to stitch; to solder.

Tanḳhwáh, *s. f.* wages, salary; an order for money.

Tanḳhwáhdár, one who receives salary, a holder of an order for wages.

Ṭánkí, *s. f.* a chisel for stone-work; a venereal chancre, or shanker; a square piece cut out of a melon to examine its quality.

Tankíh, *s. f.* deciding disputes, investigation.

Ṭanká, *v. n.* to be stitched.

Ṭánkná, *v. a.* to stitch, to cobble.

Tanná, } *v. n.* to stretch, to pull, to
Ṭanná, } sit upright.

Ṭánná, } *v. a.* to extend, to stretch,
Tánná, } to pull, to row or pull an oar.

Tannáná, *v. n.* to have a sharp pricking pain from inflammation; to twang, to tingle,

Tannúr, *s. m.* an oven, a stove.

Tan o man márná, to restrain one's desires and be silent.

Tánt, *s. f.* catgut, sinew, the string of a musical instrument.

Ṭanṭá, } *s. m.* wrangling, altercation,
Ṭanṭal, } squabble, strife; *adj.* heinous.

Ṭan ṭan, a sound.

Tantanáhaṭ, *s. f.* sharp, pricking pain from inflammation.

Tantanáná, *v. n.* to pain. See Tannáná.

Ṭánṭhá, *adj.* powerful, strong, firm, [solid.

Tanṭhái, *s. f.* solidity.

Tántí, *s. m.* a weaver.

Tán toṛná, to crack a joke, to strike up a tune.

Tantr, } *s. m.* name of a Hindú scrip-
Tantra, } ture; charm, enchantment.

Tanuk, see Tanak.

Tanúr, *s. m.* an oven, a stove.

Tanwín, *s. f.* nunation.

Tanz, *s. f.* mirth, joking, pleasantry; ridiculing, sneering, taunting.

Tanzím, *s. f.* ordering, arranging.

Táo, *s. m.* a sheet of paper; heat, passion, rage; twist, coil; proof, trial.

Táo dená, to twist; to stroke the whisker; to heat (as iron.)

Táo kháná, to be heated; to be angry.

Táoná, *v. a.* to heat, to raise heat by blowing with bellows, to prove, to assay.

Ṭap, *s. m.* the fly of a tent.

Táp, *s. f.* fever, warmth, heat.

Tap, *s. f.* warmth, heat; a fever; the hot season; devout austerity, religious penance.

Ṭáp, *s. f.* a stroke with the forefoot of a horse; the sound of a horse's hoof in travelling; a frame made of bamboos for catching fish.

Ṭápá, *s. m.* a hen-coop; a musquito screen for babes.

Ṭapak, *s. f.* pain, throbbing; sound made by dropping.

Ṭapakná, *v. n.* to drop when ripe; to drip, to distil; to throb, to palpitate; to leap over.

Ṭapak paṛná, to drip.

Ṭápá márná, to repair a tiled roof.

Tapan, *s. f.* heat, glow, farvour, warmth; the hot season.

Ṭapáná, *v. a.* to cause to jump over, to cause to leap or bound.

Tapáná, *v. a.* to make another warm himself at the fire or in the sun, to heat, to warm; to cause to oover; to pour a libation.

Tapas, *s. f.* religious austerity, penance, self-denial.

Tapashshí, *s. m.* see Tapasí.

Tapashshiyá, *s. f.* see Tapasiyá.

Tapasí, } *s. m.* a devotee, a performer
Tapassí, } of austere devotion; *adj.* devout, practising austere devotion, ascetic.

Tapassí machhlí, *s. f.* the mango fish.

Tapasyá, *s. f.* austere devotion, religious penance, mortification of self.

Ṭápáṭoí karná, } to grope, to rum-
Ṭápáṭoiyá karná, } mage.

Ṭap chaṛhná, to come on (a fever.)

Tapí, *s. m.* a devotee, a worshipper.

Tápí, *s. f.* a bricklayer's wooden beater.

Tap i diqq, *s. f.* a hectic fever.

Tap i larza, *s. m.* an ague.

Tapish, *s. f.* heat, warmth; affliction.

Ṭap jáná, *v. n.* to jump over.

Ṭapká, *s. m.* a drop of rain; fruit falling when ripe (particularly mangoes); a windfall. [distil.

Ṭapkáná, *v. a.* to cause to drip, to

Ṭapkáo, *s. m.* distillation, dripping.

Ṭapkí, *s. f.* a small drop.

Tapná, *v. n.* to glow, to be heated; to burn with pain or heat.

Ṭapná, *v. n.* to jump over.

Tápná, *v. a.* to bask in the sun or before a fire, to warm one's self at or over a fire; to warm, to heat.

Ṭápná, *v. n.* to paw with the forefeet (as a horse that is impatient.)

Ṭappá, *s. m.* the name of a mode in music; the bound of a ball, &c., a jump, a bound. [(a shot.)

Ṭappá kháná, to bound or ricochet

Ṭappá márná, to sew or stitch with intervals; to read in a desultory manner.

Tapsí, *s. m.* and *adj.* see Tapasí.

Táp tillí, } *s. f.* a disorder of the
Tap tillí, } spleen.

Ṭápú, *s. m.* an island.

Tap utarná, to go off (a fever.)

Táq, *s. m.* a recess in a wall, a shell, a niche; odd (not even); fold, ply.

Taqaiyud, *s. m. f.* diligence, assiduity, superintending, overseeing.

Taqarrur, *s. m.* confirmation, ratification. [ability.

Táqat, *s. f.* strength, power, force,

Taqázá, *s. m.* dunning, urgency, importunity.

Taqázá i shadíd, inexorable dunning.

Taqázá karná, to dunn or teaze.

Táqcha, *s. m.* a small recess in a wall.

Taqdír, *s. f.* fate, destiny, predestination, lot; the Divine decree.

Taqdís, *s. f.* sanctification, sanctity, purity.

Táqí, *adj.* defective (a horse), having the eyes of two different colours.

Táq juft, *s. m.* the game of odd or even.

Táq par rakhná (to lay on the shelf); to refuse; to neglect.

Taqríb, *s. f.* recommendation, mentioning one to another before meeting.

Taqríb karná, to commend, to recommend, to prepare a person for the reception of another.

Taqrír, *s. f.* recital, narration, detail.

Taqrír karná, to relate.

Taqsím, *s. f.* division (in arithmetic); distributing, sharing, partition, dividing.

Taqsím karná, to divide, distribute, share, apportion.

Taqsír, *s. f.* fault, error, crime.

Taqsírát, *s. plur.* crimes, &c.

Taqsírdár, } *adj.* blamable, crimi-
Taqsírmand, } nal, guilty, culpable.
Taqsírwár, }

Taqwá, *s. m.* piety, abstinence, the fear of God.

Taqwíyat, *s. f.* strength, invigoration; reliance, confidence, trust.

Tar, *adj.* moist, damp, wet, fresh, green, juicy; a particle which affixed to adjectives form the comparative degree: *postpos.* under, beneath. See Tale.

Taṛ, *s. m.* an imitative sound.

Ṭar, *adj.* intoxicated, like one intoxicated. [palm-tree.

Táṛ, *s. f.* understanding: *s. m.* the

Ṭár, *s. f.* see Ṭál.

Tár, *s. m. f.* a thread; a wire, the string of a musical instrument; the warp or threads placed lengthwise in weaving; a piece of cloth.

Tárá, *s. m.* a star.

Tará, *s. m.* see Talá.

Taraddud, *s. m.* deep consideration, contrivance, debating.

Taraf, *s. f.* side, quarter, direction; towards.

Tarafdár, *s. m.* a partisan, an assistant; *adj.* partial, prejudiced.

Tarafdárí, *s. f.* partiality, attachment to a party, assistance.

Tarah, *s. f.* manner, mode; position.

Tarah ba tarah, *adv.* various sorts, in various ways.

Tarahdár, *adj.* beautiful, well-shaped.

Tarái, *s. f.* a marsh, mead, meadow; the low ground at the foot of mountains.

Taráin, *s. m.* stars.

Taraiyá, *s. f.* a star.

Táráj, *s. m.* plunder, devastation.

Táráj karná, to lay waste, to spoil.

Tarájú, *s. f. prop.* Tarázú, a pair of scales, a balance.

Tarak, *s. m.* a beam, a rafter; see also Tark.

Taṛáká, *s. m.* the sound of striking a blow; *adj.* pretty, showy, gaudy.
Taṛakná, *v. n.* to be cracked, to be split; to burst, to crack.
Tárámanḍal, *s. m.* the firmament, the starry sphere.
Táran, *s. m.* salvation, deliverance.
Taran, *s. m.* passing over; escaping, being saved.
Taráná, *v. a.* to cause to pass over or swim; to save.
Tarang, *s. f.* wave, emotion.
Taranjubín, *s. m.* honey mixed with lime-juice, &c.
Taṛap, *s. f.* agitation, fury; leap, jump.
Taṛaphná, **Taṛapná**, *v. n.* to flutter, to palpitate; to be agitated, to writhe, to jump, to bound.
Taráq, *s. m.* a crack, the sound of anything splitting or breaking.
Taṛáqa, *adj.* pretty, showy, gaudy; see Taráq.
Taṛaqná, *v. n.* see Taṛakná.
Taraqqí, *s. f.* promotion, preferment, advancement; increase; making progress in learning, proficiency.
Tarás, *s. f.* thirst.
Tarásh, in *compos.* cutting: *s. f.* cutting, paring, cut, shape, form, fashion (of clothes. &c.)
Tarásh ḍálná, to pare off or away.
Taráshná, *v. a.* to cut, to clip, to prune; to shape, to cut out.
Tarashná, to be cut or pared.
Tarashwáná, *v. a.* to cause to be cut or pared.
Tarás lagná, to be thirsty.
Tarasná, *v. n.* to long, to desire anxiously.
Taṛáwá, *s. m.* jeering; show, ostentation.
Taṛáwá márná, **Taṛáwá phenkná**, to reproach, to blame.
Taráwat, *s. f.* freshness, verdure, moisture, humidity, dampness.
Tarázú, *s. f.* a scale, a balance.
Tár bándhná, to continue or repeat an action without interruption.
Tarbatar, *adj.* completely wet.
Tarbatar honá, to drip with wet (but generally) to be covered with blood.
Táṛbáz, *adj.* intelligent, quick of apprehension.
Táṛbází, *s. f.* quickness of apprehension.
Tarbiyat, *s. f.* education, instruction, tuition, bringing up, correction.
Tarbiyat karná, to educate, to instruct.
Tarbúj, *s. m.* see Tarbúz.
Tarbújá, *s. m.* see Tarbúza.
Tarbúz, **Tarbúza**, *s. m.* a water-melon.
Tare, *adv.* under, see Tale.
Táre ginná, *v. a.* to count the stars, *i.e.*, to get no sleep.
Tareṛá, *s. m.* the falling of water from a spout, or from any height; a float of a fishing line, a float or buoy.
Tarf, *s. f.* see Taraf.
Tarfain, *s.* both sides, both parties.
Targhíb, *s. f.* exciting desire, incitement, stimulation.
Targhíb dená, to set agog, to excite, incite, tempt, entice, induce.
Tarh, *s. f.* manner; see Tarah.
Tarí, *s. f.* moisture, freshness; water (in opposition to dry land.)
Tárí, *s. f.* the clapping of hands; a key.
Táṛí, *s. f.* the juice of the palm-tree, *vulg.* toddy.
Tạríf, *s. f.* praise, praising; a table of rates of export and import duties.
Tạrífí, *adj.* commendable, notable.
Taríḳ, *s. f.* way, road; manner, custom.
Táríḳ, *adj.* dark, obscure.
Táriká, *s. f.* a star; apple of the eye.
Táríḳh, *s. f.* date, the day of the month; annals, history.
Táríḳhwár, *adv.* daily; at stated periods, periodically, according to dates.
Táríkí, *s. f.* darkness, obscurity.
Tarín, a particle added to Persian adjectives, to form the superlative degree; most, very.

Taríq, } Taríqa, } Taríqat, } *s.f.* manner, custom; rite, religion, sect; way, path.

Tarí se, *adv.* by water.

Táṛíwálá, *s. m.* a man who climbs palm-trees and extracts their juice, or who sells the juice.

Tarjama, *s. m. prop.* Tarjuma, translation, interpretation.

Tarjíh, *s. f.* gaining a superiority, preference, pre-eminence.

Tarjíh dená, to prefer.

Tarjíh rakhná, to excel, to surpass.

Tarjuma, *s. m.* translation, interpretation.

Tarjuma honá, to be interpreted or translated.

Tarjuma karná, to interpret, to translate.

Tarjumanavís, *s. m.* a translator.

Tark, *s. m.* abandoning, leaving, deserting, abdication.

Taṛká, *s. m.* dawn of day.

Tarka, *s. m.* the estate of a deceased person.

Taṛkáná, *v. a.* to cause to be cracked.

Tarkárí, *s. f.* esculent vegetables.

Tarkash, *s. m.* a quiver.

Tárkash, *s. m.* a wire-drawer.

Tárkashí, *s. f.* a kind of needlework; wire-drawing.

Tárkashí karná, to draw wires, to wiredraw.

Taṛke, *adv.* in the morning early, at dawn of day.

Tarkhá, *adj.* rapid (a stream.)

Tark i adab, disrespect.

Tarkíb, *s. f.* composition, mixture, cement, make, form, mechanism.

Tarkíbdár, *adj.* well-formed.

Tarkíbí, *adj.* composed, mixed, artificial, artful.

Tarkíb karná, to organize.

Tark karná, to abandon, leave, forsake, cease, desert, resign.

Tarkul, *s. m.* the fruit of the táṛ tree.

Ṭarná, *v. n.* to disappear, pass away, retire.

Ṭárná, *v. a.* to move out of the way, see Ṭálná.

Tarná, *v. n.* to pass over, to be ferried; to be saved.

Tárná, *v. a.* to free, to rid, to exempt from further transmigration, to absolve from sin, to save.

Táṛná, *v. a.* to understand, to conceive, to comprehend, to guess.

Tarní, *s. f.* a ship, a vessel, a boat.

Tarotáza, *adj.* new, fresh, cheerful, verdant, fresh and frisky.

Tarotázagí, *s. f.* newness, freshness.

Taṛpáná, } Taṛpháná, } *v. a.* to put in great agitation; to cause to flutter or stumble: to throw over, to cause to jump over.

Taṛphaṛáhaṭ, *s. f.* act of fluttering, palpitation.

Taṛphaṛáná, *v. n.* to flutter, to palpitate.

Ṭarrá, *adj.* wicked, vicious (particularly a horse): stout.

Ṭarráná or Tarráná, *v. n.* to grumble, murmur; to chatter.

Tarrár, *adj.* eloquent, fluent of speech.

Tarrára, *s. m.* quickness, expedition, rapidity.

Tarrára or Tarrárá bharná, to gallop, to rush on at full speed.

Tars, *s. m.* fear, terror; compassion, mercy.

Tarsáná, *v. a.* to cause to long, to tantalize, to teaze.

Tarsh, *s. m.* thirst, wish, desire.

Tars karná, to compassionate.

Tars khánâ, to compassionate, to pity.

Tarsnák, *adj.* timid, cowardly.

Tarsoṉ, *adv.* the third day past or to come (not including the present, *i.e.* two days intervening.)

Ṭarṭar, *s. f.* chattering.

Tartará, *s. m.* a kind of dish.

Taṛtaṛáhaṭ, *s. f.* the act of dropping, the sound of warping or cracking.

Taṛtaṛáná, *v. n.* to warp or crack with noise (as a plank exposed to the sun); to trickle, to drop.

Ṭarṭaráná, *v. a.* to chatter.
Ṭartarátá, *adj.* very greasy.
Tartíb, *s. f.* arrangement, disposition, order, method.
Tartíb dená, to put in order, arrange, compose, assort, &c.
Tartíbí, *adj.* orderly, methodical.
Tár ṭúṭná, to be disjointed, to be separated.
Tárú, *s. m.* the palate.
Tarun, *adj.* young, juvenile, adult: *s. m.* a young man.
Tarunáí, *s. f.* } adolescence,
Tarunápan, *s. m.* } youth, puberty.
Tarwár, *s. f.* a sword, a scimitar.
Tarwariyá, *s. m.* a sword; a swordsman, a fencer.
Tarz, *s. m.* form, manner, fashion.
Tás, *s. m.* a cup, goblet, a leaden vessel in which water is cooled; the cards; a game at cards; brocade.
Tása, *s. m.* a kind of drum.
Tasadduq, *s. m.* giving alms (particularly with a religious view); alms; sacrificing, sacrifice, devoting.
Tasadduq honá, to become a sacrifice.
Tasadduq karná, to devote, to sacrifice.
Ṭasak, *s. f.* shooting pain, stitch, throb.
Ṭasakná, *v. n.* to have pain; to move, to shake. [lace.
Tasallí, *s. f.* consolation, comfort, solace.
Tasallí dená, to comfort, to animate, to exhilarate, to console.
Tasallí honá, to be consoled or comforted.
Tasallut, *s. m.* domination, sway, absolute rule.
Tasáníf, *s. plur.* compositions, books.
Tasannun, *s. m.* the being or becoming a sunní.
Tasar, } *s. m.* a kind of coarse silk,
Ṭasar, } the produce of a particular worm.
Tasarruf, *s. m.* possession; use, expenditure, extravagance.
Tasarruf karná, } to take or get
Tasarruf meṉ láná, } possession of, to apply to one's purpose.
Tasauwar, *s. m.* imagination, contemplation, meditation, reflection, conception, apprehension.
Tasauwar karná, to imagine, to fancy.
Tasbíh, *s. f.* praising God; a rosary of beads.
Tasdí, } *s. f.* affliction, trouble, annoy-
Tasdíạ, } ance, vexation, perplexity, toil.
Tasdíạ dená, to incommode, trouble, vex, tease, harass, distress, pester, plague, annoy.
Tasdíạ karná, to take the trouble.
Tasdíát, *s. plur.* troubles.
Tasdíq, *s. f.* verifying, attesting, attestation, acknowledging as true.
Tásh, *s. m.* cloth of gold, brocade.
Tashaffí, *s. f.* consolation, calmness.
Tashbíh, *s. f.* a simile, comparison, metaphor, allegory.
Tashbíh dená, to assimilate, liken, compare.
Tashdíd, *s. f.* the orthographical mark ّ, which shows that the letter underneath must be pronounced double.
Tashhír, *s. f.* proclaiming, publishing; marking a criminal, public exposure (of a criminal, &c., by carrying him on an ass, &c., through the city.)
Tashhír honá, to be publicly exposed (as a criminal) in the streets.
Tashḳhís, *s. f.* distinguishing perfectly (a word much used by physicians to denote their having ascertained the disorder of a patient); diagnosis.
Tashḳhís karná, to ascertain (a disease.)
Tashríf, *s. f.* honouring; visiting.
Tashríf arzání farmáná, } (means
Tashríf farmáná, } simply) to go, or to come.
Tashríf láná, to come, *i.e.*, to honour

with one's presence (never said of one's self except by a king.)

Tashríf lejáná, to go, or honour by going.

Tasht, *s. m.* see Tast.

Tashtarí, *s. f.* a salver, a small plate, a saucer.

Tashwísh, *s. f.* confusion, distraction, anxiety, grief, disquietude.

Tásír, *s. f.* the making an impression, an effect, an impression, operation, penetration.

Tásírát, *s. plur.* of Tásír, impressions, effects.

Taskín, *s. f.* consolation, comfort, pacifying, soothing, assuaging.

Taskín dená, to appease, to pacify, to soothe, calm, assuage.

Taslá, *s. m.* a brass vessel used by Hindús to dress their victuals in.

Taslíb, *s. f.* crucifixion.

Taslím, *s. f.* saluting most respectfully, homage, obeisance.

Taslímát, *plur.* of Taslím, salutations.

Taslímát bajá láná, to make obeisances.

Taslím karná, to salute (most respectfully), to make obeisance, to do homage.

Tasma, *s. m.* a thong, a strap of leather.

Tasníf, *s. f.* invention, composition; writing (of a book, &c.)

Tasníf karná, to compose, write (a book, &c.)

Tasríf, *s. f.* conjugation, declension, inflection (in grammar.)

Tasríf karná, to conjugate, decline, inflect (in grammar.)

Tassur, *s. m.* $1\frac{1}{8}$ths of an inch.

Tast, *s. m.* a large flat hollow copper utensil in the form of a basin.

Taswír, *s. f.* a picture, a portrait, an image.

Taswír banáná, Taswír khainchná, to draw, &c., to paint.

Taṭ, *s. m.* a shore or bank.

Tat, *s. m.* an element, a principle, the essence: *pron. dem.* that.

Ṭáṭ, *s. m.* canvas, sackcloth; a counter; a very coarse kind of cloth made of hemp, gunny.

Tát, Tátá, Tátal, *adj.* hot, warm, heated.

Ṭaṭáná, *v. n.* to be dried.

Tatáná, *v. a.* to warm, to heat.

Ṭáṭbáfí, *s. f.* embroidery.

Táte or Táten, from that, thence, thereby.

Tathá, *s. f.* power, ability, might.

Tathápi, *adv.* nevertheless, then, even.

Ṭáṭí, *s. f.* a matted shutter, a screen.

Ṭaṭíhrí, *s. f.* a sandpiper.

Ṭaṭíl, *s. f.* vacation, holiday.

Ṭaṭíl ká roz, Friday; the weekly holiday of Muhummadan schoolboys.

Ṭaṭiyá, *s. f.* a screen, a matted shutter.

Taṭká, *adj.* fresh, new, recent.

Tatkál, *adv.* at that time, then.'

Ṭaṭolná, *v. a.* to feel for, to grope, to search for by feeling, to touch.

Ṭaṭpúnjiá, *adj.* bankrupt, or reduced in circumstances (a merchant.)

Taṭrí, *s. f.* a fence, a hedge.

Tatt, *s. m.* an element, a principle, the essence.

Tattá, *adj.* hot, fiery, passionate, furious, outrageous, wrathful.

Ṭaṭṭar, *s. m.* a matted shutter.

Ṭaṭṭí, *s. f.* a screen, a matted shutter; a necessary office; a frame for illumination.

Ṭaṭṭú, Ṭaṭṭúá, *s. m.* a pony, a small horse.

Ṭáṭ ulaṭná, to become bankrupt.

Tatwa, *s. m.* reality, the essential element, principle.

Ṭaṭwání, *s. f.* a pony mare.

Tau, *adv.* then, that time, in that case, moreover, that, also, for, yes, well.

Tauba, *s. f.* penitence; promising to sin no more.

Taubadháṛ, *s. f.* the sound of punishing, &c.
Taubah, *s. f.* see Tauba.
Tauba karná, to repent (of sin.)
Tauba tauba, *interj.* tush! fy! foh!
Tau bhí, *adv.* even then, still, yet, nevertheless.
Taufíq, *s. f.* the divine grace, the favour of God.
Taufíq bakhshná, to grant favour.
Tauhí, *adv.* then even, still, in that case, at that very time.
Taul, *s. m.* weight, weighing.
Tau lag, *adv.* till then, so long.
Tauláí, *s. f.* the price for weighing.
Tauláná, *v. a.* to cause to be weighed.
Taulná, *v. n.* to weigh, to balance.
Taulná nazron meṉ, to estimate the worth of any one.
Tau loṉ, *adv.* till then, so long.
Taul tál, weighing and measuring.
Taulwáí, *s. f.* the price of weighing.
Tauṉ, *adv.* so, in that manner, then.
Taun, *pron. correl.* that, that same.
Tauṉsná, *v. n.* to be affected or overcome with heat.
Tauq, *s. m.* a collar, a yoke; chain (for the neck, whether by way of ornament or of punishment.)
Tauqír, *s. f.* honouring, reverence.
Taur, *s. m.* mode, manner, fashion, way; condition, state.
Tauret, *s. f.* the Pentateuch, the five books of Moses.
Táús, *s. m.* a peacock.
Tausíf, *s. f.* description, commendation.
Táw, *s. m.* see Táo.
Tawá, *s. m.* the iron plate on which bread is baked; the part of a huqqa to which the tobacco is fixed; a frying-pan.
Tawáf, *s. f.* pilgrimage, making the circuit of Mecca or of some other holy place.
Tawáí, *s. f.* distress, misfortune.
Tawáif, *s. f. plur.* of Táifa, troops, bands (particularly of dancing girls.)
Tawajjuh, *s. f.* turning towards, attending to; kindness, favour, condescension.
Tawakkul, *s. m.* trust in God, reliance, faith in, or resignation to, the divine will or destiny.
Tawakkul karná, to resign to God.
Tawallud, *s. m.* birth, nativity: *adj.* born, generated.
Tawallud honá, to be born.
Tawán, *s. m.* power, strength, ability.
Tawáná, *v. a.* to heat (as metals): *adj.* powerful, able, strong.
Tawánáí, *s. f.* power, ability.
Tawángar, *adj.* rich, wealthy.
Tawaqqụ, *s. f.* expectation, hope, desire, trust, reliance.
Tawaqquf, *s. f.* delay, pause, hesitation; patience.
Tawaqquf karná, to pause, hesitate, wait, delay, dally.
Tawaqqụ rakhná, to expect, to hope, to put trust in.
Tawárikh, *s. plur.* of Táríkh, dates, histories, annals, chronicles.
Tawassul, *s. m.* means, intervention.
Tawátur, *s. m.* continuation, succession.
Tawázá, **Tawázụ**, *s. f.* humility, attention, civility.
Tawelá, *s. m.* a stable, a stall.
Tawíl, *adj.* long, prolix; tall.
Tawíla, *s. m.* a stable, a stall.
Tạwíz, *s. m.* a charm, an amulet.
Táwná, *v. a.* see Táoná.
Tawwá, *s. m.* see Tawá.
Tayammum, *s. m.* purifying before prayer with sand or dust when water cannot be had.
Táza, *adj.* fresh, new; fat, young, tender, green; happy, pleased.
Táza ba táza, *adj.* fresh and blooming.
Táza dam, good spirits, hilarity.
Tázagí, *s. f.* freshness, newness; fatness, tenderness, greenness; pleasure.

Táza honá, to be in good case, to increase, to flourish.
Táza karná, to renew, to refresh, to recreate.
Táza wárid, new comer.
Tází, *adj.* Arabian, or Arabic; Arabian (horse.)
Tází kuttá, *s. m.* a greyhound.
Tạzím, *s. f.* reverence, respect, honour, treating with ceremony and respect, honouring.
Tạzím karná, to honour, to reverence, to show respect.
Tá zindagí, during life.
Tạzír, *s. f.* punishment, correction, reproof, censure, reprimand.
Tạziya, *s. m.* the representation of the tomb of Hasan and Husain, which is thrown into the river at the anniversary of the Muharram.
Tạziyadár, one who observes the mourning in the Muharram.
Tạziyadárí, *s. f.* the observance of the mourning in the Muharram.
Tạziyaḳhána, *s. m.* a place of Tạziya.
Táziyána, *s. m.* a whip, a scourge.
Táziyána lagáná, } *v. a.* to apply the
Táziyána márná, } whip, to scourge.
Tạziyat, *s. f.* condolence, lamentation, mourning.
Tazkír, *s. f.* masculine gender; bringing to memory, mentioning.
Tazkira, *s. m.* memory, remembrance.
Te, *postpos.* from, by, with,
Tegh, *s. f.* a scimitar.
Tehí, *adv.* exactly then.
Teís, *adj.* twenty-three.
Tej, *s. m.* splendour, glory, refulgency; energy; also *vulg.* for Tez, which see. [energetic.
Tejaswí, *adj.* glorious, splendid,
Tejmán, *adj.* glorious, splendid.
Tejpát, } *s. m.* the leaf of the
Tejpattá, } Laurus cassia, cassia.
Tejwant, *adj.* see Tejaswí.
Ṭek, *s. f.* a prop, a pillar; reliance; a promise, a vow.
Ṭekan, *s. m.* a prop, a support.
Ṭekar, *s. m.* an island; a height, a rising ground.
Ṭekná, *v. a.* to support, to prop.
Ṭekrá, *s. m.* see Ṭekar.
Ṭek rahná, to lean upon.
Tel, *s. m.* oil, lard, unctuous matter.
Tel chaṛháná, to anoint the head, shoulders, hands, and feet of the bridegroom with oil mixed with turmeric.
Telí, *s. m.* an oilman; name of the oilman's caste.
Telin, *s. f.* wife of an oilman.
Teliyá, *s. m.* name of a colour, dark bay.
Teliyásurang, *adj.* light bay coloured.
Tel malná, to anoint with oil.
Ṭelná, *v. a.* to remove.
Ṭem, *s. f.* snuff of a candle, the flame of a candle or lamp.
Teṇ, *pron.* thou: *postpos.* from, by, with.
Ṭená, *s. m.* a cock of the breed of fowls called ṭení.
Tenḍúá, *s. m.* a leopard.
Ṭengrá, *s. m.* } the name of a fish.
Ṭengrí, *s. f.* }
Ṭení, *s. f.* a particular breed of fowls: *adj.* tiny, small.
Ṭenṭ, *s. m.* the ripe fruit of karíl; a speck on the eye.
Teṇtális, *adj.* forty-three.
Ṭeṇṭeṇ, an imitative sound, inarticulate sound.
Ṭenṭí, *s. f.* a large ripe fruit of karíl.
Teṇtís, *adj.* thirty-three.
Tenṭúá, *s. m.* the wind-pipe, the throat.
Ṭeo, *s. f.* habit, custom.
Teohár, *s. m.* a holiday, a festival.
Ṭeoná, *v. a.* to sharpen.
Ṭeoráná, *v. n.* to have a swimming in the head, to fall down senseless from a blow.
Teoras, *s. m.* the third year past or to come, year before last, year after next.

Teorhí,
Ṭeorí, } s. f. frown.
Teorí,
Teorí chaṛháná, to frown.
Teorí chaṛhná, a frown to come on.
Tepchí, s, f. a kind of stitch.
Terá, pron. 2d pers. sing. thy, thine.
Terah, adj. thirteen.
Terahán, adj. thirteenth.
Teras, s. f. the thirteenth day of the lunar fortnight.
Terawán, adj. thirteenth.
Teṛhá,
Ṭeṛhá, } adj. crooked, bent, awry, uneven.
Ṭeṛhá berá,
Ṭeṛháí, s. f. crookedness, obliquity.
Ṭeṛhá karná, to bend, to crook.
Ṭeṛhá maghz, adj. obstinate, headstrong.
Ṭeṛhí, s. f. perverseness.
Ṭerná, v. n. to bawl, to call loudly, to shout, to holla; to tune.
Terus, s. m. see Teroas.
Ṭesú, s. m. the blossoms of the palás tree; a kind of play.
Tetá, adv. so much, that much.
Tetális, adj. forty-three.
Tetís, adj thirty-three.
Ṭew, s. f. habit, custom.
Tez, adj. sharp, keen, pungent; hot, acute, fiery, caustic, acrid, strong, impetuous, violent, swift.
Tezáb, s. m. nitric acid, aquafortis.
Tezaql, adj. intelligent, quick of apprehension, acute.
Tezdast, adj. dexterous.
Tezfahm, } adj. intelligent, quick of
Tezhosh, } apprehension, acute.
Tezí, s. f. sharpness, keenness, pungency, strength, swiftness, impetuosty, fleetness.
Teznákhun, adj. sharp-nailed.
Tezpát, s. m. the name of an aromatic leaf (Laurus cassia.)
Tezqadam, adj. swift, fast-going.
Tezraftár, } adj. fast-going, rapid,
Tezrau, } swift.
Tezrauí, s. f. rapidity.

Thá, v. n. past tense, was.
Ṭhá, s. m. a sound made by striking one thing on another.
Ṭhag, s. m. a robber, an assassin by strangling; a cheat, a swindler, an impostor.
Ṭhagáí, s. f. robbery, theft, cheating, swindling, extortion.
Ṭhagáná, v. n. to be cheated.
Ṭhagaurí, s. f. cheat, trick.
Ṭhagbází, } s. f. cunning, fraudu-
Ṭhagbidyá, } lent, art, dexterity.
Ṭhagin, s. f. a female robber or cheat.
Ṭhagiyá, s. m. a cheater, a robber.
Ṭhag láná, v. a. to rob, to cheat.
Ṭhag lená, v. a. to cheat.
Ṭhagná, v. a. to cheat, to deceive.
Ṭhagní, s. f. see Ṭhagin.
Ṭhagorí, s. f. cheat, trick.
Tháh, s. f. bottom, ford.
Ṭhaháká, s. m. a peal, a succession of loud sound, an explosion.
Ṭhaharná, v. n. to be stopped, to be fixed, to stop, to stay, to remain, to abide, rest, stand, to last, to be fixed on, to be determined, to be proved.
Ṭhahráná, v. a. to fix, stop, determine, appropriate, settle, to ascertain, appoint, fix on, demonstrate, to prove, conclude or consider, ascribe.
Ṭhahráo, s. m. settlement, fixture, permanence, proof.
Thailá, s. m.
Thailí, s. f. } a purse tied round the waist; a bag.
Thailiyá, s. f.
Thaká, adj. tired, weary. [weary.
Thakáná, v. a. to harass, to tire, to
Thakit, adj. wearied; astonished.
Thak jáná, v. n. to be wearied, to tire.
Thakká, s. m. clot, lump (congealed.)
Thakke ko thakke, congealed, thick, conglomerated.
Thakná, } v. n. to be wearied, to
Thákná, } tire, to be fatigued.
Ṭhak ṭhak, s. m. a sound; hard work.

Ṭhakṭhakáná, *v. a.* to tap, to pat.

Ṭhakṭhakiyá, *s. m.* a stickler, a wrangler.

Ṭhákur, *s. m.* the divinity; an idol; a lord, a master, chief (among Rajpúts); a landholder, a barber.

Ṭhákuráí, *s. f.* divinity, lordship, chiefship, mastership.

Ṭhákuráyan, *s. f.* a female divinity or idol.

Ṭhákurbárí, *s. f.* } an idol temple.
Ṭhákurdwárá, *s. m.* }

Thal, *s. m.* place, firm or dry ground, table-land.

Thál, *s. m.* a large flat dish.

Thálá, *s. m.* the place at the root of a tree for holding water; the excavation in which a tree is to be planted; a large flat dish.

Thálí, *s. f.* a platter, a flat dish.

Thaliyá, *s. f.* a salver, generally of brass.

Ṭhám, *s. m. f.* place, place of residence.

Thám, *s. m.* a prop, a pillar.

Tham, *s. m.* a pillar, a post; a stem of a plantain tree.

Thamáná, *v. a.* see Thámbhná.

Thamb, }
Thambá, }
Thambh, } *s. m.* a pillar, a post.
Thámbh, }

Thambhná, *v. n.* to stop, to cease, to be restrained, to be supported.

Thámbhná, } *v. a.* to support, to
Thámbná, } prop; to shield, to protect; to restrain; to stop, to pull up (a horse); to assist.

Thamná, *v. n.* see Thambhná.

Thámná, *v. a.* see Thámbhná.

Thán, *s. m.* a piece of cloth; a stall for cattle, a manger.

Than, *s. m.* the udder.

Ṭháṇ, *s. m. f.* } place, place of resi-
Ṭhán, *s. m.* } dence.

Thánả, } *s. m.* a station, a guard, a
Thána, } police guard-house.

Thánádár, *s. m.* the keeper of a guard-house; a constable, the headman of a Thána.

Thánádárí, *s. f.* the office of a constable; the superintendence of a Thána.

Thanák, *s.* a jingle, tinkle, clink.

Ṭhanakná. *v. n.* to throb, to shoot (as the pain of headache.)

Ṭhanḍ, } *s. f.* coldness, cold, a cold;
Thanḍ, } (*met.*) a refreshing sensation.

Ṭhanḍá, } *adj.* cold, refreshing, cool-
Thanḍá, } ing.

Ṭhanḍá honá, to become cold, to cool; to be comforted, to be pacified; to rest.

Ṭhanḍáí, *s. f.* refrigerant medicine; the intoxicating drug made of bhang; refreshing or cooling things.

Ṭhanḍak, } *s. f.* coldness, coolness.
Thanḍak, }

Ṭhanḍá karná, *v. a.* to make cold, to extinguish; to pacify.

Ṭhanḍá paṛná, to abate (anger, virility, wantonness, &c.)

Thandár, an animal with a large udder, or having an udder.

Ṭhanḍí, *adj. f.* cold.

Ṭhanḍí sáṇs bharní, to sigh.

Thanelá, *s. m.* inflamed breast (of a woman.)

Tháng, *s. f.* a den of thieves.

Thángí, *s. m.* a receiver of stolen goods.

Ṭhanká, *s. m.* a thunderbolt.

Ṭhanná, *v. n.* to be fixed, to be ascertained.

Ṭhánná, *v. a.* to resolve or fix (in the mind), to determine, to be intent on, to intend, to set one's heart on; to settle, to perform.

Ṭháṇoṇ, *s. f.* see Ṭháṇw.

Ṭháṇsná, *v. a.* to stuff, to cram.

Ṭhanṭhanáná, *v. n.* to jingle, to rattle.

Ṭhánṭhú, *s. m.* the report of a musket.

Ṭháṇw, } *s. f.* a residence, a place.
Ṭháoṇ, }

Tháp, *s. f.* a tap, a pat, a flap, paw; the sound of a small drum.
Thapak, *s. f.* a pat, a tap.
Thapeṛá, *s. m.* a slap, a box, a clout.
Thápí, *s. f.* the instrument with which potters beat their earth, or with which terraces are beaten.
Thápná, *v. a.* to patch (as a wall with cow dung); to tap.
Ṭhappá, *s. m.* an instrument for stamping leather with, a die, a stamp.
Thappaṛ, } Thapṛá, } *s. m.* a box, a slap, a cuff.
Thapṛáná, *v. a.* to slap.
Thapṛí, *s. f.* the clapping of hands.
Thapṛí bajáná, to clap the hands.
Thapṛí márná, to hoot.
Thár, *s. m.* a large flat dish, a tray.
Ṭhár, *s. m.* snow, frost.
Ṭháṛá, *adj.* erect, standing.
Ṭháṛh, *adj.* steep, lofty.
Ṭháṛhá, *m.* } Ṭháṛhí, *f.* } *adj.* erect, standing.
Ṭháṛhná, *v. n.* to be fixed, to stand.
Ṭhariyá, *s. m.* a kind of huqqa.
Ṭharrá, *s. f.* a kind of wine or spirituous liquor.
Tharráná, *v. n.* to tremble, to quiver.
Tharthar, *adj.* trembling.
Tharthráhaṭ, *s. f.* tremour, shaking, trembling, quivering, shivering.
Tharthaṛáná, *v. n.* to tremble, to quiver, to shiver, shake, quake.
Tharthari, *s. f.* see Tharthaṛáhaṭ.
Ṭhas, *adj.* deficient (in weight, measure, quality, &c.)
Ṭhasak, *s. f.* state, dignity.
Ṭhasáṭhas, *adj.* filled, crowded.
Ṭhásná, *v. a.* to stuff, to cram, to ram down the charge of a gun.
Ṭhasní, *s. f.* a rammer.
Ṭhassá, *s. m.* a mould or form into which plates of metals, &c., are beat to take the form of pastes of ornaments, &c.; pride, vanity.
Ṭháṭ, *s. m.* the frame of a roof on which the straw is laid; arrangement, adjustment.
Ṭhaṭh, *s. m.* throng, crowd; pomp.
Ṭháṭh, *s. m.* state, dignity, equipage, pomp.
Ṭhaṭhak jáná, } Ṭhaṭhakná, } Ṭhaṭhak rahná, } *v. n.* to stop short, to stand amazed, to draw back in surprise.
Ṭhaṭháná, *v. a.* to strike, to beat; to beat one's own head, &c. (in token of vexation); to harass one's self.
Ṭhaṭherá, *s. m.* a brazier, a tinker; the stalk of the joár.
Ṭhaṭherí, *s. f.* a female brazier or tinker.
Tháthí, *s. f.* a trust, what is given in charge, a charge.
Ṭhaṭhol, *adj.* banterer, waggish, jocular, jocose, jester, wag.
Ṭhaṭholí, *s. f.* fun, humour, sport, joking, jesting, jocularity, derision.
Ṭhaṭhor, *adj.* see Ṭhaṭhol.
Ṭhaṭhrí, *s. f.* the frame of a matted screen, the frame (bamboo work) of a thatched roof; shell of a house, a bier; a skeleton, a very thin person.
Tháti, *s. f.* see Tháthí.
Ṭhaṭṭhá, *s. m.* fun, joking, jest.
Ṭhaṭṭhábáz, see, Ṭhaṭṭhebáz.
Ṭhaṭṭhá karná, } Ṭhaṭṭhá márná, } to jest, joke, crack a joke, deride, ridicule.
Ṭhaṭṭhar, *s. m.* the frame made of bamboo for thatching, shell of a house.
Ṭhaṭṭhebáz, a jester, a humorous person, a funny fellow: *adj.* jocular.
Ṭhaṭṭhebází, *s. f.* jesting, sporting, joking, jocularity, fun.
Ṭhaur, *s. f.* place, residence: *adv.* upon the spot.
Ṭhaur rahná, to be murdered, to be knocked down lifeless upon the spot.

Thawa'í, *s. m.* a mason, a bricklayer, an architect.
Theglí, *s. f.* a patch (on a garment.)
Theí theí, *s. f.* merry-making, mirth.
Ṭhek, *s. f.* a support, a prop; a large sack filled with grain.
Ṭheká, *s. m.* a plug, a stopper.
Ṭhekí, *s. f.* act of resting on the way (by a porter carrying a load); a platform for resting loads on.
Ṭhekí dená, } to rest (a porter
Ṭhekí lagáná, } carrying a load.)
Ṭhelá, *s. m.* a push, a shove.
Ṭhelam ṭhelá, *s. m.* } the pushing
Ṭhelá ṭhelí, *s. f.* } and shoving of a crowd.
Ṭhelná, *v. a.* to shove, to push, to move forward by pushing.
Ṭhengá, *s. m.* a stick, a staff, a bludgeon.
Ṭhengná, *adj.* short, dwarfish.
Ṭhenṭh, *adj.* pure, genuine; contentious.
Ṭhenṭhí, *s. f.* a ball of ear-wax.
Ṭheoná, *s. m.* the knee; the pastern, (of a horse.)
Ṭhepí, *s. f.* a cork, a plug, a stopple.
Ṭhepí munh men dená, to be silent.
Ṭhes, *s. f.* a knock, a blow, tripping against a stone, &c., a shove, a push, a thrust.
Ṭhesná, *v. a.* to pierce, to knock against; to stuff, to cram, to ram in, to eat ravenously.
Ṭhewná, *s. m.* see Ṭhioná.
Thiglí, *s. f.* a patch (on a garment.)
Ṭhík, *adj.* exact, even, accurate, complete, just, fit, meet, proper, reasonable, true, regular, right: *adv.* exactly: *s. m.* sum, addition.
Ṭhíká, *s. m.* hire, fare, fixed price; work done by contract, a task.
Ṭhíkam ṭhík, *adv.* exactly, truly, rightly, quite right.
Thikán, } *s. m.* residence, place,
Ṭhikáná, } abode; the address of a letter; certainty; a vestige of anything, a place where any person or thing is to be found, boundary, limit, fixing.
Ṭhík áná, *v. n.* to fit, correspond, suit, answer, apply.
Ṭhikáná ḍhúnḍhná, to seek a residence or employment.
Ṭhikáná karná, to search or trace an affair to its commencement.
Ṭhikáná lagáná, to establish, to settle, to find out one's residence.
Ṭhikáne lagáná, to put to death, to kill, to waylay, to make away with, despatch, assassinate.
Ṭhikáne lagná, to be killed, to die, to be put an end to, to be terminated.
Ṭhík dená, *v. a.* to sum, to add or cast up, to reckon.
Ṭhík karná, to put to rights, to correct, to adjust; to beat.
Ṭhík lagná, to hit a mark, to fit (as clothes.)
Ṭhikrá, *s. m.* a fragment of an earthen vessel, a sherd, a potsherd, a vessel for carrying fire, such as faqírs use.
Ṭhikrá, *s. m.* } a broken piece of
Ṭhíkrí, *s. f.* } earthenware, a potsherd, a sherd.
Ṭhíkrí chunná, to be mad.
Ṭhík ṭhák, *adj.* exact, fit, accurate; properly, accurately.
Ṭhík ṭhák karná, *v. a.* to put to rights, correct, adjust, fit.
Ṭhiliyá, *s. f.* a waterpot.
Ṭhinakná, *v. n.* to sob.
Ṭhioná, *s. m.* the knee; the pastern (of a horse.)
Ṭhíp, *s. f.* a kind of chafing dish.
Thir, *adj.* fixed, stable, settled.
Thirakná, *v. n.* to dance with expressive action and gesture.
Thiráná, *v. n.* to settle (as liquor.)
Ṭhirná, *v. n.* to freeze, to be chilled.
Ṭhiṭharáhaṭ, *s. f.* numbedness, torpor, torpidness.
Ṭhiṭharná, *v. n.* to be numbed or benumbed, to be chill.

Ṭhiṭhiráná, *v. a.* to chill, benumb, numb.
Ṭhiṭhirná, *v. n.* see Ṭhiṭharná.
Ṭhiṭhur, *s. f.* numbness, chilliness.
Ṭhiṭhuráná, *v. a.* to chill, to benumb.
Ṭhiṭhurná, *v. n.* see Ṭhiṭharná.
Thok, *s. m.* a prop.
Ṭhokar, *s. m.* a blow, a stroke; tripping or striking the foot against anything; a kick, a stumble; a stumbling-block.
Ṭhokar khání, to trip, to stumble; to meet with a loss or misfortune.
Ṭhokar lagná, to strike against the foot (a stumbling-block or obstacle.)
Ṭhokná, *v. a.* to beat, to strike, to drive (as a stake.)
Ṭhonk dená, to hammer or drive down, to knock.
Ṭhonkná, *v. a.* to knock, to hammer; to drive (as a stake); to beat, to thump.
Ṭhonsná, *v. a.* to cram, to stuff.
Ṭhonṭh, *s. m.* a bird's beak or bill.
Thopí, *s. f.* box, thump.
Thopiyáná, *v. a.* to thump, to slap.
Thopná, *v. a.* to support, to prop; to plaster, to pile, to heap.
Ṭhor, *s. f.* beak, bill (of a bird.)
Thor, } *adj.* a little, small, scarce,
Thoṛá, } few, seldom, some, less.
Thoṛá bahut, *adj.* more or less.
Thoṛá thoṛá, *adj.* a little, by degrees.
Thoṛe se thoṛá, *adj.* very little.
Ṭhoṛhí, } *s. f.* the chin.
Ṭhoṛí, }
Ṭhos, *adj.* solid, compact, firm.
Ṭhosná, *v. a.* to cram in, to stuff.
Thotlá, *adj.* blunt, not sharp.
Thotrá, *adj.* toothless; bruised and spoiled (as the head of a mallet.)
Ṭhuḍḍí, *s.f.* the chin; parched grain.
Ṭhuḍḍí pakaṛná, to flatter, to curry favour.
Thúhar, *s. m.* the name of a plant.
Thúk, *s. m.* spittle.
Thukáná, *v. a.* to cause to spit; to cause to reproach.
Thúk chāṭná, to break one's promise.
Thúk dená, to leave, to give up.
Thukhái, *adj.* base, contemptible, (*i.e.*, fit to be spit upon.)
Thúk lagákar chhoṛná, to treat with sovereign contempt
Thúk lagáná, to apply spittle (a term of abuse and most indecent meaning.)
Thúkná, *v. a.* to spit.
Ṭhukráná, *v. a.* to kick or strike with the toes.
Thuk thukáná, *v. n.* to spit, on the mention of any disease, as a preservative against it.
Ṭhumak, *s. f.* the act of waving or walking with a graceful easy air.
Ṭhumak chál, a dignified pace, stately gait, graceful carriage.
Ṭhumakná, *v. n.* to walk with grace and stateliness, to strut, to walk with dignity.
Ṭhumká, *adj*, short, of low stature.
Ṭhumkí chál, see Ṭhumak chál.
Thúní, *s. f.* a post, pillar, column.
Ṭhunkáná, *v. a.* to cause to knock or hammer.
Ṭhúnṭh, *s. m.* a stump, a branch of a tree (broken off at the end and leafless); an amputated hand.
Ṭhúnṭhá, *adj.* having the hand amputated; having its branches lopped and leafless (a tree.)
Ṭhúnṭhí, *s. f.* stubble.
Ṭhunukná, *v. n.* to sob.
Thupáná, *v. a.* to cause to be supported, propped or plastered.
Ṭhus, an imitative sound, as of a musket ill-charged or flashing in the pan.
Ṭhusakná, *v. a.* to weep, but not loud.
Ṭhusáná, *v. a.* to cause to stuff.
Ṭhuskí, *s. f.* ventris crepitus surdus.
Ṭhuskí chhoṛná, to backbite.
Ṭhusná, *v. n.* to be stuffed, to be crammed.
Ṭhúsná, *v. a.* to cram, to stuff.

Thúthná, *s. m.* } the mouth of a horse, camel, &c.
Thútbní, *s. f.*
Thuthní, *s. f.*
Thúthṛá, *s. m.* the mouth.
Thutkárná, *v. a.* to drive away scornfully.
Ti, *adj.* (in Braj.) three.
Tibára, } *adj.* thrice.
Tibárá,
Tibb, *s. f.* medicine.
Ṭibba, *s. m.* a height, rising ground.
Tidarí, *adj.* three-doored.
Ṭiḍḍá, *s. m.* a grasshopper.
Ṭiḍḍí, *s. f.* a locust.
Tidhar, *adv.* there, in that direction.
Tidhárá, *s. m.* the meeting of three streams.
Tifl, *s. m.* an infant, a child.
Tiflí, *s. f.* infancy, childhood.
Ṭighalná, *v. n.* to be melted, to rarefy.
Tiguná, *adj.* threefold.
Tiháí, *s. f.* the third part; the third part of a piece of cloth for making trousers.
Tihál, *s. f.* the spleen, the milt.
Tihárau, *pron.* (in Braj.) your, of you.
Tihattar, *adj.* seventy-three.
Tihí, *adj.* empty, vain.
Tihídust, *adj.* empty-handed, poor.
Tihídastí, *s. f.* poverty, penury.
Tihrá, *adj.* triple, threefold.
Tihráná, *v. a.* to tertiate, to do the third time, to triple.
Tihwár, *s. m.* see Teohár.
Tíj, *s. f.* the third day of a lunar fortnight.
Tíjá, *s. m.* the third day after the death of a relation, on which oblations are offered; (used among Muhammadans.)
Tijárat, *s. f.* trade, commerce, traffic.
Tijárat karná, to trade.
Tijárí, } *s. f.* a tertian fever or ague.
Tijarí,
Ṭíká, *s. f.* a commentary; a mark or marks made on the forehead by Hindús; an ornament worn on the forehead; the nuptial gifts; inoculation, vaccination.

Ṭíká bhejná, to send the nuptial gifts, which are presented by the relations of the bride to the bridegroom.
Ṭíká lená, to accept nuptial gifts.
Ṭikáná, *v. a.* to retain, to fix in any place, to stop, to lodge, to billet.
Ṭikáo, *s. m.* stability, residence.
Ṭikáú, *adj.* durable, lasting.
Tíkhá, *adj.* angry, passionate; pungent.
Ṭikhná, *v. n.* the calling (of a partridge), to call (a partridge.)
Tíkhur, *s. f.* a starchy substance obtained from the root of the Curcuma angustifolia.
Ṭikí, *s. f.* a small loaf of bread.
Ṭikiyá, *s. f.* a small cake, a little cake of charcoal for the huqqa, a wafer, a bolus.
Tikká, *s. m.* a small piece of flesh, a steak, chop, a collop, a slice.
Ṭikkar, *s. f.* a thick loaf of bread.
Ṭikkí, *s. f.* see Ṭikí.
Ṭikkí lagáná, to earn a scanty livelihood.
Ṭiklí, *s. f.* a wafer, a small round cake; an ornament worn on the forehead.
Ṭikná, *v. n.* to stop, to remain in any place, to be detained; to lodge, stay, to tarry.
Tikoniyá, *adj.* triangular.
Ṭikrí, *s. f.* a wafer; a small round cake.
Tik tik, a sound used in driving a cart.
Ṭikṭikí, *s. f.* a lizard.
Tikúr, *s. f.* see Tíkhur.
Til, *s. m.* the seed of the sesamum, or name of the plant; a mole on the face; a moment, an instant.
Ṭíl, *s. f.* a young hen; a woman (so named in contempt.)
Ṭílá, *s. m.* a rising ground, a small hill, mound, a ridge, a hillock.
Tilá, *s. m.* gold; gold fringe; an ointment, liniment, embrocation.
Tiláí, *adj.* golden: *s. f.* a small frying-pan.

Tilak, *s. m.* the mark which Hindús make on their foreheads; a dowry; a gown.
Tilá karná, to anoint, to embrocate.
Tilakná, *v. n.* to be gray (the hair.)
Tilangá, *s. m.* a soldier; a paper kite.
Tilangí, *s. f.* a kind of child's kite.
Tilaṛá, *s. m.* } a necklace of three
Tilaṛí, *s. f.* } strings.
Tiláwat, *s. f.* meditation, reading (particularly the Qurán, as an act of religion.)
Tilcháolí, *s. f.* mixture composed of rice and sesamum seeds.
Tilchaṭṭá, *s. m.* a cockroach.
Tilendá, *s. m.* see Tirendá.
Tílí, *s. f.* a bar (as of a cage, &c.)
Tilism, *s. m.* a talisman.
Tilismátí, *adj.* talismanic, magical.
Ṭiliyá, *s. f.* a young hen.
Til ká tel, *s. m.* sesamum oil.
Tilkuṭ, *s. m.* the name of a sweetmeat composed of pounded sesamum and sugar.
Tillá, *s. m.* a golden border of a turban.
Tilládání, *s. f.* a housewife or small bag for holding needles, thread, &c.
Tilláná, *s. m.* a kind of song.
Tillí, *s. f.* the spleen or milt.
Tilmuṉhá, *adj.* (spoken of a lamp) sloped so that the oil may reach the wick.
Tilúá, *s. m.* a kind of sweetmeat.
Tilwáṉsá, *adj.* see Tilmuṉhá.
Ṭímṭám, *s. m.* dressing.
Ṭimṭim, *s. m.* a sound.
Ṭimṭimáná, *v. n.* to give a faint light.
Tín, *adj.* three.
Tin, *pron. plur. inflect.* whom, them, those.
Tínat, *s. f.* nature, disposition.
Tinheṉ, to them, to those, &c.
Tinká, *s. m.* a straw, a bit of the stalk of grass.
Tinoṉ thán, *s. m.* the private parts.
Tín terah, *adj.* dispersed, scattered, ruined.
Tín thán, *s. m.* the private parts.
Ṭíp, *s. f.* a note of hand, a cheque; raising the voice in singing; the act of pressing, compressing.
Tipárí, *s. f.* the Indian gooseberry.
Ṭípná, *v. a.* to press, to compress, to squeeze, to grope, to feel.
Ṭípṭáp, *s. f.* ornament, the act of pressing or compressing.
Tír, *s. m.* an arrow; the bank of a river, the shore of a sea; near.
Tirá, *contract.* of Terá, thy, thine.
Tiráju, *prop.* Tarázú, which see.
Tiráná, *v. a.* to cause to pass over or swim; to save.
Tiránawwe, *adj.* ninety-three.
Tírandáz, *s. m.* an archer, a bowman.
Tírandází, *s. f.* archery.
Tirás, *s. f.* thirst.
Tirás áná, to be thirsty.
Tirásí, *adj.* eighty-three.
Tirás lagná, to be thirsty.
Tírath, *s. m.* see Tírth.
Tír chaláná, *v. a.* to shoot an arrow.
Tirchhá, *adj.* crooked, across, bent, awry, askant; perverse.
Tirchhá dekhná, to squint.
Tirchhí ánkh karná, to look angrily, to cast unkind looks.
Tirchhí nazar, leer, ogle, side glance, squint.
Tirchhiyáná, *v. n.* to edge, to go obliquely.
Tirendá, *s. m.* the float of a fishing line, a float or buoy.
Tirhut, *s. f.* name of a district.
Tirhutiyá, *adj.* belonging to Tirhut, produced in Tirhut.
Ṭiṛí, *s. f.* a locust.
Tirí birí, *adj.* dispersed.
Tiriyá, *s. f.* a woman, a female.
Tiriyá charitr, *s. m.* female wiles.
Tiriyáráj, *s. m.* petticoat government.
Tirkhá, *s. f.* thirst; desire.
Tirlok, *s.* the three worlds, *i.e.*, heaven, earth, and the regions under the earth; the universe.
Tirmirí, *s. f.* vertigo; darkness.

Tirná, *v. n.* to swim, to cross over.
Tirpan, *adj.* fifty-three.
Tirsaṭh, *adj.* sixty-three.
Tírth, *s. m.* a sacred place, a place of pilgrimage, pilgrimage.
Tírthjátrá, *s.* the going to a sacred place on pilgrimage.
Tírthjátrí, *s.* a pilgrim.
Tírthráj, the city of Aláhábád.
Tís, *adj.* thirty.
Tis, *inflect. pron.* that, which, &c.
Ṭís, *s. f.* a throb, throbbing, a shooting pain.
Tishna, *adj.* thirsty: *s. f.* thirst.
Tishnagí, *s. f.* thirst.
Tísí, *s. f.* flax, flax-seed.
Ṭís márná, *v. n.* to throb.
Tis pa, } besides, over and above,
Tis par, } moreover, yet, nevertheless, still, then, after that, thereon, whereat.
Tis par bhí, thereupon, nevertheless, yet, still, notwithstanding.
Tísrá, *adj.* third.
Tisráyat, *s. m.* a third person, an umpire.
Tísre, in the third place, thirdly.
Tíswáṉ, the thirtieth.
Títá, *adj.* bitter, pungent, hot, acrid.
Titaggí, *s. f.* a thread of three strings.
Títar, *s. m.* a partridge.
Titar bitar, *adj.* dispersed.
Tith, *s. f.* a lunar day.
Titimbá, *s. m.* an obstacle, an impediment; stratagem.
Ṭiṭkárí, *s. f.* the noise made by drawing the tongue from the roof of the mouth, to make horses, &c., proceed.
Ṭiṭkárná, *v. a.* to urge an animal by [Ṭiṭkárí.
Títlí, *s. f.* a butterfly.
Titná, *adj. m.* so many, so much.
Titne meṉ, in so much (time), in the meanwhile.
Titní, *adj. f.* so many, so much.
Títrí, *s. f.* a butterfly.
Tittar bittar, *adj.* dispersed.
Tiwásí, *adj.* stale, three days old.

To, a conjunction introducing the answer to a conditional proposition, then, that; an adverb denoting asseveration, indeed, in, fact; then, that time, in that case, moreover, that, also, for, yes, well.
Ṭoá, *s. f.* act of feeling or groping.
Ṭoáṭái, *s. f.* searching, feeling for, feeling (with the hand.)
To bhí, *adv.* even, then; still, yet, nevertheless.
Tobṛa, } *s. m.* the bag out of which
Tobṛá, } horses eat their corn; a portmanteau.
Ṭoh, *s.* spying, watching, espionage.
Ṭok, *s. f.* hindrance, prevention; the influence of an evil eye; a promontory, a cape.
Ṭokáṭokí, *s. f.* hindrance, prevention.
Ṭokná, *v. a.* to interrogate, to prevent, to challenge; to look at with an evil eye.
Ṭoknewálá, *adj.* narrowly inspecting.
Ṭokrá, *s. m.* a large basket without a lid.
Ṭokrí, *s. f.* a small basket without a [lid.
Ṭok ṭák, *s. f.* hindrance, prevention.
Tol, *s. m.* weight, weighing.
Ṭol, *s. m.* a company, a society.
Tolá, } *s. m.* a rupee weight; a
Tola, } weight of 100 ratís.
Ṭolá, *s. m.* a quarter or particular part of a town.
Ṭolí, *s. f.* a company, society, crowd.
Ṭol márná, *v. a.* to dash one top against another while in motion.
Tolná, *v. a.* to weigh, to balance.
Tomṛá, *s. m.* } a hollowed gourd.
Tomṛí, *s. f.* }
Toṉ, *adv.* so, in that manner, then.
Ṭoná, *s. m.* enchantment, fascination, sorcery, witchcraft: *v. a.* to feel, to grope, to handle.
Ṭoná ṭáman, *s. m.* } hocus - pocus,
Ṭoná ṭání, *s. f.* } juggling, magic, sorcery, witchcraft.
Tond, *s. f.* a large belly, potbelly.

Tondail, Toudailá, Tondálá, } *adj.* potbellied, gorbellied, corpulent.

Tondí, *s. f.* the navel.

Ṭonhá, *s. m.* a juggler, a conjurer; a wizard.

Ṭonhái, *s. f.* a female juggler or conjurer; a witch.

Tonhín, *adv.* exactly then.

Ṭonṭá, *s. m.* a joint of bamboo; a cartridge; a cracker, a serpent in fireworks: *adj.* handless.

Ṭonṭí, *s. f.* a spout; a round tile fixed on the eaves. [a stitch.

Ṭop, *s. m.* a hat, a cap, helmet, cover;

Top, *s. f.* a cannon, a gun.

Ṭopá, *s. m.* a helmet, cap, hat.

Topak, *s. f.* a small cannon.

Topáná, *v. a.* to have buried, to cause to cover.

Top chaláná, Top chhoṛná, } *v. a.* to cannonade, to fire a cannon.

Top chhúṭná, Top daghná, } to be fired (a cannon.)

Top dághná, to cannonade, to fire a cannon.

Ṭopí, *s. f.* a hat, a cap, a cover.

Ṭopíwálá, one who wears a hat; an European in general.

Topkháná, *s. m.* a park of artillery, the place where cannon and artillery stores are kept, an arsenal.

Top lagáná, Top márná, } to cannonade.

Topná, *v. a.* to bury, to cover.

Tor, *s. f.* a net thrown over a woman's pálkí: *pron.* thy, thine.

Toṛ, *s. m.* the strength of a current; a net thrown over a woman's pálkí.

Torá, *pron.* thy, thine.

Tora, *s. m.* a number of trays, containing various dishes of food, presented to others by great men.

Toṛá, *s. m.* a purse, a bag containing one thousand rupees; the match of a gun; an ornament like a chain; scarcity, want.

Torabandí, *s. f.* the arrangement or sending out of trays of food as presents.

Toṛadár, a matchlock.

Toṛáná, *v. a.* to cause to be broken or changed (as money.)

Toraposh, *s. m.* a covering for dishes, &c. [pull down.

Toṛ ḍálná, to break and destroy, to

Toṛ dená, to break to pieces, to spoil.

Toṛedár, a matchlock.

Torhí, *s. m.* a trumpet.

Torí, *s. f.* a kind of cucumber.

Toṛí, *adv.* till, up to: *s. f.* a kind of mustard seed. [mode.

Ṭorí, *s. f.* the name of a musical

Toṛjoṛ, *s. m.* cutting out (as cloth by a tailor); arranging a speech, &c.

Toṛ karná, to make a breach (as a ball.)

Toṛ lená, to gather, to pluck (fruit.)

Toṛná, *v. a.* to break, tear, rend, burst, split; to change (as coin); to pluck or gather (fruit, flowers, &c.)

Toṛphoṛ, *s. m.* breaking, plain speaking. [ing.

Toṛtáṛ, *s. m.* breaking and destroy-

Toṛwái, *s. f.* price paid for changing money.

Toṛwáná, *v. a.* to cause to be broken or to be changed (coin.)

Tosak, *s. f. prop.* Toshak, which see.

Tosdán, *s. m.* a cartridge-box.

Tosha, *s. m.* provision (particularly of a traveller, or that which is carried with the funeral of a deceased person, to support him during his journey to the other world), viaticum.

Toshak, *s. f.* a bed, a mattress.

Toshakháná, *s. m.* a wardrobe, a place where furniture is kept.

Toshdán, *s. m.* a pouch, a cartouch-box. [gun.

Totá, *s. m.* a parrot; the cock of a

Toṭá, Ṭoṭá, } *s. m.* loss, deficiency; a cartridge; a candle's end.

Totí, *s. f.* a female parrot.
Toṭká, } *s. m.* a charm, an amulet,
Ṭoṭká, } a superstitious remedy.
Totlá, *adj.* lisper, stutterer, stammerer, speaking imperfectly (as a child.)
Totláná, } *v. n.* to lisp, to speak im-
Totráná, } perfectly (as a child.)
Tráh, } *interj.* mercy! save!
Tráhi, }
Tráhi tráhi karná, to cry out for mercy; to repent of a sin.
Trán, *s. m.* safety, salvation.
Tránkartá, *s.* a saviour, a deliverer.
Trás, *s. f.* thirst; alarm, dread.
Trás lagná, to be thirsty.
Tretá, *s. f.* the name of the second Hindú jug, the silver age.
Tribeni, *s. f.* the conflux of three sacred rivers.
Tribhuwan, *s. m.* the three worlds, viz., heaven, earth, and the infernal regions: the universe.
Trilok, *s. m.* see Tirlok.
Trin, *s. m.* grass.
Tripauliyá, *s. m.* a building with three doors or arches.
Triphalá, *s. m* the name of a medicine composed of three kinds of myrobalans.
Tript, *adj.* pleased, satisfied, gratified.
Trisúl, *s. m.* a trident; a three-pointed pike or spear.
Triyá, *s. f.* a woman, a female.
Tú, *pron.* thou.
Tuchh, *adj.* contemptible, despicable, worthless.
Tuchh karná, to despise, to contemn, to disregard.
Tuchh samajhná, to think lightly of.
Túda, *s. m.* a mound, a heap, a stack; a target.
Túda e túfán, accusing, charging with crime; a calumniator.
Tuf, *s. m.* spittle, saliva; a curse.
Tufail, by the means, through, for the sake.
Túfán, *s. m.* a storm, a tempest, a hurricane; calumny, defamation.
Tufang, *s. f.* a musket, a tube for discharging arrows, &c.
Túfání, *adj.* quarrelsome, boisterous.
Túfán lagáná, to calumniate, to defame.
Tufúliyat, *s. f.* infancy, childhood.
Tuhfa, *s. m.* a curiosty, rarity, the best or beauty (of a thing); a present: *adj.* rare, uncommon, excellent, beautiful, wonderful.
Tuhfagí, *s. f.* excellence, rarity, beauty, neatness, elegance.
Tuhfaját, *s. plur.* of Tuhfa, rarities, curiosities, presents.
Túhí, thou thyself, thou even.
Tuhmat, *s. f.* suspicion of guilt, false accusation, calumny, slander, falsely charging one with a crime, aspersion, imputation.
Tuhmat dená, to belie, to calumniate, slander, asperse, traduce, accuse falsely.
Tuhmatí, *adj.* suspicious, ignominious; a calumniator.
Tuhmat lagáná, see Tuhmat dená.
Ṭuhukná, *v. n.* to cry.
Tujjár, *s. m.* a merchant.
Tuk, } *s. f.* a moment.
Ṭuk, }
Ṭúk, } *s. m.* a piece, a little, a par-
Ṭúká, } ticle, an atom, a bit.
Tukam, *s. m. prop.* Tukhm, which see.
Tú karná, *v. a.* to thou.
Tuk ek, for one moment.
Ṭuk ek, a little way.
Tukhm, *s. m.* seed; an egg; sperm.
Tukhm i bálangú, *s. m.* a seed of a cooling quality.
Tukká, *s. m.* a sort of arrow blunt at the end.
Tukkal, *s. f.* a kind of paper kite.
Tukkash, *s. m.* a quiver.
Tuklá, *s. m.* a kind of paper kite.
Tuklí, *s. f.* a child's kite.
Tukma, *s. m.* a loop, an eye-loop, a button.
Ṭukrá, } *s. m.* a piece, a portion, a
Ṭukṛá, } bit, a division, a morsel.

Ṭukṛápurza, *s. m.* scraps, clippings, shavings.

Ṭukṛá ṭukṛá, *adv.* piecemeal, in pieces.

Ṭukṛá ṭukṛá karná, to cut to pieces, to shatter, to smash.

Ṭukrgadá, a beggar for a bit of bread, &c.

Ṭukṛí, *s. f.* see Ṭukṛá.

Túl, *s. m.* length, prolixity: *adj.* long, tall, lasting long.

Tul, *adj.* alike, like, resembling.

Tulá, *s. f.* the sign Libra of the zodiac.

Tuláná, *v. a.* to cause to be weighed; to tar, oil, or grease (wheels.)

Tuláwá, *s. m.* part of a Hindústání carriage, which rests on the axle-tree arm and supports the body of the carriage.

Tul baiṭhná, to sit straight and compact (as in a boat which might be overset by sitting uneven or carelessly.)

Túl i kalám, prolixity, length of discourse, many words.

Tulná, *v. n.* to be weighed or balanced.

Tulsí, *s. f.* the name of a shrub worshipped by Hindús.

Tulsídás, *n. prop.* name of a Gosáiṉ.

Túltawíl, *adj.* lasting long.

Tultuláná, *v. n.* to become soft (as a sore or boil when suppurating.)

Tulụ́, *s. m.* rising (as the sun, &c.)

Tulụ́ honá, to rise (the sun.)

Tum, *pron.* you.

Ṭúm, *s. m.* trifles.

Tumáí, *s. f.* the price of carding.

Tuman, *s. m.* troop, squadron.

Tumáná, *v. a.* to cause to be carded.

Tumandár, *s. m.* the commander of a Tuman.

Tum áp, you yourself.

Tumárá, *pron.* your.

Túmbá, *s. m.* a hollowed gourd; the rind of a gourd, in which beggars and faqírs carry water, &c.

Túmbí, *s. f.* a small túmbá; a kind of pipe (chiefly used by those who exhibit snakes.)

Tumeṉ, see Tumheṉ.

Tumhárá, *pron. 2nd pers. mas. gen. plur.* yours, your, of you.

Tumheṉ, *pron. plur. object. case*, to you, you.

Tumhoṉ ko, to you.

Túmiyá, *s. m.* thread made of carded cotton, in opposition to that made of what has been beat only.

Tum ko, to you.

Túmná, *v. a.* to card or separate wool or cotton with the fingers, preparatory to combing.

Túmrí, *s. f.* the snout of a crocodile, alligator, &c.

Ṭúmṭám, *s. m.* a few trifles; an ornament.

Tumtaráq, *s. m.* magnificence, grandeur, pomp.

Tumtaráqí, *adj.* pompous, ostentatious.

Tun, } **Tún,** } *s. m.* name of a tree from the timber of which furniture is made.

Túṉ, *pron.* thou.

Ṭúṉ, *s. m.* ventris crepitis.

Tunak, *adj.* slight, weak, delicate, thin.

Tund, *adj.* active, quick, swift, violent, fierce, spirited, hot, acrid.

Ṭunḍ, *s. m.* a hand or branch that has been cut off.

Ṭunḍá, *adj.* handless, one born without hands.

Tund honá, to be angry, to be displeased,

Ṭunḍí, *adj. f.* handless: *f.* the navel.

Túnḍí, *s. f.* a small branch or stump of a tree broken at the end and leafless; the navel.

Tundí, *s. f.* fierceness, activity, impetuosity.

Ṭunḍí bándhná, } **Ṭunḍí chaṛháná**, } **Ṭunḍí kasná**, } to tie the hands behind the back.

Ṭundiyáṉ bándhná, | Ṭundiyáṉ chaṛháná, | Ṭundiyáṉ kasná, } to tie the hands behind the back.
Tundḳho, *adj*. irascible, of a fiery disposition, furious, passionate.
Tundmizáj, *adj*. hot-headed, passionate.
Tundraftár, *adj*. fast-going.
Ṭúng, | Ṭungár, } *s. f.* pecking, nibbling of fruit, &c., more for amusement than from appetite.
Ṭúngá ṭángí, *s. f.* pecking and nibbling.
Ṭúngná, *v. a.* to peck, to nibble, to chew straws, &c., for amusement.
Ṭuṉiyá, *adj*. tiny.
Ṭuṉiyá totá, a kind of parrot.
Ṭunkí, *s. f.* a fine kind of bread or wafers thin as muslin.
Tunn, *s. m.* see Tun.
Túṉ táṉ karná, to dispute, to wrangle, to abuse.
Ṭunṭunáná, *v. a.* to tune slowly.
Ṭunuk, *adj*. slight, weak, delicate, thin, brittle.
Tunukmizáj, *adj*. whimsical, captious, peevish, fretful.
Tunukmizájí, *s. f.* peevishness, captiousness.
Tupak, *s. f.* a small cannon.
Tupáná, *v. a.* to have buried, to cause to cover.
Túr, *s. m.* a mountain; Sinai.
Tura'í, *s. f.* the name of a kind of cucumber.
Tuṛáná, *v. a.* to cause to break, to change (as money.)
Turang, *s. m.* a horse.
Turant, *adv.* instantly, quickly, directly.
Turapná, *v. a.* to sew (in a particular manner), to stitch.
Turat, *adv.* see Turant.
Turbat, *s. f.* a tomb, a sepulchre.
Turfa, *adj*. wonderful, strange, rare, agreeable (anything.)
Turhí, *s. f.* a trumpet, a clarion.
Turk, *s. m.* a Musalmán, a Turk.
Turkan, | Turkaní, } *s. f.* a Turkish woman.
Turkí, *adj*. Turkish: *s. m.* a kind of horse.
Turkin, *s. f.* a Turkish woman
Turksawár, *s. m.* a horseman, a cavalier.
Turpan, *s. f.* a kind of stitch.
Turpáná, *v. a.* to stitch, to hem.
Turra, *s. m.* an ornament worn in the turban; a ringlet, a curl.
Tursh, *adj*. sour, harsh; ill-tempered, crabbed.
Turshái, | Turshí, } *s. f.* sourness, acidity. harshness.
Turshmizáj, *adj*. sour-tempered, harsh, morose.
Turshrú, *adj*. cynical, morose, surly, stern; ugly.
Turt, *adv.* instantly, quickly, immediately, presently, directly.
Turtí phurtí, *adv.* hastily, quickly.
Turt phurt, *adv.* see Turt.
Turunj, *s. m.* a citron.
Tuṛwáná, *v. a.* to cause to break, &c., to cause to be changed (money.)
Ṭusakná, *v. n.* to cry, to weep, to sob.
Túsí, *s. f.* a colour so called, a kind of purple colour.
Ṭúsí, *s. f.* a bud, a young flower.
Tút, *s. m.* a mulberry.
Ṭúṭ, *s. f.* fracture, breaking; misunderstanding between friends; harm, loss deficiency; a passage omitted in the writing of a book which is afterwards written in the margin.
Ṭúṭá, *adj*. broken, decayed.
Ṭúṭan pháṭan, *s. m.* chips, clippings, filings, fragments.
Ṭuṭá phúṭá, *adj*. fragments, broken to pieces.
Ṭúṭí, *s.* loss, failure, deficiency.
Túṭí, *s. f.* a parrot, a paroquet.
Tútiyá, *s. m.* blue vitriol, tutty.
Ṭúṭ jáná, to be broken; to pine.
Ṭuṭká, *s. m.* a charm, a superstitious remedy.

Tutlá, *adj*. lisping.
Tutláná, *v. n.* to lisp, to speak imperfectly as a child.
Tutlí, *adj. f.* lisping.
Ṭúṭná, *v. n.* to break, to be broken, to burst, to fail, to break forth, or rush upon, to assault; to be helpless or destitute.
Ṭúṭ paṛná, to break in upon, to rush in, to be collected in crowds.
Ṭúṭ rahná, to be distressed, to be weary, to be reduced to poverty, to pine away; to be separated.
Tutráná, *v. n.* see Tutláná.
Tú tú, sound of calling a dog.
Tuzuk, *s. m.* retinue, pomp.
Tyág, *s.m.* abdication, abandonment, leaving, renunciation.
Tyág dená, **Tyág karná**, **Tyágná**, *v. a.* to leave, to abandon, to desert, to forsake, to quit, to abdicate, to resign.
Tyág patr, *s.m.* a bill of divorcement.
Tyauṉ, **Tyoṉ**, **Tyúṉ**, *adv.* so, in like manner; at the same time, then.

U.

U, a short vowel pronounced invariaby as *u* in bull.
U', a long vowel, pronounced invariably as *u* in tube.
Ubá, *s. f. prop.* Wabá, which see.
Ubachhná, *v. a.* to throw up water, to bale.
Ubakná, *v. n.* to vomit.
Ubalná, **U'balná**, *v. n.* to boil or boil up.
Ubálná, *v. a.* to boil, to make boil.
U'baṛ khábaṛ, *adj.* uneven, rugged.
Ubarná, *v. n.* to be set at liberty; to remain over and above, to exceed.
Ubárná, *v. a.* to set at liberty; to economize, to reserve, to keep in reserve.
Ubasná, *v. n.* to rot, to putrefy.
Uḅharná, *v. n.* to swell, to overflow; to be unladen (a cart or boat.)
Ubhárná, *v. a.* to undo, to unravel.
Ubhrá, *part.* unladen (as a cart or boat.)
Ubhrá honá, to be unladen.
Ubhráná, *v. a.* to lighten, to unload (a boat); to fill a vessel till it runs over.
Ubkáí, *s. f.* nausea.
Ubláná, *v. a.* to cause to boil (by the hands of another), to boil anything with such violence that it is spilled.
Ubráná, *v. a.* to reserve, keep remaining, or in store.
Ubṭan, **Ubṭaná**, *s. m.* a composition of perfumes, flour, &c., used to rub the body with.
Uchakká, *s. m.* **Uchakkí**, *s. f.* a thief, a pickpocket, a swindler.
Uchakná, *v. n.* to rise, to be raised or lifted, to leap, bound, spring up.
Uchalná, *v. n.* to separate, to be separated: *v. a.* to toss up (as corn in a sieve.)
Ucháná, *v. a.* to lift up a burden; to wash the hands after eating.
Ucháṭ honá, to be tired, to be disgusted; to be broken (sleep.)
Ucháṭí, *s. f.* the act of vexing or rendering sorrowful, vexation.
Uchaṭná, *v. n.* to be alienated; to separate, to be separated (as plaster from a wall); to slip, to slide, to bound (as a sword striking a hard body obliquely); to be broken or interrupted (sleep.)
Ucháṭná, *v. a.* to divide, to separate.
Uchchá, *adj.* high, lofty.
Uchchán, *s. f.* height, elevation.
Uchchár, **Uchcháran**, *s. m.* pronunciation, utterance, articulation.
Uchcharná, *v. n.* to separate (as the skin from the flesh, &c.); to be uttered or pronounced: *v. a.* to speak, utter, pronounce.
Uchchárná, *v. a.* to pronounce, to speak out, articulate, express.
Uchcháṭná, *s. m.* see Uchháṭí.

Uchhalná, } v. n. to leap, to bound,
Uchhalná, } to spring or spout up (as water in a fountain), to spring or fly up; to bounce up, to ascend, to beat (as a pulse.)

Uchhálná, *v. a.* to throw up, to toss up a thing (as a ball, &c.), and catch it in the hand.

Uchal parná, *v. n.* to become enraged.

Uchhkún, *s. m.* anything placed under a vessel, &c., to prevent its oversetting; a prop, a support.

Uchhláná, *v. a.* to cause another to throw up anything.

Uchit, *adj.* proper, fit, suitable.

Uchkáná, *v. a.* to lift or raise up.

Uchláná, *v. a.* to order a person to separate (one thing from another.)

Uchoṭ, *s. f.* a trip, a stumble.

Uchoṭ kháná, to trip, to stumble.

Ud, *s. m.* an otter.

Ụd, *s. m.* the wood aloes.

Udá, *adj.* of a light brown colour.

Udáhaṭ, } *s. f.* brownness.
Udáí, }

Udai, *s. m.* the rising of the sun or any of the heavenly bodies.

Udai honá, to rise (the sun, &c.)

Udar, *s. m.* the belly.

Udar píṛá, *s. f.* dysentery, a diarrhœa.

Udás, *adj.* lonely, forlorn, dejected, sorrowful, sad.

Udásí, *adj.* dejected, out of spirits, sad, lonely; a class of faqírs.

Udásín, *adj.* dejected, out of spirits, sad.

Udaya, *s. m.* see Udai.

Udbhav, *s. m.* act of springing up (as plants from seed.)

Udbiláo, *s. m.* an otter.

Uddhár, *s. m.* rescue, deliverance, salvation; debt, loan, credit.

Uddim, *s. m.* exertion, endeavour, labour; calling, employment, trade.

Udes, } *s. m.* news, intelligence.
Udesá, }

Udham, *s. m.* noise, impudence, rebellion, disturbance.

Udhamí, *adj.* making noise, impudent, rebellious.

Udhár, *s. m.* sale on credit.

Udhar, } *adv.* there, thither, on that
Udhar, } side, that way.

Udhárná, *v. a.* to liberate, to discharge, to save.

Udhar se, from that, or the other side.

Udheṛná, *v. a.* to undo, to unravel, to unfold, to strip off, rip, skin, excoriate.

Udhir, *adv.* see Udhar.

Udhrá, *adj.* opened, undone, unrolled (as the seam in a garment, or thread which has been rolled up in a clue.)

Udhrá pudhrá, *adj.* see Udhrá.

Udit, *adj.* rising (as the sun); distinguished, conspicuous.

Ụdsoz, *s.* an utensil to burn wood of aloes (or gum benzoin) in.

Ụdúl, *s. m.* deviation, declining, refusing, disobeying.

Ụdúl hukmí karná, to disobey orders.

Ụdúl karná, to deviate from, disobey, decline, refuse.

Udveg, *s. m.* agitation, consternation, anxiety, uneasiness, perplexity.

Udyam, *s. m.* see Uddim.

Uf, *interj.* fye! poh! for shame! alas!

Uf karná, to lament, to disapprove of.

Uftáda, *adj.* waste (land), fallen, lying (on the ground.)

Ugáhí, *s. f.* usury; the trade of lending money on interest of one-fourth, the payment of which is received by instalments.

Ugáhná, *v. a.* to gather, to collect, to accumulate.

Ugairá, *prop.* Waghaira, which see.

Ugál, *s. m.* that which is spit out after chewing anything (as betel-leaf, &c.)

Ugaldán, } *s. m.* a spittoon, a vessel
Ugáldán, } for spitting in.

Ugalná, *v. a.* to spit out, to vomit; to refund property surreptitiously obtained.

Ugáná, *v. a.* to cause to grow, &c.
Ughaṛná, *v. n.* to be uncovered, discovered, opened, pulled off.
Ughárná, *v. a.* to uncover, discover, unveil, open, pull off, unclose, bare.
Ugháṛú, *s. m.* one who uncovers or unveils.
Ugná, *v. n.* to grow, to be produced, to spring (as plants), to rise (as the moon.)
Ugte hí jaljáná, to be withered immediately on springing up (is applied to a hope or expectation which is blasted in the bud.)
Uh, an exclamation denoting pain,&c.
Uhár, *s. m.* a covering, a cover of a pálkí for women.
Uharná, *v. n.* to subside (a swelling or inundation.)
Ụhda, *s. m. vulg.* Hudda, a commission; business, office, post, appointment.
Ụhdadár, } entrusted with a business, employed, holding a commission, an officer.
Ụhdedár, }
U'í, *interj.* oh! oh fie!
Ujaḍḍ, *adj.* inconsiderate, rash, ignorant, clownish.
Ujágar, *s. m.* splendour: *adj.* splendid, famous.
Ujálá, *s. m.* } splendour, brightness, light.
Ujálí, *s. f.* }
Ujalná, *v. n.* to become clean, to shine, to be bright.
Ujan, *s. m. prop.* Wazn, which see.
Uján, *s. m.* the direction or part of a river which is opposite to the course of the stream, up the stream.
Ujar, *s. m. prop.* Ụzr, which see.
Ujáṛ, *adj.* desolate, ruined, demolished, deserted, abandoned.
Ujaṛná, *v. n.* to become desolate.
Ujáṛná, *v. a.* to lay waste, desolate, injure, expose to loss.
Ujaṛwáná, *v. a.* to lay waste by the hands of a third person.
Ujhakná, *v. n.* to peep, to spy.
Ujhalná, *v. n.* to flow or be poured from one vessel to another: *v. a.* to throw or pour quickly from one vessel into another.
Ujhálná, *v. a.* to pour from one vessel to another.
Ujhaṛ, *adj.* ignorant, clownish, clumsy, awkward.
Ujír, *s. m. prop.* Wazír, which see.
Ujírí, *s. f.* see Wazírí.
Ujjal, *adj.* clear, pure, shining, luminous, bright, splendid, white.
Ujjhaṛ, *adj.* ignorant, illiterate, clownish, clumsy, awkward.
Ujlá, *adj.* white. See Ujjal.
Ujláná, *v. a.* to cause to cleanse, to brighten.
Ujṛápujṛá, *adj.* in ruins, desolate.
Ujrat, *s. f.* reward, wages, hire.
Ụjúba, *s. m.* wonder, miracle, prodigy: *adj.* wonderful.
Ujwáná, *v. a.* to cause a person to pour from one vessel into another.
Ukálat, *s. f. prop.* Wakálat, which see.
Ukálatnáma, *s. m. prop.* Wakálatnáma, which see.
Ukasná, *v. n.* to be excited, to be moved, to try to move.
Ukaṭná, *v. a.* to dig up slowly a thing buried in the ground, to extract a secret gradually and artfully, to pump.
U'kh, *s. f.* sugarcane.
Ukhaṛná, *v. n.* to be rooted up, raised up or plucked up, to slip out (as a bone, &c.)
Ukháṛná, *v. a.* to root up, to eradicate, to extirppate, to break or pluck up; to dislocate.
Ukhaṛná pukhaṛná, to be plucked or rooted up.
Ukhaṛwáná, *v. a.* to cause to pluck or root up.
Ukheṛná, *v. a.* see Ukháṛná.
Ukheṛwáná, *v. a.* to cause to pluck or root up.
Ukhlí, *s. f.* wooden mortar.
Ukhmaj, *s.* insects produced by heat; musquitoes, gnats, flies, &c.

Ukhṛáná, *v. a.* to pluck up, to eradicate.
Ukíl, *s. m. prop.* Wakíl, which see.
Ukílí, *s. f.* see Wakílí.
Ukná, *v. n.* to miss, to err, to trip, to mistake.
Ukṛú, *s. m.* the posture of sitting on the hams with the soles of the feet on the ground.
Uktáná, *v. n.* to be uneasy, to be dejected, to fret; to be tired of.
Ukṭáná, *v. a.* to extract a secret gradually and artfully, to pump.
Ulá, *adj.* best.
Ulachná, *v. a.* to throw out the water from anything, to drain.
Uláhná, } *s. m.* a complaint (not
Ulahná, } judicial), accusation; reproof, chiding.
Ulahná dená, to reproach, complain (to), accuse, blame.
Ulajhná, *v. n.* to be entangled, to ravel, to be involved (in difficulties); to be embroiled.
Ulajh pulajh jáná, *v. n.* see Ulajhná.
Ulák, *s. f. prop.* Uláq, which see.
Ulamá, *s. plur.* of Álim, the learned.
Ulang, *adj.* naked.
Ulangná, *v.n.* to bound or spring over.
Uláq, *s. f.* a kind of small boat.
Ulár, *adj.* laden too much behind (a cart or boat.)
Ularná, *v. n.* to lie down, to rest.
Ulash, *s. m.* leavings of a superior.
Ulaṭná, *v. a.* to pervert, to subvert, to reverse, to overturn: *v. n.* to be reversed, turned over or back.
Ulaṭpulaṭ, *adj.* higgledy piggledy, topsy turvy, upside down: *s. f.* confusion, interchange.
Ulenḍná, *v. a.* to pour water.
Ulfat, *s. f.* friendship, familiarity, intimacy, affection, attachment.
Ulfatí, *adj.* friendly, affectionate.
Ulfatí banda, attached from friendship.
Ulfat karná, to form friendship, to be intimate.

Ulgáná, *v. a.* to cause to leap over.
Ulichná, *v. a.* to throw up water, to bale.
Uljhan, *s. f.* entanglement, complication.
Uljháná, *v. a.* to entangle, to ravel (as thread), to involve (in difficulties, business, &c.), to embroil.
Uljháo, } *s. m.* entanglement, per-
Uljheṛá, } plexity, intricacy.
Ullanghan, *s. m.* transgression.
Ullú, *s. m.* an owl; (*met.*) a stupid fellow, a blockhead, a fool.
Ullúpan, *s. m.* stupidity, folly.
Ulṭá, *adj.* reversed, turned back: *s. m.* reverse, opposite, contrary.
Ulṭáná, *v. a.* to overturn, turn over, overset, upset, invert, reverse.
Ulṭáná pulṭáná, *v. a.* to put into disorder or confusion; to reverse.
Ulṭá pulṭá, *adj.* topsy turvy, higgledy piggledy.
Ulṭí samajh, *s. f.* a perverse or absurd idea.
Ulú, *s. m.* a kind of grass.
Ulúá, *s. m.* an owl; a kind of grass.
Ulúhíyat, *s. f.* divinity, deity.
Ulwá, *s. m.* a kind of grass.
Umaḍná, } *v. n.* to overflow, abound,
Umanḍná, } fall (as tears), gush, swell, increase, or be poured out (as a river, clouds, an army, the heart, &c.) [exultation.
Umang, *s. f.* excessive joy, transport,
Umangná, *v. n.* to advance with joy.
Umará, *s. plur.* of Amír, nobles, grandees, a noble (generally.)
Umaráí, *s. f.* nobility, greatness.
Umaráo, see Umará.
Umaṛná, *v. n.* see Umaḍná.
Umda, *adj.* excellent, great, noble.
Umḍá dená, *v. a.* to overflow.
Umdagí, *s. f.* greatness, &c.
Umed, } *s. f.* hope, expectation,
Ummaid, } trust, dependence.
Ummaidwár, *adj.* see Ummedwár.
Ummat, *s. f.* people, sect, a people of the same religion.

Ummed, *s. f.* see Ummaid.
Ummed se, pregnant.
Ummedwár, *adj.* hopeful, hoping, expecting : *s.* an expectant, a candidate.
Ummedwár honá, to hope, to be hoping.
Ummedwárí, *s. f.* expectation, hope, dependence.
Ummí, *adj.* unable to read or write; uneducated, illiterate, stupid.
Umr, *s. f.* age, life-time, period of life.
Umr bhar, all lifetime.
Umr daráz honá, *v. n.* to be old.
Umrá, *s. m.* a noble or opulent man.
Umráí, *s. f.* grandeur.
Umuq, *s. m.* depth, profundity.
Un, a *pron. plur.* in the *oblique case*, those, them.
Un, *s. f.* wool.
Unásí, *adj.* seventy-nine.
Unch, *adj.* high, tall, lofty.
Unchá, } Unchá, } *adj.* high, tall, lofty, above, steep; loud.
Unchá bolná, to speak with pride.
Uncháhaṭ, *s. f.* height, elevation.
Uncháí, } Uncháí, } *s. f.* height, elevation, eminence, tallness.
Unchákání, *s. f.* deafness.
Unchális, *adj.* thirty-nine.
Unchán, *s. m.* height.
Uncháná, *v. a.* to raise, to take up.
Unchá nichá, *adj.* rough, uneven.
Uncháo, *s. m.* height.
Unchás, *s. f.* height, elevation.
Unchás, *adj.* forty-nine.
Unchá sunná, *v. n.* to be hard of hearing,
Uncháú, *s. m.* height, elevation.
Unchnich, unevenness, ups and downs of life, vicissitude, high and low, uneven; inequality.
Unḍelná, *v. a.* to pour out water.
Uneṇ, *pron.* they, those; he, she.
Ungal, *s. m.* a finger's breadth.
Ungh, } Unghái, } Unghás, } *s. f.* nodding, dozing, drowsiness, sleepiness, drooping.
Unghná, *v. n.* to nod from sleepiness, to doze, to droop.
Unglí, *s. f.* a finger; a finger's breadth.
Unglí káṭná, to be astonished.
Unhattar, *adj.* sixty-nine.
Unhíṇ, for Wonhíṇ, exactly in the manner, even so.
Uní, *adj.* woollen, made of wool.
Unídá, *adj.* sleepless, unshut (eyes.)
Unís, *adj.* nineteen.
Unjálá, } Unjiyálá, } *s. m* light.
Unmatt, *adj.* mad, insane, crazy.
Unoṇ, *pron.* they, them, he.
Uns, *s. m.* friendship, love, affection.
Unsaṭh, *adj.* fifty-nine.
Unsau, *adj.* ninety-nine.
Unṭ, *s. m* a camel.
Untális, *adj.* thirty-nine.
Untís, *adj.* twenty-nine.
Unṭ kaṭárá, *s. m.* name of a thistle of which camels are fond.
Unṭní, *s. f.* a female camel.
Unwán, *s. m.* mode, manner.
Upa, *prep.* near, by, by the side of, with; secondary to.
Upades, *s. m.* exhortation, admonition, instruction, preaching.
Upadesak, } Upadesí, } *s. m. f.* instructor, monitor.
Upádh, *s. f.* violence, injury, injustice, tyranny.
Upádhí, *adj.* violent, unjust.
Upadrav, injustice, tyranny, violence.
Upáe, *s. m.* expedient, plan, contrivance, remedy, method, means.
Upahás, *s. m.* laughter, fun, sport.
Upaj, *s. f.* the chorus of a song.
Upajit, *adj.* produced, propagated.
Upajná, *v. n.* to spring up, to grow, to be produced, shoot forth.
Upakár, *s. m.* assistance, benefit, kindness, favour.
Upakárí, *adj.* assisting, helping; benefactor, beneficent.
Upamá, } Upamán, } *s. f.* resemblance, comparison, simile; that thing to which another is likened.

Upapati, *s. m.* a gallant, a paramour.
Upar, } *prep.* above, on, up, upon,
Úpar, } upwards, over, atop.
Uparáwarí, *adj.* quarrel, wrangling.
Úparí, *adj.* upper or external; foreign, strange.
Uparlá, *adj.* superficial; upper, the outside of a garment (opposed to the lining): *s. m.* the moon.
Upaṛná, *v. n.* to be rooted up, to be pulled out; to be imprinted with the mark of anything.
Upáṛná, *v. a.* to root up, to extirpate, to eradicate.
Úpar se, from above, over.
Uparwálá, *s. m.* the moon.
Upás, *s. m.* a fast, fasting.
Upásá, *adj.* hungry, one who fasts.
Upásak, *s. m.* a worshipper.
Upásaná, *v. a.* to reverence, to worship: *s. f.* reverence, worship.
Upásik, *s. m.* a worshipper.
Upasná, *v. n.* to become musty, to rot.
Upasthit, *adj.* present, ready.
Upáya, *s. m.* see Upáe.
Uphanná, *v. n.* to boil over.
Upjáná, *v. a.* to produce, to make to grow, to cultivate.
Upjáú, *adj.* fertile, productive.
Uplá, *s. m.* } cakes of dried cow-
Uplí, *s. f.* } dung.
Upránt, *adv.* after which, afterwards.
Uprauncha, *s. m.* a towel or cloth for wiping the body.
Úprí, *adj.* foreign.
Upṭan, } *s. m.* a composition of per-
Upṭaná. } fumes, flour, &c., used to rub the body with.
Upṭan malná, *v. a.* to apply or rub (the upṭan.)
Ųqbá, *s. m.* futurity, future state.
Ųqda, *s. m.* a knot.
Ur, *s. m.* the breast.
Uṛá dená, *v. a.* to leave off, abandon; to squander.
Uṛák, *adj.* capable of flying, fledged.
Uṛán, *s. f.* act or manner of flying.
Uṛáná, *v. a.* to cause to fly, to squander or spend extravagantly; dissipate, blow up or away, disperse, filch, entice.
Uṛáná puṛáná, *v. a.* to squander.
Uṛánchhú hojáná, } *v. n.* to fly away,
Uṛánchhú honá, } to disappear.
Uṛaṛná, *v. n.* to become abandoned (a woman.)
Uṛas, *s. m.* a bug.
Uṛáú, *s. m.* a spendthrift, an extravagant person, prodigal.
Urbasí, *s. f.* name of one of the courtezans of Swarga, or Indra's heaven.
Uṛ chalná, *v. n.* to walk with a stately or affected gait; to surpass, to excel.
Urdabeganí, *s. f.* a female armed attendant in the harem,
Urddhabáhu, *adj.* with arms aloft or raised up (a posture of Jogís.)
Urdh, *s. m.* a kind of vetch.
Urdhsáns, *s. m.* deep inspiration, gasp.
Urdí, *s. f.* livery.
Urdú, *s. m.* the dialect spoken by the Muhammadans in India.
Ųrf, *adj.* known (by the name), commonly called, alias.
Uṛhaiyá, *s.* a wearer or putter on of a dress.
Uṛhakná, *v. n.* to overset.
Uṛháná, *v. a.* to put a cloak, shawl, &c., on a person; to cause to clothe.
Uṛhauná, *s. m.* clothing.
Uṛhná, *v. n.* to put on clothes.
Urihná, *s. m.* reproach, reproof.
Uṛis, *s. m.* a bug.
Uṛ jáná, to fly away.
Ur lená, to embrace, to caress.
Uṛná, *v. n.* to fly, to soar.
Ųrs, *s. m.* oblations, offerings to a saint.
Us, *pron. dem. sing. inflect.* of Wuh, that, him, her, it.
Usáná, *v. a.* to boil; to winnow.
Usanná, *v. n.* to boil, to simmer.

Usanwáná, *v. a.* to cause to boil (meat, &c.)
Usar, *adj.* barren (land.)
Usárá, *s. m.* a porch, portico, shed.
Usarná, *v.n.* to retreat, recede, shrink from.
Usárná, *v. a.* to remove, to put out of place.
Usaṭ, *adj.* barren (land.)
Use, *pron. object. case. sing.* of Wuh, him, to him.
Usevná, *v. a.* to throw out the water from boiled rice, &c.
Usíjhná, } *v. a.* to boil, (food, &c.)
Usijná, }
Usijná, *v.n.* to boil, to simmer.
Usísá, *s. m.* a pillow, head of a bed.
Uskáná, *v. a.* to light a fire or candle, to blow up a fire, to trim a lamp; to excite, to instigate, to stir up.
Uslúb, *s. m.* manner, mode, method; order, arrangement, form.
Uslúbdár, *adj.* well-arranged, well-proportioned; symmetrical.
Us meṇ, in that (time), meanwhile, meantime.
Usná, *adj.* boiled.
Usnáná, *v. a.* to cause to boil.
Us ne, *pron.* he, she, it.
Us par, on that, on it, on him, thereupon.
Ustá, *s. m.* a barber.
Ustád, *s. m.* a master (in any art), an adept, a teacher, preceptor, artist: *adj.* skilful, competent.
Ustádí, *s. f.* teaching, instruction, mastership, skill, art: *adj.* masterly (as workmanship, &c.)
Ustakhwán, *s. m.* a bone.
Ustará, *s. m.* a razor.
Ustarah, in that manner.
Ustáz, *s. m.* see Ustád.
Ustura, *s. m.* a razor.
Ustuwár, *adj.* strong, firm, stable, powerful.
Ustuwárí, *s. f.* strength, firmness, stability, resolution.
Usúl, *s. plur.* of Asl, roots, causes.
Us waqt, then, at that time.
Us wáste, on that account.
Uṭ, *s. m.* a camel.
Ut, } *adv.* there, thither.
Utá, }
Utá, so much, that much.
Uṭakkarlais, *adj.* precipitate, rash, acting without consideration.
Után, *adj.* lying on the back.
Utáolá, *adj. m.* swift, quick, speedy, precipitate, rash.
Utáolepaná, *s. m.* haste, rashness, precipitation, urgency.
Utáolí, *adj. f.* swift, &c.: *s. f.* haste, speed, rashness, impatience.
Utar, *s. m.* an answer; the north.
Utár, *s. m.* descent, declination; a copy, a duplicate, a letter.
Utárá, *s. m.* a descent; cast off clothes; ransom; an answer (of a letter); a copy, a duplicate.
Utáran, } *s. f.* anything taken off; cast off clothes.
Utaran, }
Utaran honá, to be freed (from debt.)
Utár dená, to bring down; to disgrace, to dishonour.
Utargáh, *s. f.* a halting-place.
Uṭárid, *s. m.* the planet Mercury.
Utarná, *v. n.* to descend, to alight, to halt, disembark, land, dismount, subside, decrease, pass over, to cross, to go off (as flavour, &c.). to decay, to fade, to flag, to be freed from debt, to become insipid, to fall in value or dignity.
Utárná, *v. a.* to cause to alight or descend, to bring down; to degrade; to cause to pass over, to convey over; to take off, to strip off, to tear off, to cut off or break off (a portion of anything); to unload, disembark, dismount, discharge.
Utarwáná, *v. a.* to cause to descend or alight, &c.
Uṭhábaiṭhí, *s.f.* act of frequently rising up and sitting down; restlessness, inconstancy.
Uṭhá dená, to remove away, abolish, abrogate, exterminate.

Uṭháígírá, *s. m.* a pilferer, a purloiner, a petty thief.
Uthalná, } *v.n.* to turn over,
Uthalná puthalná, } to overset, to be spilt.
Uṭhán, *s. m.* expense; an area or court, rising.
Uṭháná, *v. a.* to lift, take or raise up, to elevate, to hoist, to take or bear away, to produce, invent, gain, get, enjoy, abolish, rouse, awake, support, bear, carry, remove, suffer; to contract debts or purchase on credit, to expend.
Uṭhangan, *s. m.* see Uṭhgan.
Uṭhbaiṭh, *s. f.* restlessness.
Uṭhgan, *s. m.* anything placed under a vessel to prevent its oversetting; a prop, a support.
Uṭh jáná, *v. n.* to depart.
Uṭh khaṛá honá, *v. n.* to stand up.
Uthlá, *adj.* shallow, shelving.
Uthláná, *v. a.* to cause to turn over, or overset.
Uṭhná, *v. n.* to rise up, be raised, spring; to be abolished.
Uṭhwáná, *v. a.* to cause to lift or raise up, or remove, &c.
Utíran. *adj.* worn, cast off (clothes, jewels, &c.)
Uṭkáná, *v. a.* to half shut (a door.)
Utná, *adj.* as much as that, so much, so many, that much.
Utpann, *adj.* produced: *s.* proceeds, profit, produce.
Utpát, *s.m.* violence, injustice, injury.
Uṭpaṭáng, *s. m.* absurdity, nonsense, what is without meaning or foundation.
Uṭpaṭángí, *adj.* one who speaks inconsiderately.
Utpatt, } *s. f.* birth, origin, creation,
Utpatti, } production.
Utran, *s. f.* cast off clothes: liquidation of a debt.
Utráná, *v. a.* to take down or pull down (by the hands of a third person; as, to do it one's self is Utárná.)
Uttá, that much or many.
Uttam, *adj.* excellent, best, principal, first, chief.
Uttamkarm, *s. m.* a good or excellent work.
Uttampurush, an excellent man.
Uttar, *s. m.* an answer; the north.
Uttará, *adj.* northern, northerly: *s. f.* north wind.
Uttaráhá, *adj.* of, or belonging to, the north.
Uttarstán, *s.* an inn.
Uttú, *s. m.* plaits of cloth.
Uttú karná, to plait.
Uzak túzak, *s. m.* pomp, splendour.
Uzbak, *s. m.* name of a Tartar tribe or nation; a clown, a blockhead, a simpleton.
Ụzo, *s. m.* member, limb, joint.
Ụzr, *s. m.* excuse, apology.
Ụzr karná, to apologize, to make an apology or excuse, to ask pardon.
Ụzrḳhwáh, *adj.* an apologist.
Ụzrḳhwáhí, *s. f.* apology, excuse.
Ụzrḳhwáhí karná, see Ụzr karná.

V.

Va, *conj.* or, either.
Vachan, *s. m.* see Bachan.
Vaidya, *s. m.* a doctor, a physician.
Vais, *s. m.* a Vaisya, or man of the third, or agricultural and mercantile tribe; age.
Vaisá, *adv.* or *adj.* in that manner, so, such.
Vaishnav, *adj.* relating or belonging to Vishnu: *s. m.* a sectary or follower of Vishnu.
Vaishya, } *s.m.* a Hindú of the third
Vaisya, } class.
Vastra, *s. m.* cloth, clothes.
Vastu, *s. f.* thing, matter, substance.
Ved, *s. m.* see Bed.
Vedánta, *s. m.* see Bedánt.
Vedántí, *s. m.* see Bedántí.
Vesyá, *s. f.* a harlot, a prostitute.
Vidyá, *s. f.* see Bidyá.
Vidyárthí, *s. m.* student, pupil.
Vishnu, *s. m.* the name of the second

person in the trinity of the Hindús, and the preserver of the universe.

Vishnu purána, *s. m.* one of the sacred works of the Hindús.

W.

Wa, a copulative conjunction equivalent to our and, with, but, now; it is used in connecting words and phrases from the Arabic and Persian. When it merely connects two words it is sounded *o*, thus, Shab o roz.

Wá, (in Braj.) *pron. 3rd. pers. sing. inflect.* him, her, it, that.

Wabá, *s. f.* the plague or any pestilential disorder, pestilence.

Wabál, *s. m. f.* plague, vexation, misfortune.

Wábasta, *adj.* related, connected, depending on.

Wáchhire, *s. m. plur.* praising, applauding; bravo! well done! alas!

Wáda, *s. m. prop.* Wạda, which see.

Wạda, *s. m.* a promise, a vow, an engagement, agreement, bargain.

Wạda karná, to promise, to appoint, make an appointment, &c., make a bargain.

Wạdakḥiláf, a false contract, a person who does not keep his promise.

Wạdakḥiláfí, *s. f.* breach of promise.

Wạdawafá, observing one's promise, punctual, true to one's word.

Wádí, *s. f.* a valley.

Wafá, *s. f.* observation of faith, good faith, fidelity, sincerity.

Wafádár, *adj.* faithful, sincere.

Wafádárí, *s. f.* sincerity, fidelity.

Wafái, *s. f.* fidelity, sincerity.

Wafá karná, to suffice, to perform (a promise.)

Wafát, *s. f.* death, decease.

Wagar, *conj.* and, if, but.

Wagarna, and, if, not.

Waghaira, et cetera, and so forth.

Wah, *pron.* he, she, it, that, the.

Wáh, *f. interj.* bravo! well done! excellent! alas! fy!

Wahán, *adv.* there, thither, yonder.

Wahán ká wahán, everywhere, in that very place.

Wahán se, thence.

Wahdáníyat, *s. f.* unity; belief in the unity of the Deity.

Wahí, *pron.* he himself, that very (person): *s. f.* divine revelation, inspiration.

Wáhí, *adj.* weak, crazy, ill-founded (premises.)

Wáhid, *adj.* one, sole, individual, single, singular.

Wáhid sháhid, God is my witness.

Wahín, *adv.* that very (time, place, &c.), immediately, exactly there.

Wáhí tabáhí, } *s. f.* absurdity, nonsense.
Wáhí wáhí, }

Wáhiyát, *s. plur.* of Wáhí, absurdities, fiddle faddle.

Wahm, *s. m.* conjecture, opinion, imagination, idea, fancy.

Wahmí, *adj.* imaginary, conjectural, visionary, fanciful, ideal.

Wahm karná, to indulge in whims, conjectures, &c.

Wahsh, *s. m.* a wild beast.

Wahshat, *s. f.* timidity, dread, terror, loneliness; a desert.

Wahshatnák, *adj.* frightful.

Wahshatzada, *adj.* aghast, terrified.

Wahshí, *adj.* wild, savage, ferocious; a wild beast, a savage.

Wahshípaná, *s. m.* wildness, ferocity, the savage state.

Wáh wáh, *f. interj.* bravo! how excellent! well done! admirable! ha!

Wail, *s. m.* reprisal, revenge.

Wainchná, *v. a.* to skin.

Wairán, *adj.* desolated, depopulated, ruined.

Wairána, *s. m.* a solitude, a desolate spot.

Wairání, *s. f.* desolation, destruction, desert places.

Wairán karná, to lay waste, depopulate, desolate.

Waisá, *adv.* or *adj.* in that manner, so, that like, such.

Waisáhí, *adv.* in the same manner, even like that.
Waise ká waisá, such as before.
Waiseṉ, freely, without cost.
Wáịz, *s. m.* a monitor, a preacher.
Wajan, *s. m. prop.* Wazn, which see.
Wajaní, *adj.. prop.* Wazní, heavy, weighty.
Wajd, *s. m.* ecstacy, rapture.
Wajh, *s. f.* cause, reason; mode.
Wajh i tasmiya, the cause of giving any particular name.
Wájib, *adj.* necessary, incumbent, obligatory, expedient, worthy, reasonable, fit, meet, just.
Wájib honá, *v. n.* to be necessary, expedient, worthy, proper.
Wájibí, *adj.* necessary, right, expedient: that which is necessary or expedient.
Wájib ul qatl, deserving death.
Wakálat, *s. f.* embassy, agency, deputation, attorneyship.
Wakálatan, *adv.* by delegation.
Wakálatnáma, *s. m.* a power of attorney.
Wakat, *s. m. prop.* Waqt, which see.
Wakíl, *s. m.* an agent, an ambassador, attorney at law, deputy.
Wakílí, *s. f.* the business of an attorney or ambassador.
Wakíl i mutlaq, a vicegerent, invested with full powers.
Wakílkharcha, *s. m.* fees of an attorney.
Wál, } *m.* in *compos.* denotes an
Wálá, } agent, doer, keeper, inhabitant, master, lord, possessor, owner.
Wálá, *adj.* exalted in dignity, sublime, high.
Walad, *s. m.* a son, an offspring.
Wálájáh, of exalted dignity.
Wáláqadr, } of high rank or dignity.
Wálásháu, }
Waladuzziná, a son of a whore; illegitimate.
Walekin, *conj.* but, yet, however.

Walí, *s. m.* a prince, lord, master; a friend; a saint.
Wálí, *fem.* of Wálá, which see: *s. m.* a prince, a chief, a governor, sovereign, master.
Walíạhd, an heir.
Wálid, *s. m.* a father.
Wálida, *s. f.* a mother.
Wálidain, *s. m. plur.* the two parents.
Walíniạmat, a title of respect by which a father is addressed; a benefactor.
Walte, *s. f.* eaves of a house.
Wám, *s. m.* debt, credit, lending, borrowing.
Wáṉ, *adv.* there, that place.
Wán, } in *compos.* possessing, en-
Want, } dowed with, having.
Wantá, *m.* } a particle in *compos.* See
Wantí, *f.* } Wán.
Wápas, *s. m.* restitution, returning.
Wápas dená, to return, to give back, to restore.
Wápasín, *adj.* latter, last, hindmost.
Wápas karná, see Wápas dená.
Wápas lená, to take back.
Wápas milná, to get again.
Wápas rakhná, to detain, to retard.
Wáq, *s. m.* name of a bird.
Waqáị, *s. plur.* of Wáqiạ, news, events.
Waqáịnavís, an intelligencer.
Waqat, *s. m.* see Waqt.
Waqfa, *s. m.* delay, pause.
Wáqị, befalling, happening, occurring, appearing; situate.
Wáqiạ, *s. m.* an event, occurrence; news, intelligence; death.
Waqiạ honá, *v. n.* to befall, to happen.
Wáqiạ navís, a news writer.
Wáqiát, *s. f. plur.* accidents, events, occurrences; intelligence.
Wáqif, *adj.* acquainted, experienced, knowing, conversant, learned, sensible.
Wáqifdár, see Wáqif i hál.
Wáqif honá, *v. n.* to be acquainted with, to be intelligent.

Wáqif i hál, *adj.* experienced, intelligent, expert, connoisseur.
Wáqifíyat, *s. f.* experience, knowledge, intelligence, acquaintance.
Wáqif kár, *adj.* see Wáqif i hál.
Wáqifkárí, *s. f.* experience, intelligence, knowledge.
Wáqiʿ, *adv.* really, truly, verily, in fact, certainly: *adj.* true, real.
Waqr, *s. m.* dignity, honour, character.
Waqt, *s.m.* time, season, opportunity; adversity.
Waqt ba waqt, from time to time.
Waqt be waqt, in season or out of season, constantly, perpetually.
Waqt i názuk, delicate times.
Waqtíya, *adj.* timely, seasonable.
Waqt káṭná, to pass away the time.
Waqt ke waqt, at all times.
Waqt ná waqt, occasionally, without any stated time.
Waqt par, at (proper) time, seasonable, betimes; in the nick of time.
Waqt paṛná, to suffer misfortunes, to be distressed.
Waqú, *s. m.* see Wuqú.
Waqúf, *s. m.* see Wuqúf.
Waqúfdár, see Wuqúfdár.
Wáṛ, a termination in *compos.* denoting place or enclosure.
Wár, in *compos.* like, resembling; worthy of; having, possessing, endowed with: *s. f.* leisure: *s. m.* a blow, a wound, a gash; a day of the week; the near bank of a river; on this side.
War, added to nouns, implies possessing, enjoying, having: *conj.* and if, but.
Wárá, *s. m.* cheapness, benefit, gain: *adj.* cheap.
Waram, *s. m.* a swelling, a tumour: *adj.* inflated, enraged.
Waram honá, to be inflated, to be enraged.
Waram karná, to swell (any part of the body.)
Wáran, *s. m.* offerings, oblations, sacrifices.
Wárápár, *adv.* on this side and that, on both sides; across.
Waraq, *s. m.* a leaf (of a tree, book, &c.), a card, a slice.
Waraqí, *adj.* leaf-like.
Ware, *adv.* on this side, near.
Ware girná, to fall short.
Warghaláná, *v. a.* to deceive, to inveigle, to decoy, seduce, tempt.
Wáṛí, a termination denoting place or enclosure.
Wárid, *adj.* being present, coming, arriving, approaching.
Wáridát, *s. f.* events, accidents, incident, occurrence, casualty.
Wárid honá, to arrive, to come.
Wárí pherí honá, to go round anybody (as a sign of being an offering or sacrifice for his welfare), to devote one's self for any one (a practice chiefly of women.)
Wáris, *s. m.* an heir; master, lord, owner.
Wáris honá, to inherit.
Wárisí, *s. f.* heritage.
Wárná, *v. a.* to offer (in sacrifice, &c.)
War na, and if not, otherwise, although.
Wárpár, *adv.* see Wárápár.
Warsa, *s. m.* heritage, bequest.
Warsadár, *s.* an heir.
Warzish, *s. f.* labour, exertion, exercise.
Wasálat, *s. f.* see Wasátat.
Wasṭ, *s. f.* see Wusṭ.
Wasat, *s. m. f.* the middle, the centre: *adj.* centrical.
Wasátat, *s. f.* means, mediation, medium, channel.
Wasf, *s. m.* praise, encomium, description, quality, attribute.
Wasf karná, to praise, to describe.
Wasí, *s. m.* an executor, administrator (of a will), preceptor.
Wasíʿ, *adj.* extensive, large, spacious, roomy.

Wasíla, *s. m.* a medium, means (of effecting anything), cause, mediation, intervention; affinity.

Wasíladár, a client, dependent.

Wasíladárí, *s. f.* clientship, dependence.

Wásilbáqí, collections and balances.

Wásilbáqí karná, to state an account.

Wasíqa, *s. m.* a bond, obligation, written agreement.

Wasíyat, *s. f.* a last will or testament; making a will.

Wasíyat karná, to bequeath, devise, leave by will.

Wasíyatnáma, *s. m.* a last will or testament.

Wasl, *s. m.* meeting, union, conjunction.

Waslí, *adj.* copulative, conjunctive; two pieces of paper, &c., pasted together for the purpose of practising writing on.

Wasl karná, to unite, to paste, to conjoin, annex, cement.

Wasma, *s. m.* the leaves of indigo (with an extract of which the natives stain their beards, &c.)

Wásta, *s. m.* account, sake, cause, reason; connexion, relation.

Wáste, *postpos.* on account of, for the sake, for; in behalf.

Wástí, *s. f.* a reed, a pen.

Waswás, *s. m.* the temptation of the devil, distraction of mind; doubt, suspense, hesitation, suspicion, fluctuation (of mind.)

Waswása, *s. m.* temptation, evil suggestion.

Waswásí, *adj.* doubtful, causing suspense, distracting, apprehensive, scrupulous.

Watá, *adj.* that much, so much, so many.

Watan, *s. m.* native country, country.

Watani, *adj.* belonging to one's country.

Watíra, *s. m.* manner, habit, custom.

Wáwailá, *s. m.* lamentation, bewailing: *interj.* alas!

Waz, *s. m.* advice, admonition, exhortation, preaching, sermon.

Waza, *s. f.* state, condition, manner, mode, procedure, position, conduct, behaviour.

Wazáif, *s. plur.* of Wazífa, daily tasks or duties.

Waza karná, to deduct, to subtract.

Wazan, *s. m.* see Wazn.

Wazí, *adj.* ignoble, base, plebeian, low.

Wazífa, *s. m.* a daily performance, duty or task.

Wázih, *adj.* evident, apparent, manifest, clear, obvious.

Wazír, *s. m.* a minister of state; prime minister.

Wazírí, *s. f.* the office of a minister of state, ministry.

Wazn, *s. m.* weight, weighing, measure; metre, rhyme, verse; reputation, esteem, honour.

Wazní, *adj.* heavy, weighty.

Wazú, *s. m.* ablution (performed before prayer; and it consists in cleaning the teeth, washing first the hands, then the mouth inside, then throwing water on the forehead, washing the whole face, the arms, and lastly the feet.)

We, *pron. plur.* they, those.

Wetá, } *adj.* so much, that much,
Wetná, } that many.

Widá, *s. m.* farewell, adieu, bidding farewell.

Widágí, } *adj.* bidding farewell.
Widáí, }

Widá karná, to bid farewell or adieu, to dismiss.

Wiládat, *s. f.* nativity, birth.

Wiláyat, *s. f.* an inhabited country, a kingdom, a foreign country, abroad; Europe.

Wiláyatí, *adj.* European, foreign.

Wiláyatí baingan, the tomata or love-apple.

Wiláyatí khatt, a kind of Persian Nastalíq character.

Wiláyatí pání, soda-water.

Wiláyatí sem, beans.

Win, (in *Braj.*) *pron.* 3rd *pers. plur.* (same as *un*) them, those.

Winhen, *pron.* 3rd *pers. plur.* them, those, to them, or those.

Wírán, *adj.* desolate, laid waste, depopulated, ruined.

Wírána, *s. m.* a solitude, a desolated or desolate place.

Wírání, *s. f.* desolation, depopulation, destruction, desert places.

Wírán karná, to lay waste, depopulate, desolate.

Wird, *s. m.* daily use, practice, task; a portion of the Qurán fixed for reading at a certain time.

Wird karná, to repeat.

Wis, *pron.* 3rd *pers. sing. inflect.* (same as *us*) him, her, it, that, &c.

Wisál, *s. m.* meeting, interview, connexion, union.

Wise, *pron.* 3rd *pers. sing.* him, her, it, to him, to her, &c.

Witná, *adj.* that much, as much as that, so much, so many.

Wizárat, *s. f.* the dignity of Wazir; the office of prime minister or grand vizier; ministry.

Wo, for Wuh, *pron.* that, he, those, &c.

Wohí, Wohin, } *adv.* see Wunhín.

Won, *adv.* in that manner, so.

Wonhí, Wonhín, } *adv.* see Wunhín.

Won ka wonhí, exactly the same as before or originally.

Wuh, *pron.* he, she, it, that, the.

Wuhí, *pron.* he himself, that very.

Wujúd, *s. m.* existence, essence, being, body.

Wujúhát, *s. plur.* of Wajh, causes, reasons.

Wún, *adv.* in that manner, so.

Wunhín, *adv.* that very (time, place, &c.), immediately, exactly there, on the spot, in that very manner.

Wuqú, *s. m.* a contingency, accident, event, occurrence, the happening.

Wuqúf, *s. m.* understanding, information, sense, experience, wisdom.

Wuqúfdár, informed of, experienced.

Wuqúfí, *adj.* sensible, intelligent.

Wurúd, *s. m.* arrival, coming, appearing, approaching, descending, alighting. [space, extent.

Wusat, *s. f.* latitude, amplitude,

Wusúl, *s. m.* arrival, conjunction, acquisition or enjoyment (of anything desired); realization of revenue, &c.

Wusúl honá, to get, to be arrived.

Wusúl karná, to collect.

Wutná, *adj.* that much.

Wuzará, *s. plur.* of Wazír, ministers of state.

Wuzú, *s. m.* see Wazú.

Y.

Yá, *pron.* this: *conj.* or, either; a vocative particle, oh! O! In *compos.* a dealer or agent in anything, as Kapriyá, a cloth merchant.

Yáb, in *compos.* finding, getting.

Yábí, *s. f.* in *compos.* attaining.

Yábú, *s. m.* a pony, a galloway.

Yáchak, *s. m.* a mendicant.

Yáchná, *v. a.* to want, to need, implore, solicit, ask, beg.

Yád, *s. f.* memory, recollection.

Yád áná, to come to mind, to recur.

Yádash bakhair, an expression used when mentioning an absent friend.

Yáddásht, *s. f.* a memorandum.

Yád diláná, to remind.

Yádfarámosh, name of a game.

Yádgár, *s. m.* anything given as a memorial, a memorial.

Yádgárí, *s. f.* a keepsake, token, remembrance.

Yadi, *conj.* if, when, since.

Yád karná, to recollect, to remember, to call to mind, to commit to memory.

Yadyapi, *conj.* if, even if, when.

Yáft, *s. f.* perquisite, earnings, gains, income, profit, fees.

Yagána, *s. m.* kindred: *adj.* single, sole.
Yagáníyat, *s. f.* kindred; unanimity.
Yah, *pron.* this, he, she, it, the.
Yahán, *adv.* here, hither, at the abode, near, with.
Yahán ká yahín, in the very same place, exactly here.
Yahán lag, see Yahán tak.
Yahán se, hence.
Yahán tak, } to this pitch, to this
Yahán talak, } degree, thus far, hitherto.
Yáhi (in *Braj.*) *pron. dem. object. case*, [this, to this.
Yahí, this very, the same, itself.
Yahín, *adv.* this very, in this very place, here.
Yahín se, hence.
Yahúd, } *s. m.* a Jew, a Hebrew.
Yahúdí, }
Yahúdíya, the land of Judea.
Yahún, thus, in this manner.
Yájak, *s. m.* an officiating priest.
Yájúj májúj, Gog and Magog.
Yak, *adj.* one, a, an.
Yaká, one, singular.
Yakád, } *adj.* a few, one or two.
Yakádh, }
Yakáwan, *adj.* fifty-one.
Yakáyak, all at once, suddenly.
Yakáyak áná, to come immediately.
Yakbár, }
Yakbára, } immediately, all at once,
Yakbárgí, } once.
Yakbárí, }
Yak ba yak, successively, one by one.
Yakchoba, one-poled (a tent.)
Yakdil, *adj.* of one heart or mind, unanimous.
Yakdilí, *s. f.* unanimity, accord.
Yakelá, *adj.* alone, solitary, singular.
Yakhaṭṭá, in one place, together.
Yakhattar, *adj.* seventy-one.
Yak hí, the same, equal, alike.
Yak͟hní, *s. f.* gravy, sauce, stew.
Yak͟hní puláo, a kind of puláo prepared with gravy.
Yakís, *adj.* twenty-one.
Yakjá, together, in one place.
Yakján, of one soul, a friend.
Yakjoṛ, *adj.* equal, even.
Yakká, *adj.* single, solitary: *s. m.* a one-horse vehicle: *adj.* unique, unequalled.
Yakká sipáhí, a single soldier.
Yaklái, *s. f.* a breadth of cloth worn over the head and shoulders.
Yaklakht, all at once, altogether, all; one piece, entirely, wholly.
Yaklauṭá, *adj.* a single child (without brother or sister.)
Yaklohí, *s. f.* a vessel made of one piece of iron.
Yakmartaba, one time, once.
Yakmunh, unanimous.
Yakmusht, } all at once, prompt
Yakmúṭh, } payment; a handful.
Yak na yak, one or other.
Yak qalam, all, altogether, total.
Yakráh, going on the same road.
Yakrang, *adj.* of one colour; uniform.
Yak rangí, *s. f.* uniformity.
Yakrú, *adj.* unanimous.
Yakrúí, *s. f.* unanimity, friendship.
Yaksán, } equal, alike, even, in the
Yaksár, } same manner, the same, plain, level, uniform, parallel.
Yaksar, *adj.* single, in a body, altogether.
Yaksaṭh, *adj.* sixty-one.
Yakshamba, *s. m.* Sunday.
Yaktá, *adj.* single, unique, singular, incomparable.
Yaktái, *s. f.* the being unique, single or unequalled, unity.
Yaktális, *adj.* forty-one.
Yaktára, *s. m.* a kind of guitar with one string.
Yaktaraf, aside.
Yakṭhá, *adj.* collected, assembled in one place, together: *s.* a boat hollowed out of a tree.
Yakṭhán, } *adj.* collected, assem-
Yakṭháun, } bled in one place, together.
Yakzabán, of one voice, unanimous.

Yakzát, of the same caste or tribe.
Yál, *s. f.* a horse's mane.
Yam, *s. m.* the angel of death.
Yamuná, *s. f.* the river Jamuná.
Yán, *adv. contract.* of Yaháṇ, here, hither; at the abode.
Yane, } *adv.* videlicit, viz., that is to
Yaní, } say, i. e., namely, to wit.
Yaqín, *s. m.* certainty, assurance, truth: *adj.* certain, true: *adv.* with certainty, truly.
Yaqínan, *adv.* certainly, assuredly, infallibly, verily.
Yaqín honá, to become certain.
Yaqíní, *s. f.* certainty, truth: *adj.* true, indisputable.
Yaqín karná, to ascertain, to believe.
Yaqín láná, to believe, to credit.
Yá qismat, oh destiny! an exclamation of one who in distress resigns himself to the will of God.
Yaqúb, *n. prop.* Jacob.
Yáqút, *s. m.* a ruby, a precious stone.
Yáqútí, *adj.* of or relating to the ruby: *s.* name of a medicine.
Yár, *s. m.* a friend, a lover, a paramour; an assistant; companion.
Yárá, *s. m.* power, strength.
Yárána, *adv.* friendly, like a friend.
Yárbásh, *adj.* voluptuous, sensual.
Yárbáshí, *s. f.* sensuality, &c.
Yárbáz, a wanton woman, a whore: *adj.* wanton.
Yárbází, *s. f.* fornication.
Yárí, *s. f.* friendship, love, assistance.
Yár i ghár, a sincere friend.
Yár i wafádár, a faithful friend.
Yární, *s. f.* a female friend, a mistress, a sweetheart.
Yarqán, *s. m.* the yellow jaundice.
Yás, *s. f.* despair; fear, terror.
Yásaman, *s. m. f.* jasmine.
Yashm, *s. m.* a sort of agate.
Yásmín, *s. m. f.* jasmine.
Yatá, *adj.* this much or many, so much.
Yathá, *adv.* as, according to, like.
Yathájog, *adv.* as is proper, properly, sufficiently.
Yathárth, see Jathárth.
Yathásakti, according to power, to the utmost ability.
Yatím, *s. m.* an orphan.
Yatn, *s. m.* carefulness, remedy, care, effort, endeavour.
Yátrá, *s. f.* pilgrimage, departure, march, journey; a procession.
Yátrí, *s. m.* a pilgrim, a traveller.
Yattá, *adj.* this much, so many, &c.
Yaumiya, *s. m.* daily food, allowance, pay, &c.
Yauṇ, thus, in this manner.
Yauvan, *s. m.* youth, manhood.
Yáwa, *adj.* absurd, vain, futile.
Yáwa bakná, to talk nonsense.
Yáwago, an absurd talker.
Yáwagoí, *s. f.* absurdity, talking nonsense, babble.
Yáwar, *s. m.* an assistant, coadjutor.
Yáwarí, *s. f.* aid, assistance.
Yazíd, *adj.* wicked, cruel, execrable.
Ye, *pron.* (*plur.* of Yih), these, they.
Yehí, these very (persons, &c.)
Yih, *pron.* this, he, she, it, the.
Yihí, this very, the same, itself.
Yoddhá, *s. m.* a warrior, combatant.
Yog, *s. m.* see Jog.
Yogí, *s. m.* see Jogí.
Yoginí, *s. f.* see Jogní.
Yoṇ, thus, in this manner.
Yoṇhíṇ, in this very manner, thus, accidentally, by chance, causelessly, easily, cursorily.
Yoṇ toṇ, in various ways, somehow or other.
Yotikh, *s. m.* see Jotikh.
Yotishí, *s. m.* see Jotikhí.
Yuddh, *s. m.* battle, war, fight.
Yug, *s. m.* see Jug.
Yukt, *adj.* fit, proper, right, joined: *s. f.* contrivance, skill.
Yúṇ, thus, in this manner.
Yúnán, *n. prop.* Ionia, Greece.
Yúnání, *s. m.* a Grecian.
Yúnas, *n. prop.* the prophet Jonah.
Yúṇhíṇ, see Yoṇhíṇ.

Yún na yún, in one way or other, somehow or other.
Yúsuf, *n. prop.* the patriarch Joseph.
Yuvá, *s. m.* a young man.

Z.

Zabah, *s. f.* a sacrifice, slaughter.
Zabán, or Zubán, *s. f.* the tongue; language, dialect, speech.
Zabán baṛháná, to chatter, to prattle.
Zabán chaláná, to give abuse.
Zabán dábná, to hold one's tongue.
Zabán ḍálná, to ask, to put a question.
Zabándaráz, *adj.* abusive.
Zabándarází, *s. f.* abuse.
Zabán dená, } to promise.
Zabán hárná, }
Zabán hiláná, to speak.
Zabání, *adj.* traditional, oral, verbal, by word; from the statement (of any one.)
Zabán káṭná, to interrupt one's speech.
Zabán kholná, to let the tongue loose, to speak out.
Zabán pakaṛná, to prevent one from speaking, to criticise.
Zabán paluṭná, to retract, to equivocate.
Zabán par láná, to speak, to say, to mention.
Zabar, *adj.* above, superior strong: *s. m.* the vowel point *fatah* pronounced *a.*
Zabardast, *adj.* upperhanded, powerful. strong, oppressive.
Zabardastí, *s. f.* violence, force, oppression: *adv.* forcibly, violently.
Zabardastí karná, to oppress, to force, to act with violence.
Zabardastí se, with violence, forcibly.
Zabar honá, to have the upper-hand.
Zabarí, *s. f.* violence, oppression.
Zabarín, *adj.* superior.
Zabar karná, to oppress.
Zabh, *s. f.* a sacrifice, slaughter.
Zabh honá, to be sacrificed or killed.
Zabh karná, to sacrifice, to kill, to slaughter.

Zábita, *s. m.* canon, ordinance, rule, regulation.
Zabt, *s. m.* possession, control, confiscation.
Zabt honá, to be taken possession of, to be seized.
Zabtí, *s. f.* confiscation, sequestration: *adj.* confiscated, seized.
Zabt karná, to take possession, to restrain, to control, to confiscate.
Zabún, *adj.* bad, evil, ill, wicked, depraved.
Zabúní, *s. f.* violence, badness, wickedness, vice.
Zabúr, *s. f.* the psalms of David.
Zachá, *s. f.* a lying-in woman.
Zád, } in *compos.* born: *s. m.* a son,
Záda, } a child.
Zada, in *compos.* stricken, smitten, affected by; arrayed.
Zadagí, in *compos.* striking.
Zádí, in *compos.* born: *s. f.* a daughter.
Zád i ráh, provisions for travelling, way charges.
Zad o kob, *s. m.* beating.
Zafar, *s. m.* victory.
Zạfarán, *s. f.* saffron.
Zạfarání, *adj.* of saffron, yellow: *s. f.* a yellow colour.
Zafíl, *s.* a whistling.
Zahar, *s. m.* poison. See Zahr.
Záhid, *s. m.* a monk, a hermit: *adj.* religious, devout.
Zahín, *adj.* sagacious, ingenious.
Záhir, *adj.* apparent, manifest; the outward or external appearance.
Zahír, *adj.* reduced (by sickness), thin, emaciated.
Záhiran, *adv.* outwardly, apparently, openly, evidently, seemingly.
Záhirdár, *adj.* specious, plausible.
Záhirdárí, *s. f.* speciousness, plausibility.
Záhir honá, *v. n.* to become public or manifest, to be revealed or disclosed, to appear, to be evident.
Záhirí, *adj.* external, apparent.
Záhir karná, to publish, to disclose,

to discover, to reveal, manifest, explain, to tell.
Záhir men, openly, apparently, in public.
Záhirparast, *adj.* a superficial observer. [grief.
Zahmat, *s. f.* affliction, trouble,
Zahmatí, *adj.* afflicted, sick.
Zahr, *s. m.* poison.
Zahrdár, *adj.* poisonous.
Zahrí, *adj.* venomous, poisonous.
Zahr i haláhal, } *s. m.* deadly poison.
Zahr i qátil, }
Zahrmuhra, *s. m.* the bezoar, an antidote to poison.
Záj, *adj.* lost, destroyed, ruined, injured.
Záj karná, to lose, to destroy.
Záid, *adj.* redundant, superfluous.
Zaif, *adj.* weak, infirm, emaciated, feeble, frail, old.
Zaifí, *s. f.* weakness, emaciation.
Záiqa, *s. m.* the sense of tasting, the palate, relish, taste.
Zaitún, *s. m.* an olive, an olive-tree.
Zak, *s. f.* injuring, deceiving, disappointing. [see.
Zakam, *s. m. f. prop.* Zakhm, which
Zakar, *s. m.* membrum virile; the masculine gender.
Zakát, *s. f.* alms.
Zak dená, to injure, to deceive.
Zakhám, *s. m.* see Zukhám.
Zakhíra, *s. m.* treasure, provisions.
Zakhm, *s. m. f.* a wound, a sore, scar, cut.
Zakhmí, *adj.* wounded.
Zakhmí honá, to be wounded.
Zakhm i kárí, a mortal wound.
Zakhmí karná, to wound.
Zakhm kháná, to be wounded.
Zakí, *adj.* acute, ingenious, clever.
Zak uthháná, to suffer loss.
Zalal, *s. m.* deficiency, loss.
Zalíkhá, *n. prop.* the name of Potiphar's wife.
Zalíl, *adj.* abject, mean, contemptible, base, wretched.
Zalíl honá, to be disgraced.
Zalíl karná, to abase, to debase.
Zálim, *s. m.* a tyrant, an oppressor: *adj.* tyrannical, cruel, oppressive.
Zálimí, *s. f.* tyranny, oppression.
Zalzala, *s. m.* an earthquake.
Zamána, *s. m.* time, an age; the world; tense.
Zamána muwáfiq, *adj.* fortunate.
Zamánan, *adv.* by way of security.
Zamánasáz, a turn-coat, a time-server.
Zamánasází, *s. f.* turning with the tide, time-serving.
Zamánasází karná, to turn with the tide, to temporize.
Zamánat, *s. f.* suretyship, a bailbond.
Zambíl, *s. f.* a purse, a wallet.
Zambúr, *s. m.* an instrument for drawing teeth, forceps; a hornet.
Zambúra, *s. m.* a hornet.
Zambúrak, *s. f.* a small gun or swivel, usually carried on a camel.
Zamídár, *prop.* Zamíndár, which see.
Zámin, *s. m.* a surety, a sponsor, security, bail, bondsman.
Zamín, *s. f.* the earth, ground, soil; a region; the ground of a picture or chintz, &c.
Zamíndár, *s. m.* a landlord, a landholder, a farmer.
Zámindár, *s. m.* a surety.
Zámindárí, *s. f.* suretyship. [fief.
Zamíndárí, *s. f.* a landed estate; a
Zamíndární, *s. f.* the wife of a landholder or farmer. [earth.
Zamíní, *adj.* of or relating to the
Záminí, *s. f.* surety, bail.
Záminí qabúl karná, to admit as bail.
Zamín par se kuchh pará páná, to be overjoyed at finding unexpectedly the object of one's wishes.
Zamír, *s. f.* a personal pronoun.
Zamm, } *s. m.* the short vowel *u*,
Zamma, } like *u* in push.
Zamurrad, *s. m.* an emerald.
Zamurradín, *adj.* of the colour of an emerald. [at Mecca.
Zamzam, *s. m.* the name of a well

Zan, *s. f.* a woman, a wife; in *compos.* beating, striking, smiting.

Zanaḳh, } *s. m.* the chin, the pit
Zanaḳhdán, } in the chin.

Zanána, *adj.* female, feminine, effeminate, womanly: *s. f.* a wife.

Zanánaḳhána, } *s. m.* female apart-
Zanánamakán, } ments, seraglio.

Zanání, *adj.* of or relating to women of the seraglio, effeminate.

Zang, *s. m.* rust; a small bell.

Zangál, *s. m.* canker (of copper), verdigris, rust.

Zangálúd, *adj.* rusty, covered with [rust.

Zangár, *s. m.* see Zangál.

Zangárí, *adj.* rusty, the colour of rust; covered with verdigris.

Zangázorí, *s. f.* strife, quarrelling.

Zangí, *s. m.* Ethiop, negro, Moor.

Zang lagná, to become rusty or cankered.

Zání, *s. m.* an adulterer, a whoremonger, a fornicator.

Zániya, *s. f.* a whore, a strumpet.

Zanjabíl, *s. f.* dry ginger.

Zanjír, *s. f.* a chain, fetters.

Zanmurída, *adj.* hen-pecked.

Zánú, *s. m.* the hip, the lap.

Zár, in *compos.* place, multitute; a groan, lamentation: *adj.* afflicted.

Zar, *s. m.* gold, riches, wealth, money.

Zaráfat, *s. f.* wit, humour, jocularity, facetiousness.

Zarar, *s. m.* damage, injury, detriment, loss; affliction, anguish.

Zarar karná, to injure.

Zarb, *s. f.* a blow; violence, multiplication; stamping, coining (money.)

Zarbáfí, *adj.* brocaded, embroidered.

Zarbáft, *s. m.* brocade, cloth of gold.

Zarb dená, to coin.

Zard, *adj.* yellow, pale, wan, livid.

Zarda, *s. m.* a kind of puláo, dressed with saffron.

Zardálú, *s. m.* an apricot.

Zardár, *adj.* wealthy.

Zardchob, *s. f.* turmeric.

Zardí, *s. f.* yellowness; the yolk of an egg; the jaundice.

Zardoz, *s. m.* an embroiderer.

Zardozí, *s. f.* embroidery.

Zard rang, *adj.* yellow.

Zardrú, *adj.* infamous, shameless.

Zarf, *s. m.* an adverb; a large vessel.

Zarf i makán, an adverb of place.

Zarf i zamán, adverb of time.

Zargar, *s. m.* a goldsmith.

Zargarí, *s. f.* business of a goldsmith.

Zárí, *s. f.* crying, sighing, lamentation, crying for help.

Zarí, *s. f.* anything woven with gold thread.

Zaríbáf, a gold-lace worker.

Zaríf, *adj.* witty, jocose, comical, waggish.

Zar i naqd, ready money, cash.

Zarḳharíd, } *adj.* purchased (as a
Zarḳharída, } slave.)

Zarḳhez, *adj.* rich (a country); fer- [tile.

Zarnigár, *adj.* gilt.

Zarnigárí, *s. f.* gilding.

Zarníḳh, *s. m.* orpiment.

Zarq barq, *s. m.* glitter, show; splendid clothes, gaudy apparel.

Zarrá, *s. m.* } an atom, a particle, a
Zarra, *s. m.* } little, a jot, a tittle: *adj.* little, a small quantity.

Zarrá sá, a very little.

Zarrí, *s. f.* see Zarra.

Zarrín, *adj.* golden.

Zarúr, *adj.* necessary, expedient, [unavoidable.

Zarúrat, *s. f.* want, indigence, necessity, exigence.

Zarúratan, *adv.* necessarily, of or by necessity, per force.

Zarúr honá, to be necessary.

Zarúrí, *adj.* necessary, a thing needful.

Zarúriyát, *s. f. plur.* of Zarúrí, necessaries, requisites.

Zárzár, great lamentation.

Zástí, *prop.* Ziyáda, which see.

Zát, *s. f.* the essence, nature, substance, race, breed, tribe, caste.

Zaṭal, *s. f.* chattering, talking much and foolishly, tattle.

Zaṭal hánkná, } to chatter, to talk
Zaṭal márná, } nonsense.
Zát bhái, a relative, a kinsman.
Zát dená, *v. a.* to give up one's caste.
Záti, *adj.* essential, natural, innate.
Zát jáná, *v. n.* to become an outcast.
Zát lená, } *v. a.* to deprive another
Zát márná, } of caste, by touching his food, &c.
Zauj, *s. m.* a husband.
Zauja, *s. f.* a wife.
Zauq, *s. m.* taste, delight, pleasure, voluptuousness.
Zauq se, *adv.* with pleasure, willingly, with all one's heart.
Zawál, *s. m.* decline, wane, declination.
Zeb, *s. f.* ornament, elegance, beauty.
Zebá, *adj.* adorned, beautiful.
Zebáish, *s. f.* ornament, adorning, elegance.
Zeb dená, to suit, to become.
Zer, *adv.* under below: *adj.* inferior, lower: *s.* the vowel point pronounced like *i* in pin.
Zerandáz, *s. m.* the cloth or carpet which is spread under a huqqa.
Zerband, *s. m.* a martingal.
Zerbár honá, to be indebted, to undergo a great expense.
Zerbiryáṇ, *s. m.* name of a kind of dish or food.
Zerdast, *adj.* powerless, under command: *s. m.* a subject, a vassal.
Zer hukm rahná, to be in subjection.
Zer karná, to overpower, to subdue.
Zermashq, something placed under paper for writing on.
Zer o zabar, *adj.* topsy-turvy, overturned, ruined.
Zewar, *s. m.* jewels, ornament (of gold or silver.)
Zewarát, *plur.* of Zewar, jewels.
Zewar pahinná, to put on jewels, to adorn.
Zhiyán, *adj.* formidable, rapacious, terrible.

Zí, a lord, a master; in *compos.* possessed of, endowed with.
Zibaski, in as much as.
Zidd, *s. f.* the contrary, the opposite, contrariety, opposition, perversity.
Ziddí, *adj.* perverse, contradictory, naughty and unmanageable (as a child.)
Zidd karná, to persist, to persevere.
Zí hayát, endowed with life (an animal.)
Zí hijja, *s. m.* the name of the last month of the Muhammadan year.
Zihn, *s. m.* understanding, memory, genius, ability.
Zihnnishín, impressed on the mind.
Zihnnishín karná, to impress on the mind.
Zí hosh, *adj.* sensible.
Zikr, *s. m.* remembrance, mention, commemoration, praise, reading of the Qurán and recital of the praise and names of God.
Zikr karná, to recite, to mention, to relate, express, &c.
Zíl, *vulg.* Jíl, *s. f.* the treble (in music.)
Zilạ, *s. m.* a district, a division, [Zillah.
Zilạdár, an officer who has charge of the revenues of a district; a person who superintends the fulfilment of engagements of agriculturists.
Zillat, *s. f.* baseness, meanness, contemptibleness, dishonour.
Zillú, *s. f.* a leech.
Zimma, *s. m.* trust, charge, obligation.
Zimme karná, to give in charge.
Zimme lená, to take in charge, to take care of, to take upon one's self.
Zín, *s. m.* a saddle.
Zína, *s. m.* stairs, steps.
Ziná, *s. f.* adultery, fornication.
Zinákár, *s. m.* an adulterer, a fornicator.
Zinákárí, *s. f.* fornication, adultery, harlotry.

Ziná karná, to commit adultery.
Zínat, *s. f.* ornament, beauty, elegance, decoration.
Zín bándhná, to saddle.
Zinda, *adj.* alive, living.
Zindagání, } *s. f.* life, living, existence.
Zindagí, }
Zinda karná, to bring to life.
Zindán, *s. m.* a prison, a jail.
Zindání, *adj.* imprisoned, prisoner.
Zíngar, *s. m.* a saddler.
Zinhár, } *interj.* take care! beware: *adv.* by no means.
Zínhár, }
Zinjif, *s. f.* fringe, border.
Zínposh, *s.m.* a saddle-cloth, housing.
Zír, *s. f.* the treble (in music.)
Zíra, } *s. m.* cummin-seed,
Zírá, }
Ziráạt, *s. f.* agriculture, husbandry, sown field, sown land, tillage.
Zirah, *s. f.* iron armour made with rings.
Zirahposh, a man clad in armour.
Zírak, *adj.* ingenious, intelligent, sagacious, acute, shrewd.
Zírúh, a rational being.
Zisht, *adj.* deformed, ugly, hideous.
Zishtkho, of ugly habits or disposition.
Zishtrú, *adj.* ugly, ill-favoured.
Zíshuụr, *adj.* intelligent.
Zíst, *s. f.* life, living, existence.
Zíst karná, to live.
Ziyád, } *s. m.* augmentation, increase, excess: *adj.* more, too much, too many, excessive.
Ziyáda, }
Ziyáda honá, to exceed, to surpass; to be increased.
Ziyáda karná, to augment, to increase; to take away the dinner and table cloth.
Ziyádatí, *s. f.* see Ziyád.
Ziyáfat, *s. f.* a feast, a banquet, hospitality; invitation.
Ziyáfat karná, to entertain, to feast, to treat.
Ziyán, *s. m.* injury, hurt, harm, loss, damage, mischief, deficiency.
Ziyán karná, *v. a.* to cause the harm, hurt, injury, damage, &c. (of), to injure, &c.
Ziyárat, *s. f.* pilgrimage, visiting.
Ziyárat karná, to go on pilgrimage.
Zor, *s. m.* force, strength, power, vigour; violence, effort: *adv.* forcibly, violently.
Zoráwar, *adj.* powerful, strong.
Zoráwarí, *s. f.* power, force.
Zorázmáí, *s. f.* trial of strength, wrestling.
Zor dená, *v. a.* to aid, to support.
Zor karná, to compel, to exercise, to use effort, to exert one's self.
Zormand, *adj.* robust, powerful.
Zormandí, *s. f.* strength.
Zor márná, to endeavour, strive, toil, struggle.
Zú, a lord, master; in *compos.* possessed of or endowed with.
Zubán, or **Zabán**, *s. f.* the tongue, language, dialect, speech.
Zubán chaláná, to give abuse.
Zubándaráz, *adj.* abusive.
Zubándarází, *s. f.* abuse.
Zubán dená, } to promise.
Zubán hárná, }
Zubání, *adj.* traditional, oral, verbal, by word.
Zubán kátná, to interrupt one's speech.
Zubán pakarná, to prevent one from speaking, to criticise.
Zubán palatná, to retract.
Zubán par láná, to speak, to say, to mention.
Zúd, *adj.* quick, swift, soon.
Zúdranj, *adj.* irascible, soon irritated.
Zúdtar, more speedily, very soon.
Zúdtarín, with all speed.
Zụf, *s. m.* infirmity, weakness, imbecility of mind or body.
Zuhal, *s. m.* the planet Saturn.
Zuhr, *s. m.* a little after mid-day.
Zuhra, *s. f.* the planet Venus.
Zuhúr, *s. m.* appearing, arising, becoming visible.

Zukám, } *s. m.* defluxion, rheum,
Zuḳhám, } catarrh, a cold.

Zulál, *adj.* pure, limpid, wholesome (water.)

Zulam, *s. m.* see Zulm.

Zulf, *s. f.* a curling lock, a ringlet, a side lock (of hair.)

Zúl jalál, possessed of glory, glorious, splendid.

Zulm, *s. m.* oppression, injustice, tyranny, injury, extortion.

Zulmat, *s. f.* darkness.

Zulmát, *s. f.* a dark place where the water of immortality is said to be.

Zulm honá, to befall one (a misfortune.)

Zulmí, *adj.* oppressive, tyrannical, unjust; addicted to tyranny.

Zulmíyal, *s. f.* see Zulm.

Zulm karná, to oppress, to tyrannize.

Zumurrud, *s. m.* an emerald.

Zunnár, *s. f.* the Bráhmanical thread.

Zuráfa, *s. m.* the giraffe.

Zurúf, *s. plur.* vessels; adverbs, &c.

THE END.